BOLSHEVIK IDE[illegible]
THE ETHICS OF SO[illegible] [illegible]BOR

1917-1920: THE FORMATIVE YEARS

by FREDERICK I. KAPLAN, Ph. D.

This book deals with Bolshevik ideology as a fundamental attitude toward the world and with the ethics of Soviet labor as a morally colored approach to life and work. The ethics of Soviet labor are regarded as having grown out of the Communist ideology and the revolutionary situation alike. The book begins with an account of the root basis and theoretical framework of the ideology and its political and psychological significance. An exhaustive history of Russian labor from 1917-1920 follows, showing the relationships among the Communist Party, the trade unions, the factory committees, the state and its bureaus. Differing notions of workers' control as well as the conflict between the chiliastic striving of labor and the goal-postponing demands of the Bolsheviks

(*Continued on back flap*)

sity.

BOLSHEVIK IDEOLOGY AND THE ETHICS OF SOVIET LABOR

1917-1920: The Formative Years

BOLSHEVIK IDEOLOGY AND THE ETHICS OF SOVIET LABOR

1917-1920: The Formative Years

Frederick I. Kaplan
Michigan State University

PHILOSOPHICAL LIBRARY
NEW YORK

15 East 40 Street, New York, N. Y. 10016

Library of Congress Catalog Card No. 67-17636

Printed in the United States of America

Contents

Acknowledgments

Now that my book is about to appear in print, it is saddening to remember that those to whom I owe most for their teaching are no longer alive. My debt to them remains, however, and I wish to acknowledge it. Professor George M. McCune was the first of my teachers of history on the graduate level and it was from him that I first learned the methods and uses of history. Professor Robert J. Kerner, Sather Professor of History and Director of the Institute of Slavic Studies at the University of California, Berkeley, was my major professor while I worked for the doctoral degree. He insisted upon a discipline which was sometimes hard to render and even when we sometimes differed in opinion. I profited from his training. Professor George V. Lantzeff also taught me Russian history and demanded a painstaking devotion to detail in my scholarly writing. I want to thank Professor Else Frenkel-Brunswik with whom I studied psychology for two years on the graduate level and whose teaching not only enriched and deepened my insights within the field of history but also broadened my knowledge of the social sciences in general. I wish that all these scholars could see the book their teaching has influenced.

Professor Philip E. Mosely of Columbia University encouraged my work and after the death of my professors kindly and generously assisted me in ways they might have done. Some of the work for this book was completed while I was a traveling research associate for the Research Program on the History of the Communist Party of the Soviet Union, which Professor Mosely headed. I want particularly to acknowledge the kindness he showed me.

After the death of Professor Kerner, Professor Gregory Grossman of the Department of Economics of the University of California, Berkeley, was the most active member of the committee on the thesis from which this work was drawn.

My friends George Harjan and Professor Evelyn Bristol helped me in matters of translation, James Bogen in problems of epistemology, and Professors Donald M. Lowe and Alexander Vucinich read and discussed the manuscripts with me. Professor Daniel Freedman answered questions on matters of psychology. Norma Werdelin not only typed the first manuscript carefully but was my first reader and critic.

At the libraries at which I worked I was kindly assisted in their use by Mrs. Uridge of the Inter-Library Borrowing Service at the University of California, Berkeley, Mrs. Arlene Paul and her staff at the Hoover Institution, Miss Elizabeth Tokoi at the University of Helsinki and Professor Bruno Kalnins at the Slavic Institute of the University of Stockholm.

Michigan State University assisted in the preparation of the manuscript through its All-University Grants.

Prefatory Notes

NOTE ON THE USE OF ITALICS, PARENTHESES AND BRACKETS IN QUOTATIONS

All italics are those of the work cited except when otherwise stated. All parentheses are of the work quoted. All brackets are mine.

NOTE ON TRANSLITERATION

The system of transliteration used here is that of the Library of Congress without diacritical marks or ligatures. Where certain spellings are more common in English than the Library of Congress system, they have been used: for example, Trotsky instead of Trotskii.

NOTE ON CHRONOLOGY

From the year 1700 until the Gregorian calendar was adopted by the Soviet government in February 1918, the Julian calendar, which during the twentieth century was thirteen days behind the Gregorian, was in use in Russia. Here, except for the dates of the factory committee conferences and meetings, where both dates are not given, the new is used. The Bolshevik Revolution took place on 24 October-6 November 1917. It is therefore referred to as either the October or November Revolution. Either designation is used here depending upon the context.

NOTE ON SOVIET

The word "Soviet" as used here refers to the councils of the state, or to what became the councils of the state in the center, or to all the councils of the state inclusively. The word "soviet" is used here to refer to the councils of the state on the various territorial-administrative levels.

Prospect

It is the purpose of this study to add to an understanding of Soviet labor through an analysis of its historical development; for in order to understand the role of labor in the Soviet state it is necessary to know what it used to be and how it came through the course of time to derive the shape, form and substance of its present existence. In the sixth decade of the twentieth century Russian trade unions are organizations bound to the Soviet state and, like the state, are guided and directed by the Communist Party. All Russian workers, whether organized into unions or not, are employees of institutions of the state, which has nationalized all sectors of the economy. Therefore, both the unions of which they are members and the organizations by which Soviet workers are employed are branches of the state, and the trade unions as state institutions are prohibited from striking against the other state institutions which employ them. It is one of the primary functions of the unions, however, to draw ever larger numbers of workers into the building of socialism and to guide their social and even personal lives. At the factory level the factory committees—organizations of workers at a particular factory—are basic units of the trade unions. But if a meaningful understanding of the organization and function of Soviet labor is to be attained, it is necessary to acquire a knowledge of the inclinations and aspirations which it held in its past and which it no longer manifests. In order to understand the development of Soviet labor, therefore, it is fruitful to follow historically the events and circumstances in which Russian workers acted during the Revolution of 1917 and the subsequent Bolshevik order.

The story of the Bolshevik Party and even the stories of some of the opposition parties and groups have been told. The achievements of Russian labor in contributing to the growth of the Russian economy are known, but the deeds of many Russian workers who, in the revolutionary years, opposed the new Communist regime have not found their place in history. Yet their story, too, is worthy of remembrance.

THE AUTHOR'S METHOD AND IDEA OF HISTORY[1]

If the story of Russian labor is to be fully understood and appreciated, it cannot be approached in terms of success or failure; nor may success and failure be regarded as the "objective" verdict of history. The words and deeds concerning Russian labor must be investigated for the meaning found within them, and their singularity and peculiarity must not be allowed to disappear into what is sometimes regarded as a universally imperative process of industrialization, progress, or "history." An attempt will therefore be made to present the special and separate causes of events and occurrences important to the history of Soviet labor. Thus the general meaning and significance of causes and events will not be engulfed or enveloped in the assumption of an inevitable underlying process of which they are merely a somewhat adventitious expression.

The aims and purposes of the actors in the events will be sought for in words and deeds in so far as the source materials make them available to the perception of the author. And through an analysis of the source materials the author intends to show, as far as possible, what really happened among Russian laborers and workers in the revolutionary situation from 1917 to 1920.

This is an historical and political study and not an economic one. There are several good studies of Soviet labor, making use of statistics, which approach the organization, management and discipline of labor from the point of view of productivity. The political reasons for the measures taken to increase productivity will be under discussion here. Even if it is admitted that industrialization and economic development are universal imperatives or that they were a necessity for the Soviet Union, it must also be admitted that there were various ways toward that development. Certainly time and economic growth have augmented the economic rewards of Russian labor, but its share of political power and freedom have not appreciably multiplied. Looking backward from the present at statistical evidence of Soviet industrial productivity, the record may be regarded as impressive. However, statistics do not deal directly with the relations of production, relations which the Marxist-Leninists themselves value so highly, and if these relations are examined, outside of the Marxist framework, their political meaning becomes manifest through the recorded word and deed. Statistics is a language which no one speaks and only experts understand. To acquire a knowledge of the relationship between the Bolshevik Party and Soviet labor in the years during which they were shaped and formed one must return through the medium of the source materials to that time. And if the issues seem largely political, ideological and even polemical, in deed and in fact, they were.

The concern in this study is largely with politics and the ideas that motivated action. Not only the goals and objectives of the Party and its adherents but also the aims and purposes of those who opposed the Bolshevik order will be presented. In making known the aspirations of that portion of Soviet labor that was successfully opposed by the Party, the intention is not to show what, in the future, might have been, but what in all its complexity really happened at the time.

Thus this story of Russian labor and its relations with the Bolshevik Party will present the conflicting welter of intentions, goals, standards and values held variously among Russian workers who, at times and to degrees, acted with or against each other and the parties. What did happen will therefore be regarded as happening not as the result of some force or trend exerting itself independently of the goals, aspirations and awareness of the actors in the events, but primarily as the result of their actions. This does not mean that all the actors in this history acted always with full awareness of their goals. Nor does it mean that they knew or could know the consequences of their actions even when they were acutely aware of the intentions with which they performed them. By acting, the actors, in our history as in all history, started something new, something unpredictable, the end and the meaning of which they could not know.

Moreover, it is in retrospect that the author of a history writes. From his perspective he can comprehend more fully and more clearly the meaning of the events with which he deals than could the participants who at the time were engaged in them and were unaware of the story's end. For historians, in dealing with the past, project themselves backward into time and from their historical vantage point see both the past and future of the situation they examine. The individuals involved in this situation, however, know only their own present and their own past. The time through which the historian has projected himself backward does not yet exist for them. The historian, therefore, must resist the temptation to investigate with too great an emphasis on the future of an event the documents which were produced within it.

Every attempt, therefore, was made to place the source materials used here into the situational and ideological context in which they were spoken or written. Words were related to action and action to words so that as far as possible the intentions of those who spoke and acted would become manifest. Words were not only related to the situation in which they were enunciated but they were also placed within the ideological context within which they were thought out. The fundamental assumptions and theoretical framework of communist ideology were carefully examined so that the author would avoid interpreting from his own frame of reference the words written or spoken within the Bolshevik framework. Instead the author has interpreted the source materials with reference to the criteria of validity imposed by Bolshevik ideology itself and to the systematic theoretical basis of that ideology. The purpose of integrating the words into their own framework is not to "unmask" the intentions or purposes of the Bolsheviks or to reveal lies; nor is the author's purpose to show that the Bolsheviks did not say what they meant or mean what they said. It is the aim of the author, on the contrary, to show what was really meant by what was actually said.

In placing the relationship between Russian labor and the Bolshevik party within its situational context between 1917-1920 various problems arise that would not be present if the author were investigating a more stable period of time in which political and economic connections among institutions and social ties among groups of the population were well formed and set within a definite framework. During a time of war, revolution and civil war, the connections among institutions become disturbed or broken, the ties among social classes become unbalanced and conflicted, and the competition among political parties becomes more severe. In the Russia from 1917-1918 pre-revolutionary relationships in the realms of politics, economics and society had for the most part ceased to be workable, the old framework of society had been broken down or been destroyed, and the control exerted from a center was not effective over the whole of the former Empire. This must be borne in mind when evaluating the documents of the time, especially the orders, decrees, laws and administrative instructions of the Bolshevik party and the Soviet state. In spite of the wealth of source materials available, it remains difficult to determine with anything like exactitude just how powerful the Bolsheviks were after the seizure of power and to what areas their authority extended. The decrees, of course, may be compared with speeches, articles and accounts of action not only of Bolsheviks and their adherents but of their opponents as well. Thus the various kinds of source materials help to illuminate each other and, weighed one against another, help in the solution of the problem being investigated.

Another problem arises, however, and that is how far the acts and decrees of the Bolsheviks were the result of their particular techniques, their ways of dealing with reality as they saw it, and how far they were the result of the chaotic conditions in Russia after their seizure of power. For the Bolsheviks established their authority in a country that was engaged in a difficult war from which they withdrew in the Treaty of Brest-Litovsk only by sacrificing rich parts of its territory and resources and large parts of its population. The Party established its authority in a country suffering from the breakdown of its economy, rent by the beginning of civil war, and burdened by the failure of transport and the dislocation of population. Under such conditions it is difficult to enforce orders; plans come to be a concrete response to the given situation rather than abstract designs for socialism in the future. Nevertheless the Bolsheviks had just seized power and desired to maintain and increase it. Their acts and decrees reflected that desire.

A statement on objectivity is needed, for certainly any work on the Soviet Union is open to charges of sympathy or antipathy toward the Soviet state. The conservative may regard understanding as praise and the liberal may regard the revelation of an unattractive truth as prejudiced blame. It is not uncommonly a mark of enlightenment and sophistication to believe in the Soviet Union as a force of human "progress" and to view its technological advancement as "objective" proof of this. The technological goals and ends of the Soviet state are allowed to obscure the meaning of the events and acts which produced that advance. And technology, rather than the possession of freedom, action or power by its citizens, sometimes becomes the standard for judgments of the Soviet state by social scientists.

In this work objectivity is regarded by the author as an awareness and realization of his own viewpoints and judgments so that by controlling them he may prevent them from distorting or coloring his perception and understanding. But his detachment and distance from the events he is narrating does not preclude a strong interest in them; nor has he failed to be moved by the story he is telling. Indeed he hopes the reader will also be moved by it. Moreover, it has been the author's intention to present impartially what is worthy of either praise or blame among any of the participants in the story. And it must be borne in mind, where either praise or blame appears to fall on a particular group, that the opposite need not necessarily fall upon those who opposed that group. Further, where a valuation falls upon the Soviet order, it does not mean that the contrary must fall upon any other system.

What the Book Contains

This work will begin with a description of Lenin's epistemology, or theory of knowledge, and Lenin's theory of history, since they provide the ideological basis of Bolshevik thought and since they contain the fundamental assumptions and provide the theoretical framework of Bolshevik ideology as developed by Lenin from Marx and Engels. It is within this ideological context that the bearers of the ideology explain or elaborate, justify or rationalize, their action. Indeed Soviet politics has made ideology a principle of action, and both act and thought must be understood in order to adequately comprehend either. Lenin's theory of knowledge will be compared to his theory of history to see to what extent they parallel each other—to what extent they conform to each other—and to see if they share a fundamental approach to the world.

Lenin's theory of perception will be criticized and the author will investigate the political and psychological significance of the ideology.

Having presented the ideological context of Bolshevik thought, attention will be focused in Chapter II upon labor under the Provisional Government and especially upon the organization of factory committees and the demand for workers' control. Chapter II also correlates labor and Bolshevik action with Lenin's revolutionary words.

Chapter III will complete the study of Russian labor in 1917 and will discuss the conditions and emotional climate of Petrograd as they influenced labor's adherence to the Bolshevik overthrow of the Provisional Government.

The study of Russian labor under the Soviet state from 1918 to 1920 is begun in Chapter IV. From this study it becomes evident that the revolutionary goals and objectives of the workers differed from those of the Bolsheviks and Mensheviks as well. Here the concepts of "consciousness" and "spontaneity" in Bolshevik ideology and their function as a means of persuading and convincing labor to follow Bolshevik aims and purposes is discussed, and the author explains the conflict between the chiliastic strivings of labor and the goal-postponing demands of the Bolshevik party.

Chapter V contains an analysis of the interrelationships between labor, the Anarchists, the Bolshevik party and the Soviet state. It will include an explanation of the Anarchist view of goal-postponement and spontaneity and of the workers' understanding of anarchism.

Chapter VI and VII investigate the relationships between the factory committees, the trade unions, the state and the party as well as the effect of nationalization and centralization upon workers' control in 1918.

After a reconstruction in Chapter VIII of the temper of labor in the post-revolutionary situation with reference to the suppression and violence used in addition to the persuasion necessary to bring labor into conformity with Bolshevik goals, Chapters IX and X will deal with the organizational relations of labor to the state and their political implications in 1919 and 1920. They will follow the intricately changing relationships of the unions to the Soviet state and its branches as well as the relationships of the unions and the state to the party. These chapters also present the quarrel between Trotsky and his supporters on the one hand, and Lenin and Zinoviev on the other, insofar as the struggle forms part of the history of Soviet labor. The problem of workers' control and its fate in these later years, especially with reference to one-man management and bureaucracy, shall be discussed.

Chapter XII contains an account of labor discipline, of the *subbotniks* and *voskresniks,* and discusses their function of increasing labor productivity and instilling into labor habits and attitudes necessary to the political as well as economic order. This chapter is concerned with Bolshevik policy towards wages, hours and social insurance and the significance of free labor in relation to forced labor.

A brief retrospect of the previously presented history of Russian labor is presented in Chapter XIII so that the relationship of the ethics of Soviet labor to the deeds and events through which it passed, as well as its relationship to Bolshevik ideology, will be clearer.

The final chapter will then deal with ethics as the morally colored approach to life and work that the Bolshevik Party attempted to inculcate into labor through Marxist-Leninist ideology. It will discuss the demand of the Party for the close identification of the worker with the state and will show how the ideology was to be comprehended, experienced and integrated into the life of Soviet workers. Thus the author will show how the ideology functioned psychologically in forming the ethics of Soviet labor.

Although the author, in delineating the scope of his work has of necessity selected his material, he has nevertheless tried to bind together all the threads of action in the deeds and events about which he is writing. He has also refrained from imposing a pattern of his own making upon the facts provided by the source materials; rather, he has intended to tell the history of Russian labor in terms of the actual human relationships, the events, and the deeds that compose it. And if the reader is to understand the history of Soviet labor, he must listen to these words, and he must follow the intricate maze of action and the welter of events in which the words were articulated. Moreover, it is the intention of the author to clarify, but not to simplify his subject; for clarification illuminates, simplification distorts.

The author asks the reader's patience in listening to the words and following the deeds he has found worthy of remembrance and hopes the reader will persevere with him in untangling the web of the story.

CHAPTER I

Bolshevik Ideology: Lenin's Theory of Knowledge and Lenin's Theory of History

ACTION AND IDEOLOGICAL CONTEXT

In February/March 1917, the tsarist government was overthrown and replaced by a Provisional Government functioning in cooperation with the councils or soviets of workers, soldiers and peasants that had grown up during the revolutionary days. In October/November 1917, the Bolshevik party, supported largely by labor, seized power from the Provisional Government and established the Soviet state in its first stage, the dictatorship of the proletariat. Since it was by the action of the Bolsheviks and labor that the workers' state was founded, it is fruitful to see where the goals of labor and the party coincided and where they might have diverged. To do this, it is necessary to determine first the configuration of Bolshevik thought and its meaning as an ideological pattern; for the Bolsheviks were the leaders of the seizure of power and, as the rulers of the Soviet state, theirs became the dominant ideology in Russia. When the fundamental concepts and theoretical framework of Bolshevik ideology are known, it will be possible to understand within its own context the reasoning of the Bolsheviks regarding their relationship to labor. It will be possible to understand accurately the meaning of the single judgments, explanations and statements of Bolshevik party leaders. This will, in turn, illuminate their action since political action and speech are inextricable. After Bolshevik ideology has been explained, attention will be turned in subsequent chapters to the deeds of labor and the party.

The systematic theoretical basis and framework of Bolshevik thought may be found in Lenin's materialist philosophy, especially in his theory of knowledge and theory of history; for Lenin's discussions of the relationship between consciousness and being, between subject and object, man and his environment, society and history, serve to clarify and define the ideology of the party.[1]

Lenin and the Empirio-criticists

Lenin's theory of knowledge was set forth and elaborated principally in his attacks against the philosophy of empirio-criticism as developed by the Austrian physicist Ernst Mach and adopted and elaborated by his Russian admirers, such as Bogdanov and Lunacharsky. Lenin, in his work *Materialism and Empirio-criticism,*[2] attacks the empirio-criticists on the grounds that their philosophy leaves room for both fideism and idealism, and formulates his own theory of knowledge to avoid both.

The asperity of Lenin's attacks against the empirio-criticists is directed therefore not only against whatever weakness Lenin might find in the reasoning and methodology of his opponents, but even more against what he considers their fideism, their articulate or passive acknowledgment of a spiritual realm beyond this world. Lenin charges that the epistemology of the empirio-criticists is a fideist philosophy whereas ". . . materialism closes the door to every species of fideism. . . ."[3] In his attack upon other-worldliness, Lenin seems to have been concerned not only with creating a future but in destroying a past. Since a Christian faith formed the basis of tsarist ideology, his attack upon fideism served to undermine the ideological foundation of tsarism itself. It shall be shown later that Lenin, by shutting the door to the other world, deprived the many of individual immortality and made such immortality possible only for the few.

Materialism and Idealism

Also, Lenin separates philosophy into two principal divisions: ". . . the fundamental philosophical trends are materialism and idealism. Materialism regards nature as primary and spirit as secondary; it places being first and thought second. Idealism holds the contrary view."[4] The materialist starts from nature, matter, the external world; the idealist, from the sensations. "For the materialist the 'factually given' is the outer world. . . . For the idealist the 'factually given' is sensation."[5] Lenin insists that the existence of the world outside us is not dependent upon our sensations, that "Things exist independently of our consciousness, outside of us. . . ."[6]

The Unknown and the Unknowable

Moreover, for Lenin, there can be no absolute boundary between the appearance of a thing as it is perceived and the thing as it exists outside us, the thing-in-itself. He asserts that the very idea of . . . a boundary *in principle* between the appearance and the thing-in-itself is a nonsensical idea.[7] Lenin is so intransigently opposed to a theory of knowledge which admits of an inseparable boundary in principle between the appearance and the reality because once this boundary is recognized the knowability and even the existence of things-in-themselves may be cast in doubt. Further, if such a boundary is recognized, the existence of the unknowable may be posited and there is room for faith. The postulate that beyond the world of phenomena a "world-in-itself" exists is, according to Lenin, "a sort of impassable gulf created by the priests."[8] The only difference between the phenomenon and the thing-in-itself ". . . is between what is known and what is not yet known."[9] Being beyond the point where our observations ends, as for example, the existence of men on Mars, is always an open question for Lenin, but this, he asserts, is far different from the belief in the existence of an unknowable being beyond perception.[10] "Indeed," he says, "fideism positively asserts that something does exist beyond the world of perception. The materialists vigorously deny this."[11] For Lenin, then, beyond perception there can be only the unknown, not the unknowable.

The External World is Independent of Sensation

At the same time, however, that Lenin denies that anything exists beyond the ultimate reach of perception or that a boundary exists between appearance and reality, he denies also that sensation is the reality existing outside us. "One asks, how can sane people in sound mind and judgment assert that 'sense perception' (within what limits is not important) *is* the reality existing outside us?"[12] According to Lenin, the equating of things with sensations is a basic premise of idealism which begins with the assertion that "things" are our sensations.[13] Both idealists and agnostics, Lenin says, claim that we cannot know of the existence of anything beyond the bounds of sensation nor know anything certain about the things-in-themselves.[14]

Sensation as Connection to the Outside World

The materialist, according to Lenin, goes beyond sensation to its external source, the outside world: "things" exist outside our minds[15] and sensations are produced by the action of "things on our sense organs,"[16] by the ". . . transformation of the energy of external excitation into a state of consciousness."[17] Lenin claims that in contradistinction to the idealists who, he says, know only sensation and the agnostics who know nothing certain, it the materialist line ". . . that the outer world acts on our sense organs,"[18] that sensation is the direct connection between consciousness and the external world.[19]

Objective Absolute Truth

Nevertheless it is not sensation upon which we depend as the source or determinant of our knowledge or its ultimate validity, for to do so, according to Lenin, would lead to subjectivism or relativism.[20] Each man would be the measure of his own knowledge, whereas for Lenin man's knowledge must have an objective measure or model in external reality. The external world, with which we are connected by sensation, becomes that model. And the world which exists independently of our sensations becomes, for Lenin, the measure of objective truth. "To be a materialist," he says, "is to acknowledge objective truth which is revealed to us by our sense organs. To acknowledge objective truth, i.e., truth not dependent upon man and mankind is in one way or another to recognize absolute truth."[21]

The Theory of Reflection

Our sensations, perceptions or ideas do not give us direct knowledge of the objective absolute truth outside us but rather provide us only with *images* or *copies* of "reality."[22] Lenin insists that ". . . a deduction which materialism deliberately places at the foundation of its epistemology is that . . . our perceptions are *images* of the external world."[23] When our perceptions, sensations or thoughts reflect external reality as accurately as possible, they provide us with objective truth; for the objective truth of thinking *means* nothing else than the existence of objects (i.e., things-in-themselves) truly reflected by thinking."[24] According to Lenin, then, the world outside us is the external model which, correctly reflected, provides objective—and absolute truth.

Test of Reality

Our sensations, perceptions and ideas, then, are the reflections or images of "things" outside us. "Verification of these images is given by practice."[25] The degree of correctness of our sense impressions, therefore, is verified by our actions. Quoting Engels, Lenin insists: "The proof of the pudding is in the eating. From the moment we turn to our own use these objects, according to the qualities we perceive in them, we put to an infallible test the correctness or otherwise of our sense perceptions. If these perceptions have been wrong, then our estimate of the use to which an object can be turned must also be wrong, and our attempt must fail. But if we succeed in accomplishing our aim, if we find the object does agree with our idea of it, and does answer the purpose we intended it for, then that is positive proof that our perceptions of it and its qualities, so far, agree with reality outside ourselves."[26] Thus, according to Lenin, ". . . the success of human practice proves the correspondence between our ideas and the objective nature of the things we perceive."[27]

Matter, Law and Causality

The philosophical concept for the objective reality reflected by man's sense perception is, according to Lenin, matter.[28] However, if Lenin insists upon the concept of matter as objective reality existing independently of men and which men comprehend through sensation and experience, it is because this objective reality is guided by law. This law, according to Lenin, is not determined by a God or found only in the minds of men. It is a law found within matter itself. "The world," says Lenin, "is matter moving in conformity to law . . ."[29] and it is fundamental to materialism that this law is "reflected with approximate fidelity" in the minds of men.[30] By thus insisting upon an objective law independent of men, Lenin provides a final and ultimate authority for all events, both natural and human. For the Law of Nature is an absolute and universal law which applies to all of nature and all of humanity.

The law that Lenin claimed to discern in nature was one of motion and change, for the law is rooted in matter itself and there is no matter without motion.[31] Moreover, according to Lenin, the movement of men's ideas reflects the movement of matter, for "To the movement of ideas, perceptions, etc., there corresponds the movement of matter outside me."[32]

Cause and effect, according to Lenin, are part of a single universal world process in which the particular cause and particular effect lose their peculiar significance and meaning. Thus the specific cause and effect tend "to merge and dissolve" in universal action where what was here an effect becomes there a cause, and vice versa.[33] Lenin contends, therefore, that in grasping the meaning of a single cause or effect, men lose sight of its universal significance and of its function in the process as a whole. Thus he says that the concept of men reflect cause and effect only in a limited fashion, artificially isolating one or another aspect of a single world process.[34] Cause and effect are reflected in men's minds only relatively and approximately.[35]

Dialectic: The Relationship of Relative to Absolute

Moreover, the law that guides cause and effect and all of nature is a dialectical law; therefore, even though it is universal, it reveals itself in a relative fashion. Each new scientific discovery, for example, adds to the sum of absolute truth, but each new scientific proposition itself is absolute only within certain limits which expand and contract with the growth of knowledge.[36] Various sums of relative knowledge contribute to produce absolute truth. The mutability of knowledge, therefore, is not a refutation that man's mind reflects objective reality; nor does it cast doubt upon absolute truth.[37] On the contrary, to deny change in the world is to deny the dialectic.[38] However, in accordance with the dialectic of the Law of Nature, men do not know all of nature's truths all at once, nor are they known by each man or by all men.[39] Each man is limited in his capacity to comprehend absolute truth at any particular moment; but human thought itself, the thought of mankind, approaches nearer to that goal in time. It is time and distance, therefore, that determine the extent to which knowledge of the absolute is made known to man. And although our knowledge of absolute truth is limited, the existence of the truth and the fact that we approach it more closely by the acquisition of relative truths are not to be doubted; for, Lenin reiterates, "Human thought, then, by its nature is capable of giving and does give absolute truth which is compounded of a sum total of relative truths."[40]

For Lenin, the importance of the dialectic lies in this relationship of absolute to relative truth and is, of course, distinct from the concept of the thesis and antithesis as static polar opposites; for the opposition of one concept of a static object to another results only in the grasping of the concept of an equally static object. The dialectic, on the other hand, in thought, is the reflection of process in the external world, the contradictions of which have only relative validity and are not irreconcilable and insoluble. In all his most theoretical work on materialism, Lenin mentions the thesis and antithesis only once, and then to point out that the dialectics ". . . deal precisely with the inadequacy of polar opposites."[41] The latter are too rigid to reflect the movement and flux of nature, the dynamic relationship of the relative to the absolute.

Dialectics in Propositions and in Nature

Lenin regards dialectics as a description of the dynamic relations of things and claims that dialectics are found in the most common propositions. "John is a man," says Lenin, "Fido is a dog, etc. Here already we have dialectics," for the individual is the universal and every universal is a fragment, or an aspect, or the essence of an individual. "Every individual is connected by thousands of transitions with other *kinds* of individuals (things, phenomena, processes, etc.)"[42] In any proposition, Lenin then claims, there are the component parts of dialectics, the conflicts of opposites, negation, negation of the negation,[43] the change from quantity to quality. Further, Lenin claims that science has observed the dialectic objectively existing in nature and declares that it is part of the process of knowing.[44]

Dialectics and Relativism

Dialectics for Lenin is the relationship between the present and the future, the known and the unknown, ignorance and knowledge, absolute and relative truth; he asserts, for example, that we must ". . . learn to put and answer the question of the relation between absolute and relative truth dialectically."[45] Materialist dialectics, he says, recognizes the relativity of all our knowledge but the limits of this knowledge in its approximation to objective truth are historically conditional.[46] Moreover, dialectical materialism recognizes the existence of absolute truth as well as the relativity of knowledge; it is therefore " . . . not reducible to relativism."[47] By Lenin's definition, "relativism" differs from dialectical materialism, not in the recognition of the relativity of our knowledge but in a denial of absolute truth as an objective model for that knowledge.[48] It is this dialectical relation of the relative to the absolute that distinguishes dialectical materialism from what Lenin considers relativist philosophies, such as empirio-criticism. "For Bogdanov," says Lenin ". . . recognition of the relativity of our knowledge *excludes* even the least admission of absolute truth. For Engels absolute truth is compounded from relative truths. Bogdanov is a relativist; Engels is a dialectician."[49]

Necessity and Freedom

It has already been pointed out that the law and causality which Lenin finds in nature and which he believes to be revealed in a historically conditioned fashion are "reflected only with approximate fidelity" in the human mind.[50] And although nature is independent of man's concepts of it, man himself is part of nature and subject to its laws. The ". . . laws of external nature," says Lenin, and " . . . those which govern the bodily and mental existence of men themselves [are] two classes of laws, which we can separate from each other in thought but not in reality"[51]

Since men are governed by the same laws as nature itself, Lenin insists that they must adapt themselves to the necessity of nature and fulfill its laws; for "the recognition of necessity in thought is materialism."[52] To Lenin, sensation and thought are secondary—they are products of matter—but nature is primary—it has an objective, independent existence of its own. The things of the external world acting upon our sense organs produce sensations which are reflections of those things.[53] Therefore, our minds, being secondary, must reflect the laws existing in nature, which is primary. Further, our minds must adapt to necessity in nature. Lenin, citing Engels as an authority, examines the knowledge and will of man, on the one hand, and the necessity of nature on the other, and says that "the necessity of nature is primary and human will and mind secondary. The latter must necessarily and inevitably adapt themselves to the former."[54] According to Lenin, just as an unknown thing-in-itself becomes, through knowledge, a thing-for-us, an unknown necessity becomes through knowledge necessity-for-us. "The development of conciousness in each human individual and the development of the collective knowledge of humanity at large presents us at every step with examples of the transformation of the unknown 'thing-in-itself' into the known 'thing-for-us,' of the transformation of blind, unknown necessity, 'necessity-in-itself,' into the known 'necessity-for-us.' "[55] Lenin therefore avers that as our minds reflect objects they also reflect nature's law. When this law is known it must be consciously fulfilled. However, it is a dialectical law and it is never known to any man or all men as a whole or at once. "The laws of external nature

. . . are fully knowable to man but can never be known to him *with finality*."[56]

Furthermore, according to Lenin, man's freedom of action is derived from the recognition of nature's necessity. Freedom consists in knowledge of the laws of nature and acting in accordance with them; for the materialists hold that the human mind can apply these laws consciously.[57] Lenin, quoting Engels, who in turn is referring to Hegel, points out that ". . . freedom is the result of necessity. 'Necessity is *blind only in so far as it is not understood*. Freedom does not consist in the dream of independence of natural laws, but in the knowledge of these laws and in the possibility that gives of systematically making them work towards definite ends.' "[58] Freedom, according to Lenin, then, consists of putting natural laws to use. But since natural laws function independently of our minds, we must submit to them, even unconsciously. Once this submission becomes conscious we are free and capable of using those laws. "For until we know a law of nature, it, existing and acting independently and outside our mind, makes us slaves of 'blind necessity.' But once we come to know this law which acts . . .independently of our will and mind, we become the masters of nature."[59] Obedience, therefore, is not blind; rather it is the recognition of necessity, and for Lenin, dominance of nature is the result of compliance with it and is in turn proof that nature is, as far as possible, correctly mirrored in the mind. Thus in the knowledge that they will be bound by hunger and driven by its necessity if they do not eat, it is possible for men regularly to partake of food before hunger arises and so derive freedom out of necessity. By recognition of this natural need, by obeying its demands men can master it. The "I must" become the "I will" and the "I will" becomes the "I can." However, the necessity of hunger is found within us and is easy to comprehend, whereas the necessity of which Lenin speaks is found outside us and is more difficult to grasp. As an example, Lenin states that although we do know the existence of necessity in the weather, we do not know what necessity is, and so we are, therefore, "slaves of the weather." If that necessity were understood, if our minds could correctly reflect the phenomenon of the weather, we could "master" it.[60] As Lenin asserts, "The mastery of nature manifested in human practice is a result of an objectively correct reflection within the human head of the phenomena and processes of nature and is proof of the fact that this reflection (within the limits of what is revealed in practice) is objective, absolute and eternal truth."[61]

Thus according to this world view it is the function of thought not merely to describe the world, not to explain it by reference to general principles, but to reflect, participate in, and master the changes taking place in external reality. The "I know" becomes the "you must," the "you must" becomes the "I must"; the "I must" becomes the "I will," and the "I will" becomes the "I can."

TIME AND SPACE

Furthermore, according to Lenin, no power beyond the law within nature itself may exist, for the world is circumscribed by time and space and there is nothing outside them. Time and space for Lenin are objectively real forms of being and our changing notions of them are merely a dialectical process by which we acquire an increasing knowledge of objective, absolute truth.[62] And Lenin asserts that ". . . the materialists, by recognizing the real world . . . as an objective reality, have the right to conclude therefrom that no human concept . . . is valid if it goes beyond the bounds of time and space. . . ."[63]

PSYCHOLOGICAL SIGNIFICANCE OF LENIN'S EPISTEMOLOGY

If Lenin's epistemology is regarded from the *psychological* rather than the philosophical point of view, further light may be thrown upon fundamental Bolshevik attitudes toward the world. In particular, the significance of Lenin's concept of law existing in external reality and demanding the conformity of men will be clarified.

For Lenin, men are entities distinct from the external world, and the law or necessity in it demands submission of them. Thus, authority is externalized in Lenin's view; it is found outside men in a law of nature not within men themselves. Men, according to Lenin, must reflect the external world and its law as accurately as possible. A close identification with external authority is thus demanded psychologically by Lenin's theory, especially his theory of reflection.

MATTER, SENSATION AND SCIENCE

Lenin's theory of reflection is, of course, integral to his epistemology which he says, in its insistence upon the materiality of the outside world, coincides with naive realism, the view of ordinary men who do not bother themselves with philosophy in order to prove that the world outside them is really there.[64] Further, Lenin insists that matter must be the starting point of epistemology since ". . . sensation depends . . . upon matter organized in a definite way."[65] But Lenin does not attempt to show how sensation becomes a property of matter or how matter devoid of sensation is related to matter capable of sensation; he contents himself merely with saying that this problem remains to be "investigated and reinvestigated."[66] However, Lenin is not deterred in his epistemological beliefs by this unanswered problem, since he asserts: "Materialism in full agreement with natural science takes matter as primary and regards consciousness, thought, sensation as secondary, because in its well-defined form sensation is associated only with the higher forms of matter."[67] He therefore insists that there can be no sensation disassociated from matter and also refers to science to defend his view. "Light rays," he says, "falling upon the retina produce the sensation of color. This means that outside us and of our minds, there exists a movement of matter, let us say of ether waves of a definite length and of a definite velocity, which acting upon the retina, produce in man the sensation of a particular color. This is precisely how natural science regards it."[68]

The Reliability of the Senses

However, regardless of how true and scientifically valid this description of seeing may be, it does not answer the question of whether our senses are reliable. A theory of knowledge investigates our beliefs in material things, beliefs based upon seeing and touching. It may seem, therefore, that science, particularly physiology, can tell us enough about seeing and touching and our other senses to explain what seeing and touching are in order to shed light upon our beliefs in material things. Science itself, however, is derived from observation based primarily upon seeing and touching and the other senses. Thus science cannot help in providing a justification for our beliefs concerning material objects or for a particular belief regarding a specific material object. The very truth of scientific descriptions depends upon the validity of empirical observations; therefore, such descriptions can not justify trust based upon empirical observations, nor can scientific descriptions ever allay doubts as to whether empirical observations are ever reliable. For to justify beliefs based upon observation means answering the question of whether or not beliefs based upon observation are themselves trustworthy.

All Lenin has done by appealing to science is to provide certain beliefs based upon observation regarding a retina and a brain. These beliefs themselves must be justified in the same way as our beliefs concerning the material objects we see and touch. The appeal to physiology cannot yield a method by which beliefs in physical objects can be justified; for epistemology must question the premises of physiology in the same way it questions knowledge about material objects. Physiology, or science in general, describes the causes of sensation. It does not provide an answer to the question of whether our senses are ever reliable. This is a problem for epistemology and Lenin's appeal to science does not solve it.[69] It merely reinforces his view that there is an external world existing objectively and independently of consciousness. Thus, Lenin must presuppose not only an objectively existing world but a world of objects of which we have knowledge. The individual, the subject, mankind, becomes a receptor and the existence of the knowing human subject and the sensations and ideas of which he is a receptor are based upon objective factors. The subject is fastened in a world the knowledge of which is seemingly accessible, without ambiguity, to all. In this way Lenin seems to eliminate the possibility of differing viewpoints or interpretations being equally valid. Science, which for Lenin is derived from the external world and provides accurate reflections of it, becomes an authoritarian principle to provide uniform criteria of validity—objective measures or standards to which the subjects must conform. However, Lenin's appeal to science, as previously pointed out, does not support his using the external world as a point of departure for his epistemology.

Social Being and Social Consciousness

Integral to Lenin's concept of freedom and necessity is his theory of reflection. This theory, when applied by Lenin to the social realm as he conceives it, is embraced by his concept of social consciousness. Although the concept of "consciousness" shall be further discussed in a description of Lenin's idea of history, here it shall be presented primarily as an extension of his epistemology in general and his theory of reflection in particular. This concept is the bridge between Lenin's epistemology and his theory of history; for the relationship between Lenin's philosophical materialism and his historical materialism may best be seen in the parallel between the relationship of matter to mind and social being to social consciousness. "Consciousness in general," says Lenin, "*reflects* being. It is impossible not to see its direct and *inseparable* connection with the principle of historical materialism; social consciousness *reflects* social being."[70]

Just as matter has an objective and independent existence outside of the minds that reflect it, social being has an objective and independent existence outside of its reflections in the mind. "Materialism in general," says Lenin, "recognizes objectively real being (matter) as independent of [the] consciousness, sensation, experience, etc., of humanity. Historical materialism recognizes social being as independent of the social consciousness of humanity. In both cases," he adds in order to make clear the distinction between objective reality and our concept of it, "consciousness is only the reflection of being, at best an approximately true (adequate, ideally exact) reflection of it."[71] Furthermore, just as sensation is not the reality existing outside us but only an image of it, social consciousness is merely an image of social being. It is not identical with it. "Social consciousness," Lenin repeats, "reflects social being. . . . A reflection may be an approximately true copy of the reflected but to speak of identity is absurd."[72]

Thus, even though the mind must reflect and "master" external reality, it can never reflect it exactly.

Berkeley and Lenin's Theory of Reflection

A significant part of Lenin's epistemology is given over to the theory of reflection, the theory that man acquires knowledge of the external world through copies, images or reflections of it. Berkeley, the eighteenth-century idealist philosopher to whom Lenin was so intransigently opposed, presented arguments against the theory of reflection to show that it is incompatible with a materialist philosophy. It was Berkeley's intention that idealist philosophy should then be left as an alternative to materialism. Berkeley's arguments cast doubt upon the claim, such as Lenin makes, that a theory of reflection can be used to justify the belief in an objectively, independently existing natural world and man's ability to acquire a knowledge of it. However, Berkeley's arguments are directed against the theory of reflection, and are destructive of the theory of reflection, not of materialism itself. Since Lenin was familiar with these arguments against the theory of reflection, it is extremely interesting that he did not reply to them.[73] He chose rather to reject Berkeley's idealism, claiming that the premises on which it is based lead to solipsism, the view that the self is the only thing really existing.[74] Even if it is true, however, that idealism does lead to solipsism, as Lenin charges, this does not affect the validity of Berkeley's arguments against a theory reflection. It is of the utmost significance, therefore, that Lenin did not reply to Berkeley's arguments, which show that the theory of reflection is incompatible with materialism.[75]

Significance of Lenin's Theory of Reflection: Doubt and the Need for a Mediator

It should be noted that an insistence upon the concept that sensations are images or reflections of material objects does not necessarily follow from beliefs in an objectively and independently existing external world. There are alternate views of perception which do not conflict with this concept of reality.[76] It should be borne in mind, however, that Lenin arrived at his epistemological position most directly through Marx and Engels, whose materialist conceptions formed the basis for his own. Lenin also worked out, clarified, and presented his theory of knowledge in *Materialism and Empirio-Criticism* after having first adopted and elaborated his Marxist political standpoint within the Russian revolutionary movement and the tsarist state. Lenin's theory of knowledge, therefore, may be assumed to be closely interwined with his politics and revolutionary activity. Moreover, as he himself states, his epistemology provides the basis for his theory of history.[77] His theory of history, in turn, is bound to his political action. It is therefore not unreasonable to assume that his epistemology, in its relationship to other tenets of Lenin's philosophy, has a political function. This statement is not intended in any way to imply that the concept of sensations as a reflection of an external world, must, or always does, function as for Lenin.[78] It merely means that within the dynamic relationship of all parts of Lenin's philosophy or ideology, within the dynamic relationships that form the whole of Lenin's philosophy or ideology, the theory of reflection, as he presents it, has a particular function. An attempt will therefore be made to show that this tenet of Lenin's epistemology functions politically and psychologically both to reinforce the authoritarian principle by which there can be only one view of the world and at the same time to engender doubt and uncertainty concerning the knowledge that can be acquired of that world. Although Lenin's theory of knowledge demands that man's consciousness reflect the external world of nature, it should be noted that man can never have a perfectly accurate copy of what he reflects. According to Lenin, this copy must be as accurate as possible a reflection of the objective model. That Lenin states the copy should be as accurate *as possible* indicates that degrees of accuracy exist and that inaccuracy of reflection is also possible. There is always room for error and therefore always room for doubt.

Further, it has also been pointed out that the world, in Lenin's theory of knowledge, is matter in motion governed by laws of development and change. Lenin's theory of reflection, therefore, demands that the mind reflect a constantly changing reality sometimes immanently containing dialectical growth and development. Thus the mind must dynamically grasp the ever unfolding moment and comprehend it by regarding the particular as part of a dynamically changing whole. This is far different from applying general principles to particular instances; it also leaves greater room for doubt.

Lenin's criterion of practice by which the validity of our perceptions of objects and processes is put to the test by human action provides a means by which doubt concerning perceptions may be allayed. This test, however, although theoretically possible for Lenin, is not always practically possible. In such cases the complexity of the observations required, the training or knowledge necessary to make them, and the skill demanded in order to interpret them, result in the need for a mediator between the object or the event and the ordinary man. This, however, does not mean that only a theory of perception such as Lenin's permits the need for a mediator. It merely suggests that his epistemology functions in this way and the fact that other theories of knowledge may make room for a mediator, or the fact that Lenin might have used another means to do so, does not lessen the significance of mediation in Lenin's theory. Further, an examination of Lenin's theory of history seems to support this view.

Therefore, having investigated Lenin's theory of knowledge as a source for fundamental concepts of Bolshevik ideology and having shown the significance of such concepts, attention will now be focused upon Lenin's theory of history. His theory of history will also be examined as a part of Bolshevik ideology and the significance of his idea of history shown. The author's concept of ideology will be more fully discussed and the significance of Lenin's theory of knowledge and theory of history as components of ideology will be presented. In doing this, parallels between the two theories will be revealed.

Lenin's Theory of History

Lenin's chief philosophical interest is not his theory of knowledge but his theory of history. His ultimate concern is with "the crowning structure of philosophical materialism . . . not with materialist epistemology but with the materialist conception of history."[79] The former is the basis of the latter[80] and historical materialism provides the ideological foundation for Lenin's revolutionary activity and for communist action.

In his theory of history, which he believed to be a "scientifically proven proposition," the only scientific conception of history,[81] Lenin regards society as having its basis in an economic formation which develops in accordance with a law of nature. Every historical period past and present, having its own particular economic base, has its own laws which are regarded as organic laws of natural history.[82] For economic life constitutes a phenomenon analogous to the history of evolution in other branches of biology and "social organisms differ among themselves as fundamentally as plants or animals."[83] Therefore, the scientific value of an inquiry into economic life, Lenin claims, "lies in disclosing the special (historical) laws that regulate the origin, existence, development and death of a given social organism and its replacement by another and higher organism."[84] In this way the laws of capitalist development lead to its evolution into communism. "The whole theory of Marx," says Lenin, "is an application of the theory of evolution in its most consistent, complete, well-considered and fruitful form — to modern capitalism. It was natural for Marx to raise the question of applying this theory both to the coming collapse of capitalism and to the future evolution of future communism."[85]

This evolution may or may not be, according to Lenin, a dialectical one. For in describing his materialist outlook he makes it clear that the method of historical materialism[86] does not consist of applying to history the Hegelian dialectic, the laws of the triad, i.e., thesis, antithesis, synthesis, or the negation and the negation of the negation. Lenin insists that materialists ". . . never dreamed of proving anything by Hegelian triads . . . and that the sole criterion of theory . . . [is] its conformity to reality. If, however, it sometimes happened that the development of some particular social phenomenon fitted in with the Hegelian scheme, namely, thesis, negation, negation of negation, there is nothing surprising in that, for it is no rare thing in nature at all."[87]

Lenin claims, therefore, that when the materialists analyze a natural or historical phenomenon in terms of the triad, it is because the triad objectively exists within the phenomenon. But, says Lenin, "to prove anything by triads is absurd," and "nobody ever thought of doing so."[88] Insofar as the historical materialist is concerned, Lenin asserts ". . . that not the idea but the external objective phenomenon alone can serve as its point of departure."[89] Lenin claims that an example of the negation of the negation is found in the development of capitalist's society and describes this process, according to Marx and Engels, as follows: Before capitalism there was petty industry based upon the ownership by the laborer of his means of production. Petty industry, however, became incompatible with the expansion of production and brought forth the material means for its own annihilation. The individual and scattered means of production were transformed into socially concentrated ones. The individual producers were expropriated and they who formerly worked individually now work together in factories where their labor is socialized. After the establishment of capitalism, the further socialization of labor, the further transformation of the means of production into capital, and the further expropriation of private proprietors take a new form. It is now the capitalists employing many laborers, rather than the individual producers who are expropriated. The ownership of the capitalist means of production thus becomes further concentrated. The number of capitalists grows smaller and their exploitation of the workers increases. As a result of capitalist production the working class grows in numbers and through employment in capitalist production becomes "disciplined, united and organized."[90] Capitalism, however, impairs the usefulness and fullness of production for all society. "Capitalism becomes a fetter upon the mode of production. . . . Concentrations of the means of production and socialization of labor at last reach a point where they become incompatible with their capitalist integument. The integument is burst asunder. . . . The expropriators are expropriated."[91] Such is what Lenin claims to be the historical development of capitalism.

Within that development dialectical and historical materialists claim to discern the negation of the negation. Lenin, quoting Engels, who in turn is quoting Marx, continues: "It is only . . . after Marx completed his proof on the basis of historical and economic facts that he proceeds, 'The capitalist mode of appropriation, the result of the capitalist mode of production, produces private property. This is the first negation of individual private property as founded on the labor of the proprietor. But capitalist production begets with the inexorability of a law of Nature, its own negation.' "[92] It is then pointed out that the negation of the negation was discovered through Marx's scientific investigation as existing immanently in the historical process. It is explained that Marx did not propose to demonstrate that the negation of the negation had to occur. It merely did occur. "Thus, by characterizing the process as the negation of the negation, Marx does not intend to prove that the [dialectical] process was historically necessary. On the contrary: only after he has proved from history that this process has partially already occurred, and partially must occur in the future, he in addition characterizes it as a process which develops in accordance with a definite dialectical law."[93] Therefore there is a claim that Marx does not apply a dialectical law to history but presents what he finds in the process of history as operating in accordance with a law he describes as dialectical. "The dialectical method does not consist in triads at all. . . ."[94] Rather ". . . the dialectical method . . . requires us to regard society as a living organism in its functioning and development."[95]

From Quantity to Quality

Associated with the dialectic is what Lenin claims to be another phenomenon which is sometimes found in nature and in history: the phenomenon of the change from quantity to quality. The world develops, according to Lenin, in such a way that quantitative changes taking place in it result in an organically qualitative transformation. An example of such transformations from quantity into quality is the development of capitalism into imperialism. "We have produced detailed statistics which reveal the extent to which bank capital, etc., has developed . . . showing . . . the transformation of quantity into quality, of developed capitalism into imperialism."[96] Another example of this transition from quantity into quality may be found, according to Lenin, in the transition from "bourgeois democracy" to the dictatorship of the proletariat: "Here 'quantity turns into quality,' such a degree of democracy is bound up with the abandonment of the framework of bourgeois society and the beginning of its Socialist reconstruction."[97] Thus, a sum of quantitative changes may result in a qualitative change in a thing, in a difference in its nature. These changes from quantity into quality are changes, Lenin claims, from a lower to a higher stage of development, so that change does not take place in a straight line of development but spirally. These changes, according to Lenin, may take place in leaps or in a sudden or violent transition from one form into another, from quantity into quality. Dialectical development, then, is described as "repeating the levels already passed through but repeating them differently on a higher basis (the negation of the negation), development, so to speak, in spirals and not in a straight line — development by leaps, castrophe, revolution — 'breaks in gradualness,' the transition of quantity into quality."[98]

"The internal impulses" to the development of society, the contradictions and conflicts in it, are expressed in the class struggle, which is the motive force of events.[99] Thus, in the constant changes in history, "Marxism provided a guiding thread to regularity . . . namely, the theory of the class struggle," which brings about the changes from quantity to quality in history and society.[100]

Spiral Development From Past To Future

The significance of the theory of the transition from quantity to quality, and especially of leaps, is that it does allow for development in a "spiral" fashion. The changes which take place immanently in society in accordance with the laws of nature and history do not lead merely to growth and development but to changes in kind. To use the organic analogy of historical materialism, it may be said that this type of change leads to the transition or transformation of one organism into a qualitatively different, more highly developed one. It permits evolution by sudden change — in the historical sense, by revolution, "days in which 20 years are concentrated."[101] Motion, therefore, is regarded ". . . not in the banal understanding of 'evolutionists' visualizing only slow changes, but dialectically. . . ."[102] Such changes, however, have their roots in the previously existing organism as it unfolds into the future, for "movement is regarded not only from the point of view of the past but also from the point of view of the future."[103] Hence, in the development of society the dialectical materialist discovers processes which have already occurred and others which (he believes) must occur; for "... if any social phenomena is examined in its process of development, relics of the past, foundations of the present and germs of the future will be found in it."[104] The future is bred by the present and the present dies within the future. "On the basis of what data can the future evolution of future Communism be considered?" asks Lenin, and replies: "On the basis of the fact that it *has its origin* in capitalism, that it develops historically from capitalism, that it is the result of the action of a social force to which capitalism *has given birth*."[105] Thus the question of communism is treated in the same way ". . . as a naturalist would treat the question of the evolution of, say, a new biological species, if he knew such was its origin, and such and such the direction in which it changed."[106] Lenin claims that in this way Marx, "while proving the necessity of the present order of things . . . at the same time proves the necessity for another which must necessarily grow out of the preceding one. . . ."[107] Moreover, the movement from one order to another, such as the development from capitalism to communism, is, according to Lenin, "governed by laws not only independent of human will, consciousness and intentions but rather, on the contrary, determining the will, consciousness and intentions of men."[108]

INEVITABILITY

Since the transition from capitalism to communism is governed by laws which also determine the consciousness of men, the question arises of why a party is necessary to lead, or organize, or teach, or guide the proletariat to bring about what is inevitable. Karl Federn, in his critical study of historical materialism, has argued: "If such laws (social laws) did exist, and if socialism were bound to come according to a law, then it would be quite unnecessary and in a sense impossible to demand what is bound to come to pass of necessity; if socialism really were the inevitable next stage in the evolution of society, there would be no need of a socialist theory and still less of a socialist party. Nobody is likely to found a party to bring about spring or summer."[109] Mr. Federn points out, therefore, in a particular context, that a claim to bring about the necessary is self-contradictory. However, Federn seems to overlook another context from which inevitability derives a meaning necessary to the understanding of Lenin, in which it is not contradictory to assert that the inevitable may be affected, accelerated or retarded. For example, it is inevitable that each human being must die, but he may commit suicide and so die before it is organically necessary, or in case of illness he may behave in such a way as to prolong his life or hasten his death. Further, it is necessary by the law of gravity that a man jumping from an airplane will fall, but he may use a parachute or not and so retard his speed or not. Thirdly, it may be said that the rate of colonization in North America during the nineteenth century was such that the

Indians would have necessarily lost their extensive hunting grounds and that because of the superior numbers of the settlers—the army, weapons and technology upon which they could draw—it might have been obvious both to settlers and Indians that the settlers would inevitably deprive the Indians of a large part of their lands. However evident this fact might have been, the settlers persisted in fighting to establish themselves while the Indians struggled against the intruders. It might also be added that if those settlers did not acquire the land others would have. In this sense, then, it may be argued that it is not contradictory to form a party to bring about the inevitable. If it is claimed that necessity or inevitability, in the Leninist sense, may be obviated if all members of society cease to function, it should be pointed out that, for Lenin, society devoid of motion ceases to be society at all, and laws of history are held to apply only to society.[110]

Since it is possible within the Leninist framework for man to bring about the inevitable, it is fruitful to examine Lenin's concept of the role of the individual in history. It has already been pointed out that for man, subject as he is, according to Lenin, to natural and historical laws, "Freedom is the result of necessity," and that this means man's will is not "free" unless subordinated to natural and historical law.

Nevertheless "the idea of historical necessity does not in the least undermine the role of the individual in history: all history is made up of the actions of individuals who are undoubtedly active figures."[111] Thus, man is no mere passive instrument of historical law, but must rather be an active participant in the fulfillment of those laws. Therefore, even though man does not possess free will, that is, the freedom to mold society in accordance with his desires rather than with the laws of nature, Lenin insists that man must still act in accordance with his reason and his conscience. He must be aware of natural and historical law and feel responsible for his role in their unfolding. Lenin asserts: "The idea of determinism which postulates that human acts are necessitated and rejects the absurd tale about free will, in no way destroys man's reason or conscience or appraisal of his actions. Quite the contrary, only the determinist view makes a strict and correct appraisal possible instead of attributing everything you please to free will."[112] The individual, then, according to Lenin, can appraise his acts with reference to their conformity with the objective model and law outside him. The concern of the individual should be, Lenin claims, to assess the concrete situation as it dynamically develops and unfolds itself so that he may act in such a way as to advance natural law. The individual must correctly reflect reality so that his conscious action will not be lost or nullified in the mass of non-conscious, spontaneous activity. "The real question," Lenin asserts, "that arises in appraising the social activity of an individual is: what conditions ensure the success of his actions, what guarantee is there that these actions will not remain an isolated act in a welter of contrary acts?"[113] Thus, for Lenin, as the use to which an object may be put is a test of the validity of our perceptions, so the success of our social actions are a test of our reflection of, our knowledge of, our understanding of, and our consciousness of the laws of history in the present moment and their development in the future. It is through consciousness that a knowledge of "necessity" is acquired and "freedom" obtained.

The Concepts Of Consciousness And Superstructure

Fundamental to the understanding of Lenin's concept of freedom and necessity, therefore, is an understanding of his concept of consciousness—especially of social consciousness, to which again attention will be turned. It has already been pointed out that Lenin insists that social consciousness reflects social being. Consciousness, however, differs from a mere reflection or from the process of perception itself. It comprises sensations, perceptions, ideas and thoughts. Consciousness is more than the sum of these; consciousness implies the purposive, practical activity of man, his anticipation of the future, and of the conditions and actions arising out of the objective reality his mind reflects. Consciousness, therefore, implies action, and the action it implies is the action by which natural or historical necessity may be obeyed and so controlled. To understand Lenin's concept of consciousness, however, it is fruitful to describe briefly his concept of the basis of society and its superstructure. Lenin, following Marx, makes a distinction between the economic structure of society, which he regards as its real foundation, and its legal, political, ideological, philosophical, etc., superstructure.[114] The economic structure of society is comprised by the relations of production, i.e., the relations into which men enter with one another in the processes of production; the processes of production in turn correspond to a definite stage in the development of the material forces of production. Since it is the sum total of the relations of production which forms the basis of society on which the legal, political, ideological, etc., forms rest, and to which consciousness corresponds. Lenin, quoting Marx, claims: "The mode of production of material life conditions the social, political and intellectual life process in general."[115] However, Lenin does not make the distinction between basis and superstructure because he believes the life of ideas and action played out in the superstructure have no effect upon history or no significance in it. Rather, he claims that the superstructure cannot serve as the point of approach for the study of history, for the superstructure is a result of consciousness, and he asserts that in the study of civilization "not the idea but the external objective phenomenon alone can serve as its point of departure."[116]

Although Lenin claims that changes in society are a process of natural history governed by laws which are independent of human consciousness and which determine the will, consciousness and intentions of men,[117] there is not, as previously pointed out, an identity between these laws and men's consciousness: "From the fact that in their intercourse men act as conscious beings it does not follow that social consciousness is identical with social being."[118] There is a dialectical relationship between them. According to Lenin, a man is aware of his own particular action in the social process but does not comprehend social being as a whole; nor does he comprehend his effect upon the whole. "Every individual producer in the world economic system," says Lenin, "realises that he is introducing a certain change into the technique of production; every owner realises that he exchanges certain products for others; but those producers and these owners do not realise that in doing so they are thereby changing social being."[119] An individual man, because his individual consciousness does not reflect social being as a whole, is not aware of how his individual action changes social being. Just as man does not comprehend the laws of nature all at once or in their entirety, but only in a relative, historically conditioned fashion, so man's social consciousness does not comprehend the complete significance of every change in social being. According to Lenin, "The sum total of these changes in all their ramifications could not be grasped even by seventy Marxes."[120] The sum total of the changes in social being which in their totality would equal social being in its absolute truth is reflected, then, only in relative truths. And the welter of these truths in all their meaning remains somewhat obscure when reflected in the intellectual or ideological life of society which are parts of the superstructure.

Nevertheless, even though the superstructure is subordinate to the material forces of production, it remains important and not to be underestimated in its significance. For when, according to Lenin, the economic foundations of society are changing and there is a conflict between the means of production and the relations of production, it is in part of the superstructure, the ideological form of society ". . . in which men become conscious of the conflict and fight it out."[121]

Such consciousness, however, does not imply a full realization or a foreknowledge of the particular events to take place.[122] Nevertheless if the welter of changes cannot be reflected in consciousness in their entirety, the general course and direction of these changes are known. "The paramount thing," says Lenin, "is that the laws of these changes have been discovered, that the objective logic of these changes and their historical development have at the bottom and in the main been disclosed. . . ."[123]

Consciousness, therefore, is a means of action which effects change, a means by which the general course and development of history is assisted towards its end. It is the means by which historical law is reflected and "mastered," the means by which "freedom" is derived from necessity.

The antithesis of consciousness, according to Lenin, is spontaneity. the lack of consciousness. Spontaneous action, such as strikes of workers for better conditions, strikes which have no political objectives intending to advance the class struggle or to assist in bringing about socialism, are deficient in consciousness. They are at best "consciousness in an embryonic form."[124]

Consciousness and the Class Struggle

Consciousness, however, is not a necessary and direct result of the proletarian class struggle; nor does it arise directly out of the structure of capitalist society. The class struggle and changes in the economic base merely create the conditions for socialist production, but they do not produce the consciousness of the necessity for socialism. Lenin quotes Kautsky[125] to assert that socialism, like the class struggle, is derived from the capitalist relations of production: "Of course, Socialism, as a theory, has its roots in a modern economic relationship in the same way as the class struggle of the proletariat has. . . . But Socialism and the class struggle arise side by side and not one out of the other."[126] Both arise out of the social process of capitalism but are parallel to each other, for socialist consciousness does not arise out of the class struggle itself. Continuing to quote Kautsky, Lenin asserts: "Modern Socialist consciousness can arise only on the basis of profound scientific knowledge."[127] This scientific knowledge, whether technological, economic, or political, is necessary for socialism and cannot be derived from the proletariat. "Indeed, modern economic science is as much a condition for Socialist production as, say, modern technology, and the proletariat can create neither the one, nor the other, no matter how much it may desire to do so. . . ."[128] It was not the proletariat that developed socialist consciousness but the middle class intellectuals who introduced it into the class struggle from outside. "The vehicles of science are not the proletariat but the bourgeois intelligentsia. . . . It was out of the heads of the members of this stratum that modern Socialism originated and it was they who communicated it to the more intellectually developed proletarians, who in their turn introduce it into the proletarian class struggle where conditions allow that to be done. Thus socialist consciousness is something introduced into the proletarian class struggle from without and not something that arose within it spontaneously. . . ."[129] Without the mediation of the intelligentsia, the proletariat, under capitalism in the last decade of the nineteenth century, according to Lenin, could not develop socialist consciousness. Lenin affirms, that Social Democratic[130] consciousness among the workers . . . could only be brought to them from without. The history of all countries shows that the working class, exclusively by its own effort, is able to develop only trade union consciousness. . . . The theory of Socialism, however, grew out of the philosophic, historical and economic theories that were elaborated by the educated representatives of the propertied classes, the intellectuals."[131] Lenin supports his assertions by reference to "objective conditions." The founders of modern scientific socialism, Marx and Engels themselves, he says, ". . . belonged to the bourgeois intelligentsia. Similarly, in Russia the theoretical doctrine of Social Democracy arose quite independently of the spontaneous growth of the labor movement; it arose as a natural and inevitable outcome of the development of ideas among the revolutionary intelligentsia."[132] However, it must be borne in mind that these ideas, according to Lenin, are derived from an independently existing, objective, external reality, for ". . . the course of ideas depends upon the course of things."[133]

Nevertheless it is very difficult to correctly reflect the course of things because of the complex, highly convoluted and ever changing nature of reality. In developing its consciousness, for example, the working class must comprehend not only its own class position but that of other classes of society in the actual conditions of their lives. Thus, "The consciousness of the masses of the workers cannot be genuine class consciousness unless the workers learn to observe from concrete and above all from topical political facts and events, every other social class and all the manifestations of the political and ethical life of these classes."[134] Further, these observations of the manifestations of the political and ethical life of other classes must be analyzed and evaluated by means of the materialist theory, for "the proletariat must learn to apply practically the materialist analysis and the materialist estimate of *all* aspects of the life and activity of all classes, strata and groups of the population."[135]

According to Lenin, therefore, the proletariat must correctly reflect the complex reality of the activity of all classes by means of the theory derived from that "reality." In order to act with consciousness, Lenin insists that ". . . a working man must have a clear picture in his mind of the economic nature and the social and political features of the landlord, of the priest. of the high state official and of the peasant, of the student and of the tramp."[136] The difficulty of comprehending the economic, social and political character of the various social strata is enhanced, however, because the real nature of these strata, according to Lenin, is disguised and hidden. Nevertheless the working man must penetrate below the manifestations to the reality. "He [the working man] must understand all the catchwords and sophisms by which each class and each stratum camouflages its egotistical strivings and its real nature; he must understand what interests certain institutions and certain laws reflect and how they are reflected."[137] This understanding and knowledge, Lenin asserts, is obtained from the concrete event, for the worker can procure this knowledge "only from living examples and exposures following hot after their occurrence of what goes on around us at a given moment."[138] "Exposure" of the workers to the activity and ideas of all strata, of all classes, according to Lenin, is an essential condition for training them in revolutionary activity.[139] This training of the workers is necessary because their spontaneously developing action or ideas, as already stated, do not lead to socialism or socialist consciousness. Therefore, "the spontaneity of the masses demands a mass of consciousness from the socialist intellectuals."[140] And as the workers rise against their employers and the state, this Marxist party of proletarian socialism must increase its efforts to imbue the workers with consciousness and to increase its own. "The more spontaneously the masses rise, the more widespread the movement becomes," says Lenin, "so much the more rapidly grows the demand for greater consciousness in the theoretical, political and organizational work of Social Democracy."[141]

According to Lenin, the worker, in struggling against his employer, would learn to oppose the capitalists as a class. For the ". . . struggle aimed at satisfying his immediate economic needs, at improving his material conditions . . . inevitably becomes a war not against individuals, but against a *class*."[142] Lenin claims that because "the exploitation of the factory proletariat is on a large scale, socialized and concentrated . . . the worker cannot fail to see that he is oppressed by *capital*, that his struggle has to be waged against the bourgeois *class*. . . . That is why the factory worker is none other than the foremost representative of the entire exploited population. And in order that he may fulfill his function of representative in an organized, sustained struggle . . . all that is needed is simply *to make him understand* his position, to make him understand the political and economic structure of the system that oppresses him, and the necessity and inevitability of class antagonisms under this system."[143]

Lenin therefore contends that in order for the proletariat to become the leader of all the "exploited" against the "class which opposes and crushes the working people, not only in the factories but everywhere, it must be made to understand its position in capitalist society and the necessity for the class struggle."[144] It was, according to Lenin, the function of the then Social Democratic Party to bring the consciousness of that struggle to the workers. Then, when the advanced representatives of the working class "have mastered the ideas of scientific socialism, the idea of the historical role of the Russian worker, when these ideas have become widespread . . . then the Russian WORKER . . . will lead the RUSSIAN PROLETARIAT (side by side with the proletariat of ALL COUNTRIES) . . . to THE VICTORIOUS COMMUNIST REVOLUTION."[145]

The transition from capitalism to communism is regarded by Lenin as a law of development of all capitalist countries. He also finds a development into capitalism from what he designates as earlier forms of society, for example, ". . . first there was primitive communism, then private property and then the capitalist socialization of labor. . . ."[146] The transition from capitalism to communism thus becomes a universal historical phenomenon. The diversity and variety of different European and non-European countries are reduced by Marxism to a common basis, where it exists, the capitalist social formation.[147] By reducing the complexity of society to its basis—the relations of production—Lenin claims that it is possible to apply to these relations the criterion of recurrence, for "the analysis of material social relations at once makes it possible to observe the recurrence and regularity and to generalize the systems of the various countries in the single fundamental concept: *social formation*."[148] Therefore the various nations can be compared with reference to features which recur in each of them, features common to the material forces of production. And such comparisons with reference to the claim that in the process of development of social phenomena there are germs of the future, lead the historical materialists to the belief that the capitalist formations of all countries will develop into communism through a "conscious" struggle led by a "conscious" party formed by socialist intellectuals whose "profound scientific knowledge" makes them the leaders of the proletariat.

Thus the socialist intelligentsia stands as mediator between the proletariat and external reality interpreting "the course of things." Bringing to the proletariat a knowledge of historical laws, it endows it with a consciousness which the proletariat cannot acquire *directly*. This consciousness gives rise to the action necessary to implement and fulfill the laws of history. However, even though consciousness assists in the fulfillment of historical laws, consciousness itself is a universal historical necessity, for Lenin, quoting Marx, asserts that "consciousness is a thing which the world must acquire whether it likes it or not."[149]

The Withering Away of the State

In capitalist society, which is characterized by the class struggle between the bourgeoisie and proletariat, "the state is the product and the manifestation of class antagonism."[150] The state is necessitated in this view because "class antagonisms cannot be reconciled."[151] Therefore, "the state is an organ of domination of a definite class . . .";[152] under capitalism it is the organ of domination of the bourgeoisie over the proletariat. As an organ of domination the state places itself above society and becomes ever more separated from it.[153] After the socialist revolution and the establishment of the dictatorship of the proletariat, the state remains but becomes an organ of domination by the proletariat over the bourgeoisie. The bourgeois state may be brought to an end by revolution, for ". . . force is the midwife of every old society which is pregnant with the new. . . ."[154] The proletarian state, however, cannot be brought to an end by revolution; it withers away.[155] Thus there is a final revolution and a state is established which will eliminate antagonisms among classes, since all its citizens will have the same relationship to the means of production.[156] Further, the state begins to wither away when armed forces separated from "the people" are no longer needed to subdue their suppressors; a majority dominates a minority. "And once a majority of the people itself suppresses its oppressors a 'special force' for suppression is no longer necessary. In this sense the state begins to wither away."[157] However, under socialism, before the "withering away," since human nature is what it is, the need for "subordination, control and managers" cannot be eliminated.[158] But, quoting Engels, Lenin argues: "All socialists are agreed that the state and political authority along with it will disappear as the result of the coming of the social revolution, i.e., that the public functions will lose their political character and be transformed into simple administrative functions of watching over social interests."[159] These administrative duties, when the state has withered away, will be performed by all citizens. There will be no division of labor into special bureaucratic functions but each man will be his own bureaucrat.[160] In this way, "Socialism . . . will develop into communism . . . side by side with this there will vanish all need of force, for the subjection of one man to another, and of one part of the population to another," for people will become habituated to doing without compulsion what society requires; "People will grow accustomed to observing the elementary conditions of social existence without force and without subjection."[161] No state, therefore, will be needed to provide an apparatus for compulsion because people will want to do what is required by society, they will have internalized external authority to such an extent that no compulsion will be necessary. Compulsion will have become self-compulsion and the state will have "withered away."

Thus Lenin, in his theory of history, regards society as having its basis in an economic formation which develops in accordance with a law of nature, spirally from lower to higher forms. These changes may occur dialectically and may take place in revolutionary leaps from quantity to quality. Each economic formation has a superstructure corresponding to it. Men, by conscious reflection of the laws of social being and through purposive action in the superstructure, may bring changes demanded by historical necessity. Capitalism, through the agency of the class struggle—in this case the struggle of the proletariat against the bourgeoisie—will lead ultimately to communism and the withering away of the state. Moreover, Lenin affirmed that the withering away would be a protracted process of unknown length.[162] Thus the goal of history and mankind in Lenin's theory, though not other-worldly, is future-oriented.

The Political Significance of Lenin's Theory of Knowledge and Lenin's Theory of History

If Lenin's theory of history is compared with his theory of knowledge, certain threads will be found to run through both. In his epistemology Lenin claims that nature has an objective existence outside men, that men must reflect the laws existing in nature and that they can never attain a knowledge of them directly. In his theory of history, Lenin claims that the economic formation of society develops in accordance with laws of nature, laws of which men acquire a knowledge not directly but, again, through reflections or copies in the mind. The independently existing laws governing both nature and history form an objective model to which their thoughts or perceptions must conform. This leads to an insistence upon correct reflections of reality and eliminates the possibility of equally valid but differing points of view. Nevertheless both Lenin's theory of knowledge and his theory of history demand that the reflections of the external objective model in consciousness be as accurate as possible.

Moreover, dialectics is the key to consciousness, for though Lenin insists that the materialist does not apply dialectics to a study of the external world, he also claims that it is often found in nature and society and that the "scientific" investigator examining objective reality should find it there when it exists. It is this task of consciousness also, the task of recognizing the dialectic process in nature and society, of grasping the dynamically unfolding moment and anticipating its future development, that makes the possession of a "correct" consciousness so difficult to acquire, especially since nothing can be perceived directly or exactly. Because of the intolerance of ambiguity which demands that consciousness reflect as accurately as possible an objective model, knowledge of which is often so difficult to acquire, doubt is engendered concerning the accuracy of the reflection perceived.

By the criterion of practice, by pragmatic test, Lenin claims that the accuracy of perception can be tested; but although this is theoretically possible, it is not always possible in practice. It is a simple matter to test the validity of the perception of a common everyday object; to test the accuracy of reflection of social consciousness and its correct anticipation of the future is a much more difficult task. Before the Revolution, in his theory of history, Lenin claimed, for example, that the proletariat could not foresee the coming of socialism; nor could it develop a socialist consciousness directly. Socialist consciousness had to be brought to the proletariat from the outside by a mediator—the socialist intelligentsia. In a subsequent chapter the political function of the concept of consciousness in relation to labor after the Revolution will be discussed. However, now in the socialist soviet state, "The leaders of the Communist Party can see not only how events unfold today but in what direction they shall unfold tomorrow."[163] The ordinary Soviet man, nevertheless does not possess a consciousness equivalent to that of his leaders, for "the party is the supreme embodiment of communist consciousness"[164] whereas "a lag is inherent in particular in the ordinary consciousness arising, forming and changing spontaneously in people under the influence of the surrounding conditions of life."[165] Those whose superior consciousness, therefore, provides them with a correct reflection of the present and a foresight of the future serve as mediators, or an elite, between reality and the minds of those who reflect it less successfully. The existence of an elite also supposes the existence of a large body of those who are less initiated. However, the consciousness of these ordinary men affects the acceleration or retardation of historical goals and they bear a share of the responsibility, not for the direction of history, but for the manner in which it reaches its goals. How this share of responsibility placed upon labor in the building of socialism is related to the formation of a moral approach to life will also be discussed subsequently.

Psychological Implications Of Lenin's Theory Of Knowledge And History

On the psychological level, Lenin's theory of knowledge and theory of history both demand obedience to a power outside man himself. In this way Lenin externalizes authority and the world seems to be seen in terms of dominance and submission, the dominance of external natural laws which serve as a model men must reflect and obey. An example of the emphasis upon the demand for identification with an external model is provided by the concept that the state shall wither away when compulsion or external authority become self-compulsion or internalized authority. There is difficulty, however, in closely identifying with the external model because knowledge of it cannot be directly or exactly acquired. Further, the model is often in a state of dialectical flux so that a degree of foresight is needed to comprehend and follow the process of its development.

The attempt to act in conformity with or to identify with a will or model that can never be wholly known can lead to feelings of insecurity since the identity demanded can never be fully achieved.

Also, since the reality of the world is increased for each of us by the knowledge that it is seen from different vantage points by others, the intolerance of ambiguity demanding that only one view of reality be regarded as correct serves to isolate and alienate man from the world and to increase his insecurity. One of the ways to attempt silencing this insecurity is to increase dependence upon external authority, to seek for a mediator, a teacher, guide or leader. In this way doubt can be removed concerning the knowledge of external authority so that *he knows* may precede the "I know," "I must," "I will," "I can." However, because the mediator himself presumably reflects an ever changing model, feelings of security could be more fully acquired by submission to his authority than by comprehension of his changing demands. Thus the "I know" may be eliminated and it becomes sufficient that *he knows, therefore I must, I will, I can.*

Another chapter will deal with modes by which Russian labor could allay its psychic insecurity.

Bolshevik Ideology

Lenin's theory of knowledge and his theory of history may be regarded as basic component parts of his ideology, and these component parts may be regarded as a set of theoretical assumptions for Bolshevism itself. Bolshevik ideology like other ideologies is given form and structure by its basic assumptions and theoretical framework. The assumptions and framework may differ from other ideologies on a basic or surface level.[166]

Ideologies which differ on a surface level have common assumptions and a common frame of reference, but may vary in particular judgments and particular explanations within that shared framework. Ideologies which differ on a basic level are built upon a different set of assumptions and have a different theoretical frame of reference, although their component parts need not be uniquely or discretely different from each other.

Further, the structure of an ideology sets limits and bounds to the thought framed within it, for the framework not only provides shape and form for the thinking of those who hold the ideology, but it provides boundaries beyond which it is difficult for their thought to go. Moreover, the basic assumptions of the ideology determine the criteria of validity in judgments applied to objects and events. The problems dealt with by an ideology are fitted into its basic structure and molded to fit into its theoretical gridwork. The data dealt with within the ideology are viewed from the vantage point of its own foundation. Moreover, there are data which the ideology tends to exclude because only with great difficulty could they be fitted into the theoretical structure.

Action is also explained and justified within the ideological framework and acquires within it a coherence and consistency that is not always apparent from the outside.[167] Indeed even seemingly contradictory explanations of action may be consistent and coherent within the structure of the ideology within which they are made. The Bolshevik assumption, for example, that the world is matter in motion constantly unfolding and changing lends itself particularly well to changes in line of action which can be consistently explained as being in conscious accord with the laws of nature and history. Seemingly contradictory but ideologically consistent interpretations of the past for the sake of present policy are facilitated by Lenin's concept of causality as part of a universal process in which the particular event may seem here to be a cause and there to be an effect. At the same time, however, arguments made within an ideology may be used in a manipulative manner to persuade or deceive. Thus it will be noted that the arguments, explanations and justifications made by the Bolsheviks to defend or advance their position in reference to Soviet labor were consistent with their ideology but were also sometimes in addition meant to manipulate labor toward party goals.

Having presented a description and discussion of Bolshevik ideology and its political and psychological significance, attention will now be turned to labor under the Provisional Government and particularly to the factory committees, the trade unions, workers' control and Bolshevik labor policy. Subsequently, the role of labor in the seizure of power and the conflict between labor and the party after the October Revolution will be discussed. The manner in which the Bolsheviks acted in conformity with Leninist ideology will also be clarified. In addition, through the history of Russian labor from 1917 to 1920 it will be possible to see how Russian labor experienced Bolshevik ideology and finally how a labor ethic in the sense of a morally colored conduct of life was developed.

CHAPTER II

Labor Under the Provisional Government

The Provisional Government and the Soviets of Workers' Deputies

When the tsarist government was overthrown Russia was engaged as one of the Allied Powers in the conduct of the First World War. The power that unseated the imperial government was generated by the action of all classes demanding a share in the power of the state that tsarism, ruling through bureaucracy, did not sufficiently allow them.

The revolutionary overthrow took place in the capital city of Petrograd—the city's garrison troops and workers who had organized themselves into the soviets (or councils) were directly instrumental in bringing about the revolution. The Provisional Government that was established was to govern until such time as a Constituent Assembly would be convoked to institute a new and permanent form of government. Since the Provisional Government functioned in conjunction with the revolutionary councils or the Soviets of Workers', Soldiers' and Peasants' Deputies, there was not one integrated state organization; rather, there were two sources of power by which the government was directed. The Provisional Government was the heir of the tsarist state and its administration. The Soviets of Deputies provided representation in the revolutionary government for those classes such as factory workers, which had been largely excluded from the representative institutions of the imperial government by the tsarist law of suffrage.[1] Thus, under the Provisional Government, franchise for the workers in the absence of a Constituent Assembly or other regularly constituted parliamentary body in which workers were represented was provided by the counciliar organization, the Soviets of Workers' Deputies. Since the Soviets of Deputies were led by the socialist parties, the Soviets also comprised the organs of those parties.

The two exponents of state power, the Provisional Government and the Soviets, at first pursued a policy of cooperation with one another and maintained direct liaison by means of a Contact Commission.[2] Not until 2 May did a conflict occur. Furthermore, this conflict was resolved by the decision of the Executive Committee of the Soviets, and a policy of cooperation seems to have been resumed.[3]

However, the coordination of wills that had made the February Revolution possible began to falter and the interests of the workers began to collide with those of the Provisional Government; for it did not implement the will of labor alone. The revolutionary goals of the government and the workers ceased to coincide. Thus the question arises: what were the revolutionary expectations of labor?

The Anticipation of Socialism

Unlike the Bolsheviks, the workers of Russia as workers did not leave behind them an articulated ideology by which their view of the world and their aims and purposes as a political group may be determined. It is fruitful nevertheless to discover what attitudes might have existed among the workers themselves during the revolutionary situation of 1917. Although it is not possible to determine accurately what those attitudes were, it is possible to infer what they were likely to have been by examining the influences to which the workers were exposed. Aside from the church and family, the principal influences among the workers, especially the workers of Petrograd, seem to have been those of the revolutionary intellectuals. Predominant among these revolutionary intellectuals were the Mensheviks and Bolsheviks who taught that the workers, because of their particular relations to machines and to each other, would be instrumental in bringing about a socialist order. Since factory production, they said, is not the result of individual effort but of the combined effort of many men tending machines together, this combined effort of the workers schools them for the social—or socialistic—means of production and assists in the process by which socialism inevitably emerges. Since both Mensheviks and Bolsheviks believed that the workers were an agency by which socialism would be introduced, both vied to lead the working class. Both Mensheviks and Bolsheviks, therefore, brought to the workers a single idea. To the revolutionary intellectuals this idea could have been sophisticated and complex, but to the uneducated workers it probably appeared simple and direct. One day socialism would inevitably arrive. One day the machines and factories would pass from the hands of the owners to the hands of the workers themselves. One day political power, too, would pass from the hands of the masters to the hands of the workers. On that day the workers would inherit the earth. The kingdom (*tsarstvo*) of socialism would begin. By such teaching, the Bolshevik and Menshevik intellectuals probably served to generalize the anticipation of socialism among the working class.

The Bolsheviks and Mensheviks, however, were not alone in bringing to the workers the anticipation of socialism. The Social Revolutionaries and the Anarchists, deriving their conclusions from different premises, also conveyed to the workers the hope and expectation of a new order in which all the rewards of labor would be theirs. The Social Revolutionaries, (or Socialist Revolutionaries) it is true, propagated their ideas chiefly among the peasants. However, peasant and worker very frequently maintained close ties in Russia[4] and the peasant background of the worker often served to prepare him for the socialist preachings of the Marxists. Nor should the teachings of the Anarchists be underestimated, even though they lacked a disciplined party organization.[5] There is reason to believe, then, that anticipation of socialism by 1917 had become general and widespread.[6]

Origin of the Factory Committees

More important than socialist teachings in determining the aims and purposes of labor in the revolution is the action taken by the workers themselves. However, since the workers acted often with the socialist parties, care must be taken to see where their purposes were the same and where they differed.

In addition to the soviets, labor organized for joint action in factory committees and trade unions. Since the factory committees played a decisive role in the seizure of power, attention will be focused first upon them.

The first factory committees seem to have been formed during the February Revolution in an attempt by workers to take administration of some state-owned and-managed enterprises, notably those of the Artillery Department, into their own hands. The Artillery Department, under the Provisional Government, refused, however, to provide the factory committees with the funds to operate industry as managers and the managerial staffs were maintained in their functions.[7]

In a conference of representatives of the Artillery Department—the owners and managers of factories under its jurisdiction, and representatives of the Ministry of Labor and the Soviets of Workers' and Soldiers' Deputies— the conflict between the factory committees and the Artillery Department was mitigated. The factory committees were recognized as bargaining agents for workers employed in factories under Artillery Department jurisdiction but they were deprived of the administrative scope they had tried to assume. Moreover, a resolution passed by the conference asserted that: "Until the time of the complete socialization of all the social economy, state and private, the workers do not take upon themselves the responsibility for the technical and administrative-economic organization of industry."[8] Thus it is evident that though the workers might look forward to a share in management under some future socialist order, they were not, at the time, to assume the direction of technical and administrative affairs of industry. Nevertheless, this statement implies that, in the anticipation of socialism, the workers did look forward to a share in managerial functions. It is indicative also of the apprehension of management concerning the administrative ambitions of labor.

Nor did labor abdicate its ambitions. At a conference of state factories invoked on the initiative of the workers of the Artillery Department on 15 April, the problem of workers' share in industrial management again appeared. In the resolutions passed at this conference, the factory committees were given a voice in the hiring and employment of managerial personnel and were permitted to examine the accounts and correspondence of the enterprise. However, administrative decisions remained in the hands of management and the factory committees could participate in them only by means of an "advisory vote."[9]

Nevertheless the resolution made it possible for the factory committees to become an effective overseer of management, although it is difficult to assess whether many of them actually became so. Furthermore, since the division between the advisory and practical functions of the committees was not clearcut, arguments might easily have arisen.

In addition, the factory committees of the state enterprises were to be united by a coordinating center, the Chief Committee which was empowered to call general meetings of the factory committees in state industry.[10] Thus it would have been possible for the Chief Committee to canalize or direct the policy of the member committees. By so doing, they could influence not only labor and managerial policies of state factories but through that influence could exert pressure upon the state itself in the political as well as economic sphere.

By April, collegial administration, or *kollegial'nost'*—defined as administration by factory committees whose members elected by the workers themselves were subject to recall—was established as a principle, though not a fact, of factory organization by the Organizational Bureau of the workers of the Artillery Department.[11]

Factory committees were established officially and legally by the Provisional Government, acting with the Soviets, in a decree of 23 April/6 May 1917. The committees were a modification of the law of 1903 which had legalized the institution of factory elders (*starosty*).[12] The purpose of the Provisional Government in issuing this decree seems to have been to increase the participation of the workers in the administration of the factories that employed them and to secure their cooperation in the solution of the difficult economic problems that faced the nation in the war and revolutionary situation.

Provisional Government Statutes on Factory Committees

According to the Statutes of the Provisional Government on Workers' Committees in Industrial Enterprises issued on 6 May 1917, workers' committees were to be instituted in all industrial establishments of every type, both state and privately owned.[13] It permitted that workers' committees could be established both for the entire institution as well as for various parts and branches, such as workshops, etc. (*tsekh, masterskaia*). The individual committees could be united into a chief committee and the workers' committees could be established either by the proposal of not less than one tenth of the workers or by a proposal on the part of the administration.[14]

The factory committee was to consist of members selected by the workers of the establishment on the basis of universal, direct and secret voting including women and minors.[15] For the elections to be valid not less than half of all the workers of the factory or a given branch of it had to participate in the voting and a list of the members elected had to be turned over to the administration.[16]

Members of the committee could be fired by the administration only by the decision of the conciliation or mediation commissions and by the consent of the committee itself. In the absence of a permanent conciliation commission the problem was to be decided by arbitration.[17]

The factory committees were to work out the instructions for the composition, scope and activity of the committee including its relations with the administration and arrangements for the elected members of the committee to be relieved of work while they were carrying out their obligations as members of the committees. These instructions had to be approved by a general council of workers.[18]

The instructions concerning the relations between the factory committees and the administration and the instructions concerning the relief of committee members from work for the sake of their duties on the committee were to be worked out at a joint meeting with representatives of the administration and established by mutual agreement of both sides.[19]

Under the competence of the workers' factory committees were: workers' representation in questions of wages, hours and conditions of labor; representation of labor with government and social institutions; cultural education work among the workers, and other such areas of activity. But according to Paragraph 10 of the statutes, individual workers were not deprived of the right of entering personally, for themselves, into negotiations with the administration.[20]

The factory committee retained the right to convoke meetings of the workers and the administration was responsible for providing it with a meeting place at the establishment.[21]

With the decision of the committee or the chairman of the meeting, individuals such as trade union representatives could attend,[22] but meetings were to take place outside working hours.[23]

The employees, or *sluzhashchie*—a term which in general refers to white collar workers but which can also include such employees as janitors—could form their own committees or, with the consent of the workers, participate on the same basis in the elections of the workers' committees.

The Statutes of the Provisional Government were intended, it seems, to bring about increased cooperation between labor and management. It would appear that the factory committees as established by the government were to increase the communication between the workers and administration, to give the workers a greater representation in matters affecting them such as wages and hours, and to permit the workers to take a more active role generally in the life of the factories. However, there is no indication that these statutes intended the workers to assume managerial functions or control the factories. Nor were the factory committees set up as the sole bargaining agents for labor, since, according to Paragraph 10, any laborer was permitted to bargain with the administration individually. It is probable, however, that the Soviets of Workers' Deputies, which seem to have been influential in promoting the statutes, intended not only that they increase the scope of labor in industry but that they train the workers for their new role under a bourgeois democratic state and for the future establishment of socialism.[24]

Since the factory committees seem to have been formed in both state and private enterprises and maintained relations with both the soviets and the parties, they were potentially key vehicles for political assaults by the parties upon the Provisional Government. Moreover, the committees could be manipulated into strengthening the power of the Soviets or they could be used as alternative organizations, as a source of power outside the Soviets.

To understand the function of the factory committees for the Bolshevik party, it is fruitful to present briefly the relationship of the party to the Provisional Government and to the Soviets.

The Bolsheviks and the Provisional Government

An examination of the writings of Lenin in the months immediately preceding the November Revolution indicates his goal was the overthrow of the Provisional Government and the seizure of power if possible by the Bolshevik party.[25] Lenin sought to prove by reference to the principles of historical materialism that the March Revolution, which had established the Provisional Government, was not an end of revolution but a beginning, and he advanced the idea that the March Revolution had ushered in only a transitional revolutionary stage which was to lead through a democratic republic to a socialist state.[26] Lenin, therefore, was advocating transfer of "All Power to the Soviets."[27] He argued that the transfer of power from the Provisional Government to the Soviets would signify the transfer of power from the landlords and bourgeoisie to the proletariat and poor peasantry.[28] It would represent a transition from the first stage to the second stage of the revolution. To reach the second stage, however, the Provisional Government would have to be removed. Moreover, Lenin argued by reference to the Soviets of Workers' Deputies and to the natural evolutionary law of history that the bourgeois-democratic stage—the Provisional Government—dialectically contained within itself, in embryo, the type of state that was to supersede it. He insisted that "Side by side with the Provisional Government, the government of the *bourgeoisie,* there has developed another government, weak and embryonic as yet, but undoubtedly an actually existing and growing government — the Soviets of Workers' and Soldiers' Deputies."[29]

To provide evidence for his claim that the Soviets were an embryonic form of the proletarian state, Lenin turned to history to interpret the contemporary situation; for by his theory of history the present can be expected to hold relics of the past and seeds of the future. He maintained, therefore, that a knowledge of the past stages of history and their development would reveal the significance of the present and its future development. Lenin advanced the idea that the Paris Commune of 1871 was the precursor of the proletarian state and the model upon which the future proletarian state was to be built. He saw, too, in the Soviets of Workers' and Soldiers' Deputies, the heirs of the Paris Commune. "This power," said Lenin, speaking of these Soviets, "is of exactly the same type as the Paris Commune of 1871."[30] Hence it was Lenin's intention to set the Soviets alone at the head of the state, in place of the Provisional Government and Soviets acting together. Thus, before the convocation of the Constituent Assembly, if it were indeed to meet as promised by the Provisional Government, the Soviets, within which the Bolsheviks had a voice, would control all the institutions, offices and properties of the state. The scope and function of the Bolshevik Party itself, therefore, would then be increased within the Soviets and, if the Bolsheviks could dominate the Soviets, it would be possible in that way to capture the state.

However, for the first few months after the March Revolution, the Bolshevik Party maintained only a minority position in the Soviets. At the All-Russian Congress of Soviets that had assembled on 16 June 1917 in Petrograd: "Out of 777 delegates giving information as to their party allegiance, 285 were Social Revolutionaries; 248, Mensheviks; 105, Bolsheviks; a few belonged to less important groups. The left wing — the Bolsheviks and Internationalists adhering to them — constituted less than a fifth of the delegates."[31]

Moreover, just as the Bolshevik Party maintained only a minority position in the Soviets, it was also outnumbered in the trade unions. At the Third Conference of Trade Unions, the Mensheviks and their adherents constituted 55.5 per cent and the Bolsheviks 36.4 per cent.[32] Thus it was particularly important for the Bolsheviks to find some organization of industrial workers from which they could derive political strength, for until the fall of 1917, they had only minor proletarian support. As Lenin pointed out, in May of 1917: "We are at present in a minority; the masses do not trust us yet."[33] Ideologically, however, as previously pointed out, the function of the Bolsheviks was not to express the spontaneous will of the proletariat but to bring it a Bolshevik consciousness of its historical position and to interpret the laws of nature and of history for the correct manipulation of events and conditions. The party was not to implement the demands of its adherents, but as a mediator between the workers and the laws of history was to act as ". . . the teacher, guide and leader of the toiling and exploited. . . ."[34] In this way it was to guide the proletariat to its historically inevitable goal.

However, even though popular support was not ideologically necessary for the seizure of power, from the point of view of the implementation of the program of the Party, lack of support of the existing proletarian organizations was a practical obstacle to the Party's objectives.

In this situation, the factory committees, interrelated as they were with the Provisional Government, the Soviets, and industry, could be of great value to the Bolsheviks.

Moreover, unlike the trade unions organized by trade, the factory committees were organizations of workers in various trades employed at the same factories. If the Bolshevik Party could unite the factory committees along industrial lines, they could then establish an organization functioning alongside the trade unions. This organization could be used to rival or gain control of the trade unions. United factory committees might also be used to dominate the Soviets and undermine the Provisional Government.

The First Conference of Factory Committees

The Central Committee and the Petrograd Committee of the Bolshevik Party, therefore, seem to have been the chief initiators of the First Conference of the Factory Committees of Petrograd and its Environs, which took place from 12 to 18 June 1917.[35] Furthermore, Bolshevik influence at the conference seems to have been preponderant; for it is claimed their Resolution on Measures for Struggle with the Economic Disorder was adopted by 297 votes out of 362.[36] At this conference the Bolsheviks strove to create a united organization of factory committees through which to implement their policies. The proclamation urging the workers to form factory committees and to unite them into a common center at the First Conference of Factory Committees of the City of Petrograd and its Environs suggest that only the workers can solve the economic difficulties of the nation; for "They who man the work-benches must save Revolutionary Russia. . . ." In order to eliminate economic disorder[37] the proclamation urges that the factory committees unite with other workers' organizations to institute workers' control of industry and to prepare for the First Factory Committee Conference.

The representation at the Conference was determined by its Organizational Bureau as follows: "The factory committees of all factories, shops and enterprises where the number of workers does not exceed 1,000 send 1 representative; factory committees with from 1,000 to 10,000 send 2 representatives; and more than 10,000, 3 representatives, all with the right of a deciding vote."[38] Railroad and postal telegraph committees were represented on the same basis.[39]

In addition to the factory committees, the representatives of other workers' organizations such as the cooperatives, the socialist parties, and the Central Bureau of Trade Unions attended the conference. Since these organizations, however, possessed only about ten votes in all, their representation was only nominal.[40]

One of the first objectives of the First Conference of Factory Committees of Petrograd and its Environs was the unification of factory committees through a common and permanent center of administration composed of 25 men.[41]

The Organizational Center of the factory committees was also to work together with the Central Bureau of Trade Unions for the purpose of instituting workers' control.[42]

Without defining the ways and means for the factory committees to cooperate with the Central Bureau of Trade Unions, the Resolution on the Organizational Center of Factory Committees adopted at the Conference stipulates that they are to work in close union with it. A close association of the Organizational Center of the factory committees with the trade unions could have served the factory committees and their Bolshevik leadership beneficially in two ways. First, it would have made it possible to acquire trade union support for various measures of factory committee policy. Secondly, it would have permitted the Bolsheviks to gain a greater hold in the trade unions themselves by bringing the two organizations closer together.

The attempt to work in unison would have tended to obscure the conflicts arising between the trade unions and the factory committees. These conflicts will be discussed below as they occurred in other conferences where the antagonism grew more intense. Even during the First Conference of the Factory Committees, however, trade union leaders suggested that the factory committees be subordinated to the unions.[43]

The principal problem to arise at this conference, aside from the unification of the committees, was the implementation of workers' control of industry. The two chief points of view on workers' control expressed at this conference are those of the Mensheviks and Bolsheviks.

The Mensheviks And Workers' Control

The Menshevik stand on workers' control is bound up with their view of the March Revolution and its function. The Mensheviks regarded the March Revolution as a bourgeois democratic revolution for the fuller development of capitalism. They believed it was and should be a revolution of the bourgeoisie to free itself from the restrictions of a bureaucratic state that hindered the accumulation of capital and impeded the development of production and exchange. Since socialism could be achieved only on the basis of a sufficiently well developed and centralized capitalist economy, they believed it was the function of labor to assist in the bourgeois democratic revolution. The Mensheviks maintained that once the bourgeois democratic state had been established, the proletariat could strive to organize as fully as possible to wage its necessary struggle with capital. Within the framework of the bourgeois democratic state, they believed, labor could prepare for the eventual proletarian revolution. However, the Mensheviks insisted that the proletariat could not achieve a political victory over the bourgeoisie until history should have created the material factors which in turn give rise to the actual and present necessity, and not merely the possibility, of putting an end to bourgeois methods of production. Moreover, they did not believe that such material conditions existed in the Russia of 1917. Any political victory of the proletariat over the bourgeoisie under premature conditions, the Mensheviks asserted, would be only a point in the process of the bourgeois revolution itself. It would be a victory *for* the bourgeoisie, not *over* the bourgeoisie. It could not be a starting point for a socialist transformation. Nor was the mere conquest of power itself proof of what they considered the maturity of society for the socialist revolution.[44] The Mensheviks thus placed more emphasis on the economic basis than the political superstructure whereas Lenin was to reason that the germ of the future state, the Soviets, could not have been found in the superstructure unless it had developed by historical necessity from the economic base.

Further, the Mensheviks believed the Provisional Government was a bourgeois democratic republic, and that the Constituent Assembly would also establish such a state. They believed, therefore, that this new republic should advance the work of centralizing and regulating industry in order to pave the way for the eventual proletarian socialist order. Although they had previously taken the position that capital should be freed from the restrictions of the state, the Mensheviks proposed, after the March Revolution, as a remedy for economic difficulties and in opposition to Bolshevik-sponsored workers' control, that industry should be controlled and regulated by the government in cooperation with the industrialists, management, and workers' organizations. Industry was to be subject to state control, not workers' control. "The regulation and control of industry," said the Menshevik Skobolev, Provisional Government Minister of Labor, speaking at the First Conference of Factory Committees, "is not a matter for a particular class. It is a task for the state. Upon the individual class, especially the working class, lies the responsibility for helping the state in its organizational work."[45]

Therefore, according to Skobolev—a spokesman for the government and his party—the workers were not to take control functions upon themselves. On the contrary, they were to cooperate with the bourgeois state in its industrial reorganization. Skobolev's speech indicates that the workers, in some cases, had already begun taking possession of the factories at which they had been employed and he declaims against this practice: "We are in the bourgeois stage of the revolution," he said, "The transfer of an enterprise into the hands of the people does not assist this revolution at present. By seizure of the factories and plants, by partial victories we can improve the economic position of the workers in a particular place but this does not solve the problem of the labor conditions of the working class."[46] Skobolev thus insisted that the workers must act in unison as a class, and that the confiscation of particular factories by particular groups of laborers could not improve labor conditions for the laboring class as a whole.

The Menshevik Dallin also expressed this view at the First Conference of Factory Committees, insisting that the factory committees and the government should work together to end the industrial crisis. He also warned against the appropriation of factories by the factory committees: "The factory committees must see only that production continues but they should not take production and the factories into their own hands. . . . If the owner discards the enterprise it must pass not to the hands of the workers but to the jurisdiction of the city or central government."[47] Thus Dallin emphasized that industrial enterprises were to be expropriated only in default of ownership and in such cases were to become the responsibility of either local or national authorities, not of the factory committees.

The resolution introduced by Cherevanin for the Organizational Committee of the Menshevik Party and for the Executive Committee of the Petrograd Soviet of Workers' and Soldiers' Deputies further elucidated the Menshevik point of view on the control of industry, a point of view supported by the Soviets.[48] In this resolution the Mensheviks insisted that "We can stop this growing catastrophe and return economic life to normal only by the planned interference of the state in economic life . . ." and demanded a regulated distribution by the state of raw materials, fuel and equipment to industry.[49] They also called for the regulated distribution of consumer goods to the population, control over banking, and the compulsory formation into trusts of basic branches of industry. They demanded the fixing of prices, profits and wages, and an increase of taxation on capitalist income.[50]

State regulation was to be by means of a system of central and local government control, i.e., a system of state control on a geographical basis. In addition, the Mensheviks proposed that other state organs regulate branches of production on an industrial basis and that not less than half of the members of these regulating institutions belong to the representatives of the workers and peasants.[51] These representatives, however, were to be drawn not only from the factory committees alone, but from all the workers' organizations and cooperatives.

The Mensheviks also demanded that the factory committees be integrated into the Soviets of Workers' Deputies and perhaps subordinated to it.[52] Through the Soviets, in which they then predominated, the Mensheviks claimed they would exert pressure upon the state, i.e., the Provisional Government, and force it into the regulation of industry.[53]

United Internationalists on Workers' Control

B. V. Avilov, a member of the United Internationalists, presented a viewpoint similar to that of the Mensheviks.[54] Avilov called for state control and regulation of prices, wages and distribution of goods. It was necessary, he said, to satisfy the capitalists and assure them their necessary profits. Otherwise, he charged, they would refuse completely to operate their enterprises. He urged that the factory committees work hand in hand with the Provisional Government. This, said Avilov, was the best way to preserve industry so that it would be transferred whole and strong to the hands of the "revolutionary" democracy at the proper time.[55] His resolution proposed also that: "All branches of heavy industry must be united into compulsory trusts under the control of the state and revolutionary democracy. . . . All trade and banks must be placed under the control of the state. . . ."[56] Avilov's resolution demanded that the factory committees oversee or "control" the administrative acquisition of raw materials, fuel and equipment, all of which were difficult to obtain in the wartime economy. The factory committees were also to take part in the wartime economy. The factory committees were also to take part in the supervision of production. They were to look after the production norm of the factory branches (*tsekh*) and were to participate in determining the price and net cost of products. They were also to assist in clarifying the conditions under which the enterprise was to be transferred to peacetime work.[57] But the resolution of the United Internationalists, like that of the Mensheviks, called for the cooperation of the factory committees with the state regulating organs and with the factory owners.

The Bolsheviks and Workers' Control

At this time, however, the Bolsheviks, did not consider that the control and regulation of industry should be in the hands of the state, namely, the Provisional Government. This was not the "control" of which the Bolsheviks were speaking. Lenin, for example, opposing Avilov's resolution, stated: "At present very many people speak about control; even those who earlier were ready to shout, 'Beware,' at the word control now recognize that control is necessary."[58]

Further, Lenin pointed out that there were varying concepts of control. The control about which his opponents were speaking was the nullification of control as Lenin conceived it. "But by means of this general word 'control' they actually want to bring it to nothing. The coalition government of which the 'socialists' are now part do nothing to achieve this control, and therefore it is completely understandable that the factory committees want real workers' control and not workers' control on paper only."[59]

Lenin explained that control was not to be exercised by the Provisional Government, which he regarded as an organ of domination by the bourgeoisie. "Arriving at an explanation of the concept of 'control,'" he said, "and also of the problem of when and who will achieve this control, we must not lose sight for a minute of the class character of the present state, which is only an organization of class domination."[60] For control over industry to be achieved, Lenin insisted that it should be implemented by workers' organizations, not the then existing state. "In order that control over industry really be achieved," he said, "it should be workers' control by which a majority of workers enter into all responsible institutions and in which management gives an account of its actions before all the most authoritative workers' organizations."[61]

Workers' control, therefore, as Lenin proposed it at the First Conference of Factory Committees, was to be a means by which the workers' organizations could hold management in check. It was a control which under the Provisional Government would be in opposition to state control rather than in conjunction with it.

The Bolshevik Resolution on Measures for Struggle with Economic Disorder also denied the possibility of alleviating what were considered to be the catastrophic economic conditions in wartime Russia. They denied that these conditions could be improved by working with state institutions and industrialists. This resolution was introduced by Zinoviev and adopted by 297 votes, with 21 votes against it and 44 abstentions. The resolution rejected the assistance of both the state and capital in the alleviation of economic disorder and asserted that if the workers and peasants were to acquire faith in the state, it would have to confiscate capitalist income and property and transfer that income and property into the hands of "the people,"[62] i.e., the workers and peasants.

The resolution also spoke equivocally of central institutions, rather than state institutions, managing control. "The road to salvation from catastrophe," it read, "lies only in the establishment of real workers' control over the production and distribution of products. For such control it is necessary (1) that in all central institutions managing this matter there be assured a majority for the workers' organizations. The trade unions, Soviets of Workers' Deputies and the Center of Factory Committees must be allotted not less than two-thirds of all votes with the compulsory participation of those enterprise owners who have not left their businesses and also with the participation of the technically and scientifically trained personnel. . . ."[63] The resolution defended the prerogatives of the factory committees as opposed to the trade unions, stating "that the factory committees as well as the trade unions receive the right to participate in the control over each enterprise. All trading and banking books must be open to them and all facts communicated to them."[64] Workers' control was to be extended to the financial and banking operations of the enterprise,[65] and was to embrace "the full regulation and distribution of products by the workers."[66]

Workers' management, however, posed a problem. It was the problem of how workers lacking in specialized managerial techniques could administer the industries they were supposed to "control." The Bolshevik Levin, for example, states: "The fact of the matter is that the control achieved by the factory workers' organizations in the majority of cases is extremely inferior and primitive because the workers do not have the appropriate technical and commercial knowledge that would allow them really to control industrial enterprises. . . ."[67] Levin proposed to remedy this situation by creating a bureau of technicians to be attached to an All-Russian Soviet of Factory Committees. These technicians were to be chosen from those who were devoted to the revolution rather than to capitalism and the principles of private property.[68] Thus even in practical matters the workers, according to the Bolsheviks, were in need of a mediator.

THE WORKERS' MILITIA

The resolution in effect proposed that, under workers' control in the hands of the factory committees led by the Bolsheviks, general labor service was to be instituted.[69] General labor service demanded the formation of a workers' militia that was to grow into a militia of all "the people." Such a labor service and militia, regarded as popular rather than bureaucratic, would serve as the foundation of the proletarian dictatorship and would characterize the new type of state, one like the Paris Commune that was to be formed, according to the Bolsheviks, by the Soviets of Workers' and Soldiers' Deputies. "Its fundamental characteristics," said Lenin, "are: (1) The source of power is not a law previously discussed and passed by parliament, but the direct initiative of the masses from below, in their localities—outright 'seizure,' to use a popular expression; (2) The direct arming of the whole people in place of the police and army, which are institutions separated from the people and opposed to the people; order in the state under such a power is maintained by the armed workers and peasants themselves, by the armed people itself; (3) Officials and bureaucrats are either displaced by the direct rule of the people or at least placed under special control. . . . "[70]

It has already been indicated that the factory committees by direct initiative were in some cases taking possession of their factories. The Bolsheviks' Resolution on the Measures for the Struggle with Economic Disorder proposed that workers' control by the factory committees was to eliminate bureaucratic administration.

Armed patrols of workers, the workers' militia known as Red Guards which came into being at the very beginning of the revolution, were closely associated with the factory committees.[71] An extract from the protocol of a factory committee states, for example: "The factory committee, after debate, unanimously accepts the following resolution: The commander (*sotnik*) of the militia, in his duties, is considered to be a full-fledged member of the factory committee."[72]

In this way, the workers' armed guards were becoming an integral part of the factory committees and the factory committees were building up a military arm with which to exert their authority.

Thus a centralized and unified organization of committees under the Bolshevik Party would not only have assisted the Bolsheviks in establishing an economic and organizational base for their power, but it would also have given them control of the armed guards or factory militia which were organized by the factory committees. Through these armed units of workers, workers' control could be enforced against managerial opposition, and by means of this militia, pressure could be exerted upon the Provisional Government. In making their decisions, the Provisional Government and the Soviets themselves, it would seem, would have had to keep the factory militia in view.

A resolution of the Central Bureau of the Central Committee of the Bolshevik Party proposed the support and extension of the workers' militia by the soviets. The resolution, dated 8 April 1917, stated: "The next and most important task of the Soviets . . . the party considers the general arming of the people and in particular the immediate creation of the workers' Red Guards throughout all the country."[73]

Bolshevik support for the workers' militia—the armed people—was opposed, however, by the Menshevik Party. An article appearing in *Rabochaia Gazeta* of 12 May 1917 is directed against Lenin's thesis that the police and army stand above the people and must be replaced by a militia defined as the armed people themselves. The Menshevik article asserts, ". . . we already pointed out that the militia, as the armed *people,* does not stand on the order of the day, since the army standing on the side of the people is in the present situation that armed people which guards the victory of the proletariat."[74]

An earlier article in *Rabochaia Gazeta* also opposed the Leninist thesis. It stated: "If by the militia one means *the armed people* replacing the army . . . then such a militia now is impossible and even unnecessary since we have already armed the people in the person of the . . . army adhering to the revolution."[75]

Ultimately, however, this quarrel hinged not upon the distinction between the armed people and the army, but upon fundamental political realities. The question was whether armed forces that were not integrated into the state structure of the Provisional Government should be allowed to function. The question was whether the workers' organizations, especially the factory committees, should be permitted to maintain armed forces outside of the direct jurisdiction of the state. It was a problem that was to be intimately involved with the factory committees, workers' control, and the Bolshevik Party.

The Bolsheviks and the First Factory Committee Conference

Thus the chief problems to be discussed at the First Conference of Factory Committees were those of workers' control, the militia, and the unification of the factory committees. In all cases, according to the sources available, the Bolshevik resolutions were supported by large majorities. It is significant to note here that, according to the Bolshevik Riazanov, at least half the factory committees represented at the conference were from the metal-working industry,[76] for it was among the metal workers that the Bolsheviks found their principal support.[77] In any case, the Bolsheviks successfully dominated the conference, and it may be said to have become a vehicle for their policy.

The Third Conference of Trade Unions

From 3 to 11 July 1917, shortly before the "July days" of 16-17 July and shortly after the First Conference of Factory Committees of Petrograd and its Environs, the Third Conference of Trade Unions met in that city. The decision to convoke this session was made at a meeting of the Workers' Section of the All-Russian Council of Soviets that took place in Petrograd in April 1917.[78] The initiative for reaching this decision was provided by the members of the Organizational Committee elected by the Second Conference of Trade Unions in 1906 for the convocation of trade union congresses. This committee actually ceased to exist in 1909. After the Revolution of 1917, however, those members of the committee who had returned from exile and emigration decided to fulfill the obligations laid upon them by the trade union organizations eleven years earlier.[79]

The Branch of Labor of the Petrograd Soviet was entrusted with the implementation of the decision to convoke the Third All-Russian Conference of Trade Unions and in the middle of July a meeting of the Petrograd and Moscow Central Bureaus of Trade Unions was called. Here a new organizational committee was formed under the chairmanship of the Menshevik Kol'tsov.[80]

At the time of the Third Conference of Trade Unions there were 967 unions and 5 Bureaus of Trade Unions.[81] At the conference, as previously pointed out, 55.5 per cent of the representatives were made up of Mensheviks and their supporters, while the Bolsheviks and their adherents composed 36.4 per cent. The conference was marked by a bitter struggle between the factions (or fractions).[82] One of its most important concerns was the relationship between the trade unions and factory committees.

The Trade Unions and Factory Committees

A Resolution on "The Mutual Relations between the Trade Unions and Factory Committees" adopted by the Third Conference and presented by the Mensheviks Garvy and Astrov in accordance with the report of the Bolshevik N. Glebov (Glebov-Avilov) seems to represent a compromise of Bolshevik and Menshevik views.[83] This resolution emphasizes the role of the factory committees in enforcing the rights acquired for labor by the trade unions. It relegates the economic-administrative control functions of the factory committees to a secondary place. As the Menshevik Garvy pointed out, if the trade unions functioned to control and regulate the economy, they might cease to protect the interests of labor. "Imagine," said Garvy, "that we shall take all the regulation of the economy under our jurisdiction and give the guiding role to the trade unions—what would happen? I think that the union would then try to see that there are no strikes. In other words, I am afraid that the activity of the unions as organizations [having as their purpose] the defense of labor will be paralyzed."[84]

Furthermore, the Resolution on the Control over Production and Distribution and the Organization of Production in Russia adopted by the largely Menshevik Third Trade Union Conference did not attempt to arrogate the economic control functions of the factory committees to the trade unions. On the contrary, it provided that the factory committees would share their control functions over management with representatives of the government, soviets, trade unions and even the representatives of trade and industry.[85]

The Resolution on the Mutual Relations between the Trade Unions and the Factory Committees adopted by the Third Conference of Trade Unions states in Paragraph 3: "In the matter of control over production, an exceptionally significant role falls upon the factory committees. The trade unions, defending the rights and interests of hired labor . . . cannot take upon themselves administrative-economic functions in production.[86] Thus the resolution acts upon Garvy's thesis that the trade unions, assuming administrative-economic functions, might neglect the defense and advancement of the rights of labor. It seems to regard the trade unions as spokesmen for the interests of the working class, particularly in a political sense.

Paragraph 4 of the same resolution regards the control functions of the factory committees as the enforcement of labor legislation and collective agreements. Executing these duties, they were to be the basic cells of the trade unions, and according to Paragraph 5: "The factory committees are the first instances of control both over the observations of the laws for the defense of labor and for the observation of the collective agreements concluded by the union."[87]

The resolution also provided that the elections to the factory committees were to be conducted under the guidance of the trade unions. The unions were to attempt to enroll all the members of the factory committee who were not union members. The factory committees, in turn, were to agitate for the entrance of all the workers of the enterprise into the union. They were also to "increase the authority of the unions in the eyes of the unorganized workers."[88]

Thus the factory committees, according to the Menshevik resolution, insofar as they were distinct from the trade unions, were to engage in control over the economic and administrative aspects of their factories. Insofar as they were to be the lower organs of the trade unions, however, they were to execute union policy for the protection of labor. Consequently, this resolution on the whole tended to minimize the functions of control to be fulfilled by the factory committees.

In his thesis on the relationship between the trade unions and factory committees, Glebov-Avilov proposed for the Bolsheviks that the function of labor in the control and regulation of industry should be fulfilled by an economic control apparatus made up of representatives of factory committees attached to the trade unions. "For the correct and successful implementation of workers' control," said Glebov-Avilov, "we must create an economic control apparatus attached to the trade unions to carry out the control and regulation of production. But . . . this economic control apparatus must consist of the representatives of the factory committees."[89]

The Bolshevik Theses on the Role and Relationship of the Trade Unions and Factory Committees in the Regulation of Industry attempted actually to define workers' control as well as the role and function of both the factory committees and trade unions in that control. Paragraph 5 of the theses requires that for the conduct of workers' control, economic control commissions were to be attached to the central administrations of the unions. These commissions were to be made up of the members of the factory committees and were to cooperate with the latter at the individual enterprises.[90] Thus the trade unions were to make use of the factory committees as a means of directing workers' control on the factory level.

The factory committees were to be the basic cells of the trade unions and their work at the individual enterprises was to be under the direction of the economic control commission of the unions.[91]

In his speech on the relationship of the factory committees to the trade unions, Glebov-Avilov emphasized that the factory committees should be integrated into the trade union functions of control, but he warned against the alienation of the factory committees.[92] Thus it would seem that Glebov-Avilov was not only trying to gain the leadership of the trade unions for the Bolsheviks through the factory committees but was also attempting to absorb the utility of the factory committees by integrating them into the trade unions.

The Bolshevik Glebov-Avilov therefore made objections to the attempt of the Bolshevik-led Central Soviet of Factory Committees to acquire independent financial support for itself. He indicated that the factory committees were not only to perform control functions for the trade unions but were to be financially dependent upon the unions as well.[93]

According to Paragraph 3 of the Theses on the Role and Relationship of the Trade Unions and Factory Committees, workers' control was to be achieved by alloting a majority of votes to the workers' organizations in the Economic Council, the state organ created by the Provisional Government for the regulation of industry. The Economic Council, which began its work early in August, was to function as a kind of legislative body for all questions of economic policy. It provided representation for the various ministries of the government, organizations representing trade, industry and banking, as well as other economic agencies and institutions. Labor was represented by delegates from the Central Bureau of Trade Unions and the Soviets of Workers' and Soldiers' Deputies. The factory committees were not represented at all.[94]

Paragraph 3 of the Bolshevik Theses read: "Control over production cannot be achieved by bureaucratic means, nor by the creation of institutions where the majority is in the hands of the capitalists. It is necessary to establish real workers' control over production and distribution. For this a majority of votes must be reserved for labor in the Economic Council which is at the head of the organization of the national economy and labor."[95] Thus, according to this proposal, workers' control was to be carried out through an agency of the state in which the workers were to have majority representation.

According to the theses the factory committees were to be organizationally subordinate to the trade unions, for the factory committee conferences were to be convoked by the local or central organs of the trade unions, not by the Central Council of Factory Committees.[96] Workers' control on an All-Russian scale was to be carried out by the All-Russian organs of the trade unions and the economic control commissions attached to them.[97]

The theses took care explicitly to safeguard the role of the trade unions in workers' control even on the factory level. According to Paragraph 4, workers' control in each particular enterprise was to be exercised not by the factory committees independently, but by the factory committees through the trade unions. Workers' control, however, was to require that all the books of the enterprise and all data concerning it were to be made available to the factory committees.[98]

Furthermore, according to Paragraph 8, the factory committees were to "carry on the work to strengthen and extend the trade unions and to contribute to the unity of their fighting action."[99]

Thus, if these theses are valid, at the trade union conference Glebov-Avilov as a Bolshevik sought to minimize and obscure the threat the factory committees could be to the primacy of the trade unions. The Glebov-Avilov resolution seemed to be extending the functions of workers' control into the province of the unions, for the factory commttees were to be the means by which the unions were to implement workers' control at the individual factories. Nevertheless, the Bolsheviks seem to have been simultaneously fostering the formation of an independent centralized organization of factory committees under the Bolshevik-led Central Soviet of Factory Committees. While seemingly attempting to assuage trade union fears of factory committee rivalry, the Bolsheviks appear, however, to have been confronting labor with a problem of divided loyalty, loyalty to the factory committees and loyalty to the trade unions.

The Menshevik Grinevich, speaking of Glebov-Avilov's theses, warned that the policy enunciated in them would undermine the trade unions by creating an organization of factory committees independent of them.[100]

Grinevich objected to the unification of the factory committees and objected simultaneously that the committees unified only workers of individual factories rather than all the workers of a trade or industry;[101] for by their very system of organization, based on the unification by enterprise rather than by trade, the factory committees, if unified, could set up a competitive workers' organization. This was further complicated by the fact that the Third All-Russian

Trade Union Conference itself had promulgated its intention to form industrial rather than trade unions. Grinevich himself had supported this policy and the conference had adopted a Resolution on Organizational Structure, in accordance with the report of his fellow Menshevik, P. Kolokol'nikov, Paragraph 4 of which stated: "The workers must be organized not by division and branch but by industry so that all the workers of an enterprise, even those belonging to different trades and even industries, will belong to the union."[102]

However, both Bolshevik and Menshevik delegates at the Third Trade Union Conference emphasized the necessity of restricting the scope and area of the industrial unions. They asserted that the process of converting trade unions into industrial unions had of necessity to be slow, and they pointed out that the assignment of various disputed trades to the appropriate unions had to be dealt with carefully.[103]

Grinevich, however, charged the factory committees with being more inclusive than the industrial union. He seems to have assumed that a union of factory committees would unite labor into one general union rather than into unions based on specific industries.[104]

Trade Unions and Factory Committees at the Second Conference

The relationship between the trade unions and the factory committees remained a problem at the Second Conference of Factory Committees of Petrograd, its Environs and Neighboring Provinces, which took place at the Smolnyi Institute from 20 to 25 August 1917.

Lozovsky, then a Bolshevik trade union leader, pointed out at this conference that "the boundaries between the activity of the factory committees and trade unions are not clear to us and we must define them exactly, since, in practice, the disagreements which are constantly possible can do great harm."[105] Lozovsky further pointed out that the trade unions were broader organs uniting the workers by trade in a horizontal fashion, whereas the factory committees were smaller, local organs uniting them by industry vertically.[106] Thus, according to Lozovsky, the factory committees functioning chiefly within the individual factory ". . . are part of the trade union movement. They carry out the decrees of the union in the localities and must draw the broad masses into the trade unions."[107]

The Second Conference of Factory Committees made a definite

attempt to construct an efficiently working center of united factory committees by resolving that a deduction of 1/4 of 1 per cent of the wages of the workers represented by factory committees was to be made for the support of the Central Soviet of Factory Committees.[108] This was to give the Central Soviet a means of support independent of the state and the trade unions.

The Central Soviet of Factory Committees

The Second Conference also validated Instructions to the Central Soviet of Factory Committees. These instructions determined the organization and operation of the council (soviet).

Nevertheless, the initiative and enthusiasm for unifying and centralizing the factory committees does not seem to have grown from below. Skrypnik, a Bolshevik, in speaking of the difficulties facing the organization of a Central Council, pointed out the indifference of the factory committees to the central organ. He stated: "The work of the Central Soviet is seriously hindered by the lack of personnel. However, this in turn is caused by many reasons depending partly upon the workers themselves."[109] Skrypnik charged that the factory committees had been reluctant to free their members for work in the center. He also observed that "Some members of the factory committees . . . refrained from participation in the Central Soviet because of Bolshevik predominance in it. . . ."[110] Skrypnik's remark therefore indicates that some of the factory committees might have hesitated to join the unified factory committee organization for fear of supporting Bolshevik objectives thereby. It also seems to indicate that the factory committees might have been reluctant to decrease their effectiveness in the individual factories by delegating their members to the central organ.

Building up the Central Soviet seems to have been a serious problem. Kozitskii, in agitating for delegation of personnel to work permanently at the center, stated that "without permanent workers it is impossible to maintain our prestige. We must give every thing to the Central Soviet; we must send active people there . . . we must provide means for the payment . . . of specialists."[111] Thus the available sources indicate that the Central Soviet of Factory Committees was created by the Bolshevik leadership in spite of a noteworthy resistance to the center on the part of the individual factory committees. The Bolsheviks, however, seem to have wanted to strengthen the Central Council so that they could manipulate a workers' organization capable of taking a place alongside the trade unions and in opposition to other non-labor organizations. As the Bolshevik Rosenstein pointed out: ". . . there must be a center regulating all the activity of the committees. It will also send representatives to various commission . . . where by regular attendance we can achieve some measure of success."[112] The Central Soviet, therefore, was to be a stable and permanent organization, taking its place in the political and economic life of Russia.

Paragraph 6, Part 1, of the Instructions to the Central Soviet passed by the Second Conference of Factory Committees provides that all members of factory committees who are members of the Central Soviet must be detached from their committees, "members of the praesidium for permanent work and the remaining members for daily attendance. . . ."[113] In this way a permanent, fulltime staff was to be created for the Central Soviet.

Note 2 to this paragraph provides that the members of the Central Soviet be paid by the enterprise at which they had worked. Their salaries were to be on the same scale as those of other members of their factory committees.[114] This system of payment led to conflicts between the factory committees and the factory administrations, conflicts which had arisen even before the Second Conference; for the factory owners had begun to demand that the members of the Central Council return to their work at the factories. Since almost all the members of the council, as skilled workers, were deferred from military service, the factory managements threatened to cancel these deferments unless the council members returned. This, indeed, became such a serious problem that a special conference was called to attempt to solve it.[115]

The Central Council of Factory Committees, however, was presumably to keep in close touch with the individual factory committees, for Note 1 to Paragraph 6, Part 1 of the Instructions to the Central Council stipulated: "Each member of the Central Council must periodically make a report to his own factory committee and region [*raion*] on the course of work of the Central Council."[116]

The Central Council itself was to be guided by its praesidium. Paragraph 7, Part 1, of the instructions provided: "The Central Council of Factory Committees elects from among its members a praesidium composed of the chairman of the Central Council, a treasurer, two secretaries and three members of the praesidium whose number is established by decree of the Central Council."[117]

A note to Paragraph 7 stipulating that the secretary need not be a member of the Central Council but might be an individual who enjoyed their trust may again be indicative of the factory committees' need for personnel possessing administrative skills. Such council members could also be individuals drawn from the party membership.

It was the function of the praesidium to convoke the meetings of the Central Council, to determine the business it was to discuss[118] and to execute the decrees of the Central Council.[119] Between meetings of the Central Council, it was to take care of all urgent matters that arose.[120] In addition, the praesiduim was "to represent the Central Council in various institutions and conferences except when the Central Council entrusts its representation in any institution or conference to a special elected individual."[121] These individuals, however, were not to act without the sanction of the Central Council itself;[122] and were to keep the praesidium of the Central Council informed of the work of the conferences or institutions in which they participated.[123]

The Central Council of Trade Unions was empowered with the right to convoke "conferences of factory committees by branch of production together with the corresponding trade unions."[124] Specifically, this was the function of the Central Council Commission on Communication and Personnel. The council also included an Economic Commission which was to manage its economy and purchase its inventory. A Financial Commission was to draw up the budget and manage other financial matters. In addition, there was a Literary Editorial Commission for composing and editing the proclamations and appeals of the Central Council, and an Agitation Commission to deliver lectures, reports and speeches concerning the problems of workers' control and the Central Council of Factory Committees.

In accordance with the resolution of the Third Conference of Trade Unions, however, the unions were to leave the administrative-economic functions of control to the factory committees,[125] for Paragraph 20 of the Instructions to the Central Council provided that the unions were to handle conflicts between labor and management, and the factory committees were to intervene only where workers' control of the enterprise became imminent.[126] In such cases, after preliminary investigation, if the praesidium or all of the Central Council considered it necessary, a commission for the control of the enterprise was to be formed. This commission was to act in accordance with specially worked out instructions.[127]

Although the trade unions and factory committees were to work together, the particular sphere of activity of each was to be kept separate and distinct.[128] The Central Council was also to be guided by the decisions of the trade union organization in all questions concerning the trade union struggle, and delegates of the Central Bureau of Trade Unions were to participate in the work of the Central Council of Factory Committees.[129] Moreover, Paragraph 29 provided that "All members of the Central Council of Factory Committees must be members of the trade union of their own branch of production."[130]

For the purpose of the fusion of the activity of the factory committees and their Central Council with the trade unions and their Central Bureau, these two central organizations were to organize conferences of factory committees by industry[131] and the trade unions were to participate in these conferences.[132]

Thus, according to the Instructions to the Central Council of Factory Committees, close relations were to be maintained between the trade unions and the factory committees. They were to coordinate their work, yet each type of organization was to have a special sphere of its own. It must be borne in mind, however, that in the constantly changing and uncoordinated conditions of the revolutionary era, it was easier to form resolutions and instructions than to execute them. Such documents should serve, therefore, as evidence of the intentions of the groups that formulated them, rather than as descriptions of situations that were actually created.

The instructions provided also that the Central Council was to be politically guided by the Soviets of Workers' and Soldiers' Deputies for: "In the analysis of problems . . . having a political character the Central Council is guided by the decisions of the political organization of the working class, in every way avoiding coming out in the role of an independent guide."[133] But the Central Council, since it could nevertheless not turn away from the political life of the workers, was to set itself the task of unifying the factory committees.[134] It will become apparent later in this account of the factory committees, however, that the Bolsheviks did not hesitate to use the committees in a concrete and real political sense.

Even before the Second Conference of Factory Committees the Central Council had participated in the work of various economic organizations and state agencies concerned with the regulation of the economy. It is claimed that its constant policy was to object to a minority position and to attempt to secure two-thirds of the representation.[135] It was a member of the various official organizations concerned with labor, defense and supply.[136]

Statutes on the Factory Committees

In addition to the formulation on the Instructions to the Central Council of Factory Committees and the consequent strengthening of the labor organization, another major accomplishment of the Second Conference was the adoption of statutes for the regulation of the committees. The statutes as they are presented in *Oktiabr'skaia Revoliutsiia i Fabzavkomy* are not those actually adopted by the conference; they are, rather, an edited version belonging to the Central Council.[137] A preface appended to the statutes also emphasizes the auxiliary role the factory committees were to play in reference to the trade unions and the Soviets.[138] The statutes, therefore, may serve more to illustrate what the Bolsheviks believed the factory committees should have been before October than as an example of what they actually were at the time of the Second Conference.

The organs of the workers and employees of a factory, according to Paragraph 3 of the Statutes on the Factory Committees, were defined as: (1) the general council, i.e., the meeting of the workers and employees as a whole; (2) partial councils, which were councils of various departments of the factory; (3) the factory committee; and (4) the special committees set up by the factory committee itself.[139]

Paragraph 4 defined the general council as the highest organ of the workers' factory organization to which all parts of that organization were to be subordinate. The general council was invested with full power to decide all problems concerning the workers and employees of a given enterprise,[140] but its decisions could be set aside, according to Paragraph 32, by the Central Council of Factory Committees.[141]

Paragraph 5 stipulated that the general council could be convoked by the factory committee, by the committee of one or more of the departments, or at the demand of one-fifth of the workers of the enterprise. If the factory committee refused to convoke the general council, it could be convoked by special initiative.[142] Thus, the factory committee presumably could not maintain its own power by suppression of the general council. The latter could always be convoked through workers' initiative.

If, however, a meeting of the general council was dissolved because of insufficient attendance (less than one-third of all the workers), a second meeting became valid no matter how small the number of workers present.[143] Hence the workers could not boycott a meeting of the general council without making the second meeting valid. The decrees of such a meeting would also have been binding since such decrees could be passed by a simple majority.[144]

The factory management, in a manner similar to the statutes of the Provisional Government, was obliged to provide the space for the meeting of the general council. The meeting was to take place after working hours; only in exceptional cases could the meeting occur during working hours.[145]

Furthermore, ". . . individual experts, representatives of the trade unions, of the parties, and other workers' organizations, could participate in the general council with an advisory vote by invitation of the factory committee or of the general council itself."[146] This went beyond the statutes of the Provisional Government which provided merely for the attendance of such individuals at factory committee meetings.

Factory Committee Elections

The elections to the factory committees were to be conducted in accordance with the decree of the general council of the factory or at the meeting of the general council or by department.[147] All the workers and employees had the right to participate in the elections, "without distinction as to sex, age, nationality, race, or faith."[148] A note to Paragraph 2, however, provided that "Employees occupying administrative posts attached to the factory management cannot participate in the factory organization."[149]

By decree of the general council, the employees (*sluzhashchie*) had the right, according to Paragraph 14, to participation in the election of the factory committees together with or separately from the workers.[150] This also was similar to the statutes of the Provisional Government.

The employees, it appears, were in some cases to be represented in the factory committees.[151] The fusion of both workers and employees into the same representative organs, however, seems to have been a relatively late development. Originally, the employees seem to have had their own organizations separate from the workers. In the *Izvestiia* of the Petrograd Soviet of Workers' and Soldiers' Deputies, No. 8, March 1917, there is an announcement of the Elders of Employees of the Petrograd Metal Working Factory, making known, ". . . the election of the Central Council of Elders for the defense of their own interests and proposing to all the employees of other industrial institutions to organize and elect councils of elders and to join with other councils of employees for the formation of a Central Council of Elders of Employees."[152]

A Central Council of Elders does seem to have been organized. According to a notice in the *Izvestiia,* No. 71, 20 May 1917, the formation of this organization united 50,000 employees of more than 200 enterprises.[153]

By August 1917, however, there were indications that the separate councils of employees were being abolished. A resolution of the Tentel'evskii Chemical Factory of 1 August 1917, states, for example: "We the employees and workers of the Tentel'evskii Chemical Factory, at a general meeting of 322 individuals, having debated the problem of the existence of individual Councils of Elders both for the employees and also for the workers, and having taken into consideration that with the existence of a single factory committee, defending to an equal degree the interests of both workers and employees, a separate Council of Elders should not exist, have resolved by a majority vote: to abolish the Council of Elders, transferring all their functions to the Factory Committee. . . ."[154]

Although it is not possible to determine from the material at hand how common this practice was, the Statutes on the Factory Committees adopted by the Second Conference provided for committees representing both workers and employees.

The manner by which a general council of workers elected a factory committee was left to the determination of the individual factory committee, but the statutes provided for an electoral commission to supervise the validity of an election.[155] However, the statutes do not make clear whether the electoral commission could invalidate an election. For the elections to be valid not less than one half of the workers of the enterprise were to participate in them. As in the case of meetings of the general council itself, however, if elections were not held because of insufficient attendance, a second election meeting was designated to elect a temporary factory committee regardless of the number of workers attending the elections.[156] Thus the elections of the factory committees could not be indefinitely postponed and a minority of the enterprise could elect a temporary committee. No limitations to the functions of a temporary committee seem to have been set.

The ratio of the members of the factory committees to the number of workers in a factory was as follows:

No. of workers in a factory	*No. of factory committee members*
up to 500	5-7
500-1000	9-11
1000-3000	11-13
3000-6000	13-15
6000-10,000	15-20
more than 10,000	20-25

This ratio, by decision of the factory council, could be changed to meet particular conditions of the factory.[157]

The elected factory committee was to be "the executive organ of the factory organization of the workers and employees of a given enterprise."[158]

Again, in a manner similar to the Provisional Government statutes, Paragraph 25 provided that "the factory committee regulates the relations of the employees and workers

a) among themselves
b) with the factory administration
c) with the government and with social institutions and organizations."[159]

Members of the factory committee were to be elected for a six-month period after which they could be reelected. Alternates or substitutes were also elected to replace regular members if necessary.

A meeting of the factory committee was valid if not less than half the members attended, and extraordinary sessions could be called either by the chairman or by one-third the members of the committee.[160]

Recall of the factory committee as a whole and the holding of new elections was possible at the demand of not less than one-third of the workers employed at the enterprise. The demand to recall an individual member of the committee and elect a new member in his place had to be proportional. Thus, if 1,000 workers participated in the elections and 10 were elected to the factory committee, 100 workers could demand the reelection of one member of the committee. This rule also applied to the departments within the factory.

Political Relations of the Factory Committee

The provisions of the statutes that were to regulate the relations of the employees and workers with political and social organizations provided that the factory committees were to coordinate their political demonstrations (*vystuplenie*) with those of the Soviets of Workers' Deputies.[161] Also, each factory committee was to organize elections to send representatives of the factory council to the Soviets and other institutions in which the workers as a whole were represented.[162] In addition, the factory committees were to coordinate their activity with the decisions of the trade unions, the Central Bureau of Trade Unions and the Central Council of Factory Committees.[163] Conversely, any party that gained control of the factory committees could influence the Soviets and other workers' organizations.

Also, any organization that could control the Central Council and successfully impose the authority of that Council on the factory committees, could control them; for all decrees of the factory committees were ultimately dependent on the sanctions of the Central Council, and the Council could abolish any decree of the factory committees. Paragraph 32 of the Factory Committee Statutes provided: "All decrees of the factory committees are compulsory for the factory administration as well as for the workers and employees—until such time as those decrees are abolished by the committee itself, by the general council, or by the Central Council of Factory Committees."[164]

Workers' Control

The factory committee was to regulate some of the most important aspects of the life of the factory—for example, wages, hours, and employment. Thus "it was the obligation of the factory committee to . . . work out the rules of internal order (the organization of working time, wages, the hiring, firing and leave of workers and employees, etc.)."[165] In addition, it was to see that the rules concerning the above conditions were observed by the workers, employees and management. The factory committee was also to see that the management carried out all the applicable provisions of social insurance. It was to supervise sanitary conditions in the factory and was to manage all the institutions of the enterprise which dealt with the welfare of the workers, such as nurseries, schools, etc.[166]

Perhaps the most important function of the factory committee, and the one to affect the revolutionary situation most significantly, was its control over the personnel of the enterprise. Subparagraph *f* of Paragraph 21 provided for factory committee "control over the composition of the administration and over the dismissal of those personnel of the administration who cannot guarantee normal relations with the workers or who are incompetent for other reasons."[167] In addition, a note to this subparagraph stipulated that "all administrative personnel of the factory administration can enter into service only with the consent of the factory committee, which is obliged to announce their hiring either at a general council of all the factory or through the subdivision committees (by department, workshop, etc)."[168]

These provisions empowering the factory committee to control the hiring and firing of managerial personnel, if misused, could seriously have hampered the efforts of the Provisional Government to maintain the productivity of industry. The war and revolutionary situation, which had been complicating and disorganizing economic life, made the services of managers and technicians even more than ordinarily crucial. The Bolsheviks, therefore, in their attempt to undermine the Provisional Government, seem to have manipulated the factory committees against management. The Bolshevik Amosov, for example, plays upon the animosity and suspicion of labor by speaking of the "technical and administrative personnel who are always ready to be servants of the entrepreneurs and at present assist in every way in the sabotage and closing of the factories."[169] Thus, under conditions of conflict, factory committee control over administrative and technical personnel could have led to an impasse between labor and management.

The factory committees themselves, if they were successfully to manage their affairs and carry out control, were in need of personnel with a knowledge of administrative and specialized techniques. A note to Paragraph 30, for example, provided that the subcommittees of the factory committee could elect or invite specialized personnel to serve with them. Those elected were to have a decisive vote and those invited an advisory vote.[170] The need for specialists is also demonstrated in Note 1 to Paragraph 33, which states: "The secretary of the factory committee can be an invited individual who enjoys the trust of the committee."[171] And, "Specialists may be invited to the meetings of the factory committee, but only with the right of an advisory vote."[172] Thus it would seem that specialists, technicians or managers who did not offer resistance to the factory committees but consented to serve them were not opposed, whereas those who identified with the interests of ownership or industry were.

The workers and employees were not only to have control over the hiring and firing of management but were to share in its most vital and complex functions; for the factory committees were also to exercise control over the production and distribution of the factory output in conjunction with the representatives of the Central Council of Factory Committees, of the trade unions, and of the Central Bureau.[173] It seems, therefore, that another attempt was being made to centralize control under the factory committees and trade union organizations.

Connections between the factory committees and the political and other organizations of labor were also to be maintained.

Management and the Support of Factory Committees

Provisions of the statutes that would seem to have aggravated the antagonism between the workers and their employers or managers were those relating to the conduct and support of committee members and the location and time of meetings. The statutes provided that notice to the appropriate administrative personnel was sufficient to free a member of the factory committee from work so that he might fulfill his obligations to the committee.[174]

Members of the factory committee elected to the Central Council were freed from current work in the factory committees and received the right to a median wage from their employers and to deferment from military service.[175] Thus the burden of supporting factory committee representatives fell upon the owner or manager with whose work they interfered.

Moreover, unlike the statutes of the Provisional Government, the statutes of the Second Conference stipulated that the factory committee was to be convoked regularly during working hours on days designated by the committee itself. In the period between meetings, members of the factory committees were to hold office hours, during which they were to receive information from the workers and employees and attend to other matters.[176] Thus the time needed for the conduct of factory committee business was also provided by the enterprise, and an even greater burden was placed upon the latter by the stipulation that the factory administration was to provide funds for the maintenance of the committee and the conduct of its affairs.[177]

The factory committee was to have its own press and was to "inform the workers and employees of the enterprise concerning their resolutions by posting an announcement in a conspicuous place. . . ."[178] It was to inform the workers and employees of more important questions by convoking a general council.[179]

Thus the Statutes on the Factory Committees, as presented in the documents selected by the editors of *Oktiabr'skaia Revoliutsiia i Fabzavkomy,* seem to have been an an attempt at providing a more or less uniform organization for all factory committees. The statutes were also intended to give the factory committees a measure of control over industrial production and distribution. They provided also that the workers control the hiring of the administrative and technical personnel. Through these means, the factory committees would have been able to exercise workers' control over the management and its policies. It must again be pointed out, however, that such statutes should be regarded as examples of Bolshevik intention. They should not be regarded as necessarily having produced the reality they were intended to create.

The attitude and policy of management and the Provisional Government toward the factory committees must also have tempered the application of the statutes. As the Bolshevik Skrypnik pointed out: "Adopting this statute, we must not forget that it is not a normal statute confirmed by the government. It is only our platform, on the basis of which we will fight. This statute cannot in any way be compulsory for the factory administration."[180]

The preface to the statutes also points out that they have no juridical validity. Rather they are founded on the force of revolutionary right, for "The given statute is implemented on the basis of customary revolutionary right, on which the very existence of the factory committees themselves is founded."[181] The preface continues to state, however, that "For us, the workers of the factory committees, our All-City Conference is a legal organ. . . . We will be guided by its decrees whether or not they are recognized by the opposite side. Cooperative and energetic work . . . is necessary to force recognition of our decrees, even if they are contradictory to official acts."[182] Hence the Bolshevik leadership of the factory committees overtly recognized and explicitly stated that the efficacy of the factory committees lay in the extra-legal power they could exert.

At the Second Conference of Factory Committees both Bolsheviks and Mensheviks presented resolutions regarding workers' control. The Menshevik resolution, introduced by Cherevanin, varied little from that presented at the First Conference. Calling for cooperation with the bourgeoisie for the alleviation of the economic crisis, it demanded that "The production, transportation, and distribution of products must be subordinated to a general economic plan. . . ."[183] The resolution insisted also that the Provisional Government compel industry gradually to form trusts and syndicates under the state.[184] Banks also were to be placed under governmental control. The working class was to participate in the process of this control through its political and trade union organizations.[185] The resolution also demanded that the soviets, the trade unions and the factory committees occupy not less than half the places in the organs formed by the state for the regulation of economic life. In addition, the resolution proposed that the factory committees, along with the technical personnel and factory owners, should form factory councils which should be put together along geographic lines.[186] Cherevanin's resolution, however, made the cessation of the war a precondition for alleviating the economic crisis.[187]

The Bolshevik Miliutin's Resolution on the Current Moment and Workers' Control also made economic rehabilitation conditional upon the cessation of the war.[188] The provisions of this resolution were also similar to the Bolshevik resolution concerning workers' control passed by the First Conference of Factory Committees. It demanded also that the state power be placed "in the hands of the proletariat and the stratum of poor peasantry supporting it."[189] Under such conditions, it required the nationalization and centralization of banking and the nationalization of syndicates and trusts.[190]

Miliutin's resolution stipulated also that for the establishment of active workers' control, the representatives of the Soviets, trade unions and factory committees should form a majority in the organs of control. These organs were also to include representatives of the scientifically educated technical personnel.[191]

Control itself, according to Paragraph 12 of Miliutin's resolution, demanded the "abolition of commercial secrets; the books of the trader-industrialists, and the banks must be opened to control"[192] and Paragraph 15 reiterated that, with the transfer of power to the hands of the proletariat and poor peasantry, the introduction of universal labor service was necessary.[193]

Thus both Mensheviks and Bolsheviks now demanded nationalization and centralization of industry. Whereas the Mensheviks demanded that not less than half the representation in the economic organs of the Provisional Government belong to the workers, the Bolshevik resolution provided for a majority representation for the workers' organizations. Both assigned a place in workers' control to technicians and specialists; but while the Mensheviks requested cooperation among classes, the Bolsheviks demanded that the proletariat and poor peasantry take over the state. The Bolshevik resolution also provided for the introduction of universal labor service under a proletarian government.

The chief accomplishments of the Second Conference of Factory Committees, therefore, were to adopt the Instructions to the Central Council of Factory Committees and to reaffirm the policy of workers' control over industry. The relationship between the trade unions and the factory committees seems to have remained ambiguous.

The Moscow Conference of Factory Committees

Although the Bolsheviks had a large majority in the factory committees of Petrograd, they did not have support in the All-City Conference of the Factory Committees of Moscow, which convened on 5 August 1917. Of the 682 members of the conference with a deciding vote, at the last meeting the Bolsheviks, together with the non-party voters, mustered 191 votes.[194]

The resolutions of the Moscow Conference of Factory Committees seem to have supported the Provisional Government and Soviets and to have shown a desire to work through them.[195] There also seems to have been an attempt by the Moscow Regional (*Raion*) Council of Factory Committees to centralize control of the local committees under the Regional Council in matters of demonstrations, factory committee representation in other organizations, and in general political, economic and jurisdictional matters. Conflicts not solved by the individual factory committees were also to be referred to the Moscow Regional Council.[196]

Only a small amount of material on the regional councils seems to have been preserved.[197] By the end of August, the Central Council of Factory Committees tried to group the committees by region as well as by industry.[198] Thus, the Bolsheviks seem to have intended to organize the factory committees in two interlocking ways. Nevertheless, the local centers of factory committees do not appear to have been well unified and seem to have worked without contact with one another.[199]

By the time of the October Revolution, however, local Councils of Factory Committees seem to have been formed in many parts of Russia, as follows: Northwest—Petrograd, Pskov, Revel'; Central Industrial Region—Moscow, Ivanovo-Voznesensk; Volga Provinces—Saratov, Kazan, Tsaritsyn; Ukraine (Southern Mining Region)—Kharkhov, Kiev, Odessa, Iuzovka; Southwest and Caucasus—Rostov, Nakhichevan-on-the-Don, Ekaterinodar; Urals and Siberia—Irkutsk.[200] The factory committees in these areas, however, do not seem to have had nearly the same importance as those in Petrograd and Moscow.

The Second Conference of Factory Committees closed on 25 August, just as the Moscow Conference of about 2500 representatives of all the parties, organizations and institutions of importance in Russia was convoked by the Provisional Government. The government seems to have intended this Moscow Conference as a means of resolving—as far as possible—the various conflicting interests of the population, and thus forming a stable base for its own power. The Moscow Conference, however, seems to have exacerbated rather than to have ameliorated opposing interests and points of view.[201]

Calling upon the workers of Petrograd and Moscow to declare a one-day strike in protest against the Moscow Conference, the Bolshevik-led Second Conference of Factory Committees passed the following resolution: "Regarding the Moscow Conference as an attempt at the organization of counter-revolutionary forces, as an attempt to mislead public opinion and as the first decisive step on the part of the counter-revolutionary bourgeoisie to disrupt the Constituent Assembly, the Second Petrograd Conference of Factory Committees, considering the participation in this conference harmful, has resolved to propose to the factory committees that they unmask before the workers the real anti-people's character of the conference in question and to condemn decisively the policy directed to its support."[202] Thus the Second Factory Committee Conference chose to emphasize class conflict and to condemn the Moscow Conference in the name of the Constituent Assembly, which was not yet convoked and which the Bolsheviks were later to dissolve.

About two weeks after the end of the Moscow Conference there occurred the Kornilov Affair (8-12 September), a conservative response to the course of the revolution.[203] This affair not only weakened the government and the army, but increased the power of the Soviets. Furthermore, it directly contributed to the renewed growth of the Red Guards attached to the factory committees; for the factory militia, which had been formally abolished by the first half of August, were again armed and called upon by the Provisional Government and the Soviets to defend Petrograd from Kornilov. It seems that as a result of the Kornilov Affair the Red Guards were increased from about 10,000 to 20,000 armed men within the city of Petrograd.[204]

A special commission for arming the workers was attached to the Petrograd Soviet, and the Central Council of Factory Committees was a part of this commission.[205] Moreover, the Regional (*Raion*) Soviets of Factory Committees made an audit of the number of factory workers fit for military service and of the number possessing arms, and on this basis they requested weapons of the Central Council of Factory Committees. A transition thus seems to have been made from the concept of the defense of the factories to the concept of a general arming of the workers.[206]

Further, by the middle of September, when the Kornilov incident had come to an end, the factory committees possessed considerable military power with which to support their political demands and actions. Also, the Central Council of Factory Committees began to request a greater share in the power of the revolutionary organizations. Pointing to the importance of the factory committees in the Kornilov Affair, for example, it requested representation in both the Petrograd Soviet of Workers' and Soldiers' Deputies and in the Executive Committee of this Soviet.[207]

Conversely, even before the Kornilov Affair had ended, the Provisional Government had taken steps, the effect of which would have been substantially to curtail the functions of the factory committees in workers' control. The Ministry of Labor, in Circular No. 421, dated 10 September, prohibited the convocation of the workers or their factory committees during working hours, and the Statutes of the Provisional Government had previously stipulated that the meetings of the general council should take place after working hours, unless exceptional circumstances made necessary the convocation during the hours of work. From the circular of the Ministry of Labor and the reaction to it by the Third Conference of Factory Committees, it would seem that it was usual, nevertheless, for the factory committees, in accordance with the Statutes of the Second Conference, to meet during working time.

The Ministry's circular supported the right of management to deduct from the wages of workers payment for the amount of time spent in workers' meetings during working hours.[208] In addition, the Ministry seems to have issued another circular on 11 September, providing that the right of hiring and firing of the workers and employees of an enterprise (except for the firing of members of the factory committees elected on the basis of the law of 6 May) belonged to the owners of the enterprise. Other methods of hiring and firing could be used only by the mutual consent of workers and owners.[209] Thus, if this circular had been enforced, the control of the factory committees, insofar as it existed over the hiring and firing of all factory personnel, would have been brought to an end and one of the principal aspects of workers' control would have been erased. Hence the Provisional Government seems to have been making a definite attempt to curtail the power of the factory committees. It was making this attempt, however, at the very time when the powers of the factory committees, through their Red Guards, had reached a new height.

The Third Conference of Factory Committees, which met on 23 September 1917, was largely concerned with these attempts of the Provisional Government to make more definite the limits and bounds of factory committee activity. No Social Revolutionary or Menshevik representatives were present at this conference. The Menshevik Kolokol'nikov attended as the representative of the Ministry of Labor. As such, he spoke in defense of the circulars issued by the Ministry on 10 and 11 September. In defense of the circulars, Kolokol'nikov stated that they ". . . were merely the result of a faithful observance of the law. They do not introduce anything new but are only a summary of the existing regulations issued in answer to the innumerable inquiries of the industrialists concerning the rights of the factory committees."[210] He explained further that the circulars did not deprive the workers of the right of *control over* the hiring and firing of the workers, but only of the right itself of hiring and firing.[211] Thus, Kolokol'nikov, as the Bolsheviks were themselves to do at a later time, defined control as supervision over policy, as opposed to the right of making and implementing policy.

The Third Conference of Factory Committees, however, was not convinced by Kolokol'nikov's justification of the circulars issued by the Ministry of Labor on hiring and firing, and on meetings during working hours. In its resolution on the Report Concerning the Attack on the Factory Committees and the Policy of the Ministry of

Labor, the conference decreed that it would try to effect the immediate abolition of the circulars.[212] It also resolved to try to obtain "the confirmation by legislation of the rights of the factory committees which they enjoy already on the basis of customary revolutionary law."[213] The conference also claimed that factory committee members and militiamen were being deprived of their deferments from military service and that wages were being curtailed because of time spent in factory committee duties. The resolution on the attack on factory committees also stipulated, therefore, "not to allow comrades in the committee to be deprived of their deferments and to demand that they be paid an average wage."[214]

The Evacuation of Industry

In addition to its resolution concerning the decrees on the attack upon the factory committees, the Third Conference passed a Resolution on the Problem of the Evacuation and Moving of Petrograd. Since Riga had fallen and the front was drawing nearer, Petrograd seemed to be in danger of attack and some industrial establishments were leaving Petrograd to reestablish themselves in the provinces. This was being done also because of the difficulties in feeding the Petrograd population and in securing raw materials for manufacture. Moreover, the evacuation might have been a means for ownership and management to escape from workers' control and the pressure of the Red Guards, the factory committees, the Soviets of Workers' and Soldiers' Deputies, and the socialist parties in Petrograd. For these latter reasons the factory committees, it seems, objected to evacuation. The Resolution on the Problem of Evacuation and Moving of Petrograd charges that the evacuation "only decreases to an insignificant degree the size of the population and therefore cannot in any case affect the solution of the food supply crisis in Petrograd."[215]

It was charged that the proposed evacuation would be unplanned and chaotic and that because of the difficulties of reestablishing industry in new localities industrial productivity would be curtailed. This curtailment of production, the resolution insisted, was the purpose and objective of "world capital," which it thus identified with the owners and managers of Russian industry.[216]

Russian industrialists were also accused of making use of state funds in order to move their factories nearer to supplies of raw material and fuel. This latter purpose the Bolsheviks did not attribute to the exigencies of Russia's wartime economy but to the "general course of capitalist development."[217] Since the evacuation was to be carried out at the expense of the state, they claimed that the moving of industry from Petrograd would damage the economy and lead to imminent bankruptcy.[218]

The Conference in its resolution also charged that the proposed evacuation threatened the workers with insecurity, unemployment and hunger, and claimed that the disorganization of railway transport would not permit the evacuation of factory equipment. It also insinuated that plans for moving the industrial enterprises by water in the spring did not arise from military considerations, stating: "The shipping of the enterprises by waterways in the spring signifies only the closing of the enterprise by the capitalists for the struggle with the working class."[219] The conference thus construed preparation for evacuation by water as an excuse for lockouts.

Paragraphs 8 and 9 of the resolution state that since the plans for the evacuation of Petrograd were drawn up by government commissions, without the participation of the workers' organizations, the evacuation was a means by which the propertied classes intended to demolish "the advanced detachments of the revolution, the revolutionary proletariat of Petrograd,"[220] and claimed that "the plan of the general moving and evacuation of Petrograd is a counterrevolutionary plot against the working class."[221]

To implement the evacuation of individual enterprises under the existing regime, the resolution demanded that "a decree . . . worked out by the Central Council of Factory Committees and by the trade unions must be adopted and carried out."[222]

The resolution demanded also that the moving of an enterprise could be authorized only after a suitable site was found for it and suitable quarters could be provided for the workers. It provided also that the factory workers who wanted to move with their factories should be evacuated with them.[223]

Thus the Third Conference of Factory Committees sought to prevent the measures taken by the Provisional Government and industry to evacuate various factories from Petrograd. It used the opportunity to attack both the industrialists and the government. It further demanded that the evacuation be directed by the proletarian organizations and that the state itself be transferred to the hands of the proletariat and poor peasantry.[224]

This conference also dealt with the matter of the representation of the Central Council of Factory Committees in the Democratic Conference. The latter, like the Moscow Conference, was called to establish a more stable and representative government to support the executive Council of Five formed during the Kornilov Incident.[225] It was to meet only four days after the Third Factory Committee Conference. On 22 September, only one day before the Third Conference, the Bolshevik majority in the Petrograd Soviet was formally ratified.[226] Bolsheviks, therefore, were increasing and solidifying their power.

Emphasizing that the tasks of the factory committees were "essentially different" from those of the trade unions, the Bolsheviks also requested 25 places in the Democratic Conference for the Central Council of Factory Committees.[227] This was the same number of places allotted to the trade unions. By September, however, the Petrograd Council of Trade Unions had adopted a resolution supporting the Bolsheviks. Thus, Bolshevik influence in trade unions had been augmented even further. By requesting 25 places at the Democratic Conference for the solidly Bolshevik Central Council of Factory Committees, the Bolsheviks would have been represented there not only as a party but also through the factory committees and part of the trade unions.

Conversely, the Resolution of the Third Conference of Factory Committees on the Democratic Conference accused the Central Executive Committee of the Soviets of narrowing down "the representation of the really revolutionary workers', soldiers', and peasants' organizations and broadening and inflating artificially the representation of the all-class organizations of city self-government, the *zemstvos,* cooperatives, etc. . . ."[228]

At the same time, therefore, that the Bolsheviks were attempting to increase their representation in the Democratic Conference, they were accusing the Central Executive Committee of packing that conference with delegates who did not represent "revolutionary democracy."[229]

The resolution stated that the Third Conference of Factory Committees was, however, giving up the attempt to increase the representation of the proletariat and poor peasantry at the Democratic

Conference. The program for the Democratic Conference which was presented in the name of the factory committees was similar to the Bolshevik declaration presented at the Democratic Conference itself.[230] In its demand for the "abolition of all repression against the revolutionary socialists," the resolution would seem to have been directed particularly towards the elimination of the charges that, since the July days, had been keeping Lenin in hiding. The resolution demanded an immediate peace, the abolition of private property, and that the land belonging to the landholders, monasteries and churches be transferred to the jurisdiction of the land committees before the convocation of the Constituent Assembly. The poorest peasants were to receive the livestock and equipment. It further demanded workers' control over production and distribution, all possible taxation upon large capital and property and the confiscation of military profits.[231]

The Resolution of the Third Factory Committee Conference thus presented in outline the Bolshevik program for the current situation. The conference itself, as an organ of the Bolshevik Party, dealt with the problems which were confronting the factory committees in the new conditions created by the Kornilov Incident.

Factory Committee and Bolshevik Achievement

By September the factory committees seem to have become ensconced. They seem to have acquired far more power than they had requested in their beginnings. The Instructions for the Factory Committees drawn up in March by the Conference of Workers at State Enterprises had asserted that the factory committees did not want to undertake the responsibility for the administrative-economic organization of production until the complete socialization of the economy had taken place; therefore, the committees would participate in factory management only with an advisory vote. A resolution of a Petrograd gun factory drawn up on 10 September states, however: "Until the moment of the socialization of all the social economy, both state and private, begins, the workers' organizations are part of the factory administration. They are constructed on a democratic basis and have the right of control over the action of the administration in factory management, over the order of internal relations, over all problems on the way of life of the workers and over control of the general course of production of the given factory."[232] Thus it would seem that by September some factory committees no longer participated in management merely in an advisory capacity but had become part of the administration itself and had control of its most important functions.

Such a situation, however, was not without its disadvantages. Those factory committees that were engaged in managerial functions, and were presumably in control of production and distribution, themselves were open to attack because of the prevalent economic distress. The Bolshevik Chubar', a member of the Petrograd Central Council of Factory Committees, stated, for example, that ". . . with the introduction of the workers into the factory administration . . . the worker masses turn all their displeasure upon the factory committees, accusing them of not having taken steps to prevent all the confusion in production."[233] Thus the factory committees began to bear the responsibility for the conditions with which they were supposedly to deal. A tendency to avoid this responsibility was also displayed. The Bolshevik Antipov, pointing out that "we have already noticed an exacerbation of the relations between the worker masses and their elected organs," added: "Recently in Petrograd there was a meeting of all the representatives of the labor organizations, which debated the problem of the introduction of workers into the factory administration and decided against it."[234] Workers' control does not seem to have been without its disadvantages for the Bolsheviks and their Central Council of Factory Committees.

Nevertheless, in October, Bolshevik power was visibly growing, and that of the Provisional Government waning. On 22 October the Petrograd garrison refused to obey the orders of the Supreme Commander in Chief to move part of the garrison to the front. This resulted in the garrison's denunciation of the Provisional Government and to a demand for "All Power to the Soviets."[235] Consequently, on 23 October steps were taken to form the War Revolutionary Committee, the organization which, in effect, enabled the Bolsheviks to control the Petrograd troops.[236]

The First All-Russian Conference of Factory Committees

On 23 October, when the Bolsheviks began to implement their plan to gain military control of the capital, the almost exclusively Bolshevik Fourth Conference of the Factory Committees of Petrograd and its Environs took place, lasting only one day. This conference, judging from the source materials now available, bears little importance in itself; for the chief business on its agenda seems to have been the convocation of the First All-Russian Conference of Factory Committees.[237]

The First All-Russian Conference of Factory Committees, also very largely Bolshevik in composition, probably reflected, like the Fourth Conference, the popularity of the Bolshevik policy of workers' control. It met from 30 October to 4 November, closing three days before the October/November Revolution. It shall be shown below that the conference itself contributed to the success of that revolution. It seems to have been a means by which the Bolshevik Party could further attempt to organize, unite and direct the factory committees and thereby implement its goals. The appeal by the Organizational Bureau for the convocation of the All-Russian Conference states that it was being called to combat the lack of coordination of factory committee work and the vagueness of their spheres of operation. If this were true, it would indicate that the Bolsheviks had had little success with their program of factory committee unification and centralization.[238]

Asserting that an economic crisis was approaching, the appeal insisted upon the necessity of labor's solving it, implying thus that the Provisional Government itself could not do so.

The Organizational Bureau also established the following scheme of representation:

Councils and conferences uniting

20,000-40,000	workers	— 1 representative
40,000-80-000	workers	— 2 representatives
more than 80,000	workers	— 1 representative

Councils and conferences with fewer than 20,000 workers were allowed one representative with an advisory vote. The All-Russian Conference itself, however, could present such an organization with a participating vote.[239]

The All-Russian trade unions—i.e., the unions organized on a national scale—plus the All-Russian Council of Trade Unions and the central committees of the socialist parties were invited to send one representative each with a participating vote. An advisory vote was also allotted to the local delegates sent in excess of the stipulated representation and to the representatives of the various workers' organizations.[240]

The representation of the 137 delegates to the First All-Russian Conference of Factory Committees was divided as follows according to party affiliation:[241]

Party	*No.*	*%*
Bolshevik	86	62
Menshevik	8	6
Social Revolutionary	22	16
Maximalist	6	5
Anarcho-Syndicalist	11	8
Non-party	4	3

Thus, even though the Bolsheviks were in the majority, their representation at the All-Russian Conference of Factory Committees was proportionately smaller than their representation at the Petrograd Factory Committee Conference.

At the First All-Russian Conference of Factory Committees, the Bolsheviks emphasized the necessity of unifying the policies of the factory committees and of subordinating them to a single centralized controlling organ. They also further insisted upon the need for workers' control over industry.

A resolution of the First All-Russian Conference, on "The Factory Committees, Their Tasks and Activity, Their Local and All-Russian Unions" states: "The tasks of workers' control cannot be fulfilled by the kinds of workers' organizations which have existed up to the present time, but by . . . the factory committees and their local unions, the local councils of factory committees."[242]

The resolution formulates the centralizing function of the Central Council of Factory Committees as follows:

"The All-Russian Central Council of Factory Committees has on an All-Russian scale the tasks of the local councils of factory committees. It unites and directs their activity and takes measures to work out a general plan of demobilization of industry, the distribution of raw materials, fuel, etc. It represents the factory committees and their councils in all institutions and in all questions concerning their activity, and executes other tasks and commissions laid upon it by the All-Russan Conference of Factory Committees."[243]

Workers' control was also to be centralized and ". . . the economic life of the country subordinated to a single plan" which was to be executed through the factory committees by state institutions, presumably the Soviets, when "all power" was acquired by them.[244]

The labor unions were to have it seems, only a subordinate role in workers' control, being restricted to control functions primarily on the labor market,[245] and were to confer with the factory committees concerning control activities.[246]

All problems and conditions affecting the internal order of the enterprise, such as "hiring, firing, wages, conflicts between labor and management," after the introduction of workers' control, were to be decided only with the consent and confirmation of the factory committee, which also was to have the right of dismissing all the administrative personnel of the enterprise.[247]

The factory committees were to form control commissions for the purpose of control over "supplying the enterprise with materials, fuel, orders, labor and technical forces (also equipment) and all needed articles and measures . . . and were also to coordinate all the activity of the enterprise with the general economic plan."[248]

Nothing was to be hidden from the control commissions since, according to Paragraph 15, "The management of the enterprise is obliged to communicate to the workers' controller all facts for the purpose of control and information, and to open to him all business books of the enterprise."[249]

And if, through the process of workers' control, any discrepancies were uncovered in the management of an enterprise, ". . . factory committees turn for assistance to the conferences of all the factory committees in the appropriate branch of production of the given locality . . ."[250] which could take punitive measures leading even to the confiscation of the enterprise. An example of how such a confiscation was effected may be found in the case of the Gel'ferikh factory in Kharkhov. The event described occurred about a month before the First All-Russian Conference of Factory Committees took place. On 22 September the management of the Gel'ferikh factory announced that the factory would close, but on 26 September a general council of workers declared that it would stand its ground against the board of directors that the workers would continue to work, and demanded that the factory be placed under state control or that it be transferred to the state in full.[251]

Although the Provisional Government had adopted a policy of state regulation of industry, it did not sponsor a program of nationalization of private industrial enterprises or of the direct management of private industry by the government.[252] It was also obligated to recognize the private property rights of the factory owners. The

Provisional Government had no choice, therefore, but to reject the request of the Gel'ferikh factory council, and was thus forced into creating greater misunderstanding between itself and the workers.

It is possible that this was exactly the situation which the leaders of the council intended to create, for the account of the situation at the Gel'ferikh plant continues to relate that the council also declared it would seize the factory if the government refused to take it over.[253] By means of such action the factory council seems to have tried to place the ultimate responsibility for the seizure of the factory upon the Provisional Government by claiming that its confiscation was in default of the government's doing so. Seizing the factory, therefore, as the property of the workers and employees, the factory council evicted the board of directors and announced that the workers refused to leave the factory under any conditions.[254]

The procedure of the factory committees reveals another means of attack upon industry and commerce in its insistence upon cash payment for goods delivered.[255] In ignoring the function of credit in a money economy, this policy, which seems to have been adopted by many factory committees, undermined the structure of existing economic institutions. It placed an extremely serious obstacle in the path of commodity exchange. Moreover, if demands for cash payment were not met, the Gel'ferikh committee resolved to sell the stocks of raw material at hand,[256] thus acquiring cash and losing the means to manufacture.

The workers also requested the Soviets of Workers' and Soldiers' Deputies, the political organ of its own class, to recognize the legal status of the personnel they had elected to conduct factory business.[257] Since the Provisional Government did not, in any way, recognize the legality of the workers' confiscation, the factory committee requested the Soviets to recognize the seizure. Politically, then, workers' control could dichotomize the Provisional Government and the Soviets. It could alienate the workers from the Provisional Government and the Provisional Government from the workers. Moreover, it seems to have brought the factory committees and the workers into further dependence upon, and support of, the Soviets of Workers' and Soldiers' Deputies.

A notice posted by the Gel'ferikh factory committee on 5 October indicates that the committee lacked the wholehearted support of the workers. The notice was an appeal to the workers not to interfere as separate groups with the decree of the factory committee. A warning against leaving the factory was also issued and the committee inveighed against workers who absented themselves from the factory without valid reason. The committee also declared that anyone neglecting work or spreading false rumors would be placed under boycott.

Such measures for effecting workers' control indicate that they were not always entirely an expression of all workers' demands but perhaps measures imposed in the name of the workers.

These measures, which illustrate the process of "outright seizure" of which Lenin had spoken, were beginning to be feared by the Bolsheviks themselves. Such confiscation was an effective weapon against the Provisional Government and considerably trammeled the latter's struggle with economic disorder. Partly for this reason, it would seem, the Bolsheviks encouraged workers' seizure of industrial enterprises. By the time of the First All-Russian conference, however, the Bolsheviks, or Lenin, Trotsky and others at least, had begun to expect to seize the state itself. They therefore seem to have begun to emphasize workers' control on a national scale and to denounce factory committee confiscation of single enterprises by the workers themselves. Paragraph 19 of the Resolution of the Bolshevik Faction adopted by the First All-Russian Conference of Factory Committees states: "Demanding workers' control on a nation-wide scale, it rejects workers' control as the seizure by the workers of individual enterprises for their own use."[258] The Bolsheviks, it seems, were beginning to fear that if the workers seized industry, such seizure could not be used to attain Bolshevik ends.

The First All-Russian Conference of Factory Committees supported the Bolshevik slogan and goal of transferring "All Power to the Soviets" in its Resolution on the Current Moment.[259]

In October, however, when the First All-Russian Conference of Factory Committee passed this resolution in support of "All Power to the Soviets," the slogan was equated by Lenin, as leader of the Bolshevik Party, with a call to revolt. Lenin had abandoned this slogan in July, not only because of the minority position of the Bolsheviks in the Soviets at that time but also because of the power superior to that of the Soviets manifested during the July days by the factory committees, the Red Guards, and the Bolshevik organizations in the army.[260]

Lenin believed the July days had demonstrated that "it was possible to seize power by an armed uprising."[261] In his "State and Revolution," written while in hiding after the July days, he argues against the policy of those Marxists or liberals who believed the bourgeois-democratic state could evolve into the socialist state and gradually "wither away." "Progress," Lenin holds, "does not march onward simply, smoothly and directly 'to greater and greater democracy' as the liberal professors and petty bourgeois opportunists would have us believe."[262] Citing Engels, he obdurately contends that "The bourgeois state does not 'wither away,' . . . but is 'put an end to' in the course of the revolution. What withers away after the revolution is the proletarian state. . . ."[263]

Thus, in contradistinction to those socialists and liberals who believed in the gradual development of bourgeois democracy towards socialism, and in contradistinction also to the Anarchists, who believed in the complete annihilation of the state,[264] Lenin maintained that the "bourgeois state . . . cannot be replaced by the proletarian state (the dictatorship of the proletariat) through 'withering away' but, as a general rule, only through a violent revolution."[265] Thus, he insisted upon both a revolution and a proletarian dictatorship. In discussing the possibilities of this revolution, Lenin, according to the Bolshevik Ordzhonikidze, asserted: "We must shift the center of gravity to the factory committees. The factory committees must become the organs of insurrection. We must change our slogan and say, instead of "All Power to the Soviets," "All power to the Factory Committees."[266]

Iaroslavskii claims that ". . . the factory committees were under the undivided leadership of the party. It was not by accident after the July days when the question was raised as to which [organization] was to stand at the head of the movement instead of the bankrupt Soviets, Lenin fixed upon the factory committees."[267]

And according to Trotsky: "After the July raids Lenin declared: 'The power can be seized henceforth only by an armed insurrection; we must obviously rely in this operation not upon the Soviets . . . but on the factory committees. The Soviets as organs of power will have to be created anew after the victory.' "[268]

In his theoretical justification for this projected insurrection to be made by the factory committees and their Red Guards, Lenin turned to the events and conditions of past revolutions as he conceived them. His analysis of history led to the belief that all revolutions previous to that of the Paris Commune of 1871 had attempted to take over the "state machine" and to perfect it.[269] The Paris

Commune, however, as a more advanced form of revolutionary activity, attempted not the capture of the bourgeois-democratic state machine but its annihilation.[270]

Lenin had equated the Commune with the Soviets; and though he had rejected the latter as an instrument for the seizure of power in July,[271] when the Bolsheviks in September had received a majority in the soviets of Petrograd and Moscow he revived the former slogan, "All Power to the Soviets."[272] But whereas previous to July that slogan had implied a peaceful transfer of power, in September it was equated with a call to insurrection. "The slogan, 'All Power to the Soviets,' " said Lenin, "is a call to revolt."[273] It has been said of Lenin that ". . . in his single-track insistence on the organization of insurrection at the earliest possible moment, he was somewhat too contemptuous of the expediency of linking up the uprising with the meeting of the Second Congress of Soviets. . . ."[274]

That Lenin seems somewhat to have disregarded the soviets is more understandable if it is borne in mind that he believed in transferring the center of gravity from them to the factory committees, the Red Guards, and the Petrograd troops. Trotsky asserts that Lenin, who was in hiding during the weeks immediately preceding the October Revolution, intended that "the preparation and completion of the revolution was to be done by the party and afterwards accepted by the Congress of Soviets."[275] Furthermore, Lenin made it clear that "our party . . . is striving to secure political domination *for itself.*"[276] It was realized, however, that this seizure of power could not be made in the name of the party. It was made, therefore, in the name of the Soviets, whose popularity as organs of political action for the formerly disenfranchised classes was deeply rooted among the workers' and soldiers' organizations.[277] Members of the party were aware that though the troops would freely support the Soviets in an uprising, it was far from certain that such support would be given the party itself.[278] "Attempts to lead the insurrection directly through the party," says Trotsky, "nowhere produced results."[279] The insurrection, therefore, was to be carried out under the pretext of instituting and protecting the Second Congress of Soviets against those who were opposed to it.[280] "To prepare the revolution and carry it out under cover of the preparations for the Second Congress of Soviets and under the cry of defending it," Trotsky explains, "was of inestimable advantage to us."[281] "Under a cry of a fight for the Second Congress, we succeeded better than we could have expected in catching our enemies . . . in this trap of the constitutional position of the Soviets."[282]

The function of the First All-Russian Conference of Factory Committees, which closed three days before the October/November Revolution, may thus be more clearly seen. It was here that the Bolsheviks attempted to solidify their control over the factory committees and prepared to use them as a basis for their insurrection.

It is now time to turn attention to the relationship between labor, the Bolsheviks and the Provisional Government in the seizure of power.

CHAPTER III

Labor and the Seizure of Power: Hunger, Cold and the Dark Forces

It was with the support of labor organized in the factory committees and Soviets of Workers' Deputies that the Bolsheviks seized power from the Provisional Government in 1917. Although it is not the function of this chapter to investigate fully the seizure of power, attention will be focused upon the temper and mood and conditions in the city of Petrograd and the manner in which they affected the relationships between labor and the Bolsheviks. With the structure of Bolshevik ideology in mind, Bolshevik reasoning in explanation of Bolshevik action shall be presented.

The Soviets, formed by the workers themselves and having their devoted support as their principal agency of political action, were used by the Bolsheviks as a mask for seizure of political power. The factory committees formed by the workers for participation in industry were used by the Bolsheviks as a mask for the seizure of economic power.

Workers' Control

The economy was to be disorganized by means of "workers' control" of industry. Workers' control was to have a dual function: (1) to undermine the economy of the country so that the Provisional Government could not efficiently function; (2) to establish the basis for Bolshevik control over that economy. Therefore, just as "All Power to the Soviets" became the slogan of the Bolsheviks in the political sphere, "Workers' Control" became their slogan in the economic sphere. The organizations which were to implement workers' control were the factory committees.

As Lozovsky, before his temporary separation from the Bolshevik Party, pointed out: ". . . One of our fundamental problems is to snatch the regulation of industry from the Provisional Government. . . . A wide field is opened here for the factory committees. . . ."[1]

One of the quickest and most effective ways of disrupting the economy was to remove the trained technicians and administrators from their posts and so leave Russian industry technologically bankrupt. The Bolsheviks, impressed by the necessity of the machine for socialist society, do not seem to have attempted to undermine the economy by destroying them. However, they seem to have attempted to deprive the Provisional Government of the productivity of these machines by removing or rendering ineffective those techniques and administrators who were necessary to run them. Not only were the factory committees urged by the Bolsheviks to institute workers' control over such administrators, they were also induced to regard them with suspicion, distrust and apprehension. Under workers' control, administrative and managerial personnel who were retained by the factory committees were to be completely responsible to them and dependent upon them. They were to be both hired and fired by the factory committees.

Thus the Bolshevik policy was, it seems, to remove or paralyze the efficiency of administrative and technical personnel who were operating industry to fill the needs of the national economy. Their purpose would have been defeated, therefore, if the workers themselves had continued, by means of workers' control, to fulfill those needs. For this reason, it seems, they tried to introduce into the enterprises under workers' control administrative and technical personnel who would support the Bolshevik program.

At the Fourth Petrograd Conference of Factory Committees, 10 October 1917, a speaker stated, for example, that "The future All-Russian center must work out a concrete plan for the organization of industry and to attract to this work the whole of the technical force which is prepared to assist us."[2]

The Employees and the Factory Committees

Furthermore, this technical force could have been made up of persons filling analogous technical posts previous to the implementation of workers' control. They also could have been any other specialists who were willing to accept the new conditions of managerial employment. Or they could have been persons advanced from the lower ranks to posts of greater responsibility. Since the employees (*sluzhashchie*) as well as the workers were, it seems, most often members of the factory committees, and since most of the workers were generally of a low level of literacy, those functions of workers' control which required any sort of academic training were probably filled by the *sluzhashchie,* some of whom, as clerks and white-collar workers, possessed the characteristics of a marginal class. They were equivalent to the low-ranking bureaucrats, or *chinoviniki,* who belonged neither to the ranks of the workers nor to the prestigeful ranks of management. The *sluzhashchie,* however, probably had a knowledge and understanding of both these groups. They possessed to a degree, in particular, a knowledge of the techniques of administration. Thus, in the revolutionary movement of workers' control, they were probably able to step forward into positions of authority, responsibility and dominance which were not theirs under normal conditions.

In explaining that the Bolsheviks would take over intact the economic apparatus of the state, while destroying its political machinery, Lenin pointed to the importance of the *sluzhashchie* in the Bolshevik acquisition of the economic apparatus: "Capitalism has created an apparatus of registration and accounting in the shape of the banks, syndicates, the postal service, consumers' societies, and unions of employees. . . . This 'state apparatus' (which under capitalism is not wholly a state apparatus, but which will be wholly so with us under socialism) we can 'lay hold of' and 'wield' at a single stroke, by a single decree; for the actual work of bookkeeping, audit, registration, control and accounting is performed by employees [*sluzhashchie*] most of whom are themselves in the position of proletarians or semi-proletarians."[3]

It may be hypothesized, therefore, that the Bolshevik revolution received some of its most ardent support from what may be considered, within the framework of the Russian social structure, the marginal bureaucratic or managerial class.[4]

The Demobilization of Industry

An even more destructive aspect of workers' control than its policy toward administrative and technical personnel was the Bolshevik program of the demobilization of industry. The effect of this campaign was to place serious obstacles in the way of the use of resources of the nation for the military needs of the Provisional Government during the war. To achieve this the Bolsheviks carried on a campaign among the workers exhorting them to convert their factories from military to non-military production. This demobilization of industry was one of the primary functions of workers' control. It was a means by which the already overwhelming tasks of the Provisional Government in regard to military transport and supply were further magnified and complicated. Since the Bolsheviks seem to have intended to withdraw from the war as it existed if they could successfully seize power, they do not appear to have feared the consequences for them of the military failures of the Provisional Government. On the contrary, the Bolsheviks probably did fear the salubrious effects of a military victory upon the temper of the nation. Perhaps they chose to agitate for their program of demobilization through the agency of workers' control because their "anti-defensist" demand for a withdrawal from the war did not have majority support in either the Second International or the First Congress of Soviets.[5] The Bolsheviks conjured up before the workers engaged in military production the threat of unemployment at the war's end. They exhorted these workers to solve this problem before it arose by converting to peacetime production while the war was still in progress. If this suggestion had been made at the conclusion of the war, it would have had a rational basis. During the war, however, the execution of such a program, involving the conversion of machinery and the need for different raw materials and new markets, could have resulted in chaos and devastation for the war effort, and probably for industry. In all likelihood, it would have resulted also in the very unemployment the workers were urged to avoid. Nevertheless, a Bolshevik proclamation addressed to the workers in May 1917 tells them: "The question of the reorganization of production from war to peace, that is, the question of the demobilization of industry, is raised before all Russian industry. Guns, bullets, shells, and all other objects necessary for war are unnecessary in peacetime. And all workers manufacturing these objects will be thrown out into the streets. In order to prevent this, it is necessary to participate actively in the demobilization of industry."[6]

Demobilization tended to become a panacea for all current economic ills and the Resolution of the Commission on Unemployment adopted at the First All-Russian Conference of Factory Committees demanded: "4. The immediate working out of a plan of demobilization by means of participation of the factory committees and the trade unions."[7]

Thus, workers' control could function not only to remove Russian industry from the guidance of technicians and specialists who could help to solve the problems of Russia's wartime economy, but also to deprive the war effort of the nation's industrial resources.

The Economic Crisis

That the Bolsheviks were aware of the seriousness of the economic problem facing the country may be illustrated by the Bolshevik resolution in accordance with Miliutin's Report concerning the Current Moment and Workers' Control. This resolution, presented at the Second All-Russian Conference of Factory Committees in August 1917, reads:

> "1. The basic reason for the economic collapse is the incompatibility between the conditions of productive strength and the demands made by imperialistic war. This incompatibility is especially sharp in Russia because of the low level of the development of its productive strength and the backwardness of its economic and technical organization.
>
> "As a result after three years of war, our economic position may be presented in the following way: the complete exhaustion in the sphere of productivity of labor, the disorganization of production, the universal collapse and disintegration of the transportation network, the impending conditions of the final crash of state finances, and as a consequence of this a crisis verging on starvation in the matter of food supplies, the absolute lack of fuel and means of production in general, the progressive unemployment, the vast impoverishment of the masses, etc."[8]

Sabotage and Lockouts

However, the realization of the reasons for the economic difficulties oppressing Russia did not prevent the Bolsheviks from reiterating charges of sabotage. The resolution in accordance with Miliutin's report goes on to say: "2. This crisis, aggravated day by day, is increased by the politics of the bourgeoisie, who, fearing to lose either their political power or their power over production, not only do not organize it, but conduct political sabotage, resorting to surrepetitious lockouts, the cessation of production, etc., consciously promoting economic chaos in order to use it for counter-revolutionary purposes."[9]

The way for such declarations had been paved at the very beginning of the revolution when the same sort of accusations were made by the Menshevik and Socialist Revolutionary majority in the Soviets of Workers' and Soldiers' Deputies. The Soviet *Izvestiia* of 20 March 1917, for example, stated:

"The comrades must not forget that the refusal of an employer, for personal motives, to go on with production cannot serve as a reason for stopping work. In such cases, they must insist resolutely that the work be turned over to them, under the direction of a commissar of the Soviets of Workers' and Soldiers' Deputies, a representative of the trade unions involved, and the party organization of the district."[10]

It is to be noted, however, that here the workers are asked to resist work stoppages which are the result only of the employers' personal motives. But the *Izvestiia* does not charge that every work stoppage is a conscious attempt to promote economic disorder. Also, it requests that in case of unnecessary cessation of work, the factories be turned over to a coalition group made up of three different labor or socialist party organizations. This also differs from the Bolshevik policy of unilateral workers' control by the workers at the factories.[11]

The Dark Forces

Nevertheless, the Mensheviks and Socialist Revolutionaries probably contributed to the insecurity in which Bolshevik agitation could flourish because of the apprehension and suspicion which might have been evoked by statements such as this: ". . . The workers must bear in mind that tsarism is overthrown, but not completely vanquished. Its followers are still trying, and will continue to try, to harm the people in every possible way by disorganizing whatever is still accessible to their scattered forces."[12]

The Bolshevik Miliutin, however, goes beyond the Mensheviks and the Socialist Revolutionaries by making the charge of sabotage, not only against the bourgeoisie but against the government as well. The two are equated. Government resistance to the Bolshevik-sponsored policy of workers' control is also blamed for the economic crisis. The Provisional Government, in addition, is censured for its attempts to achieve inter-class cooperation in industry. Miliutin's report claims: "3. . . . The tactics of sabotage, on the part of the state power . . . and also the . . . steps which they have taken to put economic life in order, in practice cannot but lead to still greater disorder. They have not made one serious reform in the sphere of social or state economy."[13]

Furthermore, all who stood in the way of the establishment of the new socialist state were regarded as the class enemies of the workers, and this consciousness of a class struggle, joined with the anticipation of socialism, could lead to a class-centric point of view in which the world was divided into mutually antagonistic poles. In the words of Lenin, when describing what he believed to be the attitude of a Petrograd worker, "The whole world is divided into two camps, 'we' the toilers and 'they' the exploiters."[14]

The exploiters — the bourgeoisie, the capitalists, the landlords, all who opposed socialism — were referred to by their revolutionary opponents as the dark forces.[15] This term itself was in common usage in socialist and non-socialist literature and speechmaking.[16] The workers of Russia, and of Petrograd in particular, were constantly made to feel the impending threat of dark forces. Fear of the dark forces seems to have impregnated the revolutionary atmosphere of Petrograd. The dark forces, the socialist opposition, were suspected of unscrupulously blocking the progress of the revolution and of trying to turn it along a backward course. Although such a group probably did exist, socialist and Bolshevik propagandists seem to have used indiscriminately the threat of the dark forces upon any occasion on which they wanted to rally the workers to their support. By such usage, the term dark forces tended to become an all-pervasive threat removed from any rational basis in reality.

This was especially true since the dark forces were suspected of using spies and agents-provocateurs and of working their will by means of conspiracy and sabotage. The dark forces, then, were not conceived as being easily recognizable or discernible, but as secretive and disguised. The workers, therefore, had always to be on guard against an omnipresent but hidden enemy. Such an attitude could contribute to produce an atmosphere haunted by disembodied insecurity.

The Mensheviks, for example, speak of ". . . the secret as well as open enemies of the revolution, beginning with the Black Hundreds,[17] agents-provocateurs, and German spies, and ending with the bourgeoisie and bourgeois press who are anxious to restrain, stop, and even turn back altogether, the revolution. . . . The peril which endangers our revolution and our freedom is the union of all the dark forces, of all the secret and open counter-revolutionists."[18]

The dark forces were thus not only the monarchists, the landlords, and the anti-socialist bourgeoisie; they were also the Germans. The enemy was not only within but also without. The Germans, too, it was feared, would restore the old government and deprive the workers of the victories of the revolution. Among these victories were the workers' factory committees, the newly constituted and growing trade unions, and the eight-hour day.[19] By agreement between the Petrograd Association of Manufacturers and the Petrograd Soviet of Workers' Deputies, the eight-hour working day with extra pay for overtime was introduced in the Petrograd area on 23 March 1917.[20] The Moscow Soviet of Workers' Deputies on 3 April sponsored the introduction of the eight-hour day in their area, too, by an agreement reached with the association of manufacturers there. Subsequently, the eight-hour day seems to have spread throughout all Russia. The Provisional Government, however, was reluctant to legalize the eight-hour day in advance of the Constituent Assembly. It did not, therefore, acquire the force of law.[21]

Fear of losing such fruits of the revolution, moreover, was joined with apprehension that the Germans might conquer Russia, or that the solidarity and power the workers had acquired in Petrograd would be dissipated by the moving of industry or the dismissal of the revolutionary Petrograd troops from that city. The German victory at Riga and the consequent debate over the evacuation of Petrograd punctuated and intensified the fear of the dark forces. The fall of Riga on 4 September was closely followed by the Kornilov Affair, during which both the Soviets and the Provisional Government called upon the workers for support against counter-revolutionary plots.

All these occurrences the Bolsheviks wove into a counter-revolutionary web spun by the dark forces. In their propaganda and agitation, the Bolsheviks carried the threat of the counter-revolution one step further than the socialist parties. In Bolshevik agitation, not only German spies, but all "imperialists" — Russia's allies as well as enemies — were part of the dark forces. Not only the antisocialist bourgeoisie, but all the bourgeoisie, and all bourgeois governments, especially the Provisional Government, were components of these forces. A Bolshevik declaration, for example, states: "The Provisional Government itself has become the tool of the counter-revolution and the international reaction."[22]

A resolution of the Petrograd Soviet, issued on 4 October 1917, reads: ". . . the country is in danger of an attempt by the counter-revolutionists. International imperialism, working closely together with the Russian bourgeoisie, is preparing measures to crush the revolution of the workers, soldiers and peasants. . . . The Provisional Government by its decrees is striving to disorganize the revolution. All these facts . . . bring the proletariat, soldiers, and peasants face to face with the question of preparing for a possible counter-revolutionary attempt in the near future."[23]

Such agitation and propaganda, whether Bolshevik or otherwise, does not seem to have relied upon a rational analysis of factual information, but rather to have sought to destroy any rational guideposts for the working class and to manipulate the workers by instilling into them a constant apprehension of deceit and trickery.

The Bolsheviks were especially aware of the usefulness of propaganda and agitation as a manipulative technique and valued it highly as a revolutionary weapon. Lunacharsky said of it: "Cultural-educational work is as necessary as other forms of the labor movement . . . it is the working out of an active structured world conception—party propaganda and agitation are unconditionally cultural-educational work. Propaganda is carried out calmly, systematically; it influences the mind; agitation passionately influences the emotions and the will. The agitator must communicate enthusiasm. This is an art for which it is necessary to be an artist—every artist is an agitator. Socialistic agitation influences us for the most part by its eloquence and is for us socialistic music."[24]

Bolshevik policy, as Lenin conceived it, sought to shatter the state machine; Bolshevik agitation to shatter trust. As Lenin stated: "The proletarians must teach the people to distrust the bourgeoisie."[25]

Suspicion Engendered by the Past

However, Bolshevik and other such agitation and propaganda—their threats of deceit, trickery and violence by the dark forces—would probably have been less effective, despite the real fears engendered by the Kornilov Affair, the fall of Riga and the possibility of the evacuation of Petrograd, if it had not been for the history of the Russian labor movement itself. It was probably because deceit and broken faith had played a part in the Russian labor movement that more credence was lent to accusations of conspiracy and sabotage than might have been otherwise.

As recently as 1901, for example, the workers had experienced the "police socialism" of Zubatov in labor unions organized and led by the secret police itself.[26] In January 1905 the Imperial soldiers had fired on a peaceful demonstration, before the Tsar, of unarmed workers led by the priest Gapon.[27] This Bloody Sunday seems to have shaken deeply the trust of some of the workers in the integrity of governmental authority.

In the spring of 1915, war industries committees were being formed by Russian factory owners for the purpose of instituting a voluntary mobilization of industry.[28] The Central War Industry Committee, partly in order to obtain the cooperation of labor for increased productivity, decided to grant representation to labor on these committees. Under the existing laws, however, such representation was inadmissible for factory workers. The Central War Industry Committee, therefore, obtained governmental permission to carry out an election of workmen's representatives to these War Industry Committees.[29]

The elections, by bringing up as they did the questions of Russian labor's role both in the tsarist state and the World War, served to delineate sharply the policy of the two principal political parties providing the leadership for Russian labor. The Mensheviks, on the whole, for the sake of labor's self-interest, supported participation in the war industries committees.[30] The Bolsheviks, however, completely opposed to Russian prosecution of the war, refused to give their support to any institution that would facilitate the conduct of hostilities or to measures which would increase national solidarity by mitigating class conflicts.[31] Lenin announced: "We are against participation in the war industry committees which insist upon carrying on the imperialist war. We are for making use of the election campaigns, for example, the participation in the first stage of the elections, only for the purpose of agitating and organizing."[32] The Bolsheviks had avowed their intention of taking part in the elections merely for the purpose of agitating against the war and for the overthrow of the existing regime. Further, even though the tsarist government had given its permission for holding the elections, the tsarist police remained interested in what occurred at those elections. On 14 October 1915, an election meeting of 4,000 Lessner factory workers in Petrograd was interrupted by the police, who attempted to disperse the workers. When proof of the legality of the meeting had been provided by the president of the War Industries Committee and by members of the Duma (the national parliamentary assembly), the police allowed the meeting to continue. But they remained to listen.[33]

Thus, these elections illustrate the three-cornered struggle between Bolshevism, the tsarist government, and the liberal and socialist parties for the support and adherence of labor. It was a struggle that divided the ranks of labor and diverted it from its own interests. If such events and situations as Bloody Sunday, police socialism, and the supervision of the labor elections to the war industries committees are kept in mind, it is not difficult to understand that under conditions of strain and tension, labor might easily be led to fear and distrust the state authorities, whether those authorities represented the tsarist order or its successor, the Provisional Government. Any agitation that could succeed in identifying the Provisional Government with its predecessor might also have been able to make the Provisional Government heir to the distrust and suspicion that labor felt for the old regime.

Hunger and Cold

Perhaps one of the most important elements in the atmosphere of Petrograd, in particular, and other Russian cities removed from the source of agricultural and fuel supply, was the discomfort, insecurity and disorganization engendered by the lack of food and fuel.[34] In order to conserve and distribute equitably the food available, the Provisional Government maintained a system of rationing.[35] This, however, sometimes aggravated the bitterness of the population by resulting often in the necessity of waiting in line for long hours in order to receive a ration of bread. During the fall and early winter, the process of standing in queues was made more difficult by the cold. A proclamation of the factory committees, issued in the fall of 1917, stated: "The working class in the cities and the peasants in the villages are living through hard times. In the cities there is a great lack of bread and other food products. We have to spend whole hours waiting in lines and queues before receiving our dole of food: the working man must in this way waste a great deal of time which could be put to more profitable use. In wind and foul weather the working people, men, women, and children, catch cold and grow ill. As a result death is increasing among the population. And all because of a piece of bread."[36]

This lack of food and fuel, the hunger and the cold, which greatly augmented discomfort, probably served to generalize and intensify feelings of insecurity which in all likelihood made threats of conspiracy and sabotage seen more imminent and real. Hunger, in Bolshevik appeals to workers, became the result of bourgeois machinations. A proclamation issued by the Central Council of Factory Committees and appearing in *Pravda* on 30 June 1917 reads, for example, as follows:

"To all Comrade Workers and to all Factory Committees of the City of Petrograd.

"Comrades!

"The Working Class is forced to live and fight in incredibly difficult conditions at the present time.

"The continuation of the war is ruining our lives. There is a lack of food. There is disorganization in production. There is disorder throughout the economic life of the country. Prices are rising. We are exhausted and hungry.

"At the same time, the bourgeoisie are secretly organizing a counter-revolution. Capital is beginning its reactionary campaign against the workers. . . . Lockouts, retail retrenchment and even damage to production create an unendurable situation in the country. Every day there grows the danger of a crash in finances, the economy and the food supply.

* * * * * * *

"Comrades!

"A terrible cloud of counter-revolution, both political and economic, hangs over the working class.

"The Dark Forces are forging new chains for the proletariat, pushing us over the precipice of beggary and exhaustion, hunger, unemployment and despair."[37]

The Problem of Transportation

The problems of hunger, unemployment and despair, however, were directly dependent upon the problems of supply and transportation, and the success or failure of the Provisional Government rested largely upon its solution of these problems.[38]

Participation in the First World War had placed an acute strain upon the Russian economy, especially in the sphere of supply and transportation. Although the Imperial Government had built, and was building, thousands of miles of railway, the vastness of the Russian empire dwarfed the extent of this construction.[39] During the war, when Russia had to take its place with, and compete with, more highly industrialized nations and when, because of its vastness, it faced more complex problems of supply and transportation than they, the Russian railway mileage was pitifully inadequate.[40] Inland waterways have always played an important part in Russia's transportation network, but such transportation is slow and limited by the number of ships and barges. In the winter the northern rivers are frozen and unnavigable.[41] Roads were poor, trucking negligible, and horse transport slow and difficult.[42]

In addition to transporting huge numbers of troops and huge quantities of military materiel, the government also had to supply the population with food and the factories with raw materials for manufacture. It had to transport a greater quantity of supplies at a more accelerated pace than peacetime life demanded.

A lack of raw materials threatened to result in a work stoppage at the factories; a lack of provisions threatened the population with hunger, cold, and bitterness. This economic and administrative problem of the tsarist government, against a background of discontent with the autocracy which existed among all strata of the population, became imbued with an intense political significance and was one of the immediate contributions to its downfall. It is to be remembered that the cause of rioting which on 12 March led to the abdication of the Tsar and the establishment of the Provisional Government was the lack of food in Petrograd.[43]

The population which had established the Provisional Government, especially the population of the cities, and particularly of Petrograd, expected that the Provisional Government would solve the problem of supply and transportation in order to make fuel and food available.[44] Unfortunately, it had no more transportation facilities, and no more skilled labor at its disposal than did the Imperial Government. A political change, no matter how popular, could not quickly solve a problem for which there was no immediate solution.

By granting concessions to labor in hours and wages, by permitting the eight-hour day, the Provisional Government increased the problem of supply. The problem could have been eliminated—but not solved—by withdrawal from the war. This could not have been done without endangering Russia's national interests, its status as a great power, and its national and international security. Having decided to carry on its military obligations under trying and painful economic conditions, the Provisional Government therefore had no choice but to ask of the nation patience, cooperation, and endurance. In this way it could have directed economic and political life as best it could, under the obstacles which faced it.

To overcome these obstacles, the support and cooperation of labor were particularly necessary. For this reason also the Bolshevik agitation concerning the dark forces and the Bolshevik encouragement of workers' control was disruptive of the economy under the Provisional Government. And since the Provisional Government had come to power in part as the result of the difficult economic problems that faced the nation, the Bolshevik policy of shattering the economy attacked the government in an especially vulnerable area.

Peace and Bread

Since the war was the chief cause of the disorganization of the economy, the Bolsheviks, it may be argued, in their proposal to end the war, did have a positive program for alleviating economic conditions. However, the war they promised to end was the "imperialist" war, and for this they intended to substitute a civil war. In shattering the state machine, the Bolsheviks had every expectation that the bourgeoisie would resist and could be overcome only by force. Trotsky, for example, said: "There is no example, Comrades, of the propertied classes not protecting their position by every means and by every violence, but the worker masses awakened by the revolution never stop, never halt halfway, and never give up without fighting for their own victory or revolutionary rights. This is a law of history. These laws the party does not write, but studies. It is impossible to direct historical development artificially along a peaceful road. It is necessary to be conscious of and to admit openly to oneself that civil war is inevitable. It is necessary only to organize it in the interests of the worker masses. This single road makes civil war less bloody, less painful. . . . The proletariat must seize power . . . and your organization, the factory committees, must become the bearer of this idea."[45]

In spite of the fact, however, that the expectation of violence and civil war was inherent in Bolshevik policy, the equivocation of the Bolshevik slogan, "Peace, Land, Bread, and Power," does not seem always to have been understood by those who gave the Bolsheviks their support.

Through their policy of workers' control and their domination of the factory committees, the Bolsheviks seem also to have intended to manipulate and direct the Red Guards. Moreover, having successfully unified the factory committees, the Bolsheviks could control a unified workers' militia. Conversely, a workers' militia that opposed subordination to a center could make the centralizing efforts of the Bolsheviks more difficult.

The factory militia also had a particular significance within the Marxist-Leninist ideology. Such a significance, however, could be discerned, according to Lenin, only by the trained mind of a mediator possessing a high degree of scientific knowledge, for: "There are no miracles in nature and history. But every abrupt turn in history, and this applies to every revolution, presents such a wealth of material, unfolds such unexpected and specific combinations of the forms of struggle and the alignment of forces of the contestants that to the lay mind there is much that must appear miraculous."[46]

According to Lenin, the trained and scientific mind could discern in the creation of a factory militia that an incipient proletarian state was being reborn in Russia. Lenin iterates that ". . . Marxism recognized *the necessity of the state* for the purpose of the transition to socialism; but . . . not a state of the type of the usual parliamentary, bourgeois-democratic republic, but a state like the Paris Commune of 1871 and the Soviets of Workers' Deputies of 1905 and 1917. . . . The course of events, the revolution, has already actually established in our country, although in a weak and embryonic form, this new type of 'state' which is not a state in the true sense of the word."[47]

According to Lenin, the Paris Commune and the embryonic state based upon the Soviets of Workers' Deputies were not true states because a "state in the true sense of the word" is maintained by a special body of armed men exerting force against the "people," the "people" again being defined as the workers and peasants.[48] In Lenin's words, "The state in the true sense of the term is the power exercised over the masses by detachments of armed men separated from the people."[49]

By pointing to the workers' militia and armed bands of peasants, which he defines as an armed force not separated from the "people" but made up of the "people" themselves, Lenin tries to prove that this militia is characteristic of a type of state more fully developed than democracy is, in the evolutionary scale of history.[50] This new state is still a state because it employs force, says Lenin, but it is a new type of state because the force is not exerted against the "people" as in a bourgeois-democracy, but by the "people" as in the Paris Commune. "The Commune," wrote Lenin, "ceased to be a state insofar as it had to repress, not the majority of the population, but the minority (the exploiters); it has smashed the bourgeois state machine, in place of a special repressive force, the whole population itself came on the scene."[51]

Because the workers' militia was a class organ to be used by the workers against the bourgeoisie, Lenin argued that the Russian version of the Paris Commune was about to be born.

"Our new state *now in the process of being born* is also a state, for we, too need detachments of armed men. . . . But our new state, *now in the process of being born,* is no longer a state in the true sense of the term, for in many parts of Russia these detachments of armed men are *the masses themselves,* the entire people, and not merely privileged individuals, placed above and separate from the people. . . ."[52]

The Red Guards were to be these armed men; they were to form the new armed forces of the proletarian state, for until March of 1918 it seems that the Bolsheviks had not intended to create a new army out of the previously existing Imperial Army, which had also served the Provisional Government. "The 'armed people' of the future socialist state was identified with the Red Guards while the disintegrating army was looked upon as a mere reservoir of manpower on which the Red Guards could draw."[53]

"The Armed People Cannot Rule Over Themselves"

The state in the process of being born was to be the dictatorship of the proletariat over the bourgeoisie. The preceding type of state, "bourgeois-democracy," was considered to be the dictatorship of the bourgeoisie over the proletariat. Lenin wrote: "The forms of bourgeois states are exceedingly varied, but their essence is the same: in one way or another, all these states are, in the last analysis, inevitably a dictatorship of the bourgeoisie. The transition from capitalism to communism will certainly bring a great variety and abundance of political forms, but the essence will inevitably be only one: the dictatorship of the proletariat."[54]

Bourgeois-democracy was a dictatorship according to Lenin, principally because it exerted force over the people by armed bodies of men separated from the people. Therefore, since democracy, the rule of the people, was actually maintained by the exertion of force against them, when the people themselves were armed, democracy would begin to wane, for, Lenin explained, "We must look forward to the new democracy which is in the process of being born, and which is already ceasing to be a democracy. For democracy means the rule of the people, whereas the armed people cannot rule over themselves."[55]

Here the identification of the people with the state is so close that no distinction is made between them. The army being made up of the people cannot, in this view, rule over them because authority is regarded as being external, outside, different in quality from that over which it exerts its power. Once authority is equated with the will of the subject it ceases to be authority at all. Further, within this ideology members of the same class cannot rule over each other; thus the class-centric view tends also to reinforce the identification of the workers with the state. The difference in function between soldier and worker, even when an army superseded the militia in the dictatorship of the proletariat, was not recognized as setting them apart. However, even if the identification of the people with the state can be made, there still remains the problem for the worker of making his will congruent with historical necessity.

The Paris Commune and Workers' Control

Ideologically, also, the concept of workers' control is closely interwoven with the idea of the embryonic proletarian state of the same type as the Paris Commune, a state dialectically unfolding from the past into the future. Lenin believed that this was the type of government, at last discovered, which would destroy the old bourgeois state machine. It was a state in which the people—that is, the workers and peasants—would seize power, remove the bourgeois officials, and combine executive and legislative functions to administer the state themselves. In Lenin's words, it was a type of state in which ". . . The source of power is not a law previously discussed and passed by parliament, but the direct initiative of the masses from below in their localities—outright 'seizure,' to use a popular expression. . . ."[56]

The Paris Commune and the new state have as their goal the elimination of public officials who were distinguished from the "people" and existed as a class above the people. For, said Lenin, in order to destroy the state ". . . it is necessary to convert the functions of public service into such simple operations of control and accounting as are within the reach of the vast majority of the population and ultimately of every single individual."[57]

Thus, workers' control could easily be construed as an integral part of the functioning of a state like the Paris Commune. It could represent the transfer of the operations of control and accounting from the hands of those who formed a class above the people to the hands of the people themselves. It may represent the new democracy in the economic sphere, a democracy which claimed to reform not only the political but also the economic areas of life. As Lenin wrote: "Taken separately, no kind of democracy will yield to socialism. But in actual life democracy will never be 'taken separately' with other things; it will exert *its* influence in economic life, stimulating its reorganization; it will be subjected, in its turn, to the influence of economic development, and so on. Such is the dialectics of living history."[58]

It is reasonable to assume, then, that ideologically, workers' control was meant to represent, on the economic level, the operation of a state modeled after the Paris Commune.

Centralization and Workers' Control

Centralism, too, was regarded as a characteristic of the Paris Commune and Lenin warned against confusing the abolition of the state with the abolition of centralism.[59] For the Leninists, the function of the commune was, first, to destroy capitalism, and second, to unite into a centralized structure.

"But will it not be centralism," said Lenin, ". . . if the proletariat and the poorest peasants take the power of the state into their own hands, organize themselves freely into communes, and unite the action of all communes in striking at capital, in crushing the resistance of the capitalists, in the transfer of private property in railways, factories, land and so forth to the entire nation, to the whole of society. Will that not be the most consistent centralism? And proletarian centralism at that?"[60]

It would seem that the factory committees in this scheme were to be a means by which industry was to be seized from ownership and centralized under the new Bolshevik state. It will be shown subsequently, however, that it was not through promises of centralization but partly through the encouragement of workers' control that the Bolsheviks attracted adherents among the workers.

CLASS REPRESENTATION

One of the aspects of the revolutionary situation which contributed to the success of the Bolsheviks in November 1917 was the artificial political segregation of the working class into the Soviets of Workers' Deputies. The leadership in the Soviets of Workers' Deputies, and in the Soviets of Soldiers' and Peasants' Deputies with which it was joined, was provided by the revolutionary intellectuals. Since the workers, for the most part, were of low level of literacy and probably did not possess a knowledge of the techniques necessary for parliamentary procedure or for the composition of resolutions, regulations, orders and statutes, the workers themselves were overshadowed by the intellectuals who did possess such techniques. Although the workers were not articulate, influence in the soviets would also have had a tendency to gravitate towards those who had a better command of language and were better and more experienced speakers than the workers themselves. As a result of the caucus system prevailing in the soviets, influence was also weighted in favor of the intellectuals. In describing the parliamentary procedures of Russian meetings and conventions, John Reed points out that: "Almost all the real work of the session is done in caucuses of the different groups and political factions, which almost always cast their votes in a body and are represented by floor-leaders."[61]

This system further enabled the Menshevik and Bolshevik intellectuals to dominate the Soviets in spite of the active participation of the workers in the general meetings. Because of the knowledge which they possessed, the intellectuals seem to have fulfilled the functions of floor and caucus leaders. Until about mid-September the Mensheviks were the predominant influence upon the workers. Partly by wresting predominance over labor from the socialist parties, the Bolsheviks were able to achieve the success of the November Revolution.

The Bolsheviks and the Immediacy of Revolutionary Goals

The Bolsheviks seem also to have acquired labor support largely by undercutting Menshevik, Socialist Revolutionary, and Provisional Government policy. The Provisional Government had recognized the factory committees and under it the eight-hour day had been widely established. The Mensheviks had formed an effective labor union organization, had sponsored the factory committees, and promised the coming of socialism. Because of the extreme difficulties engendered by a wartime economy, however, the Provisional Government and the Mensheviks were also forced to request of labor patience, cooperation and endurance.

A July proclamation of the Minister of Labor, Skobolev, a Menshevik, explains that workers' self-interest must be coordinated with the general economic situation. Skobolev advised the workers that they could not divorce their own interests from the general welfare. Explaining that wages are dependent upon a number of related conditions, he spoke out against unreasonable requests for increased wage rates. The proclamation warned against the seizure of factories and the assumption of managerial functions by the workers. However, it was not self-sacrifice that Skobolev requested of labor; he asked only for moderation.[62]

But the program of the Bolsheviks, having as its primary objectives the acquisition of power through the disruption of the economy and the state machine, sought to manipulate labor for the implementation of Bolshevik objectives. It thus offered the solution of economic problems not through cooperation but through the destructive process of workers' control; for in their demands for workers' control, the Bolsheviks made use of the confidence and assertion acquired by the workers in their new freedom to act together in the great deeds and extraordinary events of the revolution. And through their sponsorship of workers' control the Bolsheviks took advantage of the revolutionary tide and the chiliastic mood of Petrograd, a mood which looked to the immediate realization of revolutionary goals and demanded to achieve in the present what the Provisional Government and socialist parties strove to realize in the future.[63] A worker at the Third Conference of Factory Committee (10 September 1917) stated, for example: "All parties, not excluding even the Bolsheviks, entice the workers with the promise of the Kingdom of God on earth a hundred years from now. . . . We do not need improvement a hundred years from now, but now, immediately. . . ."[64] By its sponsorship of workers' control, however, the Bolshevik party seemed to champion fulfillment of socialist goals in the here and now.

In its agitation prior to the November Revolution, the Bolshevik party attributed to deceit and trickery the postponement of those goals, no matter how unavoidable the postponement might have been. The Bolshevik program, in place of equality, offered domination. In place of support to the Provisional Government and in place of the Menshevik promise of socialism in the future, the Bolsheviks promised a sudden and spectacular change. They promised a state like that of the Paris Commune; a state which would draw socialism near. In an atmosphere of apprehension and of fear, in unavoidable conditions of hunger and of cold which tried patience and endurance to the utmost, the Bolsheviks did not ask of the workers patience and endurance, but encouraged resentment and violence against the existing order. They prevented the alleviation of the economic problems which caused the lack of fuel and food and they manipulated for their own purposes the fear of the dark forces, a fear that they themselves had helped to spread.

Labor, the Provisional Government and the Seizure of Power

By disrupting the trade unions and dominating the factory committees, the Bolsheviks gathered the threads of influence among labor into their own hands and in this way increased their power in the political organs of the working class.

As a result of their predominating influence among the factory committees, the Bolsheviks also had at their disposal the factory militia. By means of agitation in the army they disorganized the military branch of the Provisional Government.[65]

When the political domination of the Soviets of Workers' and Soldiers' Deputies had been achieved and the economic base and military arm of the Provisional Government had sufficiently disintegrated, the Bolsheviks seized power. The seizure of power attests to the success of their tactics. The degree to which Bolshevik policy was understood and accepted by Russian labor, however, is best discerned by an analysis of conditions immediately after the Bolshevik government was established.

CHAPTER IV

The Bolshevik Party, Workers' Control and the Factory Committees after the Seizure of Power

SOVIET STATUTES ON WORKERS' CONTROL

Almost immediately after the Bolshevik revolution, sometime between the second and fifth day (8-13 November) after the seizure of power, a draft Statute on Workers' Control was drawn up by Lenin.[1] In addition, a Proposed Law on Workers' Control was submitted to the Commission of Labor for its consideration on 16 November 1917.[2] And on 27 November, Statutes on Workers' Control, signed by Lenin as chairman of the Council of People's Commissars and by Shliapnikov as Commissar of Labor, were passed by the All-Russian Central Executive Committee of the Soviets of Workers', Soldiers' and Peasants' Deputies of the second convocation.[3] These statutes attest to the Bolshevik preoccupation with the problems of workers' control and to the importance of workers' control for the Bolshevik revolution. It has already been pointed out in a previous chapter that it was with the support of the factory committees (which implemented workers' control) and with the Red Guards (which enforced workers' control) that the Bolsheviks seized power in the name of the Soviets. For two reasons, then, the Bolsheviks seem to have found it necessary to reiterate their policy of workers' control: (1) because their popularity among the factory committees and Red Guards was indissolubly connected with their policy of workers' control; (2) because of the smallness and weakness of the party, the Bolsheviks had been, and immediately after the revolution still were, dependent upon the factory committees and the policy of workers' control to capture the economy of the country.

Thus, workers' control, according to the statute of 27 November, was to extend to all possible enterprises, large and small, throughout the nation.[4] The statute indicating the intention of centralizing workers' control on a national scale proclaimed that it was introduced "In the interests of a systematic regulation of the national economy. . . ."[5]

Control was to be centralized by the Central Council which, presiding over all councils of workers' control, was to work out a general plan for its execution.[6] According to the statutes there was to be a distribution of power among the central and local institutions. The regional councils were to be left free to act within the framework of the decrees issued by the center. They were to mediate between the lower organs of workers' control and to consider the appeals of the factory owners issuing instructions within the limits imposed by the All-Russian Council of Workers' Control.[7]

The decree of 27 November claimed the factory committees would be united into regional councils in which other workers' organizations would be represented. These regional councils would be organs of the Soviets of Workers', Soldiers' and Peasants' Deputies. "For each important city, *guberniia,* or *raion,"* reads Paragraph 3 of the Statute, "a local council of workers' control is created, which, being an organ of the Soviet of Workers', Soldiers' and Peasants' Deputies, is composed of representatives of the trade unions, factories, shops and other workers' committees and workers' cooperatives."[8] Thus, the revolution which was supported by the factory committees in the name of the Soviets resulted in a decree calling for the creations of councils of workers' control under the jurisdiction of the Soviets themselves. Workers' control, it seemed, was being integrated into the structure of the new state.

However, the power of the factory committees was to be weakened. Lozovsky, especially, whose political power was derived from his trade union leadership, was opposed to any measure that would increase or maintain the power of the factory committees. He put forward the point of view that the trade unions had to be part of the organizations instituting workers' control so that general proletarian interests could be properly cared for. "It is obvious," said Lozovsky, "that the trade unions must enter the institutions created by this decree in order to regulate the matter of control so that it corresponds to the interests of the working class."[9] According to the statute of 27 November, it was no longer the factory committees which were to execute workers' control, for only five out of 26, or about one-fifth, of the organizations sending a definite number of delegates in the All-Russian Council of Workers' Control were to represent the factory committees. The rest of the representatives belonged to other workers' organizations, to the All-Russian Council of Trade Unions (which had representation equal to that of the factory committees), to the peasants, and to technicians and specialists.[10]

Thus, in effect, workers' control was removed from the hands of the factory committees where it had formerly lodged. There was, indeed, even at the First All-Russian Conference of Factory Committees, immediately before the Bolshevik seizure of power, evidence that the factory committees were to be subordinated to the trade unions. The decrees on workers' control issued after the November Revolution do not seem, however, to have accepted this as an accomplished fact. Neither, it seems, did the factory committees.[11]

If the factory committees were being eliminated from the process of workers' control, the owners nevertheless seemingly continued to be subject to that control. The final decisions relating to an individual enterprise, however, were subject to review by higher organs, for according to Paragraph 8, "The decisions of the organs of workers' control are compulsory for the owners and can be abolished only by the higher organs of workers' control."[12]

A tenuous concession to ownership and management was also made by granting to the owners and managers a three-day period of appeal.[13]

Although the brevity of the time allowed for the appeal seriously limited the value of this concession, the concession itself, in the light of the vitiation of the rights of the factory committees, is significant. The enterprise owners themselves, it seems, were being used to weaken the role of the factory committees in workers' control.

Miliutin, however, at the meeting of the Central Executive Committee at which the statute was passed, claimed that the factory committees were being protected through the limitation to a three-day period of the factory owners' right of appeal: "We limited, to a three-day period, the right of the enterprise owner to appeal the decrees of the organs of workers' control. Objections were made to us, that *if the organs of workers' control were the factory committees,* and if their decrees were compulsory, it could result in the violation of the decrees of the economic plan as a whole and, therefore, it would be better to make the decisions of *the city organs of workers' control* compulsory for the factory owners."[14]

According to Miliutin, then, there was a viewpoint among the framers of the statute that if the factory committees were permitted to form and enforce policy on workers' control, it might violate the policy of the center. Therefore, they seem to have demanded that the control of workers' control be taken out of the hands of the workers' committees at the factories and placed in the hands of a central organ such as the city units of workers' control removed from the individual factories themselves.

The statute, moreover, did modify the power of the factory committees over the owners by allowing the right of appeal of the decisions of the factory committees to city and to national organs of workers' control.

"We have recognized," Miliutin pointed out, "that the decisions of the factory committees are compulsory for the owner, but the owners of the enterprise have a three-day period for appealing these decisions. The owners can appeal the decisions of the factory committees to the city organs of workers' control, and, if they remain dissatisfied with this, to the All-Russian organ of workers' control so that, in general, they have nine days for appeal."[15]

At the same meeting of the Central Executive Committee, Lozovsky objected to the statute on the grounds that it did not sufficiently centralize workers' control. "The basic defect of this legislation," he is reported as saying, "is that it is outside of any connection with a planned regulation of the people's economy and atomizes control over production instead of centralizing it."[16]

Miliutin, however, explained that the decree was issued in recognition of an existing situation. The statute attempted to encompass or to cover workers' control as it existed. After workers' control had been centralized, Miliutin maintained, it could then be fitted into a broader, more general economic plan. "We must work out the legislation on workers' control," he said, "so as to provide a general framework for the actual situation which exists in reality. The objections which were made boil down to the fact that we established workers' control without having established, at first, a general economic plan."[17]

Miliutin, however, agreed that to issue statutes on workers' control before the promulgation of a general economic plan was a violation of the order in which legislation should be formulated. "But life has outstripped us," Miliutin said. "In life, control was worked out in the struggle against sabotage, lockouts, etc. And violating the definite order in which legislation ought to develop, we must unite into one orderly statewide apparatus—that workers' control which is being put into effect locally. Therefore, our proposed legislation on workers' control appears earlier than the proposed legislation on the economic plan. . . ."[18] Centralization, therefore, is actually the first step in molding workers' control to a plan for the economy.

Workers' Control and the Supreme Council of the National Economy

Paragraph 13 of the Statutes on Workers' Control of 27 November provided for subordinating workers' control to the economic plan, stating in its second article that "The Statute on the mutual relations between the All-Russian Council of Workers' Control and other institutions regulating the people's economy will be issued separately."[19]

The statute determining this relationship between the All-Russian Council of Workers' Control and other economic institutions is the Statute on the Supreme Council [Soviet] of the National Economy, which was adopted at the meeting of the Central Executive Committee on 14 December 1917, about two weeks after the adoption of the Statute on Workers' Control. Paragraph 5 of this provides: "The Supreme Council of the National Economy is formed (a) out of the All-Russian Council of Workers' Control, the composition of which is defined by the decree of 14/27 November 1917;[20] (b) of the representatives of all the people's commissariats; (c) of experts with an advisory vote."[21]

Thus the representatives of the factory committees, who comprised only about one-fifth of the All-Russian Council of Workers' Control, would be further proportionately reduced in the Supreme Council of the National Economy.

Paragraph 9 of the Statutes on the Supreme Council of the National Economy stipulated that all matters relating to the economy of the nation as a whole were to be submitted to the Council of People's Commissars by the Supreme Council of the National Economy.[22]

Thus the Council of People's Commissars became the final arbiter of all decisions concerning economic life, including those directly relating to workers' control.

Paragraph 10 adds that all economic organs of the Soviets of Workers,' Soldiers' and Peasants' Deputies (one of which was the All-Russian Council of Workers' Control) are subordinate to the Supreme Council of the National Economy. The local councils of workers' control are also subject to this supreme organ, for "The Supreme Council of the National Economy unites and directs the work of the economic branches of the Soviet of Workers,' Soldiers' and Peasants' Deputies, including the local organs of workers' control."[23]

The All-Russian Council of Workers' Control, therefore, did not have complete jurisdiction over its subordinate local organs. The latter were also subject to the Supreme Council of the National Economy.

Thus, after the Bolshevik Revolution, the Bolshevik Party attempted to remove workers' control from the purview of the factory committees. It placed workers' control ostensibly in the jurisdiction of the Soviet of Workers', Soldiers' and Peasants' Deputies, but actually made it subordinate to the Supreme Council of the National Economy. The latter, however, was itself subject to the Council of People's Commissars, for according to Paragraph 1 of the Statute of the Supreme Council of the National Economy, "the Supreme Council of the National Economy is attached to the Council of People's Commissars."[24]

The Council of People's Commissars, with Lenin as its chairman, was made up entirely of leading members of the Bolshevik Party. They made no pretense of submitting their decrees for the ratification of the Soviet of Workers', Soldiers' and Peasants' Deputies.

On 17 November 1917 the Left Social Revolutionaries, the only party supporting the Bolsheviks in the soviets, charged that the commissars had been publishing decrees without submitting them, for preliminary debate and sanction, to the Central Executive Committee of the Soviet of Workers', Soldiers' and Peasants' Deputies. The Left Social Revolutionaries, charging that this was in direct violation of the power of the Central Executive Committee, which had been established by the second Congress of the Soviets as the supreme organ before which the government was responsible, issued the following statement:

"We made this demand to the chairman of the Council of Commissars [Lenin]:

"1. Upon what basis were the bills, decrees, and other acts not presented for the examination of the Central Executive Committee?

"2. Does the government intend to refrain from its arbitrarily established, completely inadmissible practice—the decreeing of laws?"[25]

In reply to this charge Lenin stated that "the new power could not take into account, in its activity, all the rigamarole which would set it on the road of the meticulous observation of all the formalities."[26] Lenin's disdainful reply to the Social Revolutionary charge indicates that expediency was the guide to his policy as head of the new Soviet state, and he seems to have implied that he was not bound by law or regulation, by juridical, institutional or customary limits, to the governing power. Acting, as he claimed, in accord with historical necessity, he would rule by decree.

Thus, expedience rather than law seems to have been the guiding principle of Bolshevik policy. Therefore, even though the factory committees, insofar as they were involved in workers' control, were juridically subordinate to the Council of People's Commissars through the agency of the Supreme Council of the National Economy, their juridical position was even less important than the ability to exert power and to maneuver in the political situation.

Although Bolshevik explanations of Bolshevik action were consistent within the framework of the ideology, the decrees concerning workers' control manifested a notable change in tactics and indicated an attempt on the part of the party to manipulate the factory committees and subordinate them to Bolshevik policy. Thus, almost immediately after the November Revolution, workers' control over all the economic life of Russia was proclaimed. Simultaneously, however, the Bolshevik Party leadership removed that control from the factory committees, the organizations that before November had executed the policy of workers' control partly under Bolshevik leadership. The Bolsheviks then placed that control, through consecutive decrees, under the jurisdiction of the Supreme Council of the National Economy, dominated by the Council of People's Commissars.

Conflicting Concepts of Workers' Control

Workers' control, as it had been carried out in an appreciable number of cases before November, consisted of the control of individual factories by the individual factory committees. It was the factory committees, the organs consisting of representatives of the workers and employees, that not infrequently seem to have supervised the accounting, the manufacturing, the buying and selling, and the hiring and firing at their own factories. It is true that the Bolsheviks had intended to centralize and dominate control in order eventually to regulate all of industry. However, it was sufficient for the Bolsheviks, before their seizure of power, that workers' control could function to hinder, obstruct and trammel the activity of ownership and management. This, in turn, would undermine the Provisional Government. At the Sixth Party Congress of July 1917, Miliutin explained that workers' control was only in its first stage: ". . . the supervision of the capitalists. . . . In its future development it will be turned into control over industry."[27] But under the conditions then prevailing, it was sufficient that the activity of the workers be used as a weapon against the existing governmental order. "We will ride on the crest of the economic wave of the movement of the workers and we will turn this spontaneous movement into a conscious political movement against the existing state power."[28]

There seems to have been, however, a significant difference between the movement that actually existed and the movement that the Bolsheviks sought to create. Almost at the beginning of the control movement a fundamental difference between the worker and the Bolshevik concept of workers' control was noticed. At the eleventh meeting of the Sixth Congress of the Bolshevik Party, for example, Lomov urged the party to formulate a concrete plan of centralization and, even more importantly, to convince the workers that non-centralized individual units of workers' control at individual factories were not desirable. "It is necessary to point out," said Lomov, ". . . how to coordinate self-instituted and un-supervised control with control on an All-Russian scale, in order to avoid creating the illusion, among the masses, that workers' control, carried out in individual factories, can lead to an improvement in the situation, either economically or politically."[29]

At the Second Conference of Factory Committees of Petrograd in August 1917, V. M. Levin asserted that the workers ". . . did not distinguish between the conception of control and the conception of taking possession (*zakhvat*). . . ."[30] The Bolsheviks, however, did make this distinction. Control, to the Bolshevik, did not mean the workers were to take possession of the factories for themselves. The Bolsheviks seem to have intended that the workers would control the owners but that they, in turn, would control the workers. Workers' control for the Bolsheviks was to be a means by which the workers, under the Provisional Government, could exert pressure against the state and industry and hold industry in readiness for nationalization and centralization after a Bolshevik seizure of power.

The workers, however, especially those organized in factory committees, do not seem to have accepted this Bolshevik concept. The Bolsheviks, therefore, continued to inveigh against workers' control, as construed by the workers themselves, as ownership. Miliutin, on the eve of the Bolshevik Revolution, at the First All-Russian Conference of Factory Committees, tried to make it clear to the workers that "Our control proposes the nationalization of the important branches of industry. The seizure of individual factories, their transfer into the hands of individual groups of workers, will not draw us closer towards socialism."[31]

The workers, however, in spite of the amount and intensity of the polemic directed against the process, continued to take possession of the factories for themselves. In his objections, therefore, to the Statute on Workers' Control of 27 November 1917, Lozovsky asserted: "It is necessary that the workers of each individual enterprise do not receive the impression that the enterprise belongs to them. This must be stipulated categorically and with absolute clarity."[32]

In January 1918, the Menshevik Cherevanin also claimed that workers' control, as a means to the centralization and nationalization of industry, had failed. "Workers' control," he said, "has merely changed the masters of the factories from one man to a group at individual factories, which, as formerly, are unconnected with one another."[33]

Lozovsky was most vehement in pointing out the difficulties of integrating workers' control, as it existed, into a communist system.[34] He polemicized insistently and ardently against joint ownership and insisted: "Merely because there will be a thousand instead of ten factory owners in a particular enterprise, it still does not become socialistic."[35]

Indeed, once the Bolshevik Revolution had been accomplished, the Bolsheviks found it imperative to put an end to a movement in which the workers could succeed in obtaining joint ownership of the factories in which they had been employed. Before the seizure of power, the factory committees instituting workers' control, by undermining the Provisional Government, were able to serve immediate Bolshevik goals even if they did not adhere to the Party's further objective of transferring industry to the state. With the removal of the Provisional Government, however, the previously existing juridical sanctions against workers' control were also removed. It remained to be seen, then, whether the concept of workers' control as conceived by the Bolsheviks would triumph. No longer could differences of goal or purpose be hidden by a common attack on the former social or juridical order. No longer could definitional ambiguities of "workers' control" conceal the distinction between the reality which the Bolsheviks on the one hand, or the factory committees on the other, had been striving to create. Implicit in the differing concepts of workers' control was a difference in the concept of socialism itself.

Conflicting Concepts of Socialism

Maiskii, a Menshevik, charged that: ". . . in my observation it is not some of the proletariat but most of the proletariat, especially in Petrograd, who look upon workers' control as if it were actually the emergence of the kingdom [*tsarstvo*] of socialism."[36] He complains and laments that, among the workers, "the very idea of socialism is embodied in the conception of workers' control,"[37]—that is, in the form of workers' ownership.

The conception and interpretation of workers' control as socialism itself was evident even before the Bolshevik Revolution; on 2 November 1917 the Bolshevik Skrypnik warned the factory committees that "Workers' control is still not socialism; it is only one of the transitional measures drawing us near to socialism."[38]

Writing in the *Trade Union Herald* (*Professional'nyi Vestnik*) of 5 January 1918, Lozovsky made it clear that workers' control was not to be equated with socialism: "Is workers' control a principle of socialistic production? . . . Is it the immediate realization of socialism or is it nothing more than a radical measure of transitional times clearing the way to socialism? We must at the very outset state that the workers' control is not socialism. Workers' control . . . does not mean the immediate socialization of the factories and shops, and much less the transfer of enterprises into the hands of individual groups."[39]

Over and over again speeches and articles addressed to the workers by both the Bolsheviks and Mensheviks emphasize the fact that workers' control is not equivalent to group ownership and that group ownership is not equivalent to socialism.[40] For the Bolsheviks, the problem of making a distinction between workers' control and socialism was of particular importance. It was far from a problem of abstract conception, of definitions, or of doctrine. It was a problem deeply pervading, and involved in, the revolutionary situation. It was a problem of power. If workers succeeded in maintaining their ownership of the factories they had seized, if they ran these factories for themselves, if they considered the revolution to be at an end, if they considered socialism to have been established—then there would have been no need for the revolutionary leadership of the Bolsheviks. There would have been no need for the centralized administration and economic planning, the formation of syndicates and trusts the Bolsheviks intended to create. If the Bolsheviks had acceded to the workers' conception of socialism, they could have functioned only as representatives of the working class, abiding by its values and fulfilling its goals. If they could enforce their own conception of socialism upon the workers, they could lead and direct the working class to fulfill the goals and values of the party.

The Bolsheviks could not, however, repudiate the workers so soon after the November Revolution, for they had risen to power on the crest of the workers' movement. They had manipulated the chiliastic strivings of the proletariat for the immediate realization of socialism—for socialism in the present. Largely by promising a new order—a state like the Paris Commune—the Bolsheviks had won their adherents. Even more importantly, their opponents had lost support partly by insisting that socialism must be postponed. The Bolsheviks had promised to bring the workers closer to socialism, but for the workers socialism was not the socialism which the Bolsheviks had promised.

Workers' Control in Action

Before investigating further how the Bolsheviks dealt with this problem, it would be fruitful, bearing in mind previously presented information, to describe briefly workers' control as the workers seem to have conceived it. Bolshevik historiography, however, has tended to overlook, to obscure, or to conceal the process of workers' control as it was put into effect by the workers. The conception and the manner in which it was realized may, therefore, be reconstructed only in a skeletal fashion from the contemporary articles and speeches, mostly of the opponents of workers' control, and from brief references to it in retrospective accounts of the period. From these it becomes clear that the workers conceived of control as ownership.[41]

Having seized the factories, the workers instituted "a type of cooperative association, a shareholding workers' society,"[42] in which all the workers and employees of a particular factory owned a portion of the enterprise and shared in the profits. In most cases, after the initial disorganization and disruption occasioned by workers' control, the workers seemed to have realized the advantages of maintaining the technical personnel and often did so. Sometimes they seem to have maintained the owners, as well as the managers, in administrative or technical capacities. Many factory committees seem to have realized that the owners' knowledge of how and when to obtain raw materials or to sell manufactured articles, for example, was as necessary as the skill of the workers. At any rate, workers instituting workers' control were often accused of being in concealed (*nesoznanyi*) contact with the owners.[43] Mention is ironically made of a "touching union of the owners and workers."[44] It is difficult to determine, however, how much of this contact was hidden, how much overt, or whether this accusation was merely an attempt to discredit workers' control from the communist point of view.

Even under the Provisional Government, cooperative administration and shared ownership of factories seems to have existed. The Commission to Study the Trade Union Movement in the SSSR claims that there were ". . . individual attempts of owners to conspire with their workers and employees concerning their participation in the profits of the enterprises and in the management of production. This was done by giving a part share to the workers and employees who, in this way, received part of the profits. In addition, it was proposed to introduce the representatives of the workers into the management. . . . The newspaper *Delo Naroda* No. 74 [a publication of the Social Revolutionary Party] announced that the Ministry of Trade and Industry granted the petitions of several owners concerning changes in their statutes applicable to this situation."[45]

The sharing of ownership and management, moreover, often seems to have instilled into the workers a devotion to their factories. It seems to have produced in the worker an identification of the factory interest with his own self-interest, for many workers seem to have become intimately concerned with the welfare of their factories. An article in the *Herald of the People's Commissariat of Labor* (*Vestnik Narodnago Kommissariata Truda*) in February 1918 asserts from the Bolshevik point of view that ". . . the factory committees often, and even in the majority of cases, adhered to the narrow interests of a particular enterprise. For the committee it was important that its factory functioned normally, that it was supplied with orders and funds. Individual members often acted in the capacity of expediters to satisfy these needs of the enterprise."[46] Since the interest of the owner, as well of the worker shareholders, were identified with the welfare of the factory, the article claims that "Often these committees were involuntarily converted into a kind of appendage to the owner, defending his interests. . . . The factory committees adhering to their 'factory interests' developed their own parochial patriotism and local pride."[47]

Each factory, pursuing its own self-interest in disorganized and disrupted times, seems to have tried to procure for itself the commodities it needed, for "A competition began among the workers of individual factories to assure 'their own factories' of deliveries of coal or metal. The factory committees delegated their emissaries to the provinces, for example, to the Donets basin, where they exerted pressure to obtain coal or steel, trying to assure 'their own' factories of it. For example, the Obukhovskii factory . . . delegated about 50 worker-expediters who tried to obtain coal for their own factory."[48]

Thus the workers executing workers' control tended, it seems, to try to insure the security and prosperity of the factories at which they were employed. A Bolshevik representative at a conference of metal workers' unions and factory committees claimed that a solidarity arose between the workers and the administration, and the factory committees interceded for the industrialists before the government. He charged that each factory committee exalted its own factory in respect to its technical excellence and its importance to the economic life of the country. Representatives of the factory committees, taking upon themselves the tasks of securing orders for the respective factories, went to the various ministries at Petrograd, where they praised their factories in order to solicit orders. Several factory committee representatives went to Petrograd from Kharkhov, for example, to assist the factory management in securing a subsidy.[49]

It was in the absence of strong centralized control that the factory committees were able to work autonomously for their own welfare. Nevertheless the Bolsheviks accused the factory committees of engaging in decentralizing and discoordinating activity and of thereby sacrificing the interests of the country to self-interest. The Bolsheviks, however, at the end of 1917 and the beginning of 1918, were not capable of exerting very extensively the authority necessary for centralized control. Therefore, the autonomy of the factory committees was not only a matter of inclination on their part, but seems to have resulted also from the inability of the party to exert its centralized program.[50] When the party spokesmen. then reiterated such statements as, "The workers with all their might must fight against the gradual conversion of the factory committees into private property entrepreneurial [*khozaiskopredprinimatel'skii*] organizations," they were seeking principally to ward off resistance to the program of nationalization and centralization which they intended to enforce. They do not seem to have had concern here for the success with which the enterprises were being conducted, or with the restoration of the economy. A Soviet political economist, writing within the communist framework, points out that in that epoch, as in any epoch, it is necessary to look at various systems of industrial management not only from the point of view of technical suitability and excellence but also from the standpoint of revolutionary strength.[51] Private property ownership by the factory committees would have placed the control of the economy largely in the hands of the workers. It would have escaped the total control through state trusts and syndicates that the party intended to exert.[52] It would have prevented the ". . . conversion of *all* citizens into workers and employees of *one* huge 'syndicate'—the whole state. . . ."[53] The party would thus have feared the restoration of industry if it meant the restoration of private property.

Workers' control, therefore, had to be diverted or transformed into a process of state control. A new order instituting state control conflicted with the workers' conception of socialism, but in imposing the communist conception of socialism upon the workers, the Bolsheviks were faced with the problem of alienating the workers. They had ridden to power on the revolutionary current; how, then, were they to canalize this tide toward Bolshevik objectives? How were the Bolsheviks, as the vanguard of the proletariat, to lead the workers where they did not want to go? How were they to harness to Bolshevik goals the chiliastic energy which had played an important role in the revolutionary outburst?

Chiliasm and Goal Postponement

On the psychological level, this answer may be found in the Bolshevik conception of the Paris Commune. The state which the Bolsheviks had promised to establish was to be one like the Paris

Commune, a dictatorship of the proletariat. The new order under this type of state was neither socialism nor communism; it was to be a transitional period between capitalism and the new future order. It was not the function of this state to introduce socialism immediately, for when Lenin had promised the proletariat a state like the Paris Commune, he had promised them not the Being of Socialism but the Becoming of Socialism. He had promised them the Negation of Capitalism or, more accurately, the destruction of capitalism as it previously existed. Before the Bolsheviks came to power, the concept of the Paris Commune as a new state drawing socialism near probably appealed to those revolutionary workers among whom chiliastic strivings prevailed. The promise of a new type of state, realizable in the here-and-now, might have overshadowed Lenin's modification that such a state was only transitional to socialism, not socialism itself.

Furthermore, in the light of the predominant role of workers' control in the Bolshevik program, there would seem to have been little reason for the workers to think that the Bolsheviks, after the revolution, would seriously modify workers' control as it was practiced. Even the clearly stipulated policy of the centralization of workers' control, proclaimed by the Bolsheviks on the eve of the revolution, would not necessarily have convinced the workers of what the Bolshevik policy was. There are many ways to centralization and many reasons for it. Also, the Bolshevik policy, immediately after the revolution was over, strove to go beyond centralization to total domination. It is not unlikely then, in view of the policy which the workers themselves had been carrying out, that they believed the Bolshevik revolution would enable them to carry on workers' control without restraint. They might have conceived of socialism as a time when workers' control would be extended to each individual enterprise, when industry was restored and prosperity reached. If the Bolshevik Party, however, were to dominate the economy, the solidification of workers' control as it existed could not be permitted. The workers had to be deprived of their control. This deprivation and subordination of the workers the Bolsheviks presented as a stage on the way to socialism. The process of depriving the workers of property and power, the Bolsheviks integrated into the goals of socialism itself. Workers' control was not socialism. Socialism could not immediately follow capitalism. "There is not one socialist, Comrades," said Lenin, "who would not recognize the obvious that between socialism and capitalism there lies a more or less difficult transitional period. . . ."[54] This transitional period became one in which workers' control, as understood by the workers, was to be abrogated—the workers were to become the employees of the state instead of the owners of industry.

The idea of the Paris Commune, which itself had attracted the socialistic workers and Marxist intellectuals to the Bolshevik cause, was used, after the revolution, to reconcile them to the new transitional order. The idea of the Paris Commune was utilized to restrain the revolutionary enthusiasm and chiliasm which demanded the immediate realization of socialism. By claiming to have created a state like the Paris Commune, the Bolsheviks tried to convince those who had supported their revolution that they had indeed brought about a revolutionary change in the present and earthly life of man. The Paris Commune represented a leap into a new stage of history. But by designating that leap as one into a transitional period before a more perfect and ideal earthly existence, it was possible to store and maintain the revolutionary energy. Though the leap had been made, the ultimate goal was still to be reached.

The Marxist intellectuals themselves had to be warned that their goals must be postponed, that their objectives could not immediately be achieved, and that only devotion to the Bolshevik cause could realize the socialist goals in the future. "The reason," said Lenin, "why the present position seems peculiar to many of those who would like to be regarded as Socialists is that they have been accustomed to contrasting capitalism and socialism abstractly and that they profoundly put between the two the word 'leap' . . . The majority of these so-called Socialists . . . have never stopped to think that by 'leap' the teachers of socialism meant changes in world history and that leaps of this kind extended over decades and even more."[55]

After the unfettered leap, after the revolution, Lenin insists, there is no longer need for outbursts of revolutionary enthusiasm. "Moments arise," he warns, "when enough has been blown up and the next task is to perform the prosaic (. . . the boring) work of clearing away the fragments. . . ." A rigid attention to detail was to follow the release of chiliastic zeal, for after the unfettered leap, after the revolution, there was no need for outbursts of revolutionary enthusiasm. The explosive burst of energy had to be disciplined and rationalized into a persistent and measured procession toward Bolshevik goals. Lenin, referring to his chiliastic supporters in November and to demands for the realization of socialism in the present, concludes: "Fits of hysteria are of no use to us. What we need is the steady march of iron battalions of the proletariat."[56]

The idea of the transitional era helped to dam the chiliastic strivings. It preserved them, however, as a reservoir which the Bolshevik order could canalize into the demands it would make in the name of the future and ultimate goals of communism. There was still a goal for which to strive, but the striving was being harnessed by the Bolshevik regime. The goal was integrated into time and into history. It thus retained an aura of nearness and reality, a sense of conviction for the chiliastic mind. But the goal projected into future time ceased to be disruptive of the existing order.

After the revolution, therefore, the idea of the Paris Commune served not only to postpone revolutionary goals but to provide enthusiasm, energy and incentive for the Bolshevik program. Early in 1918, for example, Lenin referred to the Paris Commune as something almost outmoded. He equated the Commune of 1871 with the revolutionary accomplishments of 1793. In 1917 he had referred to the Soviet of Workers', Soldiers' and Peasants' Deputies as an embryonic form of the Paris Commune of 1871. In 1918 he indicated, however, that the Soviet was more advanced than the Commune was, but that Russia had to progress still more to overtake Western Europe. "If we measure our revolution by the scale of West European revolutions," Lenin said, "we will find that at the present moment we are approximately at the level reached in 1793 and 1871. We can be legitimately proud of having risen to this level, and in one respect we have certainly advanced somewhat further, namely: we have decreed and introduced in the whole of Russia the highest type of state—the Soviet state."[57] In establishing the highest type of state, revolutionary enthusiasm had its present and tangible rewards. However, in spite of revolutionary achievements, the goal of socialism remained unattained. Russia could not be content with its accomplishments, for it had to devote its energies to passing through the transition to socialism. "But under no circumstances," said Lenin, "can we rest content with what we have achieved, because we have only just started the transition to socialism, we have not yet done the most decisive thing in *this* respect."[58]

For Lenin the most important thing in the transition to socialism seems to have been workers' control as the Bolsheviks conceived it. He insisted upon the regulation of industry on a national scale. The

Bolsheviks, therefore, had to make it clear to the workers that they could not retain possession of the factories they had seized. They had to convince, or force, the workers to subject their factories to centralized Bolshevik regulation. Decisive to the introduction of socialism, then, was the introduction of Bolshevik control over industry, including the factories the workers had acquired.

Continuing his analysis of the transition to socialism, Lenin advised that "The most decisive thing is the organization of the strictest accounting of control of production and of the distribution of goods. And yet we have *not yet* introduced accounting and control in those enterprises . . . which we have confiscated from the bourgeoisie and without this there can be no thought of creating the material conditions for the introduction of socialism."[59] Thus, for the Bolsheviks, workers' control, as the workers conceived it, was only a means to the confiscation of industry. It was a precondition for the implementation of the Bolshevik concept of workers' control.

According to a resolution of the Bolshevik-dominated First All-Russian Congress of Textile Workers, held in Moscow at the end of January and the beginning of February 1918, ". . . the measure of workers' control is only a transitional step to the planned organization of production and distribution; it must be nothing but the first step in the complete regulation of economic life."[60]

Workers' control thus becomes merely the preliminary to nationalization and nationalization then becomes a condition for socialism, for: "The realization of workers' control on a statewide scale must be . . . conducted simultaneously with a planned system of measures having as their aim the organization of production on a socialist basis."[61]

The nationalization of industry and a planned economy were, therefore, necessary before socialism could be established. Hence, the abandonment of the workers' conception of workers' control and the implementation of the Bolshevik concept of it were indispensable conditions of socialism in the future.

Socialism and the International Proletariat

Not only was the realization of socialism relegated to future time, it was made dependent also upon the participation of the international proletariat, which existed outside and beyond the experience of the Russian workers. Socialism did not depend only upon what the Russian workers themselves could do; by instituting the transitional period, they could lead and clear the way, but they could not reach the goal.

"We are far from ending the transitional period from capitalism to socialism," said Lenin. ". . . We never deluded ourselves with the hope that we could end it without the help of the international proletariat. We never deceived ourselves on this score and we know how difficult is the road leading from capitalism to socialism, but we are obliged to say that our republic of soviets is socialistic because we have started out on this road, and these words will not be empty words."[62]

Although the Russian workers could not establish socialism by themselves, it became their responsibility before all the workers of the world to preserve and maintain the revolution. It was their responsibility to guard and protect the transitional period—the order and regime the Bolshevik sought to establish. Thus, Trotsky declaimed: "Let us then, Comrades, remind the less conscious of us that we stand as a city on the mount and that the workers of all countries look at us and ask themselves with bated breath whether we shall tumble off or not, whether we shall fail, or stand our ground. And we, on our part, call out to them: 'We vow to you that we shall stand our ground, that we shall not fail, that we shall remain in power to the end.' "[63]

No matter how devoted to the Bolshevik cause, however, no matter how determined to maintain and augment Bolshevik power without the assistance of the world proletariat, socialism could not be established. "But you," exhorts Trotsky, ". . . workers of the other countries, you brothers, do not exhaust our patience too much, hurry up, stop the slaughter, overthrow the bourgeoisie, take the power into your hands, and then we shall turn the whole globe into one world republic of Labour. All the earthly riches, all the lands, and all the seas—all this shall be one common property of the whole of humanity, whatever the name of the parts: English, French, German, etc. We shall create one brotherly state: the land which nature gave us. This land we shall plough and cultivate on associative principles, turn into one blossoming garden, where our children, grandchildren and great-grandchildren will live as in a paradise."[64]

Although the goal is postponed and the earthly paradise is projected into the future time, where it transcends the existing order and ceases to be disruptive of the Bolshevik regime, its earthly orientation emphasized a kinship to reality and a nearness to the present, for "Time was when people believed in legends which told of a paradise. These were vague and confused dreams, the yearnings of the soul of the oppressed Man after a better life. There was a yearning after a purer, more righteous life and Man said: 'There must be such a paradise, at least, in the "other" world, an unknown and mysterious country.' But we say we shall create such a paradise with our toiling hands, *here* in *this* world, upon earth, for all, for our children and grandchildren and for all eternity."[65]

Paradise is to be established on earth rather than in heaven, but only in the future, not in the present. With dialectical contradiction, therefore, socialism is postponed while it is made to seem within reach.

Socialism and Spontaneity

Thus far, evidence has been presented to show that the Bolshevik view of workers' control and of socialism differed from the conception held by the workers. There existed, therefore, a basic and fundamental disagreement between the workers and the Bolshevik Party regarding the goals and objectives of the revolution. Further evidence of this divergence in viewpoint is provided by the Bolshevik use of the words *stikhiinost'* (spontaneity) and *soznatel'nost* (consciousness), words which have been referred to in the previous discussion of Bolshevik ideology. In order for the words to be properly understood in the context of the relations between labor and the Party, they should be viewed within the Bolshevik frame of reference and in the historical context in which they were used. Indeed, the meanings of these words seem to have become sharpened and refined in the revolutionary situation. It would be fruitful to place the words in their situational and ideological contexts in order to avoid the confusion and misunderstanding that may result from a mere transposition of the words into our own framework, for the concepts which these words encompass in relation to Russian labor and the Party are peculiar to, and specific for, the framework of Bolshevik ideology. In this respect, it is significant to note that what is perhaps the major pre-Bolshevik dictionary, *Dal'*, does not include *stikhiinost'* either as a noun or adjective.[66] The meanings these words now possess arose in part, historically, in the Bolshevik revolution and reflect the mutually antagonistic world conceptions of the Bolsheviks and the workers.

A major Soviet dictionary, the *Tolkovyi Slovar',* defines *stikhiinyi,* the adjective from *stikhiinost'* (spontaneity), as follows: ". . .unorganized, not regulated by anything, developing without any guidance." It gives an example of the usage, quoting from Stalin: ". . . to laud the spontaneous process of the workers' movement and to deny the guiding role of the party, reducing its role to the role of a registrar of events—means to preach *khvostism* [tailism], to preach the conversion of the party into the tail of the spontaneous process, into a passive force of a movement capable only of contemplating the spontaneous process and letting it take its own course."[67]

Thus, immanent in the very definition of "spontaneity" is the Bolshevik concept of the relationship of the party to the working class movement. That workers' movement is spontaneous which rejects the leadership of the party. That workers' movement is spontaneous which would have the party play a passive role, which would have the party follow the direction and goals of the workers themselves.

So important is the concept of spontaneity to communist ideology that the word *stikhiinost'* was included in the *Politicheskii Slovar'* (Soviet Political Dictionary) of 1940. *Stikhiinost'* (spontaneity) is there defined as follows: "lack of organization, the quality of being self-moving. In social life that mass movement is called spontaneous in which consciousness is absent, where there is no political guidance. . . ." Quoting Stalin, the Political Dictionary explains that: ". . . The theory which worships spontaneity is decisively opposed to giving the spontaneous movement a conscious, planned character. It is opposed to the party's going ahead of the working class, to the party's raising the masses to a conscious level, to the party's drawing the movement after it,—it is for the conscious elements of the movement not hindering the movement from going its own way, it is for the party only serving the spontaneous movement and for trailing behind at its tail. Lenin and Stalin, delivering a devastating blow to the . . . propagation of spontaneity which denies the role of the revolutionary theory in the class struggle of the working class, pointed out that without revolutionary theory there can be no revolutionary movement."[68] This indicates the importance to communist policy of a knowledge of what is believed to be the laws of nature and of history, and their development. It indicates also the importance of that theory for the explanation and justification of political action.

It would be a mistake, however, to overestimate in actuality the role of theory in the revolutionary movement. The theory itself is an elaboration of a kind of action. The action in turn is motivated by basic intentions, goals and values, for the achievement of which the bearers of the theory seek to manipulate social reality. The Bolshevik concepts of spontaneity and consciousness themselves, to a degree, seem to have grown out of the conflict arising between the workers and the party concerning the aims and purposes of the revolution. The conflict, after 1917, concerned essentially the realities of the post-revolutionary situation. The action taken by the Bolsheviks within that situation was made coherent and meaningful—was rationalized and justified—within the Bolshevik theoretical framework; but the workers, unlike the Bolshevik intellectuals, had not formulated an explicit, articulated theory of their own. This is not to say, however, that the workers, as a group, did not have their own approach to reality, their own world conception which organized their aims and purposes into a meaningful whole. For the workers to accept Bolshevik theory, however, meant to adopt Bolshevik goals and values. It meant the workers would, without resistance, partake of the action to implement those goals.

Knowledge of Bolshevik objectives and adherence to them, as previously mentioned, is termed "consciousness" by the Bolshevik Party, in contradistinction to "spontaneity," which designates action taken without adherence to Bolshevik aims. Consciousness is the evaluation of reality in accordance with the Bolshevik conception of the world. The Soviet dictionary *Tolkovyi Slovar'* defines consciousness as: ". . . the ability, the knowledge to take account of the surrounding reality, and of how it is necessary to act in it."

Consciousness comprises a knowledge of the Marxist-Leninist laws of social development—the knowledge, that is, of what Bolshevik aims are and how to reach them. The Soviet Political Dictionary provides the following definition of this term: "The precise understanding by social classes or individuals of their position and tasks in the historical development of society." Thus, consciousness is the awareness of each class, or by individuals, of their function and duties in the movement of society through the historical stages to the historical end which Marxism-Leninism deems inevitable. A knowledge of class or individual function and duty is derived not only from science and philosophy but also from the experience of proletarian struggle. Implicit in this assertion, then, seems to be a reference to workers' control and the conflict over it. The Political Dictionary elaborates: "The socialist theory, created by Lenin and Stalin, on the basis of all achievements of science, philosophy, and the experience of the struggle of the proletariat, arms the working class and the toilers with a knowledge of the laws of social development."

The Communist Party inculcates into the workers an awareness of these laws of social development, a familiarity with Marxist-Leninist theory; the party, acting as mediator between historical necessity and Russian labor, determines the methods to be used for the inculcation of these historical laws. Having instilled this knowledge into the workers, spontaneity is overcome and the Bolshevik dictatorship assured. The Political Dictionary adds: "The Communist Party instills consciousness of Marxist-Leninist theory into the workers' movement, the party of Lenin-Stalin arms the working class with the revolutionary theory of Marxism-Leninism and assures the victory of the dictatorship of the proletariat and socialism in the SSSR."[69]

The greater the working class knowledge of Marxist-Leninist theory and how to put it into effect, the greater the consciousness of the working class, for: "The more profoundly the toilers master Marxist-Leninist theory by a knowledge of the laws of social development, the higher the level of their consciousness." In short, consciousness is the awareness, the knowledge of how to behave, how to perform in order to attain Bolshevik goals. The more closely the workers adhere to this theory and concept, as law inherent in social reality, the Bolshevik means taken to reach the Bolshevik end, the more consciousness they possess.

Those workers, after the Bolshevik Revolution, who resisted the Bolshevik process of control were said to be lacking in consciousness and ignorant of socialism. "The consciousness of the individual groups of workers," said Shliapnikov, the Bolshevik Commissar of Labor in January 1918, ". . . is extremely low. Many go no further than to demand an increase in wages and present various plans for sharing in the profits. But this is not their fault. It would be strange if in a country reared in darkness, in ignorance, in the absence of organization, suddenly everyone became socialists."[70] When the workers conceive of socialism, then, as an era of profit sharing and greater material rewards for labor, they are lacking in consciousness, deficient in their comprehension of socialism.

Lozovsky, in pointing out early in 1918 that workers' control had a meaning for the workers which was at variance with that of communism, attributed the workers' conception of control to lack of consciousness and to a misunderstanding of socialism. "What are the contents of workers' control?" he asked; he answered rhetorically: "At the very beginning it is necessary to point out that with the idea of workers' control there arose among the less conscious workers the concept of the transfer of the enterprise to the hands of a particular group of workers. This idea is doubly false and least socialistic, because it breeds a species of capitalism. . . . Each representative of our congress must implant within the consciousness of the workers that if confiscation was completed somewhere, then it was transferred to the hands of all the toiling people and not to a new owner individually or collectively."[71]

Thus, one of the primary problems of the Bolshevik regime was the problem of persuading, convincing or forcing the workers to give up their joint factory ownership and to accede to the nationalization and centralization of industry. Solutions to this problem were found upon the basis and within the framework of Bolshevik ideology. Because the ideology considers history to be an organic process leading to a known and definite goal, it becomes necessary, within this view, to guide the actions of men toward that goal. Historical action is thus no longer the result of deeds and events brought about by the coordination and conflict of men's wills, but is rather the result of means taken to reach a predetermined end. Hence it becomes necessary to restrict freedom—so as to eliminate divergent action—by teaching, guiding or leading men to what is considered to be the goal of history itself. This in turn leads to a point of view which regards all men whose goals differ from the accepted one as being, at least, politically immature and in need of tutelage. Tutelage, in turn, becomes a means of manipulating men towards the objective of their tutors. Spontaneous action was thus regarded as being bred by ignorance of historical ends, and the Bolsheviks attributed to spontaneity and a lack of consciousness the insistence of the workers upon owning the factories they had seized. The following chapter will show that the worker shareholding ownership was also simultaneously labeled as capitalistic and anarchistic.

CHAPTER V

Workers' Control and Anarchism

Property Seizure and Anarchy

It has already been shown that many workers of the factory committees conceived of socialism as an era in which they themselves would share in the ownership and management of industry. Their interest, however, was focused upon the factories at which they themselves worked and which, under a system of workers' control, they hoped to own. Their resistance to the nationalizing and centralizing industrial policy of the Bolsheviks, therefore, represented the resistance of both the individual local industrial units and of the workers employed at them. This resemblance of such a proletarian industrial localism to the Anarchist idea of socialist society was apparent to both the Anarchists and Bolsheviks. The conflict between Bolsheviks and workers over concepts of workers' control was, therefore, complicated by the resemblance of workers' control, as the workers conceived it, to socialism, as the Anarchists conceived it.

Lozovsky at the First All-Russian Congress of Trade Unions asserted that ". . . the transfer of the enterprise into the hands of individual workers solves absolutely nothing and produces an extremely harmful illusion that the transfer of the business of the factory to a particular group of workers solves the problem for the given group of workers. This is an anarcho-syndicalist illusion, that a social question, i.e., a question which concerns the existence of capitalist means of production can be separately decided at each individual factory . . ."[1]

Thus, that practice was called anarchistic by which the workers made the factories into their own private possessions. However, although such a practice could function for the Bolsheviks, before October, to hinder Russian industry and the Provisional Government, after October, when the Bolsheviks were striving to form a socialist state, workers' seizure of factories served only to place a hindrance in the way of Bolshevik nationalization. Workers' seizure, the Bolsheviks insisted, would lead not to socialism but anarchy.

The *Trade Union Herald* as early as December 1917 published a declaration by the Provisional Central Committee of the foremost Bolshevik union, the Union of Metal Workers, which spoke of ". . . displays of anarchistic tendencies which are disorganizing industry. . . . The attempts at seizing the individual enterprises by the workers cannot in any case be considered an act towards the conversion of the individual and scattered means of production of many producers into a socially concentrated one [*obobshchestvlenie*]. Such attempts will inevitably lead either to the destruction of entrepreneurial initiative or to the degeneration of this form of seizure of the enterprise to simple stock-holding ownership."[2]

Here again the conflict between two basically different concepts of socialism is apparent. The concentration of production—that is, socialism as the Bolsheviks saw it—was diametrically opposed to the ownership of individual factories by the workers employed at them. The latter type of stock holding ownership the Bolsheviks termed an anti-socialistic anarchism. Such an industrial system, according to the Bolsheviks, would lead only to what they regarded as the anarchy of independent, individualistic, competitive enterprise. The Metal Workers charged: "Under present conditions of state intervention in economic life . . . attempts at seizure have that negative aspect which isolates the workers of one enterprise from the others; it leads to the necessity of competition with the same type of enterprises. . . ."[3]

Fearing the confiscation and administration of industrial enterprises by the workers themselves, and insisting upon the necessity of state ownership and centralization, the First All-Russian Congress of Commissars of Labor, a congress in which the Bolsheviks were predominant, adopted a resolution on 1 February 1918 which stated:

"4) Confiscation is carried out not in the interests of the workers of a given enterprise but in the interest of the general nationalization of industry.

"5) Confiscation is carried out through a central institution."[4]

Paragraph 1 of the resolution reads: "The administration of all confiscated enterprises is entrusted to the Councils of National Economy."[5] Thus, all confiscated factories were destined to be within the purview of a governmental institution controlled by the Bolshevik party.

The warning against local and independent confiscation by the workers, however, was directed not only against the practice of the workers but also against the policy of the Anarchists who supported the workers in their practice of confiscation.

An Anarchist appeal to the Third All-Russian Congress of Soviets in January of 1918 states: "We consider that the Congress must: First of all, in the most decisive and definite manner, establish that the only important task of the moment is the direct, immediate and energetic expropriation of private property—not only of land but of mines, factories and shops, railroads, steamships, post and telegraph, dwellings, etc."[6]

Anarchism and Centralization

Not only did the Anarchists support an active and decisive confiscation and expropriation of property, but, as opposed to the Bolsheviks who wanted the nationalization of property through a central institution, they also sponsored confiscation through workers' groups locally, within the sphere of their own geographical and political interests. They insisted that ". . . to effect this task, the complete independence and unlimited creative initiative of the workers' organizations in the localities is alone necessary."[7]

The Anarchists spoke out against the Bolshevik policy of suppressing the independent confiscations of the workers. They condemned efforts to dominate workers' activity and to subordinate it to centralized party control: "The Congress," they asserted, "must . . . refute all attempts to suppress the will and initiative of the workers' organizations. It must suppress all attempts to subordinate their activity to the political dictatorship of the party in the center."[8]

Bolshevik fear of workers' confiscation and workers' ownership is illustrated in "The Program of the Communists" (*Programma Kommunistov*), written in 1918 by Bukharin as spokesman for the party. This pamphlet is largely devoted to an attack upon workers' ownership, upon workers' control as the workers conceived it. Workers' ownership, says Bukharin, is based upon the dividing-up theory, and he further identifies Anarchism with this kind of division and sharing. "Some people," Bukharin wrote, "think that which is taken away from the rich should, in a 'God-like,' just and equal fashion, be divided among everyone and then everything will be all right . . . Each will take care of himself, having everything at his disposal, and the power of man over man will disappear, thanks to this equal sharing, to the general redistribution and allotment of wealth among the poor."[9]

The Communist Party, as Bukharin pointed out, does not uphold such a view, for it would lead, the party claimed, merely to the re-establishment of capitalism.[10]

A redistribution of property, Bukharin warned, would restore private property and small-scale production, whereas it was the intention of the communists to abolish private property and create large-scale concentrated production. "Let us imagine," Bukharin suggested, ". . . that by a miracle someone succeeded in dividing, more or less equally, everything taken away from the rich. . . . It would mean that in place of a few large owners there would be many small ones. It would not signify the *abolition* of private property, but the *extension* of it; in place of large ownership, there would be petty ownership.[11]

A large number of petty owners, such as in the system of ownership-sharing created by workers' control, according to the communists, would lead to competition and strife. The more powerful would inevitably swallow up the less powerful, for according to Bukharin, "We know very well that capitalism and the big capitalists arose out of the struggle of the small owners with one another. If, by our division, we would produce small owners, the following would occur —the richer would overcome the poorer. The poorer would be ruined and would be turned into proletarians. Their lucky rivals would increase their own wealth, they would ensnare the workers and would thus gradually become true capitalists. Thus we would return after a short time to that very structure which we had just abolished. We would again find ourselves before the old trough of capitalistic robbery."[12]

Bukharin insisted that such would be the fate of workers' control by the factory committees, of workers' control by workers of individual factories. "Among some strata of workers," he explained, ". . . who are lacking in consciousness such an understanding of the matter [of workers' control] is dominant: we, they say, will take our factories into our own hands—and that is the end of the matter. . . . Such a viewpoint, of course, is false. It very strongly reminds us of dividing-up. Indeed, if such a situation would occur in which each factory would belong to the workers *only of that factory,* then competition would arise among the factories . . . they would try to take customers away from one another. Thus the workers of one factory would be ruined, the others would become rich, and would hire the workers from the ruined enterprise . . . just as in the case of division, in a short time, capitalism would arise again."[13]

Bukharin identified this process with anarchism. The Anarchists too, he said, advocate separate communal enterprises, for: "The Anarchists believe that people will live best and freest of all when they divide all industry into small commune societies of labor."[14] But, he insisted, "It is not enough that the capitalists should go. . . . All small enterprises that aren't getting anywhere must die out. . . . There must be a single working plan. The greater the area embraced by this plan the better. . . . *In order to give production this forward impetus, we must not only not parcel out the industry which we have inherited from capitalism,* but on the contrary we must *strengthen and augment* it even more."[15] Therefore, Bukharin explained, "It is now obvious why the anarchist preachings lead to *division* instead of to the correct communist order of society."[16]

Enterprises from which the former capitalist owners had been removed, enterprises that were then privately owned by the workers and operated independently of each other, were regarded as anarchistic.

By anarchism, however, the Bolsheviks meant the workers' insistence upon joint but private-property ownership of industry. By anarchism they meant the individualistic leanings of the workers, they meant the workers' refusal to submit to Bolshevik control of industrial enterprises in which the workers were employed. In justifying their fight to wrest the factories from the workers and to place them under the control of a state dominated by the party, the Bolsheviks claimed the sanction of an historically necessary proletarian order.

Anarchism, Capitalism and Spontaneity

Even before the October Revolution, however, Lenin was aware of the importance among "the masses" of custom and habit, of their prevalent goals and values, and of deeply rooted ways of interpreting experience in the former "bourgeois" society. He realized these were factors that had to be dealt with in creating a revolutionary change. Nevertheless he considered that the habits that existed among the masses in a "bourgeois" society existed because of the lack of "consciousness," lack of the knowledge of the regime which the Bolsheviks were striving to create. He seems also to have believed that fear of bourgeois authority partly prevented the masses from expressing their will to create a communist way of life. Lenin seems to have assumed, however, that once the masses were organized and led, once they became aware or "conscious" of Bolshevik purposes, they would embrace a Bolshevik order. ". . . We have always known and repeatedly pointed out," he said, "that the bourgeoisie maintains itself not only by force but also by the lack of consciousness, by the force of custom and habit among the masses and because the masses are beaten down and not organized."[17]

Lenin does not seem to have been concerned, however, with how basic and fundamental were the habits of "the masses" he sought to lead or how close to those of the bourgeoisie were the attitudes of the workers toward property. Neither was he willing to accede to the demands arising from these attitudes, nor to sacrifice or adapt the Bolshevik program to them. However, the conflict inherent in the post-October revolutionary situation in which the workers, adhering to the concept of workers' control, resisted the process of state regulation and nationalization, forced Lenin to acknowledge the perseverance of what he regarded as bourgeois attitudes.

After October, however, when it was no longer possible to attribute the continuation of such attitudes in any way to bourgeois compulsion, they were denounced as vestiges of the outmoded bourgeois order and as manifestations of anarchist spontaneity. Anarchism, in turn, was identified with bourgeois attitudes. The Bolshevik struggle to institute control by the party and state, instead of by the workers themselves, became a struggle against "bourgeois anarchism." The workers were charged with persevering in an individualistic and self-centered mode of thought that disregarded the welfare of society as a whole. They were, in effect, urged to renounce their own self-interest and to merge with a universal socialist movement. A consciousness among the workers of the Bolshevik concept of socialism was considered so necessary by Lenin that he regarded the Bolshevik attempt to inculcate into the workers a loyalty to Bolshevik aims as a struggle of "world historical significance."

In March of 1918 Lenin stated, for example: "It is now being clearly demonstrated to us how correct is the Marxian postulate that anarchism and anarcho-syndicalism are *bourgeois* trends, that they irreconcilably contradict socialism, proletarian dictatorship and communism. The fight to instill into the minds of the masses the idea of Soviet control and accounting, and to carry out this idea in practice, the fight to break with the cursed past which taught the people to regard the gaining of bread and clothes as a 'private' matter, as buying and selling, as a transaction 'which concerns only myself'—is a great fight of world historical significance, a fight between socialist consciousness and bourgeois-anarchist spontaneity."[18]

By the words of Lenin himself, then, it would be a great mistake to underestimate or overlook the importance, intensity and significance of the conflict between the workers and the Bolsheviks concerning the meaning of socialism and the objectives of the revolution. It would be a mistake also to consider the "anarchistic" tendencies of the workers as anything more than bourgeois individualism on the part of the proletariat. These workers do not seem to have intended to abolish private property; rather, they strove to acquire property of their own, for they seem to have intended to establish joint ownership over the factories of which they had seized control.

This movement among the workers was very similar to the movement among the peasants who seized the land in order to take possession of it for themselves. Riazanov, for example, at the First All-Russian Congress of Trade Unions in January of 1918 stated: "For if we act as crudely as our comrades in power—I am speaking of the peasants—if we should deal with the socialization of industry as crudely as they sometimes deal with the socialization of land. . . . If we place the principle of seizure first, if we assume that control by the workers must be achieved first in a given enterprise then we fall into the position of the poor peasants, who seized the land in their own hands. . . ."[19]

This similarity between the peasants and workers, who conceived of socialism as a society in which they themselves would own the farms and factories, was identified by the Bolsheviks, as previously mentioned, with both anarchism and capitalism simultaneously. In a Bolshevik attack upon the Anarchists, the following charge is found: "The Russian Anarchists have nothing in common with the workers' struggle for socialism but have very much in common with the *kulak* struggle for capitalism."[20]

The Anarchism of a *kulak* struggle for peasant ownership of land and of the factory committees for workers' ownership of industry were regarded by the Bolsheviks as alien to socialism. The socialism of the Bolsheviks, however, was one in which goals were postponed and relegated to the future in a schematized and rationalized fashion. In the revolutionary present, Bolshevism concentrated upon the conscious reconstruction of society from above. The Bolsheviks were seeking to regulate and control all facets of factory and industrial life, and by such regulation to pave the way to what they conceived as socialism. Within the context of the revolutionary situation, such regulation also served to maintain the primacy of the party.

ANARCHISM AND GOAL POSTPONEMENT

To the Bolshevik concept of the dictatorship of the proletariat—of the transitional centralized state which preceded socialism—the anarchists opposed the concept of ". . . a progressive but immediate passage to a true communality, economic and federative."[21] Thus the socialism of anarchism was one in which the future flowed out of immanent and immediate change in the present, change created by the workers from below. By acknowledging the factory committees as the industrial nucleus of a new society and by recognizing workers' implementation of workers' control as a present and immediate achievement of socialism, the Anarchists recognized the attainment of the revolutionary chiliastic goal. Thus, whereas the Bolshevik concept of socialism and the transitional period served to dam the chiliastic tide and harness it to Bolshevik goals, the socialism of Anarchism presumably represented a cessation of revolutionary struggle. The Anarchist championship of the free and independent initiative of worker and peasant, however, was inextricably interwoven with its antagonism toward the power and authority of the state.[22] Thus, Anarchism contrived to wage against the dictatorship of the proletariat the struggle it had waged against tsarism and the Provisional Government. Within the context of the revolutionary situation, therefore, it was destructive of the power of the Bolshevik party.

Furthermore, just as the Bolsheviks identified the Anarchists with the bourgeois past because of the Anarchist stand on workers' ownership, the Anarchists identified the Bolsheviks with the previous bourgeois order because of the Bolshevik insistence upon the present necessity of the state.[23] Partly as the result of the Bolshevik policy of wresting the control of the factories from the workers, the Anarchists accused the communists of blocking the revolutionary process, of seizing the revolutionary power in their own hands. The Anarchists charged that ". . . characteristic for this [Bolshevik] power which as a whole belongs to the bourgeois past is the concept of the finiteness, of the limitation of the revolutionary process, the tendency to build a bulwark around, to ossify this process and again to concentrate future evolution in the hands of power and a few of the privileged instead of leaving to the laboring masses the free and independent advanced creativity of the moment."[24]

Conversely, the Anarchist concept of an unbroken, self-unfolding, post-revolutionary evolution, which denied the necessity of a special demarcated transition to revolutionary goals, evoked the Bolshevik charge that "All types of this 'pure anarchist communism' are united by the basic theoretical premise . . . the denial of the necessity of any kind of transitional stage from capitalism to complete anarchy."[25]

In spite of their rejection of the transitional period, however, the Anarchists realized that much would have to be done before the transition could be made to the new order which they envisaged. The Anarchists were most influential and probably most active in the Ukraine, particularly in the southern region of Gulai-Polia from 1918 to 1920. In those areas dominated by the partisan leader Makhno, the Anarchist activist Voline, under Makhno's protection, assisted peasants and workers in the formation of Anarchist communes as the basis for evolution to a new Anarchist society.

A resolution on the current moment, of the First Congress of the Confederation of Anarchist Organizations of the Ukraine, declares the Congress for example, as "Recognizing the social revolution as a long protracted . . . process . . ." However, the Anarchists believed in the organic growth of the new society and that the impetus for this growth shoud be the will immanent in the social units, such as the villages or factory committees. They opposed, therefore, any direction by a governmental authority outside and above these units. According to an Anarchist newspaper, "It is harmful for the revolution to await the decisions and decrees of the government. This kills the people's initiative, the people's creativity. Each village, each town, each factory or mine is an independent unit for carrying out all the tasks which face it. And when it is necessary these units will unite to decide matters where local decision will not apply. . . ."[26] The article then points to the factory committees and trade unions as examples of such units.[27] Thus, perhaps, even stronger than the Anarchist denial of the transitional period was the denial that this transition should be directed from above.

The workers who resisted state control and ownership of industry and who were, therefore, supported by the Anarchists, wanted, it seems, to rehabilitate their factories without restriction. They wanted to run their establishments unhampered and unrestrained by governmental regulation. Considering itself a spokesman for the workers, an anarchist newspaper asserted that as a result of the revolution of 1917 "The factories and shops were in the hands of the workers, the land belonged to the peasants. . . ."[28] The workers and peasants, therefore, says the paper, should finally have been the masters. But this was not so. "The Soviets (the Soviets or Bolsheviks, they are one and the same) declare themselves to be the fully empowered masters who have monopolized the factories and land and force the workers and peasants to be their hired slaves. Previously, the workers had to hire themselves out to private entrepreneurs—factory owners, landlords whom they could leave, declaring a strike. Now the only master is the State to which the workers and peasants cannot present demands without being declared counter-revolutionaries, because they do not want to be exploited by the many-headed hydra of bureaucrats which is called the State."[29]

The Anarchists opposed external power and authority in the form of what they regarded as a bureaucratic Soviet state imposed over the will of the people. This led, therefore, to anarchist opposition to the dictatorship of the proletariat and to anarchist support of the workers, who resisted the nationalization of industry.

Anarchism and the Revolution

In order to understand more fully what the Bolsheviks meant by their charges of Anarchism against the workers, it is necessary to try to determine what the politics of Anarchism were; it is necessary, also, to try to determine the relationship between the Anarchists and the workers. This, in turn, should throw light upon the relationship between the workers and the Bolsheviks. To do this, however, many threads must be untangled and many knots untied.

The Bolsheviks charge that "essentially the history of Russian anarchism, as an active factor in the revolution and counter-revolution, may be begun in the spring of 1918."[30] The Anarchists, however, place the beginning of their work during the revolutionary period, in the summer of 1917.[31] To understand when and how Anarchist activity began, however, it is necessary to distinguish between the concept of a movement and a party.[32] Anarchism as a movement did not so much represent the interests of a particular group or class within the existing order; it propagated an ideal. It emphasized the innate justice, righteousness, moral superiority and efficacy of proletarian and peasant action, and propagated the idea of immanent, organic rather than external, principles or laws of social behavior; insisting upon the rights of the local units, it demanded the abolition of all centralized control. The most fundamental political attitudes of the Anarchists seem to have been their intransigent opposition to a state of any kind, their contempt for constitutional parliamentarism, and their disdain for the political party systems of the national "bourgeois" state. The Anarchists, therefore, did not make use of their ideology to build a well-defined organization.[33] Anarchism constituted a movement, but it had not formed a political party in the sense of a disciplined, definitely constituted organization.

A 1920 declaration of the Overseas Bureau of the Russian Confederation of Anarcho-Syndicalists, entitled "In Place of a Program," stated, for example, that ". . . in Russia there is no organized Anarchist movement among workers and peasants. . . . Anarchists in general were little interested in the organizational side of their movement; they were satisfied with merely primitive forms of unification—with groups in the majority of cases not connected, or in the best case very weakly connected. The connection among them was concretely expressed in congresses, at which in the majority of cases, people convened who did not fully represent groups or were simply random elements. . . ."[34]

In their battle against the state the Anarchists seem to have assisted in the overthrow of tsarism and of the Provisional Government. In their great contempt for constitutional parliamentarism they proudly claimed the honor of dispersing the Constituent Assembly.[35] A little less than a month after the October Revolution, Maximov, one of the foremost Russian Anarchists, declared for the dispersal of the Constituent Assembly. The Constituent Assembly had been elected by free, equal and secret suffrage. Its purpose was to replace the existing, provisionally governing organs and to establish a new constitutional government. At the time of the convocation of the Constituent Assembly, the Provisional Government had fallen and the Soviets of Workers', Soldiers' and Peasants' Deputies, dominated by the Bolshevik party, had become the governing organ of the state. Displaying complete disdain for representative parliamentary democracy, as opposed to a soviet or counciliar organization, Maximov wrote, in the publication of the Union of Anarcho-Syndicalist Propaganda, the *Golos Truda* (*Voice of Labor*) of 22 December 1917/4 January 1918, as follows:

"But now when we have the Constituent Assembly, what should we do and where shall we be, if this supreme 'star chamber' comes out *against* the Soviet organization?

"If this should be, then it is our duty, the duty of honest revolutionaries—to stand in the ranks of defenders of the Soviet to brand the attempt of the Constituent Assembly as counter-revolutionary. . . . If the Constituent Assembly comes out against the people's will, the Constituent Assembly will be dispersed."[36] Maximov, as an Anarchist, declared against the Constituent Assembly and for the Soviet.

With the abolition of the Constituent Assembly and the governing bodies which had preceded it, the Anarchists were faced with the problem of how to bring about the ideal society which was the goal of their destructive action. Also, even though the Anarchists conceived of their political function as one of assistance to, rather than leadership of, the proletariat and peasantry, they were, after October, confronted with the problem of gaining mass adherence for their movement, or of defaulting to the Bolsheviks. This problem was made more acute by the fact that after October the proletariat and peasantry were, in theory, no longer the disinherited of bourgeois society, but the sole bearers, along with the intelligentsia, of political power. Furthermore, the Bolsheviks by their strength and success seem to have demonstrated to the Anarchists the desirability of party organization.

However, even though it was not until sometime near the spring of 1918 that the Anarchists seem to have attempted to act as an organized and coherent political party, it would be a mistake to ignore their influence upon the revolution prior to that time. They acted, previous to 1918, as organizationally unfettered individuals or voluntarily formed independent groups with loose connections. They carried out propaganda and ideological work among the proletariat and peasantry without attempting to organize the workers, the peasants or themselves into a disciplined political party.

The Moscow Federation of Anarchist Groups, which was one of the first groups of Anarchists organized during the Revolution, was, as its name indicates, a federation rather than a party. The Bolsheviks disdainfully claim that the "Anarchist Federation declared that any registration of its members, control over its composition, and discipline in its ranks was a bourgeois fiction."[37] Displaying profound contempt for the Anarchist indifference to organization, the Bolsheviks charged that "Russian Anarchism came to life with one organizational principle on its banner 'no organization of its own ranks.' "[38]

Nevertheless, the Anarchists claimed that "No matter how weak and organizationally unprepared they were—they nevertheless, persistently and consistently held the line of the true social revolution. . . . They were with the workers constantly when the latter long before the October Revolution, in various parts of Russia, seized the enterprises in their own hands and tried to organize production on the basis of the workers' self-administration."[39]

The Anarchists claimed, then, that in spite of their lack of party organization they were instrumental in encouraging the establishment of factory committees and in carrying out the policy of workers' control. Even though the Bolshevik influence and leadership was predominant in the conferences of the factory committees, the anarchists also exerted their influence in these organizations. The Revolutionary Center of Factory Committees, under the aegis of the Anarchists, was established between February and October 1917.[40] According to the Communist view, this Revolutionary Center existed directly in opposition to the Bolshevik Central Council of Factory Committees.

In spite of the antagonism between Anarchists and Communists in the area of workers' control, there were other areas of revolutionary activity in which there was a coincidence of Anarchist, Bolshevik and worker action. In these areas, it was possible for the Anarchists, while themselves remaining loosely organized, to profit from the more disciplined organization of the Bolshevik Party. Often, however, these areas of coincidence in specific, short-range objectives existed along with fundamental differences in ultimate goals.

In their opposition to the national and "bourgeois" state, for example, the Anarchists found themselves in agreement with the Bolshevik attack against the coalition Provisional Government.[41] The congruence of Anarchist and Bolshevik policy here is illustrated by Lenin's statement: "To oppose the coalition is *in practice* to support the Bolsheviks."[42]

The Anarchists were of assistance to the Bolsheviks not just in their attack on the Provisional Government; they also seem to have defended those Bolsheviks who were charged with being German agents. "When in the summer of 1917," so the Anarchists claimed, ". . . the Bolsheviks took a more revolutionary position in respect to the bourgeoisie, in comparison with other political parties, the

Anarchists, in a certain sense, welcomed them and considered it also their revolutionary duty to unmask the lie of the bourgeois-socialist government which called Lenin, and other Bolsheviks, agents of the German government."[43]

As a result of congruent policies towards the Provisional Government, the Anarchists and Communists were able to work together during the pre-October period. They worked, however, toward different goals. After the October Revolution, when the Bolsheviks began to implement their program of centralization and one party control, the conflict which arose between the workers and Bolsheviks arose also between the Bolsheviks and Anarchists. An Anarchist group writing retrospectively in 1922 charged: "In the days of the revolution the tactics of the Bolsheviks towards the Anarchists boiled down to the formula: the maximum use of the Anarchists as a fighting element destructive to the bourgeoisie, assisting them in every way to arm, etc. This was done in the first days of the revolution. However, *with the seizure of power by the Bolsheviks,* the relationship began to change. The Bolsheviks tried to capture the revolution, to take it into their own hands. Instead of leaving the working masses independent and free to construct and defend their new life, limiting their role only to the necessary assistance to the working masses—the Bolsheviks wanted to become the directors, rulers, the masters of the workers. They began to castrate the revolution. In addition, they began systematically to take a series of measures to weaken their former comrades in arms—the anarchists who had a different perspective of the revolution and now were in the way of the Bolsheviks."[44]

The Anarchists, the Soviets, and the Bolsheviks

Although this Anarchist description of Bolshevik policy towards the Anarchists, before and after the Bolsheviks seized power, seems to be substantially valid, the Anarchist policy towards the Bolsheviks seems to have been much the same. Each group made use of the other, hoping that its ultimate goals would be served by the other's action. In the *Golos Truda* of 22 December 1917/4 January 1918, Maximov, in his article entitled the "Soviets of Workers', Soldiers' and Peasants' Deputies and Our Relationship to Them," presents an anarchist view of the problem of support for the Soviets and for the Bolsheviks after the October Revolution. Maximov claimed that "Before 'the second, October Revolution,' the Soviets were a political, non-power class organization with the admixture of an extra-class element, the *intelligentsia.*"[45]

The article states that the Soviets had been the center in which the will of the "masses" became transformed into a "law," which was not enforced by external pressure but was put into effect without compulsion. The law of the Soviets took into consideration the unique needs and rights of the localities which could, with impunity, reject the law. This concept of law and compulsion differs from that of Lenin, for whom compulsion, having become internalized, ceases to be compulsion at all. In Maximov's view, it is the will of the people which becomes externalized into law; it therefore need not be imposed by compulsion or enforced where the will of the masses is not congruent with it.

The Soviets, Maximov said, ". . . were the center in which the will of the proletariat crystallized . . . where it was converted into a completely real mass 'law' arising out of the will of the proletariat without being based on force or compulsion, because this crystallized will, this 'law' is put into effect, not as compulsion, not as force, but as a proposal, as the will of the majority without violating the will of the minority."[46]

The Soviets, then, were the institution in which the will of the people would be expressed in "law." And Maximov insisted again upon the protection of the particular, concrete, variegated customs and rights of the individual localities against the unifying tendencies of the centralization which he foresaw.[47] Thus, essential to the Anarchist concept of the revolutionary order was the freedom for the immanent, inherent and intrinsic action of the local units. Such a political orientation was diametrically opposed to that of the Bolsheviks, who believed in rigid control from the center.

The Anarchists had also insisted upon the full responsibility of the elected to the electors. Before the October Revolution, asserted Maximov, the Soviets were the best of political institutions which had yet existed because, by the device of recall, the voters could constantly control their elected candidates. "The Soviets," Maximov claimed, ". . . made it possible for the electors to control the deputies they elected."[48]

In spite of the political excellence of the Soviets, however, Maximov pointed out that Anarchists did not consider them a permanent institution, for *"The Soviets were a temporary form of a representative, parliamentary structure transitional to complete democracy."*[49]

Furthermore, perhaps the most significant function of the Soviets, in Maximov's view, was their opposition to the previous structure of the state; he avers that "They were revolutionary in essence, since they strove to destroy the existing form of state and to substitute another more perfect form for it—the Republic of Autonomous Soviets."[50]

The Soviets, because they strove to destroy the state, were considered by the Anarchists as revolutionary and progressive, whereas those who strove to preserve the previously existing state and its branches of authority—those who opposed the Soviets—were considered reactionary and counter-revolutionary.[51]

The Anarchists, therefore, supported the Soviets as a more progressive revolutionary institution than the Provisional Government, which they identified with the revolution. They supported the Soviets because, in spite of the fact that the latter were a central organ, they seemed to be satisfying some of the Anarchist demands for decentralization and local autonomy, and direct participation in politics.[52]

This alliance was to last, however, only so long as the allies of the Anarchists did not themselves become the wielders of power, for Maximov claims that once a revolutionary force becomes a ruling power, it ceases to be revolutionary. The ruling force strives to preserve the control it has acquired and, according to Maximov, a new force then arises, opposing the authority in power and striving to broaden the revolution.[53]

Applying this view concretely to the relationship between the Anarchists and the Bolsheviks, Maximov says that before their rise to power the Bolsheviks were a revolutionary force, but having seized power they became a force arresting revolutionary progress, a force trying to mold and shape the revolution for Bolshevik ends. The Anarchists, on the other hand, continued in their attempt to enlarge the revolution.[54]

"That is why," continued Maximov, ". . . the Bolsheviks, before the victory over Menshevism, defencism, and opportunism, were a revolutionary force; now after victory in virtue of the law of progress, they have become a stagnant force—a force striving to arrest the revolutionary pressure of life, a force trying to squeeze life into the framework of their own program. This naturally calls forth a new force, progressive, revolutionary, which strives to destroy the framework set up and to increase the sphere of revolutionary activity. Anarchism is such a force at the given moment."[55]

With Anarchistic hatred for the state—bourgeois or proletarian—Maximov declared that at the point at which the Bolsheviks began to build the state the Anarchists had to turn against them.

"Our assistance to the Bolsheviks . . . must stop where their victory begins.

". . . We remain on the field of battle and go no further, with the Bolsheviks, because further begins their 'constructive' work directed toward strengthening that against which we are fighting, which is an obstacle to progress—the strengthening of the *State*.

"It is not our business to strengthen that which we think should be destroyed.

"We must go underground to organize work for a third and final revolution. . . ."[56]

Participation in the state Maximov insisted, ". . . means to recognize the parliamentary tactic . . . to believe in the power of decrees and laws, to lose faith in the self-directed creativity of the masses."[57]

In their fight against the establishment of a state and its centralization, the Anarchist policy was to fight against the existing organization of Soviets. The Anarchist aim was to see that the Soviets acted only as connecting links between autonomous workers' organizations without exerting power over them.[58]

The struggle for communes of Soviets, which were to be the veins and arteries in a network of individual, independent and self-governing local organizations, was to be waged by the Anarchists both within and outside of the Soviets, but most important was to be the opposition outside the Soviets.[59]

Thus Anarchist policy, as presented by one of the foremost Russian Anarchists, in one of the leading Anarchist publications of the time, makes it clear that just as the Bolsheviks were willing to make use of the Anarchists, the Anarchists had made use of the Bolsheviks. Maximov's article indicates that once the Bolsheviks had seized power, however, many members of the Russian Anarchist movement began to turn against the Bolshevik party.[60] It also became clear that the significance and influence of the Anarchist movement in the revolutionary situation cannot be gauged or measured by the strength of the Russian Anarchist parties or by the representation they acquired in political institutions. As previously stated, to understand Russian Anarchism, it must be approached as a movement, not a party.

Anarchists, Bolsheviks and the Third International

The conflict and antagonism between the Bolsheviks and Russian Anarchists which arose in accordance with their different perspectives of the revolution led to a serious problem for the Bolsheviks in the Third International and in the Red International of Trade Unions. It seems that the Bolsheviks, to prevent a weakening of their influence in the international proletarian movement, had to alienate and isolate the Russian Anarchists from other non-Bolshevik groups, without, at the same time, alienating the non-Russian Anarchist groups in the international labor movements. Perhaps the Bolsheviks wanted also to retain the support of the Anarchists outside Russia, hoping they would be as valuable in bringing about communist revolutions in their native countries as they had been in Russia.

It seems that to remove the Anarchist threat to Bolshevik control of the international movements, as well as to deprive Anarchism of popularity in Russia, Russian Anarchism was identified with the "*kulak* struggle for capitalism."[61] There was an attempt to obscure the relationship between the Russian Anarchists and the Russian workers, and Anarchism was identified with an agrarian rather than a proletarian movement. A Communist publication addressed principally to European and American Anarchists asserted: "Russian anarchism, not having roots in the workers' movement, was converted in Russia into one of the tendencies of the middle and rich peasants. The Western European worker, whose idea of Anarchism is connected with the revolutionary trade union movement, has difficulty in understanding this singular phenomenon."[62] Continuing his attempt to disassociate Anarchism from the workers' movement and trying to avoid a breach between the Anarchists and the Bolsheviks in the Third International, the author stated: "We ask you constantly to bear in mind that the open struggle of the Soviet power with the Russian kulak-anarchist elements does not, in any way, signify a struggle of the Third International with Western European revolutionary anarcho-syndicalists."[63]

Thus, by seeking to remove any identification of the Russian Anarchism with the Russian labor movement, the Bolsheviks sought to mask their struggle both against the workers who strove to maintain joint factory ownership and against the Anarchists who supported those workers. Furthermore, it seems that the Bolsheviks intended, in this way, to cut off support by the international labor movement to the Anarchists and to the workers to whom the Anarchists adhered. In doing so, the Bolsheviks sought also to win the support of the non-Russian Anarchists in the trade union international.

The author of a Bolshevik pamphlet on Anarchism stated: "There are many profound divergences between us and the European and American revolutionary Anarchists and revolutionary Syndicalists. But these divergences cannot hinder us from getting along with them in a comradely fashion, in a single international trade union movement."[64]

It seems obvious, therefore, that in the first years after the Revolution, the Bolsheviks were anxious to have the support of the foreign Anarchist movement in the international trade union organization.[65]

Anarchism and Anarchist-Bolshevism

The relationships of both the Bolsheviks and the workers to the Anarchists were further complicated by the fact that there existed anarchist groups which supported the Bolsheviks.These Anarchists who supported or did not oppose them, the Bolsheviks referred to as the *ideinyi* Anarchists or Anarchists of ideas, whom the Bolsheviks regarded as the true Anarchists. Furthermore, whereas it was natural for the Bolsheviks to claim that those Anarchists who supported them were the true Anarchists, it was equally natural for the Anarchists who opposed the Bolsheviks to cast out of the Anarchist movement those who supported the Bolsheviks. A resolution of the First Congress of the Confederation of Anarchist Organizations of the Ukraine says: ". . . the congress considers it necessary to state openly and directly. . . .

"a) that in its opinion the representatives of the so-called 'Soviet Anarchism' standing on the platform of recognition and support of the Soviet power, by that very fact automatically cease to be Anarchistic."[66]

Even more confusion for the proper identification of Anarchism was the use of the Anarchist name by groups of brigands and criminals. The *Voice of Anarchism* (*Golos Anarkhista*) of 15 March 1918, for example, stated: "Each day the papers bring us news of the fact that in various cities of Russia there are frequent armed robberies sometimes accompanied by murders. The individuals committing those robberies often call themselves Anarchists, Maximalists, etc. . . . The Anarchists do not have any relationship to all these robberies. . . . Those who commit these robberies . . . call themselves Anarchists in order more conveniently to conduct their robberies and to hide themselves under the name of a revolutionary organization."[67]

The use of the Anarchist name to cover criminal activity was further complicated by the existence of the Black Guards attached to the Moscow Federation of Anarchist Groups. These Black Guards functioned also in Petrograd and other cities. They were probably the Anarchist equivalent of the Red Guards and seem to have been used to make confiscation and requisitions of property for the use of Anarchist communes. Such practices would have interfered, of course, with Bolshevik nationalization. On 11 and 12 April 1918 the Bolsheviks, through the use of force, suppressed the Black Guards.[68]

Trotsky, speaking on 14 April 1918 about this suppression of the Anarchists, made a distinction between the *"ideinyi"* Anarchists, i.e., the idealist Anarchists, and all other Anarchists who engaged in anti-Bolshevik action. The latter he identified with the criminal element. "But, Comrades, during the revolution, under the flag of anarchism—as everybody knows, and the honest idealist anarchist better than anybody else—a host of all sorts of hooligans, jail birds, thieves and night bandits have crowded in."[69]

Trotsky asserted that the "idealist" anarchists were conscious of the infiltration of criminals into their movement, for he said, "Comrades, I have talked about it to the idealist anarchists, and they themselves say: 'A lot of these jail birds, hooligans, and criminals have smuggled themselves into our movement.' "[70]

In Trotsky's further charges, however, there are indications that it is not the criminal activities of "pseudo-anarchists" that are of concern to the Bolsheviks but rather the political and military attacks of the Anarchists upon communist institutions.

"You all know," continued Trotsky, ". . . what occurs in Moscow. Buildings are seized over the heads of the Soviets, of the labor organizations, and it happens also that when the Soviets occupy a building these hooligans under the masks of Anarchists break into the building, fix up machine guns, seize armoured cars and even artillery."[71]

Such exploits, which might indicate Anarchist obstruction to Bolshevik nationalization, resistance to Bolshevik labor policy, or opposition to the formation of a state, are identified solely with the work of a criminal element, for according to Trotsky: "Lots of plunder, heaps of gold have been discovered in their nests. They are simply raiders and burglars who compromise the Anarchists. Anarchism is an idea, although a mistaken one, but hooliganism is hooliganism, and we told the Anarchists: you must draw a strict line between yourselves and the burglars . . . The Soviet regime . . . took power not in order to plunder like highwaymen and burglars, but in order to introduce a common labour discipline and an honest labour life."[72]

Thus the idea of anarchism was placed in opposition to the armed action which attempted to implement that idea itself. The Anarchists were warned that a distinction would be made between criminals and Anarchists only so long as the Anarchists did not engage in armed activity and opposition to the Bolshevik order. Trotsky continued by addressing the pseudo-anarchists, but delivered a message that might easily have applied to the Anarchist opposition. "I hold that the Soviet authorities acted quite correctly when they said to the pseudo-anarchists: don't imagine that your reign has come, don't imagine that the Russian people and the Soviet state is now a carrion upon which the crows alight to peck it to pieces. If you want to live together with us on the principles of common labour, then submit with us to the common Soviet discipline of the labouring class, but if you put yourselves in our way, then don't blame us. if the labour government, the Soviet power handles you without kid gloves."[73]

Hence the Bolsheviks presented the anarchists with an ultimatum: Submit or prepare for punishment. "It is said," Trotsky continued, "that among the hooligans there are a few who are honest Anarchists. If this is true . . . you must put between you and the hooligans . . . a hard line in order that you should not be mixed up with one another, and that we should know once and for all, who is a burglar and who is an honest idealist."[74]

It was the Bolsheviks, however, who from their position of power, could obscure the boundaries and dim the distinctions between a burglar and an honest idealist. Furthermore, it must be borne in mind that there would also have been a fundamental distinction in the term "anarchist of ideas" (or idealist anarchist, *ideinyi*[75] *anarkhist*) for the Bolsheviks and for the Anarchists. To the Bolsheviks, an idealist anarchist would have been, to paraphrase Trotsky, one who did not get in the way of the Bolsheviks. To the Anarchist, an idealist would be one who devoted himself to the achievement of Anarchist goals. Nevertheless, it is also likely that each group was at least partly aware of this difference in meaning the phrase bore for the other. At any rate, these two concepts of the term "anarchist of ideas" must be borne in mind when the Anarchist Emma Goldman claimed that Lenin assured her: "'Anarchists of ideas [*ideinyi*] are not in our prisons,'" and added, "Yet at that very moment numerous Anarchists filled the jails of Moscow, Petrograd and of many other cities in Russia."[76]

Although the Bolsheviks could arrest individual Anarchists and break up Anarchist organizations, they could not as easily eradicate the Anarchist movement or the Anarchist idea. The loose organizational connections of the movement and its lack of party structure probably made it less susceptible to disruption by Bolshevik repression.

Anarchism, the Factory Committees and Trade Unions

It was largely because of Anarchist support of workers' control at the individual local units and because of Anarchist support of factory ownership by the factory committees that the Bolsheviks feared and oppressed the Anarchists.

The Anarchist support to the factory committees, as opposed to the trade unions, was evident, for example, at the First All-Russian Congress of Trade Unions which took place at the beginning of January 1918. At that Congress, Maximov asserted: "We must not forget that the factory committees, as the organizations introduced directly by life itself by the course of the revolution, are the closest of all the working class, much closer than the trade unions."[77]

Not only did Maximov insist upon the close and natural connection between the workers and their factory committees, he also regarded them as the basic units of the future socialist society. "We must not forget," he said, "that the factory committees are the nuclei of the future socialist order. . . ."[78]

Thus, whereas the Bolsheviks attempted to deprive the factory committees of their ownership of factories where that ownership existed, the Anarchists, taking a diametrically opposite point of view, regarded these factory committee enterprises as the basic and fundamental cells of socialism.

The Bolshevik objective was centralization and state ownership. The Anarchists, however, saw no advantage for the workers in the substitution of the state for the individual employer.

"It is not the liberation of the proletariat," said Maximov, "when many individual plunderers are changed for one very powerful plunderer—the state. The position of the proletariat remains the same."[79]

Maximov asserted that as employees and employer, the worker and the state would have conflicting interests. This conflict, he asserted, would be expressed also in the antagonism between the local enterprises and the production center.

"We must not forget," Maximov warned the Congress of Trade Unions, ". . . that the state as the adversary of the organization of the working class movement, will try to maintain its own interests at the expense of the interests of the workers. There is no doubt that we will be the witnesses of a great conflict between the state power in the center and the organizations composed exclusively of workers which are found in the localities."[80]

The Anarchists, therefore, were the proponents of a federated rather than centralized order, in the economic as well as the political sphere, and Maximov admonished the Congress that any state would inevitably tend to impose the will of the center upon the localities. The goal of the proletariat, he said, was to create a center of coordination, not of subordination. Such a center, protecting local interests, could then regulate Russian industry on a national scale, for according to Maximov: "The working class as the class which strives for its complete freedom, not only in the sphere of politics but in the sphere of economics, should not forget that power, as such, even though it does not call itself such, will always try to subordinate the interests of the locality to the interests of the center. The aim of the proletariat is to coordinate all activity, all local interest, to create a center but not a center of decrees and ordinances but a center of regulation, of guidance—and only through such a center to organize the industrial life of the country."[81]

Anarchism, therefore, looked forward to a society in which all the parts would be organically related and coordinated from below. Seeking after an orderly, balanced and harmonious society, it held that this order and balance could be achieved only through the destruction of the centralized state. However, Anarchism did not seek to destroy the immanent organic bonds that welded individuals into communities and communities into the social organizations which, for the Anarchists, formed society as a whole. It sought to destroy the state so that an orderly society might flourish. "Anarchism," an Anarchist writer asserted, "does not in any way signify disorder."[82]

"It is a mistaken teaching which states that anarchists are trying to destroy society. Anarchists know very well that people have lived and will live in communities . . . [and] are always striving to weld it together. They are striving to create a harmonious, comradely society of free and equal people."[83]

The order and harmony which the Anarchists looked forward to in the economic sphere, therefore, were to grow out of the relationships established by the spontaneously acting organizations which themselves were spontaneously created in the revolutionary situation. Production was to be regulated by the factory committees which had been an outgrowth of the "order of anarchy" produced by the revolution,[84] but the planned economy of the Anarchists was to be planned from below, not from above.

Production, therefore, according to the Anarchists, should have been reorganized, as a result of the revolution, not by a central power, not by means of a definite center dictating from above; for the Anarchists held that it was possible to achieve a true, planned organization of production only "by means of the spontaneous, independent, self-directed masses."[85]

Just as the Bolsheviks, therefore, execrated any activity on the part of labor that was not organized or led by the communist party, the Anarchists idealized any activity on the part of labor which was not led, directed or instituted by a party or the state. An Anarchist Resolution presented at the First All-Russian Congress of Trade Unions in January of 1918 decried the disorganization and decline in the industrial life of Russia, stating: "There is only one way out: to allow the toiling people themselves to carry on the struggle with disorder. This is the only correct road. Because the people, creating the most excellent and most perfect forms of organization, girded with energy and initiative, exerting themselves to the utmost, will quickly put an end to disorder and to the state capitalist system of contemporary society."[86]

What was necessary for ending this disorder, the resolution states, was "real workers' control, not state workers' control."[87]

According to the Anarchist resolution, order could be restored only by the abolition of state capitalism, the system the Bolsheviks were striving to intensify and accelerate.[88]

Again the Anarchists insisted that control of production had to be in the hands of the workers and not in the hands of any other class, especially a bureaucracy of any kind, for the Resolution of the Anarcho-Syndicalists ". . . it is necessary that the organization of production, transport, distribution, etc., be immediately transferred to the hands of the toiling people themselves and not to the hands of the state or some other state civil service machine made up of one kind or another of the class enemies of the proletariat because it is impossible for the workers to expect any good of them."[89]

The resolution proposed an economic order in which the factory and village committees would be the basic units of a federation. The federation formed by these committees were, in turn, to join in multi-industrial councils of autonomous units regulating the industrial life of Russia. The resolution read: "The toiling people through the assistance of their own basic organizations, in the villages—village committees, in the cities—factory, railroad, bank, commercial-industrial, house committees, etc., should be united on the basis of federalism, by industry, into an industrial federation. The industrial federations should unite among themselves forming poly-industrial soviets of national economy in whose duties shall lie the regulation of the economic life of the country. . . ."[90]

Thus, for the Anarchists the factory committees are no mere organization of workers for revolutionary purposes only. They are the very core of the future socialist order. Maximov, in his speech on the Regulation of Industry at the First All-Russian Congress of Trade Unions in January 1918, stated, therefore, that the function of the factory committees was no longer to protect and improve conditions for the worker. The factory committees were to seek a predominant position in the industry and economy of Russia. Completely independent from any kind of party grouping, it was necessary, said Maximov, for the proletariat to create its own forms of organization. These forms would be the heirs of capital. They would create a new production on a new basis, and the trade unions, according to Maximov, were not such a form. but the factory committees as the offspring of the revolution were.[91]

Although the Bolsheviks, after October, turned away from the factory committees toward the trade unions, the Anarchists continued to support the factory committees and oppose the trade unions. Maximov, at the First All-Russian Congress of Trade Unions, asserted: "It is necessary . . . for the Congress to listen to the voice of life and to find a place for the trade unions as organizations of the old type which fully corresponded with the old economic relations of tsarist times. They are now living out their time as fighting organizations of the proletariat, as organizations which can regulate and direct production. They have already lived out their time."[92]

Here, too, as it shall be demonstrated shortly, the Anarchists were diametrically opposed to the Bolsheviks. The Bolsheviks, having made use of the factory committees against the trade unions before October, were to make use of the trade unions against the factory committees after October. Thus, the emphasis which the Anarchists placed upon the factory committees in the socialist order, as they envisioned it, was likely to hinder the Bolshevik program.

Anarchist Organization

From all the evidence presented above, it is possible to reach the following conclusions concerning the inter-relationship of the workers, the Anarchist movement and the Bolshevik party. To the Anarchists, the factory committees instituting workers' control seemed to be the protagonists in the initial stage of an industrial community to be composed of autonomous local production units. The Anarchists regarded the factory committees as the Anarchist idea come to life, as Anarchist communes bred spontaneously and immanently in the revolutionary situation. They regarded the workers' implementation of workers' control as proof that to realize the Anarchist idea, the Anarchists need only assist, not lead, the workers. This, in turn, seems to have strengthened the Anarchist belief that party organization was the betrayal of spontaneous, anarchic order. Indeed, within the conceptual framework of Anarchist ideology, which rejected and contemned law and authority, it would have been a fundamental contradiction to require Anarchists to submit to the rules and regulations which party organization and procedure necessitate.[93] There was, therefore, a lack of organization in the Anarchist movement and the absence of a party to lead and guide it. This was coupled with the juxtaposition and congruence, before October, of the immediate objectives of the Anarchists and Bolsheviks regarding the factory committees and workers' control; this congruence seems to have given to the Bolsheviks leadership of a movement which the Anarchists helped to formulate and encourage, but which they would not organize and direct. In their seizure of power, therefore, the Bolsheviks seem to have been the leaders of an Anarchist as well as a Communist movement.

It was only after Anarchism had witnessed the post-October Bolshevik policy toward the factory committees and workers' control, and had itself been subject to Bolshevik repression, that it attempted to fight the Bolshevik party and the Soviet state by means of a united movement, if not by a united party.

A Resolution, taken in April 1919, of the First Congress of the Confederation of Anarchist Organizations in the Ukraine—the region which seems to have become the stronghold of Anarchism. for it was being driven out of the Petersburg and Moscow areas—stated:[94]

"The Congress proposes that it is necessary

"1) to increase propagandistic and organizational work to spread the idea of 'a single anarchism,' . . .

"2) to more clearly illuminate the idea of a single anarchism not as a new tendency broken off other tendencies, but on the contrary, as a movement striving to unite organizationally for the purpose of fruitful joint work."[95]

Hesitating to impose a central authority upon its adherents, however, the Confederation permitted particular differences to exist as long as the basic Anarchist premises were not assailed. The Resolution continued: ". . . in addition, the congress finds it necessary to emphasize, that under the union of Anarchists of various tendencies, it is necessary, of course, to understand not a purely mechanical union, but a union in work on the basis of ideological agreement on the basic principles . . . with the full freedom of each to defend his own point of view in all those problems in which he disagrees with his comrades in work."[96] The principal bonds uniting the Anarchists were thus to have been fundamental ideological agreement and common work for the Anarchist cause.

However, the Anarchists still did not feel at home in imposing authority upon each other, nor were they successful in directing a constructive social movement, except, perhaps, under the aegis of Makhno. Anarchist energy and activity had been directed principally towards destroying the old order. In addition, the Anarchists bore the conviction that the removal of state and governmental authority and its juridical institutions would leave the "masses" free spontaneously to form a new society. Disdaining the law and institutions of the modern nation state, Russian Anarchism had nothing to offer in place of them except the conviction that "the masses" would in some way form a better order than the tsarist state or "bourgeois" democracy.

There is something of pathos in that part of the Anarchist Resolution which states that the Anarchists were faced with ". . . the necessity of transferring the center of gravity of ideological work from the purely critical sphere to the positive sphere. The masses now expect of us chiefly not criticism, not an answer to the problem how and where one must not go, but a definite and clear answer to the problem: where and how are the masses to go from here?"[97]

The Anarchists, however, do not seem to have successfully provided any more comprehensive answer for the positive organization of an Anarchist society than the local commune.[98] Ultimately, however, the fundamental inefficacy of Anarchism lay not in the questions for which it had no answer, but in the question it did not ask. What was to preserve a society based on the lack of power? Anarchism did not raise this question. Its class-centric conviction in the talent for social organization inherent in "the masses" and its faith in the innate goodness of the worker and peasants led to the assumption that the governmental institutions of organized political life had only to be removed in order to allow the burgeoning of peace, order and prosperity.[99]

Worker Understanding of the Anarchist Idea

Although the Anarcho-Syndicalists did speak of industrial federations and unions of these federations, there is no indication that the workers instituting workers' control intended to form such federations out of their councils or were concerned with doing so. From all the indications presented here, it would seem that the workers seized the factories and instituted workers' control not for the purpose of establishing Anarchist communes, nor to destroy the state. Their soviets were a form of political, not apolitical organization. Moreover, those workers who persisted in maintaining workers' control against Bolshevik opposition seem to have been intent upon their ownership and operation of industry. They were concerned not with the order of anarchy, but with their rights to the property they had seized and sometimes shared. It would seem, therefore, that there was not necessarily any greater or more permanent correspondence of final goals between the Anarchists and workers than between the Bolsheviks and the workers. Nor is there any reason to believe the workers had a clearer idea of Anarchist than of Bolshevik aims and purposes. A Resolution on the Current Moment, taken at the First Congress of the Confederation of Anarchist Organizations of the Ukraine 'Nabat' in April of 1919, complains of a lack of understanding of the Anarchist world-view on the part of the workers. "On the one hand we have the conceptual [*ideinyi*] blindness of the broad masses of the population," the resolution stated, "who still do not see a definite way out of the situation which has been created. . . . On the other hand, we observe: (1) the instinctive strivings of the masses devoid of a clear view. . . ."[100]

However, it is not strange that at this time, among the workers, there was a lack of understanding of the totality of the Anarchist as well as Bolshevik ideology. The ideologies of both Bolshevism and Anarchism seem to have been formulated and borne most largely by Russian intellectuals, not by Russian workers. The world conceptions of these intellectuals, insofar as they were determined by the specific social milieu of the intellectuals themselves, would have tended to reflect the specific outlook of their group. Further, the basic mode of life and common experiences of the intellectuals as a stratum in society probably gave rise to an approach to the world that differed from that of the workers. There is little need to wonder, then, that the workers interpreted, within their own conceptual framework, the ideas and concepts of the intellectuals. Since this framework would seem to have been formed at least in part by a way of life significantly different from that of the intellectuals, it is also probable that their goals and values should have differed in some significant ways. Nevertheless, there is also reason to believe that the Anarchist movement, in its championship of the factory committees and workers' control, both before and after October, was a vital influence among the workers.

As the movement existed among the workers, however, it is best described in the words of its Bolshevik enemies, who referred to it as "bourgeois anarchism." For insofar as the Anarchist movement existing among the workers insisted upon private property ownership, shared though that ownership was, the movement was bourgeois. Insofar as it might have rejected parties, parliamentarianism, constitutions and juridical institutions, it was anarchistic.

The Bolsheviks and Anarchism

The Bolshevik designation of the workers' control movement as both bourgeois and anarchistic served as a two-pronged weapon against it. By labeling as bourgeois the workers who defended their joint ownership of individual factories, the Bolsheviks placed those workers in disrepute among the adherents of socialism. By simultaneously labeling the workers' control movement as anarchistic, the Bolsheviks placed it in disrepute among the defenders of private property who might, in some cases, have made the best of a bad bargain by recognizing the right of revolutionary seizure in return for a share of the property seized. The charge of Anarchism might also have served to isolate the factory committee workers engaged in workers' control from possible non-Anarchist support from abroad. Thus the label bestowed upon this movement of workers' control served to cut it off from the support of both the right and left and to isolate it from the assistance of any but the Anarchists.

Having attempted to clarify the relationship among the workers, the Anarchists, and the Bolsheviks, it is desirable now to turn our attention once again to the Bolshevik policy toward the factory committees.

CHAPTER VI

The Factory Committees, Centralization and the Trade Unions

CONTROL VS. REGULATION

In attempting to convince the factory committees to give up workers' control as the committees themselves conceived it, the Bolshevik Party did not explicitly state its intention of annulling factory committee power. They claimed, rather, that it was their policy to broaden workers' control and to increase its scope.

The role of the factory committees and of workers' control were two of the principal problems dealt with by the First All-Russian Congress of Trade Unions, which met 20-27 January 1918. Shortly before the opening of this congress, on 18 January, the Bolshevik troops and the Bolshevik Red Guards had fired upon those workers who demonstrated in favor of the Constituent Assembly, which met for the first and last time on that date.[1]

This shooting could not but have served as concrete evidence for the workers that opposition to the Bolsheviks might be suppressed by violence. The delegates to the congress could not have attended it, therefore, without some degree of apprehension and fear of the consequences that might follow upon disagreement with the Bolshevik Party.

The incident of 18 January was not the only case of Bolshevik violence against labor. Lozovsky, before his temporary expulsion from the Party, wrote in the *Trade Union Herald* on 2 January 1918 protesting against the Bolshevik use of repressive measures and violence against the workers.[2] Thus, by the opening of the First All-Russian Congress of Trade Unions—the first major meeting of labor organizations after the Bolsheviks seized power—labor had already been subjected to Bolshevik repression.

Nevertheless, the party did not attack the factory committees and their policy of workers' control directly. The Bolsheviks attempted to persuade the committees to give up their control of the individual industrial units for the promise of participation in the regulation of nationalized industry.

"At present," said the Communist Kozelev at the First All-Russian Congress of Trade Unions, "the working class is faced with the regulation of industry, with the organization of the people's economy as a whole, rather than with workers' control in the enterprise."[3]

Kozelev adds, however, that workers' control is not to be abandoned but is to serve as a means towards the regulation of all industry. As regulation in the individual enterprise, he explained: ". . . workers' control is not, of course, to be abolished—it has become a propeller, a lever, a tentacle in this universal apparatus which is passing now to the working class. . . . It must be said that all the forces of the working class have now to be directed to the sphere of the regulation of industry."[4]

If industry was to be nationalized and centralized, it was important to the Bolsheviks that workers' control be taken out of the hands of the factory committees and the workers; for if the latter retained control of nationalized industry, they would also have retained a dominant place in the state, and, in fact, the Bolsheviks were to insist upon a distinction between the organized workers and the proletarian state. The workers, therefore, were promised broad participation in nationalized factories only so long as they maintained an identity separate from ownership and management. Kozelev said: "We understand workers' control not only as the definite independence of the masses in the sense of their intervention within the individual enterprise, both in the technical aspects and in the commercial side of these enterprises, but also as intervention in social and administrative relations. We say that, in the end, the administration itself must be transferred to workers' control, and we do not restrict it by even one reservation."[5] Thus the Bolsheviks made a distinction between the functions of workers' control and the administration and regulation of industry. Once this distinction was made and the workers were separated or "became independent" of the factory administration, they could be promised the right of intervention in an administration which they did not run.

It became obvious, therefore, that for the opponents of workers' control there was a distinction between control and regulation. Workers' control was to be turned away from the management of industrial enterprises. "Control," according to Osinskii, "is not concerned with administration. Control is the examination of how the fulfillment corresponds to the task."[6] It was presumably to be a check upon the efficacy with which administration fulfilled the tasks assigned to it. It was in this sense that workers' control was to be turned into the general regulation of all industry.

Thus the factory committees were not to decide what to do but, deflected from administration, were to do what had been decided upon. The power they had created by acting together was being wrested from them and they were being deprived of the possibility of continuing their own course or of finding and taking new directions. Hence they were relegated to following, carrying out, and fulfilling. Politically, this is a distinction between those who rule and those who are ruled.

Lozovsky claimed that centralized state planning was actually equivalent to workers' control. Moreover, in spite of the fact that Lozovsky attacked the factory committees for a purpose differing from that of the Bolsheviks, his attack was ultimately to serve Bolshevik ends. For this reason the expulsion of Lozovsky from the Bolshevik Party served the latter in good stead. The most vehement opponent of workers' control as the workers conceived it was, during the period of his attack upon the factory committees, excluded from the party.

"What exactly is workers' control?" Lozovsky asked at the First All-Russian Congress of Trade Unions, answering rhetorically: "Workers' control is an attempt to introduce definite planning by an organized scheme, the definite idea of standardization in the sphere of production. . . . "[7] This, of course, was not the workers' conception of workers' control, but, as Lozovsky said, "Just because the workers misunderstand and falsely interpret workers' control is no reason to repudiate it."[8]

The Resolution on Workers' Control introduced by the Bolsheviks and passed by the First All-Russian Congress of Trade Unions, however, clearly defines workers' control as the means by which the centralized economic plan is carried out in the local enterprises. Paragraph 4 of the Resolution stated: "Workers' control is indissolubly connected with the general system of the regulation and is the instrument by which the universal economic plan is put into effect locally."[9]

The implementation of workers' control as the workers conceived it was beginning to be indicative not only of misunderstanding but of a clear-sighted opposition to Bolshevik policy. Many factory committees continued to be concerned with the care of their own factories and regarded workers' control as workers' ownership and management. The Bolsheviks charged, therefore, that ". . . the factory committee management has shown, that, unfortunately, it cannot stand for an all-state or even an industrial-wide point of view."[10] The workers adhering to workers' control were reluctant to give up the factories they held. They feared, perhaps, the loss of their voice in the general chorus of what the Bolsheviks called the voice of all the working class. They preferred workers' control, as they conceived it, to state control. A significant number of committees seem to have been concerned more with the welfare of their own enterprises than with the problems of political economy.

Control vs. Centralization

Therefore, Riazanov insisted, the workers' government—that is, the dictatorship of the proletariat, which was regarded as the representative of the working class as a whole—should exert its control over the factory committees. "Before us," he said, ". . . stands . . . the question of control by the workers' government, by the whole working class over the workers in individual factory enterprises . . . they forget that there may be a thousand times the metallists, a thousand times the shoemakers, a thousand times the textile workers, but that this does not give any right to the textile worker, to the shoemaker, to the metallist to consider himself the single, exact and manifest expression of the interests of the whole of the working class."[11]

Unless the factory committees were controlled by the central government, the national economy, Riazanov insisted, would be despoiled. "Without such control on the part of all the working class, on the part of all the proletariat—and for this we need a whole network of organs which control the activity of each such individual cell in each factory, in each enterprise—without such a network of organs we will have only a pillage of the people's economy, a pillage of the economy which we want to socialize and organize into a whole out of many parts. We will have a mass of atomized cells."[12]

The factory committees, however, do not seem to have believed that their interests would be served best by the centralized state acting in the name of labor as a whole. "The factory committees," said Riazanov, "identify the interests of a particular factory with the interests of the national economy, with the interests of all the working class."[13] It seems, therefore, that the workers of the factory committees believed that the interests of the working class would be served best if each factory attended to its own self-interest rather than by sacrificing that interest in the name of the "working class a whole."

It has been demonstrated previously, however, that immediately after the October Revolution the Bolshevik Party, constituted as the revolutionary government, took steps to undermine workers' control and the factory committees. It has also been pointed out that the Bolshevik Party in the first months after the revolution seems to have been reluctant to alienate the factory committees and the Red Guards. The Red Guards had helped them to power and they were still dependent upon them for support.

However, in addition to the fear of alienating the Red Guards before communist power was consolidated, the Bolsheviks were not in a position during the first months after the revolution to control industry on a nationwide scale by themselves. For this reason, perhaps, the factory committees and workers' control would continue to perform a useful function for the party. The committees could perform the first step in the state control of industry that the Bolsheviks were planning. Lozovsky, writing in the *Trade Union Herald* two days before the First All-Russian Congress of Trade Unions, pointed out that the factory committees could be permitted to execute workers' control only if the prime objective of such a policy was the immediate institution of control at each enterprise, with the hope of statewide control in the future.[14] He concluded, however, that "Workers' control . . . must be centralized. Otherwise it loses all meaning, otherwise it atomizes the energy of the worker masses. . . . It is very obvious that workers' control would lose nine-tenths of its significance if each factory committee would begin to solve everything in its own manner."[15]

The Menshevik Cherevanin, at the First All-Russian Congress of Trade Unions, also charged that the Statutes on Workers' Control had not succeeded in centralizing and organizing industry, that the government had not been able to enforce its unifying decrees, that ". . . so far this has been only talk."[16]

In the three months after the revolution and the promulgation of a centralized economic order, little progress seems to have been made in that direction. Lozovsky charged that "The factory committees are so much the owners and masters that they, to a significant degree, are independent of the general controlling organs which 'should not interfere where they are not wanted.' "[17]

Lozovsky therefore insisted upon two concrete measures that would deprive the workers of effective control of their factories. One measure was to acquire possession of the products of the factories and the other was to control their finances. "If the given enterprise is not the property of the individual group of workers," insisted Lozovsky, "then its products of manufacture also belong to all, and not to the individual group of workers."[18]

The problem of whether the workers or the state were to dispose of the products of an enterprise was an even more concrete one than the problem of ownership. The abstract recognition by the workers of state ownership would have had little advantage for the Bolsheviks if the workers continued to sell and receive the profits of the products of their enterprises.

Along with the problem of the disposition of articles of manufacture went the problem of the finances of the factories. The factory committees could not maintain their independence and function as self-reliant institutions if their profits, and their funds for purchasing raw materials, for paying workers and employees, and for overhead expenses, were taken out of their hands. If they were deprived of the financial control of their enterprises, the very basis of their control functions in general would be destroyed. This, therefore, is what the opponents of the factory committees proposed to do.[19]

Thus, whereas before October it was the function of the factory committee control commissions to control the finances of the enterprise, Lozovsky, after October, proposed that this function be removed from their competence. Claiming that finance was too complex a matter for the factory committees to handle, Lozovsky insisted that only the center, not the individual enterprise, could deal with what he considered to be the financial machinations and trickery of the capitalistic trusts. "I repeat," he said, "that . . . the individual cells independently can do nothing, only through the center can they ascertain what the financial sources of the enterprise are, how the syndicates and trusts cover up for the firm. That is why we must state that the financial side of the business is deleted from the functions of the control commission."[20]

At the First All-Russian Congress of Trade Unions, Lozovsky insisted that financial control of the individual enterprises should be vested in the Supreme Council of the National Economy and its departments. "I have declared most categorically," he said at this congress, ". . . against the idea of those comrades who entrust financial control functions to the lower organs of workers' control. This sphere does not lie in the lower organs of workers' control, since it does not enter into the limits of their competence. . . . This, in each case, is in the competence of the highest organs of control . . . which are connected . . . with the general apparatus of management, with the Supreme Council of the National Economy and its various branches. Only when all branches of financial control will be centralized can we be sure that we will have real control."[21]

Lozovsky cites an instance of the dependence of the central government upon the factory committees to determine the financial status of industrial enterprises. Pointing to this as a sign of weakness and debilitation on the part of the communist state, Lozovsky declared: "When the government took possession of the banks, it issued a proclamation signed by Obolenskii [Osinskii] and another comrade, to all the factory committees, with the request that they verify the demands of the administration of the factory concerning its need for money, how much they needed, whether they really needed it, and whether they needed it to pay the workers or not. This appeal from the State Bank to the individual factory enterprises to determine how much money a given enterprise needed to settle its accounts could be issued only in a period of disintegration, in a period of struggle, during the very time of the transfer of power. . . ."[22] Such a system, Lozovsky charged, "could lead to collusion between the administration and individual factory committees which are insufficiently conscious of their obligations."[23]

This dependence of the central government upon the factory committees seems also to illustrate what Lozovsky neglected to mention—the fact that the factory committees, in many cases, had worked out a means of acquiring the cooperation of the factory management. Even more importantly, it illustrates that workers' control could be effective as a system of federally coordinated independent units. It demonstrates also that the factory committees were useful to the Bolshevik regime in its earliest stages. Nevertheless, Lozovsky insisted that, in the sphere of finance, ". . . everything must be left to the higher organs of workers' control."[24] This was the policy adopted at the First All-Russian Congress of Trade Unions in January 1918. Paragraph 8 of the Resolution on Workers' Control adopted at this congress read: "The control commission does not deal with the financial problems of the enterprise and when such questions arise they are transferred to the state regulating institutions."[25]

Factory Committees and Trade Unions

The question of finance, however, was only one problem in the centralized control of the factory committees. It was a part of the broader problem facing the Bolsheviks—the problem of wresting control of industry from the factory committees. The struggle of the Bolshevik Party with the factory committees was waged, however, largely through the trade unions.

It has been pointed out that the Third All-Russian Conference of Trade Unions had resolved that unions should be formed on an industrial basis. Thus the claim that the factory committees should supersede the unions because of their organization by industry rather than by trade could no longer be effectively upheld. Furthermore, at the First All-Russian Conference of Factory Committees an attempt was made to bring the committees under the aegis of the trade unions. A Resolution of the Commission on the Problem of the Relations between the Factory Committees and the Trade Unions, adopted at the First All-Russian Conference of Factory Committees, stated in Paragraph 5 that the Center of the Factory Committees would be a branch of the regulation of industry and workers' control in the All-Russian Council of Trade Unions. The factory committee center was also to include representatives of the trade unions.[27] The local councils of factory committees and the local trade unions, according to Paragraph 6, were to be similarly related.[28]

According to the Commission to Study the Trade Union Movement in the SSSR, the general resolutions of the First All-Russian Conference of Factory Committees are unobtainable. Only the resolutions of the special commission on the question of the relations between the factory committees and the trade unions are available.[29] "Basically," says the Commission to Study the Trade Union Movement, "a temporary dualism with a rather definite division of functions between the two organizations was preserved."[30] It then explains that the two organizations could not fuse so long as there were ". . . defensist and collaborationist elements in the trade unions, attempting through the trade unions to subordinate the factory committees to themselves and to direct their work. It is clear that at first this was one of the basic motives for the independent organization of the factory committees. But by September, in Petrograd, this movement withered away with the formulation in the Petrograd Soviet of the majority trade union resolution supporting the Bolsheviks."[31]

The designation of *defensist* was applied by the Bolsheviks to those who had advocated Russia's continued participation in the world war; *collaborationist,* to those who advocated that the workers share political power with other classes. The names apply, among others, to the Mensheviks and Right Social Revolutionaries, to all those socialist parties who participated in the Provisional Government. As long as the Mensheviks maintained a majority in the trade unions and attempted to defend the primacy of the unions against the encroachment of the factory committees, the Bolsheviks pitted the factory committees against the trade unions. When, however, the Bolsheviks gained a majority in the Petrograd Soviet of Trade Unions, and when they could no longer direct the factory committees towards Bolshevik goals, they supported union opposition to the factory committees. Having gained a majority in the First All-Russian Congress of Trade Unions and having discovered that the factory committees were becoming centers of resistance to Bolshevik domination of the economy, the Bolsheviks began to subordinate the factory committees to the trade unions. Still retaining a majority at the First All-Russian Conference of Factory Committees, which took place on the eve of the October Revolution, the Bolsheviks attempted to undermine the activity of the factory committees by eliminating the central institution it had striven to place above them. The independent center of the factory committees, says the Commission to Study the Trade Union Movement, abolished itself.[32]

Riazanov, speaking to the First All-Russian Congress of Trade Unions, also claimed that at the First All-Russian Conference of Factory Committees, the committees represented there agreed, after a stubborn struggle and resistance, to yield their place of predominance to the trade unions. They agreed, Riazanov claimed, to their death warrant.[33]

Lozovsky's account of the struggle between the trade unions and factory committees at the First All-Russian Conference of Factory Committees seems to be more realistic than either of the two reports presented above. Lozovsky emphasized the compromise character of the solution reached. He did not assert that the factory committees accepted the predominance of the trade unions, but that: ". . . we succeeded . . . in coming to a compromise solution which concluded that the center elected at the All-Russian Conference, filled in with representatives of the All-Russian union of factory committees, would become the branch regulating the people's economy within the All-Russian Council of Trade Unions. . . . The conference recognized that its center was only part of the All-Russian Council of Trade Unions."[34]

Even this compromise, however, does not seem to have been accepted by the factory committees. Riazanov stated, for example: "These committees [the First All-Russian Conference of Factory Committees] after this, in practice, completely disclaimed this compromise and returned to their old point of view."[35]

This renunciation of the resolution, which the Bolsheviks interpreted as the subordination of the factory committees to the trade unions (unless the significance of that resolution was retrospectively exaggerated by the Bolsheviks), may be illustrative of two conditions. First, it indicates that though the Bolsheviks were, by far, in the majority at the First All-Russian Conference of Factory Committees, and as representatives of the factory committees could force a resolution through this conference, they could not enforce that resolution against the opposition of the factory committees themselves. Secondly, it suggests that the factory committees accepted Bolshevik leadership only so long as the divergences in their goals were not brought to the test. That the Bolsheviks, in the first months immediately following the October Revolution, did not insist upon the enforcement of the resolution subordinating the factory committees to the trade unions, may indicate again their reluctance to alienate the factory committees.

The fact that little was accomplished by the resolution subordinating the factory committees to the trade unions may also indicate that the Central Council of Factory Committees, as a creation largely of the Bolshevik Party itself, was not necessary to the individual, local factory committees. The local units, it seems, could continue to function without the direction of the center, especially since this center seems to have been superimposed from above and was not the result of organic growth from below. Thus, in spite of the resolution passed at the First All Russian Conference of Factory Committees, the struggle to subordinate the factory committees to the the trade unions had to be fought subsequently. It is one of the chief problems of the First All-Russian Congress of Trade Unions of January 1918.

Since the factory committees identified with interests of their own factories, they were accused by the Bolsheviks of localism and separatism. Since the Bolsheviks regarded a socialist economy as a centralized economy, they further accused the factory committees of being incapable of instituting a socialistic order. Riazanov, for example, referred to the factory committees as "the separatist opposition to the reorganization of the economy on a socialist basis."[36]

The Bolsheviks and Lozovsky claimed that the factory committees were to be superseded by the trade unions. Lozovsky asserted that, unlike the trade unions, the Central Council of Factory Committees understood workers' control as separate control at each individual factory.[37] "But how are we to implement the execution of workers' control?"[38] Lozovsky asked, after indicating the inability of the factory committees to execute this task. "How are we to weld the individual control cells into one statewide chain so that they all act according to a single plan?"[39] And he answered, "Only the industrial unions can fulfill this task."[40] Lozovsky represented the trade unions, therefore, as exponents of centralized workers' control. He brought them forward as the organizations ready to implement workers' control on a country-wide scale.

The industrial unions, on the ground that they represented workers of all industries, in all factories, on a nationwide basis, were regarded as having, implicitly, a perspective capable of encompassing all industry. Weinberg, speaking for the Bolsheviks at the First All-Russian Congress of Trade Unions, stated that ". . . the trade unions—or, more correctly, the industrial unions—espouse the point of view not of the individual factory, not even of the workers of a particular city, but the point of view of the working class of all industry."[41] Therefore, Weinberg insisted, "the factory committees must be subordinated to the trade unions."[42]

Reasoning from the above arguments for the purpose of depriving the workers of control of the factories they had expropriated, and for the purpose of placing the economy securely in their own hands, the Bolsheviks converted the factory committees into the lowest organs of the local trade unions. The Statute of the All-Russian Union of Textile Workingmen and Workingwomen, a Bolshevik-dominated union, stated, for example, that "The lowest cell of the union is the factory committee, whose obligations consist of putting into effect in a given enterprise all the decrees of the union."[43]

Resolution, Decree and Practice

The subordination of the factory committees to the trade unions was determined, in general, by resolutions adopted by the First All-Russian Congress of Trade Unions. It must be pointed out again here, however, that such resolutions and decrees passed in the first year or two after the Bolshevik seizure of power often functioned more as examples of Bolshevik intent than of Bolshevik achievement. In some cases, the Bolsheviks did not have the power to enforce their decrees; in other cases, they were able to go further in achieving their aims than the resolution allowed. The Bolsheviks, as Lenin had pointed out, were not bound by legalistic formalities. In his introduction to the Stenographic Report of the First All-Russian Congress of Trade Unions, Tomsky apologized for the departures, made by actual practice, from the resolutions: "In the period when everything stored up by the centuries was literally turned upside down by the relations of the proletarian revolution, to take into account and to foresee not only the general direction of this advance, but to foresee exactly all its details beforehand would be hopelessly pedantic."[44] Tomsky insisted that reality itself, not theory, be the determinant of action. The theory the Bolsheviks claimed to derive from reality had to be adaptable to the needs of each "moment," to each change demanded in accordance with the general line of Bolshevik directions and goals. Resolutions and theory, said Tomsky, cannot force reality into their mold. Life must put them to the test, and Tomsky asserted that the very changes made to the resolutions of the First Congress merely proved that the direction the Congress had originally taken was the only right one.[45]

Tomsky indicated that the trade unions had passed to their function in nationalized industry more quickly than the resolutions of the First All-Russian Congress of Trade Unions had anticipated. He claimed that the preliminary stages of nationalization (which would seem to be workers' control) were not as necessary as they were thought to have been. This seems to indicate that it was not the decrees and resolutions which determined the course of Bolshevik action, but that expediency determined the means by which goals were reached.

In order to justify the departure from the resolutions, Tomsky claimed that the corrections and modifications to them merely served as proof of their validity. The fact that the resolutions had been superseded, said Tomsky, bore witness to the progress labor was making: "If the resolutions on workers' control, demobilization, and regulation, are in part at the present moment already significantly outmoded it is only because the working class, in its process of active, self-directed construction of the new life, progressed considerably faster and, advancing through preliminary forms, closely approximated the organization of production by means of the nationalization and direct administration of production."[46]

According to Tomsky, then, resolutions passed by the First All-Russian Congress of Trade Unions were outmoded by the time of their publication in the Stenographic Report of the congress because nationalization of industry had proceeded more quickly than had been expected. As previously stated, it would therefore be both naive and misleading to present the resolutions of the early labor, as well as other, congresses and conferences as examples of situations and relationships which were actually created. They are useful, however, in presenting Bolshevik intent and the rationalizations for the course the Bolsheviks planned to take. This does not mean, however, that the Bolsheviks did not achieve their objectives. In most cases they seem even to have exceeded their expectations. It means only that the goals embodied in the decrees and resolutions of the early post-October period may not always have been attained in the systemized and formalized fashion the decrees and resolutions would indicate. Tomsky's statement also acts as a justification for the non-fulfillment of decrees that the Bolsheviks repudiated.

Trade Unions and Control

From the decrees and resolutions it is clear that the Bolsheviks intended to subordinate the factory committees to other organs which would direct labor and industry. The manner in which the Bolsheviks intended to subordinate the factory committees, and their justification for this action, is found, for example, in the Resolution on Workers' Control and in the Resolution on the Trade Unions and Factory Committees.

Paragraph 1 of the Resolution on the Trade Unions and Factory Committees explains that during the revolutionary upsurge the factory committees merely appropriated the function of the trade unions: "1. The Great Russian Revolution, bringing to life all the creative forces of the working class, created in its first days, at the factories and shops, organs of workers' representation which took upon themselves the tasks usually fulfilled by the trade unions."[47] Paragraph 2, however, claimed that since the trade unions had grown stronger, they had to absorb the factory committees,[48] for two forms of workers' organizations, having intersecting functions, hindered the tasks of labor. These tasks, it said, could best be fulfilled under the single direction of the industrial unions.[49]

Recognizing that the authority of the Trade Union Congress could not, at that time, be extended throughout all Russia, the fourth paragraph of the resolution requested that where factory committees continued to exist they cooperate with the trade unions: "In those places where the factory committees still have not been transformed into organs of the corresponding industrial trade unions, they can play an outstanding role by putting into practice and achieving the designated tasks, if they will work in full union with the trade unions."[50]

Thus, the Bolsheviks were willing to continue to make use of the factory committees where necessary, encouraging them, at the same time, to pave their way to absorption by the trade unions.

It has been pointed out above that the administrative and executive organs of the factory committees were the control commissions. These control commissions, according to the Regulation on Workers' Control of the First All-Russian Congress of Trade Unions of January 1918, were to be subordinated to the economic control commissions, a control institution established by the trade unions in each branch of industry. Paragraph 11 of the Resolution on Workers' Control adopted by the First All-Russian Congress of Trade Unions in January 1918 read: "In order to carry out workers' control correctly in the localities, it is necessary that the control commissions or the factory committees substituting for them are subordinated to the economic control commissions, which are established by the trade unions in each branch of production. . . ."[51]

Actually, these economic control commissions do not seem to have been very prevalent. It is possible that such a transitional step was discovered to be unnecessary and the factory committees became, as determined by the resolution and statutes of the textile workers' union, simply the basic cells of the unions locally. However, according to the Resolution on Workers' Control of the First All-Russian Congress of Trade Unions, the commissions were the trade-union organs of workers' control, organs spoken of in Parapraph 8 of that resolution: "The trade unions, organized according to production, must enter into the creation on the spot, and in the center, of organs of workers' control taking upon themselves the task of their ideological and organizational guidance."[52]

One of the principal tasks of the economic control commissions of the trade unions was to inculcate into the workers the Bolshevik concept of workers' control. The commissions were to convince the workers that their own concepts of control were erroneous, for, in accordance with Paragraph 8: "The trade unions must go over each decree of the factory committees in the sphere of control, explain through their delegates at the factories and shops that control over production does not mean the transfer of the enterprise into the hands of the workers of a given enterprise, that workers' control does not equal the socialization of production and exchange but is only a preparatory step towards it."[53] Hence, it was to be the task of the trade unions, in effect, to convince the workers that they were to give up the factories of which they had taken possession.

Historical Function of Factory Committees and Trade Unions

Since, however, the Bolsheviks themselves had sponsored the factory committees in opposition to the trade unions, it was necessary for them to explain why they were, after October, attempting to subordinate the factory committees to the trade unions. Arskii, in an article on "The Trade Unions and the Factory Committees," (*"Professionalnye Soiuzy i Zavodskie Komitety"*), tries to rationalize this change in Bolshevik tactics. He reasons that it was the lack of discipline and experience on the part of the workers that resulted in their organization into factory committees. It is significant that Arskii makes no mention of the fact that the organization of the factory committees and their policy of workers' control was propagated and encouraged by the Bolshevik Party. The trade unions, he says, make more demands upon the worker, whereas the factory committees catered to their needs. Arskii claimed that before the Bolshevik Revolution, ". . . there was not sufficient discipline or organizational experience among the masses. Participation in the trade union movement demands from the masses a certain activity and consciousness, a subordination to the discipline of the union, etc. The factory committees made significantly fewer demands upon the masses, supporting them in their demonstrations. . . . The committees from the first days of the revolution took care of the workers, making it possible for them to work, regulating the relation with the masters, trying to raise wages, organizing deliveries of foodstuffs, etc. It is natural that in such conditions the committees increased and grew strong, especially in view of the fact that the trade unions at this time were only just growing again and could not take upon themselves all these tasks."[54]

It is not without reason that Arskii pointed to the permissive and nurturing qualities of the factory committees, and to the discipline and demands of the trade unions. As the latter grew stronger in the Bolshevik order, they were to exact much from the worker. Tomsky, in his introduction to the Stenographic Report of the First All-Russian Congress of Trade Unions, wrote that "the trade union movement . . . demands from the workers not only not less constant discipline, but more, to get them used not only to individual self-sacrifice but also to group self-sacrifice in the universal class interest."[55] Bolshevik progress demanded the renunciation of self-interest.

It is significant also, especially within the Leninist framework, that the factory committees are identified with the past and the decadent, while the trade unions are identified with the future and the strong. The logic of Bolshevik ideology should have led the communists to support the factory committees and to reject the trade unions. The factory committees as a newer form of workers' organization might, within the Bolshevik ideology, have been considered as superior to the trade unions, as the soviets were to parliaments. However, to rebut this argument and to forestall its repetition, the Bolshevik Gastev asserted that in spite of the fact that many thought the factory committees were a new type of workers' organization, they were not so. They arose in Russia only in the absence of a strong trade union movement, but in Europe, where the trade unions were strong, it is they that would probably take over the enterprises in the communist revolutions that were to come.[56]

Workers' Control, Capitalist Ownership and the Formation of Trusts

The Bolsheviks and Lozovsky also attempted to convince the workers that workers' control was never supposed to have been opposed to state control. Lozovsky at the All-Russian Conference of Trade

Unions and Factory Committees of Textile Workers, insisted that workers' control arose not in opposition to state control but in the absence of any control. He interpreted workers' control itself as an attempt to institute the control which the previous governments had refused to take.[57]

Since the Bolshevik program was directed toward a concentration of industry that many workers were opposing, the Party attempted to convince the workers of the superiority of trusts versus individual enterprises. Bolshevik ideology, however, had also pointed out, especially in its opposition to the war, that the war itself had been caused by the competition of national capitalist syndicates for foreign markets. They had called upon the workers to oppose the war because it was a struggle of syndicates and trusts. The Bolsheviks had, of course, declared their intention of increasing the concentration of industry under the dictatorship of the proletariat. Nevertheless, after the seizure of power, in their opposition to the decentralization of workers' control, the Bolsheviks felt it necessary to convince the workers that syndicates had caused war. They therefore now had to convince the workers that it was not concentrated, centralized industry itself but rather capitalist ownership of that industry that brought conflict about.

The Bolshevik Resolution on the Regulation of Industry adopted at the First All-Russian Congress of Trade Unions in January 1918 states in Paragraph 7: "The reaction of the wide democratic masses against the war, is not, at the same time, a reaction against the principle of contemporary organization and distribution of production, as a whole, that is, not against the regulation of industry . . . but against the use of this regulation by the capitalist class for their own interests and to the detriment of the interests of the working class."[58]

The resolution goes on to explain that any measures of the former governments to regulate the production and distribution of goods were attempts to undermine the opposition of the workers to the war and its effects. Such efforts, because they spread capitalist ownership, were impossible of success and merely convinced the "masses" that regulation of the economy was possible only under another, more "democratic" regime.

The Bolshevik Revolution made the regulation of industry possible by instituting a political system in which capitalist methods of regulation were to be employed against capitalism itself. Paragraph 9 of the resolution states: "The revolution in Russia, for the first time, raised the question of the regulation of industry and other branches of the people's economy under political conditions in which methods of regulation created by the capitalist class against the masses of the people can and must be used for these masses and against the capitalist system as a whole."[59]

Thus, again, the Bolsheviks made it clear that they did not oppose the industrial system worked out by capitalism. They opposed capitalist ownership only.

Regulation at individual enterprises—that is, the kind of workers' control executed by the factory committees—was regarded as being incompatible with the system of syndicates. Paragraph 10 states: "The all-embracing process of forming syndicates and trusts in the various branches of production, transport, and finance characteristic of the new stage of capitalism, completely excludes the possibility of regulation only in individual enterprises. This process directly connects all, or at least the most important enterprises of each branch of industry into one whole, then unites the syndicates of various branches together, carrying out this connection and union on an international scale."[60]

The Soviet Government, said the resolution, could not renounce the concentration of industry which it had inherited from capitalism without disorganizing economic life. It had, on the contrary, to increase the formation of trusts.[61]

The concentration and centralization of industry was represented as the solution to Russian post-revolutionary economic disorder. Any departures from this projected centralization, such as the independence of the factory committees, were represented as contributing to Russia's economic disintegration. Hence, throughout most of the speeches and writings addressed to labor after November and through the early part of 1918, there was a noticeable attempt on the part of the Bolsheviks and Lozovsky to convince the factory committees to give up their control of the factories they had seized. Much pressure was exerted upon the workers to submit to government regulation of industry, and the individual factories instituting workers' control as separate entities were accused of a narrow egoism and localism. The Bolsheviks and Lozovsky claimed to speak for the proletariat as a whole in their efforts to convince factory committees to renounce control of their enterprises. In this way, control could pass from the workers to the Bolsheviks or to the trade unions. At times, the bounds of persuasion were exceeded, and Lozovsky, for example, warned the workers: "If anywhere the local patriotism of the individual factories conflicts with the interests of all the proletariat, we must unconditionally state that we do not hesitate before any measures for the suppression of tendencies harmful to the toilers."[62]

The Mensheviks and Workers' Control

However, in addition to the Bolsheviks and Lozovsky, other voices were raised with other proposals for labor. The Mensheviks also had a particular point of view and were, like the Bolsheviks, proponents of state regulation. In his speech on the Regulation of Industry and Workers' Control, Cherevanin said, for example: "The socialist order toward which the Mensheviks are striving is characterized by the planned organization of all social industry."[63]

The Mensheviks, therefore, also looked forward to the establishment of a systematized and rationalized economy. Like the Bolsheviks, they also believed that the more highly developed capitalism is, the easier the transition to the planned organization of production. The planned organization of production, in turn, is considered the basis of socialism.[64] Therefore, they opposed the individualistic tendencies of the factory committees in whose activities they saw the cause of economic disorganization. Paragraph 7 of the Menshevik Resolution on the Regulation of Industry proposed at the First All-Russian Congress of Trade Unions states, for instance: "An inevitable crash is accelerated by the specific features of so-called workers' control which is splitting the dictatorship of the proletariat into the dictatorship of individual factories that are operating uncoordinatedly and which by their own fracturing activity, are increasing the anarchy and destruction of economic life."[65]

The Mensheviks thus opposed the autonomy of the local economic units and stood for a centralized economy, but they also believed that the solution to the economic problems facing the revolution was to be found in the cooperation of all classes. The guiding role, however, was to be played by the group from which many of the Mensheviks themselves seem to have been recruited—the intelligentsia or the professions. "The kind of organs necessary" to regulate the economy, said Cherevanin at the First All-Russian Congress of Trade Unions, ". . . are those in which there will be workers, factory owners, and other strata of democracy. The organs should include the professional intelligentsia whom the present government has forced into resistance and sabotage. The representatives of the cooperatives and of the peasantry should also be included because the regulation of industry is something in which all classes of the population are interested. The way out of the problem seems to be in those regulating organs in which the middle strata of democracy, standing between the workers and factory owners, occupy a conspicuous place."[66] The Mensheviks thus proposed that all classes of the population share in the administration of industry. They seem to have suggested also that the largest share of this administration be apportioned to the intelligentsia.

The Workers' and Workers' Control

At the First All-Russian Congress of Trade Unions, the voice of the workers engaging in workers' control was also heard. Belousov, a delegate to the congress, in defense of the factory committees, protested against the constant criticism to which they were subjected. He charged that they had not been given any clear-cut program to guide them.

"First of all, I shall turn to the speech of Comrade Lozovsky. We expected to hear from the speaker a plan which had been drawn up regarding the factory committees and control, but this we did not hear. We heard only criticism of the work which we are now carrying on. Comrade Lozovsky criticized the local factory committees which are doing this work. He said they are not doing the job. The reason for this is that from the very beginning of our work we could never act according to rules and regulations—it is necessary to recognize this—. . ."[67] Hence Belousov, claiming to represent the point of view of the local factory committees, declared that the center did not provide the factory committees with standards and rules by which they were to abide.

In refutation of the Bolshevik thesis that by a process of industrial concentration and centralization capitalism had paved the way for socialism, Belousov asserted that capitalism had not yet evolved in Russia. The prevalent industrial disorganization, he said, was the result of the war and the absence of a capitalist organization; he thus seems to have implied that the disorder in industry was not the result of workers' control. On the contrary, he said, workers' control was the solution to Russia's economic disintegration: "If we make an industrial survey of the industrial movement in Russia, we must admit that capitalism did not develop in Russia. Capitalism was not organized among us; now in time of war everything is disintegrating because it was not organized. If anyone does not recognize this, he is blind. Whoever looks at things with open eyes must recognize that the only way out remaining to the workers is to take the factories into their own hands and manage them."[68]

Therefore, just as the Bolsheviks attributed economic disintegration to the factory committees in order to justify depriving them of their control functions, the factory committees, in order to preserve those functions, insisted that workers' control was the only way out of economic disorder. Belousov also insisted that the factory committees were in need of constructive assistance but received, instead, only hostile criticism.

"It is pointed out to us all the time that the job is not being done and that we [the factory committees] cannot do it, but we are not given a definite plan so that the workers can say, 'Yes, this plan is really good.' Here we have heard only that we do not know anything and therefore we cannot do anything. But then, this will freeze local work, we then will have to stand still locally and do nothing. Only then will we make no mistakes, since only that which does nothing does not make mistakes. Comrades, the mistakes will be corrected; the gaps will be filled later. The congress should not be frightened at this."[69]

Belousov seems to have recognized that only by the abdication of action could the factory committees avoid "mistakes." And, indeed, mistakes according to the Bolshevik view would have consisted of any independent action continuing the former course taken by the factory committees or beginning a new one.

Attempting to reassure the Trade Union Congress of the efficacy and success of factory committee control, Belousov requested that the congress draw up a plan by which the factory committees might enter the trade unions. He reiterated again that this plan should indicate how the factory committees were to conduct their work within an explicitly defined framework: "I thought that at this All-Russian Congress, the first in Russia, a law would be worked out in respect to the trade union movement, but here I see it is completely the other way round. No definite plan is pointed out to us and we have to leave defeated. We came here in order to collect material, to become acquainted with a plan by which we could enter into the trade unions in order to conduct our affairs within a specific framework, as it is necessary to do. We have not heard anything from the speakers here about this definite plan. . . . Therefore, I propose to you, Comrades who will speak after me. . . tell us what we should hear . . . about the plan which it is necessary to put into effect." Thus, Belousov pointed out that the factory committees were willing to confine their activity to the limits set for them within a general plan. Within that plan, however, they wanted freedom of action. They wanted not merely to follow but to do.

It is significant, also, that Belousov conceived of the amalgamation of factory committees and trade unions in such a way that the function and activity of the factory committees would be preserved. He did not, in any way, interpret this amalgamation as the obliteration of factory committee power. It is even more significant for the fate of the factory committees and labor in Russia that he expected a plan, asked for instructions, and was willing to be told what role labor should play in the proletarian dictatorship. The workers of the factory committees themselves do not seem to have worked out their own program. They do not seem to have attempted, actively and assertively, to take the leadership of the labor movement upon themselves. Belousov, for example, asked for leadership; he did not, at the Congress, provide it.

Workers' Control Allocated to the Trade Unions

Bolshevik labor leadership, however, which after October was to replace the leadership of all other parties, planned that the factory committees would be absorbed into the trade unions. The trade unions were then to execute workers' control as the communists conceived it. Lozovsky, the foremost labor leader outside the Bolshevik party, was in agreement with the Bolshevik intention of depriving the factory committees of workers' control, but was in conflict with them over the relationship of the unions to the state. Like the Bolsheviks, he proposed transferring the function of workers' control to the trade unions. Thus, he asserted that control had to be continued, and he warned that if the trade unions did not take upon themselves the functions of workers' control, the factory committees would assume them. "What can you propose instead of workers' control?" asked Lozovsky. "What other organizations [beside the trade unions] can introduce planning into the problems of control and regulation of production? And if the trade unions refuse to participate in control, other workers' organizations will arise, namely the industrial organizations, the factory committees who are interested in this question."[71]

Thus with the threat of the factory committees, the trade unions were urged to take up workers' control functions. These functions however, were to change the unions into governmental organs. To investigate workers' control further, therefore, it is necessary now to turn to the trade unions and their relationship to the Bolshevik Party and the Soviet state.

CHAPTER VII

The Trade Unions, the State, and the Party: 1918

The Trade Unions and the Party

Almost immediately after the October revolution there was brought forward the problem of the relationship of the trade unions to the Bolshevik party and to the Soviet state. The question arose: If the October Revolution was to establish the workers' state—the dictatorship of the proletariat—which of the workers' organizations was to form, or to be, that state? The grounds upon which the factory committees were rejected for the role of state organs have already been demonstrated. The trade unions, however, as alternate workers' organizations, were naturally claimants to the headship of the workers' state. Such a claim, however, threatened the political role of both the Soviets and the Bolshevik party.

It was necessary for the Bolsheviks, therefore, to prevent the unions from acquiring state functions. As the party seeking to dominate the state, however, it was also necessary for the Bolsheviks to capture the unions for the support of the party.

The *Trade Union Herald* (*Professional'nyi Vestnik*) of 20 December 1917/2 January 1918, No. 8, published a "Resolution Concerning the Trade Unions and the Political Parties" in which it claimed that the trade union movement, in addition to engaging in the work common to all the laboring class, had a mission of its own—the leadership of the economic struggle of the proletariat. To accomplish this mission, the trade unions had to be organized into a separate and distinct apparatus.[1]

Thus the trade unions were to maintain an organizational identity separate from the rest of the workers' movements. At the same time, however, the unions were warned that they could not act independently of the rest of the working class. It was especially emphasized that the activity of the trade unions had to be coordinated with the activity of the political parties; for ". . . the trade unions cannot fulfill independently the historical mission laid upon them . . . Therefore all the activity [*vystuplenie*] of the trade unions must ideologically and actually connect with the activity of other proletarian organizations, as for example, the political parties, etc. . . ."[2]

Insisting, therefore, upon the cooperation of the trade unions with the political parties, the resolution asserted that the trade unions were not to absorb the political functions of a party. Political functions, according to the resolution, were outside the scope and beyond the strength of the unions. The resolution stated: ". . . the trade unions cannot substitute themselves for party organizations or take upon themselves the functions laid upon the latter which are beyond the strength of, and inappropriate for, the trade unions, in the very essence of their historical destiny. This relates especially to the political forms of struggle with the organs that fulfill it—to the political parties."[3]

Steering the trade unions between independence from the political parties and the absorption of party functions, the resolution exhorted the unions to take a part in the political struggle, for ". . . without turning into independent organs of political struggle, into independent political parties, or appendages of them, the trade unions, at the same time, cannot remain indifferent to the problems advanced by the political struggle of the proletariat. . . ."[4]

The trade unions, as an organization, however, had to join with a political party and support the program of that party: "But joining its destiny organizationally with some political party, the trade unions, as fighting class organizations of the proletariat, must support the political slogan and tactics of that proletarian political party, which at the given moment approaches more closely than others the solution of the historical tasks of the heterogeneous working class movement."[5]

There can be little doubt that the Bolsheviks, who dominated the All-Russian Soviet of Trade Unions which published the *Trade Union Herald,* regarded themselves as the political party which most closely approached the solution of the historical problems of the working class. They therefore requested that the trade unions, while remaining separate from the party and while refraining from taking over the political functions of the party, give the party their support.

This, in essence, with various elaborations, as shall be shown below, was the policy of the Bolshevik party toward the trade unions during 1918 and 1919. The Bolsheviks demanded that the trade unions maintain a separate identity while fufilling the goals of the party. Since the Bolshevik party, after October, was erecting a state machine based upon the soviet structure, the relationship of the trade unions to the party was inextricably bound up with the relationship of the trade unions to the Soviet state.

THE TRADE UNIONS AND THE STATE: LOZOVSKY

In the same issue of the *Trade Union Herald* (20 December 1917, No. 8) in which the resolution quoted above is found, Lozovsky wrote an article discussing the relationship between the trade unions and the state;[6] and partly because of this article, Lozovsky was expelled from the Bolshevik party.[7] For a fuller understanding of the labor movement at that time, therefore, it is necessary to understand the differences and divergences between Lozovksy and the Bolshevik party regarding the trade unions.

Lozovsky began his article by saying that the accession of the Soviets to state power raised the question of the relationship between the Soviets and the trade unions, for "The October Revolution, raising the Soviet power to the helm of the state, at the same time raised to the order of the day, the problem of the relationship between the Soviets and trade unions."[8]

Before the October revolution, according to Lozovsky, the relationship between the soviets and the trade unions was one between the political and economic organizations of the workers striving to influence the state. After October, Lozovsky asserts that since the Soviets themselves had become the state, the trade unions should have been concerned with their relationship to the Soviets in the latter's capacity as governing organs of the Republic. "Earlier," said Lozovsky, ". . . the matter concerned the relationship between purely economic workers' organizations and the worker-peasants' fighting organs, struggling for influence on the state apparatus, but now when the Soviets themselves have become organs of state power, we are concerned with the relations between our organizations and the central and local organs of the Soviet Republic."[9]

Lozovsky claimed that, early in the revolution, the local soviets carried out functions properly belonging to the unions. As a consequence of this, some soviets regarded the trade unions as organizations subordinate to them, and they intervened in the internal organization of the unions. Lozovsky claimed that since such intervention on the part of the soviets was deleterious to the trade unions, the All-Russian Central Council of Trade Unions sought to delimit the functions of each of the organizations.

"First of all," he wrote, "it is necessary to point out that the soviets and trade unions, in the first days of the revolution lived in a comparatively neighborly relationship. The soviets directed the strikes, organized the courts of conciliation and the arbitration courts, and assisted in the organization of the trade unions whose work they were forced to fulfill. This replacement of the trade unions by the soviets, resulting from the special conditions of development of the Russian Revolution, had as its consequence that several soviets began to look upon the trade unions as institutions 'under their jurisdiction,' intervening not only in the economic struggle but even in the internal life of the trade union organization. However, it was completely obvious that with the development of the trade union movement, the intervention of the soviets in the economic struggle, could lead to nothing except disorganization and therefore, the All-Russian Central Council came out for the establishment of an exact boundary or 'zone of influence' of these organizations different in construction and tasks."[10]

The field of economics, Lozovsky wrote, should be relegated to the trade unions, and the soviets should enter that field only where the trade unions did not exist, or where the unions requested the help of the soviets. This was the point of view, according to Lozovsky, which was put into effect. "The sphere of the economic struggle," he said, "should be transferred to the full and unlimited jurisdiction of the trade union organizations and the interference of the soviets should be allowed only in the absence of the economic organizations of the proletariat or in cases in which theese organizations turn to the soviets for assistance. In general, and on the whole, this point of view was put into practice. . . ."[11]

Lozovsky asserted, however, that the trade unions, while defending their prerogatives, had not intended to confine themselves to a narrow corporative framework. The trade unions, on the contrary, said Lozovsky, working closely with the soviets, took an active part in revolutionary activity. He maintained, however, that when the soviets assumed a defensist and opportunistic role (that is, pursued a policy of cooperation with all classes and supported the continuation of the war), the trade unions opposed them. Bolshevism began to conquer the trade unions and by October the rift between the trade unions and the Central Executive Committee of the First Soviet was complete.[12]

Lozovsky maintained, however, that the October Revolution bridged the gap which had been forming between the trade unions and the soviets. Again there was cooperation between the two organizations. Lozovsky favored the trade union support of the soviets in post-October conditions, but he contended that union functions should be clearly marked off from those of the Soviet state.

"The October Revolution," he wrote, "removed the gulf which had been forming between the trade unions and the soviets: again close cooperation and common work was established, but in new conditions and on new bases. Now the time had arrived for the trade unions to put into effect the resolution of the Third All-Russian Conference which prescribed 'to support completely the activity of the Soviets of Workers' and Soldiers' Deputies, directed towards extending and deepening the victories of the proletariat.' The Soviets have this support from the trade unions, but . . . it is necessary to establish with perfect exactness, the limits of this support and to mark off the trade unions from the state power."[13]

Thus insisting upon a separate and distinct existence for the trade unions, Lozovsky posed the following questions concerning the relationship of the trade unions to the state and especially to the Council of People's Commissars.

"It is necessary for us the organizers [*deiatel'*] of the trade union movement," wrote Lozovsky, ". . . to give a clear and categorical answer to the following questions facing the trade union movement: 1) Whether the trade unions consider it necessary to preserve the independence of their class organization or not? 2) Should the trade unions become organs of power and take state functions upon themselves? 3) What are the limits and conditions of support to the Council of People's Commissars?"[14]

Having posed the question of whether the trade unions should remain independent of the state and its institutions, Lozovsky asserted that ". . . the independent existence of the trade unions is absolutely necessary" not only for theoretical but for practical reasons.[15] He pointed out that the trade unions had to obtain an identity distinct from the state, which was to be the employer of labor. As the representative of labor, he asserted, the trade unions should not fuse into the state; for, in that case, they would be both employee and employer, and in their functions as employee, the trade unions would not be able to make demands upon their employer, the state, of which the trade unions themselves would be a part. Lozovsky, in his *Trade Union Herald* article, wrote that the ". . . independence [of the trade unions] is dictated not only by general theoretical considerations, but also by considerations which are highly practical. The worker masses may present unfulfilled demands to the state and in this case the trade unions cannot come forward as a representative of the workers because it will be that 'employer' to whom the demands are presented."[16]

Lozovsky warned against the fusion of the trade unions with the state by threatening, as he was so often to do, that such a policy would encourage the Anarchist and factory committee movement. He wrote that ". . . such a fusion of the unions with the state power would give food to the Anarchists for opposing the factory committees to the trade unions and would inevitably lead to the decline of the trade unions and possibly of all the trade union movement in Russia."[17]

Lozovsky not only insisted, however, upon the independence of the trade unions from the state and upon their definite separation into different organizations, he also insisted that each was to act upon different assumptions. He claimed for the trade unions the sphere of economic activity: ". . . if it is true," he said, "that the independence and preservation of the economic organizations is now a historical necessity, and that is absolutely true, then it is necessary to erect a very definite barrier between the trade unions and the existing power. This barrier must be one of both organization and principle."[18]

As institutions independent of the state both in organization and principle, the trade unions, said Lozovsky, had to be allowed the right to criticize the Council of People's Commissars. "Our independence of the Council of People's Commissars," he wrote, "must be expressed in the free and open criticism of its power. . . ."[19]

In a charge that is reminiscent of the attack of the Left Socialist Revolutionaries upon the Council of People's Commissars at the meeting of the Central Executive Committees of the Soviets, Lozovsky stated also that the Council of People's Commissars acted without any restriction by the Central Executive Committee—the guiding branch of the Soviets.[20] Speaking of the trade unions as the economic organizations of the proletariat, Lozovsky proposed that the Soviets and the trade unions together, rather than the Commissars, control the state, and concluded his article with the statement that: "Because the Central Executive Committee functions incorrectly, the Council of People's Commissars at present acts in nine-tenths of the cases without control. . . . The duty of the economic organizations of the proletariat is to organize, together with the Soviets, real workers' control over the worker-peasant government. By criticism and strict comradely control, the Russian workers' movement and along with it, the Russian revolution, can only gain."[21]

In considering Lozovsky's opposition to the Soviet of People's Commissars, it must again be borne in mind that in the months immediately following the October Revolution, the source of Lozovsky's political strength lay in the trade unions rather than in the Bolshevik party. Lozovsky himself, although a Bolshevik when it was founded, was not one of the members of the Council of People's Commissars. He, as well as other Bolsheviks, had spoken out against Bolshevik attempts at complete domination of the state. Lozovsky had written on 17 November/1 December 1917 in *The New Life* (*Novaia Zhizn'*), the organ of the United Social Democrat Internationalists: "I cannot, in the name of party discipline, pass over in silence the discontent of the toiling masses that fought for a Soviet government only to discover that for reasons not clear to them, this government has turned out to be a purely Bolshevik one."[22]

Lozovsky's charges against the Bolshevik Party were based largely upon its disregard of the rights of the labor unions, its ruthless suppression of union resistance to Bolshevik policy, and its intense determination to dominate union and other aspects of Russian life.[23] Lozovsky's subsequent adhesion to Bolshevik party policy from the beginning of 1919 onward, and his position as secretary-general of the Red International of Trade Unions, may indicate, however, that his opposition to the Bolshevik party in 1918 was largely a bid for political dominance of his own, based upon his position of leadership in the trade unions.

At the First All-Russian Congress of Trade Unions, Lozovsky reiterated the opinion he had expressed in the *Trade Union Herald* of 1917, by stating: "The guidance of the economic struggle of the working class belongs exclusively to the local and central unions of the trade union organizations."[24]

Thus placing the revolutionary problems of the working class within the competence of the trade unions alone, Lozovsky insisted that in those cases in which local soviets dealt with problems of labor and economy, such jurisdictions must be transferred entirely to the trade unions. The trade unions, according to Lozovsky, had become strong enough to deal with those problems which had been within the scope of the branches of labor of the soviets.[25]

Since Lozovsky claimed that the trade unions had been consolidated to a degree which made the labor functions of the soviets superfluous, he insisted that all workers' organizations be established in accordance with trade-union regulations. Lozovsky proposed that where local trade unions had not been formed, the departments of the soviets dealing with labor should establish the requisite organizations with the consent of the trade union concerned.[26] Lozovsky, in effect, advocated not only the independence of the trade unions but that they take over economic functions that were being fulfilled by the soviets.

The conflict over whether the trade unions were to become organs of the state—that is, the conflict over the statification or independence of the trade unions—existed, however, not only between the Bolsheviks and Lozovsky. After his expulsion from the party of 11/24 January 1918, Lozovsky became, as previously mentioned, one of the leading members of the United Social Democrat Internationalists. Within this party he fought for his concept of trade union independence. The Mensheviks and Left Social Revolutionaries also took an active stand on the statification of the trade unions, and the problem was one which faced the First All-Russian Conference of Trade Unions, 7/20-14/27 January 1918, the Fourth All-Russian Conference of Trade Unions, 12/25-17/30 March 1918, and the Second All-Russian Congress of Trade Unions, 16-25 January 1919.

The Trade Unions and the State: Left Social Revolutionaries

Strazhevskii, a Left Social Revolutionary representative at the First All-Russian Congress of Trade Unions, presented a point of view similar to that of the Bolsheviks. The Left Social Revolutionaries advocated the integration of the trade unions into the Soviet state; they might have held this view because their support seems to have been found to a greater degree in the local soviets than in the trade unions. Strazhevskii asserted that since the soviets were the organs of the workers' dictatorship and were filled, just as the trade unions were, with representatives of the workers, there was no reason to maintain the independence of the trade unions.

"Just as members of the working class," said Strazhevskii, "sent representatives into the trade unions, so they are sent into the soviets, into the organs of their political dictatorship and they themselves realize the political dictatorship in the country. Therefore, it is unthinkable to imagine that the trade unions which so closely work with the soviets, work independently of the Soviet power."[27]

Strazhevskii insisted that the trade unions should not only be independent of the local soviets but as organs of the Soviet State, should be subordinate to the soviets. "We can conceive of the trade unions, at the present time," he said, "as state organizations, as organizations working in contact and cooperation with, but also in subordination to, the soviets. We can conceive of the trade unions only as merging with the soviets. . . ."[28]

Upholding, therefore, the statification of the trade unions, Strazhevskii concluded his speech with the denial of the point of view held by the Mensheviks on trade union independence. The Mensheviks held that the trade unions should remain independent since the state represented the peasants as well as workers and the trade unions would be necessary to defend the interests of the workers against the peasants.[29] Strazhevskii made his peroration as follows: ". . . we the Left Social Revolutionaries reject the idea which asserts that the interests of the toiling peasants and of the working class may differ and, therefore, the trade unions cannot beecome organs of the Soviet power."[30] Strazhevskii, therefore, denied that the claims and needs of the peasants were at variance with those of the workers, and since he held that their interests were the same, he saw no obstacle to converting the trade unions into branches of the state.

The Trade Unions and the State: The Mensheviks

The Mensheviks, who sought to maintain the independence of the trade unions, contended that, in order to maintain the special and peculiar interests of the working class in a state representing both peasants and workers, the trade unions had to be independent of the state. The Menshevik Grinevich, for example, pointed out at the First All-Russian Congress of Trade Unions that the Soviet government was a government of workers and peasants. The peasants, according to Grinevich, represented petty bourgeois interests. The unions, therefore, from the Menshevik point of view, would not be able effectively to protect the interests of labor if they were to be absorbed by the state. Grinevich charged that if the unions were absorbed by the state, they would be swamped by the numerically larger peasantry and would not be able to defend the needs of the proletariat.[31]

Since the Mensheviks believed that the revolution had been a bourgeois democratic revolution and not a proletarian one, and that the trade unions had to be independent of the state in order to fight for their rights in a bourgeois society and for the establishment of a future socialist order, the Mensheviks opposed the statification of the trade unions on those grounds also.[32]

The Mensheviks regarded the dictatorship of the proletariat which the Bolsheviks had established as a purely temporary phenomenon doomed to failure, and the Menshevik Cherevanin, in defending the independence of the trade unions, stated that "The present stage is only ephemeral, Russia must pass through a long process of bourgeois development and in this stage of development, it is necessary that the trade unions act as organs of the working class struggle."[33]

Since the Mensheviks regarded the dominance of the proletarian parties as a mere interlude in a bourgeois revolution, they believed that an adjustment of the trade unions to such a situation would destroy the efficacy of the unions once the bourgeois order again asserted its supremacy. To assign the trade unions a role in a socialist society would, according to the Mensheviks, undermine the oppositional role the unions had to play in a bourgeois state.[34]

The idea that the trade unions had to preserve their independence so that they could struggle against capital in a bourgeois order was stated even more emphatically in the Resolution of the Menshevik faction on the statification of the trade unions at the First All-Russian Congress; it also charged that the measures being carried out for the purpose of introducing socialism would only further disrupt the economy and make the lot of the working class worse.[35]

For these reasons, the Mensheviks, in their resolution, stated that the proletariat had to continue to strive toward improving its position in a bourgeois capitalist regime. The primary organization in the opposition to capitalism would be, according to the Mensheviks, the trade unions working in conjunction with "the political party of the proletariat," i.e., the Mensheviks.[36]

The Mensheviks, in their resolution, vigorously spoke out against the policy advocated by the Council of People's Commissars—a policy of subordinating the trade unions to the state. The Mensheviks concluded their resolution by proposing that the Congress ". . . in a most decisive manner repudiate the attempt of the Soviet of People's Commissars to transform the trade unions into subsidiary organs of the so-called worker-peasant government and openly proclaim that the trade unions must, even in the future, remain free and independent unions of the class struggle of the proletariat."[37]

Menshevik objection to the statification of the trade unions was motivated, however, by more than theory and principle. The Bolsheviks had acquired control of the state and had replaced the Mensheviks in the governmental organs. The Mensheviks were no longer participants in the All-Russian Soviet. The chief basis for their political power and their existence as a party seems to have been in the trade unions. If the trade unions were statified and thus brought under the domination and control of the Bolshevik party, the Mensheviks could look forward only to the deterioration of their position in the labor movement. As a consequence of this, their position and functions as a party were also threatened. Therefore, though there is every reason to believe that the Mensheviks were convinced of the validity of their theory concerning the independence of the trade unions, their vital interests as a party, in this problem, must also be borne in mind.

The Trade Unions and the State: The Bolsheviks

The Bolsheviks, as the party controlling the soviets, in advocating the subordination of the trade unions to the state in effect advocated their subordination also to the Bolshevik party. Before the subordination of the trade unions to the Bolshevik party may properly be understood, however, investigation must be made of the Bolshevik party's policy toward the subordination of the unions to the state.

At the First All-Russian Congress of Trade Unions, the Bolsheviks attempted to refute the Menshevik position on the trade unions. Zinoviev stated that the Bolsheviks never regarded it as the function of the trade unions merely to fight against capitalism. He pointed out that it was not the Bolsheviks, but their opponents, who believed the trade unions were to operate within the capitalistic structure.[38]

The Bolsheviks, said Zinoviev, regard it as the function of the trade unions to fight for socialism. They never considered that the trade unions would be confined to advancing the position of labor within the capitalist framework.[39]

Advocating that the trade unions must help to build socialism in the Soviet state, Zinoviev held that it was not necessary for the trade unions to be independent of that state. In posing the question of independence, Zinoviev twisted and corrupted the meaning of the word so that it would indicate opposition to the Soviet state. He offered, in effect, as the only alternative to independence, subordination to the Soviets or support of the bourgeoisie. The possibility that the trade unions could be independent of both the bourgeoisie and the Soviets was not recognized. Neutrality was regarded as opposition. "I ask," said Zinoviev, ". . . from what and from whom is it necessary to be independent? From your own government, from your workers' and peasants' government, from the Soviet of Workers' and Soldiers' Deputies? Let it be understood, we are also for the independence of the trade union movement, but from the bourgeoisie. We overthrew the power of the bourgeoisie and at the very moment when the working class together with the poor peasants has achieved power for the working class, when your union is part of that power, what kind of real significance has independence? It has real significance among representatives of the right wing; independence from the Soviets of Workers' and Peasants' Deputies . . . means independence in order to support those who fight against the workers' and peasants' government so that in the name of the sacred right to strike, and in the name of the freedom of coalition they may support those who strike against the working class."[40]

Hence the working class is so closely identified with the state that any independence from the state loses its meaning. Any opposition to the state, therefore, even on the part of the workers themselves, is construed as an attack upon the government of the workers and peasants.

The Bolshevik Weinberg, in discussing the problem of the independence of the trade unions, claimed that since the bourgeoisie was no longer in power, it was no longer the function of the trade unions to work merely toward the improvement of working class conditions. "I must bring to your attention," said Weinberg, "that earlier the trade unions worked only for the improvement of the conditions of the working class, for the increase of wages, but now they have passed out of that arena, because there is no other master of the economy, the bourgeoisie has been cast out of power, cast out of industry. If you hold the point of view that this is a mistake," he said, attacking the Menshevik tenet that the revolution must be bourgeois not proletarian, "then all history, all the revolution is a mistake and the Soviet too is a mistake."[41] With the proletarian domination of the bourgeoisie, the tasks that faced the working class had become broader, for, according to Weinberg: "Not only the tasks of regulating wages, the defense of the interests of the workers, the struggle for the improvement of the material economic conditions of the working class, not only these tasks lie before us but still more extensive tasks."[42]

The more extensive tasks which faced the workers lay in the organization of the economy. Since, as it has already been shown, the workers' concept of its economic role differed from that of the Bolsheviks, Weinberg recognized that many workers misunderstood the Bolshevik concept.

"Now someone must take upon himself," he said, "the task of the organization of the economy and we must recognize unconditionally that this task falls to the lot of the working class. In this respect it is not necessary for us to fear that not all the workers understand us, that they are not all members of the workers' organizations."[43] The workers, said Weinberg, in their misunderstanding and as a result of actual conditions of their lives, were making demands for their own welfare. The Bolsheviks, speaking another language to the workers than that which they were accustomed to hear, point to the obligations of labor, and this the workers would understand. "We know, comrades," continued Weinberg, "and this is a fact, that sometimes the workers present incredible demands, but they present these demands because life requires them. We speak another language to the working class, we say that other duties lie upon them and the working class understands this."[44]

Weinberg and the Bolsheviks claimed that the duties placed upon the workers in the organization of the economy were the duties encompassed by labor's "creative role" in the revolution. The "creative role" which the Bolsheviks relegate to the trade unions, however, was one which was removed from the fundamental and basic problems facing labor. The "creative role," in contrast to the work of the factory committees in managing their enterprises, was one which seems to have been designed to keep the trade unions busy and out of the way. The unions and factory committees, in conjunction with soviet organizations, were permitted to pass out questionnaires and to look over factories. Policy decisions were not mentioned as being within their purview. Moreover, the "creative role" demanded self-renunciation and sacrifice. It demanded that the workers strive to build a Soviet state rather than guard the welfare of labor. "Many workers," said Weinberg, "already are conscious of the fact that if they make too many demands now, production will suffer. The most conscious workers think over immoderate demands carefully. This signifies that the working class is conscious of its own obligations; it clearly recognizes that it is now engaged in creativity. Look at those organizations which are now being created in every city, notice how they carry out work together with the trade unions and factory committees. They distribute questionnaires to the masses, inspect enterprises and draw greater and greater numbers of workers into this work. Here we have a genuine creativity."[45]

In the process of such "creativity," according to the Bolsheviks, the trade unions could function as organizations subordinate to the state and there would be no necessity for a demarcation between the proletariat as the state and the proletariat as organized labor.[46]

The Resolution of the Bolsheviks, which presumably defined the relationship of the trade unions to the state, is ambiguous. It does not explicitly state the degree or manner in which the trade unions were to be statified. Such were the charges that Lozovsky made in opposing the Bolshevik resolution, and an examination of it will uphold the validity of Lozovsky's charge.[47]

The Resolution began by saying that the October Revolution, representing the triumph of the workers and poor peasants over other classes and parties, had brought Russia to the point where it could begin the international socialist revolution and begin also to reconstruct Russian society on a socialist basis.[48]

The Resolution claimed that the political victory of the Bolsheviks had brought with it economic tasks and international leadership, that by transferring political power into the hands of the workers and poor peasants, the October Revolution had created for the trade unions a new labor situation.[49]

The Bolsheviks stated that in these new conditions the working class had to try to carry out socialist measures and emphasized that the working class was to take the actual, practical steps towards implementing those measures. It was cautiously careful not to say that the working class was to formulate socialist measures. In the light of the fact that workers' control by the factory committees was regarded, by some workers, as the advent of socialism, the resolution was also careful to state that the proletariat is merely "close to the beginning of the socialist revolution." This statement, furthermore, had another function. It shall be pointed out that the promise of acting as organs of governmental power in the socialist state was held out to the trade unions. The postponement of socialism thus served to stave off the trade-union demand for state power, while dangling it before them as a promise. The resolution also reiterated the view that the Bolsheviks, even before the Revolution, did not regard the trade unions as concerned only with economic problems. The Bolsheviks, it said, always expected the unions to play a political role in conjunction with other organizations of the working class, a reference, it would seem, to the Bolshevik party.[50]

The Bolsheviks, in their resolution, asserted that in the new situation—in which the bourgeoisie had been overthrown and in which the working class was faced with the implementation of measures for the realization of socialism—the trade unions could not be neutral, but had to support the Soviet state headed by the Council of People's Commissars. Paragraph 4 reads: "The idea of the 'neutrality' of the trade unions was and remains a bourgeois idea. There is not and cannot be neutrality in the trade union movement in Russia, in a country living through a great revolution and having overthrown the bourgeois yoke . . . the trade unions . . . must completely and wholeheartedly support the policy of the socialist Soviet power, led by the Council of People's Commissars."[51]

The Bolsheviks also insisted that the trade unions transfer their work to the "organizational-economic" sphere. Just as the Bolsheviks were attempting to divert the attention of the factory committees from control of their factories to a semblance of participation in the organization of nationalized industry, so the trade unions were to be diverted from concern with conditions of labor in their trades to a role designated for labor in production planned by the state. The resolution proposed that the trade unions participate in the solution of problems involved in nationalized production and distribution, problems such as the exchange of products between town and country, the registration and assignment of labor, etc., for: "The center of gravity of the work of the trade unions at present must be transferred to the organizational-economic sphere. The trade unions, as class organizations of the proletariat, must take upon themselves the chief work in the organization of production and the restoration of the undermined productive forces of the country. The most energetic participation in all centers of the regulation of production, the organization of workers' control, the registration and distribution of manpower, the organization of exchange between city and village, the most energetic participation in the demobilization of industry, the struggle with sabotage, the introduction of universal labor service—such are the tasks of the day."[52]

In order for the trade unions to implement such tasks as are outlined in paragraph 6, the resolution stated that the unions had to become state organs subordinate to the Soviet government.[53]

Before the trade unions could actually become organs of socialist power they had to pass through a transitional period. During this period they had to prove their worth by joining themselves inextricably to the Soviet state. If the trade unions did this they might also absorb their rivals—the factory committees and other economic organs (as distinct from the political organs, such as the party or the state). Before this could be done, the trade unions had to join themselves inseparably to the Soviets of Workers' and Soldiers' Deputies. It should be noted, however, that the Resolution did not attempt to designate exactly what kind of connection there was to be between the trade unions and the state. The relationship between the trade unions and the state was not juridically defined or limited in any way: "The transitional measures for this, and also for the fusion of all the economic organizations of the working class [in particular the factory committees] are: the closest cooperation and indissoluble organizational connection of the trade unions with the proletarian political organizations and first of all with the Soviet of Workers' and Soldiers' Deputies."[54]

The Resolution continued to say, although vaguely, that as a result of the transitional process by which the trade unions would join themselves indissolubly with the Soviet government, the unions would, in the future, be converted into state organs. Membership in the unions would then be compulsory for all employees of each industry.[55]

The Bolshevik party, therefore, held out to the trade unions the promise of eventually becoming a branch of the state, and the trade unions were promised the acquisition of state power. By the vagueness of the promise, however, the Bolsheviks would seem to have been avoiding the possibility of being held accountable for it. The vagueness of the Bolshevik resolution is brought into relief by the Resolution of the Left Socialist Revolutionaries, which stated: ". . . the Left Socialist Revolutionaries think of the trade unions not as organs neutral and independent in relation to the worker-peasant state, but as state organizations, considering this measure as transitional to the creation of organs of socialist power out of the trade unions."[56] Here the Left Socialist Revolutionaries indicated that after a transitional period in which the trade unions would be state organizations, the socialist government itself would be created out of the trade unions. In the Bolshevik Resolution at the First All-Russian Congress of Trade Unions, such a promise is avoided.

The Bolshevik promise that the trade unions would be, in the future, not subordinate to the state, but part of the state, was made dependent upon the successful development of the international trade-union movement.[57] By thus making the scope of the trade unions international, it seems to have been the intention of the Bolsheviks not only to postpone the time when the trade unions would be state organs, but also to bind the unions to the Bolshevik cause by promising them an international scope for their activity.

Thus the Bolshevik Resolution as a whole demanded that the trade unions give up their independence and become organizations subordinate to the state. In this way, the Bolshevik party attempted, it seems, to forestall any opposition on the part of the trade unions to the policy exerted by the party upon the state. By statifying the trade unions, the Bolsheviks were able to manipulate them in their program of industrial reorganization.

The Trade Unions and the Commissariat of Labor

Integral to the problem of the independence and statification of the trade unions was the problem of the relationship between the trade unions and the Commissariat of Labor. The Commissariat of Labor was the former Ministry of Labor, which was taken over by the Bolsheviks and placed under the party member Shliapnikov, who was named Commissar of Labor. It represented the labor branch of the Council of People's Commissars, to which the trade unions were to be subordinate.[58] In the subordination of labor to departments of the state, however, there arose the problem of bureaucracy. Lenin had promised that the Bolshevik revolution would bring bureaucracy to a close, for the transitional period itself was to abolish bureaucracy. "Until the 'higher' phase of Communism arrives," wrote

Lenin in 1917, "the Socialists demand the *strictest* control, *by society and by the state,* of the quantity of labour and the quantity of consumption, only this control must *start* with the expropriation of the capitalists, and must be carried out, not by a state of bureaucrats, but by a state of armed workers."[59] One of the principal promises of the Bolshevik party to its adherents, therefore, would seem to have been the promise to abolish bureaucracy.

The theses on Soviet Power passed by the Seventh Congress of the Russian Communist Party, which took place on 6-8 March 1918, promised "A closer connection between the masses and all the apparatus of state power and state administration than previous forms of democracy."[60] These theses also looked forward to "the possibility of abolishing bureaucracy, of dispensing with it, the beginning of the realization of this possibility."[61]

The Bolshevik attack on bureaucracy was aimed not only against the old Russian order but was also directed against representative parliamentary government and its separation of executive from legislative powers. Democratic parliamentary states of that type usually retain a permanent bureaucratic civil service which remains to a large degree constant in spite of changes in the executive and legislative composition of the state. Contrary to the practice of parliamentary states, the Bolsheviks fused executive and legislative functions into one body and by so doing actually increased the importance of bureaucracy in the administration of the state. But in claiming to draw all "the people" into this administration, the Bolsheviks claimed also that they were providing a greater degree of democracy than the parliamentary state. In addition, the Bolsheviks were to make a distinction between the execution of policy and the making of policy. The "broad masses" were to be the executors of state decrees, not the formulators of legislation. There were reasons, however, that such a policy could not be explicitly stated.

Since the tsarist state itself had been to an extremely high degree bureaucratic, the revolutionary opposition to the tsarist state had been in part an opposition to bureaucracy. In addition, workers' control, as it was being practiced by the factory committees, had placed the management of industry largely in the hands of the workers themselves. The Bolsheviks, therefore, could not directly and openly take control of labor and industry out of the hands of the workers and place it in the hands of government bureaus. The Bolsheviks could openly state their policy of centralizing the control of industry but they could not always openly admit that such control would be carried out by a government institution. It was for this reason, it seems, that workers' control functions were delegated to the trade unions; for the trade unions were presumably the organs representing the workers themselves. The problem of bureaucracy and the state regulation of industry, however, is vividly illustrated by Paragraph 14 of the Resolution on the Regulation of Industry proposed by the Bolsheviks and adopted by the First All-Russian Congress of Trade Unions.

The resolution made the usual equivocating distinction between regulation and control, where regulation meant the organization and administration of industry, and control the fulfillment of regulating decrees. According to Paragraph 14, the basis of the regulation of industry by the state was to be workers' control in centralized industrial establishments. The lack of such control by the workers, the Bolsheviks admitted in their resolution, would breed a new bureaucracy. Workers' control could take place, however, only if the control regulating organs subordinated the local enterprises. The trade unions were to participate in control to avoid bureaucratic administration. Paragraph 14 reads: "The basis of state regulation is workers' control in enterprises placed under state syndicates and trusts. The absence of such control would bring to life a new industrial bureaucracy injurious to and completely unsuited for, the relations of production. But such control can take place only if there is a close connection with the chief regulating center, if the cells are soldered together and subordinated to the chief center of workers' control and if it is based on a trade union organization which will enrich the center with the necessary and most suitable forces."[62]

To avoid the charge of bureaucracy, it seems, the Commissariat of Labor, whether the chief center of workers' control or not, had to be closely allied with the trade unions. It has already been pointed out, however, that by a resolution of the First All-Russian Congress of Trade Unions, it was determined that the trade unions were to work in close cooperation with, and subordinate to, the state.

At the Fourth Conference of Trade Unions, which took place from 12-17 March 1918, the Bolshevik Resolution on the Relations between the Trade Unions and the Commissariat of Labor further defined the relationship between the trade unions and the state. According to this resolution, the October Revolution had changed "the meaning and character of state organs and the significance of proletarian organs as well."[63]

Under the Provisional Government, the resolution stated, the Ministry of Labor acted as arbitrator and peacemaker between labor and capital, but the October Revolution had made the Ministry of Labor into an instrument of the worker-peasant government. In this government the industrial proletariat itself had the leading role. Thus the Ministry of Labor, converted into the Commissariat of Labor, became not an arbitrator between employee and employer but, according to the Bolsheviks, the champion of the economic policy of the working class. As an organ of the state, the Commissariat of Labor had at its disposal all the machinery of the state and all the force of state compulsion.[64]

However, just as the Ministry of Labor in the proletarian state, according to the resolution, had become the champion of the working class, the industrial trade unions were to change "from purely fighting organizations to more and more economically productive associations of the proletariat."[65] Thus, the resolution implied that the trade unions were to cease fighting for the interests of the workers in particular trades; they were to concentrate upon increasing production. The trade unions were to represent the interests of the working class as a whole—that is, the interests of the proletarian state. The Resolution asserted that "The trade unions are acquiring national significance as the organs called upon to regulate conditions of labor and production in the interests of the working class as a whole."[66]

Under the dictatorship of the proletariat, therefore, the functions of the Commissariat of Labor as the champion of the working class and of the trade unions as champions of industrial production grow similar to one another. Carrying on similar activities separately, these two organizations were considered merely to disrupt what should have been a united economic policy, for: "Working towards the same direction independently from one another, the trade unions and the Commissariat of Labor sometimes decide one and the same question differently, introducing an undesirable dualism into the single economic policy of the working class."[67]

To avoid this dualism, the trade unions were to be the sole representatives of the proletariat, organized along industrial lines. "Only by recognizing the trade unions as the single authoritative representative of the industrially organized proletariat, called upon to carry out a single economic policy in the interests of the working class as a whole, can we once and for all put an end to the undesirable divergence of solutions on various questions in the economic sphere."[68]

Whereas the trade unions were the only representatives of the organized proletariat, it was the Commissariat of Labor, according to the resolution, which was endowed with the compulsory force of a state organ. The trade unions possessed no coercive powers or executive authority of their own. Even though they themselves might have been statified and were organs of the state, they remained subordinate and dependent, for they could execute their policies only through the Labor Commissariat. Paragraph 6 of the Resolution on the Relationship between the Trade Unions and the Commissariat of Labor defined ". . . the role and tasks of the Commissariat of Labor as a state organ making use of the authority and coercion of the state power by the will of the industrially organized proletariat under the control of its guiding economic organization."[69]

Although Paragraph 5 stated that the trade unions were to control the Commissariat of Labor, it was the Commissariat and not the unions which possessed coercive and executive power. It must also be borne in mind that control, as the Bolsheviks conceived it, was not to be confused with regulation or administration. Furthermore, in actuality, the unions directed the workers, and the Commissariat of Labor performed union functions. Paragraph 6, however, concluded: "In this way, the Commissariat of Labor is on the whole, like a state economic organ of the proletariat organized on a class scale, and responsible before its organizations."[70]

Here, therefore, the Commissariat of Labor, as a state economic organ of the proletariat, is compared to a union having state power and responsible to its locals. The unions, however, had no power to enforce responsibility upon the Commissariat.

According to Paragraph 7 of the resolution, the chief decisions of the top level organs of the trade unions were to guide the Commissariat of Labor. It stated also that all special effective decisions of the Commissariat of Labor had first to be approved by the appropriate trade union organization. This, in effect, weakened the policy-making prerogatives of the Commissariat of Labor, but it did not strengthen the power of the trade unions. Such a provision, in effect, established a dichotomy between policy-making and policy fulfillment. It allowed for the possibility that each of the organs be rendered ineffective by the other. Neither the organs of the organized proletariat nor those of the state were allowed full authority over labor. According to Paragraph 7: ". . . all decisions of principle of the higher organs of the trade unions (congresses, conferences, etc.) are binding upon the Commissariat of Labor. All legislative proposals and special binding decisions concerning the conditions of labor and production, must be preliminarily approved by the appropriate organs of the trade unions (i.e., the All-Russian and local Soviets of Trade Unions)."[71]

Therefore, it would seem that before the Commissariat of Labor could exert its coercive governmental power, it was to have the approval of the trade unions for its decisions. It will be demonstrated shortly that such was not to be the real situation.

In order formally to prevent the accusation of bureaucracy and, presumably, to assure that the preliminary approval of the All-Russian or local Councils of Trade Unions was given to the binding decisions of the Commissariat of Labor, the resolution decreed: ". . . the All-Russian and local Councils of Trade Unions organize *collegia* attached to the Commissariat of Labor as their own responsible organs in order to carry out a class-wide economic policy and to coordinate practical measures."[72]

Such trade-union *collegia* attached to the Commissariat of Labor served to divert charges that labor was being managed by the Commissariat of Labor as a state-bureaucratic institution. It is to be noted, however, that the trade-union *collegia* attached to the Commissariat of Labor, and not the Commissariat of Labor itself, were to be responsible to the trade unions. Neither was any mention made that the trade-union *collegia* would be endowed with the compulsory power of state organs, as the Commissariat of Labor was.

This Resolution of the Fourth All-Russian Conference of Trade Unions stipulated that the Commissariat of Labor was to be bound by the principal decisions of the higher organs of the trade unions, and that the trade unions had to preliminarily approve all decisions of the Commissariat concerning labor and production.[73] In May, however, there was passed a Resolution of the Second All-Russian Congress of Commissars of Labor, Representatives of the Labor Exchange and Insurance Funds, "Concerning the Relationship of the Commissars of Labor to the Councils of the People's Economy, to the Executive Committee of the Soviets of Deputies and to the Trade Unions." This resolution warned the Commissars of Labor against indiscriminately considering that all the decrees of the trade unions were binding upon them. The Commissars of Labor were reminded that they, in contrast to the trade unions, were the representatives of the working class.

"Since the Commissars of Labor," read this resolution, "are elected by the trade union workers they must, in their own work, strictly coordinate their decisions with the general decisions of the unions. Nevertheless, defending first of all the interests of the class, the Commissars of Labor cannot and should not consider *all decrees of the trade unions without exception* compulsory for them."[74]

That the trade unions were to serve purely as a façade for the Commissariat of Labor, and that the unions were to be powerless to insist upon the implementation of their decisions, is indicated by the final words of Paragraph 3 of the above resolution: "No conflict between workers and factory owners can be taken under consideration by the Commissars of Labor without the decision of the corresponding trade union, which however, cannot be considered compulsory for them."[75]

Thus, the Commissariat of Labor was to carry out a policy in the name of the trade unions, a policy over which the trade unions themselves had little control. Furthermore, it has already been pointed out that according to a resolution adopted at the First All-Russian Congress of Trade Unions, the unions were to be subordinate to the Soviet state. It has also been pointed out that it was largely through the use of the popularity of the Soviets of Workers' and Soldiers' Deputies that the Bolsheviks were able to acquire support for their revolution. A revolution in the name of the party itself would not have been as likely to acquire as much support.[76] It is likely, also, that in January of 1918, only four months after the revolution, the Soviets still retained a large degree of this popularity and that the party had gained little, if any, more appeal. The Commissariat of Labor, however, under the direct administration of a Bolshevik Commissar of Labor, even though it was an organ of the state, was more likely to be, first and foremost, an organ of the Bolshevik party. It is with this in mind that Paragraph 9 of Tomsky's "Resolution on the Relationship between the Trade Unions and the Commissariat of Labor" adopted by the Fourth Conference of Trade Unions should be read and understood. Paragraph 9 removed labor problems from the purview of the soviets and placed them in the hands of the Commissariat of Labor. Lozovsky had similarly attempted to remove labor problems from the competence of the soviets and to delegate them exclusively to the trade unions. Paragraph 9 read: "Moreover, in order to remove finally the harmful divergencies in the decisions of economic problems, the political organizations of the proletairat must once and for all give up independent decisions and conclusively abolish all 'branches,' 'bureaus' and 'commissions' of labor attached to the soviets, *dumas,* etc. The soviets and *dumas* can decide similar problems only when, for the given problem, there exists a defiinite decision of the directing trade union organization and the Commissariat of Labor."[77] Tomsky proposed, therefore, that the soviets, *dumas* and other governing organs give up any independence they had in dealing with problems of labor. They were to be guided by the decisions of the trade unions and the Commissariat of Labor.

The Resolution concluded with an administrative justification for this stand by stating in Paragraph 10: "Only by observing this basic position can the useless duplication of effort be done away with in deciding the conditions of labor of the unified working class."[78]

Local Soviets and the Trade Unions

The removal of labor jurisdictions from the soviets and local *dumas,* however, represents also another phase of the Bolshevik process of centralization and one-party domination. In the early part of 1918 Russia was still decentralized. At the First All-Russian Congress of Trade Unions, for example, Smirnov, Chairman of the central committee of the right wing of the Social Revolutionaries, stated, without evoking the objections of any of the factions: "The country is disorganized, shattered into separate fragments. Each village has its own provisional government, its own rule of people's commissars, its own unofficial village life . . . Russia has crumbled into a whole lot of little pieces. . . ."[79] Another speaker at the same congress, in discussing the disorganization of the Russian communication system, stated that "letters that should have reached their destinations in two days are taking six months to arrive and an urgent telegram required twenty-six days for delivery."[80] Whether this statement is accurate or not, there can be no doubt that there were long delays in communication. This left many outlying areas free of control from the center. In these provinces and localities the governing organs were often the soviets or *dumas,* and these organs do not seem to have been always in Bolshevik hands. Even where they were, there is little reason to believe they had, in all cases, any greater realization of Bolshevik aims and purposes than the factory committees had. If, therefore, the Bolsheviks were to attain their domination in the center and extend it into the localities, it was necessary for them to wrest from the local soviets the jurisdiction they possessed. Hence they attempted to deprive the independent local soviets of their competence in labor matters and to place these functions within the jurisdiction of the Commissariat of Labor. The latter, as a state bureaucratic organization radiating from the central power, was dependent for its welfare upon the party which was dominating the state.

THE COMMISSARIAT OF LABOR AND THE TRADE UNIONS: LOZOVSKY

It was this domination of the trade unions by a state organ that Lozovsky continued to oppose. At the Fourth Conference of Trade Unions he proposed a Resolution on the Trade Unions and Commissariat of Labor which was not adopted. Its purpose seems to have been to establish the primacy of the trade unions. Lozovsky began his resolution by stating that the Commissariats of Labor, along with the labor departments of the soviets, acted not only as mediator between capital and labor, as the Bolsheviks claim, but also acted in the capacity of trade unions.[81] The activity of the trade unions, on the other hand, was transferred, by the October Revolution, "from the sphere of the direct defense and protection of labor to the sphere of the regulation of industry and workers' control."[82]

As a result of their responsibilities in the regulation of industry, the trade unions, according to Lozovsky, from October on, sloughed off part of their former functions, presumably in the sphere of the protection of labor. They transferred these functions to the Commissariat of Labor.[83]

Thus the trade unions, according to Lozovsky, delegated to the Commissariat of Labor those of its functions which were secondary to the regulation of labor and workers' control, and "The Commissariats of Labor, converted into organs of the defense and protection of labor, began to fulfill the tasks of the trade unions, organizing bureaus and branches and taking upon themselves the standardization of wages, determining the living wage, alleviating conflicts, etc."[84] In this way, according to Lozovsky's resolution, the Commissariats of Labor fulfilled the former functions of the trade unions. The Commissariats became a peculiar kind of semi-trade union having the forces of state compulsion at their disposal.[85]

Lozovsky continued his resolution by saying that as a result of the power of compulsion possessed by the Commissariats of Labor, and the lack of such power in the trade unions, the Commissariats of Labor would naturally supersede the trade unions in the sphere of labor protection.[86]

Thus, Lozovsky charged that there was a dualism in the working class movement: that the trade unions carried out regulation and control and the Commissariats of Labor defended the interests of the workers. To avoid this dualism, he asserted, it was necessary to subordinate the Commissariats of Labor to the trade unions.[87]

Lozovsky, however, did not propose that there be a fusion of the Commissariats of Labor, as organs of the centralized state, with the trade unions, even though the commissars of labor were to be guided by the decrees of the trade-union institutions. According to Paragraph 8 of the resolution: "The commissars of labor who are guided by the decrees of the congresses and conferences of industrial and trade unions, remain nevertheless organs of central state power and this excludes any thought of fusion of the Commissariat of Labor with the trade unions."[88]

In objecting that the Commissariats of Labor could not be attached to the trade unions, Lozovsky argued, as the Mensheviks were doing, that the state represented both the workers and peasants—the latter designated as the petty bourgeoisie. Since the state represented two classes—both the peasants and the proletariat—the trade unions, Lozovsky contended, should not be adulterated by fusion with the state organ—the Commissariat of Labor. According to Paragraph 9: "As organs of state worker-peasant power representing the interests of two classes, the proletariat and petty bourgeoisie, the Commissariats of Labor cannot also become organs attached to the trade unions."[89]

Thus, coming out against the fusion of the Commissariats of Labor with the trade unions, Lozovsky stipulated in his resolution the following means by which the trade unions were to hold the Commissariats of Labor in check: "The trade unions elect or ratify the appointed local and *guberniia* commissars of labor who must: a) review conflicts only after they have gone through the trade unions; b) be guided in their decisions by the resolutions and decisions of the appropriate trade union organization; c) not interfere with the relations between labor and capital without preliminary approval of the appropriate trade unions; d) abolish all 'branches,' 'unions for the defense of labor,' etc., created by some commissariat institutions which introduce disorganization into the trade union movement; e) act in constant contact with the trade union organizations."

Having enumerated various regulations which in effect subordinated the Commissariats of Labor to the trade unions, Lozovsky emphasized again that control by the trade unions over the commissars of labor was not to lead to the fusion of the labor commissariats with the unions.[90]

For this reason, the resolution proposed that the trade unions should refrain from participating in the elections of the People's Commissars of Labor. The resolution also advised against the elections of the Commissars of Labor to the All-Russian Council of Trade Unions, reiterating that in this way the purely proletarian trade unions would be converted into ". . . organs which are not homogeneous in their class relations of power, the policy of which could diverge and often digress from the classwide tasks of the worker masses."[91]

Lozovsky then concluded his resolution by insisting that only independent unions could defend the interests of the working class.[92]

Thus Lozovsky's proposal for the relationship that was to be established between the trade unions and the Soviet state was diametrically opposed to that of the Bolsheviks. Whereas the Bolsheviks in 1918 proposed to abolish the independence of the trade unions from the state and to subordinate the unions to the Commissariat of Labor, Lozovsky proposed to maintain the independence of the trade unions and to subordinate the Commissariat of Labor to them. Both Lozovsky and the Bolsheviks, however, strove to remove the soviets from any actual jurisdiction over the trade unions. Nevertheless, whereas the Bolsheviks sought to dominate the trade unions through the state, Lozovsky seems to have been seeking to dominate the state through the trade unions. In Lozovsky's scheme, therefore, the trade unions were to remain independent and outside the state. Any fusion with the Commissariat of Labor was to be avoided. Thus the conflict seems to have centered ultimately upon whether the trade unions or the Bolshevik party was to function as a supra-state organ, guiding and directing the Soviet government. Accordingly, as early as 1918 there can be noted the conflict between the party and the trade unions—a conflict which was to pass through many events and conditions to culminate in the Workers' Opposition of 1921. To understand more fully the three-cornered struggle of the state, the party and the unions, it is necessary to follow the problem of the statification of the trade unions into the years 1919 and 1920.

CHAPTER VIII

Labor and the Party: The Temper of the Post-Revolutionary Situation

THE LABOR CLIMATE

Before the problem of statification is discussed further, it would be fruitful to investigate the temper of the relationship between Russian labor and the Bolshevik Party. It is necessary to try to determine whether problems of labor were elaborated and solved in conditions of peace and accord or amidst conflict, resentment and violence. It is necessary to convey the impression, which the sources provide, of the conflict which did exist between Russian labor and the Communist Party. Also, it would be advantageous to show, as far as the sources allow, what alternatives to Bolshevik action, other than those already discussed, were available to labor in the Soviet state. In addition, the Bolshevik reasoning by which the party chose to justify its policy or capture the support of labor shall be further examined. This chapter, however, shall not be an attempt to search out and present all the conflicts between labor and the Soviet order; nor will it be an investigation of all the alternatives to Bolshevik labor leadership. The function of this chapter is to present the background, the mood, the temper, of the post-revolutionary labor situation, a background which the reading of the sources provides.

In the presentation of the relationship of the trade unions, the state and the party thus far, the trade unions have been depicted in a passive role. The objections of non-Bolshevik representatives of the trade unions have, indeed, been presented. However, the resistance of non-Bolshevik unions to Bolshevik policy, or the opposition of parts of unions opposed to the Bolsheviks, has not yet been discussed. Here again, as in the case of workers' control exercised in the manner of joint ownership, information is scanty. The evidence of resistance to Bolshevik policy among various unions, however, cannot be denied. The Bolsheviks found their chief support among the Union of Metal Workers and in the Textile Workers' Union.[1]

Others passively supported the Bolshevik party or actively resisted it. Parts of some unions broke away to form Bolshevik branches of their own, as, for example, the Union of Communist Railwaymen, which broke away from the original All-Russian Union of Railwaymen. This latter union serves as an example of the active role the unions could take toward the Bolshevik party.

In the first days after the October Revolution *Vikzhel,* the Central Executive Committee of the All-Russian Union of Railwaymen, did not passively accept Bolshevik one-party rule but had attempted to bring about a coalition government of socialist parties.[2]

As a result of the close connection that the communists were trying to establish between the trade unions, the Bolshevik party and the Soviet state, a discussion of the conflict between the trade unions and the Bolsheviks is not complete unless the relationships of the resisting trade unions and the opposition workers to the state and to other parties, as a whole, are also taken into account.

Bolshevik Repression of Labor and Labor Resistance

Soon after the October Revolution, the conflict between the Bolsheviks and many workers in Petrograd, Moscow and other cities of Russia was to become intense and violent. As already mentioned, on 18 January 1918, shortly before the opening of the First All-Russian Congress of Trade Unions, workers who demonstrated in favor of the Constituent Assembly, which met for the first and last time on 18 January, were fired upon by Bolshevik troops and Bolshevik Red Guards.[3] This could not but prove to the workers that opposition to the Bolshevik Party was likely to be suppressed by violence. Nevertheless, resistance to Bolshevik policy continued. Nor did the Bolsheviks hesitate to use repressive measures against the labor opposition. It closed the opposition press and prevented the dissemination of opposition literature among the workers.

Lozovsky, while still a Bolshevik, writing in the *Trade Union Herald* on 20 December 1917/2 January 1918, protested against the Bolshevik policy of suppressing, by violence, workers' strikes against the new government. He protested also against punitive measures used against the leaders of the opposition among the workers. Speaking, it seems, of the strikes of workers in government offices and enterprises who opposed the Bolshevik seizure of power, Lozovsky wrote: "Exerting all the power of our organizational influence on those proletarian elements entangled in the web of defensism who thought to oppose the October Revolution by means of the strike, and battling against the hare-brained policy of sabotage of the Soviet power, the trade unions must, at the same time, protest in the most decisive manner [the use of] violence against the strikers. The task of the trade unions and the Soviet power is the isolation of the bourgeois elements who lead strikes and sabotage but this isolation should not be achieved merely by mechanical means, by arrests, by shipping to the front. or by deprivation of bread cards. . . ."[4] Thus Lozovsky charged that the Soviet power, in addition to using violence against strikers, used also the devices of assignment to front-line duty and the recall of bread cards. This latter would, in effect, deprive those subject to it of the legal right to rations, of the right to eat. Individuals deprived of their bread cards, therefore, would consequently tend to be forced into efforts to obtain food on the black market or by other illegal means. Thus, they would also be forced into subsequent crimes against the state.

Speaking against these repressive measures by which opposition was being overcome, Lozovsky also protested against the deprivation of free speech and of the freedom of agitation. "The trade unions," he wrote, "should not in any case sanctify violence against the press. Preliminary censorship, the destruction of newspapers, the annihilation of freedom of agitation for the socialist and democratic parties, is for us absolutely inadmissible. . . . The closing of the newspapers, violence against strikers, etc., irritates open wounds. There has been too much of this type of 'action' recently in the memory of the Russian toiling masses, and this can lead to an analogy deadly to the Soviet power."[5]

Thus Lozovsky reminded the Bolsheviks that their policy, in its disregard of the basic civil rights of the workers, could not but remind the latter of the worst days of the tsarist regime. Such a policy would evoke distrust and suspicion. Nor was Lozovsky wrong in his prediction. Riazanov, one of the foremost communist party members and labor leaders, in January 1919 simultaneously admitted and apologized for the lack of faith the trade unions felt in the Bolshevik party. "Since the political party of the proletariat," he said, "has to manage its affairs under such huge difficulties, it is completely natural that mistrust in the role of the party toward the trade unions arises."[6] This mistrust was sometimes expressed in very concrete ways.

An opposition newspaper, *Our Age* (*Nash Vek*), of 15/28 March 1918, reported a meeting of 170 representatives of 56 industrial enterprises. The paper claims the workers charged that the working class organizations had been turned into bureaucratic organs of the Soviet power, and did not meet their obligations to labor. The meeting moved that the workers should demand strict responsibility from their representatives, both in the soviets and in trade union organizations, so that their representatives should not act contrary to the wishes of their electors.[7]

Our Voice (*Nash Golos*), a Menshevik newspaper, reported that a Resolution of the Moscow Committee of the Menshevik Party condemned the support given by the workers' soviets and trade unions to the new Bolshevik state, in disregard of the welfare of the workers. The resolution stated: "The Soviets of Workers' Deputies and the trade unions have turned into organs of state power and cease to express the will of the working class."[8]

A council of workers' representatives adopted the following resolution, reported in the Menshevik newspaper *The Spark* (*Iskra*) of 14/27 June 1918: "The offenses of the Soviet power are continuing. People are executed with and without a trial. Workers meetings are dispersed and arrests are made. Prisons are overflowing. . . . Workers of many towns have come forward against political violence. It is impossible to keep silent any longer. The council of representatives, having debated the problem of the impossible position of the proletariat of the whole country, has decided to call the Petrograd workers to a one day strike as a political protest under the slogans Down with Capital Punishment! Down with Executives! Down with the Civil War. Long live Freedom of Speech, Assembly and of Strikes! Long live the Constituent Assembly!"[9] The resolution was adopted and a strike was announced for Tuesday, 2 July 1918.

It thus becomes obvious that there were groups of workers who actively opposed not only the Bolshevik policy toward the trade unions but the political dictatorship of the Bolsheviks as well. This opposition to the Bolshevik dictatorship was often conducted under the leadership of labor.

Expulsion of Opposition from the Moscow Soviet

The same edition of *Iskra* from which quotations have been presented above contains a Declaration of the Menshevik Fraction read at a meeting of 12/25 June of the Moscow Soviet of Workers' Deputies. In this declaration the Mensheviks accused the Bolshevik party of counter-revolutionary action for expelling the Social Revolutionaries and Mensheviks from the Moscow Soviet of Workers' Deputies. It condemned the Bolsheviks for arresting workers' representatives and delegates. "The arrest of the council of workers' representatives of the Moscow factories and shops, of the Tula delegates, of the Petrograd and Briansk workers,[10] the decision of the Central Executive Committee [of the Soviet] to expel the opposition fractions from the Soviet, and also the hypocritical decision of the Moscow Soviet to expel the entire fraction of Social Revolutionaries and the Russian Social Democratic Workers' Party [Mensheviks] from the executive organs of the representatives of the party of the working class, is the last act of that counter-revolutionary policy which the Bolshevik party is waging."[11]

The declaration went on to accuse the Bolsheviks of denying free speech to the workers, of turning the soviets into organs which suppress rather than protect the working class, and of filling the soviets with Bolshevik party appointees: the Mensheviks charged the Bolsheviks with distorting the working class movement.[12] Their declaration expelled the Bolsheviks from the ranks of proletarian leadership and charged the Bolsheviks with eliminating all the workers' organizations that did not support them. By destroying the independence of the workers, the Mensheviks charged that the Bolsheviks destroyed the cornerstone of the revolution and the goals for which it was fought.[13] They resolved upon four means by which they would fight their expulsion. The first was to publicize the Bolshevik measures and to propose that the workers send delegates to the Soviet demanding that it rescind its expulsion.[14] Unfortunately, there was little likelihood that the pressure of workers' delegates would have had much effect upon a party that was bound to historical goals, not workers' demands. The Mensheviks, in effect, proposed to send delegates to ask a Bolshevized Soviet to readmit delegates it had expelled. In the light of their own accusations against the Bolsheviks, it seems they could have had little faith in the efficacy of such measures.

Secondly, the Mensheviks resolved to retaliate against the Bolsheviks by expelling those soviet representatives who had voted for the exclusion of the Mensheviks. They intended to use, therefore, the same measures against which they were fighting. Unlike the Bolsheviks, however, they were dependent upon the force of workers' opinion, not upon the state or its arms. In their opposition to their expulsion from the soviet, they proposed that the workers ignore the decree excluding the Menshevik representatives from the soviet and that the workers continue to recognize the expelled deputies as their representatives.[15]

If the Moscow Soviet or Bolshevik party resisted this action which the Mensheviks proposed that the workers take, the Mensheviks would then begin a campaign among the Moscow workers to recall all their representatives from the Moscow and regional (*rai*) soviets which, they charged, had been "completely transformed into Bolshevik party institutions."[16] The Mensheviks, however, did not make clear exactly how this recall was to take place. Was it to be a formal process and did they imply there was a juridical basis for this? The Mensheviks could hardly hope to recall the Bolsheviks by what the latter would consider to be "legislative rigamarole" or, as the Bolshevik Tomsky at the Second All-Russian Congress of Trade Unions had pointed out: "It would be ludicrous if we refrained from using violence, or repudiated it or the force of state coercion for the purpose of strengthening the new society we are building. . . . This would mean to conceive of the transition from capitalism to socialism . . . by passing time in voting. . . ."[17] It seems, therefore, that a demand for recall could have imposed no limitations upon Bolshevik action. The Mensheviks could have removed the Bolsheviks from control of the unions and the state if they had had at their disposal the use of a greater degree of force, but this demand for recall seems to have accomplished nothing.

The Mensheviks also hoped to by-pass the Moscow Soviet and create another workers' organization independent of both the Soviet and the Bolshevik party. There was, however, a plethora of workers' organizations for the workers to support and not a lack of them. There were the trade unions, the factory committees, the soviets of workers' deputies, the Anarchist communes, and the various proletarian parties. What good was one more; especially when the Bolsheviks were steadily acquiring the control of a state apparatus?

The fourth measure which the Mensheviks proposed to take against the Soviet, however, was contained in Paragraph 4 of their resolution, which read: "The Conference recognizes that the last decision of the Moscow Soviet provides a stimulus for the most urgent and immediate unification of the Moscow proletariat into independent mass workers' organizations. Therefore the Conference of the Moscow Organization of the Russian Social Democratic Workers' Party appeals to the Moscow workers not to be discouraged by the political repressions of the Bolshevik power and to continue energetically to fight for the creation of an independent proletarian organization. . . ."[18]

Thus the Menshevik party called upon the workers for support in the political struggles that arose between the Mensheviks and Bolsheviks both before and after October. Since the Mensheviks as well as the Bolsheviks were leaders of part of the trade union movement, and since the relationship between the trade unions and the soviets as a state was a close one, the political movement and the trade-union movement became entangled with one another. Menshevik supporters in the trade unions, therefore, could not consolidate their forces and work solely within the trade unions for trade-union independence, if such were their objective. They were also called upon to extend their forces and support their party in its conflicts with the Soviet state and the Bolsheviks.

Protest of 14 June 1918

The Bolsheviks, however, were able to use to good advantage the protests of the workers against the Soviets. Just as the Mensheviks and the workers protesting Bolshevik policy in the Soviets tried to set themselves up in opposition to the Soviet organs, the Bolsheviks tried, and with more success, to exclude the opposition workers from the workers' organizations. An incident which occurred at the Fourth All-Russian Congress of Soviets, which took place in Moscow in June 1918 concomitant with the expulsion of the Mensheviks and Social Revolutionaries from the Moscow Soviet, will illustrate this. The arrests of which the Menshevik papers speak in the citations above took place on 13 June 1918. On that day the Soviet state arrested workers' delegates to a conference that was to take place in Moscow on the general problems of the working class. To protest that action, on 14 June the workers' representatives of many Moscow factories attempted to send their representatives to a meeting of the All-Russian Central Executive Committee of the Soviets, which was taking place that day.

This action, it seems, would have presumably supported the right of the trade unions to determine their own representatives and the right of the non-Bolshevik socialist parties to represent the workers in the trade unions. The result of the dispute which had been waging between the Bolsheviks and the Left Social Revolutionaries on the one hand and the Mensheviks and Social Revolutionaries on the other hand, was the complete victory of the Bolsheviks. Significantly enough, it was on that day also that the Central Executive Committee excluded the Mensheviks and the Social Revolutionaries of the right and center fractions from the Central Executive Committee.[19] Martov, the Menshevik leader, charged at that meeting of the All-Russian Central Executive Committee that "By a specially issued order, no one was allowed through today except Bolsheviks and Left Social Revolutionaries. The other comrade workers are now standing in the street, vainly waiting on the court steps so that those elected by hundreds and thousands of workers may be allowed to be present at this meeting where our fraction is trying to raise the question of this new act of arbitrariness and violence against the proletariat."[20] He proposed to bring before the congress the problem of workers' resistance to the government policy, charging that in other places these conflicts had led to the use of violence against the workers.[21]

Sosnovskii, the Bolshevik chairman of the All-Russian Central Executive Committee, at its meeting of 14 June, in reply to Martov's condemnation of the arrests, denied the validity of Martov's charges. He did not, however, deny the arrests. He merely refused to admit that those arrested represented the working class. He based this denial on the grounds that the representatives were opposed by the Moscow Soviet of Workers' Deputies and its regional soviets, which had expelled the Mensheviks and Right Social Revolutionary representatives.[22]

The Bolsheviks, therefore, recognized as representatives of the Moscow workers only those who were members of the Moscow Soviet of Workers' Deputies. By excluding the Mensheviks and Social Revolutionaries from the Moscow Soviet, the Bolsheviks thus deprived the Moscow workers of representation by these parties. Furthermore, the fight to defend this right of representation led to the isolation of the workers defending the excluded parties. Moreover, it seems to have assisted in the expulsion of those parties from the All-Russian Soviet of Workers' Deputies. This, in turn, deprived the workers of all Soviet Russia from representation by the Menshevik and Social Revolutionary parties.

Proletarians and Non-Proletarians

The struggle between the Bolsheviks and other proletarian parties concerning who were the real representatives of the working class led also to a struggle over what the real working class itself was. Lenin, at the Second All-Russian Congress of Trade Unions, expelled from the ranks of the proletariat all those who, by an open resistance to the statification, supported the independence of the trade unions. "It seems to me," said Lenin, ". . . the declaration of those under the flag of unity or independence of the trade union movement . . . led the groups supporting this slogan to an open struggle against the Soviet power and this attempt placed them . . . outside the ranks of the working class."[23]

A year earlier Sosnovskii had made much the same statement at the First All-Russian Congress of Trade Unions when he asserted that, though the trade union movement should not be split, the trade unions had "to differentiate between those who stand for the proletarian and peasant revolution and those who do not."[24] Since ultimately the Bolshevik party was to be the final arbiter of who and what stood for the proletarian revolution and who and what did not, those who opposed Bolshevik policy would be excluded from the ranks of the proletariat. This, according to the Bolsheviks, would not cause a split in the trade union movement, it would merely differentiate those who supported the revolution from those who opposed it.

This distinction was made in the Statutes of the All-Russian Central Council of Trade Unions adopted at the First All-Russian Congress of Trade Unions. The Statutes provide, in Paragraph 11, that "At the congress of trade unions only those workers of the trade unions have the right to representation, who in their activity are guided by the principle of the class struggle of the proletariat. . . ."[25]

Hence by the Statutes of the Congress of Trade Unions itself the membership in the central organization of the unions was restricted to those who accepted the fundamental assumptions of the socialist parties. The Bolshevik party, from its position of power, was able to interpret just how the principle of the class struggle was to be interpreted. Indeed, the Bolsheviks lost no time in doing so. Shliapnikov, the People's Commissar of Labor, at the First All-Russian Congress of Trade Unions in January 1918, explained that all those workers' organizations taking part in the October All-Russian organization of trade unions were invited to send representatives into the Collegia of the Commissariat of Labor. He added, however: "The All-Russian Council of Trade Unions of the old composition was not invited principally because the majority of the old council was in the enemy camp."[26] Thus, it was Bolshevik policy to eliminate from representation in both the trade unions and state organs those who disagreed with their program.

Also, the Bolshevik party, through its policy of demobilization, made it possible to eliminate from the ranks of the working class all or part of the workers of an enterprise that resisted Bolshevik policy. The process of demobilization of industry included the reconversion and relocation of industrial enterprises to meet the program of a centralized economy that was planned by the Bolshevik controlled state. The Bolsheviks, by this means, acquired the possibility of uprooting and distributing the workers of whole factories. Furthermore, it would be naive indeed to believe that the Bolsheviks were guided in this process purely by the consideration of economic planning. The political implications of the process of demobilization do not seem to have been overlooked. It was a weapon which could have been used with particular effectiveness against those factory committees that sought to maintain the ownership and management of their factories. The workers were given no voice in the demobilization of their own enterprises, especially where the decision concerned its continued existence or its closure. Paragraph 5 of the Resolution on Workers' Control adopted by the First All-Russian Congress of Trade Unions stated: "In order that workers' control may be of the maximum use to the proletariat, it is absolutely necessary to refrain from any idea of atomizing workers' control by leaving to the workers of individual enterprises the right to make final decisions on questions touching upon the existence of the enterprise."[27] Enterprises, therefore, which contained particularly recalcitrant groups of workers could be closed, and the trade unions allowed to the workers no means of recourse against such closures.

That demobilization was used to rid factories of groups of undesirable workers seems to be definitely indicated by the communist Arskii in his article "Piece Rate Wages and the Raising of Productivity," in which he makes it clear that ". . . the proletarian government carried out the demobilization of industry which made it possible to work under new conditions and to free industry from the semi-proletarian and non-proletarian elements who were often a burden to the workers' movement. After the demobilization there remained at the factories only the true proletarian elements."[28] Here, however, Arskii designates as non-proletarian and semi-proletarian those workers who came from the villages to work in the factories during the war. He distinguishes them from "the true proletariat," whose entire lives are spent as factory workers. "During the war," wrote Arskii, "the composition of the proletariat was changed by the influx of new and alien elements attracted to work at factories and shops only during the war.

"These elements were not in any way connected with the factories and shops. They did not take into account their significance for the life of the country. They looked upon the factories and shops as upon a place of labor far from home which made it possible for them to work temporarily.

"It was not a true proletariat which had grown up and was trained at the factories and was closely connected with it, whereas the true proletarian wholly belongs to the factory, having been connected with it all his life."[29]

The semi-proletarians or non-proletarians, therefore, according to Arskii were those who were temporarily deriving their livelihoods from industrial employment, whose lives were not devoted to factory work, and who did not realize the significance of the worker to the life of the state. The true proletarian, on the other hand, devoted himself wholly to the factory.

There can be no doubt that the large industrial cities of Russia did contain many workers whose livelihood was entirely dependent upon factory labor and, in this sense, formed a "true proletariat." Nevertheless, it can also not be denied that significantly large numbers of industrial workers in Russia retained close contact with their farms and village communities. About twenty years before Arskii wrote his article, the economist and labor leader of the Trudoviki Party, Peshekonov, wrote: "The Russian worker and the Russian peasant are united by a strong economic bond, in many of their interests not only do they not oppose one another but even fuse together, and namely because the Russian worker, in the mass, is also the Russian peasant, and the Russian peasant is often also the Russian worker. Our worker, insofar as he is a seasoned industrial worker and insofar as he is part of the peasant family continuing to carry on his household economy for its sake,—is not a proletarian. The interests of the 'bourgeois' peasant are not indifferent to him because he himself was one yesterday and perhaps tomorrow will be one again; because his father, wife, children, brothers live by these interests; because his wages are part of the general budget of the family, and the extent of the satisfaction of his demands is defined not only by the fact that he himself earns but also by how much his family receives from its own household earnings. . . . The separation of the worker from the peasant, the opposition of one group to the other is possible only in theory and has no place in reality."[30]

There was, therefore, according to Peshekonov, almost an inextricable connection between the Russian worker and the Russian peasant. If he were not the same, his economic ties with his family served to identify the interests of the peasant and the worker. Twenty years had elapsed, however, between the time Peshekonov had written his article and Arskii his. These twenty years might very well have brought into being considerably larger numbers of workers who had severed connection with their village communities. There can be little doubt, nevertheless, that the situation which Peshekonov described continued to exist to a high degree. Solomon Schwarz, in his study of Soviet Labor, states that, after World War I, "Industrial labor moved farther from its farm background, yet strong country connections remained even after 1917."[31] The communist Rudzutak also stated at the Second All-Russian Congress of Trade Unions in January 1919: "We observe that in many industrial centers the workers, because of the curtailment of production at the factories, are dissolving into peasant states and tendencies and the working population is becoming half peasant, and often purely peasant."[32] And Lenin, writing in June 1919, affirmed that ". . . in backward capitalist countries like Russia the majority of the population consists of semi-proletarians, i.e., of people who regularly live in a proletarian way part of the year who regularly eke out their livelihood as wage workers in capitalist enterprises."[33] There would, therefore, have been in Russia large numbers of "non-proletarian" or "semi-proletarian" workers, as Arskii, speaking for the Bolsheviks, defined them.

Furthermore, based on the distribution of candidates by political parties at the First All-Russian Congress of Trade Unions, it would seem that those unions which were likely to have contained the largest number of "true proletarians" were the Menshevik, rather than Bolshevik, unions. The Mensheviks seem to have derived their greatest support from the older and more highly organized unions—from the nationally organized, All-Russian unions. The distribution of Menshevik and Bolshevik representatives from among the All-

Russian unions at the First All-Russian Congress was as follows:[34]

Bolsheviks	9
Mensheviks	12

From the unions on the next level—the provincial (*oblast'*) unions—the distribution of Bolshevik and Menshevik representatives was:

Bolsheviks	12
Mensheviks	9

The local soviets of trade unions, that is, the local councils of various trade unions, presented the following picture of their representation:

Bolsheviks	28
Mensheviks	12

In the local unions, however—the unions which had been largely organized after the February Revolution—the distribution of representatives between the two parties was as follows:

Bolsheviks	232
Mensheviks	34

Nor were these latter unions established on a very firm foundation. Lozovsky pointed out, at the First All-Russian Congress, that it was difficult to tell if a local union had as many members as it claimed or if they were all paying members.[35]

At any rate, it would seem that the greatest part of the Bolshevik strength in the trade union movement was derived from the newer, smaller, local unions, which, it seems, would have had larger numbers of "semi-proletarians" and "non-proletarians" than the national, more well established unions in which the Mensheviks found their support.

This digression into the relative strength of Bolsheviks and Mensheviks among the "true" and "semi-proletarians," however, should not obscure the point at issue. The point is, that in their process of demobilization, the Bolsheviks would hardly have inquired into the relationship of the worker to his peasant origins. In the light of Bolshevik usage of the concepts of "consciousness," "spontaneity" and "bourgeois-anarchism" there can be little doubt that the Bolsheviks would have used politically the concept of non-proletarian and semi-proletarian. There can be little doubt that to the Bolsheviks a true proletarian was one who possessed "consciousness" of Bolshevik goals, one who was devoted to factory work under Bolshevik discipline. Indeed in speaking of the "true proletarians" who remained at the factories after the demobilization of the non-proletarians, Arskii pointed out: "It was much easier to talk to these elements [the true proletarians] concerning the necessity of proletarian discipline and the revolutionary order."[36] Again, therefore, the Bolshevik usage of a word is equivocal. There existed in Russia a large group of semi-proletarians or non-proletarian workers whose attachments to the village were as the Bolsheviks described. Such a situation, however, was not produced merely by the war, as the Bolsheviks claimed, it was a long standing phenomenon of the Russian socio-economic scene. The Bolsheviks, moreover, manipulated the word into a term of censure and used it against workers who resisted Bolshevik policy.

Organizational Means of Bolshevik Trade Union Control

An analysis of the organizational structure set up for the All-Russian Central Council of Trade Unions in 1919 will show how difficult it was for the trade unions included in it to resist the policy it made. The highest organ of the All-Russian trade union movement was the All-Russian Congress of Trade Unions. The All-Russian Central Council of Trade Unions took over the supreme authority between Congresses and acted on the regulations and "principles" adopted by the Congress. (Conferences were called only when it was impossible to convoke an organized congress properly.)[37]

All the decrees of the All-Russian Central Council were compulsory for all the unions in its jurisdiction and for each member of those unions.[38] Any union violating a decree of the All-Russian Central Council was expelled from the organization. It was placed outside the only framework in which the Bolshevik regime would permit unions to exist. According to Paragraph 3 of the Resolution: "The violation of the decrees and insubordination to them on the part of the individual unions lead to their expulsion from the family of proletarian unions."[39]

The All-Russian Central Council of Trade Unions was formed on the basis of proportional representation. All the local Councils of Trade Unions were required to reflect the proportional representative changes that took place in the Central Council. According to

Paragraph 5 of the Organizational Resolution adopted by the Second All-Russian Congress of Trade Unions: "All local Soviets of Unions are constructed according to the scheme of the All-Russian Central Soviet of Trade Unions with the corresponding proportional changes in its numerical relations. All congresses of trade unions are convoked on the principle of direct proportion."[40] Thus it becomes obvious that once having obtained control of the All-Russian Trade Union Congress, the Bolsheviks were able to control the trade union organization on all levels. No other party could hope to break this hold in elections, either from below or above.

Working from above or below, however, the Bolsheviks had been striving to secure total domination of the trade unions and had tried to eliminate the influence of any other party or group. The Bolshevik Tomsky stated on 28 September 1918 that it was the task of the Communists, first, to strive to create well-knit trade unions in their own industries, ". . . secondly, to take possession of these organizations by tenacious work, thirdly, to stand at the head of these organizations, fourthly, to expel all non-proletarian organizations, and fifthly, to take the union under our own communist influence."[41]

Thus, just as Lenin had stated that it was the task of the party to secure political domination of the state for itself, so Tomsky stated that it was the task of the communists to secure their domination of the trade unions.

Bolshevik Control of Trade Union Personnel

Not only were the Bolsheviks able to use the organizational structure of the unions to uproot workers' resistance, but as those in control of the Central Council of Trade Unions, they weakened the movement itself by withdrawing leaders from the unions and assigning them to other organizations. Tomsky, at the Second All-Russian Congress of Trade Unions, made it clear that trade union leaders would be drawn away from the trade union movement. "You know, comrades," said Tomsky, ". . . that in Russia, where the trade union movement is relatively young, there is no place from which to draw an especially large cadre of experienced workers in the trade union movement who are acquainted with its practice and theory. But even those forces which are at our disposal in the process of social revolution were spent in other branches of labor which were as important for the working class, branches of Soviet work, and for this we do not reproach our comrades. Although there is no more important an organization of the workers' movement than the trade unions, we had to divide the best forces, not only to organize the people's economy, but also to participate in the organization of its state apparatus. This is what we have done and this is what we will do. It is not our fault that we cannot accommodate all organizations, that because of the lack of forces we cannot have our representatives everywhere. It is our misfortune and the misfortune of all the working class that it suffers, at present, from a lack of trained conscious workers."[42]

In addition to subordinating the trade unions to the Soviet state, the Central Soviet of Trade Unions itself was drawing the trade union leaders away from their unions. Nor was it filling these vacant posts with other personnel. It was, however, assigning the former trade union leaders to posts in the Soviet government. Since such transferred personnel would then depend both for their livelihood and their careers upon the Soviet state, only the most altruistic of them, it would seem, would have continued to protect the interests of the unions, especially when these interests competed with those of the state. Nor should the advantage of a government post, a position of security in the conditions of revolutionary instability of that time, be underestimated. In the Russia of War Communism and Civil War, any security, any status, any livelihood had a value immensely magnified by the general revolutionary insecurity and want.

Financial Control of Trade Unions

The hold of the Central Council of Trade Unions over the member unions was made secure partly by financial means. The local unions, although serving as the collectors of funds, were not to retain their own treasuries. The funds they collected were not to be at their own disposition. Paragraph 2 of the Resolution on the Organizational Structure of the Unions adapted at the First All-Russian Congress of Trade Unions stated: "In the heavy industrial centers the relations between the small cells of the trade unions and the central organs were established from the very beginning: small cells were the . . . collectors of money . . . but did not have their own treasuries."[43]

The resolution went on to say, in Paragraph 3, however, that such a "correct" procedure as the above—the remission of funds to the center—was not always practiced, for: ". . . along with such a centralized and completely correct form of relationship with the center branches, there were other forms: branches disconnected to a large extent acquired a semi-independent character, acquired their own funds, the means of which they spent on their own local needs."[44]

The disposition of the funds of the local unions for their own needs, according to the resolution, was not to continue in the future when, financially and otherwise, the local unions were to be subordinated to the center.[45]

The justification for the absorption by the central institution of all the local funds was that the centers serve all the needs of the local unions.[46] In accordance with Paragraph 6, the union of unions in the locality was to dispose of all funds, and was to be the final authority on all local matters.[47]

The center of the local unions of a given locality had to be in the same kind of relationship to the All-Russian Union of Unions as the local branch unions were to the local center. The latter, in accordance with Paragraph 7 of the Resolution, were to forward a minimum of 50% of their dues to the central treasury.[48] The local unions were to retain none of their funds, the local union centers would retain no more than 50%, and the All-Russian Union of Unions would receive at least 50%. The enforcement of such a system would leave the local unions completely dependent financially upon the central organizations, and they would be left without strike funds, insurance funds and other such guarantees of the welfare of their members.

The resolution, however, was a project for the future, not a description of the organizational conditions then existing. Actually, during the first year of its existence, Moscow paid in 76% of all the funds of the Central Council of Trade Unions. The rest were remitted by all the provinces, including Petersburg.[49] The union bookkeeping, said Tomsky, was so bad it looked like sabotage. But, he added, "I do not think it is sabotage, only Russian illiteracy."[50]

If, however, it was the policy of the Central Council of Trade Unions to draw or to attempt to draw away the funds from the localities to the center, the Central Council itself was the recipient of funds from the state and the party. The Central Council, rather than being dependent upon its branch unions for the funds which it received, was made independent of its membership by the subsidies it was granted by the state and the party. Tomsky, in his report to the Second All-Russian Congress of Soviets on the All-Russian Central Council of Trade Unions, announced that the organization had received 200,000 rubles from the Commissariat of Labor, 100,000 rubles from the Central Committee of the Communist Party for agitation and for propaganda abroad, and 500,000 rubles from the All-Russian Central Executive Committee of Soviets of Workers' Deputies for the same purpose.[51] Such subsidies, however, were not given only for agitational uses abroad. The Central Council of Trade Unions received, for example, 200,000 rubles for a railroad strike in the Ukraine.[52] Chirkin, an independent representative at the second All-Russian Congress of Trade Unions, charged that the willingness of the Central Council of Trade Unions to subordinate the unions to the state and to sacrifice union independence hinged upon the subsidy which the state provided for the Central Council of Trade Unions. Chirkin charged that "All questions concerning the dependence or independence of the trade union movement . . . boil down to the fact that they have received a subsidy on which they have existed for the past year."[53]

There are indications, then, that the leaders of the trade union movement who had not been drawn away from their posts retained them not through their devotion to the cause of labor but through their devotion to the Soviet state and the Bolshevik party. For this devotion, their power in the trade unions was maintained by financial as well as tactical assistance to their work in the unions.

Creation of Splinter Unions: The "Mixed Unions"

In addition to maintaining financial independence from its unions and attempting to subordinate the branch unions financially, the Central Council of Trade Unions attempted to reorganize, split and dominate unions that were independent of the Council and which would not abide by its organizational regulations. The most effective way of breaking the resistance of these unions and of bringing them into the Bolshevik fold was to encourage the communist-supporting element in the independent unions to set up parallel unions of their own. Such organizations would not, of course, oppose the Central Council of Trade Unions and the Bolshevik party. Having the support of the party, and of the Soviet state which the party controlled, these unions could successfully prevail over their parent organizations. The Menshevik Kammermacher charged: "The Central Council acted against the unity of the trade union movement, not only by not taking proper steps against its disorganization by the communist party, but even by lending indirect support to the criminal device of creating parallel communist unions."[54]

The practice of which Kammermacher accused the Bolsheviks, the practice of splitting off the communist or communist-supporting elements of recalcitrant trade unions, is described in the Resolution on Organizational Structure adopted by the First All-Russian Congress of Trade Unions in January of 1918. The resolution explained that there were in Russia, mostly among employees of state enterprises, over ten unions whose organizational structure contained both workers and managerial personnel. These "mixed unions" did not belong to the All-Russian Central Council of Trade Unions, and the resolution charged that they remained outside the Central Council partly because they did not want "to be subordinate to general proletarian trade-union discipline."[55]

The resolution further insisted that these unions be integrated into the Central Council but demanded that, before being admitted into the central organization, they ". . . coordinate their statutes with the statutes of the proletarian movements."[56] Finally, the resolution recommended that, in cases in which the unions refused to coordinate their statutes with those of the member unions of the Central Council and join it, the proletarian part of the mixed unions form their own union and join the national organization.

It was, nevertheless, not the mixed character of the unions to which the Bolshevik labor leadership objected; for the Bolsheviks themselves seem to have been intent upon combining both workers and managerial employees into industrial unions.[57]

For example, the 1918 Statutes of the Textiles Workers Union, a union which the Bolsheviks controlled although excluding from the unions, by Paragraph 20, all persons employed in an administrative capacity, added, in a note to Paragraph 20: "Personnel engaged in administrative duties, through election by the workers themselves or by appointment by the trade union, may be members of the union."[58] This indicates, then, that the All-Russian Central Soviet of Trade Unions permitted the inclusion of administrative personnel in their member unions. Nevertheless, the Resolution on the Organizational Problem passed by the Second All-Russian Congress of Trade Unions in January 1919 implied that the policy of admitting mixed unions into the All-Russian organization was being newly adopted by the Congress in 1919.[59]

The resolution stated that even though the First Congress of Trade

Unions had not considered feasible the fusion of higher and lower employees into one union, a year of proletarian dictatorship, having successfully removed much of the antagonism between the workers and employees, had demonstrated the desirability, or even necessity, of such a fusion.[60]

The concluding statement of Paragraph 4 left no doubt that administrative personnel were included in the category of higher employees, by stating that "Only in those enterprises and establishments, where the increase or reduction of wages of hired workers and employees is decided by individuals of the administrative personnel, such individuals cannot be members of the given union."[61]

The Second Congress of Trade Unions, therefore, provided not only that mixed unions be admitted to the All-Russian Central Soviet of Trade Unions, but also that all unions in the Central Soviet be mixed. It would seem, therefore, that the objections in 1918 to the inclusion of the mixed union in the Central Soviet were not based upon their composition. The reason for their exclusion might be found in their relationship to the state. As unions of state employees which had existed, in many cases, previous to the Bolshevik regime, they bore a special relationship to the governmental machinery. As members of state departments, as railway men, postal telegraph employees, and workers of the customs department, Ministry of Finance, etc., they were part of the state apparatus. Among these workers in nationalized enterprises and governmental departments, workers' control was even more of a problem for the Bolsheviks. If these workers, for example, took over the institutions in which they were employed, they would be, in effect, taking over branches of the state.[62] If they claimed to be not only the employees of these departments, but administrators and policy makers as well, the unions would have absorbed the functions of state power. Especially in those cases in which the unions were not Bolshevized, this was a situation which the Bolsheviks were seeking to avoid. The very policy of statification was directed toward excluding the unions from state power while identifying them with, and subordinating them to, the state. There are indications, however, that the "mixed unions" were claiming governmental functions. Evidence for this is found in their designation as "public law" and "trade union-political organizations." By public law was meant law to which the state was one of the parties. In addition, the usage of this term in the situation under discussion indicates that the mixed unions did not accept the same status in regard to the state—the same statification as other unions. Only slight evidence is available for the determination of the exact meaning of the term public law unions. They seem to have been, however, unions which actually did try to take over functions of the state, that did claim to be endowed with state power. In the case of the communist union of railwaymen represented by *Vikzhedor* (the All-Russian Executive Committee of Railwaymen), they seem actually to have been delegated in 1918 with this power by the Bolshevik party. For these reasons, too, it seems, the "mixed unions" were known also as trade union-political organizations.[63]

It therefore would indeed seem to have been the problem of status rather than of composition around which the quarrel between the mixed unions and the All-Russian Central Council of Trade Unions centered.

The device used in 1918 in attempting to force the mixed unions into the Central Council seems to have been the formation of "proletarian" unions within them, as called for by Paragraph 25 of the Statutes on Organizational Structure adopted by the First All-Russian Congress of Trade Unions, and which would be equivalent to the creation of the parallel unions spoken of by Kammermacher above. Once these splinter unions were created they would have received the support of the Central Council of Trade Unions and the Bolshevik party. In addition, they would, it seems, have been recognized as true proletarian unions in contrast to the "mixed" unions they replaced. The "mixed" unions would then have been open to the charge of being non-proletarian and subject to dispersal; for no union could officially or safely maintain itself outside the Central Council of Trade Unions. Those who still retained their affiliation with the original mixed unions might have been threatened with loss of jobs and livelihood. On the other hand, those who became members of the proletarian unions, whether workers or employees, would have had the support of an official union. The "proletarian" unions, therefore, were not necessarily formed by those convinced of the communist cause. They were composed not necessarily of the militant, of the enthusiastic, of the indoctrinated, or of the faithful, but, perhaps, of the practical and the timid.

Election and Reelection

Control over unions was maintained by the Bolshevik party also through the system of elections. The Theses on the Soviet Power, passed at the Seventh Congress of the Communist Party, in Paragraph 6, Section 10, called for: "Fuller democracy by virtue of less formality, greater easiness of election and recall."[64] This informality, this easiness of election and recall was to serve well the interests of the Party wherever the appointive principle was not substituted for the elective one. Chirkin, an Independent at the Second Trade Union Congress, stated that many officers of trade union institutions were not elected, and when they were, the principle of recall was so freely used that the elections were meaningless. Chirkin claimed: "In the majority of factories, in the majority of regions *[rai]*—and it was possible for me to travel there—there were institutions representing the trade union movement, but these institutions were not elected in any way, were not ratified in any way, and if the elections were conducted and individuals were elected who were not suitable to the needs of . . . the All-Russian Council of Trade Unions and to the local powers, then these elections were annulled very freely and those individuals were replaced by an administration more suitable to them."[65]

Aside from Chirkin's charge, there is other evidence of the Bolshevik practice of recalling these elected representatives of the workers who were opposed to the Bolshevik policy.[66]

The policy of substituting the appointment for the election of union officers seems to have been a common one. Kossior asserted, for example, in 1920, that the practice of "appointmentism" was common both in railway unions and the union of metallists.[67]

The Independent Perkon spoke out against the regulation which required that the representatives sent by the workers' organizations to the Commissariats of Labor be ratified by the Commissariat. "If at the meetings of unions or councils of trade unions," he said, "you can elect any person as a commissar; i.e., if the working class were allowed in a given case to express its will, sending definite people to the commissariat, you would think that this individual would represent your interests in the commissariat, that he would be your commissar. But no, in spite of the fact that you have expressed your will, the will of the working class—it is still necessary that the commissar you have elected be confirmed by the authorities. This line at once bears witness that we do not have a dictatorship of the proletariat, but a dictatorship over the proletariat. The proletariat is allowed the right to make a fool of itself; it is allowed to elect its representatives but the state power, whether it ratifies the elections or not, treats them however it pleases. In case he is not confirmed, it chooses a man who will follow its policy, a policy which is, perhaps, contrary to the interests of the working class, which has sent its own representative but this is necessary for the dictatorship of the proletariat."[68]

Perkon complained, therefore, that the government authorities, by their power of confirmation and ratification of candidates, did not hesitate to reject the representatives of the workers when they were not subservient to Commissariat policy. Moreover, Perkon charged that even in those cases when the Commissariats of Labor ratified the candidates elected by the unions, they did not feel bound to take the representative's power or views into serious consideration. Perkon's accusations seem to be upheld by the implications of Shliapnikov's statement as People's Commissar of Labor. "Eminent specialists," he said, "in the field of labor politics were invited to this elected organ [the *Collegium* of the People's Commissariat of Labor] and thus our work was more successful and the individual workers of the Trade Unions did not suffer from overwork in such a combination of forces."[69] The Commissariat of Labor, therefore, seems to have been so concerned for the representatives of workers that it invited specialists in labor policy to relieve the workers' representatives of some of their duties. Nor did the communists admit the existence of resistance to their system of elections. The Bolshevik Schmidt asserted: "Against the purely formal objections that candidates to responsible posts (Commissars, members of *collegia,* etc.) must be confirmed by the Central or local power, the trade unions have never quarreled. On the contrary, they have considered this extremely necessary in the interests of a single class policy."[70]

The Moscow Printers' Union, however, like the speakers above, charged the Bolshevik party with violations of free representation in the trade unions. In a surreptitiously printed article, "The Independents and the Press," the Moscow Printers charged that the Bolsheviks sometimes used the threat of arrest to convince a representative to leave his post. Sometimes the Bolsheviks, according to the article, threatened factories with reduction of rations and other articles of consumption if communists were not elected to the factory committees or soviets. Such threats, when executed, were often effective. The article further stated: "Communists sometimes use threats of arrest against the workers to oblige them to leave their posts in the board of the union voluntarily, and in practice this often happens.

Sometimes they do it otherwise; they say that if a Communist is not elected to the Board or Factory Workers' Committee, they, the Communists will arrange so that their workers will receive less food and other necessary things. And sometimes this produces its effect. This affirmation can be verified in many factories in Moscow."[71]

Although there is no means now available of verification of this accusation, it seems to confirm Lozovsky's charge that the Bolsheviks were using the rationing system as a punitive measure. It indicates that the Bolsheviks, as the party in control of the state and the central trade-union organizations, were in a position to exert many vital pressures against the trade unions. It is, at any rate, merely a logical extension of the system of preferential supply practiced by the Bolshevik regime. Preferential supply was a method by which those workers who were loyal and necessary to the Bolshevik regime were supplied with more rations than those who were less loyal and less necessary. "Would it not be better," said Lenin in December 1920, for example, "to take, say, meat from such-and-such a category of workers and give it in the form of a bonus to 'urgent' workers?"[72] "The Independents and the Press" continued: "When such measures [the deprivation of rations] have no result the Communists let the local soviets or Central Council of Trade Unions dissolve the Board of the Trade Union; such was the case with the first Central Board of the Printers' Union."[73]

The control which the Bolsheviks wielded over the Central Council of Trade Unions and over the state was an invaluable weapon against opposition on the part of the workers. This weapon gave it the advantage over all other parties and workers' organizations.

Workers' Support of Non-Bolshevik Parties

In those areas away from Moscow and Petrograd—the centers of Bolshevik power—non-Bolshevik parties continued to receive support from the workers. The Menshevik Rubtsov claimed that "The fact is that in the last elections to the Kharkov Soviet of Deputies, a large number of the workers curiae were representatives of our party. (A voice: Liar, That's not true.) At the locomotive factory there were 26 Mensheviks and 22 Bolsheviks. At the (not heard) factory 5 Mensheviks and 1 Bolshevik. (Voice: And in general?) In general, among the metallists the majority are Mensheviks, among the textile workers the majority are Mensheviks. . . ."[74]

In spite of the heckling Rubtsov's claims evoked from the floor, they seem to have been valid. The Communist Kossior, in replying to Rubtsov's speech, asserted that only the "backward" proletariat supported the Mensheviks, but while intending to damn the Menshevik policy he points out, in effect, that they had more to offer than the Bolsheviks. The Mensheviks, he says, looked after the workers; therefore, their policy had more appeal to the trade unions. Kossior admitted that there was much resistance to Commuinst unions in the Ukraine, where workers fought against them on the principle of the independence of the unions from the Soviet government. Kossior asserts that Menshevik appeals ". . . were considered only by the backward Ukraininian proletariat and their hungry stomachs. By means of the backward, they [the Mensheviks] wanted to preserve . . . their influence on the organizations, because their slogans were more concrete, more tangible, more understandable as slogans around which they could reestablish the broad working masses against us. So it was during the elections and reelections of all the trade union organizations of Kharkov, so it was in the elections of the Donets basin, so it was in the *Guberniia* Conferences of the city of Kharkhov. . . ."[75]

Thus, it would seem that trade union opposition to the Bolsheviks died hard. It would seem that where the workers wanted a concrete program to improve their lot, they supported the Mensheviks. That this support was attributed, by the Bolsheviks, to the hungry stomachs of a backward proletariat, indicates that the Communists had little more to offer than self-sacrifice and devotion to an idea. Kossior's speech indicates also that the workers defended the independence of their unions where they had the opportunity.

Resistance of the Printers' Union

The Printers' Union was one of the focal points of resistance to Bolshevik authority. When the wages of the printers were lowered in order to conform with a city-wide wage scale introduced by the All-Russian Central Council of Trade Unions, the Printers' Union refused to accept this wage scale. In this resistance, the Independent or Neutralist trade-union members and leaders were active. The Bolshevik Antsilovich, in his condemnation of the Printers' Union and its Menshevik leadership, asked: "Comrades, before mass meetings of workers who are still on a low level of intellectual and political development, is it possible to nurture demagogy, saying, 'See the Soviet power does not want to raise your wages'? Such arguments, such methods, were put into motion by the so-called neutralists of the printers union at that very moment at which we instituted a city-wide wage scale in Petrograd, at the moment at which we tried to subordinate the interests of the individual trades, perhaps to sacrifice the interests of the part to the interests of the whole."[76]

Thus the Bolsheviks constantly harp upon the lack of understanding of Bolshevik goals and methods on the part of the workers. There is continuous talk of the lack of "consciousness," of the non-proletarian attitudes, of a low level of development and of political immaturity among the workers. This talk of backwardness among the workers is often joined with mention of the workers' willingness to sacrifice their own welfare. The natural, legitimate self-interest of the workers is equated with selfishness and political and social self-centeredness.

Having stated, however, that the Central Council of Trade Unions was trying to subordinate the interests of the unions to the interests of the class, Antsilovich inquires: "And at that moment who hindered us, who undermined the authority of the Soviet Union? The Neutralists of the Printers' Union. They counted on the fact that their masters, when industry had not been nationalized,—at the expense of those who read books, of those who read newspapers, were ready to flirt with the workers, to make concessions to them. On this basis an ugly demagogy has broken out concerning wage scales."[77] Hence those who defend the independence of the trade unions, the neutralists, are accused of being in the service of "their masters," the owners. The higher wages paid to the printers before the printing industry was nationalized is referred to as an irresponsible flirtation of the owners with the workers, a device to attract and deceive. A demand for a higher wage (in this case a demand that the wage was not to be lowered) is depicted as a self-indulgent sacrifice, by labor, of the reading public. The higher wage, Antsilovich insinuates. cost the workers and owners nothing and the consumer much. This sudden defense of the consumer, however, is somewhat incongruous in light of the fact that a Resolution of the First All-Russian Congress of Trade Unions had made it a function of the unions "to defend the organs of state administration from possible attempts to satisfy consumers at the expense of producers."[78] Antsilovich, however seems to be more concerned with the effectiveness of his oratory than with the logic and reasonableness of his thought. Self-righteously, therefore, he continues by saying: "But it is clear, comrades, that these arguments [the arguments of the neutralist opposition] do not bear criticism, not only from the point of view of our contemporary revolutionary construction, but also from the point of view of the so-called truly independent movement."[79]

Since the supporters of the independence of the trade-union movement maintained an existence separate from the state and seem to have continued their functions as union representatives, organizers, or leaders under those governments and in those areas which were engaged in civil war with the communist regime, their defense of trade-union independence was identified with treason.

"However, let us admit," said Antsilovich, "that you are independent of power, that your independence goes so far that you go along with Kolchak, that you consider it necessary to support the shooters of communists in those cities where you act with our enemies. Let us admit that."[80] Having accused the Independents of giving support to the enemies of the Communist state, Antsilovich charges them with insubordination to the will of the working class. Claiming that this will is represented wholly by the All-Russian Central Council of Trade Unions, he claims the right for that organization to impose wage scales upon the Printers' Union and to take a hand in its internal organization. "If I may say so, however," Antsilovich went on, "is not the will of all the working class, the subordination to general rates, and the coordination of the interests of one trade with the interests of others, even in wage policy, is not this compulsory for you? Is it not inadmissible from the point of view of a union worker to say that the All-Russian Council does not have the right to intervene in the organizational life of the printers? Does it have that right? Why is it impossible to interfere for the interests of the whole, in the interests of the majority, in the interests of a class?"[81]

It will be noted, therefore, that the Bolsheviks seldom spoke in their own interests. They spoke most often in the interests of "the class." Thus, any interests which the Bolsheviks opposed became, it seems, special interests, particular interests, interests opposed to the common welfare. So closely did the Bolsheviks identify their own interests with those of the proletariat as a whole that the party itself seldom admitted it had any interests of its own.

Antsilovich then concluded by explaining that the Petrograd Printers' Union, after having been shut down, ousted the Independent leaders and chose another administration.

"The most non-class conscious," asserted Antsilovich, "under the influence of the lesson of the world revolution, under the influence of the revolution which is developing in Russia, are beginning . . . to say as one: 'Hands off, there is no place for you as leaders of the trade union movement.' "[82] The exultation of Antsilovich was hardly well founded, however; nor were the Bolsheviks secure in the adherence of the reorganized union. The Printers' Union was not given the right of a participating vote at the Second All-Russian Congress of Trade Unions, even though it was represented by non-elected delegates who were sent by the Printers' Union after its dispersal and reconstitution. Moreover, the Printers' Union continued to be the mainstay of the Independents as well as a focus of opposition to the Bolshevik regime. It was the Printers' Union in Moscow, for example, that raised its voice against the Bolshevik party during the visit of the British Labour Delegation to a meeting of the Printers' Union on 23 May 1920. It was at this meeting, also, that Chernov, the hunted Social Revolutionary leader, emerged from hiding to address the union and disappeared into safety at the close of his speech.[83] This, however, was to be the last organized protest of note that the Printers' Union was to make.

The Printers' Union itself, however, gives an account of the methods by which the Bolsheviks were able to bring it into subjection.[84] A report of the Printers' Union charges that, in retaliation for the Printers' meeting at which the printers spoke out to the British delegation against the Bolshevik regime, the office of the union was occupied on the morning of 18 June by the armed forces of the Soviet government, and "all those who had for any reason displeased the Communists were arrested there."[85] The printers in protest against this action went on strike, demanding that those who had been arrested be freed. To break the strike, the Printers' Union claimed, the Soviet authorities used their control of the food ration. The report states: "The privation of food is, in the present conditions, the most terrible measure against starving people,—that was used."[86] In addition the Bolsheviks, it would seem, sought to bring the strikers into submission by singling out for punishment some of the strikers whom they arrested as leaders. By thus placing the responsibility for the strike upon a few who were punished, the remainder were offered the same treatment, or absolution from punishment through submission. "At the same time [as the curtailment of rations]," the printers' report charges, "there were arrests of the supposed leaders of the strikers. . . . The strikers began to work. . . ."[87] These measures were successful. Further, the report suggests that the continued use of such a policy would bring the printers to additional acts of subordination. "Possibly under pressure of such measures," says the report, "they [the Printers' Union] will soon be compelled to invent even resolutions of condemnation against those who have led them until now."[88] Such overt action, says the report, will merely increase the hatred of the printers for the authority which is forcing them into submission.[89] Thus, it becomes evident, if the accusations of the Printers' Union are given credence, that indirect compulsion, and threats—direct and indirect—were used to force the recalcitrant Printers' Union into submission to the Bolsheviks and the Soviet state.

The Right to Strike

Although the Printers' Union made use of the strike in its fight against the Soviet state and the Bolshevik party, the strike, by 1920, had been outlawed. Even by 1918, although the strike was not explicitly prohibited in the Soviet state, its use was sanctioned only against the capitalist entrepreneur. As a weapon of the unions themselves, it was being eliminated. By depriving the unions of the strike weapon, therefore, the Bolsheviks were able to weaken union strength and effectiveness. Matrozov, at the First All-Russian Congress of Trade Unions, stated: "It is said: allow even the strike to exist. Yes, of course, as long as we have not completely overcome capitalism, as long as enterprises constructed on capitalist models exist, it is completely natural that there will even be strikes; but this does not mean, that struggling for socialism, we will not try to see that these enterprises take on a new character and that there will be a struggle different from the strike."[90] Therefore, once capitalist enterprises were socialized the strike was to give way to a new "form" of struggle. Matrozov, claiming that during the transitional period industry would belong to the state and the state to the workers, equated and identified labor and the state so completely that he asserted: "During the transfer of power into the hands of the workers and soldiers, during the struggle for socialist conditions of life, it is impossible that we [the workers] present demands to ourselves."[91] Having equated the workers with the state as entrepreneur, Matrozov asserted that a substitute for the strike had to be found to suit the new conditions. The new "form" had to be clearly defined so that the meaning of sabotage and the meaning of strike would be definitely differentiated.

". . . Once we pass the construction of a new life, it is necessary, obviously, to find new forms. What forms it is difficult to say, but we are obliged to look for them . . . otherwise we will leave a whole series of gaps which will give us the right variously to interpret the meaning of sabotage and the meaning of a strike."[92] Although Matrozov had no suggestions for the new form to be substituted for the strike, he associated the strike with sabotage. Indeed Matrozov did not hesitate to make accusations of sabotage against those who defended the right to strike. Work, according to Matrozov, was the first obligation of the new order. "Before the October Revolution," he said, "the right to strike was our sacred right in the struggle with our enemies—the capitalists, but from the moment of the October Revolution, when the power became the people themselves, the first decision, the first appeal of the Council of Commissars, was the appeal to the workers 'stay at your work benches and work hard.' You, comrades, understand why the Council of Commissars turned to you with such a request—it could not be otherwise. At the moment of the most severe disorder, at the moment when we ourselves enter into the construction of a new life, we must not abandon work. From the moment of the revolution, comrades, a crisis occurs, a change in the relationship to strike. (Laughter from the right.) They laugh and they laugh with perfect right, because the strike for them has been transformed into sabotage."[93]

In spite of Matrozov's demand that the Congress clarify the issue of the strike and sabotage, the question of the freedom to strike was not settled at the First All-Russian Congress of Trade Unions. Riazanov brought up the motion to discuss the strike under the conditions then prevailing, but the motion was voted down.[94]

Although the question of the strike was not placed upon the order of the day of the First All-Russian Congress of Trade Unions, the Bolsheviks do not seem to have permitted strikes of state employees. The Menshevik Grinevich accused the Bolsheviks of having violated the right of the postal-telegraph and other state employees to strike.[95]

With the close relationship established between the trade unions and the Commissariat of Labor, however, the state committed itself more definitely, by official word, to the abolition of the right to strike. Schmidt, as Commissar of Labor, in February 1918 wrote: ". . . it is already unthinkable . . . to organize strikes. The individual trade unions have already begun to realize this and the most important of them, the Union of Metal Workers, at its First Constituent Congress excluded from its statutes the strike struggle. The Petrograd Soviet of Trade Unions has, as of the present, not changed the decision on the inadmissibility of the strike adopted in the October days. . . . In the last analysis, the All-Russian Central Council [of Trade Unions] . . . must definitely come out either for the strike struggle, as a means of achieving the demands presented—or for state interference. The All-Russian Congress of Trade Unions and the majority elected to the executive committee have come out as partisans of the latter method."[96] Thus, by February of 1918 the Soviet Government, as well as the All-Russian Central Council of Trade Unions, was committing itself to a condemnation of the strike. By 1920, the strike had been so far obliterated that Zinoviev, at the Third All-Russian Congress of Trade Unions, said that the strike funds, having no longer any function, were to be turned over to the Red International of Trade Unions. "We propose," said Zinoviev, "that our congress decree that all the former strike funds of the trade unions in Russia, in view of the fact that these funds are no longer necessary, be used as the basis for an international fund of Red Trade Unions."[97] The unions, therefore, were not only deprived of the funds which had provided security for workers or strikers, but these funds were turned over to assist in the organization of an international communist-directed association of trade unions.

Opposition and Strife

From all the above illustrations and examples derived from Bolshevik and non-Bolshevik sources, it becomes obvious that the climate of the post-revolutionary labor situation was one of conflict and discord. There seems to have been a definite and widespread opposition by the workers to the Bolshevik order. Not all the unions accepted Bolshevik leadership, in spite of its majority at the All-Russian Congress of Trade Unions and its control of the All-Russian Central Council of Trade Unions. Many unions actively resisted Bolshevik attempts to lead them. The resistance of the trade unions, when coupled with the resistance of the factory committees and the support shown by the workers to the Menshevik and other parties, indicates that the Bolsheviks were faced with a formidable opposition among the working class for whom they claimed to speak. The

Bolsheviks, however, from their commanding heights of state power, had at their disposal forces of compulsion and manipulation which the trade unions, the factory committees, and other labor organizations lacked. This was one of the primary means by which they overcame labor resistance. It must be borne in mind that the events, conditions and situations through which labor passed occurred, therefore, in an atmosphere of controversy, conflict and violence. It is with this in mind that the decrees, statutes, and printed word in general, of this time must be read.

The question arises, however: if the Bolsheviks pursued a policy of repression and dominance, how is there so much evidence of resistance and outspoken criticism of the Bolshevik regime? The answer would seem to be found principally in the fact that in the years under discussion, the Communist Party had not yet consolidated its power. It was not then in a position to exert total domination. Transportation and communication facilities were in extremely poor condition and the Bolshevik party could not extend its power over all parts of Russia. The Civil War added further problems to the Bolshevik administration of the Russians under its command. There was, in addition, a shortage of officials whom the party could find both efficient and reliable. Then, too, resistance to the Bolsheviks was often expressed by those who did not yet know their own weakness or Bolshevik strength. Also, the resistance which was expressed against the Bolsheviks did not always act in its disfavor. Such resistance, as long as the Bolsheviks remained in control of the commanding heights, served to bring the enemies of the Bolsheviks into the open and to segregate from their ranks those who would submit to Bolshevik rule. Resistance served also to clarify Bolshevik goals and values and to make Bolshevik objectives clear. When, however, Bolshevik power was consolidated and the party had stretched its dominance and penetrated its rule throughout Russian life, the former resistance was uprooted and ceased to express itself overtly.

CHAPTER IX

The Trade Unions, the State and the Party: 1919

The Meaning of Statification

It was against a background of conflict and resistance that the labor policy of the Bolshevik party was put into effect; and it was amid turmoil and confusion that the relationships between the trade unions and the organs of the state were evolved. It is, therefore, time now to turn once again to these relationships and see how they developed in 1919 and 1920.

In spite of the resolutions passed by the First All-Russian Congress of Trade Unions in 1918, the problem of the statification of the unions had still not been solved. Schmidt, as a communist trade union leader, writing in the *Trade Union Herald* during the time of the Second All-Russian Congress of Trade Unions, referred to "the old but still far from settled quarrel concerning the statification of the trade unions."[1] As in the case of other words and terms current in that day, statification meant different things to different groups. Schmidt averred that "there is an unbelievable confusion concerning the problem and the 'statification' of the trade unions is understood in extremely various ways."[2] To understand the problem of statification, then, it is necessary to understand the varying concepts of it, as well as to have a knowledge of which concept prevailed.

A difference of opinion on statification existed within the communist party itself. Zenkovich and Nogin, two prominent Bolsheviks, "understood statification as the complete fusion with the organs of state power and the abolition of the union apparatus."[3] From this point of view, the trade unions had no reason at any time to stand in opposition to the Soviets or to limit their power or activity in any way.[4] The Soviets, as the organs of the class as a whole, were in the future to absorb the trade unions and completely dissolve them; but " 'For the immediate future all the apparatus of the trade unions is preserved, and it is the obligation of each worker to be a member of the union,' "[5] wrote Schmidt, quoting Zenkovich.

Nogin supported the view of Zenkovich by his thesis that even to the supporters of the trade unions as a party, and even before October, it was clear that the function of the Soviets was to assure the victory of the proletariat. This the Soviets were to do, by virtue of the fact that they embraced all the working classes and united all forms of its movement. In relationship to the Soviet of Workers' Deputies, therefore, all other workers' organizations, including the trade unions, were secondary. According to Nogin's scheme, the administration or management of industrial enterprise (n.b.: not the factory committees) were to be the basic cells in the production process of communist society. Above them was to be the administration of that particular industry as a whole. The supreme organization was the Council of National Economy. According to Nogin's thesis, the trade unions were to become the basis of political power for the workers, and any opposition of the unions to the Soviets or other organs of the state became impossible, i.e., inconceivable.[6] There is no indication, however, of the reasoning by which Nogin explained this inconceivability; but it is obvious from his scheme that both industry and labor were to be directed by state organs, not by the trade unions.

On the other hand, however, Schmidt explained that other communists conceived of statification as the transfer of state power to the trade unions. According to their point of view, the trade unions were to fulfill state tasks under the control of state organs. Schmidt claimed that the view of Bukharin, Rykov and Miliutin was diametrically opposed to that of Nogin and Zenkovich. The former believed the unions should acquire state functions; the latter believed the state should obliterate the unions.[7] However, just as Zenkovich and Nogin advocated the disbanding of the trade unions only in the future and called for their preservation in the present, so the advocates of entrusting state functions to the unions modified their demand by advocating the delegation of such functions only under the control of the class as a whole, that is, under the control of the state. " 'Far from the idea of wholly leaving to the industrial unions, the independent administration of production,' they are for all-class control and all-class administration of production."[8]

Neither of these two views, however, according to Schmidt, who seems to be the official spokesman for the party, encompassed the true definition of statification. According to Schmidt, "the exact definition of 'statification' of the trade unions presupposes: 1) the existence of the trade unions themselves; 2) state compulsory membership of all the toilers in some branch of industry; 3) the regulation by the state power of all the activity of the trade unions."[9]

Thus, statification demanded that all workers be drawn into the trade unions and that the unions be regulated by the state. The existence of the trade unions was insisted upon, it seems, so that the state could have a means of controlling all workers through the union organization. What is more, a distinction was made between the workers' state and the totality of workers organized in trade unions. The totality of workers was not considered as forming the state. It merely formed the trade unions. A discussion of the full implications of this distinction and of this concept of statification must wait, however, for further discussion below of the relationship of the trade unions, the state and the party.

In effect, however, the trade unions compulsorily enrolling workers were to be independent, organizationally, from the state. The trade unions and the state were to be separate and distinct organizations. Nevertheless, this organizational independence did not presuppose or admit any independence of political action, or of the defense of labor's special or particular interests. Nor were the trade unions to be neutral. They were actively to support the state. Therefore, Schmidt wrote: "We must remove still another important misunderstanding, arising out of the incorrect interpretation and understanding of the neutrality and independence of the trade unions. These two concepts are incorrectly confused. 'Neutrality' is confused with the formal non-partiness of the trade unions, and independence with organizational independence of the unions."[10]

The organizational independence of the trade unions, therefore, was not to be confused with independence in other spheres, nor was neutrality—the formal non-party status of the unions—to be confused with lack of support for the Bolsheviks.

Independence, as distinguished from organizational independence, had to be defined, said Schmidt, as the opponents of the Bolsheviks defined it. He cites as the definition of independence, therefore, the declaration of the minority of the First All-Russian Congress of Trade Unions. This resolution asserted, and Schmidt quotes, that " 'the preservation of the full *political* independence of the class organization of the proletariat is necessary to defend its daily and general interests as a class of hired laborers . . . [and consists of] the possession of the freedom of coalition and of free struggle against the factory owner, even though it might be the state.' "[11]

Thus the opponents of the Bolsheviks and their concept of statification defined independence as freedom of political action and of collective struggle against the employer, even if the latter were the state. This is a concept of independence which the Bolsheviks, in insisting upon the organizational independence of the trade unions, rejected. Schmidt's quotation illustrating the concept of independence held by the minority of the Trade Union Congress serves to outline and incise the distinction between the Bolshevik concept of statification and the opposition view of neutrality and independence. Schmidt has prefaced his quotation, therefore, with the statement: "We will let our opponents define what independence is, so that we can more graphically show our friends who confuse these concepts that the trade union movement in Russia, as a whole, is as far in its own daily practice from these definitions of the independence of the trade unions, as heaven from earth."[12]

If the Bolshevik concept of statification is to be understood, therefore, even at the danger of excessive reiteration, it must be pointed out that the distinction between the minority concept of independence and the Bolshevik concept of organizational independence must be borne in mind. With this in view, the conclusions reached by Schmidt are presented: "The trade unions," he wrote, "preserve all their own organizational independence based on the independence of the masses."[13] This organizational independence, however, did not include immunity from intervention in the internal life of the unions. Such immunity was one of the stipulations made by the advocates of the independence of the trade unions; as quoted and rejected by Schmidt, it reads: "The trade unions, preserving full independence from the organs of state power and the Commissariat of Labor, must demand from the latter, complete non-interference in their internal affairs. . . ."[14] Since the Bolsheviks decisively rejected this stipulation, organizational independence as they define it does not include immunity from interference by the state in the internal affairs of the unions. The "independence of the masses," upon which the organizational independence of the unions depends, indicates also that the masses do not form the state, but are outside of it.

The statification of the trade unions, as the Bolsheviks determined it, required that the trade unions fulfill the duties laid upon them by the state. Schmidt concluded, in his definition of statification, that: "The trade unions, serving as a trustworthy stronghold of Soviet power, take upon themselves, the fulfillment of the tasks of the Soviet power, under the guidance of the local and All-Russian Central Council of Trade Unions, and bear all the moral responsibility before the central power for the tasks entrusted to them."[15] Not only, therefore, had the trade unions, which were to enroll all the proletariat in their ranks, to carry out the tasks laid upon them by the state, but they had also to bear the moral and psychic burden of responsibility for the fulfillment of those tasks.

In addition, the trade unions had to assist in the formation and reconstitution of state organs submitting always to the direction of the state. According to Schmidt, "The trade unions assist the central power in the formation and reformation of state organs and organs of administration, subordinating themselves to the general class leadership."[16] Not only, therefore, was union organization not free from state interference, but the unions were called upon to assist the state in the latter's intervention in other organizations.

Schmidt on the Trade Unions and the Commissariat of Labor

The problem of the statification of the trade unions, in 1919 as well as in 1918, continued to be inextricably connected with the relationship of the trade unions to the Commissariat of Labor. According to Schmidt, under the conditions provided by the statification of the trade unions, as he has presented them, there was only one solution to the problem of the relationship between the unions and the labor commissariat. That solution is found in the statute adopted at the Fourth All-Russian Conference of Trade Unions held in March of 1918. This statute recognized the trade unions as "the sole representative of the proletariat organized according to industry." It thus excluded the factory committees, also organized according to industry, from a claim to the representation of the proletariat. The Commissariat of Labor was defined as a state organ fulfilling, with the authority and compulsion of state power, the will of the trade unions. The Commissariat of Labor, according to the statute, was responsible before the trade unions, but it must be pointed out, again, that since the Commissariat of Labor possessed the force and authority of state power, and the trade unions were devoid of such authority and force, there was no way to assure the responsibility of the Commissariat to the trade unions.

There was, however, a division of authority between the two organizations which could have served to check the authority of each.

All practical, administrative and executive authority was entrusted to the Commissariat of Labor. Within its scope lay labor conditions, organizations, insurance, social welfare, and propaganda. Schmidt enumerated the functions of the Commissariat of Labor as follows:

"1) Conditions of labor (working time, wages, hiring and firing, rules of internal order, labor discipline).

"2) The organization of labor (the construction of the unions on the production principle, implementation of labor service, accounting and distribution of the manpower in the country).

"3) The protection of labor (prohibition of child labor, limitation of the labor of women and minors, curtailment of working time in especially harmful industries, sanitation).

"4) The insurance of the toilers (during illness, disability, unemployment, invalidism, maternity, old age).

"5) The statistics of labor (investigation of the way of life, conditions and degree of organization of the toilers).

"6) Agitational propaganda work among the toilers for the study of the fundamentals of socialist and communist economy."[17]

Thus it becomes clear that among the functions of the Commissariat of Labor was the unilateral determination of conditions and problems which were formerly settled by means of collective bargaining between the unions and employers. The Commissariat of Labor was substituted in the settlement of such problems for both. Basic decisions on economic policy and organization were to be made by the trade-union congresses and the All-Russian Central Council of Trade Unions, but all the decisions which required state power for their enforcement were to be transferred to the Commissariat of Labor to which such power belonged. All other problems arising out of policy decisions were to be worked out by both organizations together, in full conformity with the structure of their central and local organs.

The Bolsheviks, in an attempt to make a close connection between the Commissariat of Labor and the trade unions, arranged that the personnel of the labor Commissariat were in many cases nominated by the trade unions and confirmed by the Commissariat. Such a procedure was used also to avoid charges of bureaucracy and to show a presumed responsibility of the Commissariat to the trade unions. The trade-union representatives, however, were not only confirmed by the Commissariat; it would seem that they could not be held responsible to the trade unions in the light of the latter's lack of state power. Also, the personnel sent by the trade unions to the Commissariat could function in that organization only to administer and execute the decisions of the labor Commissariat. Such personnel became dependent upon the latter, rather than upon the trade unions for the scope of their activity and for their security, status, prestige and livelihood. This procedure, then, like the practice of transferring trade-union officials to various government posts, served to deplete the ranks of trade-union leadership. However, according to Schmidt: "The most correct relationship established between the All-Russian Central Council of Trade Unions and the People's Commissariat of Labor . . . boils down to the following. 1) The candidature of the People's Commissariat of Labor is advanced by the All-Russian Central Council of Trade Unions and confirmed by the All-Russian Central Executive Committee. 2) The college of the People's Commissariat of Labor is composed of the majority of candidates of the All-Russian Central Council of Trade Unions and confirmed by the Council of People's Commissars. 3) Branches either in the majority, or as a whole—Social Insurance, Protection of Labor and Tariffs are formed of representatives of the All-Russian Central Council of Trade Unions which is guided in its work by special statutes ratified by the plenum of the All-Russian Central Council of Trade Unions."[18]

These regulations, however, since the trade unions had no means of insuring to themselves the responsibility of their representatives in the Commissariat, represent merely the delegation of trade-union nominees to a government department. But such delegation regarded as a panacea for bureaucracy, as far as the Bolsheviks were concerned, was not the abolition of government bureaus, but the delegation of trade-union representation to these bureaus. According to the Communist Rudzutak: "Only when we have succeeded in saturating our chief regulating organs with representatives of proletarian organizations, only then will that bureaucratism and red tape which we have observed till now, be eradicated."[19] In the final analysis, however, bureaucracy can be eradicated only by the abolition of bureaus, not by a change of personnel. However, for a strongly centralized state administration, bureaucracy is a most efficient means of governing. It must also be remembered that in workers' control, as the workers conceived it, a solution to bureaucracy had been achieved. However, the Bolsheviks could not accept this solution without losing their predominant position in the state.

The "correct" relationship between the All-Russian Central Council of Trade Unions and the Commissariat of Labor which Schmidt outlined, however, was not a description of how things were but, again, of how they ought to be. As Schmidt pointed out: ". . . things are far from working out so felicitously in the localities. There these relationships are extremely confused, and even such important workers' centers as Petrograd, Moscow and the Urals decide these problems in different ways."[20]

Trade-Union Independence at the Second All-Russian Congress of Trade Unions

With Schmidt's clarification on the statification and independence of the trade unions in mind, attention shall now be turned to the problem of statification as it arose at the Second All-Russian Congress of Trade Unions.

It has been pointed out that the Bolshevik concept of statification rejected the idea of the political independence of the trade unions and their freedom of coalition. Independence of this kind was not to be confused with the organizational independence of the trade unions. Organizational independence was concomitant with the subordination of the unions to the state, but it secured the independence of the state from the unions. It prevented a fusion of the two and placed the proletarian state above the proletarian unions. The Menshevik leader Martov, at the Second All-Russian Congress of Trade Unions, therefore, stated: "How strange, indeed, that in the socialist proletarian state we are told that the workers' organizations should not be independent. Independent of what? Should they not be independent of the party holding state power in its hands? But we socialists, not sharing the new truths of Russian communism, raise first of all, another more important question. Should the state power be independent of the working class and its organizations? . . . The question is whether the state power can really, and not on paper only, depend on the workers' organizations, the trade unions and other organizations of workers—this is hushed up."[21] Martov thus raised the question of whether the organizational independence of the trade unions functioned to preserve the independence of the trade unions from the state, or of the state from the trade unions. This was far from an abstract question, since there are indications that the trade unions regarded statification as a process which would make them organs of the state. They seem also to have believed that as such, they would possess executive power with which they could themselves solve the problems of labor. In speaking to the trade union representatives on the subject of statification, Schmidt declared: "You are warned against the untimely tasks which the trade unions take upon themselves as organs of state power . . . namely against those premature tasks, against those premature and unassigned tasks which the trade unions are trying to take upon themselves."[22] Hence the trade unions were admonished for engaging in activity which had not been specifically assigned to them. They were warned, too, against attempts to act in the capacity of state organs.

The Resolution on the Tasks of the Trade Unions, adopted by the Second All-Russian Congress of Trade Unions, promised "the gradual change of their organization by means of fusing the organs of the unions with the organs of state power."[23] This, however, was again a promise for the future, since the Resolution added that the unions, at that time, were not to share the state power with the state.[24] In the words of Tomsky, who uses the term statification to include state power: "If you look at our proposed resolution, you will see that not a word is said in it about the immediate statification of the trade unions. In the resolution there is not a word about the trade unions taking upon themselves the functions of state power."[25] Tomsky made it clear, therefore, that the acquisition of state functions by the trade unions was not a matter for the present.

However, the 1919 Resolution on the Tasks of the Trade Unions, like that of 1918, clearly held out the hope that the trade unions and the state would fuse together. The Resolution promised such fusion if the trade unions cooperated with the state, and if the trade unions educated the workers in their duties and obligations to the Soviet order. According to the Resolution: "The whole process of the complete fusion of the trade unions with the organs of state power (the process of statification) must be the completely inevitable result of their close and harmonious teamwork and the preparation by the trade unions of the wide masses of the workers for the task of administration of the state apparatus and all its economic regulating organs."[26] It seems obvious, then, that statification was being held out to the trade unions as a future reward in return for service rendered to the state in the here and now. The resolution used the word statification differently from the way it was defined by Schmidt in his *Trade Union Herald* article. It was used in the resolution to convey the idea of union merger with the state; in Schmidt's article it was defined as the organizational independence of the unions from the state. The process of fusion, however, was placed in the future. Organizational independence remained in the present. As Schmidt declared at the Second All-Russian Congress of Trade Unions: "Without refusing to fulfill, in the process of development of the trade unions, those explicit tasks which fall to our lot in the matter of the regulation of industry, we will only gradually fuse our organs with the organs of the state power."[27] Hence it is obvious that the Bolsheviks were scrupulously avoiding any possibility of the acquisition of state power by the unions in the present. At the same time, however, the process of statification was immediately to be one in which the trade unions were to execute a program assigned to them by the state.[28]

Lozovsky, at the Second All-Russian Congress of Trade Unions, proposed not only the organizational independence of the unions, but proposed also that they should have their own executive apparatus. The resolution he introduced for the Social Democratic Internationalist Fraction on the Tasks of the Trade Unions stated: "On the basis of richly growing negative experience, both in the center and locally, the conversion of the unions into organs of state power and the transference to them of the management of individual branches of the people's labor must be emphatically and categorically rejected. The trade unions remain, during the entire period of transition, independent class organizations with definite functions and definite tasks, having their own apparatus for putting into effect their own decrees and decisions, to defend the rights of the economic interests of the proletariat. It is not permissible for them to be either fused with organs of state power, nor subordinated to them."[29] Thus the resolution seems to insist upon a separate existence for the trade unions and upon an organizational structure which would have permitted them to implement their own policy themselves.

However, Lozovsky's view on the statification or independence of the trade unions was closer to that of the Bolsheviks than would seem on the surface. Lozovsky made it clear that by independence he did not mean neutrality, but that the trade unions were to support the Soviet power. "When I speak of independent unions," said Lozovsky, "I do not in any way say they must be independent of socialism, independent of the socialist struggle. No, the unions must work in the closest contact with the Soviet power. . . ."[30] Thus by the

Second All-Russian Congress of Trade Unions, Lozovsky's position on statification had grown quite close to that of the Bolsheviks. In effect, he proposed the organizational but not the political independence of the trade unions. He demanded that the trade unions actively support the Soviet government.

Lozovsky demanded, however, a definite, specific and exact delimitation of functions between the trade unions and the state. Asserting that it was the task of the trade unions to struggle for socialism, Lozovsky added: "But the trade unions will fulfill this task better, the more exactly the relations between the unions and the organs of power are established and the better the functions of independent and free economic unions of the proletariat are marked off from the worker-peasant power which is hybrid in its social relations."[31] Alluding in this way to what he regards as the partial peasant character of the Soviet government, Lozovsky insisted that ". . . the trade unions . . . must . . . with complete exactness delimit their own functions from the functions of the organs of state power, so that the workers know where the voluntary unions begin and where the state coercive organs of power begin."[32] The ambiguity mentioned by Lozovsky in the relationship between the trade unions and the state was in accord with the lack of juridical limitations to practical Bolshevik action, a lack which seems to have been characteristic of the early Bolshevik regime. It allowed the Bolsheviks a wider area of political maneuverability and the opportunity to depend upon power rather than law for the scope of their governmental activity. Attacking the ambiguity of the Bolshevik Resolution on the Tasks of the Trade Unions, Lozovsky, for example, stated: "If you read through this resolution again, if you try tomorrow, leaving for the provinces, or arriving at your trade union, on the basis of this resolution, to do something practical, I am sure that you will not find anything concrete."[33] The ambiguity which Lozovsky decried made it difficult for the trade unions to act with certainty or security. The Bolsheviks, it seems, usually remained the final arbiters of the interpretation of such resolutions and decrees, and ultimately their interpretations were pragmatic. Those applications of the resolution which served Bolshevik goals were "correct."

Ambiguity, however, was not as serious a deterrent to the scope of trade-union action as the acquisition of trade-union functions by the Commissariat of Labor. The first part of the Communist Resolution on the Trade Unions and the Commissariat of Labor provided for the coordinated, joint work of the unions and the Commissariat. The Resolution began by stating that the trade unions, organized by industry, and having to regulate the conditions of labor and production, were constantly acquiring greater state-wide significance.[34]

The Commissariat of Labor was said to be the agency through which the economic policy of the proletariat was enforced. It was referred to as an organ of the Soviet government in which the proletariat was said to be predominant. In that government, the Commissariat of Labor had at its disposal all the state forces of compulsion.[35] Matters of theory and principle, which were decided by the Congresses of the Unions, were to be accepted by the Commissariat and all special decrees of the Commissariat had to be approved by the All-Russian Central Council of Trade Unions, the organ functioning for the Trade Union Congresses when the latter were not in session.[36] The resolution then decreed that the local Councils of Trade Unions compulsorily take part in the work of the local Branches of Labor which dealt with social insurance, the labor market, protection of labor, etc. To do this, the local councils of trade unions sent their representatives to the *collegia* of the Commissariat. The subbranches of the Commissariat of Labor were to be formed from the union apparatus.[37] Thus the very apparatus of the unions, the local councils of trade unions, themselves were transferred intact to the Commissariat of Labor. These union branches, therefore, which formerly served union interests, were being transferred to a state department. Hence, they were becoming government bureaus dependent upon the state for their functions. The personnel of these transferred branches were no longer dependent upon the unions for their livelihood and welfare, but upon the state. It is likely, therefore, that at least in some cases their loyalties also would be transferred. In addition, the organizational structure of the unions was not only thus depleted of its personnel, but part of its organizational structure was swallowed whole by the Commissariat of Labor.

It becomes clear, however, that the trade unions would have had little need for any sort of administrative or executive branches at all. The unions were being deprived of all functions of any importance by the final paragraph of the Resolution on the Trade Unions and the Commissariat of Labor, which proposed: ". . . that the All-Russian Central Executive Committee of the Soviets and the Council of People's Commissars . . . concentrate exclusively in the People's Commissariat of Labor, the working out of norms, the regulation of labor conditions, wages, the organization of labor, the order of hiring and firing, the protection of labor, and social insurance."[38] The most important functions of the trade unions were thus taken out of their hands and placed within the sole jurisdiction of the Commissariat of Labor.

This despoliation of the rights and prerogatives of the trade unions did not go unchallenged. The fraction of Independents at the Second All-Russian Congress inveighed against the subordination of the unions to the Commissariat and their transformation "into secondary or deliberative organs attached to the Commissariat of Labor."[39] The Independents spoke out against "the substitution of decrees by the Commissariat of Labor for collective agreements."[40] The interference of the Commissariat of Labor in the internal organizational affairs of the unions also brought objections from the fraction of Independents. In their resolution, the Independents demanded that the trade unions be represented in all the organs of the Commissariat concerned with the legislative protection of labor; they also demanded the complete freedom of election of the representatives to the organs.[41] The resolution proposed to safeguard the rights of the unions in the elections by depriving the Commissariat of its right to ratify the election of the candidate or to dismiss him.[42] In this way the Independents sought to insure the representation of the unions in the Commissariat and the validity of the elections for that representation. However, since the fraction of the Independents was numerically powerless at the Trade Union Congress, its Resolution served more as a protest against Bolshevik policy than as a program of action.

The resolution introduced by Lozovsky for the party of the Social Democratic Internationalists did not attempt seriously to defend the prerogatives of the trade unions against the Commissariat of Labor. His resolution, for example, stated: "The normalization of labor and wages on an All-Russian scale must be concentrated exclusively in the hands of the Commissariat of Labor. . . ."[43] Only in the case of the disputed questions concerning such matters as wages and insurance was the primacy of the unions over the Commissariat of Labor upheld by Lozovsky's resolution. The final decision on these questions, according to the resolution, was to be made by "the appropriate representative organ of the proletariat organized in trade unions."[44] Lozovsky's resolution did not differ fundamentally from that of the Bolsheviks; in fact it made less pretense of defending the rights of the trade unions.

The Second Congress of Trade Unions had gone far beyond the First in subordinating the trade unions to the state. The Commissariat of Labor, however, was not the only state organ to subordinate and dominate the trade unions. The Heads (*Glavki*) and Centers (*Tsentri*), each in charge of a particular industry, also tried to turn the trade unions to their purposes. The Heads and Centers were themselves branches of the Supreme Council of the National [People's] Economy, which was established on 5 December 1917. Originally, it seems, this organization was to have functioned as the economic branch of the Central Executive Committee of the Soviets. The Heads and Centers, however, were not always established by the Supreme Council of the National Economy. Often the Commissars themselves would individually establish Heads or Centers of various industries without seeking the consent of one of the three governmental departments legally possessing the authority for their creation. These departments were: the Central Executive Committee of the Soviets, the Council of People's Commissars, and the Praesidium of the Supreme Council of the People's Economy.[45] The Commissars, in thus establishing Heads and Centers, acted outside the juridical bounds of the state in whose name they acted. Actually, the Heads and Centers seem to have functioned to undermine the administrative apparatus of the Soviet state. This was especially true in the localities.[46] The Heads and Centers, as organizations representing individual Bolshevik Commissars who headed the party and the central administration of the state, wrested from the local soviet institutions the jurisdictions that had been theirs. The territorial or geographical principle upon which the soviet structure had been founded was being opposed and undermined by the industrial principle of the Heads and Centers. The latter, representing the central administration of various industries, cut across the geographical, governmental and administrative divisions of the Soviet state, especially of the Council of the People's Economy. The Heads and Centers, since they were opposed to the branches of the state, allied themselves with the trade unions in order, it would seem, to secure an apparatus for their administration and a justification for their opposition to branches of the state. Since the trade unions were also organized on the industrial principle, they provided an organization by which the party could oppose the Soviets. It has been pointed out, however, that the party took great care to maintain a distinction between the trade unions and the state, and to subordinate the unions to the Commissariat of Labor—an organ of the state directed by the Bolshevik party—for the Commissariat of Labor was one of the branches of the Council of the People's Commissars.

THE COUNCIL OF PEOPLE'S COMMISSARS

The Council of the People's Commissar, by about the middle of 1918, acted in turn as the *de facto* governing organ of the state. According to Zinoviev, at the Eighth Congress of the party in March of 1919, ". . . for a half year under the leadership of Comrade Lenin a definite group was formed which for good or bad, making many mistakes, is, nevertheless, exactly like a government at present. It is a business-like institution which inspects the apparatus as a whole and is in possession of the apparatus which can guide the ship of state."[47] Sovnarkom, the Council of the People's Commissars, was taking the place of the Central Executive Committee of the Soviets as the administration of the Soviet state. The individual commissars did not hesitate, it seems, to issue directives and decrees over-riding the policy of the central or local soviet institutions. Osinskii. a leader of the opposition within the party, stated in Paragraph 4 of his resolution on the Party Structure: "In view of the fact that at present individual people's commissars disclose a tendency to issue without debate in Sovnarkom decrees contradictory to the decrees of, and encroaching upon, the competence of other central and local institutions, it is necessary to establish and put into effect a regulation that not one branch has the right to issue decrees . . . without the discussion and ratification of them by the Council of People's Commissars."[48] Thus, not only was Sovnarkom acting without reference to the Central Executive Committee of the Soviets. but the individual commissars, all of whom were prominent Bolsheviks, were acting independently of the Council of the People's Commissars itself. In so doing they were acting, it would seem, in their capacity as party members rather than as officers of the state; or, more accurately, they were acting for the party as officers of the state. Lunacharsky, replying to Osinskii, assertively defended the implementation of such a policy by the party and the commissars. "The Council of the People's Commissars," he said, "is a more decisive government insofar as it decides the more important legislative problems within the framework of the general laws established by the Central Executive Committee of the Soviets. The executive organ of the government, in the proper sense of the word, is also Sovnarkom. The Central Committee [of the Party] intervenes in policy when it is necessary to issue general directives on important questions. Can there be any doubt for the congress that we as the dominating party, that our Central Committee as the personification of the party, should issue directives in such cases?"[49] Lunacharsky thus proclaimed that it was the prerogative of the party to issue decrees to the state, and continued by asserting that it was the prerogative of the Central Committee to act through the individual commissars. Clearly the Central Committee was not bound by constitutional and juridical limitations. Lunacharsky rhetorically inquires: "And why should we concern ourselves with the problem that in emergencies the Central Committee carries out its directives not through Sovnarkom but directly through one of the People's Commissars? If you examine the constitutional aspects of the problem, you will see that the Central Executive Committee of the Soviets establishes laws, and Sovnarkom within the limits of the law executes all the governmental work. The Central Committee, as the ideological-moral dominating quantity (members of Sovnarkom are members of the party and are subordinated to the Central Committee), in decisive moments analyzes problems and issues its own morally obligatory and politically sage directives."[50] Thus, according to Lunacharsky, the members of the Central Committee of the Party were morally bound to place their obligations to the party above their duties to the state and to place party directives before Soviet decrees. By virtue of the party's moral force, the Central Committee, through the commissars of the Councils of the People's Commissars, could dominate the combined executive and legislative branch of state. Through the commissars, the Central Committee of the Party could thus dominate the Commissariat of Labor and the Heads and Centers under the jurisdiction of the various Commissariats.

The Party and the Soviets

It becomes clear also that the party acted through the state and above the state, but not as the state or in the state. Just as the party maintained a distinction between itself and the trade unions, it made a distinction also between the party and the Soviets. Nor did the party attempt to organize all the working class and poor peasants in whose name it ruled. "The party," said Zinoviev, "differs from the class in that it is the most advanced part of it. . . ."[51] The Resolution on the Organizational Problem, Part C, The Relation Between the Party and Soviets, adopted at the Eighth Congress of the Party, also stated: "The Communist party is the organization uniting in its ranks only the vanguard of the proletariat and poor peasants—that part of these classes which consciously strives to put into practice the communist program."[52] The party thus intended to unite in its ranks only those who actively supported it and its policies. The party was a restricted, select and elite organization; the Soviets, on the other hand, were to unite all the members of both classes making up the state. According to the Bolshevik Resolution, "The Soviets unite in their ranks tens of millions of toilers and must try to unite in their ranks all of the working class and all the poor and middle peasants."[53] Thus those members of the peasantry and proletariat, who were left after the vanguard had been skimmed off to form the party, constituted the ranks of the soviets. The Soviets also formed the state organization through which the dictatorship of the proletariat was carried out. "The Soviets," stated the resolution, "are a state organization of the working class and poor peasants, carrying out the dictatorship of the proletariat . . ."[54] The state, however, which unites in its ranks "tens of millions of toilers" for the purpose of wielding the dictatorship of the proletariat, was to be dominated by the Bolshevik party. ". . . The Russian Communist Party," read the resolution, "must capture for itself unshared political domination in the Soviets and actual control over all its work."[55] The unshared political domination over the Soviet state which the party strove to obtain was to be acquired by organizing in all Soviet institutions disciplined communist fractions subordinated to the party.[56]

It was through the placement of individuals who could be controlled by the party center, therefore, that the Bolshevik leadership sought to dominate the Soviet state structure. Also the party was in need of large numbers of personnel for the administration of the regime it was seeking to establish. Furthermore, even though such personnel would have been relatively very small in relationship to the total Russian population, their numbers were large enough to present a problem of control for the party. Moreover, it is very likely that the reason the party found it so necessary to expound the distinctions between the party and the state was because this distinction was previously not understood by its rank and file members. There are also indications that the explicit and forceful statement of this distinction seems also to have been motivated by the rivalry between Lenin and his supporters within the party, on the one hand, and the Left Communists on the other. This conflict, however, is not to be discussed here. In its resolution, moreover, the party leadership made it clear that party members were not to bestow their loyalties, first of all, upon the government institutions in which they were employed. Their primary loyalties were to be to the party. They were not to regard themselves, first and foremost, as servants of the state. The resolution complains that "the best forces of the party are ebbing away from the party organization into the Soviet, giving away all their energy and all their time to Soviet governmental work."[57] The party leadership also made it clear, in its resolution, that the party was not to be fused with the state. It was to retain its own identity. "It is not fitting in any case," the resolution read, "to blend the functions of the party collective with the functions of the state organs which are the Soviets. Such blending would yield ruinous results. . . . The party must carry out its own decision through the Soviet organs within the framework of the Soviet constitution. The party strives to direct the activity of the Soviets, but not to take the place of them."[58] The Soviets, therefore, were a necessary means by which the party was to govern the state, but the party was not to become the state. It was to remain above it. It will be noticed, also, that the resolution stipulated the party was to carry out its decisions through the Soviet organs within the framework of the Soviet constitution. This seems to contradict the previously presented evidence brought forward to show that the Bolshevik party did not consider itself bound by juridical limitations to the state power. It must be borne in mind, however, that it was the Central Committee of the Party that claimed the right to bypass both the Central Executive Committee of the Soviets and the Councils of the People's Commissars themselves. This prerogative of over-riding and ignoring the rights of state organs at their own initiative was not to be allowed to party members outside the Central Committee. All the lower party members were to be subordinated to strict discipline and surveillance. Although the party was to control the soviets through its party members in the soviets, these party members were not themselves to exercise a personal authority. The resolution makes it clear that ". . . the party organization must never resort to petty tutorship over the soviets. It must impress upon its members, that membership in the Russian Communist Party, does not grant any privileges but only lays a more serious responsibility upon them."[59] Party members in the soviets, therefore, were to act only as agents of the party leadership, or of the party leader, Lenin. They were not to act without the direction of the party. The resolution affirmed: "The stringent discipline of all by a single member of the party is necessary. All members of the party, even if they do not occupy important posts, are unconditionally under the control of the party."[60] Thus, all party members, from the highest echelons to the lowest, were to be undeviatingly subordinate to the single party leader. Nor were all party members to have equal rights within the party. Justifying the limitation of the rights of party members by the charge that the party had been infiltrated by insufficiently communistic elements, "careerists," and "hangers-on," the resolution stated: "This even results in the completely correct limitation of the electoral rights of members of the party at the All-Russian Party Congress."[61] Not only were the electoral votes of party members curtailed, but the resolution asserted that "A serious purging of both soviets and party organizations is necessary."[62] Thus, both party and soviet members were threatened with expulsion from the party or soviets—and the concomitant consequences of that expulsion—if they did not act in accordance with the party program.

From the above evidence it becomes clear that the party not only intended to dominate the Soviet state through the Bolshevik party, but that it explicitly stated this intention to its members. It sought also to achieve this domination through party personnel. The resoluion quoted above also indicates that even within the party there were individuals who devoted their energies to the soviet organization rather than to the party. There is also evidence to show that the soviets resisted the domination of the party.

Local Soviets and V.S.N.Kh.

Soviet resistance to party domination was especially marked on the local level. It seems that it was not until about the end of 1920 that the party was able to penetrate down into the local soviet organs sufficiently enough to control them from the center. In 1918 it could be said, with some validity, that the local soviets were almost completely autonomous. At the Fourth All-Russian Congress of Soviets, for example, Bogolepov stated "that locally the soviets do whatever they want, and, as has been said, can make a man of a woman and vice versa."[63] Clearly the Bolshevik party, as a party striving to secure unshared political power for itself, could not tolerate this independence of local soviets. At the Fourth Congress of Soviets, meeting from 20 March to 14 June 1918, the Bolsheviks expelled from the Central Executive Committee all parties but the fraction of the Left Social Revolutionaries. In this way, in effect, they achieved complete domination of the central structure of the soviet. In controlling the central state organ, the Communists also had considerable leeway and room for maneuver by virtue of the fact that the Soviet Constitution did not clearly set forth the organization of the Soviet structure.[64] In practice, however, according to the Left Communist Sapronov, there was a conflict between the local soviet organs and those at the center. "On the one hand," said Sapronov, "local soviets often considered themselves a power, completely autonomous locally, so that they were in no way subordinate but existed independently; on the other hand, it was the tendency of the central organization to take the opposite road, i.e., the abolition of all power locally."[65] Thus, in 1919, a conflict existed between the central and local soviets concerning the degree to which the localities would remain independent of the center. It has been shown above that in 1918 and 1919 there was also a conflict over power between the Central Executive Committee of the Soviets and the People's Commissars, and that the latter acted as instruments of the Central Committee of the Party. Sapronov contended that the functions of the Central Executive Committee were being appropriated by the People's Commissars and the Heads and Centers, and he objected to this appropriation.[66] He and other Left Communists sought to weaken the People's Commissars by subordinating them to the Central Executive Committee of the Soviets and making them responsible before it. Locally, also, they proposed to subordinate the branches of the Commissariats, the Heads and Centers, to the appropriate executive committees of the local soviets, i.e., to the *Guberniia* Executive Committees in the provinces, the *Uezd* Executive Committees in the districts, etc.[67] In accordance with the structure of the Soviet state, it was presumably these executive committees, and the local legislative and executive powers, that were to exercise jurisdiction over the economic matters which the Heads and Centers were administrating. These economic matters were, of course, fraught with political significance and consequence. The Heads and Centers, however, were not subordinated to the Executive Committees, but by the end of 1918 to the Supreme Soviet of the People's Economy (V.S.N.Kh.).[68] In speaking of the establishment of the Heads and Centers and their local branches which undermined the authority and jurisdictions of the Executive Committees, Sapronov charged that other government departments had started out on that road; ". . . but then V.S.N.Kh. began to take it more cleverly and more decisively. It convoked its own congress, the plenum of the Soviets of People's Economy which elected its own praesidium. This praesidium often said to the Executive Committee of the *guberniia, uezd,* or of the city, that I am not subordinate to you, that this is an economic organization which exists parallel to the Executive Committee, etc."[69] Thus the Supreme Council of the People's Economy set itself and its branches against the soviet state structure. In particular, the V.S.N.Kh. and its branches were opposed to the local Councils of the People's Economy, which were originally established as organs of the Soviet state for the purpose of administering the economy in the localities. V.S.N.Kh., however, worked through the Heads and Centers, not through the *Sovnarkhozy* (the Councils of the People's Economy [S.N.Kh.]). The Heads and Centers, operating in the localities, were not under the jurisdiction of the local Councils of the People's Economy.[70] It is natural, therefore, that conflict arose between these two different kinds of organizations. The Heads and Centers asserted their authority in the name of both the central government and the process of administrative centralization. The local Councils of the People's Economy defended their prerogatives in the name of the rights and privileges of the localities. They represented a federative rather than a centralizing point of view. They represented also, it would seem, one of the forces of the revolution; opposition to the bureaucratic centralization of tsarism and the power of the center versus the rights of the localities may be seen in conflict here. The Communist Arskii, writing on the Congress of the Councils of the People's Economy, where the matter of centralization versus decentralization was discussed, said: "The center of gravity of all problems between the so-called 'centralists' and 'decentralists' lay in the problem of the mutual relations between the Heads and Centers on one side and Councils of the People's Economy on the other. Here two definite points of view stood in conflict: one demanded the complete subordination of the local Councils of People's Commissars to the center, the other tried to preserve almost complete independence."[71]

At the Congress of which Arskii was speaking and at which the proponents of centralism fought against the proponents of local rights, it was the centralists who triumphed. "All the economic power and regulation of the local economy and economic life" was transferred by the Congress to the Supreme Council of the People's Economy and its branches.[72]

This was a victory, however, not only for the proponents of centralism, but for the Bolshevik party. It was a defeat not only for the government made up of soviets, but for the Left Communists as well.

V.S.N.Kh. and Its "Dispatched Individuals"

The means by which the Supreme Council of the People's Economy chose to enforce its authority upon the local councils of the people's economy was simple in both its conception and execution. Of its effectiveness, however, there can be little doubt. To enforce its policy upon the local councils of the people's economy, V.S.N.Kh., the Supreme Council of the People's Economy, dispatched its representatives to them bearing mandates to carry out the instructions of V.S.N.Kh. The instructions defining the mutual relations between the individuals dispatched by the Supreme Council of the People's Economy and the local councils of the people's economy stated: "Individuals dispatched by the central organ of V.S.N.Kh. and the local Councils of the People's Economy must be guided as follows: . . . "1) Upon arrival at the locality it is necessary for the individual dispatched to appear immediately at the praesidium of the local Council of the People's Economy, to present his mandate and to explain the conditions of work connected with the fulfillment of the commission entrusted to the dispatched individual."[73] Thus the individual entrusted with a commission by V.S.N.Kh. had to present his mandate to the local councils of the people's economy and explain how his instructions were to be carried out.

The same paragraph of the Instructions stated: "2) For the fulfillment of the task entrusted to the dispatched individual, he uses within the limits of his mandate and to the necessary degree, the appropriate executive organ of the local Council of the People's Economy."[74]

The bearer of the authority of V.S.N.Kh., therefore, was empowered to use the administrative apparatus of the local council of people's economy itself in order to fulfill his mission. The instructions took into account that the local councils of the people's economy might have attempted to malinger or obstruct the work of the delegate by claiming to be organizationally incapable of carrying out the instructions he gave them. To avoid this and to deal with the case, if it were actually so, the delegate was required to inform the central institution concerning the local council's presumed inability to execute the orders of the delegate. V.S.N.Kh. could then empower its delegate to create a new organization capable of carrying out his orders, for the instructions read: "3) In those cases in which it is shown that the local Council of People's Economy, in the person of its organs, is not in condition to give the necessary assistance to the dispatched individual in the fulfillment of the task laid upon him, the latter immediately informs his dispatching central institution about this.

"Note 1—By the order and direction of the appropriate central organ (the Heads, Centers, etc., or of the production branch of the V.S.N.Kh.), the dispatched individual may be allowed the right to reorganize the existing or create a new apparatus of a temporary or permanent character attached to the local Council of the People's Economy. . . ."[75]

V.S.N.Kh. and its Heads and Centers, therefore, had the power not only to carry out their policy and program through the local economic organs of the Soviet state, they had the authority even to reorganize those organs or to create new ones. None of the instructions of the delegates of V.S.N.Kh. could be annulled by the praesidia of the local councils of the people's economy, and they were binding upon the latter and their organs. An appeal to V.S.N.Kh. against the instructions could be made, but its appropriate local organ had to be informed of that appeal.[76] Thus V.S.N.Kh., as a central organ established and directed by the Bolshevik party, was directly and unrestrictedly interfering in the administration of the Soviet state, especially on the local level. It was a means by which the Bolsheviks, at the center, prevented the local soviet institutions from consolidating their power. Before the local institutions had a chance to crystallize and solidify their position and relationships in the newly formed soviet state, the very foundations of their authority were shaken.

V.S.N.Kh., Bureaucracy, and the Trade Unions

V.S.N.Kh., however, not only acted in opposition to the representative governing organs of the proletarian state itself, it acquired the jurisdiction of the syndicates and trusts existing previously to the October Revolution.[77] In addition, it presided over new syndicates formed after the Revolution. As a government bureau, V.S.N.Kh. was formed out of the old bureaucratic apparatus of the tsarist regime, an apparatus that had also continued to function under the Provisional Government. "This old apparatus," said a communist writer in *Narodnoe Khoziaistvo,* the publication of the V.S.N.Kh., "must become part of it [V.S.N.Kh.] even though it is in disorder and has almost stopped working."[78] Thus, in contrast to the soviets, which were the political representative organs of the Russian Revolution, V.S.N.Kh. and its Heads and Centers were, in part, survivals of the old bureaucratic order, or imitations of them. They represented, in addition, the continuation of the syndicates and trusts of the previous regime and of war-time Russia.[79] In the struggle with the local soviet organs, as well as with the Central Executive Committee of the Soviets and with the Left Communists, the leadership of the Bolshevik party could hardly have defended openly the sponsorship of bureaucratic state organizations in opposition to the soviets. This is especially true in view of the popularity of the soviets in many places and of the resentment which existed for the bureaucracy of the old order. To avoid, it seems, accusations of bureaucracy against V.S.N.Kh. and the Heads and Centers, the latter were closely joined with the trade unions. At the head of each branch of the praesidium of V.S.N.Kh. was a *collegium* which worked out the plan of organization for the branch. Its function was to confirm the composition of the sub-branches and to introduce (and thus determine) all the current work the sub-branches were to do. All measures and decrees of a general character or more important significance had to be confirmed by the praesidium. In effect, then, the Praesidium alone could make the policy for V.S.N.Kh. Representatives of the All-Russian Union of Unions (*obedinenie*) served on the *collegia* of the corresponding industrial branches of V.S.N.Kh. All the *collegia* of the branches had to be confirmed, however, by the Praesidium. The heads of the branches were elected by the Praesidium from among the members of the *collegia.*[80] The Praesidium of V.S.N.Kh. was composed of ten to twelve men elected at the All-Russian Congress of Soviets of the People's Economy. The Chairman of the Praesidium was a member of the Council of People's Commissars.[81] In actuality, he was always a Bolshevik leader. It has been shown above how V.S.N.Kh. could override the administration of the local Councils of the People's Economy through individuals it dispatched to them. It shall be shown below how the Chairman of the V.S.N.Kh. was the final arbiter and authority over all the work of the branches.

Having shown how the unions were represented in the branches, attention will be focused now upon the relationship between the trade unions and the Heads and Centers.

The Resolutions of the First All-Russian Congress of Workingmen and Workingwomen of the Textile Industry, which took place in February of 1918, described the Center of the Textile Industry (*Tsentrotekstil'*) as follows: "The Central Committee of the Textile Industry (*Tsentrotekstil'*) is the supreme government organ uniting and directing all activity in the sphere of industry and subordinate only to the Supreme Council of the People's Economy."[82] *Tsentrotekstil',* therefore, the Center of the textile industry, was a branch of the state subordinate only to V.S.N.Kh. According to Paragraph 2, all existing organizations for the regulation of the textile industry were subordinated to *Tsentrotekstil'*.[83] This included, of course, the Soviets of Workers' Control, the factory committees and the trade unions. According to the Resolution on the Position of the Central Committee of the Textile Industry, "*Tsentrotekstil'* was made up of: a) 30 representatives, elected by the All-Russian Congress of Workingmen and Workingwomen in the textile manufacture (Workers' group *Tsentrotekstil'*); b) 15 representatives of the enfranchised groups, who are delegated by the All-Russian Union of enfranchised groups of the textile industry."[84]

Thus, two-thirds of the Central Committee of *Tsentrotekstil'* was made up of workers' representatives and one-third of the former enfranchised democracy, that is, those who had been enfranchised under the tsarist government and distinguished from the "revolutionary" or "soviet" democracy which had not been enfranchised under the tsarist regime. This latter group, in *Tsentrotekstil',* would have been composed of owners or former owners of textile plants, technicians, administrators, and bureaucrats of various sorts. The two-thirds representation of the trade unions, however, was said to give the Heads and Centers a completely proletarian character.[85] The workers were said to play a prominent role in them.[86] This, however, was the claim of the communists. Others did not regard the representation of the trade unions in the Heads and Centers as a nullification of bureaucracy. And Rudzutak, the Bolshevik, pointed out that: "In the process of all the work of our state organs—of the

Councils of the People's Economy, of the so-called Heads and Centers of the Production Branches of the Council of the People's Economy—complaints and accusations of bureaucracy were constantly heard."[87] Rudzutak, however, did not attempt to refute these accusations; rather, he justified them and apologized for them, saying that "Insofar as we are passing into a new system of production, to a new system of organization, we must preserve the old technical apparatus. It is natural that this apparatus approached new tasks with old methods of solving technical problems because it is necessary to make use of these old methods, for we have not worked out our own ways and methods of achieving and executing our resolutions and measures."[88] Rudzutak, as a spokesman for the communist party, therefore admitted that the old bureaucratic machinery of the former state was being used in the old manner by the Bolshevik regime. His solution for this was not the abolition of bureaucratic means of administration. He proposed, rather, to solve the problem of bureaucracy by making bureaucrats out of workers or, more specifically, out of trade-union representatives. "This bureaucratism may be liquidated," said Rudzutak, "only when we succeed in filling all our organs of regulation with representatives of proletarian organizations, which, in this case, are the trade unions."[89] The Bolsheviks argued, therefore, that bureaucracy would be overcome when the bureaus were staffed by representatives of the trade unions. There was no admission or, perhaps, realization of the fact that bureaucracy could be eliminated only by the elimination of bureaucratic control. To counteract bureaucracy or charges of bureaucracy, representatives of the trade unions were to staff the Heads and Centers along with bureaucrats of the old regime. Moreover, in spite of the claim that the presence of trade-union representatives in the Heads and Centers, and other branches of V.S.N.Kh., changed their character from the bureaucratic to the proletarian, the actual connection with the trade unions, at least in the first days of V.S.N.Kh., seems to have been tenuous. Osinskii, writing about the beginnings of V.S.N.Kh., stated that "the business-like connections which should have been given the workers in the production branches by the trade unions were weak. Furthermore, the unions themselves, in most cases took a passive attitude toward V.S.N.Kh."[90] The same enthusiasm which prevailed in V.S.N.Kh., for the participation of the trade unions does not seem to have prevailed among the trade unions for participation in V.S.N.Kh.

In any case, however, the role of the unions in the Heads and Centers did not guarantee to the unions a voice in the policy-making functions of those organizations. As bureaucratic institutions, the Heads and Centers were administered by decree rather than by legislative processes. Furthermore, no decree could be issued without the sanction and signature of the Chairman of the Supreme Council of the People's Economy, who, it seems, was to be sole arbiter of all policy, for the Statute of 10 April 1918 of the Praesidium of the Supreme Council of the People's Economy, concerning the order of publication of all statutes of V.S.N.Kh., stated: "Not one branch of the Supreme Council of the People's Economy can issue statutes and publish them without the signature of the Chairman of the Supreme Soviet of the People's Economy or his delegate."[91] The Heads and Centers themselves, therefore, presumably could not act without the approval of the Chairman of V.S.N.Kh. Moreover, once the unions were statified and subordinated to the People's Commissariat of Labor, they could hardly conduct an independent policy of their own within the Heads and Centers, no matter how saturated the latter were with union representatives. Nor were the trade-union representatives to the branches of V.S.N.Kh. to be elected directly by the union membership. The representatives were actually appointees designated at joint meetings of the central committees of the unions in question and the Praesidium of V.S.N.Kh., for Paragraph 8, Section (a), of the Resolution adopted by the Third All-Russian Congress of Trade Unions stated: "The Central Committee of the appropriate trade union and the praesidium of V.S.N.Kh. designates a list of candidates which is discussed and adopted at a joint meeting of the representatives of the Central Committee of this union and of the praesidium of V.S.N.Kh. at which both sides have the right to make objections. The list thus adopted is confirmed by the praesidium of V.S.N.Kh."[92] In actuality, therefore, the trade-union candidates for the branches of V.S.N.Kh. were chosen at joint meetings of the top leadership of both V.S.N.Kh. and the union in question. Since the praesidium was in a position of supreme authority and had paramount influence in the branches, its selections of candidates were not likely to have been strenuously opposed by the members of the central committees of the unions. Indeed, the central committees themselves, in all likelihood, were controlled by the party, and probably little difference of opinion arose as to the selection of candidates. The primacy of V.S.N.Kh. was not easily threatened by such a system.

Party, State and Unions

The evidence presented thus far concerning the relationship between the trade unions, the party and the state leads to the following conclusions. The policy of subordinating the trade unions to the Commissariat of Labor, a policy begun in 1918, was continued during the early part of 1919. This policy, however, was conducted in the name of statification—the promise that the unions would wield state power; but the Bolshevik intention seems to have been that the unions would remain separate and distinct from—organizationally independent of—the state. Moreover the state itself was subordinated to the party, for the party, retaining an identity separate from the state, dominated the Soviets. To weaken the control of the local soviets (councils) over industry, the party made use of V.S.N.Kh. and its Heads and Centers. In so doing, they used the remnants of bureaucratic departments of the former state to undermine the soviets. Trade-union representatives were attached to the organs of V.S.N.Kh. to mask its bureaucratic character. In 1920 it was becoming obvious, however, that some Heads and Centers had done their work only too well and that trade-union representatives were exercising real rather than fictitious power. This situation, and the manner in which the Communist Party dealt with it, must now be investigated.

CHAPTER X

The Trade Unions, the State and the Party: 1920

The Soviets, V.S.N.Kh. and Decentralization

In 1920 the relationships between the soviets (councils), the trade unions, and the Heads and Centers radically changed. In 1919 the trade unions and the Heads and Centers had been used by the Bolshevik Party to undermine the soviets. By the end of 1920, steps were taken to undermine the authority of the trade unions and the Heads and Centers by presumably increasing the economic jurisdictions of the local soviets.

The administrative organs which had been built up by the Bolshevik Party to oppose the local soviet institutions, therefore, were transferred into the jurisdiction of the local soviets they had been instituted to oppose. A decree introduced by the communist Rykov, chairman of V.S.N.Kh., and adopted by the Eighth Congress of Soviets, proposed: "To create attached to the *Guberniia* Executive Committees . . . *Guberniia* Economic Councils [*soveshchanie*] which are entrusted with the coordination of the activity of the local organs of the People's Commissariats (the Supreme Council of the People's Economy, the People's Commissariat of Agriculture, the People's Commissariat of Labor and the People's Commissariat of Finance)."[1]

Thus the *Guberniia* Economic Councils were to have the prerogative of coordinating the local branches of various commissariats, including V.S.N.Kh. In effect, then, this decree could give the *Guberniia* Economic Councils jurisdiction over the local branches of V.S.N.Kh. Paragraph 2 of the Theses on Industry and its Restoration stated, in addition, that "The creation, in the localities, of special organs of V.S.N.Kh. outside of the *Guberniia* Council of the People's Economy, with the exception of the enterprises . . . in the direct administration of V.S.N.Kh. is not allowed."[2] It will be noted, then, that V.S.N.Kh. retained its power as a central institution but that some of its branches were made subordinate to the *Guberniia* councils.

The Heads and Centers became the organs guiding and controlling the *Guberniia* Councils of the People's Economy, according to the centralized economic plan, but the enterprises themselves were placed under the jurisdiction of the *Guberniia* Council of the People's Economy.[3] In reality, therefore, the resolution did not create a clear-cut economic administrative organization but rather increased the complexity of industrial administration by the creation of overlapping jurisdictions. The system of organization was such as to encourage jurisdictional conflict among the member bureaus. In this way, the party could have balanced and maneuvered between the various economic organizations, pitting one against the other. The party could have prevented any of the organizations from taking root. Furthermore, the various organizations would have tended to compete for party support. In spite of this, the reorganizational measures were carried out ostensibly for the purpose of rationalizing the economic organization. This improvement was to be expressed "by perfecting the apparatus of V.S.N.Kh. itself, by means of removing parallelism in work, the cessation of superfluous red tape and correspondence, and the strengthening of connections between the local enterprises and the *Guberniia* Council of the People's Economy on the one hand, and the guiding branches and Heads of V.S.N.Kh. on the other."[4] In the light of the ambiguous allocations of power by the theses, it is difficult to see how parallelism was avoided. This is especially true since the local institutions, which were formerly subordinated to the central, are now presumably subordinating the branches of those same institutions to themselves. Paragraph 6a of the theses came out for "the future development of the independence, initiative and perfection of the apparatus of the local organs."[5] While increasing the role of the local apparatus, however, the centralization of the economy was to be maintained.[6]

The Bolsheviks asserted, nevertheless, that they had been forced by the Civil War to extreme centralization. "We too easily made concessions to centralistic and ultra-centralistic demands," said Zinoviev.[7] It has been shown, however, that this policy of centralization was aimed against both local rights and privileges and the power of the soviets. The function of V.S.N.Kh., its branches, Heads and Centers, was to undermine the soviets as governing institutions. The re-establishment of the economic jurisdictions of local soviet institutions was, conversely, aimed at reducing the authority of the Heads and Centers and local branches of V.S.N.Kh. The Bolshevik party, as a party above and distinct from the state, seeking to control the nation through the state, was transferring both its support and dependence from the organs of V.S.N.Kh. to the soviets. "The Soviets," said Zinoviev, "especially in the localities, must be revitalized and we must do everything which we can for this. That which we adopted yesterday on the broadening of the rights in the localities, we adopted having the soviets in view."[8] The policy of alleged decentralization, then, is a policy also of alleged revitalization of the soviets.

The Heads and Centers, Trade Unions and Localism

It has been pointed out, however, that the trade-union organization and the organization of the Heads and Centers and branches of V.S.N.Kh. were closely joined together. It has been pointed out, as well, that the trade unions, if their role was evaluated in accordance with the decrees and statutes concerning it, would act primarily as a facade for Bolshevik bureaucracy. Yet it has also been mentioned previously that there was often a difference between the decree and the political reality of its application, and there are indications that, under civil-war conditions, the Heads and Centers sometimes became autonomous or at least somewhat independent organizations. As branches of state, organizing a particular industry, they seem to have tended zealously and jealously to guard the interests of that industry. The trade unions were even accused of having captured some of the Heads and Centers. Kaktyn, Bolshevik opponent of the Heads and Centers and defender of the Councils of the People's Economy, wrote in the spring of 1919 that "One of the reasons for all the disagreement and quarrels [between the Heads and Centers and the local Councils of the People's Economy] in my opinion is . . . the extremely strong predominance of the trade unions in the Heads and regional administrations, and in the Heads and Centers themselves, and their inevitable tendency to fight for their own group trade union interests at the expense of the interests of the whole—a tendency clearly leading to syndicalism."[9] The Heads and Centers, therefore, were being accused of advancing the specific interests of the unions attached to them.

It was the charge of localism which had been levied against the soviets in the Bolshevik campaign to wrest power from them. In attaching trade-union representatives to the Heads and Centers, it had been argued that having been organized on an industrial rather than a geographical basis, the trade unions would counteract this localism. However, in 1919, the trade unions were charged with infecting the Heads and Centers with their own kind of localism.

"Often," wrote Kaktyn, "some Head or Center or Chief Administration absolutely does not want to consider state-wide interests, or the interests of the whole, placing first and foremost the interests of its own industry—or what is still worse—of its own workers, i.e., of a group of toilers against all the masses. . . . There are cases in which the Heads and Centers consider themselves completely independent and 'autonomous'. . . . This is just as reprehensible a kind of localism albeit a localism of an industry or a union, as the localism of a locality. . . . They seek to be autonomous from the central organs, from V.S.N.Kh."[10] With these charges of autonomous leanings and localism, Kaktyn indicated that the Heads and Centers were evading the control of the center. He accused them of absorbing control of parts of the economy for their own power and aggrandizement as organs of the state. Kaktyn's charges, appearing in the organ of V.S.N.Kh. itself, indicate that V.S.N.Kh. might not have been able to control the Heads and Centers which were presumably under its jurisdiction. He asserted that "V.S.N.Kh. and its guiding organs do not themselves know how many Heads and Centers, and Central Administrations, they have under them."[11] He charged that V.S.N.Kh. was itself unsystematized and internally disorganized.[12] The reorganization of the Heads and Centers in 1920 seems to lend support to Kaktyn's charges.

Further evidence to show that some Heads and Centers evaded the control of V.S.N.Kh. may be found in a speech by Tomsky at the Third All-Russian Congress of Trade Unions in April of 1920. Tomsky indicated that some of the Heads and Centers tended to function more as organs of the unions than of V.S.N.Kh. "One often hears," he said, "reproaches against a certain looseness of the organs of V.S.N.Kh., in particular of the Heads and Centers, so that it is necessary to take into account the abnormal conditions which existed in the guiding *collegia* of these organs up to now. Up to the present there has existed a relationship in which the unions, sending their representatives to the guiding *collegia* of the Head or Center, regarded them as their direct representatives who remained subordinate to the unions. From this it followed that the members of the *collegia* of the Heads and Centers in all questions which they met in their practical activity turned for instruction to their unions.

They received directives from the unions; but on the other hand they were members of the state organ. Thus there was a diarchy and indecision, a conflict of two wills which was in evidence in the most negligible problems and sometimes in important questions having a practical character. And if V.S.N.Kh. gave directions which were guided by a general economic plan, the unions sometimes, in their directives, appeared to be and felt they were the protectors and defenders of a particular industry. Under such conditions the lack of agreement resulted in want of discipline. At the Third Congress of Trade Unions . . . we must decisively put an end . . . to the interference of the unions in the direct regulation of industry."[13]

Thus, Tomsky too charged that the representatives of the trade unions who were attached to the *collegia* of the Heads and Centers acted as representatives of the trade unions rather than as the representatives of the central state. He charged that the union representatives referred to their unions for instructions concerning their policy in the Heads and Centers and claimed that the union representatives acted as the champions of their unions. He accused them of lack of discipline and of insubordination to the center. More specifically, he insisted that such a state of affairs gave the unions a direct influence upon the regulation and administration of industry, and he made it clear that this was a role the unions were not to play.

The Party, V.S.N.Kh. and the Trade Unions

It should be noted also that Tomsky implied that it was not the primary obligation of trade-union representatives to represent the interests of the unions. The representatives in general, however, seem to have tended to foster union welfare. Others might have been tempted to carve out spheres of influence for themselves as union representatives. But, in general, it would seem to have been only the most "conscious" of them at this time who clearly realized they were to assist in the subordination of the unions to the state and to the Communist Party. Since the party itself vaunted and boasted of the representation of the unions in the state economic organs, however, it is not difficult to understand why party policy toward the unions was not always easily understood by all those who were to execute it.

Party policy would not permit either the trade unions or state institutions to obtain a grip upon the economy. The three-cornered struggle of the trade unions, the soviets and the central state economic organizations seemed to have prevented any one of these institutions from acquiring power over economic life.

From the evidence presented by Kaktyn and Tomsky, however, it seems that the unions were exerting their influence on the state organizations, Heads and Centers. If the Bolshevik party was to maintain control of the economy through the state, therefore, it had to shift its support from the trade unions and the Heads and Centers and branches of V.S.N.Kh. to other institutions. If the trade unions, Heads and Centers, and similar organs were allowed to coalesce, solidify and acquire control of the industries with which they were connected, they would have been able to exert pressure upon the state and upon the Bolshevik party itself. They could have acquired political strength, if not ascendancy. This the Communist Party leadership would not, it seems, allow, even to Bolshevised institutions. The party would identify with no institutions; it identified rather with the power above the institutions.

In the shift of Bolshevik power from the organs of V.S.N.Kh. to soviet organs, the trade unions played a vital part; for the trade unions represented an organizational base which could provide an alternative for Bolshevik dependence upon the Heads and Centers. As a result of their close connections with the Heads and Centers and with the Commissariat of Labor, their organization could have been conveniently adapted to the administration of industry. Within the party itself there existed a faction which proposed such a utilization of the trade unions.

Trotsky and Statification

Administration of industry was closely connected with the problems of statification, for if the unions were to be statified, it could easily be argued that they take over or fuse with the state organs regulating industry. In December of 1920, Trotsky and his supporters advocated a policy which would, in effect, have led to their acquisition of control over the economy through the use of the trade unions. Manipulating the concept and promise of statification, Trotsky proposed to fuse the chief organs of industrial administration with the trade unions. As in all previous usage of the concept of statification, Trotsky's usage also provided for the postponement of the actual goal—the complete acquisition of state power by the unions. Trotsky proposed to fuse the All-Russian Central Council of Trade Unions with V.S.N.Kh. He proposed also to fuse the central committees of the unions with the Heads and Centers, with the *guberniia* organs, and even with individual enterprises.[14]

Trotsky made it clear, however, that this did not imply that the trade unions be statified immediately. He stated, rather, that "It is obviously not a matter of statifying the trade unions in 24 hours. That is nonsense. It is a matter actually of *holding to the course of statification. . . .*"[15] In defense of the orthodoxy of his position, Trotsky quoted what he claimed (and he was not refuted) to be an extract from the party program. This extract, it will be noted, is in accord with previous resolutions on statification. The extract stated that the trade unions, since they already participated in the administration of industry, were to take over the administration of the national economy. In this way, according to the extract, the masses would gradually participate in the management of that economy. Trotsky quoted: " 'Being already, in accordance with the laws of the Soviet republic and established practice, participants in all local and central organs of the administration of industry, *the trade unions must arrive at the actual concentration, in their own hands of all the administration of all the people's economy,* as their single economic goal. Assuring thus the indissoluble connection between the central state administration, the people's economy, and the broad masses of the toilers, the trade unions, must to the broadest degree, draw the latter into the direct work of managing the economy' . . ."[16] This seemed to promise the trade unions, and the workers organized in them, that they themselves would some day manage the economic life of the nation. It was a thesis in accord with the earlier pre-revolutionary promise that the revolution would destroy a political and economic system in which government and industrial management were in the hands of bodies of officials separate from the "people." It was a promise which before the revolution had been used to manipulate the revolutionary chiliastic mood of the workers and which after October was used as a device to postpone the chiliastic goals and project them into the future. In December of 1920, Trotsky was using this promise against Lenin, Zinoviev and their supporters in the party. While retaining the goal-postponing functions of statification, he was claiming to approach more closely and more quickly the fusion of the trade unions with the state. In his much disputed theses on *The Role and Tasks of the Trade Unions,* Trotsky attacked Leninist policy by charging: "It is absolutely inadmissible to turn the statification of the union into a final goal beyond the clouds having no influence on present practice."[17] Trotsky was dangling the promise of statification or fusion before the trade unions while Lenin was saying, "The most correct thing to do about 'fusion' at present would be to keep quiet about it."[18] Trotsky, nevertheless, would not keep quiet. Yet his intention was not to place the administration of the Russian economy in the hands of the trade unions themselves, but to place the economic organizations of the Soviet state in the hands of communist trade-union leaders. Trotsky claimed that the workers would be schooled for their role in production if their leaders managed industry. "The unions will become true schools of communism," he asserted, "when, more and more, all the broad masses see that the guiding communists in the union are the real organizers of industry, the builders of a new communist economy, and see themselves closely connected with these leaders into a single communist structure."[19] Trotsky, therefore, proposed to place the management and administration of industry in the hands of leading communists in the trade unions. His scheme seems to have been an adaptation and extension of the system that the Ninth Congress of the Party, in April of 1920, had established for the organization of transport. The Congress had set up *Glavpolitput'* (Main Political Section of the People's Commissariat for Rail Transport) as a temporary institution functioning as an organ of both the party and the Soviet state, with Trotsky as its chief.[20] The function of *Glavpolitput'*, according to Congress, was to send Bolshevik organizers to improve discipline in the railway workers' union and to reconstitute transport. *Glavpolitput'*, presumably because of its dual function—the improvement of transportation and the tightening of discipline in the trade unions—was included on both a central and a local level—in the trade union organization of railroad workers and in the People's Commissariat of Transport. In its trade-union capacities, *Glavpolitput'* had close connections with *Tsektran* (the Central Committee of the Union of Workers in Rail and Water Transportation), established at the Congress of Railway Workers in August 1920. *Tsektran* undercut the authority of the All-Russian Central Council of Trade Unions and, in effect, centralized railway union control in Trotsky's hands.[21] Nor did *Tsektran* hesitate to exert its authority compulsorily over the railway unions by any means that were effective, such as militarization and management by decree. Particular use was made of the device of "appointmentism"—the appointment rather than the election of trade-union officials to reliably force through party policy. "It is true," said Kossior, a Trotsky supporter, "no democratic niceties were observed."[22]

Though Trotsky claimed he was willing to abolish *Glavpolitput'*, he was charged with attempting to extend the organizational system developed there to the unions as a whole.[23] And it seems that Trotsky might have intended to establish control over industry and labor by means of exerting the power of the party through state economic organs. He intended, it appears, to appoint party personnel to dual functions in the trade unions and economic-industrial institutions of the state, and seems to have proposed, for example, that one-third to one-half the members of the All-Russian Central Council of Trade Unions and of the Praesidium of V.S.N.Kh. should be members of both bodies. In the case of the *collegia,* he was credited with proposing that the inter-representation should be from one-half to two-thirds.[24] In this way, control over the unions and the economy of the state could be consolidated.

Trotsky's scheme was not, in effect, a radical departure from the system of dual representation which already existed in the sphere of labor and industry;[25] but he seems to have been attempting to manipulate the trade unions into support for his proposal by the promise of statification. Also, the issue of statification provided a rationalization and, even more importantly, a mask for the struggles for power which, in actuality, Trotsky's proposal seems to represent. The issue seems to lie in the possibility that Trotsky, as leader of this movement, could not only have controlled the Soviet economy, but would also have had at his disposal a large number of offices which derived from management of trade unions and industry. By disposing of these offices, he could have built up and controlled a powerful following of officials, functionaries, or bureaucrats dependent upon him. It would have been possible to establish a series of institutions and a body of personnel dependent upon a single leader, Trotsky. Trotsky's position in such a case would have been further advanced by his actual close connections with the army, militarized labor, and the sphere of transportation. It was probably this struggle for power within the party that lent intensity and bitterness to the quarrel between Trotsky and Lenin over the role of the trade unions in December 1920.[26]

At any rate, a decree of the Central Committee of the Party abolished *Glavpolitput'* and its equivalent in water transport—*Glavpolit-*

vod—by a decree published in the *News* of the Central Committee of 20 December 1920. The methods used by *Tsektran* (and the decree seems to be referring to "appointmentism" in particular) were to give way to "normal methods of proletarian democracy." *Tsektran* was to be reduced to the same status as other unions in the All-Russian Central Council of Trade Unions. In February a Congress of Railway and Waterway Workers was to be convoked at which "normal elections" were to be held for a new *Tsektran*. Until then, however, the old one was to continue functioning. Although the decree condemned methods of "reconstructing the trade-union organizations from above," it must be borne in mind that such practices as "appointmentism" were not the monopoly of *Glavpolitput', Tsektran*, or Trotsky.[27] Kossior does not seem to have been speaking without cause when he said: "Now a democratic wind is blowing and you are beginning to shout: not all democratic principles were observed . . . 'appointmentism,' etc."[28] and added: "If in the past our party changed some harsh methods or other, does that mean that now . . . we must sit in judgment over them?"[29] Indeed it does not seem fundamentally to have been the policies of *Tsektran* that evoked the opposition of Lenin and Zinoviev, but its powers.[30]

Lenin and Zinoviev on Statification

Moreover, Trotsky's use of the concept of statification forced the Leninist group of the Communist Party into a clarification of its stand on that issue. Lenin's assertion that the only thing to do about fusion was to keep silent about it,[31] was in itself a clarification. Nevertheless, Lenin himself did not keep quiet. He explained that the dictatorship of the proletariat was not to be a dictatorship of the trade unions; for political leadership belonged only to the vanguard of the working class, i.e., to the party. The trade unions, however, encompassed all of the workers. They could not, therefore, expect to execute the role of political leadership, which was to be played only by the few. The trade unions were to be a link between the party and the masses organized in them. They were to be an organization acting between the party and the state. "The place the trade unions occupy in the system of the dictatorship of the proletariat," said Lenin, "is, if we may so express it, between the Party and the state power. In the transition to socialism, the dictatorship of the proletariat is inevitable, but this dictatorship is not achieved by the organizations which embrace all the workers without exception. . . . What happens is that the Party, so to speak, absorbs into itself the vanguard of the proletariat, and this vanguard carries out the dictatorship of the proletariat."[32] For the very reason, then, that the trade unions were to include all the workers in their organizations, they were unfit to implement the dictatorship of the proletariat. According to Lenin, ". . . it is impossible to carry out the dictatorship of the proletariat through the proletariat organized as a whole without exception. . . ."[33] The dictatorship was not to be implemented by the unions enrolling as many workers as possible, but by a small, select, elite group—by the Communist Party. Lenin explicitly stated, also, that "The Party is the directly ruling vanguard of the proletariat, it is the leader."[34] He tried, however, to placate the trade unions by assigning them a function which was useful for the proletarian dictatorship. He did not, however, explain in his speech of 30 December 1920 what the specific relationships between the trade unions and the state were to be. Lenin indicated merely that the unions, like the state, provided an organization through which the party could exert its power.

"Without a foundation like the trade unions," Lenin declared, "it is impossible to carry out the dictatorship, it is impossible to fulfill state functions. They have to be carried out through a number of special installations, again, in their own way, of a new type, namely, through the Soviet apparatus."[35] Lenin thus indicated that the trade unions were institutions upon which the state depended in carrying out the proletarian dictatorship.

Zinoviev, in his speech of 30 December 1920, is somewhat more definite than Lenin on the relationship between the Soviet state and the trade unions. Declaring that the trade unions were the most important part of the proletarian dictatorship, he added that they were, nevertheless, not organs of state power. "The trade unions," said Zinoviev, "are the most important component parts of the dictatorship of the proletariat. But this cannot be construed to mean that the trade unions themselves are the direct implements of the dictatorship, direct organs of state compulsion. No, for this we have purely state organs, for this we have the soviets behind which the party stands."[36] Thus, the only organs of compulsion were to be organs of the state. The party, in turn, was the power behind the state. The trade unions were to fulfill tasks which were removed from the exercise of power, and they were to absorb and organize all the proletariat. In so doing, they would place labor within a framework in which the party could easily lead it. Furthermore, it must be pointed out that the trade-union task of increasing membership in the unions would, according to Bolshevik reasoning, make them less fit to rule; for it follows logically from Lenin's assertion that the trade unions were unfit for dictatorship, because they were to include workers without exception, that the more workers they included, the less fit for dictatorship they would be. In addition, according to Lenin, the proletarian masses were unfit to carry out the dictatorship of the proletariat because they were degraded and corrupt. "But it is impossible," said Lenin, "to achieve the dictatorship of the proletariat through its all-inclusive organization. Because not only among us, in one of the most backward capitalistic countries, but even in all other capitalist countries, the proletariat is still so atomized, so servile, so corrupt in some places (namely by imperialism in certain countries) that the all-inclusive organizations of the proletariat cannot achieve this dictatorship directly."[37] Lenin thus implied that the proletariat had to establish its dictatorship through the mediation of the party. Insinuating that the proletariat was not sufficiently mature to unite together for the purpose of the dictatorship, he reminded it of its supranational composition and the debasement of some of its members contaminated by capitalism. He thus emphasized again the party's role as mediator and the role of the unions as inclusive organizations of the working class, distinct from its leadership.

Zinoviev, in accord with Lenin, while denying the trade unions the function of state organs, insisted that the task of the unions was to organize the labor masses. "The trade unions . . .," said Zinoviev, "fulfill, so to speak, the manual labor in the organization of the working masses. . . . We must bear in mind that these organizations have special tasks: *not* directly to command, *not* to issue orders, not directly to dictate, but tasks which, first of all boil down to attracting mass millions into the stream of the organized proletarian movement. The drawing of millions of non-party workingmen and workingwomen into this stream in order to give them, within the framework of the unions, the elementary lessons of communism, in order to teach them the fundamentals of the proletarian movement and to lead them further and further—these are the tasks of the unions. . . ."[38] Hence, it was the function of the unions to draw the non-party members of the working class into the union framework, within which the party could direct and control it, and educate the proletariat in communism. That the proletariat was said to have been in need of education implies that it was politically immature and unfit for political action, that it was incompetent to choose its goals and the manner of reaching them. The unions, as mass organizations of the politically inept, were to be segregated from the party, which as an elite group was to remain separate and distinct from the mass organization it controlled. In so far as the proletariat was unaware of communist goals, or opposed to them, from the Bolshevik point of view, it may be said to have been in need of the education by which it would be made to accept or submit to Bolshevik leadership. However, if labor was regarded as being capable of taking its place in political life, then it would need no "education."

Lenin, clarifying the relationship between the trade unions and the party, made a distinction between the trade unions and the masses whom the trade unions were supposed to organize, and indicated that the unions were to be over the masses, not of the masses. "The trade unions," said Lenin, "create a *link* between the vanguard and the masses, the trade unions by their daily work, convince the masses, the masses of that class which is the only one in a position to take us from capitalism to communism. This is one side of the matter. On the other side the trade unions are a reservoir of state power. This is what the trade unions are, in the transition from capitalism to communism."[39] The trade unions, therefore, were to form a connection or a bond between the party and the masses. At the same time, they were to provide a reservoir—a politically inactive source of power—which the party could draw upon when needed. This, in essence, was the position of the trade unions as Lenin defined it in December of 1920. On the specific question of fusion, however, he kept silent. Nevertheless, Zinoviev, as Lenin's chief supporter in the dispute with Trotsky over the trade unions, did clarify the question of fusion.

Zinoviev, speaking on 30 December 1920, also said: ". . . we are *against immediate* statification, we are even *against* the artificial hastening and forcing of this process."[40] Since Trotsky did not advocate the immediate statification or fusion of the unions with the state, the Leninist opposition could not attack him on those grounds. They attacked, therefore, Trotsky's assertion that the road to statification had to be shortened. Zinoviev insisted that the process of statification should not be accelerated in any way. Such an acceleration, according to Zinoviev, who did not say how, would hinder the trade unions from being schools of communism.[41]

Further, the concept of the unions as schools of communism was introduced to combat the statification of the trade unions without seeming to abrogate the promise that the workers would some day administer industry. While relegating the problem of statification to the realm of silence and oblivion, the Leninists propagated the concept of the unions as schools of communism. This concept seems to have been a further goal-postponing device, one which also served to emphasize the distinction between the unions as the proletarian body of the state and the party as its vanguard. The concept of the unions as schools of communism further served to underline not only that the unions were not to exercise state power but that they were not yet ready to assume their proper role in the soviet state. A trade union, said Lenin, "is not a state organization, it is not an organization of compulsion, it is an educational organization, an organization that enlists, that teaches, it is a school, a school of administration, a school of management, a school of communism."[42] In these schools, the workers were to learn, trade-union leaders were to teach, neither were to rule. "What," asked Zinoviev, "does 'school of communism' mean? If it is taken seriously, this is the definition. It means, first of all, it is necessary to *teach* and *educate* and *not* to command in the school of communism."[43] With this statement Zinoviev attacked the Trotskyite opposition that sought to use the trade unions as a basis for controlling the economy. Zinoviev warned that the function of union leaders was to teach, not to command. The trade unions were to be schools of communism, not organs of power. As such, they could not play the role that Trotsky had designed for them.

Trotskyist View of Schools of Communism

Kossior charged that the unions as they existed could not be schools of communism because they had only negligible influence upon their members. "The unions," he further said, "were not able to give the masses economic, industrial or even practical education. . . . And in order to turn the unions into real schools of communism one must give them a field of production, practical work and the possibility of fulfilling it."[44] Kossior, as a supporter of Trotsky, insisted that the unions be given state functions in the field of production and the means to carry out those functions. "We believe," he said, "that the unions must become schools of mass production and in order to do this we must turn the unions into business-like organizations, place them close to production, join them to the work of the Councils of the People's Economy, give them definite rights and functions as organs of power. . . . We are for such schools of communism. Other schools of communism cannot be."[45] Thus, Trotsky and his adherents were proposing to join the unions with the economic councils, to exert a portion of state power through them and make them organs of industrial production as well as labor organizations. Labor unions in this way would not be "statified," would not be organs of state power, but would be a means through which the state and party would dominate industry. Perhaps the suggestion that the unions be schools of production was a popular one, for although directed against the Trotsky fraction, the party decree calling for new elections for *Tsektran* uses words reminiscent of Kossior's stating that the masses had to be drawn into "organizations and actual administration. Therefore methods of workers' democracy must be methods of production workers' democracy."[46]

The Soviets and Control of the Economy

To eliminate, it seems, any possibility of Trotsky's combining the control of the unions with the control of the state economic councils, which were part of V.S.N.Kh., the local organs of V.S.N.Kh. were placed under the control of the local soviets. Zinoviev, therefore, speaking at the Eighth Congress of Soviets on 28 December 1920, and referring to Trotsky's proposal, said: "Some of our comrades think that now, in connection with the restoration of the economy and the epoch of economic revival the chief work is to be done not in the Soviets but in the trade unions. I have heard such an opinion from eminent comrades. Since we are faced with the restoration of the economy, it would now be a mistake to dream of the restoration of the soviets. In their opinion not the soviets are to be restored, but the trade unions. Is this true? No, it is absolutely not true. The role of the trade unions will grow to be gigantic. The economic role of the trade unions will increase with every day. That is true. But the soviets must not and will not stand aside from every day work."[47]

Zinoviev made it clear, then, that the soviets and not the trade unions were to take over the economic administration of the state. Originally, however, V.S.N.Kh. had been established in order to wrest control of the economy from the same local soviets to which economic jurisdictions were now being transferred. Also, the trade-union personnel had originally been poured into the organs of V.S.N.Kh. where they allegedly served as representatives of the trade unions and as an alleged counterbalance to bureaucracy. At the end of 1920, however, many organs of V.S.N.Kh. were being removed from its jurisdiction and placed under the control of the soviets. The role of the unions and some of the branches, Heads and Centers of V.S.N.Kh. in the administration of the economy was being curtailed, and the role of the soviets was presumably being increased.

In order to fully understand, however, the political reality in which the trade unions functioned, it is necessary to investigate briefly the degree to which the soviets were able to exercise their authority.

First of all, it must be pointed out that from the first to the second half of 1920 the political composition of the *Guberniia* Executive Committees increased from 89 1/2% communist (and 12 1/2% non-party) to 91% communist.[48] This, however, does not seem to have been enough assurance to the Leninist faction in the Central Committee of the Party that the soviets would be in their control. Four principal methods seem to have been used to keep the soviets in line. One was the reduction of the number of soviet employees. Another was the right of suspension of the decrees of the People's Commissariat of Labor. A third was the continued use of "dispatched individuals" to carry out the decrees of the center directly at the localities. Worker-Peasant Inspections were a fourth method of control over the soviets and other institutions.

First Method of Dominating Soviets: Reduction of Soviet Employees

The reduction of the numbers of soviet personnel was closely connected with the problem of bureaucracy. It has already been pointed out that the pre-soviet Russian state employed a large bureaucratic force. It has been pointed out also that many of the bureaucratic departments of the previous governments had been retained by the Bolsheviks and adapted to their needs. In addition, the expanding Bolshevik state-capitalist system, and the concurrent decline in private enterprise, left the state as the principal, and in some cases the sole, institution where the *sluzhashchie* (employees, or white collar workers), technicians, and former bureaucrats could find employment. This situation was aggravated by the penalties for unemployment and the relative desirability of a state post from the point of view of its economic and social rewards. It is with this in mind that Zinoviev's speech at the 6th meeting of the Eighth Congress of Soviets shall be presented. In this same speech in which Zinoviev announced the primacy of the soviets over the trade unions, he discussed the problem of soviet employees and bureaucracy. The definite announcement of the predominance of the soviets over the trade unions would seem to have assured the employee and bureaucrat of his predominance over the proletarian. It assured him that it would be possible to preserve his status, that he need not be declassed. There was, however, a price to pay for status.

Zinoviev, in discussing the problem of Soviet employees, reminds them of both the desirability and the insecurity of their position. "You know," he said, addressing the Congress of Soviets and speaking of Soviet institutions, "that among us now, staffs are very easily created, institutions expanded, departments inflated. Thousands of new Soviet employees are gathered together who do no productive work, who puff up our apparatus, and make it less muscular, less capable, less fit for work. Why is this?"[49] Having pointed out in this way that Soviet institutions were overstaffed and inefficient, Zinoviev then reminded the Soviet employees he was addressing that they were in desperate need of their posts and of the rivalry that existed for such offices. ". . . Our social revolution," he said, "placed tens and hundreds of thousands of people who now call themselves Soviet employees into a position in which they can insinuate themselves into a livelihood in no other way except through service."[50] It was upon this stratum of the population that Zinoviev placed the onus and responsibility for what he considered overstaffed bureaus. He implied that the Soviet leaders had been helpless against the pressure of those who wanted employment in the Soviet administration: "We can make as many resolutions as possible, but if, at the same time, . . . tens and hundreds of thousands of people press upon us in many cities seeking to find some kind of work for themselves, we cannot by any means fight against the swelling of bureaucracy in our apparatus. . . ."[51] It was these individuals, according to Zinoviev, who carried the plague of bureaucracy. It was these excess, would-be employees of Soviet bureaucratic organs whom Zinoviev accused of infiltrating into Soviet institutions and of making them bureaucratic.

"From these Soviet employees there is formed . . . ," Zinoviev claimed, "a reserve army which weighs upon all our institutions and by its weight undermines our defenses, somehow or other infiltrates, and somehow or other bears with it, this bureaucracy."[52] Zinoviev made it clear that he understood well the desperation in which this "reserve army" found itself. He made it clear also that one of the avowed objectives of the Bolshevik revolution had been to destroy the bureaucratic state. Zinoviev then warned the Soviet employees that 10% and then 20% of them had to be eliminated from the service. This, he said, would solve the problem of bureaucracy. Protesting, however, that the transfer of Soviet employees to manual labor would not be a repressive measure, Zinoviev betrayed the threat involved in such a policy. ". . . We cannot take real measures, comrades," he said, "until we first transfer 10% and then 20% of our Soviet employees to other work, for until then we cannot seriously solve the problem of bureaucracy. Not in any case, however, should we, when transferring Soviet employees to other occupations regard this transfer as repression."[53] The purge of Soviet employees, Zinoviev ironically continued, was not to be carried out for the sake of unpleasantness. The transfer of Soviet employees to factories and shops, he claimed, was merely a matter of expediency.

If the full impact of Zinoviev's words upon his audience is to be understood, it is necessary to take cognizance of the fact that, at this point in the history of the Soviet state, unskilled labor was being organized into military battalions subject to military discipline. Since it would seem that very few of the Soviet employees could be classified as skilled workers, it would perhaps have been, in many cases, labor battalions to which the expelled Soviet employees would have been assigned.[54] Sardonically, then, Zinoviev continued his speech by saying: "We should not treat the matter in such a way as with the greatest possible unpleasantness to purge that stratum which is not purely proletarian. It is a matter of the more expedient use of manpower in order to give people work which is in accordance with their strength and which will be useful to the Soviet power. In our proposal we mentioned the transfer to such work of 20% of the employees, but of course, it is impossible to do this in one day, for it is necessary to carry it out coherently and systematically. It may be compared with the struggle for illiteracy with which we have to fight not only for a month and not only for a year. Other kinds of work have been found at the factories and shops where we can use the labor of the employees in order to decrease the reserve army and to begin the economic redistribution of working hands at our disposal."[55] Thus, the transfer of 20% of Soviet employees was not to take place in one operation which would leave the remaining 80% free of the dangers of the purge. The transfer was to extend over an indefinite period of time. In this way, all Soviet employees feeling that threat of transfer to factory or manual labor hanging over their heads would probably have tended to vie with each other to prove their loyalty, devotion and usefulness to the Bolshevik regime. Certainly the threat delivered by Zinoviev to the overwhelmingly communist assembly to which he spoke would have tended to reduce to a minimum, if not to obliterate, opposition by the adherents of Trotsky and others to control of the Soviets by the dominant Bolshevik fraction. Trotsky was offering to create and bestow bureaucratic posts; Zinoviev was threatening to remove from these posts those who already held them. The latter seems to have been a more effective method of ensuring allegiance than the former. One dealt with future offices and emoluments, the other with a present reality. This was the first method which the Bolsheviks used to control the soviets.

Second Method of Dominating Soviets: Suspension of Decrees

The second device to control the soviets was a clause in the decree on Soviet structure, a clause which presumably gave the local organs of the Soviets the right to suspend the decisions of the People's Commissariats. This clause, however, was merely a facade behind which the suspension of any decree was made extremely perilous. Any *Guberniia* Executive Committee of the *guberniia* soviets that suspended a decree of a People's Commissariat was responsible before the courts. A suspension not upheld by the courts became an offense. Zinoviev, speaking of the third section of the decree on Soviet structure, stated: "In this section there is a clause giving the localities the right to suspend the decision of the People's Commissariat. This is a very serious clause. If any *Guberniia* Executive Committee suspends a decision of the People's Commissariat, it must do so with the consciousness that it takes upon itself a great legal responsibility, since it will then answer to the state, . . . You have the right to suspend a legal decision but if you do it, you must do it after mature consideration since you will answer for this before the courts. And finally, if the decree of the People's Commissariat is proven to be inapplicable, it will become an offense and the [People's Commissariat] will be held legally responsible for the guilt in issuing an incorrect decree. This will hold in the exact same way for the institutions in the localities."[56] Here, Zinoviev does not seem to be referring to a mere juridical reversal of a decision. His statements seem to imply that those guilty of an unwarranted suspension would be subject to punishment. Indeed, soviet employees, according to a decree of the Eighth Congress of Soviets, were subject to administrative punishment and arrest merely for violation of service discipline.[57] However, in the light of the statement previously uttered concerning the transfer of 20% of the soviet employees to factory labor, Zinoviev's warning concerning the misapplication of a suspension could not but have been stunningly effective.

Third Method of Dominating Soviets: Plenipotentiaries

The third device for subordinating the soviets to the party, like the previous ones, was hidden behind a facade of what it was not. It may be found in the portion of the decree on Soviet structure which committed the government to abolishing the system of dispatched individuals—the plenipotentiaries sent by the center to the localities.[58] Zinoviev, speaking of the provision, stated: "Another point of the third section also possesses great importance where it is said that the central government must strive to abolish the system of plenipotentiaries. This point is connected with the problem of appointees, the use of whom we cannot immediately reject. We will give up this practice gradually because in such a huge country as Russia it is still impossible to do without them. We send them to places where they sometimes meet with hostility. But we must remember, they are sent either by the party or by representatives of the central power and each appointee can become a local worker. And at first, it would have been impossible to work without them. . . . We must move toward the abolition of this system and it is possible to begin to do this only now when we have a new generation of workers who can carry out the directions of the center."[59]

Thus, Zinoviev revealed the dependence of both the party and the central state organs upon plenipotential emissaries. He revealed at the same time, it would seem, an active and widespread opposition to Bolshevik measures; for it was that opposition that necessitated their dispatch. He made it clear also that the party would be able to do without such representatives only when the voluntary subordination of the localities to the Bolshevik center and their ability to enforce its decrees would be such that the use of special emissaries would become unnecessary.

Fourth Method of Dominating Soviets: Worker-Peasant Inspections

The fourth control over the soviets and their institutions is found in the Worker-Peasant Inspections. These organizations were established by a decree of the Seventh Congress of Soviets, which met in December of 1919. The Eighth Congress of Soviets revived and extended the activity of these inspections.[60] The Worker-Peasant Inspections were organized as organs of control connected with the local "toiling masses," both peasants and workers. The function of the inspections was purely one of control, that is, "to see how the execution corresponded to the task." The Worker-Peasant Inspections had no administrative executive, organizational or legislative functions. They were to do nothing but to oversee the work of the soviet institutions. Since they probably could not, as peasants and workers, effectively perform functions of technical review, it would seem that they were to act as harassing agents for the party.

To prevent the identification of the inspections with any of the institutions they were to observe, the inspections were prohibited from having any connections with these organizations by means of representatives or otherwise. Thy were to be completely external to the organs inspected. All soviet institutions were to be supervised by the Worker-Peasant Inspections. These inspections were supported by the central treasury and were thus made independent of the local organizations over which they were to perform functions of control.[61]

The Trade Unions and the Party

While tightening their control over the soviets, the Bolsheviks were, at the same time, placing the control of the Heads, Centers and branches of V.S.N.Kh. under the jurisdiction of the local soviet organs. In so doing they were undercutting any independence, autonomy, stability or power acquired by the Heads, Centers, or branches, and trade-union representation in them. Simultaneously, the fraction of the Central Committee of the Communist Party, supporting Lenin, was undermining Trotsky's scheme to gain control of the economy and trade unions. Trotsky had been attempting to acquire this control through a system of dual representation, i.e. by combining the functions of trade-union leaders with the functions of the administrators of the state economic institutions. In winning their struggle against Trotsky, Lenin and his supporters also succeeded in reducing the power and the expectations of the trade unions. By the end of 1920, therefore, the relationship of the trade unions to the party can best be described by the Theses of the Central Committee of the Communist Party, which had been issued earlier in the year, in March of 1920. By the end of the year, these theses seem indeed, in their broad outlines, to have become a reality. The main shift in emphasis from March to the end of December 1920 is from the organizational-economic task of the trade unions to their educational tasks. However, even in March the educational task of the trade unions had been brought forward to a position of prominence. The Theses of the Central Committee therefore stated: "The tasks of the trade unions lie, for the most part, in the organizational-economic and educational spheres. These tasks the trade unions must fulfill, not in the capacity of self-sufficient, organizationally isolated forces, but in the capacity of one of the basic apparatuses of the Soviet state, directed by the Soviet party."[62] Thus, the trade unions were to be an instrument of the Soviet state directed by the Communist Party. Although organizationally separate and distinct, they were not to be self-sufficient or independent of the state. Part II of the theses, therefore, further defined the relationship between the trade unions and the state. The theses asserted that the state included the peasantry as well as the proletariat. The Mensheviks many times used this assertion to argue for the independence of the unions, for, as previously noted, they espoused the point of view that the trade unions should be independent of the state in order to defend the particular interests of the working class against a state made up of peasants as well as workers. The Bolsheviks used the argument to indicate that the Soviet state, since it included the peasantry, was a broader organization than the workers alone. As such, they implied, it was superior to the unions.[63]

The Theses of the Central Committee of the Communist Party declared: "The Soviet state is the most manifold and universal form of workers' organizations which achieves in practice the construction of communism, ever drawing into this work broader masses of the peasantry. On the other hand, the soviet state is a kind of workers' organization which has at its disposal all the material means of coercion. Being the proletarian dictatorship, the Soviet state is the lever of the economic revolution. Therefore, there can be no talk of organs of trade unions opposing the organs of Soviet power."[64] Hence, while maintaining the peasant-worker character of the state, the theses also maintained that it was a workers' organization having a monopoly of coercive forces. By claiming to be the lever of the economic revolution, the Bolsheviks were here killing two birds with one stone. They had formerly held, in order to block the unions from state power, that the unions were the economic organs of the proletariat while the soviets were the political. When the soviets were designated as the economic lever of the revolution, however, it became the function of the state rather than the unions to attend to economic measures. Since the state also claimed to be a proletarian dictatorship, the unions, as the organization of the same proletariat, could not, according to the Bolsheviks, oppose the state.

The theses inveighed against any opposition to the single will of the proletarian dictatorship to which the unions had to be subordinated, reading that ". . . Therefore, the opposition of the trade unions as economic organizations of the working class, to the soviets as its political organizations, is, in general, absurd and is a deviation from Marxism towards bourgeoisdom, in particular bourgeois trade union prejudices. Such opposition is especially absurd and harmful in the epoch of the dictatorship of the proletariat when all its struggle and all its activity, both economic and political, must be more than ever united, concentrated, directed by a single will, bound by an iron unity."[65] Thus demanding the subordination of the trade unions to the state, the Bolsheviks defined the relationship of the unions to the party as Lenin and Zinoviev were to present it again in December of 1920. The theses referred to the trade unions as: ". . . a school of communism and a link connecting the most backward masses of the proletariat who have still not been liberated from the old guild [*tsekh*] and trade union narrowness, with their vanguard the communist party. . . ."[66] Hence, the trade unions seem to have been regarded as a burdensome impediment, hindering the unions' forward-straining vanguard—the party.

The theses, then, once again betrayed the fear that the trade unions might capture the state by asserting that ". . . the trade unions . . . must gradually be transformed into subsidiary organs of the proletarian state and not vice versa."[67] Having thus established the fundamental relationship between the Soviet state and the trade unions, the theses reiterated that "The Communist Party is the organization of the vanguard of the working class, the guide of the proletarian movement and of the struggle for the communist order," and then added that the party was to lead the trade unions by means of the communist fractions and cells in them.[68] The trade unions as a whole, however, according to the theses, were not to be communized.

"The Party," the theses read, "exerts its influence on the broad non-party strata of the toilers through the communist fractions and cells in all other workers' organizations, the trade unions first of all. Only to that degree in which the trade unions remain formally non-party, will they become communist in essence, and carry out the policy of the Communist Party—only to this degree, will the dictatorship of the proletariat and the Communist Party be assured."[69] The Central Committee of the Communist Party thereby insisted that the unions remain a non-party organization. It has already been pointed out that the Communist Party feared the unions might capture the state. The insistence that the unions be a non-party organization suggests that the Central Committee also feared that the unions could capture the party. It seems as though the party considered that if union members, as a whole, became party members, the character of the party as an elite vanguard would have changed and the leadership would have lost its hold. The party, as it existed, might have been inundated by a more representative whole determining its own goals, its own policy, and its own course of action.

The theses decreed that there had to be a communist fraction in each union. The party fractions in the local unions were to be subordinated to the local party committee. The party fraction in the All-Russian Central Council of Trade Unions was to be directly subordinate to the chief central organ of the party—the Central Committee. Having stated that the dictatorship of the proletariat could be assured only if the trade unions carried out the policy of the Communist Party, the theses continued as follows: "Therefore, there must be, in each trade union, a disciplined, organized fraction of communist. Each party fraction is part of the local organization, subordinate to the party committee, and the fraction of the All-Russian Central Council of Trade Unions is subordinate to the Central Committee of the Russian Communist Party."[70] Within this chain of command the decrees of the All-Russian Central Council of Trade Unions (itself immediately subordinate to the Central Committee of the Party) were compulsory not only for the unions, but also for the party fractions in them. The local party committees were expressly informed that they were in charge only of the ideological work of the unions and were not to take charge of any other aspects of union affairs. The relations between the local party fractions and the trade unions were defined by the party statutes: "All the decrees of the All-Russian Central Council of Trade Unions concerning the conditions and organizations of labor, are compulsory for all trade union organizations and also for members of the party working in them, and cannot be changed by any other party organ except the Central Committee . . . The local committees, completely directing the ideological work of the trade unions, should in no way have recourse to petty tutelage over them. The relations between the local party fractions and the party fractions in the trade unions are precisely regulated by the appropriate paragraph of the party statutes."[71] Only the Central Committee, therefore, could change the decrees of the All-Russian Central Council of Trade Unions, and the relationship between the local party fractions and the party fractions in the trade unions were defined and delimited by party statutes.

However, to understand more fully the various ramifications of the theses, especially the insistence that all decrees of the All-Russian Central Council be compulsory for the party members in the trade unions, the conflict of December 1920 must be borne in mind. It was probably becoming clear as early as March of 1920 that various party members in the trade unions were using their party status to manage, at their own discretion, the trade unions, or the economic institutions to which they were attached as union representatives. One of the ways in which Trotsky seems to have built up his support by December 1920 seems to have been by gaining the adherence of such communist union leaders.[72] The March theses might have been proposed partly to prevent such a situation. If so, they do not seem to have been immediately successful. The party strove also to prevent its members on the lower, local levels from exercising "petty tutelage," i.e., from guiding local unions in accordance with what they, as individuals, thought the party meant. The party fractions in the local unions were to act as "the eyes and ears of the party," but not as its brains. Instructions of the Central Committee of the Russian Communist Party state that the lower party members were to exercise no personal authority of their own. They were merely instruments of, and informers for, the party: "None of the members of the Communist Party cells at work can interfere directly in the activity or the management of the administration . . . but in case of abuses by the latter, or sabotage, or neglect of business, can appeal to the appropriate Commissariat of Labor, bringing it to the attention of his party organization at the same time."[73]

It is to be noted also that members of the party fraction in the trade unions, on the local level, appealed infringements of communist orders not to the party, but to the Commissariat of Labor. This appeal was to be reported simultaneously to the party organization. Thus, the Commissariat of Labor, as a state organ, retained jurisdiction over the problem. Simultaneously, however, the party, acting behind the facade of the Commissariat of Labor, which also served to intervene between the local party fraction and its upper levels, could follow and control the appeal. Furthermore, it must also be remembered that party cells existed in the state organs as well. Moreover, between the local party members and the higher party echelons there were intervening organizations which kept the local party personnel removed from the source of power. Not only were they prevented from acting directly, neither could they see, observe, follow or understand how the party made its decisions. They, like all others involved, could see only the result of party decisions and party actions, not the process through which party action evolved. This is especially true since party and Soviet rule was rule by decree rather than by legislation. Legislation is the result of deduction from generally accepted principles; decrees are the result of expediency and the demands of the moment. Since Bolshevik ideology itself demanded a correct reflection of an ever-changing reality, and communist consciousness implied the foresight with which to act in conformity with that reality, government by decree and in accord with expediency was not only compatible with the ideology but even encouraged by it. Furthermore, there are no intermediary stages between a decree and its application. Many, therefore, can understand and follow the legislative process. Only a few experts are cognizant of the complexities and convolutions of the ever-changing decree. Thus the local party fractions, acting as sentinels and informants for the party, were to assure speed of communication, when necessary, from the locality to the center. They were to assure the center of constant knowledge of local activity. However, the system of intervening blocks of authority, through which the lower party members communicated with the Central Committee, obstructed and denied access to how and why the party reached its decisions and made its decrees. It served to make the reasoning of the authorities abstract and remote while their decisions and actions remained immediate and real.[74]

Furthermore, in examining the relations between the trade unions, the state and the party, it must be borne in mind that as the Bolshevik Party increased its power, these relations, as well as the situations in which these institutions were involved, were increasingly determined by decree. It must also be borne in mind that it was the party center and not the party as a whole that issued decrees.

The Party, the State and the Trade Unions

From all the evidence presented above concerning the relationships among the trade unions, the party and the state, it becomes clear that the party maneuvered between the trade unions and the state, holding itself always separate and distinct from each. At the same time, however, it used each of the other two as a means of exerting its domination over the nation. It used the soviets to check the power and ambition of the trade unions or their leadership, and it used the trade unions as a check upon the power of the soviets. To diminish the role of one, the Bolsheviks increased the role of the other. The party, by decree, created, abolished, and rearranged institutions. It reshuffled their internal organization. The Bolshevik leadership would allow no institution to take root, to solidify, to rival the power of the Central Committee of the Communist Party.

In spite of the party's avowed purpose of achieving a planned and rationalized economy, the role of the trade unions and the Soviet economic organs in this economy was determined ultimately by political considerations, not by criteria of economic efficiency. "Politics," said Lenin, in speaking of the functions of the trade unions, "cannot but have precedence over economics."[75] The party ruled through bureaucracy, simultaneously attacking and threatening the bureaucracy, through which it ruled. The three-cornered struggle of the Soviets, the organs of V.S.N.Kh., and the trade unions seems to have assisted the party in balancing itself above all these institutions. The party permitted over-lapping jurisdictions while it constantly inveighed against the parallelism of the organs it used or created. Such a conflict in jurisdictions, while often injurious to the economy, was frequently advantageous to the Bolsheviks. Before the power of the party was firmly consolidated, the rivalry among various organs of the state and between those organs and the trade unions served to prevent any organization from acquiring more power than the party. Having used the trade unions and the soviets as a facade behind which the bureaucracy that managed the economy could function, the party also attached trade-union representatives to the bureaucracy to forestall the trade-union demand to become governing organizations of the state. The very promise of statification was the result of Lenin's pre-October claim that the workers themselves would perform the functions that, under capitalism, are performed by management and bureaucracy. The assertion that the trade unions were schools of communism served to keep this promise alive while further postponing the goals such "schooling" was to achieve.

Having investigated the relationships among the trade unions, the Bolshevik Party and the state, it is necessary now to examine again the problem of workers' control.

CHAPTER XI

From Workers' Control to Workers' Administration

Bolshevik Repudiation of Workers' Control

The Bolsheviks had promised the abolition of bureaucracy. They had promised that the functions which had been performed by bureaucracy and management would, in the future, be performed by the proletariat. A brief recapitulation of the problem of workers' control will show that, largely as the result of Bolshevik pre-October policy, many factory committees carrying out workers' control, as they conceived it, at the beginning of 1918 were managing or sharing in the management of their enterprises. Moreover, in view of the Bolshevik dependence upon the factory committees in the months after the October Revolution, they could not immediately and directly repudiate the policy of workers' control, especially since the appeal of workers' control had proved its effectiveness in acquiring adherents for the Bolsheviks. The Bolsheviks, therefore, seem to have chosen the expedient policy of claiming to continue and extend workers' control. Simultaneously, however, they undermined the functions of that control and undercut the factory committees at the individual enterprises.

The essence of workers' control was the power of the workers' committees within the individual factories at which they were employed. The reality of workers' control, as far as most workers seem to have been concerned, was represented by shared ownership of their own factories and by a voice in the management of them. This, to the workers, seems to have been a condition of socialism. To the Bolsheviks, on the other hand, socialism meant the centralization of all industry and its control by the Party through the state. The Bolsheviks opposed, therefore, the solidification and institutionalization of the factory committees and of the relationships demanded by workers' control within the factory, for the solidification of such control and the institutionalization of such relationships would have hindered seriously the state control the Bolsheviks were going to establish.

BUKHARIN'S SOLUTION TO WORKERS' CONTROL

In attacking workers' control as the workers conceived it, Bukharin, for example, suggested in his pamphlet *The Program of the Communists* (*Programma Kommunistov* [*bol'shevikov*]), published in 1919, that the majority of the administration of a factory be made up of workers and employees (*sluzhashchie*) who were not employed at that factory. Although such a system, in reality, would have represented none of the workers working at the factory, Bukharin nevertheless claimed that this system would have protected the interests of all the working class as a whole. "It is obvious," wrote Bukharin, "that we must create such a workers' administration of the enterprise that would accustom the workers to the viewpoint that each factory is the property not of the workers of *that* factory, but *of all the working people*. This can be achieved in the following way. At each factory and at each shop there must be a *workers'* administration, but it is necessary to constitute it so that the *majority* of this administration, is not composed of the workers of that factory, but consists of workers sent by the trade unions. . . . If the administration is composed of workers and employees . . . and the majority of the workers will not be from the given factory, that factory will be administered in accordance with the interests of all the working class as a whole."[1]

By thus reasoning that no workers owned any part of their own factories, the Bolsheviks insisted that all workers owned all factories. Bukharin suggested, therefore, that the factory administration be staffed by workers and employees who were not employed at the factories that they were presumably to manage, but be assigned, by the trade unions, the Soviet of Workers' Deputies, and the *Oblast'* (Territorial) Soviets of the People's Economy. This, in effect, would have taken the management of the factories out of the hands of the factory committees and the workers employed at the factories. It would have placed the management and administration of individual factories in the hands of the centralized trade unions and state institutions in which the Bolsheviks were consolidating their control. On the ground that the factory administrations would have been composed of workers and employees, Bukharin claimed that such a system would be the non-bureaucratic control of all industry by all workers. This scheme, however, would have placed the administration of industrial enterprises in the hands of individuals unfamiliar with the organization and the problems of the factory they were presumably to manage. Splitting the management of each enterprise among the representatives of three different organizations, Bukharin's scheme might have made it possible for conflict to develop among them. This conflict, coupled with a lack of familiarity with the enterprise on the part of the soviet and trade-union representatives, might have allowed for the possibility that the factory committees, rather than the trade-union representatives, could have continued to function as the effective factory administration. Thus, unlike the conflict among state organizations—a conflict which served to enhance the primacy of the Bolshevik Party—a conflict within the factory administrations probably would have made Bolshevik control over the individual factories more difficult. Perhaps for this reason Bukharin's proposal was not carried out.

Bolshevik Solution to Workers' Control

The Communist Party took other, more effective, means of undermining the factory committees, means which allowed the party to acquire greater control over the individual factories. The Bolsheviks removed the management and administration of the individual factories entirely from the hands of the workers, whether appointed by a central institution or not. The Bolsheviks retained the control commissions set up by the factory committees, but the management of the enterprises returned to the owners. For example, the Resolution on Workers' Control, adopted by the First All-Russian Congress of Trade Unions, stated: "Managerial [*rasporiaditel'nyi*] rights relating to the administration of the enterprise and its management remain to the owners. The control commission does not participate in the administration of the enterprise and does not bear the responsibility for its management, which remains to the owner."[2] Hence the factory committees and their control commissions had no administrative functions or rights. In addition, the financial problems of the factories and shops, as previously pointed out, were entirely removed from the competence of the control commissions, which were, in effect, deprived of any real voice in its policy.[3]

The Bolsheviks had encouraged formation of control commissions before October. These control commissions, and the factory committees of which they were a part, functioned to hamper ownership and management and to undermine the industrial base of the Provisional Government. After October, partly in order to wrest control of the factories from the factory committees where the latter had succeeded in taking them over, the Bolsheviks attempted to place management directly in the hands of the owners.

The control commissions or the factory committees were not only denied managerial functions but, according to the above-quoted Resolution on Workers' Control, the factory committees were also to be subordinated to the control-economic commissions of the trade unions. In a manner reminiscent of Bukharin's suggestion, some of the control commissions at the factories were to be individuals not employed at the factory but delegated by the trade unions of the branch of industry to which the factory belonged. The control commission not only contained representatives of the trade unions who were not employees of the factory, but these members were to keep the union informed of the activity of the control commission. Since the unions were supervisory organizations, the union representatives, through the reports they were required to submit to the trade unions on the members of the control commission, could keep the latter in subordination to the unions.[4]

As an additional and more effective means of controlling the control commission and all the workers of the factory, the Resolution on Workers' Control provided that the control-distributive commission of the trade union could demand the recall and re-election of the control commission. The control-distributive commission of the union could also request the state regulating institution to close the factory temporarily or to fire the workers if the latter resisted the decrees of the union commission. Therefore, by calling for the re-election of the members of the control commission, by temporarily shutting down the factory, and by firing all, or some, of the workers, the unions were given the means of controlling the factory committees.[5]

The control-distributive commissions of the unions were also empowered to re-allocate raw materials, fuel, machinery and personnel from one factory to another.[6] This could also have been a prerogative which, if used politically, could exert overwhelming pressure upon the factories involved. Bearing in mind Lenin's injunction concerning the precedence of politics over economics,[7] it would seem to be likely that the power to re-allocate factory resources was used to reward factories that submitted to the Bolshevik regime and to punish those that did not.

It has been previously demonstrated that many factory committees opposed centralization. They also had an existence separate from the trade unions. If, however. they resisted the fulfillment of union decrees, and if the provisions for re-allocating fuel, equipment and personnel were applied politically, the resistance of the factory committees, and of the workers loyal to them, could have been broken. Therefore, the political implications of this resolution should not be underestimated.

Partly by such threats against insubordination on the part of the control commissions and the factory workers, the authority of the trade unions and the state organs of Workers' Control seems to have been imposed upon the factory committees and the individual factory enterprises. At the same time, moreover, the control commissions themselves were used to prevent the acquisition of full and complete authority by the factory management.[8] In the early part of 1919 the Bolsheviks decreed that the control commissions were to serve as an agency to collect data concerning the enterprise and present them to both the factory administration and to the control branch of the industrial union. Paragraph 5 of the Decree on Workers' and State Control, passed by the Second All-Russian Congress of the Soviets of People's Economy, stated: ". . . in each nationalized, industrial, trading, transport, etc., enterprise, the local control commission takes upon itself the inspection over the running of the enterprise and the activity of the factory administration for whom it collects and systematizes all the facts relating to the running of the enterprise and presents them to the branch of control of its own industrial union before whom, in necessary cases, it raises the question of designating the investigation of the enterprise."[9] Thus, the control commissions were to serve both labor and management, and could suggest to the union's branch of control that the enterprise be investigated. It could, however, make no decisions of its own.

Schooling Workers for Management

It has already been shown that the factory committees were subordinated to the trade unions and that the trade unions were subordinated to the party and the state. In addition, it has been demonstrated that the Bolshevik Party, while wresting control of industrial enterprises from the factory committees, claimed to be extending the control of the workers over all industry. The Bolshevik made still another claim. They claimed that in centralizing the administration of industry and in using the trade unions to subordinate the factory committees, they were schooling the workers for their role in managing and organizing all of the industrial life of the country. Paragraph 6 of the Resolution on Workers' Control, adopted by the Second Congress of the All-Russian Soviets of the People's Economy stated: "The industrial unions . . . must take the most active part in control on a state scale in order that organizations of workers' control be created which will be united under a single plan and a single center and which would be organs of the gradual preparation of the broadest masses of the working class for the direct participation in the matter of administration and the organization of production."[10] Once again, therefore, the Bolsheviks reiterated that they were going to train the workers for the task of participating directly in the management and organization of industry. The resolution did not state that the working class would administer and manage industry directly. It stated that the workers would participate directly in that administration. However, in light of the promises the Bolsheviks had made, there was little in these words to indicate that the Bolsheviks meant to remove labor from the management of industry. Nevertheless, under the guise of training large numbers of workers, the Bolsheviks were rendering ineffectual, in the control commissions, those units made up of the workers representing the factory, for the latter formed only part of the control commission; the other part was made up of the representatives of the trade unions. According to Paragraph 10 of the resolution, "The local control commission is organized, a) of the representatives of the appropriate industrial (trade) unions, b) of individuals elected by the general council of workers of the factory who are confirmed by the committee of the appropriate industrial (trade) unions."[11] Thus, that part of the control commission which was elected by the workers at the local factory had to be confirmed by the trade union. In spite of this, however, members of the control commission delegated by the trade unions would remain the permanent core of the commission, whereas the members elected by the general council of the factory were to serve only for "the shortest possible time."[12] Moreover, the Bolsheviks claimed that by thus permitting the elected representatives of the factory workers at the individual factory to serve the control commission for only short periods of time, they were training the workers for management. In spite of the claim that this would train the largest number of workers for administration, however, this could not have been the effect of such a policy. In actuality, the workers who represented the factory would not have had time, as a result of being rotated in rapid succession, to acquire the practice and knowledge necessary for the administration of an industrial enterprise. The rapid rotation of the members of the factory who served on the control commission could have functioned to prevent any of these workers from gaining a knowledge of the problems of the factory. The practice of rotation, therefore, would have put the workers elected by the council at a great disadvantage in relation to the permanent members of the control commission who were delegated by the trade unions. The latter could have acquired an over-all knowledge of the factory problems which the factory representative would not have had the time to obtain. Also, since factory representatives were always to be replaced, the permanent members of the control commission would not have had to take the opinions of the former seriously into account. It is this kind of administrative activity—this rotation of workers in functions of control—to which Lenin seems to have referred when he claimed that the workers were being trained to take over the administration not only of industry but of the state as well. The most important task of the trade unions, said Lenin, "is to teach the masses the art of administration . . . from practical experience, so that . . . larger and larger numbers, ever newer sections of the workers, may enter departments, and that the place of each new section may be taken by ten others like it"[13] Lenin seems to have been referring to the system of rotation established by the trade-union congress at which he spoke these words, and he promised that this system of training workers in administration would one day enable greater numbers of the proletariat to assume the functions of government. Nevertheless, the measures taken to deprive the factory committees of their managerial functions, and the measures taken to replace the workers of the factories on the control commissions in the shortest amount of time, were in all likelihood designed to prevent the acquisition of managerial functions by the workers, not to foster such an acquisition.

Workers' Responsibility for the Economy

If the workers were being prevented from acquiring managerial functions, however, the pretense at administration that the control commissions were allowed served as a means by which the Bolsheviks could remove from themselves the responsibility for economic conditions. Lenin, while reiterating that the workers should be taught the administrative process, placed upon the working class the responsibility for the successful management of the economy. "We shall find," said Lenin, "that we can . . . teach vast masses of the working people the business of administering the state and administering industry, that we can develop practical activity and shatter the pernicious prejudice which for decades and centuries has been implanted among the working masses, namely, that administration of the state is the business of the privileged few, that it is a special art. That is not true. We shall inevitably make mistakes, but now every mistake will serve to teach . . . millions of working people who will personally suffer the consequences of every mistake, will themselves see that they are faced with the urgent task of registering and distributing products, of increasing the productivity of labour, and who can see from experience that nobody will help them if they do not help themselves. That is the new mentality that is awakening in the working class. . . ."[14] Thus, by claiming to be training the workers for administration, the Bolsheviks were transposing from the party to the workers the responsibility for economic conditions. At the same time, they reminded the workers, by insisting upon the necessity for "training" and "schooling," that they were unfit for the managerial tasks they were supposedly to fulfill. Labor was accused of being imbued with the ethical insufficiencies and deficiencies of the capitalist society in which it had previously lived. "The workers were never separated by a Chinese wall from the old society," said Lenin. "And they have preserved a good deal of the traditional mentality of capitalist society. The workers are building a new society without themselves having become new people, cleansed of the filth of the old world, they are still standing up to their knees in that filth. We can only dream of cleansing ourselves of that filth. It would be the height of utopianism to think that this can be done all at once. It would be utopianism which, in practice, would only postpone socialism to kingdom come."[15] According to Lenin, then, what he conceived to be the stain and defilement left upon the workers by capitalism rendered the workers incapable of realizing socialism in the present. Until the working class was cleansed of the filth in which Lenin claimed it wallowed, he implied that socialism could not be achieved. Furthermore, to act upon the assumption that capitalist stains could be rapidly eradicated from the workers would only postpone socialism all the more.

At the same time that the Bolsheviks were trying to convince the workers of their unworthiness for the fulfillment of socialist tasks, they were trying, nevertheless, to convince the workers that they were in possession of economic power. They were attempting to persuade the workers that "power is in their hands and that nobody will help them if they do not help themselves."[16] However, the workers were not placed in a position in which they themselves could exercise managerial control over industry. The control commissions and factory committees in nationalized enterprises served as a facade behind which the workers employed at the individual enterprises could be deprived of an effective voice in the management of those enterprises. The trade unions were used to deprive the control commissions of their functions and to eradicate workers' control as the workers conceived it.

Workers' Control in Private and State Enterprises

However, since workers' control was found still to be useful to the Bolshevik regime, even after October in private enterprises, a distinction had to be made between workers' control in private and state establishments. Arskii, in an article on workers' control, pointed out that the control commissions in the private enterprises were to serve as a check upon the owners and were gradually to remove the latter from the factory administration. He made it clear that this was not to be the case in the nationalized enterprises, for, he asserted, "The circle of activity and the framework of these [control] commissions actually differed from the work of the control commissions in the non-nationalized enterprises, where they gradually cut out the masters, suspending, if necessary, some of his decisions, checking each step in practical work, accounting for all income, expenditures, etc."[17] Such a check placed by the workers upon private owner was not to be tolerated, according to Arskii, where the management was an organization of the workers' state, an organization which claimed to represent the proletariat as a class.

Arskii continued: "A similar cutting out [as the control commissions cut out the owners] by one workers' organization of another similar and close to it in function and obligations is absolutely undesirable and there is no reason to hasten its gradual cutting out by means of the work of the control workers' commissions."[18] Control therefore was to be used by the control commissions over the entrepreneur, even though the latter supposedly retained managerial rights and was responsible for the management of the enterprise; but the control commissions in private enterprises had to review the measures of the owner before they were put into effect. In nationalized enterprises, measures taken by the management could be examined by the control commission only after they had been instituted. Arskii wrote: "In respect to the private master, to the entrepreneur, the control commissions use the method of preliminary control: they take into account and consideration one or another measure before putting it into effect. In the nationalized enterprises, the control commissions must take into account that which has already been done and put into effect . . . but it is completely inadmissible to leave to them the possibility of preliminary examination. . . ."[19] Hence, the control commissions in the privately-owned enterprises were to serve as a check upon the owner. They were not, however, to hinder the management of nationalized factories.

Control by Default

As a result of their attack upon workers' control, the Bolsheviks found it necessary to obscure the role the Bolshevik Party had played in encouraging the workers' control movement. The Bolsheviks, therefore, propagated the idea that it was chiefly because the factory owners and managers had run away that the workers, through their factory committees, had taken over the factories and instituted workers' control.[20] Workers' control was thus presented as having occurred by necessity and default rather than as a result of the workers' inclinations and the leadership of the Bolsheviks. The source materials, however, do not uphold this view; rather, they definitely indicate that the workers' control movement was inextricably bound up with the workers' conception of socialism. They indicate also that the Bolsheviks took a very active part in propagandizing and organizing workers' control.

Workers' control, as many workers conceived of and organized it, gave the workers a direct voice in the management and policy-making functions of their factories, through their factory committees or control commissions. It was carried out, therefore, not by single individual workers, but by a group of representatives of all the workers.

Moreover, the collegial principle seems to have been fundamental to the revolution of 1917. A Plan of Instruction, adopted as early as March 1917 by a conference of representatives of state enterprises and institutions, stated, for example, that "The principle of collegial administration and broad democracy, i.e., the election of all members of the factory organization and the right to recall them must be the basis for the factory organization of the workers at state enterprises."[21] Factory committees, since they were elected by the workers themselves, were cited as an example of collegial management or *kollegial'nost'*. Thus collegial management, in this sense, demanded factory-committee administration or its equivalent, and the anti-collegial policy of the Communist Party after October would seem to have been directed against shared and cooperative management instituted by the factory committees.

The Bolsheviks, in combatting workers' control in 1918 and 1919, attached to the control commissions representatives of the industrial union of the appropriate industry. Also, representatives of the trade unions entered into *collegia* at the Commissariat of Labor, the Heads and Centers, and other organs of the state. These bodies or *collegia* performed their functions as a joint group, and the collective administration or control by these groups was referred to also as *kollegial'nost'*—collegial or group administration. In industry, the latter was to give way to *edinovlastie,* or one-man management. *Edinovlastie* was also concomitant with the more effective subordination to the Bolshevik Party of the trade unions, the soviets and other state organs.[22] Both collegial and one-man management were subsumed under *edinovlastie* as long as administrative responsibility was concentrated in a single individual.[23]

The problem of *edinovlastie* was closely interwoven with the problem concerning the role that labor was to play in the administration of the economy and the state, and the question of collegial versus one-man management was closely connected with the divergent concepts of socialism. It was bound to the doctrine of the withering away of the state. Lenin, for example, had emphatically stated, before October, that the state could not pass out of existence until all its inhabitants had learned how to carry out functions performed by management and bureaucracy. "For in order to destroy the state," said Lenin, "it is necessary to convert the functions of public service into such simple operations of control and accounting as are within the reach of the vast majority of the population, and ultimately of every single individual."[24] The Bolsheviks claimed, however, that these functions would have to be taught to the population before the latter could carry them out. Collegial management was supposedly a means of schooling the workers for their managerial role. In actuality, however, it served as a means of undermining the power of the factory committees which themselves seem to have established collegial control. By splitting the control commissions into permanent representatives of the trade unions and temporary representatives of the workers employed at the factory, the Bolsheviks attempted to maintain collegial "control" (though not administration) while actually negating factory-committee functions.

Thus *kollegial'nost'* demanded factory-committee administration or its equivalent. This administration was, in turn, to be elected by the workers themselves and was subject to recall. The anti-collegial policy of the Communist Party after October would seem to have been directed against shared and cooperative management instituted by the factory committees.

Moreover, as early as 1918, Trotsky had tried to convince the workers that their elected *collegia* could not replace technicians and specialists. "The elected *collegia* consisting of the best representatives of the working class but which do not possess the necessary technical knowledge," he asserted, "cannot replace one technician who has graduated from a special school and who knows how to perform a special given task."[25] Trotsky made it clear, therefore, that the workers could not do without the techniques and special knowledge in the possession of members of the managerial class. However, collegial management—and the factory committee—had allowed for the participation of technicians and specialists. The Statute on Workers' Control passed by the First All-Russian Congress of Trade Unions stipulated, for example, that technicians and specialists should be members of the control-distributive commissions, the union organs immediately above the control commissions. It would seem, therefore, that Trotsky spoke not so much for the use of technicians and specialists as against the use of factory committee *collegia* in which the workers, as well as the specialists and managers, were represented. Trotsky suggested increasing the power of single specialized individuals in factory management. However, although Trotsky proposed to free technicians from the control of the *collegia,* he did not intend to free them from strict political surveillance. Trotsky insisted that although *kollegial'nost'* was a natural reaction of the "young revolutionary class" to its former oppression, "The next step must consist of the self-limitation of the collegial principle, of the healthy and salutary self-limitation of the working class which knows where the elected representatives of the workers themselves may have the decisive word and where it is necessary to give way to technical knowledge, to the specialist who is equipped with specific knowledge and upon whom it is necessary to place great responsibility and who must be placed under vigilant political control."[26] In insisting that the workers limit their collegial control over specialists and technicians, however, Trotsky did not explain how collegial control could hinder specialists any more than the vigilant political control he proposed.

Lenin, in 1918, explained that one-man management was necessary in order to make the transition from small-scale production to large-scale trusts. To build these trusts, Lenin insisted that the assistance of former capitalists was necessary. The worker, according to Lenin, would learn from the experience of the capitalist technicians how to manage industry. Further, they could appeal the orders of any technician and request the Soviet government to remove him. Also, the Soviet state itself was to determine the bounds of the capitalist-specialist's activity and be the ultimate arbiter of his authority. Thus, the capitalist-specialist was to be subjected to pressure from both above and below. The workers were to have the right to appeal against the specialist to the state organs. Moreover, the state organs, at their own initiative, could change or annul his decisions. In addition, capitalist managers were to be under the surveillance of political commissars. ". . . In the first place," said Lenin, "in placing 'management' in the hands of capitalists, the Soviet government appoints workers' commissars, or workers' committees who will watch every step of the manager, who will learn from his experience in management, who will not only have the right to appeal against his orders, but to secure his removal through the organs of the Soviet government. In the second place, 'management' is entrusted to capitalists only in regard to executive functions while at work, the conditions of which are determined by the Soviet government, by whom they may be abolished or revised."[27] Having pointed out that capitalist technicians were to work under the surveillance of the state, Lenin added that they were to show the workers the way from small proprietorship to state capitalism.

"In the third place," he stated, " 'management' is entrusted by the Soviet government to capitalists not as capitalists, but as highly paid specialist-technicians and organizers. And the workers know very well that ninety-nine percent of the organizers and first-class technicians of really large-scale and giant enterprises, trusts or other establishments belong to the capitalist class. But it is precisely these people whom we, the proletarian party, must appoint to direct the labour process and the organization of production, for there are no other people who have practical experience in this business; for the workers, having emerged from the infancy in which they could be misled by Left phrases or petty bourgeois loose thinking, are advancing towards socialism through the capitalist management of trusts, through gigantic machine industry, through enterprises having a turnover of several millions per annum—only through such a system of production and such enterprises. The workers are not petty bourgeois. They are not afraid of large-scale 'state capitalism,' they prize it as their *proletarian* weapon which *their* government, the Soviet government, will use against small-proprietor disintegration and disorganization."[28]

It would seem, then, that the policy of one-man management could often have been used against the small individual enterprise where the factory committees represented, from the Bolshevik point of view, the small proprietor. One-man management, Lenin implied, was to bring these factories into enterprises having a turnover of several millions per annum, and he made it clear that only such enterprises were of use to the Soviet state—that small enterprises and collegial management of them were, in 1918, of no use to it.

By the end of 1919, the question of substituting one-man management for collegial control was raised at the Seventh Congress of Soviets, where it was proposed by the Left Communist Sapronov to substitute a single specialist for the managerial or control *collegia*. "In practice," he said, "we everywhere have collegial administration, not one-man management. . . . But the tendency towards the transition to one-man management has existed among us for a long time, and at present it has more than ever come into the order of the day. . . ."[29] Sapronov pointed out that often the *collegia* consisted of both workers and specialists, and he inquired which of them would remain, under one-man management. "Comrades," he said, "the *collegia* are composed of five men, three workers, two specialists. If you switch over to one-man management then whom will you place in it? The worker? But he alone cannot cope with it. The specialist? It will not do; he will work not for the revolution, but for the counter-revolution."[30] Sapronov asserted, therefore, that the specialists would not foster the cause of the party. He proposed that specialists be retained as administrators, but only under the control of workers and claimed that it was for this reason that collegial management was necessary. "We will not reject the use of specialists," he said, "but they must be only under the control of the proletariat. They must administer together with the workers and under their control. Therefore, not in any case may one-man management be permitted. . . ."[31] In objecting to one-man management, Sapronov pointed to the fact that Lenin had promised to use as many workers in administration as possible. He inquired how the workers could be drawn into management if that function was to be permitted to the specialists alone. Sapronov, however, did not suggest that the workers themselves engage in managerial functions. He suggested merely that they control the specialists. "We must decisively object to the principle of one-man management, both from the point of view of the proletariat and from the point of view of our party. . . . How will you draw them into this work when at the head of the business, at the head of the administration stands a man completely foreign to them, the *spets* [specialist]? . . . The workers must be at the head of all organs of the dictatorship of the proletariat. . . . we must make use of the specialists, but under the strict control of the working class. . . ."[32] Here Sapronov made obvious the fact that one-man management was incompatible with workers' participation in the administration of industry. By proposing one-man management, the Bolsheviks were beginning to relinquish even the pretense of schooling the workers in management. The trade unions, not the *collegia,* were to be the schools of communism. There, however, the workers were to learn discipline, not management. Management was to be the realm of the specialist.

Curtailment of the Collegia and Factory Committees: 1920

At the Third All-Russian Congress of Trade Unions, in April of 1920, the policy of *edinovlastie* was put into effect by the adoption of the Resolution on the Character and Form of Participation of the Union in the Administration and Organization of the People's Economy. In stating that the policy arose from "Technical and practical considerations," the resolution avoided a discussion of the principle involved and surrendered without a struggle the idea of *kollegial'nost'* as a measure of training the workers for administration.

In arranging the transition to one-man management, the resolution did not dissolve the *collegia*. Instead, each member of the *collegium* was made solely responsible for his particular sphere of administration.[33] The *collegium* functioned jointly, then, only to discuss problems which were general for all members.[34] Each member was to make independent decisions concerning current problems of administrative action. Administrative action, however, was distinct from administrative policy. Policy was not to be formed by the members of the *collegium,* for Paragraph 3 of the Resolution stated: "The full composition of the college is personally subordinate and carries out the directives only of the economic organs. . . ."[35] The *collegia,* thus, were actually merely the executive organs of higher organizations. They bore the responsibility for carrying out the decrees of the superior organization but did not have a voice in the formation of its policy.

At the same time that the *collegia* were given executive functions and the responsibility for executing the decrees of the economic organs of state, the control functions of the factory committees were further curtailed and subordinated to the administration. The resolution provided that the factory committees were not to take part in the administration in any way but were to execute the decisions of the trade unions. The factory committees were to be organs executing, but not formulating, the decrees of the union.[36] The primary functions of the factory committees were to increase labor discipline and labor productivity by performing disciplinary and agitational functions. In the comradely courts, the factory committees were to try and to sentence workers for violations of discipline and were also to exert pressure upon management through their right to initiate trials between the workers and the administration.[37] However, although they could try workers for factory offenses, the factory committees could merely initiate trials in disputes between the factory management and the workers: in the latter cases the union organs above the factory committees were to make the decisions.[38]

In the resolution passed by the Third All-Russian Congress of Trade Unions, control functions were finally removed from the purview of the factory committees. According to the resolution, the factory committees could exert control functions only through the worker-peasant inspections—organization which existed outside the factory and were unconnected with it. Subparagraph c of the resolution stated that one of the tasks of the factory committees was "the control over the administration through worker-peasant inspection."[39] Thus, workers' control was not to be carried out by an organization integral to the factory itself. Control functions were to be fulfilled by organs made up of both peasants and workers, organs having no roots in the individual factory.

The claim that the factory committees were participating in administration was still being made, however. The resolution, for example, stated that the factory committees were to draw all workers into production and administration by presenting the factory management with reports on the activity of labor. This activity, as shown above, was confined to the sphere of productivity and discipline. According to Subparagraph e of the resolution, one of the tasks of the factory committee lay "in drawing all the masses of the workers into the process of production and administration, in educating and interesting this mass by means of establishing periodic reporting to the factory administration (inquiries and proposals). Times and forms for such reporting are established by the union in such a way as not to violate the normal work of the factory administration."[40] Therefore, an attempt was made not only to confine the so-called administrative work of the factory committees to reporting on labor's role in the factory, but these reports containing inquiries and proposals were, it seems, to be rationalized and fitted into the general managerial scheme. The reports were to be made on specific standardized forms and presented at specific times. The factory committees were becoming subsidiary and subordinate branches of the factory management.

Attack on Factory Committees or Trade Unions?

Slowly, then, from 1918 to 1920, a constant process of attrition was conducted by the Bolshevik Party against the factory committees.

The resolution of the trade unions and the decrees of the organs of the state turned factory committee functions into a contemptuous travesty of what they had been in the October days. However, it has often been pointed out that there was often a discrepancy between the decree and reality. Further, there are indications that the vigor and roots of the factory committees seem to have been strong. They seem to have remained firmly planted at many factory enterprises in spite of the measures taken to undermine them. Lozovsky, at the Third All-Russian Congress of Trade Unions in April 1920, attested to the tenacious strength of the factory committees by stating: "You know from the experience of the past two years, especially of the last year, that very often the factory committees or collectives feel that they are absolutely independent of the union. . . . The resolution must finally subordinate these cells to the trade unions. . . ."[41] Therefore, if there is any truth in Lozovsky's assertion, the factory committees, even as late as 1920, escaped union control. Glebov, speaking at the same congress, presented the same charges as Lozovsky. "It was emphasized," he stated, "that a dual power was created at the factories, that the factory committees interfered in the direct work of administration." Glebov, like Lozovsky, claimed, then, that the factory committees still contested the power of the trade unions and insisted that they should confine themselves to raising labor discipline and carrying out propaganda work.[42] Although Glebov and Lozovsky might have been exaggerating the significance of the factory committees in order to justify a further curtailment of their activities, it might also have been possible that to some degree, in some places, the factory committees had managed to preserve their former prerogatives. It must also be borne in mind, however, that by 1920 the factory committees were supposed to have been part of the unions. Also, the factory committees were collegial units in which the trade unions presumably played the principal role. The Bolshevik attack upon the factory committees in 1920, therefore, might have been masking an attack upon the trade unions and *kollegial'nost'*.

One-Man Management: 1920

The Bolsheviks, however, in their attack upon the factory committees and *kollegial'nost'*, made use of the factory committees themselves. The factory committees, subject to the approval of the factory management, were to select individuals to perform various specific tasks. All the commissions (such as the central commission) attached to the factory committees and which had formerly attended to all special business as it arose, were to be abolished.[43] In this manner, the Third All-Russian Congress of Trade Unions decreed the end of the collegial work of the factory committees. Single individuals were to be substituted for the *collegia*.

For the transition to one-man management on a higher level within the individual factory, the Resolution on the Character and Form of the Participation of the Union in the Administration and Organization of the People's Economy provided that one-man management could be instituted when, for the office of the leader, there was the undisputed candidacy of a worker who had also been a professional revolutionary. He was to be assisted by a specialist.[44] The reverse of this was also possible. A specialist could be appointed if a worker were appointed to assist him.[45] One-man management, therefore, could be exercised by a professional revolutionary worker with the assistance of a specialist or by a specialist with the assistance of a worker. It becomes obvious, then, that one-man management was actually two-man management. The two, of course, were not equals. One was to manage and the other was to keep a constant check upon him. In this way, it seems, the Bolsheviks sought to assure both the technical qualifications and the political reliability of its managers. To do this, two men were necessary for one-man management. It is difficult to see, however, how such a system could have been more efficient than the collegial system. Unless one of the individuals on the two-man one-man management teams was constantly in agreement with or in subordination to the other, it would have been difficult for them to resolve the conflicts that arose. Such conflicts could probably have been more easily settled in a *collegium* made up of several men where various shades of opinion, capable of supporting one or another view, might exist. In the case of two men, a difference of opinion could more easily lead to an impasse. If these conflicts, therefore, were presented to the higher organs of control and management for their solution, each such conflict would have weakened the management, or manager, at the individual factory. Such a situation, it would seem, could have served to subordinate the single enterprise more effectively to centralized control.

For workers who were appointed to managerial posts, the Third

Congress of Trade Unions demanded a combination of political, technical and managerial qualifications that would have been hard to find. They demanded political reliability, experience, technical training, and managerial talent. Such individuals could be appointed by the unions only with the sanction of the economic organs of the state: "The unions, naming in agreement with the economic organs, candidates for the organs of the administration of production, must pay attention to the following necessary qualifications of the worker: a) the political and trade union qualifications; b) practical experience and special technical training (irrespective of specialized education); c) administrative and organizational capabilities."[46] It is not clear what the resolution meant by "practical experience and special technical training (irrespective of education)," but it would seem that this would refer to highly skilled workers of some sort. Rank and file workers could hardly have met the stipulated qualifications for managerial functions.

Workers' Administration and One-Man Management

By all these means cited above, however, the Bolsheviks curtailed the activity of the factory committees and reduced to nothingness workers' control as it had been understood by the workers. The transition from control and management by the workers at the individual enterprises to control of the workers in all enterprises, through the trade unions directed by the state and Communist Party, is known as the transition from Workers' Control to Workers' Administration. Workers' Control existed before October, when the workers took over the factories from the owners. Workers' Administration was enforced by the Bolsheviks after October in the process of nationalization and of state and party domination of industry. The Statutes of 1919 of the All-Russian Union of Metal Workers read, "The October Revolution making completely possible the putting of workers' control into effect, raised the question of the nationalization of industry and that itself brought up the task of 'Workers' Administration.' The past year of the proletarian dictatorship is known as the epoch of the transition of the proletariat in all important branches of industry from Workers' Control to Workers' Administration and Organization of Production."[47] This transition represented, as the previously presented discussion of the sources demonstrates, a steady weakening of the factory committees and the increased centralization of the management of industry.

The radical difference existing between workers' control and workers' administration is admirably illustrated by the Statute of the Metal Workers' Union, which stated: "Being a revolutionary slogan in the period before the October Revolution, workers' control, as it is proclaimed and conducted in its original aspect, now in the period of workers' administration, is unconditionally reactionary since it deflects the consciousness of the working masses from the tasks of administration."[48] Those workers, therefore, who were intent upon running their own factories could not fulfill very well the tasks of Workers' Administration and were lacking in consciousness of their duties under socialism.

One of the logical results of Workers' Administration was the elimination of *kollegial'nost'* and the adoption of one-man management. It was natural also that this one man should be either two men, one a specialist and one a worker, or that he should be a specialist alone.

It is clear also that one-man management, as decreed by the Third All-Russian Congress of Trade Unions in 1920, was designed to eliminate all interference by any organization in managerial activity. Rykov, speaking at the Third All-Russian Congress of Trade Unions, stated that as soon as one-man management was established, the manager alone was responsible for the factory administration. He therefore was not to be subject to interference. "As soon as we have created such an an administration . . ." said Rykov, "no interference in management either on the part of the trade unions, or on the part of the party organizations, or on the part of the executive committees is admissible. . . . When it is organized, it and only it answers for the factory. The factory administration should not allow interference in the administrative functions by the representatives of any organization in any case. . . ."[49] Thus, no local organization at the factory, whether it was the factory committee, the trade union or the party cell, should, according to Rykov, take any part in factory management. Such activity was to belong to the one-man administrator alone.

The One-Man Managers

According to Trotsky, these one-man managers were to be made up of a core of party workers whom the party had been transferring from post to post since the founding of the Soviet state. Trotsky claimed that it was largely through the judicious assignment of these individuals from one place to another that Soviet rule was successful. "Our top stratum of the working class," he said, "is very thin. This stratum saw the underground, knows the revolutionary struggle, has seen Europe, part of it has read much in prison or in exile—this is the most precious part of the working class with the broadest horizons. Then, there is a younger generation of the revolution who physically participated in our revolution. It is a very valuable part of the working class. Wherever you look—at the Soviet structure, at the structure of the trade unions, at party work, at the civil war front, we everywhere and always made use of this basic capital of the workers. All the life of the Soviet Republic for the past two or three years consisted of the fact that we maneuvered and transferred this advance stratum of the workers from one front to another . . ."[50] Hence, according to Trotsky, the Bolshevik regime depended a great deal upon maneuvering its dependable force of revolutionaries from one office and function to another. It was through them, he said, that Soviet (and thus Bolshevik) policy was carried out. Trotsky asserted also that a collegial system of management was inexpedient because there were not enough such individuals to form enough *collegia*. It was necessary also, said Trotsky, that these individuals should be not only politically reliable but also administratively talented. Formal democracy and elections could not be relied upon to provide individuals with these qualifications, for according to Trotsky, ". . . we have sorted out only a few workers and we need thousands of managers of large and small enterprises. . . . Very often our administrators were selected in accordance with faith in their political capacity . . . but their capacity as administrators, as builders of industry was not taken into account. Here the principle of formal democracy, of elections, of collectivity as a principle, is impossible."[51] Since there were not enough such individuals as Trotsky described to staff *collegia,* and since he claimed that democratic elections could not guarantee their selection, Trotsky, in April of 1920, proposed that the unions and V.S.N.Kh. register, assign and transfer prominent revolutionaries with administrative talent from one managerial post to another.[52] The process of transfer would not only have made maximum use of these individuals, it would also have prevented them from entrenching their power and influence in any one place. The use of selected individuals in selected posts was also integral to Trotsky's plan for the domination of the trade unions and industry at the end of 1920.[53]

ONE-MAN MANAGEMENT AND SOCIALISM

All proposals for one-man management and all Bolshevik discussion of it reveal the objective of eliminating joint committees of workers and technicians. One-man management was to eliminate the workers as a group from the management and control of industry. It represents a retreat, in reality, if not ideologically, from Lenin's promises to the workers in 1917 that they would share in the administration of industry; and it represents a further postponement of socialist goals. In speaking of the problems of industrial administration, Lenin said: "After two years of experiece we cannot reason that we can undertake socialist construction at first. We were foolish in the *Smolnyi period* [before October]. . . . But there is nothing disgraceful about this."[54] Socialism, therefore, according to Lenin, had to be further postponed, and *kollegial'nost'* had to be given up as an immature and outmoded practice. *Kollegial'nost'*, according to Lenin, was characteristic of a period in which Russia was without power.[55] This period of powerlessness, stated Lenin, "was a period of complete *kollegial'nost'*. There is no getting out of this historical fact when it is said that *kollegial'nost'* is a school of administration . . . it is impossible to sit always at a preparatory course at school. That won't do."[56] Lenin, thus indicated that *kollegial'nost'* was a passing stage of puerile weakness which had to be given up in favor of bourgeois specialists. Under these conditions, Lenin claimed, the workers would be prepared for administration by performing any functions that were assigned to them. "We must govern," Lenin stated, "with the assistance of that class which we have overthrown. . . . In addition to this, we must recruit our own administrators from the ranks of our own class, we must use the entire apparatus of the state as an educational institution as a means of education outside of school, as practical preparation—all this is to take place under the direction of the communists, for the proletariat, for the workers, for the toiling peasants."[57] Hence the *collegia* were referred to as artificial institutions removed from the current of life. On the other hand, Lenin implied that the worker, merely by performing his labor in a communist regime, could acquire practical experience in management superior to the experience and training the *collegia* could provide. Also, in spite of the fact that Lenin retreated from his 1917 promise on the participation of workers in management, he continued to reiterate that promise again and again while postponing its fulfillment.

THE RED GUARDS

In discussing the means by which the factory committees were deprived of their power, the question of the factory militia arises. Lenin had claimed, in 1917, not only that the workers would participate in management and government, but also that these workers would be and should be armed.[58] Before October the party had demanded the formation of an extra-garrison (*vnekazarmennyi*) militia[59] made up of all citizens capable of bearing arms. By 1919, however, the Bolsheviks rejected the organization of a militia army. At the Eighth Congress of the Party, the congress declared against the use of a militia organized along factory and territorial lines. The army, like industry, was to be placed on a national rather than on an industrial or regional basis. Part III of the Resolution of the Eighth Congress of the Russian Communist Party on the Military Problems stated: "Rejecting, for the next historical period, the so-called all-people's character of the militia as it was maintained in our old program, we do not, in any way, depart from the program of the militia as such. We place political democracy on a class basis and convert it into Soviet democracy. We transfer the militia to a class basis and convert it to a Soviet militia. Our next program of work consists, therefore, in the creation of an army of workers and poor peasants on the basis of compulsory military training of an extra-garrison type as far as possible, i.e., in conditions closest to the labor conditions of the working class."[60] The party, therefore, resolved it would organize a militia made up only of workers and poor peasants composed out of industrial and agricultural units. The Resolution declared: ". . . That the very best army we could acquire would be created on the basis of compulsory training of the workers and the toiling peasants in conditions closest to their daily toil . . . companies, battalions, regiments, brigades, divisions which would coincide with the workshops [*masterskaia*] of the factories, the villages, counties (*volost'*), districts (*uezd*), and provinces (*guberniia*), etc. . . . We are going toward such an army. Sooner or later we shall reach it."[61] Thus the resolution continued to promise the establishment of an army as closely connected with the individual economic units as the Red Guards were connected with the factories. The goal of achieving a national militia, like most other socialist goals, however, was to be postponed. The Bolsheviks, claiming that civil war and foreign intervention did not allow time for the establishment of a militia, declared that a garrison army had to be formed immediately.[62] They stated also that the army should be a center not only of military training but of political indoctrination. According to the resolution: "All the forces of the military department are directed towards approximating the barracks to military schools, to make them the home not only of purely military training, but also of political education."[63]

The Bolshevik insistence upon political education within the army indicates, as the example of the factory committees also does, that a popular militia would probably have pursued political goals and objectives different from those of the Bolsheviks. Moreover, the transition to a garrison army marked the end of the Red Guards as a militia and left the factory committees without the military force to make the revolution which the Bolsheviks captured. Once the Red Guards were dispersed or absorbed into the Red Army and the workers' militia ceased to exist, the factory committees no longer had an arm with which to fight. Without the Red Guards, the factory committees lost their power and their independence. Without independent factory committees, workers' control, as the workers conceived it, ceased to exist. By the end of 1919 even the Bolshevik manipulation of the words and the concept "workers' control" had begun to diminish. Preoccupation with workers' control gave way to preoccupation with Workers' Administration and one-man management. Workers' control was turned away from the goals and objectives of the factory committees to the aims and purposes of the Party.

CHAPTER XII

Labor Discipline

Worker Ownership and Identification with the State

The Bolshevik Party subordinated the factory committees to the trade unions, the trade unions to the state, and the state to the party. The administration of the factory was taken out of the hands of the workers and placed in the hands of the specialist, technician, manager, and bureaucrat. To the Russian worker there was left the function, obligation and responsibility of increasing productivity.

It has already been pointed out that in spite of the fact that the workers were being deprived of factory-control functions, the Bolsheviks attempted to convince them that they were to have a share in the administration of all industry. The Bolsheviks, after workers' control had been eliminated, attempted to convince the workers that industry belonged to the workers themselves. Rykov, at the Third All-Russian Congress of Trade Unions, stated, after urging the establishment of one-man management, that "It is necessary to see that the workers try to look upon the factory or shop not as upon something alien, but as upon their own property—to look upon it with the eyes of a proprietor."[1] In spite of the fact, therefore, that the workers were being deprived of any share in management, Rykov, the Bolshevik chairman of V.S.N.Kh., proposed that the workers be persuaded that not only the enterprises at which they were employed but industry as a whole were their own property. Speaking at the same congress, the Bolshevik Weinstein also urged that the workers should be convinced that all industry belonged to them. "It is necessary," he said, "to instill deeply into the consciousness of the toilers that the factories in which they work, all industry with which they are concerned, and generally all industry in Russia, is their own industry."[2] Once industrial establishments were largely nationalized and safely controlled by the Communist Party, the party tried to convince the workers that industry belonged to labor. When, however, at the end of 1917 and the beginning of 1918, the workers, through the factory committees, had taken over the factories as shared private property, the Bolsheviks tried to convince the workers that they did not own the factories at which they worked. Workers' ownership, as far the Bolsheviks were concerned, was equated with nationalization. Workers' ownership, according to the Bolsheviks, was proletarian class ownership, for the state was a workers' state. In order for the workers to be convinced that they were the owners of nationalized property, therefore, they had to acquire the closest possible identification with the state; since, in many cases, the workers had been deprived of both ownership and management of industry, it was necessary for the Bolsheviks to inculcate this identification into the workers if the latter were not to continue to be resistant to, and resentful of, Bolshevik policy. The identification of the worker with the state was necessitated also by the fact that under the Bolshevik regime, labor was to lose some fundamental advances it had previously made. Wages, for example, were to be changed from daily, weekly or monthly rates to piece rates. On 3 April 1918, the All-Russian Central Council of Trade Unions decreed that the worker had to guarantee a definite norm of work and a specific minimum productivity in order to receive a definite guaranteed wage.[3]

Norm of Productivity

This productivity was to be determined by a normalization bureau which was to measure the capacities of particular branches of labor and particular categories of workers. Paragraph 5 of the Statute on Labor Discipline which was adopted by the All-Russian Central Council of Trade Unions, stated: "For this purpose [of guaranteeing a fixed norm for a fixed wage] a special commission (Bureau of Normalization) is attached to each union to define the norm of productivity of each branch [*tsekh*] and each category of worker occupied in a given production."[4] The Bureau of Normalization of the union, therefore, was to establish norms for each particular kind of work demanded by the industry. The normalization commissions, or Bureaus of Normalization, were to be attached to the factory committees themselves, and were to record and register the productivity of each worker and the productivity of each category of labor in the enterprise. Paragraph 8 of the Statute provided that: "To clarify the general productive level of a given enterprise and to define the productivity of each worker individually, there must be immediately realized a system of *registration* of productivity by means of registration cards for each individual worker and registration tables for each branch [*tsekh*], category, and enterprise as a whole."[5] Thus a record of the productivity of each worker and each type of work was to be made and the norms of productivity were to be established.

A worker producing above these norms was to receive bonus payments. This increased productivity was to be rationalized, and a maximum was to be set, above which the worker was not permitted to go. While encouraging an increase in productivity, the Bolsheviks wanted to keep that productivity within certain assessable bounds. They also wanted to prevent an increase of productivity upon one occasion which would lead to a decrease on the next. "Allow me to explain this point [concerning piece work]," said Tomsky. "The thing is that piece wages are exactly the kind of wage norm to which we always objected. It has many negative aspects. Workers working at piece rates try as much as possible to work as much as possible. Working tensely, in several months, they wear themselves out so much that they are completely thrown out of commission. If you compare the daily work of the Russian and foreign worker, you will see that the foreign worker does a particular amount of work, then stops, but the Russian worker works until he drops from fatigue. This is avarice and therefore we were always against piece work."[6]

Price Rates and Hours

It does not seem, however, to be avarice alone to which the Bolsheviks objected. The Bolshevik aim in establishing piece rates seems to have been to effect an over-all increase in productivity. The purpose of piece rates was to encourage the worker to produce above the norm. Production above the norm was to be a constant assessable and rationalized process. An over-all increase in productivity could not have been achieved by workers who increased their work as much as possible one day and did not work at all on the next. If Tomsky's claim that the workers would work to the point of exhaustion was true, the reason would seem to be found not in avarice but in other factors. Many Russian workers, as has been previously pointed out, maintained close connections with their villages and farms. In the early post-revolutionary situation, because of difficulties in transportation and because of peasant resistance to Bolshevik requisitions, it was difficult for the workers to obtain food and other articles of consumption in the cities.[7] The expropriation of land from the landlords also led the peasant-worker to expect to acquire larger landholdings. Partly for these reasons, many workers seem to have left the factories to return to the villages. Workers who had close ties with their agricultural communities, therefore, might have preferred to earn as much as possible and to return to their villages as soon as possible. The Bolsheviks, however, were trying to increase productivity on an over-all basis. The workers, therefore, had to be be prevented from working merely to earn enough to return to their farms. They had to be prevented from working to temporarily satisfy their needs so that they might leave work to return again only when they were once more in need. Perhaps for these reasons, also, the Bolsheviks set a definite limit by which the piece rate norm could be exceeded. Tomsky continued his explanation of the piece rate system established by the All-Russian Congress of Trade Unions by saying: "Where the trade unions themselves consider piece work admissible as a means of raising productivity, it can still be used, but a norm must be established more than which it would be impossible to work. With such a limitation of piece work, we approach another system, a standardized one. The system of standardized work forces [the worker] to work well and in addition deters the worker from a superfluous expenditure of energy. The worker can do 1/3 or 1/4 more than the norm, but he does not have the right to work more and does not receive wages for it. Thus a limit is set for the capable and energetic worker, more than which he cannot work under present conditions; for if the worker is allowed to act rashly, this leads, because of present poor nutrition, only to his exhaustion. Raising the productivity of labor, we must preserve it from a superfluous squandering."[8] Thus, the piece rate wages were to be established within a definite framework so that the Russian worker would strive steadily and over long periods of time to raise productivity. Tomsky pointed out also that the poor diet available to the worker likewise necessitated that a limit be set to his expenditure of energy.

The Statute on Labor Discipline, in Paragraph 10, which deals with piece rates, decreed that the lowest and highest norms of productivity and bonuses for exceeding the norms within exactly defined limits were to be set by the trade unions.[9] The purpose of the norms and piece rate wages was, again, to increase the productivity of labor as far as possible over as long a period of time as possible. However, bonuses for exceeding the norms of productivity would also have tended to encourage labor to make the norm the minimum. In accordance with Bolshevik policy, the Statutes of the All-Russian Union of Metal Workers of 1919 rejected what was regarded as the system of wages in use under capitalism and demanded the institution of piece rates.[10]

Under a capitalist economy, read the statutes, ". . . the only acceptable system of wages for the workers were periodic (daily, monthly) wages, the raising of which improved the position of the workers and at the same time forced the factory owners, in their own capitalist interests to improve methods of management and to introduce new techniques better adapted to the instruments and means of production and also to unite isolated economic units into huge trusts."[11] Therefore, according to the Union of Metal Workers, the system of periodic wages existing under capitalism served, through their impetus to technical development and the formation of trusts, to bring capitalism closer to socialism. Under socialism, however, periodic wages do not serve the functions they performed under capitalism, for ". . . as a result of the transfer of the entire economic apparatus into the hands of the proletarian state, periodic wages are already unable to play a role in the technical development of the enterprise and in the industrial life of the country . . ."[12] Piece rate wages were regarded as the most fitting for the conditions then existing. According to the statutes: "Piecework wages which have been in use for the past half year, played a very important historical role in the process of revitalizing Russian industry and must be put into practice insofar as a transition to more contemporary methods of pay seem technically impossible."[13] Although piecework wages were regarded as the most expedient form of wages in the situation then present, they were acknowledged as transitional, and a promise of a better form of remuneration was implied. Fundamental to piecework wages, however, was the concept that the worker was responsible for the productivity of the enterprise.[14] Hence, in spite of the fact that the workers were being deprived of managerial functions, piecework wages, as a form of labor discipline, were to remind the workers that they were responsible for industrial productivity.

Self-Discipline

Furthermore, it was the unions themselves which were to institute and enforce the norms of productivity and the payment of piece wages. The unions were to enforce labor discipline and to deal with violations of that discipline. Tomsky, at the Fourth Conference of Factory Committees and Trade Unions, emphasized that the workers had to fulfill the policy which he claimed they themselves had determined. "The order which we have established ourselves," he said, "we must submit to, and every worker at his workbench must see to its fulfillment. Courts of comrades must be organized in order to influence those who will violate the rules of internal order; dealing with drunkards, those who negligently carry out their obligations, those who are not punctual at work, the courts must pass sentence even going so far as removing the guilty ones from the factory and excluding them from the union."[15] Thus, the comradely courts of the unions themselves were to bring offenders to trial and pass sentence upon them.[16] "Remember, comrades," continued Tomsky, "we are the directors of the economic policy—we, the trade unions and the factory committees. . . . The policy which is being carried out now is our policy—the policy of the factory committees and the trade unions. And if we decide to carry it out, then we must be the first to be subordinated to it."[17] In this way the Bolsheviks sought to convince the workers that the authority to which they were subordinated was not alien to them, but was an authority derived from their own organizations: Labor discipline equated with self-discipline served to internalize external authority.

According to an article entitled "The Self-Discipline of the Worker" in *Izvestiia* of 13 April 1918: ". . . proletarian discipline does not have anything in common with military discipline; it does not signify blind obedience. No—it is a voluntary, democratic discipline and submission to the decisions of the workers themselves."[18] Thus, the authority of the labor organizations and the will of the workers themselves were equated. However, the article continues by pointing out that in the absence of self-imposed obedience on the part of the workers, the workers' organizations should use pressure and compulsion to exert their authority; for even though labor discipline is voluntary discipline, "this does not mean that along with labor discipline, the repressions of the union cannot be used. If there is not voluntary submission, then it is the moral right and even obligation of the workers' organizations, especially at the present significant moment of the organization of socialist economy, to make use of pressure and compulsion."[19] Even the use of compulsion, however, was regarded as self-compulsion because it was exerted by the union itself. "This will be self-compulsion," read the article, "and not a police measure, as numbers of opponents of severe measures are inclined to think. This will be active workers' self-control."[20] Compulsion, then, if it was exerted by workers' organizations was not regarded as a force exerted upon the workers from outside or from above. As compulsion exerted by the workers upon the workers, it was considered to be self-compulsion.

Along with the piece rate wage which encouraged the workers to exert pressure upon themselves to raise productivity, force, therefore, was also recognized as a means of compelling workers to submit to the demands made upon them by the unions and industry.

Regulation of Wages

The concept of self-compulsion and self-discipline, however, was bound up with the Bolshevik effort to place upon the workers the responsibility for increased productivity. The Resolution on the Normalization of Wages and Labor, introduced by Schmidt and passed by the Second All-Russian Congress of Trade Unions, stated, like the Statutes of the Metal Workers, that the purpose of piece and premium wages was to place upon the workers responsibility for production.[21] "In those branches of industry where it is impossible to standardize labor, periodic payment exactly regulated by working time and by firmly established rules of internal order, must be used."[22] In the absence of conditions in which norms of labor and piece or premium wages could be established the workers or employees were paid on the basis of time. In such cases, also, working conditions and hours were to be rigidly standardized and regulated.

The determination of wage rates, like all other labor policy, was centralized and removed from the jurisdiction of the local unions. The All-Russian Central Council of Trade Unions and the People's Commissariat of Labor, as a state organ, were to ratify all wage scales, and no local council of trade unions had the right to establish wage regulations unless it did not have an All-Russian union. Even in these cases, the wage regulations of the All-Russian Soviet of Trade Unions were to guide it.[23]

Wage Rates

The wages of the higher ranking specialized personnel, whose wages were controlled by the industrial union, were also to be regulated by the wage scales established by the All-Russian Central Soviet of Trade Unions and the Commissariat of Labor. All personnel employed by industry were divided into three basic groups: 1) the high-ranking technicians and administrators; 2) the middle-ranking administrators; and 3) the workers. The Resolution of the Second Congress of Trade Unions on the Normalization of Wages and Labor stated: "The rates of industrial unions must include the higher technical, commercial and administrative personnel who receive wages under the control of the union. In accordance with this, the rate regulations are divided into three basic parts: a) the highest technical, commercial and administrative personnel; b) the middle technical and administrative personnel; employees of boards [*pravlenie*], of offices, of institutions, and of trading establishments; c) workers."[24] Hence, a differentiation among kinds of workers and employees was established. On this scale, the workers formed the lowest rung. In 1919, four groups and twelve categories were established for each of the three orders of workers and employees. This was a change from the previously existing system of five groups and fifteen categories. The relationship of the highest wages to the lowest within each four groups was 1 to 1.75. Thus: "For the purpose of abolishing the number of categories, which is too great (5 groups and 15 categories), and for a more equitable payment of the fundamental core of workers and employees in production, 4 groups and 12 categories are established for each of the 3 orders (high personnel, middle and workers), and the relation of the highest rates to the lowest within the bounds of each of the 4 groups of the 1st to the 12th category must be 1:1.75."[25] Thus, each of the three orders was to be broken up into 4 groups and 12 categories, and within each of the 4 groups the highest wage was supposedly to be 1¾ higher than the lowest of the same category.

However, although similar wage scales comprising 5 groups and 15 categories had been previously decreed, these wage scales do not seem to have been enforced successfully. The technicians, especially, had managed to evade them, for the Resolution on the Normalization of Wages and Labor of the Second All-Russian Congress of Trade Unions was preceded by the following statement: ". . . there is, in the sphere of standardization of wages, an extreme divergence and lack of agreement of the rate regulations, making difficult not only the standardization of labor, but even its actual enforcement, and explaining such an abnormal phenomenon in this sphere by many serious defects (the absence of a definite system of wages as the basis of the rate regulations, the elasticity of groups and categories, the removal from the rate regulations of the ratings of the higher technical, commercial and administrative personnel) resulting from the hasty transition from one form of regulation of wages to another, the weakness of the unions locally and their local separatism, and, finally, the instability of the local state organs in their rate policy. . . .[26] In spite of previous attempts, then, to standardize wages and centralize the system of wage control, the Bolsheviks do not seem to have succeeded, by 1919, in enforcing a stable wage policy. Local unions often took the particular conditions of their industries and localities into account instead of merely conforming to the wage decrees of the center. Salaries for technicians and specialists seem to have been removed or excluded from the wage scales. As a result, skilled workers, specialists and technicians, because of the need of the proletarian state for their services, seem to have been able to demand high wages. Schmidt, speaking of this problem at the Second All-Russian Congress of Trade Unions, stated: "Again, a year's experience convinced us that the exclusion of these categories of employees from the general wage-scale regulations, in practice led to the fact that these specialists were dubbed with a very accurate nickname 'specialists in receiving ratings.' They found themselves outside the scope of general wage-scale regulations and being left to free competition, they ran wages up so high that the creation of a whole series of special commissions and councils was required in order to regulate the wage scale of the so-called specialists."[27] Supply and demand, therefore, seem to have functioned to the advantage of the highly skilled, the technician, specialist or administrator employed in the dictatorship of the proletariat.

Lozovsky, at the Second All-Russian Congress of Trade Unions, objected to the high salaries of the specialists and claimed that Marxism had promised that the administrative apparatus of the proletarian state, having been rid of bureaucrats, would be cheap. He pointed out that even though the ratio of the highest to the lowest rates for technicians had to be 1:1.75, the lowest rate, nevertheless, could be relatively high.

Wages of "Specialists"

"Here at the Congress," said Lozovsky, "we must say what we think of those high salaries which are given to the so-called specialists. At a time when the living wage in Moscow is 390 [rubles], you have specialists who receive 4,500-5,000 rubles a month. If we actually want to do something about this situation and make the state apparatus cheap, and Marx in his *Civil War* says that this cheap state apparatus is one of the signs of a [proletarian] state regime, then we must extend our influence even to this reserved category. Nothing has been said about this . . . . only the following has been said, that all categories are divided into 3: administrative, then employees, then workers, and it is stated here that the lower rates are related to each of these categories at 1:1.75, but nothing is said about the lowest rates of the specialists. Their lowest rates can be 1,500-2,000 rubles and still come to 1.75."[28] Thus, Lozovsky pointed out that even the wage scales adopted by the Second All-Russian Congress of Trade Unions allowed for high and preferential wages for specialised personnel, and he claimed that these high rewards were contrary to the Marxian promise of an inexpensive state machine.

Seniushkin, of the Internationalist fraction, also pointed out at the Second All-Russian Congress of Trade Unions that there was a great contrast between the high and low rates, and charged that this discrepancy in wages was creating a workers' aristocracy. In his Thesis on the Standardization of Wages, Seniushkin stated that: "A defect of the wage scale is the overextension of groups and ranks . . . too great a gulf between the top and bottom leads to the creation of a special workers' aristocracy and the ill will of the broad masses toward this upper strata which is directly reflected in the productivity of work. The same may also be said for the rates for 'technical forces,' under which is included not only specialist technicians, but in general all capable men."[29] Seniushkin thus seems to have claimed that any individual with a skill needed by industry could demand a high salary and the high salaries of these specialists evoked the resentment of the common worker. Also, according to Seniushkin, the need for specialists was so great and the salaries paid them varied to such an extent that they went from one department to another to acquire the highest wage possible. "The rates for these specialists in various departments," he said, "are entirely different and make for a situation in which these specialists rush from one enterprise to another and cause the animosity of the working masses against the over high salaries of specialists."[30] The less skilled workers, therefore, do not seem to have taken kindly to the greater advantages offered specialists in the proletarian state. Antagonism seems to have been growing up between them. The Menshevik Rubtsov, at the Third All-Russian Congress of Trade Unions a year later, in 1920, charged that specialists were still receiving wages excessively higher than those of the ordinary worker. In 1920, also, the ratio of highest to lowest wages in the groups was raised from 1:1.75 to 1:8. The Resolution of the Third All-Russian Congress of Trade Unions on the Tasks of the Tariff (i.e., wages) Policy not only made compulsory the inclusion of specialists in the union wage scales and raised the ratio to 1:8, it also provided for the sharpening of distinctions among wages.[31] The resolution stated: "The tariff scale should be constructed so that the relations will be sharper among categories, so that they will show the skilled workers to better advantage and will make possible the preservation of the number of tariff categories."[32] Thus, the wage scale was to be constructed to the advantage of the specialists and skilled workers. This indicates that the purpose of including the wages of specialists in the wage scales was not only to control these wages, but also to weaken the demands of the common laborer for higher pay by increasing the conflict of interests among the heterogeneous members of the industrial unions. Rubtsov also charged that the ratio of 1:8 was being ignored to the advantage of the specialists, and claimed that "A machinist receives 3,000, an engineer, in accordance with a higher rate, 9,000 and a ration of 50,000, 59,000 in all. This is not a relationship of 1:8."[33] Since Rubtsov's charge was not refuted at the overwhelmingly Bolshevik Congress at which he made it, his accusation indicates that such discrepancies in wages might indeed have existed.

Wages and Equality

Differentiation in wages—a scale of rewards for types of work performed—was entirely in accordance with the ideology of Bolshevism and the concept of equality found within it. Lenin, in discussing his concept of equality in 1917, stated that in the first phase of communist society, as it emerged from capitalism, equality would consist in rewarding each individual according to the work performed. Under such a system, ". . . every man having done as much social labor as every other receives an equal share of the socialist products. . . ."[34] Thus, those who have done equal amounts of work receive equal rewards, and Lenin makes it clear that such a distribution would be unequal, "for every right is an application of the same measure to different people who, in fact, are not the same and are not equal to one another. . . ."[35] Hence, if each individual is rewarded in accordance with the work he performs, and since some will perform more work or work greater in value than others, ". . . differences and unjust differences in wealth will still exist."[36] However, in spite of these inequalities, in the first stage of communism, according to Lenin, the proletariat, ". . . by overwhelming the bourgeoisie . . . takes a decisive step towards the abolition of classes . . . ," which in effect is equality, for the conception of equality must be understood to mean the abolition of classes.[37] In the Leninist concept of equality, then, classes become equal but individuals remain unequal. Nor did Lenin consider that even classes had been eliminated after the seizure of power, for he pointed out that ". . . classes *remain and will remain* in the era of the dictatorship of the proletariat." In such a society differentiated wage scales, and *edinovlastie* as well, were completely congruent with the postulation of the basic inequality of men.

Preferential Supply

The Third All-Russian Congress of Trade Unions further developed and refined the system of piece and premium wages introduced in 1918. A resolution decreed, first of all, that wages were not to be raised in spite of the economic difficulties of the workers, and the congress recognized "that in the present economic and financial position of the country, the further raising of monetary wages cannot in any way serve as a way out of the difficult economic position of the toiling masses."[38] An increase in monetary payment, therefore, was rejected by the congress as a means of increasing wages. An increase in wages was to be provided by increasing rations of food and other necessities. The resolution decreed: ". . . the establishment of a system of supplying the toilers with food products and objects of prime necessity in dependence upon the productivity and economic importance of their labor for the state (purposeful [*tselevoe*] supply)."[39] Premium payments, therefore, were to take the form of fundamental necessities, in a time when such were scarce. Moreover, the payments were to be dependent upon the importance of the workers' labor for the state. Furthermore, the payment of such premiums was dependent upon the future, or at least upon the continued increase of productivity. The resolution stated that the congress decreed "the introduction of a motivating system of wages (premiums) only in strict dependence upon its results."[40] If the system of premium payment, then, did not succeed in increasing productivity, premiums consisting of food and other necessities would not be paid. A subsequent section of the resolution explained that the premium system of wages had to be ". . . closely connected with the 'purposive' supply of the toilers."[41] Clearly, then, he who worked most would be fed and clothed best.[42] In the conditions of scarcity prevailing at that time in Soviet Russia, it would hardly seem that the premiums passed from the realm of subsistence to the realm of luxury, and the resolution explained that: "The lack of products and objects of prime necessity leads to the strict necessity of distributing as expediently as possible the fund of real wages which we have at hand, among those groups of toilers whose work is recognized as most necessary and productive in the struggle for the restoration of our ruined economy."[43] Hence, the Bolsheviks announced their intention of making use of the limited fund of real, as opposed to monetary, wages in order to increase productivity. According to the resolution: "This work [of distribution of real wages] must be closely connected with our tariff work for two reasons: 1) The former system of supplying the workers, due to its lack of connection with our tariff policy, in fact led to a rigid tariff."[44] The Bolsheviks thus stated that if the workers were supplied equally and equitably, the wage scales could not be easily manipulated to increase productivity. Wage scales under such conditions, according to the Bolsheviks, remained "rigid" rather than flexible. Since it did not raise productivity, the increase of rations unconnected with the incentive system of wages performed no function for the Bolshevik Party. The second reason provided by the Resolution for relating an increase of real wages to an increase in productivity is given as follows: "2) An increase of the rations of the workers and in some cases also of the employees which was given as an addition to the basic tariff rate, was not connected with the incentive system of wages and bears an accidental character, assisting little in raising the productivity of labor. Therefore, the premium system, as one of the best means of incentives, must be very closely connected with the system of supplying the workers, since only under these conditions can the premium system yield the greatest productivity of labor. Supplying toilers must become the basic part of the premium system."[45] Labor productivity, then, according to the Bolsheviks, was to be based upon a system of incentives—the incentive often being articles of prime necessity.

The system of purposive supply applied not only to the individual workers, or to the workers of a particular branch of an enterprise, but to whole trade unions as well. At the Third All-Russian Congress of Trade Unions, Lenin pointed out that the trade unions which were not necessary for socialism were faring ill. "It is true," said Lenin, "that the division of workers into trade unions is continuing, but of these trade unions, there were many which were necessary to the capitalists, but not necessary to us. And we know that the workers of these trade unions suffer a more severe hunger than the others. It could not be otherwise."[46] Those trade unions, therefore, which were not useful to the Bolsheviks—and this usefulness was likely to be determined on political as well as economic grounds—suffered greater hunger than the unions that supported Bolshevik policy. This hunger could have been the result of purposive supply or of lack of work. Buksin, a Menshevik, speaking for the printers at the same congress, indicated that purposive supply could be used to starve a union into submission or out of existence. Buksin urged: "Change your food supply policy, set the problem so that the worker will be more or less secure. Now there exist many trade unions which are literally dying out, the workers of which are literally starving. They do not receive payment in kind when other trade unions receive it. Do not make such a distinction. . . ."[47] Thus, the recalcitrant Printers' Union would seem to have been one of those which, being opposed to the Bolsheviks, suffered a severer hunger than the others.

It seems, therefore, that those who sought to maintain their own legitimate interests under the Bolshevik regime were cast out of the Bolshevik order. Those workers who were willing to give up their own interests and sacrifice those interests to the Bolshevik cause, if they did not fare well, at least fared better. If their hunger was not satisfied, at least they were less hungry. According to Lenin, "Those workers who are not able to make . . . sacrifices, we regard as self-seekers and cast them out of the proletarian family."[48]

Fulfillment of Norm

On the other hand, rewards in the form of basic necessities were given to those who could increase productivity by producing above the norm. The Third All-Russian Congress of Trade Unions placed at the basis of tariff work "the establishment of an obligatory norm of wages and number of working days."[49] A definite quantity of work, within a definite time, for a definite wage was to be standardized. These norms were constantly to be reviewed and revised. The resolution provided that: "In the establishment of norms worked out, under present conditions, mistakes, approximations and other errors will unavoidably be made. Therefore, the unions are obliged to publish both the norms themselves, and the degree of their fulfillment and periodically, not less than once in three months, to correct these norms."[50] With this system of frequent periodic investigation of norms, the norms could constantly be changed. A quantity of production which previously had earned a premium reward could, therefore, itself become a norm of productivity. The workers would then have had to exceed the new norm in order to receive a bonus payment. This new quantity of production could subsequently have been turned into a new norm. It would also have been possible, by means of these reinvestigations, to lower norms if they proved to be inefficient or unprofitable.

The norms established for various kinds of work were closely related to the periods of time in which the worker did not work; for, according to the resolution: "The normalization of labor is found in closest dependence upon the number of periods of idleness, therefore, in establishing norms it is necessary also firmly to fix especially for various branches of production, the number of rest days in each month."[51] Thus the number of working days and rest days were exactly standardized. The resolution having standardized norms of production and norms of working time, penalties were imposed upon the workers if these norms were not fulfilled, for the resolution provided that "Both for the non-fulfillment of the norms and for the non-observance of the number of working days . . . there must be established the strict responsibility of the toiler for the agreement, before comradely disciplinary courts and corresponding organs."[52] The workers, therefore, were responsible for the fulfillment of the norms of wages and hours and subject to penalties for their non-fulfillment. Lateness, absence and the non-fulfillment of norms were also to be penalized by the lowering of premiums.[53] The premium method of payment was also to be used in various ways. The proportional, differential and Rowan systems of premium payment were all to be employed.[54] The function of wages in the proletarian state, therefore, was not to insure to all workers the most reasonable standard of living in the conditions then prevailing; the function of wages was to increase productivity, to make the worker conscious of his responsibility for the increasing productivity, and to evaluate his worth to the state. "The form of wages," said Trotsky at the Third

All-Russian Congress of Trade Unions, "must be regarded not as a means of insuring the personal existence of the individual workers, but first of all, it must serve as a means of evaluating what the individual worker gives by his work, to the republic. Wages must be a measure of the intensity, conscientiousness, suitability, and the productivity of the labor of each given worker."[55] In this way, the worker was to be reminded that if he did not eat enough, it was because he did not work enough. Furthermore, in the conditions then existing in Russia, in which it was difficult to supply workers adequately with their minimum needs, the Bolsheviks claimed to supply them according to their usefulness and devotion to the state. "As long as we are poor," Trotsky stated, "as long as we are in want of provisions to satisfy minimum needs, we cannot distribute them equally to all the toilers. We will send objects of consumption to the chief branches of labor, to the most productive enterprises. And we are obliged to do this, in the name of saving the toiling masses. We can clothe the worker more warmly, feed him better, if the worker will work honestly, conscientiously and intensively. For this reason we use the premium system."[56] Moreover, those who resisted Bolshevik labor measures were to be subject to punishment. "Finally," said Trotsky, "we do not refrain from repression to which we will resort as long as the state continues to exist. Towards self-seekers, deserters of labor, the workers' state has the right to use the severe, heavy hand of repression."[57] Labor, therefore, was to be rewarded for what the Bolsheviks conceived to be its devotion to duty and its self-sacrifice. It was to be punished for what the Bolsheviks conceived to be its negligence and self-seeking.

Work Compulsory

In speaking of Soviet labor, however, it must be borne in mind that this labor was not free. The Russian worker did not have the right not to work, nor did he have the right to choose where to work. Although he was compelled to work by the state, he could not sell his labor openly on the free market. Russian labor was compulsory labor. Trotsky defined compulsory labor as: "Compulsory labor is labor where each worker occupies a definite place assigned to him by the territorial (*oblast'*), provincial (*gubernaiia*), or district (*uzed*) economic organs." "The regulation of labor," he added, "does not use the spontaneous means of buying or selling, but is based on an economic plan which encompasses the whole country and embraces all the working class. This is the program of labor service which has always been part of the socialist program. . . . And once we have recognized this, we thus recognize fundamentally, not formally but fundamentally, the right of the workers' state to send every workingman and workingwoman to that place in which he is needed to fulfill an economic task. In the same way, we recognize the right of the state, the workers' state, to punish the workingman and workingwoman who refuse to fulfill the orders of the state."[58] The Russian worker, then, was assigned to his job by the state. The state reserved the right to send him wherever it believed he was needed, and could punish the worker who refused to go where he was sent. Labor in the Soviet Union was juridically compulsory.

The Menshevik Abramovich, in rebuttal to Trotsky, who claimed that all labor was compulsory, pointed out the distinction between juridically compulsory labor and juridically free labor by asserting that the economic compulsion to work was fundamentally different from the juridical compulsion to work. To equate these two concepts, according to Abramovich, was merely a play upon words, and he stated: "Trotsky says: 'Without compulsion there is no labor. All labor is compulsory.' True. And therefore, it is not necessary to play with concepts. Because then the concept of compulsory labor in general disappears. When we speak of compulsory labor, we speak of juridically compulsory labor. When we speak of free labor, we speak of juridically free labor. When labor is free in bourgeois society, does it not mean that man can also not work? Juridically he has the right not to work, but hunger forces him to work. When we speak of free labor no one hides that this is compulsory economically. . . . Trotsky is convinced that those who object to juridical compulsion are wrong. . . ."[59]

In March of 1920 the *News* of the *Chief Committee of Universal Labor Service* (*Izvestiia Glavnogo Komiteta Vseobshchei Trudovoi Povinnosti*) printed the "Theses of the Central Committee of the Russian Communist Party on the Mobilization of the Industrial Proletariat, Labor Service, the Militarization of the Economy and the Use of Military Units for Economic Tasks." These theses rejected the freedom of labor and demanded that universal labor service be put into practice. According to Paragraph 11 of the Theses: "The socialist order rejects on principle the liberal capitalistic reasons for the 'freedom of labor' which in bourgeois society signifies for one the freedom to exploit, for the others the freedom to be exploited.

Insofar as the basic tasks of social organization are the conquest by man of hostile external physical conditions, socialism demands the compulsory participation of all members of society in the production of material values and sets as its task the most reasonable, i.e., the most economic and the most attractive of all forms of social labor. The principle of universal labor service, unshakably established by the basic laws of the R.S.F.S.R., must now find a broad and universal application in fact."[60] Thus, the Communist Party tried to obscure the significance of juridically free labor by arguing that it signified the exploitation of labor by another class. Further, the party claimed to be applying universal labor service in a search for better forms of social labor by which man would conquer his physical environment or nature.

Distribution of Labor Power

Labor was registered, accounted for and assigned to its employment through the labor exchanges. The labor exchanges had been set up under the Provisional Government to cope with unemployment; they were then attached by the Soviet government to the trade unions as offices regulating the demand for labor and supplying it.[61] According to Schmidt, in the middle of 1918 and the beginning of 1919 the supply of labor fell behind the demand. In reporting to the Third All-Russian Congress of Trade Unions on the work of the labor exchanges, he stated: "If we trace the curve of the number of unemployed, we will see that in the month of January 1918, the general number of unemployed in Russia would reach approximately one and a half million. Of these, we could offer a place to only 900,000, send 750,000 (62%) to work. Thus we see the number of unemployed exceeded the demand. But already in the middle of 1918 and the beginning of 1919, this relationship sharply changed: the number of unemployed on the Labor Exchange numbered 800,000, the demand for working hands reached 900,000. Consequently the supply of labor already fell behind the demand. The per cent sent to work increased almost to 90."[62] Thus, by the middle of 1918, about eight months after the October Revolution, the number of unemployed looking for jobs through the labor exchange fell, according to Schmidt, from 1,500,000 to 800,000. The demand for labor was greater than the supply. As Schmidt points out, however, this was not so much due to the absorption of labor by industry as to the reluctance of labor to enter industry and to the return of many workers to the villages. It was due also to the fact that a worker could be assigned work in a geographical area which he himself did not choose. Schmidt explained: ". . . that under the Labor Exchanges there were organized booking offices of unemployed so that there was the possibility that those who did not receive a place would leave an area most convenient to the unemployed themselves and go to an area where there was a greater need of working hands. Already in 1919 we succeeded in creating more favorable conditions in the labor market. But apart from what the trade unions did, there was another reason for the unloading of the labor market—the departure for the villages in connection with our land reform."[63] Thus, it seems, the workers preferred to return to the villages than to live and work as laborers in industry under the Soviet state. The labor exchanges, in their attempts to redistribute labor, had to make use of state compulsion. Thus, "The labor exchanges, from organs of the trade unions, were converted into organs of state power."[64] According to Schmidt, as the task of distributing manpower became more difficult, the work of the labor exchanges, formerly under the trade unions and the People's Commissariat of Labor, was taken over by *Glavkomtrud* (the Chief Committee for Conducting Labor Service), which was connected with the Military Department and the People's Commissariat of Internal Affairs. *Glavkomtrud* was formed, Schmidt stated, because: ". . . All practical work could be fulfilled with great success if, along with the accounting apparatus there functioned an apparatus of compulsion, an apparatus for the swift transfer of manpower. And when there arose the problem . . . of the compulsory mass transfer of manpower, the necessity of the integration of these functions became obvious. . . ."[65] For these reasons, according to Schmidt, *Glavkomtrud* was formed.[66] *Glavkomtrud,* however, was to handle the mobilization of unskilled labor; the trade unions were to deal with the mobilization of skilled labor.[67] Extreme measures were needed to mobilize unskilled labor because the Soviet government had few, if any, rewards to offer it. "It would be Utopia," said Schmidt, "to think that the peasant, or he who is working now on the free market, would come voluntarily to work at a lower and rate under more difficult conditions of labor although it is extremely necessary for the state. Compulsion here becomes a necessity and can be achieved by a particular organ endowed with all the fullness of state power."[68] The compulsory power of the state was necessary, therefore, to induce labor to work for state industry.

The recruitment of skilled labor was also being separated from the recruitment of unskilled labor. Not only was *Glavkomtrud* to deal with unskilled labor and the trade unions with skilled, but military units that were not needed for military duties were to be used as labor armies.

Labor Armies: Skilled and Unskilled Labor

In January 1920, Trotsky took measures to convert the Third Army, then located in the Urals, into the First Labor Army. Instead of demobilizing his troops, who were no longer needed for immediate military purposes, Trotsky, after assigning the specialists of the Third Army to the Fifth Army, was to reorganize his troops for labor service for the purpose of restoring the economy of the Urals.[68a] However, he proposed also that the revolutionary labor army be ". . . the supreme organ of control and organization of the Ural *oblast'* and its leading administrative organ.[68b] In effect, then, Trotsky as the commander of the First Labor Army would have controlled not only labor and an army, but the economy and the political administration of the rich Ural region.

Skilled laborers, unless their skill had a particular application to the work of the labor army, were to be transferred into factory work. The Decree of the Soviet of Workers'-Peasants' Defense, which directed universal labor service and which established the Third Red Army as a labor army, stipulated that: "Skilled laborers insofar as they are not needed for work in the labor army are to be transferred to factories."[69] Trotsky reported that about three thousand skilled laborers passed through the army to the disposition of the Commissariat of Labor.[70] Those who remained in the labor army engaged, however, in work, some of which required skill and training. The labor army took part in coal mining, lumbering, and food-supply work. Although it is not clear what operations were required for food supply, lumbering and coal mining are difficult and dangerous, especially for those who have not been trained in them. Nor can untrained workers work as productively in these occupations. Only large numbers of cheaply employed laborers could compensate for the lack of skill. It seems, therefore, that the Soviet government was trying to substitute unskilled compulsory labor in quantity for skilled, voluntary, and profitably employed lumbermen and miners.

Moreover, the use of compulsory labor armies made up principally of unskilled labor could not but have had the effect of reconciling skilled labor to conditions of Soviet employment, no matter how unattractive those conditions were. In the labor army itself, for example, miners and lumbermen, if they were willing to lead the operations of the unskilled laborers, would have had a relatively better position than the common laborer they directed. Also, skilled laborers would have been less recalcitrant about making use of their skills under the conditions of Soviet labor, if they were aware that the alternative was to serve as unskilled labor in the labor army. Furthermore, the labor armies served also to remind skilled labor that no matter how few the rewards of the skilled, the reward of the unskilled were fewer. The refusal of a worker to use or acknowledge the labor skill he possessed could have led to his classification as an unskilled worker. This, in turn, could have led to his employment in a militarized labor unit. The "Theses of the Central Committee of the Russian Communist Party on the Mobilization of the Industrial Proletariat, Labor Service, the Militarization of the Economy and the Military Units for Economic Needs," provided, in Paragraph 25, for: "The mass drawing in, by means of labor service, of manpower which is untrained and which is not organized into trade unions, for food supply, fuel, construction, and loading work, etc., demands, especially, at first, labor organization approximating that of the army."[71] Thus, unskilled labor which did not belong to labor unions was to be formed into labor armies for the performance of various kinds of manual labor. Expulsion from a trade union could result, therefore, in assignment to militarized labor; conversely, admission to a trade union could avoid it. The Bolsheviks, having made all labor juridically compulsory, made unskilled and non-unionized labor less free and more unattractive. In this way, undesirable working conditions, and restrictions upon the free choice of skilled labor, could be made relatively desirable by contrast.

Militarized Enterprises

In addition to the conversion of military units into labor armies and the organization of unskilled labor into units similar to the army in construction, the Communist Party also proposed the militarization of particular enterprises. Paragraph 24 of the Theses on

Militarized Labor stated that the party decrees: "The formal militarization of the individual enterprises of the individual branches of industry having special significance at the present moment or which are in particular threatened by disintegration."[72] The Communist Party, therefore, declared its intention of militarizing enterprises particularly important to them or enterprises which were not functioning efficiently under conditions imposed by the Soviet state.

The workers in militarized labor units were to be led by individuals whose leadership and communist reliability had been proved, especially those who had been trained by the communist military schools. Paragraph 26 of the theses stated: "Elements of labor organization, and the necessary discipline, both internal and also external compulsory discipline, can be introduced into the mobilization of the labor service of hundreds of thousands and millions of laborers only through the advanced, conscious, resolute and reliable workers, especially those who have been in the military schools and who are accustomed to organize the masses and to lead them under the most difficult conditions."[73] It seems, therefore, that a basic core of personnel upon whom the Bolsheviks were relying for the implementation of party policy were to be transferred to industry to enforce party policy there.

Living Conditions

Thus, the Communist Party reached the decision that what labor would not do voluntarily, it was to do by compulsion. Compulsion, which in turn was to become internal discipline, seems to have been, in part, necessitated by the fact that the Bolsheviks had very little to offer labor in terms of real wages, for real wages began to decline in the first few months of the Bolshevik regime. The *Courier* of the People's Commissariat of Labor (*Vestnik Narodnogo Komissariata Truda*) of April-May 1918 had reported that in spite of the increase of monetary wages for some workers, real wages had on the whole decreased considerably. The report stated: "The Second All-Russian Congress of Commissars of Labor, representatives of Labor Exchanges, and insuring organizations states that in spite of the fact that in a number of cases wages of individual groups of workers have reached a degree never before reached in Russia, the real wages of the working class as a whole for the last few months have declined because the increase in the cost of living, in spite of the restraining acts of the Soviet power, under conditions in which products are scarce, has far outstripped the increase in wages. An especially sharp decline in real wages has taken place in the capitals where as a result it is not possible for the proletariat to acquire products in the quantity necessary to maintain its ability to work at a normal level. . . ."[74] Thus, by the middle of 1918, the cost of living had risen to such a degree that real wages had fallen below a subsistence wage. This situation does not seem to have improved by any considerable extent by April of 1920. Rykov, at the Third All-Russian Congress of Trade Unions, reported that the daily norm of nutrition for a worker performing eight hours of work was one pound of bread and one-half pound of vegetables. One quarter of a pound of bread was provided for each two hours overtime. However, Rykov adds that 1,200,00 people could not be completely provided for.[75] In reply to the charge of a Menshevik representative of the Printers' Union that a skilled laborer could not live on the 2,000 to 3,000 rubles he received, Schmidt concurred that "They live in unbelievable conditions. We know that wages are minimal and small under present conditions. But the trade unions themselves are establishing them, openly announcing to the masses that under present conditions we are giving everything possible. . . ."[76] The Bolsheviks, therefore, did not deny the inadequacy of real wages, but by attributing the determination of these wages to the trade unions they suggested that the workers themselves had agreed to the wages and their consequences. By insisting also that they were providing for the workers as well as they could, the Bolsheviks removed from themselves the responsibility for adverse conditions. At the same time, they seem to have closed the door upon attempts to improve the situation by any methods other than their own.

Working Conditions

Not only were living conditions difficult for workers, working conditions were also onerous; for contrary to the Labor Code of the Soviet Union, the reality of working conditions placed many excess burdens upon the workers.[77] The laws which presumably provided for the protection of labor were not applied. Schmidt, at the Third All-Russian Congress of Trade Unions, in speaking of the protection of labor, stated: "First of all, we tried to proclaim it as our basic task, as our basic purpose. . . . Experience and practice, in reality, have shown, that it is one thing to talk about it . . . and another to put it into effect. . . ."[78] Further perusal of Schmidt's report makes clear that there was little in common between the Soviet labor code and the decrees and regulations by which labor had to abide. The labor code, for example, had established that the working day in industries harmful to the health of the worker should be less than 8 hours. Night work for women was prohibited. These provisions of the labor code were not observed. According to Schmidt, "We have proclaimed that the working day in those branches of production where there are harmful conditions of labor should be lower than the established maximum of eight hours, but in practice we are convinced that very often it is impossible to carry out these measures as a result of the lack of manpower and of the severe lowering of the productivity of labor. Only in case of particularly harmful production did we permit the shortening of the working day. In the rest [of the industries with harmful labor] we had to remain under the eight hour working day, i.e., the maximum under given conditions. Night work for women which was forbidden by us wholly and completely was allowed in night industries. . . ."[79] Thus, the protection of labor in dangerous occupations and the prohibition of the employment of women in night industry were permitted, in spite of the labor code.

The Eight-Hour Day

The eight-hour day, which had been proclaimed for all industry except in those dangerous occupations in which it was to have been shorter, was also violated. Schmidt pointed out that the eight-hour working day was not faring well. "The organs of the protection of of labor," he said, "are entrusted with the tasks of undeviatingly seeing that the eight hour working day is not violated. However, the economic conditions of the country force us to permit overtime work. This was done in several branches of industry, even compulsorily but again with the consent of the appropriate union."[80] Thus, overtime work was compulsorily introduced to supplement the eight-hour day. Again, the unions bore the responsibility and, again, the compulsion was presumably made less thereby. Furthermore, in spite of the fact that the Bolsheviks were constantly violating the labor code and the principles of the protection of labor which they themselves had formulated, they continued to reiterate those principles. Having stated that the Bolsheviks were forced to retreat from their stand on the protection of labor, Schmidt claimed that it was "not because of ill will, not even because we do not have an apparatus of technical strength, but because of objective necessity. And each time . . . we do not refrain from making our original declarative pronouncements for the time when the condition of the country will improve."[81]

Those conditions, then, which had been promised labor by the Bolsheviks were not provided. The promise, however, was made to serve as an ideal for the future of Russian labor, and served as a facade to attract the labor movement in other parts of the world to the communist cause.

It must also be pointed out that the overtime hours required of Russian labor were not always paid for. Seniushkin, speaking at the Second All-Russian Congress of Trade Unions in January 1919, asserted that the ten-hour working day had been introduced for railroad workers without pay for overtime.[82] There were also other ways of increasing without pay the labor demanded of Soviet workers. A decree of 29 January 1920 established that in addition to the workers' permanent employment he was compulsorily subject to supplementary labor service.[83]

Subbotniks and Voskresniks

Another means of increasing working hours may be found in the *subbotniks* or *voskresniks,* the former referring to the performance of unpaid voluntary labor on Saturday and the latter on Sunday.

Although *subbotniks* had been organized previous to 10 May 1919, the official campaign for their propagation may be said to have begun on that date with the Moscow-Kazan Railway *subbotnik,* which was given extensive publicity in the labor organizations of all Soviet Russia. The *subbotnik* was organized and led by party members who served as examples of self-sacrifice and devotion to the state. The Resolution of the General Council of Communists of the *Subraion* of the Moscow-Kazan Railway and Their Adherents, introducing *subbotniks,* stated that ". . . in order to overcome the class enemy . . . the communists and their sympathizers again must spur themselves on and extract from their time off still another hour of work, i.e., they must increase their working day by an hour, add it up and on Saturday devote six hours at a stretch to physical labor thereby producing immediately a real value. Considering that communists should not spare their health and lives for the victory of the revolution, the work is conducted without pay."[84]

Although the declaration of the Moscow-Kazan Railway provided for six hours of labor, the time donated seems to have differed with various *subbotniks,* since the Regulations on *Subbotniks,* published by the Chief Committee for General Labor Service, stipulated that "The *subbotnik* continues usually for four hours but may be prolonged each time at the discretion of the organizer of the *subbotnik* and with the consent of the administration."[85] The *subbotniks,* and *voskresniks,* therefore, were of no particular duration, although it would seem that ordinarily they lasted a minimum of four hours.

Voskresniks seem to have been regarded as having greater ethical value: a labor encyclopedia stated that "As differentiated from the *subbotniks,* the *voskresniks* demand still greater consciousness and citizen self-denial, because, if on a working day, on Saturday, one has to exert the force of his will in order to continue working without pay even for a few hours after the usual working day, it is still more difficult for each participant 'to get into the swing' of work on a day dedicated from time immemorial to rest. Thus in the matter of developing positive social habits the *voskresniks* play, doubtlessly, an extremely important role."[86]

It was the communist leadership of the *subbotniks* rather than their mass character that was emphasized. Molotov, for example, writing in 1920 when the *subbotniks* were being introduced on a large scale, stated that "The *subbotniks* and *voskresniks* . . . were a striking example of the proletarian consciousness and self-denial of the *advanced* workers but not of the worker *masses.* In the forefront and in the majority of cases, in strongly preponderant numbers, communists were the participants of the *subbotniks.* And in comparison with all the mass of workers as a whole only a very small part of the participants were non-party rank and file workers, employees and still less peasants."[87] The implication is that it was the communists who possessed more often than others the degree of consciousness necessary to contribute their labor and leisure time voluntarily and without pay for the building of socialism. Workers of non-party status, though permitted and encouraged to join in the labor of *subbotniks* and *voskresniks,* did so in a subordinate capacity—as followers not as leaders. Indeed, the pressure of the party cells would seem to have been exerted upon the non-party workers, both skilled and unskilled, to contribute their labor,[88] but the initiative for these days of extra work belonged to the party members. The official regulations emphasized that "*Subbotniks* arose as an idea of the communists; they are a form of communist labor and therefore their leadership must derive from the party committees."[89]

Also, communists reputedly worked more wholeheartedly than non-party workers at *subbotniks.* According to a *subbotnik* participant: "I observed groups working where there were communists and groups working where there were no communists. . . . In the groups where there were no communists, the greatest indifference to work was noticed as if it were some kind of conscript service one had 'to put in time for.' Consciousness . . . was absent. . . ."[90]

One of the purposes of the *subbotniks* would seem to have been to demonstrate to the workers that they possessed less consciousness, less willingness for self-sacrifice and devotion, than party members who were supposed to possess a greater insight into "necessity" and a greater dedication to socialism than they. Molotov pointed out that during the first year of their existence "the *subbotniks* could have chiefly a moral or educative significance."[91] The Regulations on *Subbotniks* stated also that *"Subbotniks* are one of the forms of propaganda of the idea of labor service and self-organization of the working class,"[92] and ". . . must be a laboratory of communist labor."[93] Moreover, the *subbotniks* were, according to the party, actual examples of communist labor; they were the only earnest of communism yet existing in the transitional period. "Communist *subbotniks,"* said Lenin, "are extraordinarily valuable as the actual beginning of *Communism;* and this is a very rare thing because we are in a stage when 'only the *first steps* in the transition from capitalism to Communism are being taken.' "[94] The *subbotniks* were communistic, according to Lenin, because of their higher productivity compared with capitalist productivity, because of their voluntary, class-conscious character, and because they were performed by labor united for a productive purpose.[95] Characteristic of the *subbotniks* also, and another indication of their communist quality, was the self-sacrifice of the laborers engaged in them. "The unskilled labourers and railway workers of Moscow," said Lenin, ". . . are toilers who are living in desperately hard conditions. They are constantly underfed, and now, before the new harvest is gathered, with the general worsening of the food situation, they are actually starving. And yet these starving workers . . . organize Communist *subbotniks,* work overtime *without any pay* and achieve an enormous *increase in the productivity of labour,* in spite of the fact that they are weary, tormented, exhausted by starvation. Is this not magnificent heroism? Is this not the beginning of a change of world historical significance?"[96]

However, Lenin not only lauds the self-sacrifice and consciousness of the ill-fed in increasing the productivity of their labor, he reminds them that unless they increase their productivity, they will continue to starve. "In order to raise the productivity of labour," said Lenin, "we must save ourselves from starvation, and in order to save ourselves from starvation we must raise the productivity of labour."[97] Furthermore, the self-sacrifice of which Lenin speaks is not only indicative of the communist spirit but its absence is construed as evidence of opposition to socialism, "of profiteers, officials and other white guards." Objections to participation in *subbotniks* could be considered as ". . . the counter-revolutionary agitation of the bourgeoisie, the Mensheviks, the Social Revolutionaries."[98] And, ". . . only the most contemptible people who have sold themselves to capitalism body and soul can condemn the fact that the great May Day holiday has been utilized for a mass attempt to introduce communist labor."[99] Self-sacrificing, voluntary, enthusiastic participation in *subbotniks,* on the other hand, was earnest of the communist. "From the point of view of principle," said Lenin, "we observe no phenomenon other than *subbotniks* that would indicate that not only do we call ourselves Communists, not only do we desire to be communists but that we are already accomplishing something that in practice is not only socialist but communist."[100]

Mass Subbotniks

Although *subbotniks* were introduced originally as examples of the higher productivity of labor performed voluntarily, enthusiastically and consciously by communists, *subbotniks* were subsequently conducted on a mass scale. The mass *subbotniks* were to be regarded as a means of eliminating the purely voluntary character of *subbotnik* labor and became a means of increasing labor productivity and of rationalizing and integrating this labor into the routine of ordinary work. "The *subbotniks,*" said Molotov, "were . . . a labor guard in the transition to general organized communist labor."[101] And, he continued, "This is a transition from a labor guard of advanced workers to the primary basis of the army of labor of the worker and peasant masses."[102] The First of May *subbotnik,* which was put into effect by the decree of the All-Russian Central Executive Committee, throughout the Soviet Republic marked the transition to the new mass *subbotnik*. In the *Nizhegorodskaia Guberniia,* the *Guberniia* Commission for the First of May *Subbotnik* reported to the *Guberniia*

Executive Committee the decision to extend the First of May *Subbotnik* to a second day, to the second of May, as well. More importantly, they decided to organize "periodic mass *subbotniks* not less than twice a month."[103] This attempt to make the work of the *subbotniks* "systematic and permanent," to sustain it and maintain it, was lauded by the party.[104] While maintaining their character of voluntary conscious expressions of devotion to the state, the *subbotniks* and *voskresniks* were to be systematically continued and were to become a regular part of the working month. Moreover, the productivity of labor at *subbotniks* was supposed to increase over the usual. Subparagraph 4, Part I, of the Regulation on *Subbotniks* stated: "*Subbotniks* must accomplish not less than the established norm but participants of the *subbotniks* must strive to exceed this norm."[105] And just as *subbotniks* themselves were to be preserved as regular events of the labor month, the productivity of labor, presumably resulting from the enthusiasm of the labor holidays, as the *subbotniks* and *voskresniks* were called, was also to be regularized and maintained. Lenin, quoting a *Pravda* article of 23 May 1920, agreed that the highly increased productivity of labor claimed for *subbotnik* workers was explained " 'by the fact that in ordinary times their work is dull and uninteresting whereas here [on the *subbotniks*] they worked with a will and with enthusiasm. Now, however, they will be ashamed to turn out less work in ordinary times than they did at the Communist *subbotnik*.' "[106] By the device of the transitional period the Bolsheviks had attempted to dam the chiliastic tide the revolution had awakened and to use it as a reservoir from which to draw for labor productivity. By the device of the *subbotniks* they sought, it seems, to draw upon this enthusiasm where it existed, to inculcate enthusiasm where it did not exist, and to use it as a means of inculcating labor discipline.

The mass *subbotniks* were not, however, carried out entirely as the result of mass enthusiasm or voluntary mass labor. Molotov points out, for example, that after the unanimous decision of the *Guberniia* Trade Union Council and the *Guberniia* Trade Union Congress in the *Nizhegorodskaiia Guberniia,* members of all the *guberniia* trade unions had to participate in *subbotniks*. It has already been pointed out that the unions were often manipulated into fulfilling Bolshevik policy, but Molotov insisted that "The non-party workers and employees are members of trade unions. They are subordinated to proletarian trade union discipline. And that is why members of the unions which have decided to participate in mass *subbotniks* . . . must participate in them. . . .In this we have the free and organized decision of the trade unions. In this we have trade union discipline so that the decisions of the guiding union organs are carried into effect strictly and undeviatingly."[107] The decision to provide an extra working day of unpaid labor, then, was made by the administration of the trade unions and was binding upon the union members.

Although the *subbotniks* and *voskresniks* were presumably voluntary and claimed to draw upon enthusiasm, they were not the result of spontaneous impulse.[108] The Regulations on *Subbotniks* carefully provided for their organization and conduct, and the practical work of organizing *subbotniks* was entrusted by the party committees to a *troika,* or committee of three, selected by them to manage labor services.[109] These *troikas* worked out a general plan along with the labor committees (*trudtroika*) of the party. In addition, the regulations stipulated that "for the close, business-like connection of the party committee, the labor committees and the commissariat of labor, one of the members of the party committee must be at the same time a member of both the commissariat of labor and the labor committee."[110] Thus, through the person of a party member who was also an official of the state in the commissariat of labor, the party work in organizing *subbotniks* would be coordinated. Further, the power of both party and state could be used in organizing them. Moreover, requests for *subbotniks* were to be directed to the local commissariat of labor. "The organizations and institutions interested in arranging *subbotniks* for themselves," the Regulation read, "direct their requests for them directly to the local commissariat of labor."[111] Not later than two days before the *subbotnik* was to take place, members of the labor committees were to call a meeting of representatives from the party cells and to assign them, other party members and non-party members to definite tasks in accordance with a plan worked out by the commissariat of labor. Organizers selected by the cells for work among women were invited to these meetings.[112] Responsibility for various tasks of the *subbotniks* was assigned to the organizers of them and to the administration of the institution in which the *subbotnik* was to take place.[113] Various skilled and unskilled workers were to be supplied with the necessary tools and assigned definite places at the *subbotniks*.[114] The technical distribution of manpower and the direction of the technical work was to belong, however, to the administration of the institution at which the *subbotnik* was to take place.[115] The guidance of the *subbotnik,* in terms of the ideas it was to instill, the responsibility for the labor of the *subbotnik* workers, and the assistance to the administration in the distribution of manpower, were placed upon the organizer of the *subbotnik* who had been selected by the labor committee. The organizer was also obliged to present a report on the *subbotnik* to the commissariat of labor not later than three days after the *subbotnik* took place.[116] It should be noted here that the responsibilities of the *subbotnik* organizers and the administration of the institutions at which they were being performed for the use and distribution of manpower could lead to a conflict of jurisdictions. Thus, regulations intended to define obligations and duties could result in confusing them.

This was further complicated by the fact that the party cell also selected an elder responsible to the cell for a particular group at the *subbotnik;* he reported to the cell on the work of its own members.[117] The general responsibility for the use of manpower was shared by the elders mentioned above and by the organizers of the *subbotnik,* i.e., the labor committees.[118] "All the complaints of the responsible organizer of the *subbotnik,*" read the regulations, "are fulfilled without dispute, but complaints can be brought up to the Central Committee [of the party]."[119] In spite of the jurisdictional ambiguities that might arise, then, there was still an authority whose orders had to be followed but against whose decisions complaints could be made.

There were various categories of workers who were exempt from participation in the *subbotniks.* These were skilled workers who were freed from work assigned to those in the labor service category or those released from participation in heavy physical labor. Labor organizers or workers in particularly responsible positions, or carrying particularly heavy work loads, or performing particularly urgent tasks, could also be released personally for a period of from one to three months by order of the local party committee. Thus, those who were more skilled, more valuable and more useful to the Soviet republic were released from the obligation of donating their labor to the state in a communist fashion.

In addition, there were the ordinary exemptions for those under 16, pregnant women, nursing mothers, and those released from general labor service because of illness.[120]

Records of all these exceptions and releases were to be kept and forwarded to the higher authorities with the reports on *subbotniks.*[121]

Thus, exemptions were recorded and there was always the possibility that they could be used as evidence of a lack of consciousness or malingering on the part cf those who received them. Also, through influence, connections or bribery, exemptions could be misused to release those who had, by the regulations, no right to them.

Party members had special responsibilities towards *subbotniks,* for, according to the regulations, "Each member of the party by his own example in labor, by propaganda, must attract the non-party working masses to participation in the *subbotniks.*"[122] Moreover, each member of the party was required to participate in *subbotniks* not less than twice a month. In the light of the fact that the same demands were made upon the non-party workers in the *Nizhegorodskaiia Guberniia,* for example, this was not an excessive obligation to be placed upon those setting an example for them.

An elder or an organizer of a *subbotnik* could bring before a party court for violation of party discipline those who refused to participate or those who were not sufficiently serious about the work they performed in a *subbotnik*. If the offender could not provide a valid reason for his absence from a *subbotnik,* the party committees could give him a warning, censure him, assign him to a week's hard labor, or change his status from that of party member to party candidate.[123] Various sanctions could therefore be used to force the less enthusiastic members of the party into exemplary communist conduct. More than that, the *subbotniks* were used to purge the party of those who were considered to be insufficiently devoted. In this way, of course, all members were disciplined. *"Subbotniks,"* said Lenin, ". . . are also significant from the point of view of the party, a significance which for us, as Party members, should not be left in the shade—it is their significance as a means of purging the Party of alien elements. . . ."[124]

The subbotniks were not only used to purge and discipline the party, they were also used to discipline labor, for sanctions could also be used against non-party offenders against satisfactory *subbotnik* behavior. The regulations provided that "Non-party members who are observed behaving with a lack of consciousness regarding *subbotniks* are deprived of their right to participate in *subbotniks* and the appropriate trade union is informed of this so that it may take the proper disciplinary action."[125]

It is interesting to note that measures seem to have been provided to force party members into participation in *subbotniks* in cases in which they violated their obligations to do so. Non-party workers, however, who did not display sufficient enthusiasm for *subbotnik* labor, were deprived of the right of participation. For the communist, therefore, the *subbotnik* was a responsibility; for the non-party worker, it seems to have been a privilege by means of which he could provide evidence of his developing consciousness. By his unpaid, voluntary, enthusiastic labor, the non-party worker could begin to approach the level of consciousness presumably achieved by the communist. Further, since deprivation of the right of participation in *subbotniks* could hardly have been a punishment for the recalcitrant, the disciplinary action taken after this deprivation was in all probability a measure which made labor at *subbotniks* seem, at least to some degree, desirable. Rewards also seem to have been given, at times, to those who participated in *subbotniks*. From the overt Bolshevik viewpoint, however, these rewards were regarded as having no significance; Molotov, for example, disdainfully rejected the suggestion that enthusiasm for *subbotniks* could be explained "merely as a striving for more food, for a pound of bread, for a scanty meal and a piece of sugar candy."[126] And Lenin, quoting an article from *Pravda* of 23 May, pointed out that the *subbotnik* workers on the Alexandrovsky Railway worked five hours overtime gratis. "The only thing they got," he says, "was the right to purchase a second dinner, for which they also paid." However, if, as Lenin himself asserted at the time, hunger was common, the right even to purchase a second meal—or extra food of any kind—could prove to be no small incentive for volunteer labor.

Nevertheless, in spite of the pressures used and the rewards bestowed, there is no reason to believe that, at least among some of the workers, the *subbotniks* did fulfill one of their principal purposes—the instilling of communist consciousness and enthusiasm into the labor force. It would be a mistake to dismiss too lightly statements such as those which claimed that each *subbotnik* worker fought not only with the external enemies of hunger, disorder and ignorance, but also with the enemies within him, indolence and laziness, and that "he sensed about him the spirit of Communist labor."[127]

The consciousness that the worker acquired by labor at a *subbotnik* was presumably a consciousness of working for a new and better order. "We will roll up our sleeves," said Zinoviev, "and begin to work on the reconstruction of Russia on a new basis, on its transformation into a country which will not know either hunger, cold, or need."[128] The new order was to be built by a state which, according to the Bolsheviks, exerted the power of the proletariat and which belonged to them with all the wealth they could produce in it. A workingwoman, writing in *Pravda* on *subbotniks,* stated: "The workingwomen became imbued with the consciousness that this was voluntary labor . . . for one's own self and not for a lot of parasites. . . . Now we are all in power and we have to take care of things, to put them right. . . ."[128a] And Lenin also asserted, "For the first time after centuries of working for others, of working in subjection for the exploiter it has become possible to *work for oneself.* . . ."[129]

Moreover, in working for itself in a communist fashion, the proletariat would win the support of the peasantry for the proletarian state. With this support, the food crisis would be alleviated and the soviet power strengthened. "It is precisely such proletarian work as is called 'Communist *subbotniks,*' the work which is done at these *subbotniks* that will serve to win completely the respect and love of the peasantry for the proletarian state. Such work and only such work completely convinces the peasant that we are right, that Communism is right and makes the peasant our loyal ally. And this will lead to the complete victory of Communism over capitalism on the question of the production and distribution of grain, it will lead to the absolute consolidation of Communism. . . ."[130] For the building of the new order and the elimination of hunger, then, the support of the peasantry was necessary and the exemplary labor of the proletariat would help to acquire that support. Thus, again, the responsibility for the coming of communism and the alleviation of present conditions was placed upon the proletariat and its labor.

The purpose and function of *subbotniks,* then, was not only to provide the state with supplementary free labor but also to increase labor productivity. It served as a means of threatening party members and non-party members alike with the punishments that could result from insufficiently developed consciousness.

Nor were the *subbotniks* entirely without disadvantages. Their often sporadic, erratic character interfered with rationalized planning, and they sometimes tended to exhaust labor and place excessive wear and tear upon machinery and equipment. They were difficult to manage and interfered with the ordinary routine of work. However, Lenin reassuringly stated that "Defects, mistakes, blunders in such a new, difficult and great task are inevitable."[131] The open recognition of the serious practical disadvantages inherent in *subbotniks* indicates also that one of their purposes was not least of all to instill communist consciousness into labor.

Subbotniks and *voskresniks,* in addition to the labor service that could be compulsorily assigned by the state for indefinite periods, in accordance with the previously mentioned decree of 29 January 1920, made a fiction of the eight-hour working day that the workers had won in the February Revolution and which had been presumably guaranteed them by the Bolshevik regime.

Social Insurance

In the sphere of social insurance, Bolshevik policy also departed far from its promises. An ambitious social insurance program was announced. It was, however, never put into effect. Schmidt stated, at the Third All-Russian Congress of Trade Unions, that: "From the very first days of the foundation of NKT [People's Commissariat of Labor], it was announced that complete social insurance to the extent of full wages at the expense of the employer, at the expense of those who hired labor would be allowed to all toilers who would be exempt from all dues and that they would be allowed complete self-administration in questions of social insurance."[132] Hence the Bolsheviks had promised the insurance of complete wages at the full expense of the employer and that the administration of social insurance was to be in the hands of the workers themselves. This promise, however, was not fulfilled. "We could not at once broaden the circle of the insured," said Schmidt, "we could not at once introduce all types of social insurance for two reasons: 1) the organs actually capable of realizing the matter of social insurance were not sufficiently developed, and 2) the resources of the state were so insignificant that it was not possible to assure the insurance funds of requisite means."[133] Schmidt does not explain, however, why the necessary administrative organs could not be created for social insurance work when innumerable other departments, agencies and administrations were formed in the Bolshevik state. Nor does he explain why the Bolsheviks had promised so much at their accession to power when they were able to give so little. Not only was the pre-October Bolshevik social insurance program not realized, but also the hospital and insurance funds which individual unions had instituted and fostered were taken away from them. The workers themselves were not to be allowed to administer their own insurance funds. They were to be administered entirely by the state.[134]

Russian workers, therefore, received few, if any material benefits from the proletarian dictatorship. They received a bare subsistence wage, and were subject to long hours of work and labor tasks in addition to their normal employment. Labor was compulsory and could be assigned where the state saw fit.

Political Implications of Bolshevik Labor Discipline

One of the results of the difficult living conditions for skilled workers, however, was that the competition for skilled labor and specialists on the part of industry tended to drive their wages up and to nullify the wage scales established by the Bolsheviks. Another result was the reluctance of the workers to enter industry located in urban areas since cities particularly were poorly supplied with food. Workers seemed to have preferred to return to or remain in the agricultural communities with which they were connected. The consequent lack of skilled workers was a serious threat to the Bolshevik industrial program. The Communist Kozelev, at the Third All-Russian Congress of Trade Unions, stated, for example, that "One of the most important reasons for the crisis in production is that, in addition to the usual lack of industrial technical specialists . . . is the decrease and even the obliteration of the number of skilled workers in Russia. . . ."[135] The lack of skilled labor was being seriously felt in the Soviet state.

It is in relationship to this need for labor that the Bolshevik policy of labor discipline must be understood. The Bolsheviks, in their attempt to totally dominate the nation, could not allow their dependence upon labor to become, for the latter, a bargaining point for political and economic concessions to the working class. Free labor could have forced the Bolshevik Party into such a dependent position. Thus, before the Bolsheviks could dominate the industrial economy of the country they had to dominate labor. Labor, therefore, had to be made compulsory. Furthermore, it had to be compelled to work under conditions set by the Bolsheviks. To have made working conditions attractive to labor, on its own terms, would have signified that labor had power over the party, whereas it was the party that was intransigently insistent upon having power over labor. The creation of militarized labor units made up of unskilled labor functioned, therefore, partly to force skilled labor into choosing work in Soviet enterprises for there it enjoyed relatively better conditions. For fear of having to do something worse, skilled labor chose to do what it was being forced to do.

To emphasize the relatively better position of skilled labor, many distinctions were made between categories of workers. Under such a system, no matter how inadequate the rewards of labor can be, the more skilled receive more rewards. Purposive supply also rewarded those who worked best within the Bolshevik labor framework.

It may be said, therefore, that the Bolshevik Party, having deprived Russian labor of workers' control and of its share in managerial functions, and having deprived the trade unions of their independence, also deprived the individual worker of his freedom. Finally, it held over the worker the threat of labor that was even less free. At the same time, the Bolsheviks placed the moral responsibility for economic conditions upon the workers and played upon the workers' sense of generosity, self-sacrifice and devotion to the state.

In formulating its measures of labor discipline, the party's practical interests in industrial productivity which were, of course, valid and legitimate, have often been retrospectively magnified at the expense of its political interests. The advantages for industry of decreased pay and increased productivity are obvious and doubtless assisted in the recovery of Russian industry from revolutionary dislocation. Also, measures to control wages and increase productivity may be taken in the freest of countries during times of emergency; the Soviet Union was not only recovering from Russian participation in the World War but was engaged in civil war. Under such conditions it is reasonable to lengthen hours and to lower pay. This, however, as the source materials reveal, was not the political issue between large segments of labor and the Bolsheviks. Economic considerations, no matter how reasonable they seem, should not obscure the conflict between labor and the party in the formative years of the Soviet state. Moreover, this conflict especially where armed force was used or determined resistance was organized, was part of the civil war. In these cases the problem for the Bolsheviks was not to secure the cooperation of labor in the civil war but to force labor into obedience—to make war upon labor. The issue was not whether economic problems were to be solved but who was to solve them and by what means they were to be solved. Only after Bolshevik power had been consolidated and secured was it possible to place economic considerations above the political, and then, of course, only within the framework of the party leadership. The party did not "lead" because it held the key to economic development; it held the key to economic development because it led.

CHAPTER XIII

Retrospect

A study of the relationship between the Bolshevik Party and Russian labor from 1917 to 1920 indicates that there was a divergence between the goals and values of large groups of laborers and the Party. Before the Bolsheviks seized power, they had encouraged labor to organize factory committees and. through these organizations, to institute workers' control over their factories. The Bolshevik policy of workers' control functioned to undermine the wartime economy of the Provisional Government and also to capture the chiliastic strivings of Russian labor for the Bolshevik seizure of power.

Conflicting Concepts of Workers' Control

After the October Revolution, however, the difference between the objectives of the Bolshevik Party and of many of the factory committees became apparent. These objectives were inherent in the concepts of workers' control and of socialism itself. There are many indications that there was a strong movement among the factory committees to institute shared workers' ownership by the factory committees at each individual factory. Along with the direction of management or a voice in it, shared ownership was considered by much of labor to be workers' control. Such a concept was diametrically opposed to that of the Bolsheviks. Thus, once the Bolsheviks had acquired state power, they took measures to end the seizure of factories by the individual factory committees. Instead, they introduced the nationalization of industry from the center, and from above. This policy ultimately placed control of the economy in the hands of the party.

Workers' control before the October Revolution had served not only to undermine the economy of the Provisional Government; the factory committees had also been used by the Bolsheviks to undermine Menshevik leadership of the trade unions. Support for the Bolsheviks was overwhelmingly strong in the factory committees, but weak in the unions. The Bolsheviks had attempted to unite and centralize the factory committees and form them into a labor organization rivaling the trade unions.

The Red Guards or workers' militia that was formed by the factory committees served, before October, as a military arm of the Bolshevik Party and undermined the former Imperial army which served as the basis of military strength of the Provisional Government. It seems that partly because of the dependence of the Bolshevik Party upon the Red Guards of the factory committees in the early days following the October Revolution, the Bolsheviks continued the policy of workers' control as the workers conceived it. Workers' control over all of the economic life of Russia was proclaimed. Simultaneously, however, the Bolshevik leadership removed the control from the factory committees. The Party then placed the control of industry, by consecutive decrees, under the jurisdiction of the Supreme Council of the People's Economy dominated by the Council of People's Commissars.

Eventually, also, the Red Guards, as a type of military organization, were repudiated, in spite of the fact that ideologically they had been used to prove the superiority of the communist over the bourgeois order. If the factory committees had been permitted to maintain their factory militia, however, they could have provided an armed resistance to the Bolshevik policy of centralization and nationalization.

The Bolsheviks opposed to the policy of workers' control as the workers conceived it, a policy of workers' control which would serve to bring about the aims and purposes of the Party. While depriving the workers and their factory committees of their control over the factories at which they were employed, the Bolsheviks claimed to be extending control of the workers over all industry. While depriving the workers of any real voice in administration or management, the Bolsheviks claimed to be training labor for a future role in the direction of industry and the state. In actuality, however, by rotating in the managerial *collegium* of a factory the representatives of the workers of that particular factory, the Bolsheviks considerably weakened the workers' voice in the administration. The permanent members of the managerial *collegia* came to be individuals who were not employed at the factory whose workers they represented. These permanent members were appointed from a central trade-union organization dominated by the Bolsheviks. By 1921, one-man management, or *edinovlastie,* was substituted by *kollegial'nost'. Kollegial'-nost',* however, the practice of group management by workers and specialists, had been a fundamental principle of workers' control as instituted by the factory committees even before October.

Consciousness and Spontaneity

The resistance to the Bolshevik policy towards industry and labor displayed by many of the workers in the factory committees was attributed, within Bolshevik ideology, to a lack of consciousness. Those workers who defended the local rights of their factories and labor's share in the management and profits of their industrial enterprises were charged with acting spontaneously, that is, without consciousness. The consciousness of which the Bolsheviks spoke, however, was the consciousness of communist goals, values and objectives. Consciousness also necessitated adherence to those goals. The spontaneity of which the Bolsheviks spoke implied a rejection of Bolshevik aims and purposes. The adherents of a spontaneous movement, according to the Bolsheviks, were opposed to the Party's leading the movement and were for assisting the workers toward their own "spontaneous" goals.

The Bolshevik concept of spontaneity as applied to the factory committees and workers' control must be understood in the sense presented above. It is not construed to mean that workers' control was an undirected movement. The Bolsheviks themselves, although always intending to centralize workers' control, had advocated workers' seizure of industry before October. Until they themselves were in power, they seem to have encouraged rather than opposed workers' control as the workers conceived it. The conflict over workers' control was a conflict over the disposition of industry and the workers' share in it. It was a conflict over the varying concepts of workers' control and the action to implement those concepts. The words, however, remained, holding different meaning for the Bolsheviks and those that opposed them.

Anarchism

The Anarchists, for example, saw in workers' control, as so many of the workers conceived it, the decentralized, federated communes of an anarchist society. They lent their support, therefore, to the workers' movement of workers' control. In this way, Anarchism and workers' control, as the factory committees implemented it, became identified with one another. Anarchism supported the workers' demands for the rewards of the revolution in the present. Bolshevism, with its goal-postponing concept of the transitional period, attempted to harness chiliastic energy to the future objectives of communism.

The Trade Unions and Factory Committees

In undermining the power of the factory committees and their implementation of workers' control, the Bolsheviks made use of the trade unions. By January of 1918 the Bolshevik Party was firmly in control of the unions. It thus had no need to oppose them, as it had formerly done, through the factory committees. On the contrary, the Bolsheviks began to subordinate the factory committees to the unions. The factory committees became the lowest nuclei of the trade-union organization. By a resolution of the First All-Russian Congress of Trade Unions, the unions were empowered to call for reelections of the control commissions of the factory committees. They could temporarily shut down the factory or dismiss all or some of the workers. The trade unions could also reallocate raw materials, fuel, machinery and personnel from one factory to another.

As a result of the removal of the factory committees from any significant voice in the management of industry, and as a result of the subordination of the unions to the state, factory management became a bureaucratic function of the state itself. Parts of the former tsarist bureaucracy were used by the Bolshevik Party to administer industry in the Soviet state.

The Trade Unions, the State and the Party

The question of the relationship of the trade unions to the state and their function within it was of primary importance during the period under discussion. The trade unions, as the representatives of organized labor, had a claim to hegemony in the proletarian Soviet state. This claim was a threat to the primacy of the Party. The promise of statification that the Party held out to the trade unions, however, indicated that the unions would share in the power of the state. Nevertheless, as far as the Bolsheviks were concerned, statification necessitated the organizational independence of the unions. Organizationally, the unions were to be separate and distinct from the state, i.e., they were not to share in the state power. On the contrary, they were to be subordinated to the Commissariat of Labor which, unlike the unions, was endowed with the compulsory power of the state. The Commissariat of Labor was itself dominated by the Council of People's Commissars. The Council of People's Commissars was, in turn, an organ through which the Bolshevik Party dominated the state. The unions were to form an organization drawing as many workers into their ranks as possible; through the unions, the state and party were to dominate labor. This was the Bolshevik concept of the statification of the trade unions.

The trade unions were not only subordinated to the Commissariat of Labor, but the Heads of Centers also tried to dominate the trade unions. The Heads and Centers were, theoretically, branches of the Supreme Council of the People's Economy, but often they were established directly by individual commissars. The Heads and Centers were used, in part, to wrest control from the local soviet institutions. Furthermore, in their attack upon the local soviets, the Heads and Centers made use of the trade unions and the organizational structure of the latter. The industrial principle of organization represented by the Heads and Centers and the trade unions was used by the Party to undermine the Soviet structure. The Council of People's Commissars, to which the Heads and Centers were subordinate, by 1919 was the *de facto* governing organ of the state. It was, however, directly subordinate to the Central Committee of the Party, and to the individual Commissars who were members of the latter.

The Party itself remained separate and distinct not only from the trade unions but from the state and its other institutions as well. The Party did not identify with any institutions. It remained above them all, identifying only with power. All members of the Party were strictly subordinated to the party leadership. As early as March 1919 the party leadership advocated a purge of what it considered to be recalcitrant party members. It threatened to purge those who considered their first loyalty to be to the state or its institutions rather than to the Party.

In addition, the Bolsheviks used V.S.N.Kh. and its Heads and Centers to undercut the authority of the soviets in the localities. V.S.N.Kh. and the Heads and Centers, however, were largely based upon or imitative of the old bureaucratic organs of the Imperial government, or of the syndicates and trusts that existed under the latter. To mask the bureaucratic character of V.S.N.Kh. and the Heads and Centers, therefore, they were closely joined in 1919, with the trade unions.

However, there are indications that by 1920 the trade unions, the Heads and Centers, and branches of V.S.N.Kh. in parts of the Soviet Union were solidifying their power over industry. Therefore, just as the Bolshevik Party had used the Heads, Centers, and branches of V.S.N.Kh. in conjunction with the trade unions to weaken the power of the soviets, in 1920 the soviets were used by the Bolshevik Party to weaken the growing power of the Heads, Centers, trade unions and V.S.N.Kh. The Bolshevik Party explained the policy on the grounds that an over-rapid and over-extended centralization was taking place. In effect, however, the Bolshevik Party set up a system of overlapping and ill-defined jurisdictions. It was thus able to maneuver among the state and trade-union organs, playing off one against the other. The Party, in this way, prevented the solidification of power in any institution or organization. Power remained in the hands of the Party itself.

In 1920, also, Trotsky attempted to manipulate the trade unions for the control of industry and of the Soviet economy. Utilizing the concept of statification, Trotsky proposed to fuse the state organs of industrial administration with the trade unions. He proposed, for example, to fuse the All-Russian Central Council of Trade Unions with V.S.N.Kh., and the central committees of the unions with the Heads and Centers. Even in this process, however, Trotsky did not promise the immediate statification of the trade unions. Moreover, Trotsky's intention seems to have been to place the management and administration of industry in the hands of the leading communists in the trade unions, and especially in the hands of the personnel loyal to him.

Trotsky was successfully opposed in his plan by Lenin and Zinoviev. In this dispute, Lenin and Zinoviev clarified the position of the dominant fraction of the party concerning the statification of the trade unions. The trade unions, encompassing as many of the proletariat as possible, were to be a link between the Party and the masses. The dictatorship of the proletariat was to be carried out by the Party through the state, not through the trade unions. The goal of statification was further postponed by the use of the concept of the trade unions as schools of communism. In these schools, workers were to learn, labor leaders were to teach, and neither was to command.

In spite of the fact that by 1920 the soviets were already largely communist and were being used against the trade unions, various devices were employed to keep the soviets themselves under the strict surveillance of the Party. The clearly stated policy of reducing the number of Soviet employees could not but have increased the loyalty of all who had hoped to retain their posts. Penalties were also imposed upon the personnel of institutions that were adjudged to have unwarrantably suspended the decrees of the People's Commissariats. The use of individuals dispatched with plenipotential powers by the Party enabled the Party to extend its authority over any local soviet institution. The Worker-Peasant Inspection also functioned to check on the activities of local organs. Soviet government became a bureaucratic rule by decree.

The unions themselves were subjected to party discipline by means of party cells within them. The Party attempted stringently to control these cells too from the center. The local party cells or personnel were to act as the eyes and ears and overseers for the Party, but were to exercise no power of their own.

Labor in the Soviet State

As the Bolsheviks continued to force the attention of labor away from the rewards the workers had expected of the revolution, they began to concentrate upon labor discipline and the workers' responsibility for economic conditions. The more the workers were deprived of their voice in worker's control, the harder the Bolsheviks tried to convince them of their responsibility for increasing productivity and improving the economy. Since industry had been nationalized and thus taken out of the hands of the factory committees, the closest possible identification of the workers with the state was demanded if the former were to consider themselves the owners of industry. The Party tried to convince labor that the authority to which it was subordinate was its own authority, and the unions became responsible for fulfilling labor discipline. The Bolsheviks made it clear, however, that if the workers did not voluntarily submit to labor discipline, force would be used against them.

Labor itself became juridically compulsory and subject to assignment at the discretion of the state Labor Exchanges or *Glavkomtrud*. Labor was made compulsory partly because the reduction in real wages, in social security, and in the protection of labor made it more profitable for the workers to return to the villages and farms with which they had connections.

The system of differentiated wages established by the Soviet government through the trade unions worked in favor of specialists and skilled labor. Skilled labor was given a relatively further advantage in the Soviet economy by the relegation of unskilled labor largely to militarized labor battalions. Thus, the lot of the skilled labor, in spite of the paucity of its material rewards, became far superior to that of unskilled labor.

To increase productivity, systems of piece rate and bonus payments were introduced. Issues of rations and the system of preferential supply of the workers in particular industries and unions were used to win or force the workers in these unions to the Bolshevik cause. The principle was also established that, for a definite wage, a definite norm of productivity had to be guaranteed. In the effort to increase productivity the Bolsheviks attempted to record the output of each worker and each branch of industry. The norms thus established were periodically revised.

By such various means the Bolshevik Party turned labor aside from its own goals and its own interests and forced or manipulated the workers into serving Bolshevik aims and purposes. *Subbotniks* and *voskresniks*, also increasing the hours of the working week, served to draw upon chiliastic enthusiasm where it existed—to rationalize it, to stimulate it and to serve as examples of the conscious communist labor of the future order.

Bolshevik labor policy from 1917 to 1920 can not be understood solely by reference to its role within a centralized economic plan, or merely by reference to goals of increased economic productivity. The political relationships between the party, the state and labor must be borne in mind.

Decrees, Party Control and the Unexpected

Although the Party could not always enforce its decrees, and although its control of the state and economy was not fully effected until years after the seizure of power, the decrees, regulations and laws issued from 1917 to 1920 indicate that the intention of the Party was to achieve political control over labor as well as to regulate the national economy. The facts of subsequent Soviet history also bear this out.

It should not be assumed, however, that because the Party intended to control labor it had a preconceived plan that worked with the fine precision of a scientific instrument. The Party often met with unexpected reactions on the part of labor or even the state institutions or party members themselves. It dealt with political and economic exigencies as they arose, and if one solution did not work it tried another. The solutions attempted were reached within a definite framework based upon definite assumptions. The problems that arose were dealt with from the vantage point of those assumptions which are concomitant with a certain way of looking at the world and are directed toward certain goals and objectives. Aside from the party leadership, there seem to have been very few Russians who understood basic Bolshevik assumptions and the theoretical framework of Bolshevik ideology. Even some of the explicit objectives of the Party were not clearly understood by others, as evidenced by the differing concepts of workers' control and socialism found among groups of workers at variance with the Bolsheviks. Indeed, it may be that this very lack of understanding of Bolshevik aims and of the Bolshevik view of the world on the part of others contributed to Party success. For, in many cases, by the time Bolshevik objections were understood by those who came, through an understanding, to oppose them, the Party had acquired enough power to crush its opposition.

Bolshevik Ideology

The explanations, justifications and rationalizations of the course of action the Bolsheviks took were made within the framework of their ideology. In this ideology man does not experience the "external, objective" world directly; he experiences it by means of images or reflections. The proletariat, in its comprehension of the very laws of history which bring about the proletarian revolution and develop it, is in need of a mediator to provide it with a correct consciousness of events and of how to act within them. It is the task of the proletariat, as of all humanity, however, to comply with natural and historical laws and, by compliance, to conquer them; for "freedom is the result of necessity."

The world tends to be seen in terms of dominance and submission and a demand is made for the closest possible identification with a constantly changing external model that can never be fully known.

CHAPTER XIV

The Ethics of Soviet Labor

It was an objective of the Bolshevik Party to provide the Soviet state with a disciplined labor force capable of working in a rationalized, organized, systematized fashion. There were various practical measures taken by the party to manipulate it into working in such a manner but beyond that it attempted to instill into labor a certain approach to the world, certain moral beliefs which would affect all areas of life including the performance of work. In this sense the attitudes the party attempted to instill may be referred to as a labor ethic.[1]

Out of the large force of semi-proletarian workers who still retained many attitudes of the peasant whose labor was exerted in conjunction with the seasons, the weather and other uncontrolled phenomena, a labor force capable of constant and sustained attention to the machine was to be created. In place of large numbers of peasant proletarians who worked in order to return to the village, a proletariat was to be formed whose way of life was closely associated with the factory and the machine. And in place of a labor force that worked principally for its self-interest, satisfaction of need and the rewards of goods, a labor force was to be molded to work for the welfare of the state, for an earthly paradise, for posterity. In place of a worker whose life was spent in the personal fulfillment of spontaneous and natural emotions and needs there was to be a worker devoted to the conscious and controlled fulfillment of the needs of the state. Lenin inveighed against "... the many newcomers who came into factory life ... with the sole end in view of making as much as possible and clearing out."[2] To create a new force of workers, the Party was prepared to devote dauntlessly and relentlessly its time and effort. "The work of creating a new labor discipline," said Lenin, "of creating new forms of social ties between men, of creating new forms and methods of getting people to work, must take many years and decades."[3] Bolshevik ideology functioned in the molding of such a labor force.

It has been seen that the ideology demanded that man was not to function spontaneously but in such a way as to anticipate the course of historical events. ". . . Our thoughts and our feelings," says a communist in an early Soviet novel, "belong to that which one calls necessity: the incontrovertible truth of history."[4] Only the trained and expert mind, however, could correctly foresee the laws of history, and the experience of a large part of Soviet labor tended to prove to it—that it had incorrectly understood the course of events and conditions. The understanding of workers' control and of socialism itself, held by many Russian workers, had been proved by the Party to be in error. For after the seizure of power, the Bolshevik Party, through its control of the state, was able to direct events or determine their interpretation. And the Bolsheviks had demonstrated to a large part of the labor force that it was lacking in communist consciousness, that it had misunderstood the events and goals of history. Moreover, the party had assigned to labor through its organizations—the unions and factory committees—the tasks of fulfilling Bolshevik policy, not of formulating it. In addition, from their position of power, the Bolsheviks continued to demand the closest identification with what they decreed the course of history to be, and they demanded a like identification with the state through whose power communism would one day be attained. This demand, which so many workers had found so difficult to meet, and the doubt generated by the ideology itself concerning the ability to identify with an ever-changing external model, served to reinforce the authority of the party as mediator. It could serve as well to generate insecurity among workers regarding their role in the building of the Soviet state. Also giving rise to doubt and uncertainty, and congruent with the ideology, was bureaucratic rule by decree arising out of the expediency of circumstances and conditions known only to the informed expert or official.

The behavior and conduct of communists themselves was depicted as being inscrutable. "The two members of the Special Commission," a Communist author, Gladkov, writes in his novel *Cement,* "were strangers. Both wore military coats and caps. One had prominent cheek-bones and was so dark he was almost black; his brow, nose and chin were dotted with grey warts. It was impossible to know whether he was smiling or in a rage. The other one was gaunt with a pale face and a beard like a besom. He was constantly taking it between three fingers and pulling it. When he sat down he shrivelled up into the smallest possible compass. When he raised his eyes they disappeared under half-closed lids. When he interrogated a Communist summoned before him, he did not look at him, but spoke as though he were addressing someone else. . . . And when the gaunt man called . . . Serge could not catch whether it was he who spoke or the man beside him."[5] The communist was often portrayed in such a way, remote and puzzling; as the personification of authority, he was often inscrutable. Thus, not only were doubts and insecurity engendered abstractly, conceptually, and ideologically, the experience and relations of the Soviet worker with communist officials would also seem, according to descriptions by communists themselves, to have engendered doubt and insecurity concerning his understanding of Soviet authority.

In the *subbotniks,* however, the Communist Party provided a means by which that insecurity could be silenced. Voluntary unpaid labor in service to the state was regarded as the only truly communist feature to exist in the dictatorship of the proletariat. "Communist labour," said Lenin, "in the narrower and stricter sense of the term, is labour performed gratis for the benefit of society, labour performed not as a definite duty, not for the purpose of obtaining a right to certain products, not according to previously established and legally fixed rates; labour performed without the expectation of reward, labour performed out of a habit of working for the common good—labour as the requirement of a healthy body."[6]

Labor becomes an end in itself and so far removed from the desire for reward, so foreign to feelings of compulsion, that it is almost reduced to a physiological need, to "the requirement of a healthy body." It is, however, more than that, for it is labor performed out of a habit of working for the common good, and therein lies its ethical content. Devoted labor, labor beyond the demands of rules and regulations, could thus be evidence of the communist spirit. Personal anxiety and insecurity on the part of the worker concerning his ability to understand and to further the demands of history, of the state, of the party, could be reduced by recourse to labor.

For, if the worker could not choose the roads toward the earthly paradise, if he could not understand why they were taken, through his sustained and conscious labor he could demonstrate his eagerness to take those roads. Insecurity itself, therefore, could become a motive force of work.

It was not sufficient, however, to demonstrate eagerness and devotion spontaneously or impulsively. It was necessary to provide a lifetime of devoted, systematic labor. "In the future," said Lenin, "everyone who calls his enterprise, institution or undertaking a commune *without having set an example* of real Communist organization achieved as a result of arduous toil and practical *success in prolonged effort,* shall be made a laughing stock and mercilessly pilloried as a charlatan or windbag."[7]

Proof of the worker's claim to be a member of the new society was a life organized around the performance of work. It should be recognized, however, that among its other uses, the *subbotnik* functioned not only to keep alive the workers' chiliastic energies and outbursts but also to encourage the rationalized organization of working time.

Although labor can be an end in itself, it acquires this character because it contributes to the building of an ideal society, an ideal world, a world of plenty. "The programme . . . ," said Lenin, "is simple, clear and intelligible to all; it is: everyone to have sound footwear and good clothing; everyone to have warm dwellings."[8] "For there is enough bread, iron, timber, wool, cotton and flax in Russia to satisfy the needs of all, if only labor and its products are properly distributed . . ."[9] However, all these possessions were the property of the state, the belongings of "the people," and were to be carefully cared for, spent and saved. "Communism begins," said Lenin, "when the rank and file workers begin to display self-sacrificing concern . . . for husbanding every pood of grain, coal, iron and other products which do not accrue to the workers personally or to their 'close kith and kin,' but to their remote 'kith and kin,' i.e., to society as a whole, to tens and hundreds of millions of people organized in a single Socialist state and then a Union of Soviet Republics."[10] The worker, then, was to care scrupulously for the goods of this world precisely because they belonged to the state and to "the people" and not to him alone. At the same time, however, the worker was encouraged to identify so closely with the state that the property of the state seemed to be his property. ". . . The Soviets are their own and not alien institutions to the masses of the workers and peasants," insisted Lenin.[11] And a model workingwoman, reflecting this view, is reported as saying, "The most important thing is that I myself am the owner of the factory. The factory is mine. The state is mine . . . I am part of all the Soviet power."[12] Having identified so closely with the state and its possessions that they seem to be hers, the speaker devotes part of her time and labor voluntarily and without pay to take special care of them. "I was put in charge of the struggle with waste," says the same worker. "You see, each little piece of cotton costs us labor and money. We must take care of it and I make that my job. First of all I go to work a half hour before the beginning of the shift. I do this, of course, because of my own consciousness. I look over the floor and pick up any bits of thread that are left on it. During working hours . . . I see that the thread on the bobbins is not knotted. At the end of the working day, I also stay behind for a while and sort out the defective goods . . . You see, now the power is ours, the factory is ours, the land is ours, who then should take care of things if we do not do it ourselves?"[13] This worker's consciousness leads her to extend her proprietorial care even further, for she tells us that "I see that the slop which goes to feed the pigs is all right. I myself look into the garbage buckets to see whether or not there are any little bits of glass or iron. Who knows sometimes a class enemy may even poison the slop. There have been such cases."[14]

Care is taken of the common goods not only because they are now the workers' own but because they are the people's property and altruism becomes identified with self-interest. Thrift is ethically desirable. "Introduce accurate and conscientious accounting of money, manage economically, do not be lazy, do not steal . . ." Lenin admonished.[15] And a Soviet bulletin stated: ". . . intensity of labor, care and consideration for machines, tools and instruments, conscientiousness in the use of materials, etc., must exist in the consciousness of the workers . . . All the population . . . must understand that the abolition of all types of labor desertion and self-seeking, lateness to work, carelessness, indolence, and misuses are problems of life and death for all the country . . ."[16]

Part of the ethic supported by Bolshevik ideology led to the condemnation of one's fellow citizen for his deviation from prescribed conduct rather than to sympathy for the weakness or perhaps integrity that would lead him to resistance. The class enemy was always present and could consist of those lacking in "consciousness," of those who did not willingly devote their lives to labor and self-sacrifice for the state, as well as those who opposed it. For ". . . it is those who violate labour discipline in any factory, in any place who are *responsible* for the starvation and unemployment . . . the guilty ones must be found, tried before the court and ruthlessly punished."[17] Not only was the shirking of duty an offense but it was construed as an offense against labor itself, a cause of the ills from which labor suffered. Shirkers were class enemies equated in their criminality with the idle, the rich, the "exploiters" and other offenders against the proletarian dictatorship. And the revolutionary violence directed against offenders was itself construed as having its basis in a disciplined labor force. "The economic foundation of . . . revolutionary violence, the guarantee of its virility and its success is the fact that the proletariat represents and carries out a higher type of social organization of labor compared with capitalism."[18] The class-centric orientation of the ideology led to the venting of resentment and violence against "the class enemy," among them those who were guilty of a breach of the labor ethic, or led at least to the surveillance or supervision of the offenders or potential offenders. And if there were a this-worldly goal, an earthly paradise to reach in the future, there was, for the enemies of the proletarian state, a this-worldly hell in the here and now. "Not a single rogue (including those who shirk their work)," said Lenin, "[is] to be at liberty; all are to be kept in prison or put to compulsory labor of the hardest kind . . . In one place half a score of rich, a dozen rogues, half a dozen workers who shirk their work . . . will be put in prison. In another place they will be put to cleaning latrines. In a third place they will be provided with 'yellow tickets' after they have served their time, so that all the people shall have these *pernicious* people under their surveillance until they reform. In a fourth place one out of every two idlers will be shot on the spot."[19]

The punishment for a worker who did not persevere in systematized and rationalized labor was a random and non-rational mode of punishment, which did not fall with equal justice upon all but threatened each: here they will be given one punishment, there another, "one out of every two will be shot." This could not but have functioned to increase insecurity, and the means of silencing that insecurity in turn could not but have been disciplined, systematized and organized labor.

To work in this systematized and organized fashion the worker had to exercise constant self-control. "Everyone of us must fulfill one and the same obligation," said Trotsky. "I work a certain number of hours a day with all the energy and all the application I am capable of . . . ,"[20] "and . . . every particle of labor should be really filled with work . . ."[21] ". . . work without rest or haste. . . ."[22] And a manager in the new soviet industry says to a workingman, in the novel *Cement,* "You musn't waste time to spit here, to wink or blow your nose . . . only . . . work. Every second is more precious to us than a whole life."[23] In the labor ethic, a consciousness of time seems to inculcate self-discipline and self-control for the purpose of leading the worker toward a rationalized, systematized, organized life. In Kataev's novel *Time Forward,* for example, time itself becomes an external authority which serves to overcome the spontaneous expression of needs and emotions and becomes not only a measure of labor but a measure of life.[24]

Obedience to management, as well as a developed sense of time, served to inculcate discipline and functioned as proof of "conscious" devotion to socialism. "In regard to . . . individual dictatorial powers," said Lenin, "from the point of view of specific tasks of the present moment, it must be said that large scale machine industry which is precisely the material productive source and foundation of socialism —calls for absolute and strict unity of will which directs the joint labor of hundreds, thousands, and tens of thousands of people. The technical, economic and historical necessity of this is obvious, and all those who have thought about socialism have always regarded it as one of the conditions of socialism. But how can strict unity of will be ensured? By thousands subordinating their will to the will of one." The willingness of the worker to submit to the authority placed above him in the performance of his work would not only be proof of his unity with the collective will but would remove the necessity of using compulsion against him. "Given ideal . . . consciousness and discipline on the part of those taking part in common work this subordination would more than anything remind one of the mild leadership of an orchestra. It may assume the sharp forms of a dictatorship if ideal discipline and class consciousness are lacking. But be that as it may, *unquestioning submission* to a single will is absolutely necessary for the success of labour processes that are based on large scale machine industry."[25] Resistance to managerial authority would testify to the worker's divergence from and rejection of the collective will, whereas obedience in the performance of his labor duty gave evidence for the worker of his fellowship with his class, of his devotion to socialism, and of his ethical conduct.

Furthermore, obedience to the technician, the specialist, the manager was to substitute for the worker's exercise of managerial responsibility through factory committee meetings. It was to these meetings the Party had attributed the disintegration of labor discipline.[26] However, meetings were to be retained as a device by which the workers might be convinced that their concern with problems of labor and management could best be served by subordination to the "people's" specialists. The task of the Communist Party, Lenin said, was to lead the masses ". . . along the path of coordinating the task of holding meetings and discussing the conditions of labour with the task of unquestioningly obeying the will of the Soviet leader, of the dictator, during working time."[27]

More than that, the worker was to internalize external authority to the point where obedience, self-control and discipline were chosen by himself rather than imposed from above. In the meetings, the worker was to identify his will with the will of the collective, which in turn was identified with communist aims and purposes. ". . . Without holding meetings," said Lenin, "the masses of the oppressed could never pass from the *compulsory discipline* of the exploiters to . . . conscious voluntary discipline."[28]

The meetings were to serve not only to unify but instill collectivism into the worker on the basis of that unification. Bogdanov, having become prominent in labor agitation and propaganda and remaining officially so until October 1920, asserted that ". . . unification is achieved in fact and [is] only gradually expressed in consciousness."[29] Here Bogdanov seems to have come over to Lenin's dictum that social consciousness reflects social being. As in Lenin, the reflection is not equated with reality, but the demand that the reflection be as accurate as possible remains. Also, it is within time and with the development of historical conditions that the relative truths of the reflection approach the absolute more closely.

Consciousness of collectivism as differentiated from *kollegial'nost'* presupposes a fusion of purposes as well as a union of forces. Nor was collectivist consciousness to be confused with democratic consciousness, which, according to Bogdanov, considers each individual will, adds them up by means of a vote, and subordinates the minority to the majority, thereby creating an individualistic authority and a mechanical subordination.[30] In contrast, "the transition from democratic consciousness to collectivist consciousness consists . . . not in the subordination of the majority to the minority but its full agreement with the majority."[31] Such subordination to the collective takes place through "consciousness."

A collectivist consciousness develops, therefore, which "works out . . . a way of life and the norms for it.[32] The previous norms of a way of life were called habits, laws, morality, but "It is entirely incorrect to designate new laws in such a way."[33] "Custom," wrote Bogdanov, "has the sanction of the past, law the sanction of state power, morals the sanction of God's will and justice, the sanction of abstract good."[34] None of these is fitting for the proletariat, which must have the sanction of ". . . expediency from the point of view of the collective."[35] Here Bogdanov seems to be rooting the norms for a proletarian way of life in collectivist consciousness rather than in nature or history. Such norms, insisted Bogdanov ". . . do not need the sanction of compulsion, the force of compulsion, for whoever belongs to the collective lives for its purposes without any compulsion."[36] The worker, then, must understand what has to be done and do it for the sake of the collective, whose ultimate aims were the building of socialism and the Soviet state. Expedience became the sanction of all action, and expediency, as has been shown, was determined by the Party. The very sanctions of ethical and moral conduct in practical labor affairs comes, in this way, to be determined for the worker by the technician, specialist or manager who, like the worker, also fulfilled the policy of the Party. The manner in which this policy would be fulfilled in specific instances, however, was discussed at meetings of the workers' collectives, and it became the obligation of each to fuse his will with the general will of the collective, to internalize that will and to do voluntarily and with enthusiasm that which had to be done. This class collectivism was enjoined as a way of life.[37]

Expedience as an ethical sanction for a way of life could be adapted with ease to the ideological demand that the mind reflect the ever-changing reality. It could be used in a practical and concrete fashion to rationalize the constant changes and shifting authority among the various Soviet institutions.[38]

The discipline that enforced collectivism was "comradely discipline," in which the will of the leader was identified with the will of the collective itself. "The leader," said Bogdanov, "is not a power, he is only a competent individual. Power gives way to competence, i.e., to subordination to an organizer within those limits in which he is more experienced and know the will of the collective."[39] Experience itself, however, was construed as a general achievement and possession of the collective in its broadest sense—the collective of man.

The leader was regarded as having a greater and better sum of such experience. In addition, the competence of the leader as an organizer or manager is based often on his political experience, on his knowledge of what position the masses should take on a given problem, for he ". . . is better acquainted than others with the will of the collective."[40]

It was, then, not only in determining general policy and major decisions that a mediator was needed to correctly understand, interpret and foresee the future event; a mediator—the specialist, technician, manager, leader, party member—was needed in the factory as well to correctly determine, through his "competence," the will of the collective itself.

Conversely, however, the workers' meetings, carried on as they were under surveillance of the party members, were also used to exert pressure upon and confine the authority of the technicians, specialists and managers. The workers could demand an increase of production over that planned by management, could offer alternative solutions to factory problems, and could make charges and accusations against management which could jeopardize its position with higher state and party authorities. Thus, the workers' meetings served not only to bring the workers into agreement with management but also as a device by which they could express their views and suggestions concerning the means to attain production goals. For such reasons, a believing worker could say with pride, "And now I am the power; if I see anything that is incorrect, I can go all the way to Kalinin [Chairman of the All-Russian Central Executive Committee of the Soviets]. Everywhere they must listen to me."[41] The believer, then, felt that his concern for production and the management of industry was respected and valued.

Moreover, if the worker had to exert self-control and discipline in unquestioning submission to the will of the dictator during working time, he himself, in relation to the machine, could play the role of organizer and manager, performing work of an intellectual and spiritual character; for, according to Bogdanov, there were two kinds of labor, the labor of the administrator and the labor of those who execute his orders. In relationship to the machine, the worker was both one and the other, for, Bogdanov claimed, "This division of labor is the broadest we know in the history of man. It may be compared with the division of functions between head and hands. . . . And in actuality the worker at the machine directs it just as the previous organizer-director managed the workers. And at the same time the worker, as previously, remains subordinate, remains the one who fulfills the task," he becomes a "worker-director."[42]

The machine is identified with the worker and the worker with the machine. "When I'm with the engines," says a worker in *Cement,* "I'm an engine myself . . . For me, there's only one thing: me and the machine, we are one."[43] And in his identification with the machine the worker is bound to it with ties of affection. "So long as the machines are alive we can't get away from them. The yearning for machines is stronger than that for a sweetheart."[44] The worker must exert discipline not only upon himself but upon the machine, for "machines need discipline and a live hand. . . ."[45] They are surrogate workers. "The machine was substituted for the previous hand worker. It thus is his own kind of iron slave. . . ."[46] Before the introduction of machines, the organizer and director of hand labor gave orders but usually did not do physical work. "But the worker-director, of course, cannot give orders—the machine does not understand, nothing happens and he himself acts on it with his hands."[47] In his attention to the machine, ". . . the worker becomes an engineer."[48] "An exertion of an intellectual character is demanded of the worker and also a longer, steadier exertion . . . an uninterrupted intellectual activity."[49] Care and knowledge of the machine endowed labor with an intellectual and spiritual character; dignified and elevated it. For the worker "has attentively to watch the movements of the machine, to control them . . . changing in some sense or other their direction, speed, force, etc., in general to regulate them. In cases of breakdown, and breakdown occurs the more often, the more complicated the machine is, he has to consider and decide what to do, to take the initiative, to think quickly and make independent decisions . . . basing his decisions on an exact knowledge of how the machine is constructed. Obviously all this is intellectual effort: attentive work is, of course, exertion of a spiritual character."[50] The worker, then, worked not only with his hands but with his mind and soul. If he had no effective voice in his government, or in the regulation of industry, he yet had decision-making powers over the machine. What is more, the intellectuals who formulated his ideology and molded his ethic endowed him with what seems to be the greatest honor they could give—the performance of intellectual labor.

To attend the machine properly, however, the worker must derive a sense of pleasure from his work, for "It is not possible to calculate steadily and well, to act exactly and quickly, if this does not become for the worker a positive factor, if he does not have all this in his soul . . . he cannot but regard it as a necessary, natural, normal and in some degree even pleasant part of his existence; otherwise he would be a bad worker."[51] Labor becomes the focus of the worker's life, it colors his very existence, elicits his devotion and fills him with pride. "The whole way of life of the working class is defined by his labor. In the thinking of the worker, the idea of labor occupies a central place, it is his point of departure. In his world of feelings there . . . is developed first of all love for labor, secondly pride in labor because he sees constantly in his work how labor conquers nature, conquers spontaneity."[52]

Labor, then, is the very force by which man, having recognized the necessity in nature and history, systematically puts its laws to use. Through systematic self-control and discipline, through submission to the will of the dictator during working hours, and at all times to the party as mediator, the worker provides the energy and power by which dominance of nature and of history is achieved. Labor discipline is not just something to which the worker must submit and make the best of, it is not merely a means of raising labor productivity; for by the conquest of his spontaneous impulses, the worker helps to free mankind from dependence upon nature and assists in the conquest of history: in this way ". . . the proletariat fights for the liberation of all humanity."[53] Thus the worker must perform his labor with a sense of comradely love and ethical responsibility. He must be conscious of the inseparable connection of the "self" with the course of world history. And the systematic fulfillment of his daily task by the worker in a lifetime of labor brings all men closer to the mastery of society, of the world, and indeed even of the cosmos. In building communism in an organic connection with his collective, the worker builds in himself a vital need for labor as a means of creativity, of fulfillment, and even of happiness.

In this sense, then, within the experience of the believing worker who assumes the responsibility, his submission to the Party becomes equated with submission to the laws of nature, and freedom is the result of necessity. Compulsion becomes self-compulsion and self-compulsion the voluntary performance of duty.

In the performance of duty, not only work but self-sacrifice itself became psychically desirable as evidence and reassurance of devotion to the state and the communist cause. In an economy in which the production of consumer goods was neglected and the barest necessities were scarce, living with a minimum of material possessions and comforts for the sake of building socialism could also serve as proof of virtue. And the greater rewards of managers and technicians could be viewed as justly distributed for greater service to the state.

This ideology and ethic not only manipulated hate and fear of the class enemy, not only fostered insecurity, but manipulated also love for mankind and its future. It not only demanded submission and compliance, it imbued the worker with pride in his labor, pride in his responsibility and pride in himself. "We shall endeavour, comrades," said Trotsky, "to erect in the nearest future on our squares, monuments to Labour, monuments to workers . . . monuments which will remind everyone of you . . . look, you were a slave, you were nothing and now you must become everything, you must rise high, you must learn, you must become the master of life."[54] Constantly reminded of his former oppression, the worker was promised that his posterity would dominate the universe. "We must see to it," said Trotsky, "that our children . . . [will] be able to live as befits a human being who calls himself 'lord of creation' and not as hitherto like a wretched slave, crushed and oppressed."[55]

Remembrance of the labor of the proletariat would be found in monuments and its everlasting life in the generations of its progeny. Individual immortality was denied the proletariat by the materialist basis of Bolshevik ideology and its repudiation of fideism and Christianity.[56] Hence the identification with both the collective and the state and with the achievement of each could be further intensified. Faced with the finality of mortality, Russian labor could find compensation in the hope or conviction that they were building the eventual communist society. In that future order the fruits of their labor would mature. "A man must know," says a scientist in a contemporary Soviet drama, "that after death he lives only in what he has done—There is no after life—Remember that everything that it is given to you to do on earth—that alone is your life. . . . Then men will begin to think. Have I done enough? Is it only for this that I was born?"[57] Yet the achievements of men of science, letters or politics are more lasting than those of laborers, the products of whose efforts remain *individually* anonymous and most often are soon consumed.[58] The anonymity of labor and its collective character was to be brilliantly illuminated after the death of Lenin. For not only were his name, his personality and his deeds to be remembered, he was to be preserved bodily in this world and on this earth. Passing generations of Soviet citizenry in all their finite mortality were to view with awe his timeless body, witnessing that it was impervious to corruption, decay or death. Their bodies, however, would return to dust, releasing no immortal soul for eternal life. Only as builders of a future order could they attain a semblance of immortality. Through their labor the state would wither away. When the state withered away their labor would flower. In a paradise on earth their descendants would be "the lords of creation."

The most important compensation to labor, therefore, to the believing and the faithful, were psychic rewards found in the acceptance of Bolshevik ideology and the ethic integrated with it. Within this frame of reference, the workers became protagonists in the earthly drama, heroic actors indispensable to the scene.

Appendix

Berkeleian Arguments Against the Theory of Reflection[1]

The arguments are as follows: first, if two things resemble each other, they must look like each other, feel like each other, taste like each other. etc. Hence, statements of the form "A resembles B" (where "A" and "B" are names of material objects—images, colors, sounds, mirages, rainbows, etc.) are verified by looking at, touching, listening to, tasting, smelling, etc., both A and B and comparing features of them. Consider a case in which we want to know if a visual sensation is an accurate image of an object. When A is a sensation and B is a material object in the external world, as it is for Lenin, the statement "I see B" means: 1) I have a sensation, 2) the sensation resembles B, and 3) the sensation is caused by B.[2] If to see B means only to have a sensation A, it is impossible to observe both the sensation and the object in order to compare the sensation to the object. Therefore, there is no way of telling whether A resembles B. Parallel arguments may be constructed to show the impossibility of determining whether sensations of the other senses resemble objects.[3] And to compare, in this way, one sensation to another in order to determine the reliability of sense images of external objects, of images produced by sensations, would be, as Wittgenstein remarks in another context, "As if someone were to buy several copies of the morning paper to assure himself that what it said was true."[4]

Second, Lenin says that when you see an object B you have a sensation A which is caused by B so that there could be no sensation without the object B.[5] However, statements of the form "B causes A" can be verified only by observing that A never occurs unless B obtains. This means that to verify statements of the form "B causes A," it is necessary to observe both A and B. Consider the case where A is a sensation and B an object. For Lenin, to observe B means to have a sensation A. That means that A and B cannot be observed independently, that the object and the sensation cannot be observed separately from each other or that it is impossible to observe both A and B, object and sensation, at the same time. Hence the statement "B causes A" cannot in principle be verified where A is a sensation and B is an object.[6]

Third, Berkeley and other theorists (some contemporary Oxford philosophers) believe that a given theory of the kind that Lenin espoused, the claim that there are material objects which resemble sensations or images is not false but literally without meaning. To resemble an image, a material object would have to have some features in common with the image, such as size, color, texture, etc. These theorists claim that within the context of a theory like Lenin's it is impossible for a material object to have such properties, just as it is impossible for a musical tone to be red or a smell to be high-pitched. It was seen above that, in Lenin's theory, statements of the form "I see (hear, touch, etc.) A" turn out to mean I have an image, the image resembles A, the image is caused by A. Accordingly, what is directly experienced is not the object A which is seen (heard, felt, etc.) *via* the image but the image itself.

Berkeley says we do not perceive anything by any sense unless we can perceive it directly.[7] A reason for saying this is that, to perceive something is to detect its presence and we cannot detect the presence of anything which is not itself directly perceived, unless we have a way of knowing that it is present whenever that which we directly perceive is present. In order to establish a correlation between two things so that we can say that the presence of one of them indicates the presence of the other, we must be able at least in one case to have a direct perception of both of them.

For example, if I hear a knock on the door, I cannot doubt whether I have had an auditory experience but I can perfectly well wonder who was knocking or, in unusual situations (e.g., if I know I am subject to hallucinations), whether what I heard was really a knock on the door at all. If I say "I hear Boris Sergeievich at the door," I must be perceiving Boris Sergeievich indirectly, since all I can be said to perceive directly is the sound. In case of doubt as to who is there or whether there is anyone there, the presence of Boris Sergeievich can be established only by opening the door and looking. If no such check could ever be carried out at any time, then I could never say "I hear Boris Sergeievich" because there would be no way of correlating the sound with his presence. Hence I cannot perceive him even indirectly unless, in principle at least, it is possible to perceive him directly.

In Lenin's theory, only images can be directly perceived; material objects cannot. Berkeley argues that nothing can be said to have a color unless it is visible and nothing can be said to be visible unless it can be perceived, and (presumably because of the kinds of considerations raised above) that nothing can be perceived unless it can be directly perceived. Further, since material objects cannot in principle be directly perceived, they are, therefore, strictly speaking, invisible; hence, by Lenin's theory, they cannot be said to have colors.[8] The same arguments may be applied to all other sensible qualities in virtue of which Lenin claims that material objects can resemble images. Berkeley argues that a sensible property (e.g., a color) can be like nothing but another sensible property.[9] Since it follows from Lenin's theory that natural objects cannot be directly perceived, it also follows that they cannot have sensible properties—which then must reside in the image. Hence, by Lenin's theory, it makes no sense to say that material objects resemble or fail to resemble images because it is logically impossible for the two to share qualities by which they may be compared.[10]

FOOTNOTES

PROSPECT

1. For his concept of history the author is most indebted to the influence of R. G. Collingwood and Hannah Arendt; especially to Collingwood's *The Idea of History,* Oxford, London, 1946, and Hannah Arendt's essay "The Concept of History" in *Between Past and Future, Six Exercises in Political Thought,* World, Cleveland, 1963 (henceforth referred to as Arendt, H., *Between Past and Future*), pp. 41-90.

CHAPTER I

1. Because of Lenin's leadership of the party, and because his theory of knowledge and theory of history still function in the training of party theoreticians, they may be considered not only an indication of the fundamental attitudes of Lenin but of the Party as well.
2. Lenin, V. I., *Materialism and Empirio-Criticism, Critical Comments on a Reactionary Philosophy,* Foreign Languages Publishing House, Moscow, 1952 (henceforth referred to as Lenin, V. I., *Materialism and Empirio-Criticism*).
3. *Ibid.* p. 126.
4. *Ibid.,* p. 94.
5. *Ibid.,* p. 108.
6. *Ibid.,* pp. 78 and 98.
7. *Ibid.,* p. 113.
8. *Ibid.,* p. 115.
9. *Ibid.,* p. 98.
10. *Ibid.,* p. 113.
11. *Ibid.,* p. 114.
12. *Ibid.,* p. 111.
13. *Ibid.,* p. 107.
14. *Ibid.,* pp. 116 and 103-104.
15. *Ibid.,* p. 115.
16. *Ibid.,* p. 85.
17. *Ibid.,* p. 44.
18. *Ibid.,* p. 103.
19. *Ibid.,* p. 44.
20. *Ibid.,* pp. 124 and 135.
21. *Ibid.,* p. 130.
22. *Ibid.,* p. 17. (Italics mine)
23. *Ibid.,* p. 99. (Italics mine)
24. *Ibid.,* p. 100.
25. *Ibid.,* p. 106.

26. *Ibid.*, p. 105.
27. *Ibid.*, p. 138.
28. *Ibid.*, pp. 127 and 276.
29. *Ibid.*, p. 170.
30. *Ibid.*, p. 155.
31. *Ibid.*, p. 279.
32. *Ibid.*, p. 276.
33. *Ibid.*, p. 156.
34. *Loc. cit.*
35. *Ibid.*, p. 157.
36. *Ibid.*, p. 133. Lenin cites as an example Boyle's Law. For the relationship of absolute to relative truth, see also p. 177.
37. *Ibid.*, p. 177.
38. *Ibid.*, p. 269.
39. *Ibid.*, p. 132.
40. *Ibid.*, p. 133.
41. *Ibid.*, p. 132.
42. Lenin, V. I., *Philosophical Notebooks, Collected Works* 38, 4th ed., Lawrence and Wishart, London, 1961 (henceforth referred to as Lenin, V. I., *Philosophical Notebooks, C.W.* 38), p. 361. The author does not subscribe to the use of the verb "to be" as it is employed by Lenin in saying that the occurrence of "is" in "Fido is a dog" and "John is a man" indicates that the individual is the universal.
43. Lenin's use of "negation" here is closer to Hegel's use of *"aufheben"* than it is to the ordinary concept of negation, according to which P=P.
44. Lenin, V. I., *Philosophical Notebooks, C.W.* 38, pp. 361-362.
45. Lenin, V. I., *Materialism and Empirio-Criticism,* p. 131.
46. *Ibid.*, p. 135.
47. *Loc. cit.*
48. *Loc. cit.*
49. *Ibid.*, p. 132.
50. *Ibid.*, p. 155.
51. *Ibid.*, p. 190.
52. *Ibid.*, p. 167.
53. *Ibid.*, p. 85.
54. *Ibid.*, p. 191.
55. *Ibid.*, p. 192.
56. *Loc. cit.*
57. *Ibid.*, p. 156.
58. *Ibid.*, p. 190.
59. *Ibid.*, p. 193.
60. *Ibid.*, pp. 192-193.
61. *Ibid.*, p. 193.
62. *Ibid.*, p. 177.
63. *Ibid.*, pp. 183-184.
64. *Ibid.*, p. 61 This assertion, however, should not be confused with the contention that common sense serves to fit the perceptions of the other senses into a world all men share.
65. *Ibid.*, p. 38.

66. *Ibid.*, p. 39.

67. *Ibid.*, p. 38.

68. *Ibid.*, p. 48.

69. For the view of the relationship between science and epistemology presented here, see Price, H. H., *Perception*, Methuen, London, 1961, pp. 1-2.

70. Lenin, V. I., *Materialism and Empirio-Criticism*, p. 337.

71. Lenin, V. I., *Materializm i Emperiokrititsizm, Kriticheskie Zametki ob Odnoi Reaktsionnoi Filosofii*, Gosudarstvennoe Izdatel'stvo Politicheskoi Literatury, n.p. 1953, p. 308, translation mine. The Russian translation into English, in the English edition of Lenin's work used throughout this paper, renders the Russian word *ideal'no-tochnoe* as "perfectly exact," which is misleading. The sense is not that the reflection is perfectly exact but as exact as possible or ideally exact.

72. Lenin, V. I., *Materialism and Empirio-Criticism*, p. 337.

73. For Lenin on Berkeley, see *Materialism and Empirio-Criticism*, pp. 14-28.

74. For Lenin on solipsism, see *Materialism and Empirio-Criticism*, pp. 34-35, 89 ff.

75. For three arguments against the theory of reflection, arguments adopted from Berkeley, see Appendix.

76. The Oxford philosophers, such as J. L. Austin, for example, contemporarily hold such views.

77. Lenin, V. I., *Materialism and Empirio-Criticism*, p. 344.

78. This theory of reflection does function differently, for example, in the philosophy of Locke.

79. Lenin, V. I., *Materialism and Empirio-Criticism*, p. 344.

80. *Loc. cit.*

81. Lenin, V. I., "What the Friends of the People Are," *Collected Works* 1, 4th ed., Lawrence and Wishart, London, 1961 (henceforth referred to as Lenin, V. I., "What the Friends of the People Are," *C.W.* 1), p. 142.

82. *Ibid.*, p. 167.

83. *Loc. cit.* Witt-Hansen, in his *Historical Materialism. The Method, The Theories, Exposition and Critique. Book One—The Method*, Munksgaard, Copenhagen, 1960 (henceforth referred to as Witt-Hansen, J., *Historical Materialism, The Method*), pp. 67-68, claims that historical materialists assert social and historical phenomena cannot be described in terms of biology. This does not seem to be true of Lenin.

84. Lenin, V. I., "What the Friends of the People Are," *C.W.* 1, p. 167.

85. Lenin, V. I., *State and Revolution*, International Publishers, New York, 1932 (henceforth referred to as Lenin, V. I., *State and Revolution*), p. 70.

86. For a discussion of historical materialism as a method, see Witt-Hansen, J., *Historical Materialism, The Method*.

87. Lenin, V. I., "What the Friends of the People Are.," *C.W.* 1, p. 163.

88. *Ibid.*, p. 164.

89. *Ibid.*, p. 166.

90. *Ibid.*, p. 172.

91. *Loc. cit.*

92. *Ibid.*, p. 173.

93. *Loc. cit.*
94. *Ibid.*, p. 183.
95. *Ibid.*, p. 189.
96. Lenin, V. I., *Imperialism, The Highest Stage of Capitalism, A Popular Outline,* International Publishers, New York, 1939 (henceforth referred to as Lenin, V. I., *Imperialism*), p. 90.
97. Lenin, V. I., *State and Revolution,* p. 83.
98. Lenin, V. I., "Karl Marx," in *Sochineniia,* 21, 4th ed., 35 Vols., Gosudarstvennoe Izdatel'stvo Politicheskoi Literatury, Moscow, 1941-52 (henceforth referred to as Lenin, V. I, *Sochineniia*), p. 38.
99. *Loc. cit.*
100. *Ibid.*, p. 41.
101. *Ibid.*, p. 58.
102. *Loc. cit.*
103. *Ibid.*, p. 59.
104. Lenin, V. I., "What the Friends of the People Are," *C.W.* 1, p. 179.
105. Lenin, V. I., *State and Revolution,* p. 70.
106. *Loc. cit.*
107. Lenin, V. I., "What the Friends of the People Are," *C.W.* 1, p. 166.
108. *Loc. cit.*
109. Federn, Karl, *The Materialist Conception of History, A Critical Analysis,* Macmillan, New York, 1939. For a counter-argument, see Witt-Hansen, J., *Historical Materialism, The Method,* pp. 70-71, and also Akademiia Nauk SSSR, Institut Filosofii, *Osnovy Marksistkoi Filosofii,* Gosudarstvennoe Izdatel'stvo Politicheskoi Literatury, Moscow, 1959, pp. 358-360.
110. However, such a concept of history as presented above depends, as Lenin's does, upon the assumption not only that history is a process that has its source of growth and development within itself, but also that it has a definite end. However, history has no known end and the changes brought about in it are caused by the actions of men. The actions of men and the events they bring about take place in a network of relations and conditions which may be structured and limited by law and government, for example, but which no one himself designs and no one himself brings to an end. That no one unequivocally begins or ends events does not, nevertheless, mean that forces or trends or laws of nature or of history do. Only to the backward glance of the historian, then, can historical events seem inevitable. To the actors within them, although their acts may be carefully planned and fraught with intentions and hopes, their actions merely bring about consequences new and unknown. For a brilliant discussion of the concept of history just presented, see Arendt, H., "The Concept of History" in *Between Past and Future,* pp. 41-90.
111. Lenin, V. I., "What the Friends of the People Are," *C.W.* 1, p. 159.
112. *Loc. cit.*
113. *Loc. cit.*
114. *Ibid.*, p. 138.
115. *Loc. cit.*
116. *Ibid.*, p. 166.
117. *Ibid.*, p. 138.
118. Lenin, V. I., *Materialism and Empirio-Criticism,* p. 337.

119. *Ibid.,* pp. 338-339.
120. *Ibid.,* p. 339.
121. Lenin, V. I., "What the Friends of the People Are," *C.W.* 1, p.139.
122. Lenin, V. I., *Materialism and Empirio-Criticism,* p. 339.
123. *Loc. cit.*
124. Lenin, V. I., *What's To Be Done? Burning Questions of Our Movement,* International Publishers, New York, 1929 (henceforth referred to as Lenin, V. I., *What's To Be Done*), p. 39.
125. Karl Kautsky was one of the foremost theoreticians of the German Social Democratic Party. Although he and Lenin were in accord when Lenin wrote "What the Friends of the People Are," Lenin was later to regard him as a renegade and inveterate opponent of communism.
126. Lenin, V. I., *What's To Be Done*, p. 40.
127. *Loc. cit.*
128. *Loc. cit.*
129. *Loc. cit.*
130. In 1894 when Lenin wrote "What the Friends of the People Are," the Socialist Democratic Party was the party of the Marxian Socialists; it later was to split into Bolshevik and Menshevik factions.
131. Lenin, V. I., *What's To Be Done,* p. 32-33.
132. *Loc. cit.*
133. Lenin, V. I., "What the Friends of the People Are," *C.W.* 1, pp. 140-141.
134. Lenin, V. I., *What's To Be Done,* p. 68.
135. *Loc. cit.*
136. *Loc. cit.*
137. *Loc. cit.*
138. *Ibid.,* p. 69.
139. *Loc. cit.*
140. *Ibid.,* p. 52.
141. *Loc. cit.*
142. Lenin, V. I., "What the Friends of the People Are," *C. W. 1,* p. 299.
143. *Loc. cit.*
144. *Ibid.,* p. 279.
145. *Ibid.,* p. 300.
146. *Ibid.,* p. 164.
147. *Ibid.,* p. 158.
148. *Ibid.,* p. 140.
149. Lenin, V. I., "What the Friends of the People Are," *C.W. 1,* p. 185.
150. Lenin, V. I., *State and Revolution,* p. 8.
151. *Ibid.,* p. 185.
152. *Ibid.,* p. 9.
153. *Ibid.,* p. 10.
154. Lenin, quoting Engels, in *ibid.,* p. 19.
155. *Ibid.,* p. 17.
156. *Ibid.,* p. 73.
157. *Ibid.,* p. 37.
158. *Ibid.,* pp. 42-43.
159. *Ibid.,* p. 53.

160. *Ibid.*, p. 65.
161. *Ibid.*, p. 68.
162. *Ibid.*, p. 79.
163. Akademiia Nauk SSSR, Institut Filosofii, *Istoricheskii Materializm*, Gosudarstvennoe Izdatel'stvo Politicheskoi Literatury, Moscow, 1954 (henceforth referred to as Akademiia Nauk, *Istoricheskii Materializm*), p. 333.
164. *Ibid.*, p. 468.
165. *Ibid.*, p. 344.
166. This distinction is based upon Karl Mannheim's discussion of the particular and total concepts of ideology in his *Ideology and Utopia, An Introduction to the Sociology of Knowledge,* Harcourt Brace, New York, 1949 (henceforth referred to as Mannheim, Karl, *Ideology and Utopia*), pp. 49-51.
167. Barrington Moore, in his *Soviet Politics, The Dilemma of Power, The Role of Ideas in Social Change,* Harvard University Press, Cambridge, 1950, p. 139, states: "The general method of questioning constitutes one of the more stable aspects of Marxist-Leninist theory.

"Reacting to the situations as they arose, Lenin continued to add new conceptions and to abandon or modify old ones. The same process of growth and attrition has been maintained since his death. Superimposed upon this simple process a cyclical tendency may be observed in the development of Bolshevik theory and also in Bolshevik practice. . . . The continuity in the general method of questioning, combined with the flexibility and variety in the answers produced is among the major factors that give Russian Marxist theory the superficial paradoxical appearance of dogmatic permanence and opportunistic change.

"Therefore if one speaks of Leninist theory, it is usually necessary to speak of it as it existed at a given point in time and at a given stage of its development." Mr. Moore's point of view tends to deemphasize the coherence and wholeness of Bolshevik ideology and to emphasize the remarkable flexibility of the dialectic and its adaptability to tactical aims and practical goals. The many changes and seeming contradictions take place, however, within the bounds of the ideology and, no matter how opportunistic, have a consistency within it.

CHAPTER II

1. For the franchise under tsarism, see Harper, S. N., *The New Electoral Law for the Russian Duma,* University of Chicago Press, Chicago, 1908, espec. p. 28, n. 16, and p. 29, n. 18. See also Gronsky, P., and Astrov, N., *The War and the Russian Government,* Yale Univ. Press, New Haven, 1929. The groups that had been represented in the local self-governing institutions of tsarist Russia and its Duma—the central representative assembly—were known as "enfranchised democracy" (*tsensovaia democratiia*). This group must be distinguished from the *soviet,* or "revolutionary democracy," which was made up of those excluded from the suffrage and who, in the revolutions of 1905 and March 1917, had formed councils, or soviets, as a means of representation outside the tsarist suffrage. Its leaders were the professional revolutionaries of

the political underground. See, for example Chernov, Viktor, *Rozhdenie Revoliutsionnoi Rossii* (*Fevral'skaia Revoliutsiia*), Iubileinyi Komitet, Paris, 1939, p. 211.

2. For the Contact Commission, see Trotsky, Leon, *The History of the Russian Revolution,* (trans. Max Eastman) (3 Vols. in 1), Simon and Shuster, New York, 1932 (henceforth referred to as Trotsky, L., *Russian Revolution*), pp. 198-199. See also Tyrkova-Williams, Ariadna, *From Liberty to Brest-Litovsk. The First Year of the Russian Revolution,* Macmillan, London, 1919 (henceforth referred to as Tyrkova-Willams, A., *From Liberty to Brest-Litovsk*), p. 60, and Tseretelli, Irakli, "Reminiscences of the February Revolution (Part I), The April Crisis," *The Russian Review,* 14, No. 2, April 1955, espec. pp. 93-96.

3. Trotsky, L., *Russian Revolution,* 1, pp. 332-339; see also Tseretelli, Irakli, "Reminiscences of the February Revolution . . . ," *The Russian Review,* 14, No. 2, April 1955, pp. 101-108.

4. See Chapter VIII.

5. See Chapter V.

6. Massaryk, Thomas, *The Spirit of Russia, Studies in History, Literature and Philosophy,* 1 (Trans. Eden and Cedar Paul), Allen and Unwin, London, 1919, pp. 150-151, contends that as early as 1870 the peasants had become receptive to the revolutionary teachings of the intellectuals. By 1917, therefore, the anticipation of socialism had had many years to mature.

7. For a description of the Artillery Department conference of 26 March drawn from the *Rabochaia Gazeta* account, see Komissiia po Izucheniiu Istorii Professional'nogo Dvizheniia v SSSR, *Oktibr'skaia Revoliutsiia i Fabzavkomy* 1, 2, VTsSPS, Moscow, 1927 (henceforth referred to as *Okt. Rev. i Fabzavkomy*), 1, pp. 27-30.

8. *Ibid.,* p. 30.

9. *Ibid.,* pp. 32-34. Aleksandrov, G., Galianov, V., and Rubinstein, N., *Politicheskii Slovar',* Gosudarstvennoe Izdatel'stvo Politicheskoi Literatury, n.p., 1940 (henceforth referred to as Aleksandrov, *et al., Politicheskii Slovar'*) define the advisory vote as follows: "Gives the right to those attending meetings, conferences, and congresses to express themselves on questions which are being debated, but does not give the right to participate in the voting."

10. Paragraph 12, Section III of the Instructions for the Organization of Workers in State Enterprises, *Okt. Rev. i Fabzavkomy, 1,* p. 35.

11. Paragraph 1, Section I of the Instructions for the Organization of Workers in State Enterprises, *loc. cit.*

12. It is interesting to note that the history of the factory committees as derivatives of the factory elders can be traced to the institution of village elders. Historically, working hands were provided for Russian industry by ascription to them of peasants, whole villages of whom were often assigned to factories. (See Mavor, James, *An Economic History of Russia, 1,* J. M. Dent, London, 1914, p. 125.) Furthermore, since even in the twentieth century it was often the village from which Russian workers came and to which they often returned, authority in the factory resembled that in the village. For this reason, the Russian has not been translated here to factory foreman, as is sometimes done.

13. For the Statutes on Workers Committees, see Moskovskii Sovet Rabochikh i Soldatskikh Deputatov, Otdel Truda, *Kak Organizovat' Zavodskii* (fab-

richnyi) Rabochii Komitet, Mamontov Moscow, 1917 (henceforth referred to as *Kak organizovat' rabochii Komitet*), pp. 14-18; Brower and Kerensky, *The Russian Provisional Government, II,* pp. 718-720; and *Okt. Rev. i Fabzavkomy, 1,* p. 24.

14. *Kak Organizovat' rabochii Komitet,* "Postanovlenie Vremennago Pravitel'stvo o Rabochikh Komitetakh v Promyshlennykh Zavedeniiakh," Article 2, p. 14.

15. Statutes, Article 3, *Okt. Rev. i Fabzavkomy, 1,* p. 15.

16. Statutes, Articles 4 and 5, *loc. cit.*

17. Statutes, Article 6, *loc. cit.* For the mediation commission and arbitration courts, see Rudin, N., *Primiritel'nyia Kamery i Treteiskii Sud,* Moskovskii Sovet Rabochikh Deputatov, Moscow, 1917.

18. *Kak Organizovat'rabochii Komitet,* "Postanovlenii . . . ," Statutes, Article 7, p. 15.

19. Statutes, Article 8, *ibid.,* pp. 16-17.

20. Statutes, Articles 9 and 10, *ibid.,* p. 17.

21. Statutes, Articles 11 and 12, *loc. cit.*

22. Statutes, Article 13, *ibid.,* pp. 17-18.

23. Statutes, Article 14, *ibid.,* p. 18.

24. For the role of the Soviets in promoting the Statutes on the Workers' Committees, see Zagorsky, S. O., *State Control of Industry in Russia during the War,* Yale University Press, New Haven, 1928 (henceforth referred to as Zagorsky, S. O., *State Control of Industry*), p. 171; also *Izvestiia,* No. 8, March 7/20, 1917, in Golder, F. A., *Documents of Russian History,* 1914-1917, trans. E. Aronsberg, Century, New York and London, 1927 (henceforth referred to as Golder, F. C., *Documents of Russian History*), p. 419.

25. For these writings, see Lenin, V. I., *Selected Works,* International Publishers, New York, 12 Vols., 1935-38 (henceforth referred to as Lenin, V. I., *Selected Works*), 6, *From the Bourgeois Revolution to the Proletarian Revolution;* see also Lenin, V. I., *Sochineniia,* 23, 24, 25, 26.

26. See Lenin, V. I., "Letters from Afar; First Letter; The First Stage of the Revolution," March 20, 1917, *Selected Works,* 6, pp. 10-12; and "Tasks of the Proletariat in the Present Revolution," April 20, 1917, *ibid.,* p. 22.

27. Lenin, V. I., "Tasks of the Proletariat in the Present Revolution," April 20, 1917, *Selected Works,* 6, p. 23.

28. Lenin, V. I., "Letters on Tactics," April 1917, *ibid.,* espec. pp. 32-33.

29. Lenin, V. I., "A Dual Power," April 22, 1917, *ibid.,* p. 27.

30. *Loc. cit.*

31. Trotsky, L., *Russian Revolution,* 1, p. 438.

32. Abolin, A., *The October Revolution and the Trade Unions,* Cooperative Publishing Society of Foreign Workers in the USSR, Moscow, 1933 (henceforth referred to as Abolin, A., *October Revolution and Trade Unions*), p. 13.

33. Lenin, V. I., "Report on the Current Situation delivered at the April Conference of the Russian Social Democratic Labor Party," May 9, 1917, *Selected Works,* 6, p. 91.

34. Lenin, V. I., "State and Revolution," August-September 1917, *Collected Works,* 21, 4th ed., Lawrence and Wishart, London, 1961 (henceforth referred to as Lenin, V. I., "State and Revolution," *C.W.,* 21), Part 2, p. 169.

35. *Okt. Rev. i Fabzavkomy,* 1, p. 68.

36. *Ibid.*, p. 107. Trotsky, in his *Russian Revolution*, 1, p. 422, states that the Bolsheviks won 335 out of 421 votes for a resolution they proposed at the conference.

37. *Okt. Rev. i Fabzavkomy,* 1, p. 76.

38. *Ibid.*, p. 80.

39. *Loc. cit.*

40. *Loc. cit.*

41. For the creation of the Central Council of Factory Committees, see *ibid.*, p. 75.

42. For the Central Bureau of Trade Unions, see *Bol'shaia Sovetskaia Entsiklopediia,* Moscow, 1926. The Encyclopedia states that the Central Bureau of Trade Unions was an organization which had grown up during the revolution of 1905. With the suppression of this revolution, these bureaus were abolished except in Petrograd and Moscow, where they maintained a semi-legal existence. After the February Revolution of 1917, the Central Bureaus of Trade Unions were reactivated. See also Kolokol'nikov, P., *Professional'nye Soiuzy v Moskve,* Novyi Mir, Petersburgh, n.d., pp. 46-48. According to Pankratova, A. M., *Fabzavkomy i Profsoiuzy v Revoliutsii 1917 Goda,* Gosudarstvennoe, Moscow, 1927 (henceforth referred to as Pankratova, A. M., *Fabzavkomy i Profsoiuzy*), p. 60, the Central Bureau of Trade Unions was converted into the Petrograd Bureau of Trade Unions and continued to exist concomitantly with the Central Council of Trade Unions. According to Abolin, A., *October Revolution and Trade Unions,* p. 8, the Bolsheviks, were predominant in the Petrograd Bureau of Trade Unions. According to Garvy, P. A., in his *Professional'nye Soiuzy v Rossii v Pervye Gody Revoliutsii* (*1917-1921*), n.p. New York, 1958 (henceforth referred to as Garvy, P. A., *Professional'nye Soiuzy*), pp. 24-25, in April of 1917 there was parity between the Mensheviks and Bolsheviks in the Central Bureau of Trade Unions of Petrograd which became the Petrograd Soviet of Trade Unions in July.

43. For the conflict between the factory committees and trade unions as manifested at the First Conference of Factory Committees, see *Okt. Rev. i Fabzavkomy, 1,* pp. 132-134, especially the speeches of Riazanov and Akashev.

44. See Martov, L., *Proletarskaia Bor'ba v Rossii* (*Predislovie P. Akselrod*) (2nd. Ed.) Glagolev, St. Petersburgh, 1904, pp. 129-131; and Martov, J., "Marx and the Dictatorship of the Proletariat" (first published 1918), in *The State and the Socialist Revolution* (trans. Integer), International Review, New York, 1938, p. 59. For the Mensheviks and their relationship to the Bolsheviks, see also Wolfe, B. D., *Three Who Made a Revolution,* Dial Press, New York, 1948, pp. 521-523 and 289; and Schapiro, Leonard, *The Origin of the Communist Autocracy, Political Opposition in the Soviet State*: *First Phase* 1917-1922, Harvard University Press, Cambridge, 1955 (henceforth referred to as Schapiro, L., *Communist Autocracy*), pp. 21-22. In 1917 Martov became the leader of the Menshevik left wing—the Menshevik Internationalists—a group which attempted to avoid a split with its own party and a defection to the Bolsheviks. Martov's disagreement with the majority of the party took place over the question of socialist participation in the World War. Martov was opposed to national defense and supported the idea of international socialist opposition to the World War. See *ibid.*, pp. 22-23. For Lenin's presentation of a comparison of the Bolshevik, Menshevik and other party policies, see "Political

Parties in Russia and the Tasks of the Proletariat," April 1917, in Lenin, V. I., *Selected Works, 6,* pp. 77-78.

45. *Okt. Rev. i Fabzavkomy, 1,* p. 83.

46. *Loc. cit.*

47. *Ibid.,* p. 100.

48. For the support of the Menshevik resolution on control by the Executive Committee of the Soviets, see *ibid.,* p. 96, n. 1.

49. *Ibid.,* p. 95.

50. *Loc. cit.*

51. *Ibid.,* p. 96.

52. *Loc. cit.*

53. *Loc. cit.*

54. Avilov, B. V. is not to be confused with the Bolshevik N. P. Avilov, known as Glebov or Glebov-Avilov. B. V. Avilov was a leader of the United Internationalists, an offshoot of the Social Democratic Party, which remained Marxian socialist while attempting to be independent of both Bolsheviks and Mensheviks.

55. *Okt. Rev. i Fabzavkomy, 1,* p. 89.

56. *Ibid.,* p. 90.

57. *Loc. cit.*

58. *Ibid.,* p. 91.

59. *Loc. cit.*

60. *Ibid.,* p. 92.

61. *Loc. cit.*

62. Paragraph 2 of the Resolution on Measures for Struggle with Economic Disorder, *ibid.,* pp. 107-108.

63. *Ibid.,* p. 108.

64. Paragraph 2, *loc. cit.*

65. Paragraph 5, *loc. cit.*

66. Paragraph 6, *loc. cit.*

67. *Ibid.,* p. 113.

68. *Ibid.,* p. 18.

69. *Ibid.,* p. 108.

70. Lenin, V. I., "A Dual Power," 22 April 1917, *Selected Works, 6,* pp. 27-28.

71. Golder, F. A., *Documents of Russian History,* p. 288.

72. Extract from Protocol No. 16, issued at the meeting of March 28, 1917 of the O-va Electric Light Co., in *Okt. Rev. i Fabzavkomy, 1,* p. 50.

73. Pravda, No. 18, 26 March/8 April 1917, in Avdeev, N. *Revoliutsiia,* p. 200.

74. "O Krasnoi Gvardii," in *Rabochaia Gazeta, Organ Organizatsionnago Komiteta i Petrogradskoi Organizatsii Rossiiskoi Sotsial-Demokraticheskoi Partii* (henceforth referred to as *Rabochaia Gazeta*), No. 43, 29 April/12 May 1917, p. 1.

75. "O Militsii," in *ibid.,* No. 2, 8/21 March 1917, p. 1.

76. *Okt. Rev. i Fabzavkomy, 1,* p. 132.

77. For the Metal Workers' Union support of the Bolsheviks, particularly in October, see Abolin, A., *October Revolution and Trade Unions,* pp. 8-11.

78. Komissiia Po Izucheniiu Istorii Professional'nogo Dvizheniia v SSSR

(Istprof V. Ts. S.P.S.), *Tret'ia Vserossiiskaia Konferentsiia Professional'nykh Soiuzov, 20-28 Iunia/3-11 Iulia 1917g, Stenograficheskii Otchet,* V. Ts. S.P.S., Moscow, 1927 (henceforth referred to as *3 Konf. Profsoiuzov*), p. vii.

79. *Loc. cit.*

80. *Ibid.,* p. viii.

81. *Ibid.,* p. vii.

82. *Ibid.,* p. ix.

83. There are two sources available for the Third Conference of Trade Unions, the *Stenographic Report of the Third All-Russian Conference of Trade Unions,* (*3 Konf. Profsoiuzov*) and the undated but probably earlier publication, *The Resolutions of the Third All-Russian Conference of Trade Unions.* (Tret'ia Vserossiiskaia Konferentsiia Professional'nykh Soiuzov, *Rezoliutsii Priniatiia na Zasedaniakh Konferentsii 20-28 Iunia/3-11 Iulia* 1917g, Petrograd, n.d. (henceforth referred to as *Rezoliutsii 3 Konf. Profsoiuzov*).) The latter publication contains a resolution on "The Mutual Relations between the Trade Unions and Factory Committees," adopted by the Third Conference and presented by the Mensheviks Garvy and Astrov in accordance with the report of the Bolshevik N. Glebov (Glebov-Avilov). According to Garvy, P. A., in his *Professional'nye Soiuzy,* the resolution he and Astrov presented was adopted by the conference and he does not mention Glebov-Avilov in connection with it (p. 21). The *Stenographic Report,* however, does not include this resolution in its collection of those adopted by the conference. Nevertheless, in its appendix the *Stenographic Report* prints the thesis of Glebov-Avilov on "The Role and Relationship of the Trade Unions and Factory Committees in the Regulation of Industry." This discrepancy between the respective inclusions and exclusions of the two sources is further complicated by the *Stenographic Report's* index reference to the thesis by the same title as that used in the *Resolutions,* "The Mutual Relations between the Trade Unions and the Factory Committees."

The absence of the adopted resolution regarding the trade unions and the factory committees, in addition to the inclusion of Glebov-Avilov's thesis in the *Stenographic Report,* may indicate that the editors of the *Report* made changes and modifications in the text to suit the political climate of 1927. The theses fall in so well with the post-October policy of the Bolsheviks toward both the workers' organizations that the position they occupy in the *Stenographic Report* seems suspect. This is especially true in comparison with the adopted resolution presented in the *Resolutions,* which, having been drawn up by the Mensheviks Garvy and Astrov in accordance with the thesis of Glebov-Avilov, would thus seem to represent a compromise Bolshevik and Menshevik view.

84. Garvy, P. A., at the meeting of 12 July 1917 of the Third Conference of Trade Unions, in *3 Konf. Profsoiuzov,* p. 334.

85. *Rezoliutsii 3 Konf. Profsoiuzov,* pp. 15-16.

86. *Ibid.,* p. 18.

87. *Loc. cit.,* Paragraph 5 of the Resolution on the Mutual Relations between the Trade Unions and the Factory Committees.

88. Paragraph 6, *loc. cit.*

89. *Ibid.,* p. 321

90. *Ibid.,* p. 485.

91. Paragraph 6, *loc. cit.*
92. *Ibid.*, p. 321.
93. *Ibid.*, p. 323.
94. For the Economic Council, see Zagorsky, S. O., *State Control of Industry*, pp. 187-189.
95. *3 Konf. Profsoiuzov*, p. 485.
96. Paragraph 7 of the Theses on the Role and Relationship of the Trade Unions and Factory Committees in the Regulation of Industry, *loc. cit.*
97. Paragraph 10, *loc. cit.*
98. *Ibid.*, p. 484.
99. *Ibid.*, p. 485.
100. *Ibid.*, p. 364.
101. *Ibid.*, p. 365.
102. *Rezoliutsii 3 Konf. Profsoiuzov*, p. 10.
103. For the point of view of the Menshevik Kolokol'nikov on industrial unionism, see *3 Konf. Profsoiuzov*, pp. 179-181; for the Menshevik Grinevich, see *ibid.*, pp. 226-227; and for the Bolshevik Riazanov, see *ibid.*, pp. 225-226. All these men favored the conversion from trade to industrial unions if the unions did not encompass too many trades. Abolin, A., in *October Revolution and Trade Unions*, p. 6, quotes a message of greeting from the Central Committee of the Communist Party to the All-Union Central Council of Trade Unions dated 23 July 1922. This message, in referring to the pre-October trade-union situation, states: "The Menshevik majority regarded it as its historical mission to divert it [the trade union movement] to the path of craft unionism. . . ." This statement, however, is contradictory to Menshevik policy at the Third All-Russian Conference of Trade Unions. Also, the Mensheviks had supported a policy of industrial unionism even before 1917. See Kolokol'nikov, P. (K. Dmitriev), *Professional'noe Dvizhenie v Rossii, I Organizatsiia Soiuzov*, Rabochaia Biblioteka Tsentral'nago Komiteta, R.S.-D.R.P. (obedin) Petrograd, 1917 (henceforth referred to as Kolokol'nikov P., *Prof. Dvizhenie*), pp. 42-51, 53-56.
104. *3 Konf. Profsoiuzov*, p. 364. It should be noted that the organization of labor into unions based on the factory committees, or even single industries which unite workers fulfilling various kinds of functions, tends to ignore the skills that differentiate and distinguish one worker from another and tends to equate them or reduce them all to mere units of labor power.
105. Lozovsky at the 8th meeting of the Second Factory Committee Conference on 24(?) August 1917, in *Okt. Rev. i Fabzavkomy, 1*, p. 228. The editors of the work cited point out that the conditions of the records of the conference make some of the dates uncertain. When this is so the questionable date will be indicated, as above, with a question mark. Lozovsky was expelled from the Bolshevik Party on January 11, 1918, and returned to the party in 1919. At the time this speech was made, he was one of the outstanding members of the party. See Bunyan, J., and Fisher, H.H., *The Bolshevik Revolution 1917-1918: Documents and Materials*, Stanford University Press, Stanford, 1934 (henceforth referred to as Bunyan and Fisher, *Bolshevik Revolution*), pp. 637-638.
106. *Okt. Rev. i Fabzavkomy*, 1, p. 228.
107. *Ibid.*, p. 229.

108. *Ibid.* p. 258.
109. Skrypnik at the 4th meeting, 22 August 1917, *ibid.,* p. 190.
110. *Loc. cit.*
111. *Ibid.,* p. 183.
112. *Ibid.,* p. 182.
113. Instructions to the Central Council of Factory Committees, *ibid.,* p. 245.
114. *Loc. cit.*
115. *Ibid.,* pp. 258-259.
116. *Ibid.,* p. 245.
117. *Ibid.,* p. 246.
118. Subparagraph a, Paragraph 8 of the Instructions to the Central Council, *loc. cit.*
119. Subparagraph c, Paragraph 8 of the Instructions to the Central Council, *loc. cit.*
120. Subparagraph b, Paragraph 8, *loc. cit.*
121. Subparagraph d, Paragraph 8, *loc. cit.*
122. Paragraph 24, *loc. cit.,* p. 249.
123. Paragraphs 24, 25 and 26 of the Instructions to the Central Council, *loc. cit.*
124. Subparagraph a, Paragraph 16, Section 6 of the Instructions to the Central Council, *ibid.,* p. 247.
125. For the trade union resolution on this point at the Third Conference of Trade Unions, see *Rezoliutsii 3 Konf. Profsoiuzov,* p. 18.
126. *Okt. Rev. i Fabzavkomy, 1,* Paragraph 20 of the Instructions to the Central Council of Factory Committees, p. 248.
127. Paragraph 22, *loc. cit.*
128. Paragraph 28, *loc. cit.*
129. *Ibid.,* p. 249.
130. *Loc. cit.*
131. Paragraph 30 of the Instructions to the Central Council, *loc. cit.*
132. Paragraph 31, *loc. cit.*
133. Paragraph 27, *loc. cit.*
134. *Loc. cit.*
135. *Ibid.,* p. 259.
136. *Loc. cit.*
137. *Ibid.,* p. 239.
138. *Loc. cit.*
139. *Ibid.,* p. 238.
140. *Ibid.,* p. 240.
141. *Ibid.,* p. 244.
142. *Ibid.,* p. 240.
143. *Loc. cit.*
144. *Okt. Rev. i Fabzavkomy, 1,* p. 240.
145. Paragraph 7, *loc. cit.*
146. Paragraph 9, *ibid.,* pp. 240-241.
147. Paragraph 11, *ibid.,* p. 241.
148. Paragraph 13. *loc. cit.*

149. *Ibid.*, p. 238.
150. *Ibid.*, p. 241.
151. See for example Statutes of the Factory Committees, Paragraph 13, in *ibid.*, p. 241.
152. *Izvestiia,* No. 8, 7 March 1917, quoted in *ibid.*, p. 43.
153. *Izvestiia,* No. 71, 20 May 1917, quoted *loc. cit.*
154. *Ibid.*, p. 260.
155. *Ibid.*, p. 241.
156. *Loc. cit.*
157. *Loc. cit.*
158. *Loc. cit.*
159. Paragraph 25, *ibid.*, p. 242.
160. Paragraphs 37 and 38, *ibid.*, p. 244.
161. Paragraphs 23 and 24, *ibid.*, p. 242.
162. Paragraph 29, *ibid.*, p. 243.
163. Paragraph 31,*ibid.*, p. 244.
164. Paragraph 32, *loc. cit.*
165. Paragraph 26, *ibid.*, p. 242.
166. *Ibid.*, pp. 242-243.
167. *Ibid.*, p. 243.
168. *Loc. cit.*
169. Amosov at the 2nd meeting, 21 August 1917, of the Second Conference of Factory Committees of Petrograd and its Environs, in *ibid.*, p. 174.
170. *Loc. cit.*
171. *Ibid.*, p. 245.
172. Paragraph 41 of the Statutes of the Factory Committees, *loc. cit.*
173. *Ibid.* p. 243.
174. Paragraph 35, *ibid.*, p. 245.
175. Note 2 Paragraph 33, *loc. cit.*
176. *Ibid.*, p. 244.
177. Paragraph 40, *loc. cit.*
178. Paragraphs 33 and 34, *loc. cit.*
179. *Loc. cit.*
180. *Ibid.*, p. 238.
181. *Ibid.*, p. 239.
182. *Ibid.*, p. 240.
183. *Ibid.*, p. 214.
184. *Loc. cit.*
185. *Loc. cit.*
186. *Loc. cit.*
187. *Ibid.*, p. 213.
188. Miliutin's Resolution on the Current Moment and Workers' Control, Paragraph 7, *loc. cit.*
189. *Ibid.*, p. 218.
190. Paragraph 8 of Miliutin's resolution, *loc. cit.*
191. Paragraph 9 of Miliutin's resolution, *loc. cit.*
192. *Loc. cit.*
193. Paragraph 15 of Miliutin's resolution, *ibid.*, p. 219.
194. *Ibid.*, p. 271.

195. See, for example, the preamble to a resolution of the conference, *ibid.*, p. 270.

196. Circular of the Moscow Regional Council, date unknown, *ibid.*, p. 95. Since this council does not seem to have supported the Bolsheviks, the circular may be evidence of an attempt of the Council to forestall Bolshevik policy in the local factories. If the circular, however, should date from the post-October period, it may have functioned to achieve Bolshevik centralization of the factory committees.

197. *Ibid.*, p. 94.

198. See the plan for the organization of the factory committees published in *Novyi Put'*, No. 3 February 1918-1919, in *ibid.*, pp. 37-38.

199. *Ibid.*, p. 130.

200. *Ibid.*, p. 111.

201. For the Moscow Conference, see Golder, F. A., *Documents of Russian History*, pp. 480-512.

202. *Okt. Rev. i Fabzavkomy, 1,* p. 253.

203. For a documentary account of the Kornilov Affair see Golder, F. A., *Documents of Russian History*, pp. 513-32. See also, for Kerensky's point of view, Kerensky, A. F., *The Prelude to Bolshevism, The Kornilov Rebellion*, Fisher, Unwin, London, 1919; Kerensky, A. F., *The Catastrophe: Kerensky's Own Story of the Russian Revolution*, Appleton, New York, 1927, pp. 297-324; Kerensky, A. F., *Delo Kornilova*, Zadruga, Moscow, 1918 (hereafter cited respectively as Kerensky, A. F., *The Prelude to Bolshevism; The Catastrophe;* and *Delo Kornilova*); and Ross, E. A., *The Russian Bolshevik Revolution*, Century, New York, 1921 (henceforth referred to as Ross, E. A., *Bolshevik Revolution*), pp. 223-244. See especially Ascher, Abraham, "The Kornilov Affair," *Russian Review*, XII, No. 4, pp. 235-252, October 1953. See also L. I. Strakhovsky, "Was there a Kornilov Rebellion—A Re-Appraisal of the Evidence," *The Slavonic and East European Review*, XXXIII, No. 8, pp. 372-395, June 1955.

204. For the expansion of the Red Guards as a result of the Kornilov Affair, see Fedotoff-White, D., *The Growth of the Red Army*, Princeton University Press, Princeton, 1944 (henceforth referred to as Fedotoff-White, D., *Red Army*), p. 17.

205. *Okt. Rev. i Fabzavkomy, 2,* p. 49.

206. *Loc. cit.*

207. See the communication of the Central Council of Factory Committees addressed to the Executive Committee of the Council of Workers' and Soldiers' Deputies on 8 October 1917, *ibid.*, p. 11.

208. *Ibid.*, p. 8.

209. *Ibid.*, p. 9.

210. *Ibid.*, p. 18.

211. *Ibid.*, p. 19.

212. *Ibid.*, p. 28.

213. *Loc. cit.*

214. *Loc. cit.*

215. Paragraph 1, *ibid.*, p. 35.

216. *Loc. cit.*, Paragraphs 2 and 3.

217. *Loc. cit.*

218. *Loc. cit.*, Paragraph 4.
219. *Ibid.*, pp. 35-36, Paragraphs 5, 6 and 7.
220. *Ibid.*, p. 36.
221. *Loc. cit.*
222. *Loc. cit.*
223. *Loc. cit.*
224. *Loc. cit.*
225. For documentary accounts of the Council of Five, see Golder, F. A., *Documents of Russian History*, pp. 533-539; for the Democratic Conference, see *ibid.*, pp. 540-567.
226. *Ibid.*, p. 578. The date here is given as 21 September in Ross, E. A., *Bolshevik Revolution*, p. 243, and as 22 September in Trotsky, L., *Russian Revolution, 3*, p. 434.
227. See the communication of the Central Council of Factory Committees of 18 September to the Organizational Bureau for the Convocation of the Conference of Democratic Organizations, *Okt. Rev. i Fabzavkomy, 2*, p. 13.
228. *Ibid.*, p. 44.
229. *Loc. cit.*
230. For the Bolshevik declaration at the Democratic Conference, see Golder, F. A., *Documents of Russian History*, pp. 549-553; for the Resolution of the Third Conference of Factory Committees on the Democratic Conference, see *Okt. Rev. i Fabzavkomy, 2*, pp. 43-44.
231. *Ibid.*, p. 44.
232. *Ibid.*, p. 67.
233. Chubar' at the evening meeting 2 November 1917, of the First All-Russian Conference of Factory Committees, *ibid.*, p. 175.
234. Antipov at the morning meeting, 2 November 1917 of the First All-Russian Congress of Trade Unions, *ibid.*, p. 17.
235. See Golder, F. A., *Documents of Russian History*, p. 587, and Bunyan and Fisher, *Bolshevik Revolution*, p. 68.
236. For the War Revolutionary Committee, see Golder, F. A., *Documents of Russian History*, pp. 587-590; and Bunyan and Fisher, *Bolshevik Revolution*, p. 69; and Trotsky L., *Russian Revolution, 3*, pp. 88-123.
237. *Okt. Rev. i Fabzavkomy, 2*, p. 12.
238. *Ibid.*, p. 138.
239. *Ibid.*, p. 118.
240. *Loc. cit.*
241. *Ibid.*, p. 114.
242. The Factory Committees, Their Tasks and Activity, Their Local and All-Russian Unions, Plan (*Proekt*) of the Resolution by the Commission on the Organizational Question, at the First All-Russian Conference of Factory Committees, *Okt. Rev. i Fabzavkomy, 2*, p. 213.
243. Paragraph 5, *loc. cit.*
244. Paragraph 8, *ibid.*, p. 187.
245. Paragraph 9, *loc. cit.*
246. Paragraph 13, *loc. cit.*
247. Paragraph 14, *loc. cit.*
248. Paragraph 15, *ibid.*, pp. 187-188.
249. *Ibid.*, p. 188.

250. Paragraph 6, *loc. cit.*

251. *Ibid.*, pp. 60-61.

252. For state control of industry by the Provisional Government, see Zagorsky, S. O., *State Control of Industry*, espec. pp. 179ff.

253. *Okt. Rev. i Fabzavkomy, 2*, p. 61.

254. *Loc. cit.*

255. *Loc. cit.*

256. *Loc. cit.*

256. *Loc. cit.*

257. *Loc. cit.*

258. *Ibid.*, p. 188.

259. *Ibid.*, p. 167.

260. For the July days and their implications, see Chamberlin, William Henry, *The Russian Revolution, 1*, Macmillan, New York, 1935 (henceforth referred to as Chamberlin, W. H., *Russian Revolution*), pp. 166-191. For the Bolshevik point of view in retrospect, see the footnote to p. 167 in Lenin, V. I., *Selected Works, 6*, pp. 562-566. For the contemporary Bolshevik political evaluation of the July days, see the Resolution on the Political Situation, Rossiiskaia Kommunisticheskaia Partiia (bol'shevikov), *Protokoly VI S"ezda R.S.-D.R.P. (bol'shevikov) 26 Iunia-3 Avgusta 1917*, Kommunist, Moscow, 1919 (henceforth referred to as *RKP(b)6 S"ezd*), pp. 218-221. For a detailed presentation and Marxian analysis, see also Trotsky, L., *Russian Revolution, 1*, pp. 3-127. See also Schapiro, L., *Communist Autocracy*, p. 52.

261. Ordzhonikidze, G.K., *Izbrannye Stat'i i Rechi 1911-1937*, Gosudarstvennoe Izdatel'stvo Politicheskoi Literatury, Moscow, 1939 (henceforth referred to as Ordzhonikidze, G. K., *Stat'i*) p. 214.

262. Lenin, V. I., "State and Revolution," *Collected Works, 21*, Part 2, p. 219.

263. *Ibid.*, p. 163.

264. For the ideology of Russian anarchism, see the works of Bakunin, Michael, and Kropotkin, Peter, especially the former's *Parizhkaia Kommuna i Poniatie Gosudarstvennosti s Pis'mom P. A. Kropotkina, k Izdateliam Anarkhicheskoi Biblioteki*, Novaiia Russkaiia Tipografiia, Geneva, 1892, and the latter's *Anarchist Communism, Its Basis and Principles*, Freedom Press, London, 1913 (cited hereafter, respectively, as Bakunin, M., *Parizhakaia Kommuna*, and Kropotkin, P., *Anarchist Communism*).

265. Lenin, V. I., "State and Revolution," *Collected Works, 21*, Part 2, p. 166. A resolution "On the Political Situation," adopted at the Sixth Congress of the Bolshevik Party, held 8-16 August 1917, states: "The slogan of the transfer of power to the Soviets advanced in the first wave of revolution and which our party propagandized, was the slogan of the peaceful development of the revolution, of the painless transfer of power from the bourgeoisie to the workers and peasants. . . . At the present time the peaceful development and painless transfer of power to the soviets has become impossible," *RKP* (b) 6 *S"ezd*, p. 220.

266. Ordzhonikidze, G. K., *Stat'i*, p. 124. Cf. Trotsky, L., *Russian Revolution, 2*, p. 315, and Chamberlin, W. H., *Russian Revolution*, p. 184.

267. Iaroslavskii, E., *et al.*, *Istoriia VKP(b), 4*, Gosudarstvennoe Izdatel'stvo, Moscow, 1930, p. 168.

268. Trotsky, L., *Russian Revolution, 3,* p. 127.

269. Lenin, V. I., "State and Revolution," *Collected Works, 21,* Part 2, p. 171.

270. *Ibid.,* p. 194.

271. Lenin, V. I., "Marxism and Insurrection," September 26-27, 1917, *Selected Works, 6,* p. 219.

272. In "The Bolsheviks Must Assume State Power," September 25-27, 1917, Lenin states: "Having obtained a majority in the Soviets of Workers' and Soldiers' Deputies of both capitals, the Bolsheviks can, and must take over the power of government." *Selected Works, 6,* p. 215. Also in "Marxism and Insurrection," September 26-27, 1917, Lenin states: "Now, we have a majority in both soviets," *ibid.,* p. 219.

273. Lenin, V. I., "A Letter to the Bolshevik Comrades," October 21, 1917, *ibid.,* p. 300.

274. Chamberlin, W. H., *Russian Revolution, 1,* p. 287.

275. Trotsky, L., *The Lessons of October 1917* (Trans. Susan Lawrence and I. Olshan), Labour Publishing, London, 1925, (henceforth referred to as Trotsky, L., *Lessons of October*), p. 59.

276. Lenin, V. I., "Compromise," September 14-16, 1917, *Selected Works, 6,* p. 209.

277. Schapiro, L., *Communist Autocracy,* pp. 520.

278. Trotsky, L., *Russian Revolution, 3,* p. 283.

279. *Loc. cit.*

280. For the issue of the Second Congress of Soviets, see Chamberlin, W. H., *Russian Revolution, 1,* p. 298, and Reed, John, *Ten Days that Shook the World,* Modern Library, New York, 1935 (henceforth referred to as Reed, John, *Ten Days*).

281. Trotsky, L., *Lessons of October,* p. 61.

282. Trotsky, L., *Lessons of October,* p. 63. In *Communist Autocracy,* pp. 52ff., Schapiro states that Lenin had rejected the soviets as organs of power and was depending upon the Bolshevik Party and the factory committees, Red Guards, and other organizations which the Bolsheviks controlled, in order to carry out the seizure of power. It was Trotsky, Schapiro claims, who directed the insurrection in Petrograd and who believed in conducting the uprising in the name of the soviets. If a comparison of the writings of Trotsky and Lenin is made, this interpretation seems to be substantially valid. There is, nevertheless, a difficulty in determining the validity of this view—a difficulty necessitated by comparing the retrospective accounts of Trotsky with the contemporary accounts of Lenin. Also, in the material available to this author, Trotsky seems to avoid an explicit assertion of the differences between himself and Lenin regarding the conduct of the uprising. He insists upon an underlying unity of principle but a difference in technique. Trotsky maintains that "there was not the shadow of thought of contrasting the two plans in principle. . . . But nevertheless the two were different approaches." (Trotsky, L., *Russian Revolution, 3,* pp. 285-286; cf. his *Lessons of October,* p. 59.) Thus Trotsky, while pointing out the distinction between his approach to the revolution and that of Lenin, seems at the same time to emphasize the accord that existed between the two leaders. Trotsky, however, might have been diminshing the difference in approach in order to capture, after Lenin's death, the

sanction of the latter for the Trotsky faction and school of thought. Trotsky's assertions concerning the manipulation of the soviets and their importance in the revolution evoked a rebuttal in the Communist Party. For this dispute, see Stalin, Joseph, "Trotskyism or Leninism," in *The October Revolution, A Collection of Articles and Speeches,* International Publishers, New York, 1934 (henceforth referred to as Stalin, J., *October Revolution*), pp. 68-94. See also Pokrovskii, M. N., *Oktiabr'skaiia Revoliutsiia, Sbornik Statei,* 1917-1927, Kommunisticheskaiia Akademiia, Moscow, 1929 (henceforth referred to as Pokrovskii, M. N., *Okt. Revoliutsiia*), espec. pp. 201-206. For a reply by Trotsky, see his *Russian Revolution, 3,* espec. pp. 287-290. This dispute is, of course, related to the political struggle between Stalin and Trotsky, which it is not the author's purpose to discuss here. It is sufficient for present purposes that the dispute has thrown light upon the October Revolution.

CHAPTER III

1. Lozovsky at the 8th, morning, meeting, August 11, 1917, of the Second Conference of Factory Committees of Petrograd, Its Suburbs and Neighboring Provinces, *Okt. Rev. i Fabzavkomy, 1,* p. 228.

2. Antipov at the Fourth Conference of Factory Committees of Petrograd, Its Vicinity, and Neighboring Provinces, *Okt. Rev. i Fabzavkomy, 2,* pp. 120-121.

3. Lenin, V. I., "Can the Bolsheviks Retain State Power?" October 14, 1917, *Selected Works, 6,* p. 266. For the original, see Lenin, V. I., *Sochineniia* (2nd Ed.), 1931, p. 260.

4. For the sociological formation of this class in the early nineteenth century, see Nechkina, M. V., *Obshchestvo Soedinennikh Slavian,* Gosudarstvennoe Izdatel'stvo, Moscow, 1927, pp. 15-17.

5. See Schapiro, L., *Communist Autocracy,* pp. 1-23, for an account of the attitude of the socialist parties to the war.

6. Proclamation to All Factory Committees of Workers, Soviets of Elders, Railroad and Transport Workers, *Okt. Rev. i Fabzavkomy, 1,* p. 77.

7. Resolution of the Commission on Unemployment and the Trade Unions, adopted at the First All-Russian Conference of Factory Committees, at the meeting of 3 November 1917, *ibid., 2,* p. 197.

8. Miliutin's Resolution on the Current Moment and Workers' Control at the Second Conference of Factory Committees of Petrograd, Its Suburbs and Neighboring Provinces, *Okt. Rev. i Fabzavkomy, 1,* p. 217. This is the same resolution as that adopted at the 6th Congress of the Bolshevik Party, 26 July-31 August, 1917. Cf. *RKP (b) 6 S'ezd,* pp. 221-23.

9. Miliutin's Resolution on the Current Moment and Workers' Control at the Second Conference of Factory Committees of Petrograd, Its Suburbs and Neighboring Provinces, *Okt. Rev. i Fabzavkomy, 1,* p. 217.

10. *Izvestiia,* No. 8, March 20, 1917, in Golder, F. A., *Documents of Russian History,* p. 419.

11. For the implementation of workers' control see Chapter II.

12. *Izvestiia,* No. 8, March 20, 1917, in Golder, F. A., *Documents of Russian History,* p. 419.

13. Second Conference of Factory Committees of Petrograd, Its Suburbs and Neighboring Provinces, August 7-12, 1917, *Okt. Rev. i Fabzavkomy, 1,* p. 217. For the Bolshevik accusation of collusion between the Provisional Government and factory owners against the workers and socialists see also Miliutin's speech in *RKP(b) 6 S'ezd,* 11th meeting, espec. p. 132.

14. Lenin, V. I., "Can the Bolsheviks Retain State Power?" October 14, 1917, Lenin, V. I., *Selected Works, 6,* p. 281.

15. For a psychological interpretation of the significance of the concept of dark forces in Russian life, see Gorer, G., and Richman, J., *The People of Great Russia,* Cresset, London, 1949, espec. pp. 130 and 156.

16. See, for example, Golder, F. A., *Documents of Russian History,* pp. 270, 308, 611, and 466; and Reed, John, *Ten Days,* p. 48; and the illustrations cited below.

17. The Black Hundreds were a political reactionary group committed to the support of autocracy and responsible on occasions in the period 1905-1917 for armed attacks on minority groups and those they considered subversive.

18. Menshevik Proclamation to the Workers, *ca.* July 8, 1917, in Golder, F. A., *Documents of Russian History,* pp. 457 and 459.

19. For the factory committees see Chapter II. For the growth of the trade unions after March 1917 see Vsesouiznyi Tsentral'nyi Soviet Professional'nykh Soiuzov, *Pervyi Vserossiiskii S'ezd Professional'nykh Soiuzov 7-14 Ianvaria 1918, Stenograficheskii Otchet c Predisloviem M. Tomskago,* Moscow, 1918, p. 351. See also *Professional'nyi Vestnik,* Nos. 9, 10, 5 January 1918, p. 2.

20. See the agreement between the Petrograd Soviet of Workers' Deputies and the Society of Manufacturers and Factory Owners in Arkhiv Oktiabr'skoi Revoliutsii, *Rabochee Dvizhenie v 1917, Godu,* (ed. Meller, V.L.), Gosudarstvennoe Izdatel'stvo, 1926 (henceforth referred to as *Rabochee Dvizhenie*) p. 40.

21. For the establishment of the eight-hour day, see Chernov, Victor, *The Great Russian Revolution,* (trans. and abridged by Philip E. Mosley) Yale University Press, New Haven, 1936, pp. 135-138, and Trotsky, L., *Russian Revolution, 1,* pp. 241-244. For the institution of the eight-hour day by the factory committees, see *Okt. Rev. i Fabzavkomy, 1,* pp. 51-52; and Brower and Kerensky, *The Russian Provisional Government, II,* pp. 712-713.

22. Golder F. A., *Documents of Russian History,* p. 509.

23. *Ibid.,* pp. 582-583, quoted from *Izvestiia,* No. 178, October 5, 1917.

24. Lunacharsky, A. V., Report on Cultural-Educational Work, at the ninth meeting, August 11, 1917, of the Second Conference of Factory Committees of Petrograd, Its Suburbs and Neighboring Provinces, *Okt, Rev. i Fabzavkomy, 1,* p. 234.

25. Lenin, V. I., "The Tasks of the Proletariat in our Revolution, Draft of Platform for the Proletarian Party," April 23, 1917, *Selected Works, 6,* p. 52.

26. For an account of Zubatovism, see Turin, Sergei, *From Peter the Great to Lenin, A History of the Russian Labour Movement with Special Reference to Trade Unionism,* S. P. King, London, 1935 (henceforth referred to as Turin S., *Peter the Great to Lenin*), pp. 56-67. See also Wolfe, B. D.,

Three Who Made a Revolution, pp. 272-274.

27. For an account of this event and its consequences for the labor movement, see Turin, S., *Peter the Great to Lenin,* pp. 68-83.

28. Zagorsky, S. O., *State Control of Industry,* p. 82.

29. For labor on the war industries committees, see *ibid.,* pp. 90-91. Romanov, F., *Rabochee i Professional'noe Dvizhenie v Gody Pervoi Voiny i Vtoroi Russkoi Revoliutsii, 1914-Fevral' 1917 Goda; Istoricheskii Ocherk,* Profizdat, Moscow, 1949 (henceforth referred to as Romanov, F., *Rabochee Dvizhenie*), p. 142, says that "Guchkov (president of the Central War Industry Committee) requested the Minister of Internal Affairs, Shcherbatov, and General Florov, Commander of the Petrograd Miiltary District, to take the election of the workers' groups under their protection. The order of elections drawn up by Konavlov (vice chairman of the Central War Industry Committee) provided that all the meetings of the workers must take place under strict surveillance of the police." In the material available to this writer, there is no evidence to support Romanov's undocumented assertion. There is contrary evidence, however, in the "Izvestiia Glavnago Komiteta po Snabzheniiu Armii," Nos. 2-3, October 14, 1915, translated in Golder, F. A., *Documents of Russian History,* pp. 127-129. The representatives were to be elected by a twofold system. First, workers at general meetings of their individual factories were to elect to a general council of delegates one delegate for each thousand workers (enterprises of from five hundred to one thousand elected only one delegate). Second, representatives to the war industry committees were to be elected at the general council of all delegates. It was decided to conduct the election at first in Petrograd and Moscow, and then in other industrial centers. For the labor elections to the war industries committees, see Golder, F. A., *Documents of Russian History,* pp. 127-129.

30. For Menshevik support of the war industry committees, see *loc. cit.* and Zagorsky, S. O., *State Control of Industry,* pp. 91-92.

31. For Bolshevik insistence at this time, upon the overthrow of the tsarist government, the international workers' fight for socialism and opposition to the war, see Lenin, V. I., "Neskol'ko Tezisov," October 1915, *Sochineniia, 21,* pp. 366-368, and Romanov, F., *Rabochee Dvizhenie,* p. 143.

32. Lenin, V. I., "Neskol'ko Tezisov," October 1915, *Sochineniia, 21,* p. 366.

33. "Izvestiia Glavnago Komiteta po Snabzheniiu Armii," Nos. 2-3, October, 14, 1915, in Golder, F. A., *Documents of Russian History,* p. 126.

34. Zagorsky, S. O., *State Control of Industry,* pp. 163-164. See also pp. 207-254.

35. For rationing under the Provisional Government, see Zaitsev, K. I., Dolinsky, N. V., and Demosthenov, S. S., *Food Supply in Russia During the World War* (Ed. P. B. Struve), Yale University Press, 1930 (henceforth referred to as Zaitsev, K. I., *Food Supply*), pp. 169-173.

36. *Okt. Rev. i Fabzavkomy, 2,* p. 83. For this situation, see also Reed, John, *Ten Days,* pp. 11-12.

37. *Okt. Rev. i Fabzavkomy, 1,* pp. 141-142, from the complete proclamation of the Central Council of Factory Committees, *Pravda,* No. 84, June 30, 1917. For the Bolsheviks on the food situation in Petrograd during the summer of 1917, see speech on Miliutin at 11th meeting, 31 July, in *Protokoly VI*

S"ezda R.S.D.R.P.(b), 26 July-3 August, 1917, Kommunist, Moscow, 1919, p. 131.

38. For the point of view which considers the Russian transportation system irremediably inadequate, see Zaitsev, K. I., *Food Supply*, pp. xiv, xvi, and xix. For a point of view which considers it to have been the tsarist government itself which was unable to deal effectively with the economic conditions of the war and for the effects of these conditions on the February Revolution, see Zagorsky, S. O., *State Control of Industry*, pp. 166ff.

39. For the situation in the Russian Railways during the war, see Greiner, J. E., "The Russian Railway Situation and Some Personal Observations," reprinted from the *Monthly Journal of the Engineers Club of Baltimore*, 7, No. 7, January 1918. Greiner was a member of the American Railway Commission for Russia, a group of railroad experts which was requested by the Provisional Government to assist in the solution of its railway problems. In his capacity as adviser, Greiner resided in Russia from May 13 to August 14, 1917. He points out that: "During the spring of 1917, the total mileage of all government and private railways in European and Asiatic Russia (exclusive of Finland) was approximately 43,000. . . . The Germans had taken possession of 4,000 miles and this left 39,300 miles still under the control of the Russian government. In addition, there was under construction and under consideration about 9,700 miles of new lines, parts of which were in temporary operation along the front" (p. 5). Mr. Greiner also notes (p. 6) that "the United States with its 258,000 miles of railways . . . has about one mile of track to each 390 people and about 8.6 miles to each 100 square miles while European and Asiatic Russia with its 43,000 miles of railway has about 1 mile to 3,930 people and only about 1/2 mile to each 100 square miles of territory." For information on the Russian Railways pertinent to the problem discussed here, see also Mamontov, S. I., *O Zhelezno-Dorozhnom Khoziaistve v Rossii*, Kushnerev, Moscow, 1909, espec. pp. 5-13; Uspenskii, Iu. E., *Budushchee Zheleznodorozhnoe Stroitel'stvo, Ego Razmery i Poriadok Osushchestvleniia*, Ministerstvo Putei Soobscheniia, Petrograd, 1916, pp. 1-50, and Oppenheim, K. A., *Rossia v Dorozhnom Otnoshenii*, Vysshii Sovet Narodnago Khoziaistva, Moscow, 1920, pp. 57-157.

40. For the difficulties of the transport of food supply by rail and how the problem was dealt with by the tsarist and Provisional Governments, see Zaitsev, K. I., *Food Supply*, pp. 61-76. For the difficulties of fuel transportation, espec. in the Petrograd region, see Zagorsky, S. O., *State Control of Industry*, pp. 79-80.

41. For the difficulties of using water transport for the wartime economy, see Zaitsev, K. I., *Food Supply*, pp. 76-78.

42. For Tsarist and Provisional Government measures for horse transport, see *ibid.*, pp. 78-81.

43. For the effect of the food and transportation crisis on the downfall of the monarchy, see Zagorsky, S. O., *State Control of Industry*, pp. 163-166; Tyrkova-Williams, A., *From Liberty to Brest-Litovsk*, pp. 1, 4, and 6; Trotsky, L., *Russian Revolution, 1*, p. 238. In the Introduction to *Food Supply*, Struve warns, however, that "the student of economic factors will not ascribe the political catastrophe that overwhelmed Russia in 1917 to the economic condition of the country in general and its food situation in particular" (p. xx).

44. See Trotsky, L., *Russian Revolution, 2,* p. 4.

45. Trotsky, L., evening meeting of the First All-Russian Conference of Factory Committees, October 18, 1917, *Okt. Rev. i Fabzavkomy, 1,* pp. 159-60. The view that civil war would replace the international war cannot be attributed to Trotsky alone among the Bolsheviks or to Trotsky as the leader of a party distinct from the Bolsheviks, although he was for a time the leader of such a party. Trotsky returned to Petrograd from New York in May 1917. At that time he reconstituted the *Mezhduraiontsy.* By mid-July, however, Trotsky was in full support of the Bolsheviks and on August 8, at the Sixth Bolshevik Party Congress, the formal union of the *Mezhduraiontsy* with the Bolsheviks took place. See Schapiro, L., *Communist Autocracy,* pp. 46-48; and Trotsky, L., *Russian Revolution,* 2, pp. 310-311. In October, Lenin and Trotsky held divergent views on the role of the factory committees, Red Guards and Soviets, but they worked in close alliance with one another. Lenin's view on turning the imperialist war into a revolutionary war may be found in his "Nes-kol'ko Tezisov," *Sochineniia,* 21, p. 368, for the promulgation of this policy by the Bolshevik Party, see Avdeev, N., *Revoliutsiia* 1917 *Goda* (*Khronika Sobytii*), *1,* 3 Vols., Gosudarstvennoe Izdatel'stvo, Moscow, 1923, (henceforth referred to as Avdeev, N., *Revoliutsiia*), pp. 200-201, presenting an extract from *Pravda,* No. 18, April 8, 1917. In November 1914, the Bolshevik Party had presented the slogan, "Turn the Imperialist War into a Civil War." See Lenin, V. I., "Farewell Letter to Swiss Workers," 26 March, 1917, *Selected Works, 6,* p. 19.

46. Lenin, V. I., "Letters from Afar; First Letter, the First Stage of Revolution," March 20, 1917, *Selected Works, 6,* p. 3.

47. Lenin, V. I., "Tasks of the Proletariat in our Revolution," April 23, 1917, *Selected Works, 6,* p. 73.

48. Lenin, V. I., "State and Revolution," *Collected Works, 21,* Part 2, p. 181.

49. Lenin, V. I., "Tasks of the Proletariat in our Revolution," April 23, 1917, *Selected Works, 6,* p. 74.

50. *Loc. cit.*

51. Lenin, V. I., "State and Revolution," *Collected Works, 21,* Part 2, p. 202.

52. Lenin, V. I., "Tasks of the Proletariat in our Revolution," April 10/23, 1917, *Selected Works, 6,* p. 74.

53. Schapiro, L., *Communist Autocracy,* p. 235.

54. Lenin, V. I., "State and Revolution," *Collected Works, 21,* Part 2, p. 177.

55. Lenin, V. I., "Tasks of the Proletariat in our Revolution," April 23, 1917, *Selected Works, 6,* p. 74.

56. Lenin, V. I., "A Dual Power," April 22, 1917, *ibid.,* pp. 27-28.

57. Lenin, V. I., "State and Revolution," *Collected Works, 21,* Part 2, p. 211.

58. *Loc. cit.*

59. For Lenin on Proudhon, federalism and centralism, see *ibid.,* p. 191.

60. *Ibid.,* p. 192.

61. Reed, John, *Ten Days,* p. xvii.

62. *Volia Naroda* (a Socialist Revolutionary newspaper), 17 July 1917.

See also "To the Comrade Workers," *Izvestiia,* No. 10, March 22, 1917, in Golder, F. A., *Documents of Russian History,* pp. 420-421.

63. For the chiliastic mood of revolutionary Petrograd after the February Revolution, see Sorokin, Pitrim, *Leaves from a Russian Diary,* E. P. Dutton, New York, 1924, pp. 25-39; Tyrkova-Williams, *From Liberty to Brest-Litovsk,* pp. 10-12; Reed, John, *Ten Days,* passim; and Schapiro, L., *Communist Autocracy,* p. 21.

64. Afinogenev at the Third Conference of Factory Committees of Petrograd, Its Vicinity and Neighboring Provinces, *Okt. Rev. i Fabzavkomy, 2,* p. 23.

65. For the disruption of the army as a fighting force, see Schapiro, L., *Communist Autocracy,* pp. 92-94, espec. note 15, pp. 92-93. See also Schapiro's sources, Brusilov, A. A., *Moi Vospominaniia,* n.p. Moscow, 1929, pp. 209-212; Fedotoff-White, D., *Red Army,* p. 21; and Kakurin, N. E., Ed. *Razlozhenie Armii v 1917 godu,* n.p., Moscow, 1925, pp. 118 and 151-152.

CHAPTER IV

1. For this statute see Orakhelashvili, M. D., and Sorin, V. G., *Dekrety Oktiabr'skoi Revoliutsii (Pravitel'stvennye Akty Podpisannye ili Utverzhdennye Leninym Kak Predsedatelem Sovnarkoma), I, Oktiabr'skogo Perevorota Do Rospuska Uchreditel'nogo Sobraniia,* Partinnoe Izdatel'stvo, Moscow, 1923 (henceforth referred to as *Dekrety Okt. Rev.*), pp. 89-90. For an English translation, see Lenin, V. I., *Selected Works, 6,* pp. 410-411.

2. *Dekrety Okt. Rev.*, pp. 90-91.

3. *Ibid.,* pp. 91-92. See also Rossiiskaia Sotsialisticheskaia Federativnaia Respublika, *Protokoly Zasedanii Vserossiiskago Tsentral'nogo Ispoln. Komiteta Soveta R.S.K. i Kaz. Deputatov II Sozyva,* V.Ts. i K.R.S.K. i K.D., Moscow 1918 (henceforth referred to as *VTSIK II Protokoly*), pp. 62-63; and *Narodnoe Khoziaistvo,* No. 1, January 1918, p. 26. For an English translation, see also Bunyan and Fisher, *Bolshevik Revolution*, pp. 308-310.

4. Statutes on Workers' Control, 27 November 1917, in *Narodnoe Khoziaistvo,* No. 1, March 1918, p. 26.

5. *Loc. cit.*

6. Paragraph 13, *loc. cit.*

7. Paragraph 11, *loc. cit.*

8. *Loc. cit.*

9. Lozovsky at the meeting of 27 November 1917 of the All-Russian Central Executive Committee, *VTSIK II Protokoly,* p. 62.

10. Paragraph 4, Statutes on Workers' Control, 27 November 1917, in *Narodnoe Khoziaistvo,* No. 1, March 1918, p. 26.

11. For a fuller discussion of the relationship between the factory committees and the trade unions as it was treated at the First All-Russian Conference of Factory Committees, see Chapter III.

12. Statutes on Workers' Control, 27 November 1917, in *Narodnoe Khoziaistvo,* No. 1, March 1918, p. 26.

13. Paragraph 9, *loc. cit.*

14. Miliutin at the meeting of 27 November 1917 of the All-Russian Central Executive Committee, in *VTSIK II Protokoly,* p. 61.

15. *Loc. cit.*

16. Miliutin at the 4th meeting, 27 November 1917 of the All-Russian Central Executive Committee, *ibid.,* p. 62.

17. *Ibid.,* p. 61.

18. *Loc. cit.*

19. Statutes on Workers' Control, 27 November 1917, in *Narodnoe Khoziaistvo,* No. 1, March 1918, p. 26.

20. See Paragraph 4 of the Statute on Workers' Control of 27 November 1917, quoted above.

21. Statutes on the Supreme Council of the National Economy, 14 December 1917, in *Narodnoe Khoziaistvo,* No. 1, January 1918, p. 24.

22. *Loc. cit.* A Plan of Instructions on Workers' Control, drawn up by a committee elected by the All-Russian Council of Workers' Control for the approval of the Supreme Council, decrees in Paragraph 23 that "All decrees of the Supreme Council of the National Economy and other state regulating organs in the sphere of the regulation of the economy are compulsory for all organs of workers' control." The date of this Plan of Instructions cannot be determined exactly, but it was issued sometime between November 1917 and March 1918. For these instructions see *ibid.,* p. 28. The statutes on the *raion, oblast',* and local councils of peoples' economy state, paragraph 9: "All the regional councils of people's economy must immediately enter into business-like connections with the Supreme Council of National Economy, subordinating themselves to its guidance in questions concerning all-state interests." *Ibid.,* p. 25.

23. *Ibid.,* p. 24.

24. *Loc. cit.*

25. Meeting of the All-Russian Central Executive Committee of the Soviet of Workers', Soldiers' and Peasants' Deputies, in *VTSIK II Protokoly,* p. 29. For an alternate English translation see Bunyan and Fisher, *Bolshevik Revolution,* p. 188.

26. *VTSIK II Protokoly,* p. 29. For the resolutions of the Central Executive Committee of 17 and 30 November 1917, which, as a concession to the Left Socialist Revolutionaries, limits the power of the Soviets of People's Commissars, see *ibid.,* p. 31, and Bunyan and Fisher, *Bolshevik Revolution,* p. 189. The resolution of 17 November, however, stating that "the Soviet Parliament has nothing in common with bourgeois parliaments . . ." undermined any hope of turning the soviets into a legislative organ to which the Council of People's Commissars, as an executive, was responsible. The Seventh Congress of Soviets of March 1918, in its Thesis on Soviet Power, Paragraph 3, came out for "the annihilation of parliamentarism (like the separation of legislative work from the executive). . . ." It advocated: "The fusion of administration with legislation." The Central Executive Committee, however, was much too large for an executive and legislative body, even if the Bolshevik Party had permitted it to become one in fact. For Paragraph 3 of the Thesis on Soviet Power of the Seventh Congress, see Tsentral'nyi Komitet RKP (bolshevik), Komissiia Po Istorii Oktiabr'skoi Revoliutsii i RKP (bolshevik) (Istpart), *Sed'moi S"ezd Rossiiskoi Kommunisticheskoi Partii, Stenograficheskii Otchet*

6-8 Marta 1918, Gosudarstvennoe Izdatel'stvo, Moscow, 1923 (henceforth referred to as *7 S"ezd Partii*), p. 205.

27. *RKP(b) 6 S"ezd,* Miliutin at the 11th meeting, 13 August 1917, p. 134.

28. *Ibid.,* p. 135.

29. Lomov at the meeting of 13 August 1917 of the 6th Congress of the Bolshevik Party, *ibid.,* p. 136.

30. *Okt. Rev. i Fabzavkomy, 1,* p. 171.

31. *Ibid., 2,* p. 184.

32. Lozovsky at the meeting of 27 November 1917 of the All-Russian Central Executive Committee, *VTSIK II Protokoly,* p. 62.

33. Cherevanin on the Regulation of Industry and Workers' Control, on the 7th day, 26 January 1918, of the First All-Russian Congress of Trade Unions, in *1 S"ezd Profsoiuzov,* p. 227.

34. It is true that Lozovsky was expelled from the Bolshevik Party on 11 January 1918, but his expulsion was due to his stand on the trade unions and their relationship to the party and state. His policy of opposition toward the factory committees coincided with that of the Bolshevik Party, however. And in his concluding speech on workers' control at the First All-Russian Congress of Trade Unions, he identifies himself with the Bolsheviks, stating, " . . . not one of us, not one Bolshevik said we understood control as pulverizing, disorganizing control," *ibid.,* p. 227.

35. Lozovsky on the Regulation of Industry, 6th day, *ibid.,* p. 193. For this same point of view expressed again by Lozovsky, see Vsesoiuznyi S"ezd Professional'nykh Soiuzov Tekstil'shchikov i Fabrichnykh Komitetov, *Protokoly I-go Vserossiiskogo S"ezda Professional'nykh Soiuzov Tekstil'shchikov i Fabrichnykh Komitetov,* Vserossiiskii Sovet Professional'nykh Soiuzov Tekstil'shchikov, Moscow, 1918 (henceforth referred to as *1 S"ezd Tekstil'shchikov Protokoly*), p. 11.

36. Maiskii on the 6th day, 25 January 1918, of the First All-Russian Congress of Trade Unions, *1 S"ezd Profsoiusov,* p. 212.

37. *Loc. cit.*

38. Skrypnik at the First All-Russian Conference of Factory Committees, morning meeting, 20 October 1917, in *Okt. Rev. i Fabzavkomy, 2,* p. 184.

39. Lozovsky, "Rabochi Kontrol'," in *Professional'nyi Vestnik, Organ Vserossiiskogo Soveta Professional'nykh Soiuzov,* No. 5, January 1918, (henceforth referred to as *Professional'nyi Vestnik*).

40. See espec. *1 S"ezd Profsoiuzov,* passim.

41. See previous references and Rosenfeld, R. S., *Promyshlennaia Politika SSSR,* n.p., Moscow, 1926 (henceforth referred to as Rosenfeld, R. S., *Promyshlennaia Politika*), p. 92.

42. See Lozovsky on workers' control in *1 S"ezd Tekstil'shchikov Protokoly,* p. 13.

43. See, for example, *loc. cit.,* and the Resolution on Demobilization, *1 S"ezd Profsoiuzov,* p. 373.

44. Filipopov at the 28 October 1917 meeting of the Tariff Conference of Metal Workers, in Vserossiiskii Soiuz Rabochikh Metallistov, *Protokoly Pervoi Vserossiiskoi Tarifnoi Konferentsii Soiuzov Metallistov Sovmestno c Predstavitelem Zavodskikh Komitetov,* Tsentral'nyi Komitet, Petrograd, 1918 (henceforth referred to as *1 Vseros. Konf. Metallistov Protokoly*), p. 15.

45. *Okt. Rev. i Fabzavkomy, 2,* p. 19. So scornful is the Commission to Study the Trade Union Movement in the SSSR of this practice of ownership and management sharing that it refers to the workers engaged in this process not only as members of the petty bourgeoisie but at deserters from the army. It states: "Here also a game was played with the non-class conscious elements, or that part of the workers who actually were military deserters to the ranks of the petty bourgeoisie." *Loc. cit.*

46. Arskii, R., "Professional'nyi Soiuzy i Zavodskie Komitety," in *Vestnik Narodnago Kommissariata Truda,* No. 2-3, February-March 1918, pp. 124-124 (henceforth referred to as *Vestnik NKT*).

47. *Ibid.,* p. 125.

48. *Loc. cit.*

49. Gastev at the 28 October 1917 meeting of the Tariff Conference of the Metal Workers' Union, in *1 Vseros. Konf. Metallistov Protokoly,* pp. 6-7. For the interest of the factory committees in their factories, see also Weinberg on the Regulation of Industry and Workers' Control, 8th day, 27 January 1918, in *1 S"ezd Profsoiuzov,* p. 243; Gastev on Demobilization of Industry, *ibid.,* p. 165; and Lozovsky on the Regulation of Industry, *ibid.,* p. 194. The above accounts were presented from the Bolshevik viewpoint, which considered the autonomy and self-interest of the factory committees undesirable. It also execrated cooperation with ownership outside of a system of state control. Therefore, in attacking the factory committees and their implementation of workers' control, the Bolsheviks might have exaggerated what they considered negative attributes. Nevertheless, if the Bolshevik frame of reference is kept in mind, a substantially valid picture of workers' control may be derived from an examination of the situation as a whole, in its various aspects, derived from various sources.

50. For this lack of centralization at the beginning of Bolshevik rule, see Rosenfeld, R. S., *Promyshlennaia Politika,* pp. 84-85, 92.

51. *Ibid.,* p. 93.

52. Lenin, e.g., on 14 October 1917 wrote: "Compulsory trustification, i.e., compulsory amalgamation into association under the control of the state, is what capitalism has paved the way for. . . . This will fully be realized in Russia by the Soviets and the dictatorship of the proletariat." Lenin, V. I., "Can the Bolsheviks Retain State Power?" in *Selected Works, 6,* p. 268. See also Lenin, V. I., "The Threatening Catastrophe and How to Fight It," published at the end of October 1917, in *Collected Works 21,* Part 1, espec. pp. 106 and 198.

53. Lenin, V. I., "State and Revolution," *ibid.,* Part 2, p. 226. In the first phase of communism, Lenin planned that "*All* citizens are here transformed into hired employees of the state. . . . *All* citizens become employees and workers of *one* national state 'syndicate.'" *Ibid.,* p. 229.

54. Lenin, on 24 January 1918, the 2nd day of the 3rd All-Russian Congress of Soviets of Workers', Soldiers' and Peasants' Deputies, in Rossiiskaia Sotsialdemokraticheskaia Rabochaia Partiia, *Tretii Vserossiiskii S"ezd Sovetov Rabochikh, Soldatskikh i Krestianskikh Deputatov,* Petrograd, 1918 (henceforth referred to as *3 S"ezd Sovetov*), p. 22.

55. Lenin, V. I., "The Immediate Tasks of the Soviet Government, the International Position of the Russian Soviet Republic, and the Fundamental

Tasks of the Socialist Revolution," April 1918, in *Selected Works, 7,* pp. 346-347.

56. *Ibid.,* p. 347.

57. *Ibid.,* p. 319.

58. *Loc. cit.*

59. *Loc. cit.*

60. Vsesoiuznyi S"ezd Professional'nykh Soiuzov Tekstil'shchikov i Fabrichnykh Komitetov, *Rezoliutsii I-go Vserossiskago S"ezda Rabochikh i Rabotnits Tekstil'shchikov Sostoiavshagosia v Moskve, 28 Ianvaria-2 Fevralia 1918,* Vserossiiskii Sovet Tekstil'shchikov, Moscow, 1918 (henceforth referred to as *1 S"ezd Tekstil'shchikov Rezoliutsii*), p. 8.

61. *Loc. cit.* The Resolution on Workers' Control at the First All-Russian Congress of Trade Unions also states: "Russia . . . can extricate itself from economic chaos only by means of a planned regulation of industry, trade, credit, agriculture and transport." 1 *S"ezd Profsoiuzov,* p. 369.

62. Lenin, on the 2nd day, 25 January 1918, of the Third Congress of Soviets of Workers', Soldiers' and Peasants' Deputies, in *3 S"ezd Sovetov,* p. 28.

63. Trotsky, L., *A Paradise in This World, An address delivered to a working class audience on April 14, 1918,* British Socialist Party, London, n. d., p. 20.

64. *Loc. cit.*

65. *Loc. cit.*

66. Vladimir Dal', *Tolkovyi Slovar' Zhivogo Velikorusskago Iazyka* (3rd Ed.), M. O. Wol'f, Petrograd, 1903-1909 (henceforth referred to as *Dal'*).

67. *Tolkovyi Slovar' Russkogo Iazyka* (Ed. Ushakov), Ogiz, Moscow, 1935 (henceforth referred to as *Tolkovyi Slovar'*).

68. These definitions are included in the 1940 edition of Aleksandrov, *et al., Politicheskii Slovar'.* The 1958 edition of this dictionary does not include definitions of either *stikhiinost'* or *soznatel'nost'.*

69. Having been published after the Stalin-Trotsky dispute, the *Politicheskii Slovar'* emphasizes the victory of socialism in the SSSR, as opposed to an emphasis upon the victory of world socialism. In the period under examination here, it was the victory of world socialism which was emphasized.

70. Shliapnikov at the First All-Russian Congress of Commissars of Labor, 29 January 1918, in *Vestnik NKT,* No. 2-3, February-March, 1918, p. 217.

71. Lozovsky at the First All-Russian Congress of Trade Unions and Factory Committees of Textile Workers, 10 February-15 February, 1918, in *1 S"ezd Tekstil'shchikov Protokoly,* p. 30.

CHAPTER V

1. Lozovsky on Regulation of Industry, 6th day, 12/25 January 1918 of the First All-Russian Congress of Trade Unions in *1 S"ezd Profsoiuzov,* p. 196.

2. *Professional'nyi Vestnik,* No. 8, December, 1917, p. 14.

3. *Loc. cit.*

4. *Vestnik NKT,* No. 2/3, February/March 1918, p. 239.

5. *Loc. cit.*

6. An appeal published in January 1918 in *Golos Truda* organ of the Petrograd Union of Anarcho-Syndicalist Propaganda, reprinted in and quoted from the *Khar'kovskii Nabat, Organ Khar'kovskii Gruppy Anarkhistov Nabat,* 16 February 1919.

7. *Loc. cit.*

8. *Loc. cit.*

9. Bukharin, N., *Programma Kommunistov (bol'shevikov)*, Petrogradskii Sovet Rabochikh i Krasnoarmeiskikh Deputatov, Petrograd, 1919 (henceforth referred to as Bukharin, N., *Programma Kommunistov*), p. 8. For an English translation, see Bukharin, N., *Program of the Communists (Bolshevik),* Communist Labor Party of America, n.p., n.d. There are also other English-language editions. Bukharin may be ranked as a Left Communist, but in spite of the charges made against him during his trial in 1938, he was one of the Party leaders in 1918.

10. Bukharin, N., *Programma Kommunistov,* p. 8.

11. *Loc. cit.*

12. *Ibid.,* pp. 8-9.

13. *Ibid.,* pp. 30-31.

14. Bukharin, N., *Programma Kommunistov,* p. 10.

15. *Ibid.,* p. 11.

16. *Ibid.,* p. 12.

17. Lenin, V. I., "Pisma o Taktike," *Sochineniia, 24,* p. 27. For an alternate translation, see his "First Letter on Tactics. An Estimate of the Present Situation," April 1917, *Selected Works, 6,* pp. 35-36.

18. Lenin, V. I., "The Immediate Tasks of the Soviet Government, The International Position of the Russian Soviet Republic and the Fundamental Tasks of the Socialist Revolution," March/April 1918, in *Selected Works, 7,* p. 328.

19. Riazanov, 8th day, 14/27 January 1918 of the First All-Russian Congress of Trade Unions in 1 *S"ezd Profsoiuzov,* p. 236.

20. Iakovlev, Ia, *Russkii Anarkhizm v Velikoi Russkoi Revoliutsii,* Iskra, New York, 1922 (henceforth referred to as Iakovlev, Ia, *Russkii Anarkhizm*), p. 89.

21. Voline (V. M. Eichenbaum), *La Révolution Inconnue (1917 -1921, Documentation Inedite sur la Revolution Russe,* Les Amis de Voline, Paris, 1947 (henceforth referred to as Voline, *La Révolution Inconnue*), p. 154. Voline or V. M. Volin, one of the leading anarchists of the revolutionary period, is not to be confused with B. M. Volin, the Bolshevik.

22. See, for example, Kropotkin, P., *Revolutionary Government,* Freedom Press, London, 1943 (first published in 1890) (henceforth referred to as Kropotkin, P., *Revolutionary Government*), espec. pp. 7-8. Here Kropotkin presents the formula of the anarchists as "Nothing good or durable can be done except by the free initiative of the people and every government tends to destroy it." See also Karelin, A., *Chto Takoe Anarkhiia?* Vserossiiskaia Federatsiia Anarkh.-Kommunistov, Moscow, 1923 (henceforth referred to as Karelin, A., *Chto Takoe Anarkhiia?*), pp. 3-4.

23. For an anarchist view of the conflicting ideas of the Bolsheviks and

Anarchists in the period under discussion, see Voline, *Le Révolution Inconnue,* pp. 153-154. For the Bolshevik view, see Iakovlev, Ia, *Russkii Anarkhizm, passim.*

24. Gruppy Anarkhistov v Germanii, *Goneniia Na Anarkhizm v Sovetskoi Rossii,* Berlin, 1920 (henceforth referred to as *Goneniia Na Anarkhizm*), p. 10.

25. Iakovlev, Ia, *Russkii Anarkhizm,* p. 53.

26. *Golos Anarkhista,* 11 March 1918, p. 5. For Anarchism in the Ukraine see especially Voline, *La Révolution Inconnue,* Chap. 7 and 13. For the relationship between Voline and Makhno see Makhno, Nestor, *Makhnovshchina i ee Vcherashnie Soiuzniki-Bol'sheviki,* Biblioteka Makhnovtsev, Paris 1928, pp. 41-46

27. *Loc. cit.*

28. *Guliaipol'skii Nabat,* No. 7, March 9, 1917.

29. *Loc. cit.*

30. Iakovlev, Ia, *Russkii Anarkhizm,* p. 3. Yaroslavsky, E., in his *History of Anarchism in Russia,* International Publishers, New York, 1937 (henceforth referred to as Yaroslavsky, E., *History of Anarchism in Russia*), p. 49, also, from the Bolshevik point of view, charges that the Anarchists took no part in the October Revolution.

31. Iakovlev, Ia, *Russkii Anarkhizm,* p. 16.

32. For the distinction between a party and a movement as used here, see Arendt, Hannah, *The Origins of Totalitarianism,* Harcourt Brace, New York, 1951 (henceforth referred to as Arendt, H., *Origins of Totalitarianism*), especially pp. 243-265.

33. There are indications that Bakunin not only did not reject the idea of organization for Anarchists but himself drew up a plan for organization. See, for example, his Secret Regulations for the League of Social Democracy, in Bakunin, M., *Rechi i Vozzvaniia,* Balshov, n.p., 1906, pp. 209ff. Bakunin's relationship to Nechaev also indicates, because of Nechaev's secret committee and its presumed affiliation with an "International Revolutionary Union," that Bakunin was not adverse to revolutionary organization and discipline. For Nechaev and Bakunin, see Steklov, Iu, *Mikhail Aleksandrovich Bakunin Ego Zhizn' i Deiatel'nost', 3,* Gosurdarstvennoe, Moscow, 1927 (henceforth referred to as Steklov, Iu, *Bakunin*), pp. 418-521; Nomad, Max, *Apostles of Revolution,* Little, Brown, Boston, 1939 (henceforth referred to as Nomad, Max, *Apostles of Revolution*), pp. 211-254; and Prawdin, Michael, *The Unmentionable Nechaev,* George Allen and Unwin, London, 1961, pp. 23-32 and pp. 43-58. It is not within the scope of this work, however, to discuss the problem of the relationship between Bakunin and Nechaev or the significance of that relationship for the Anarchist movement. It should be noted, however, that the Russian Anarchism under discussion here shows no systematized party organization.

34. Zagranichnoe Biuro po Sozdaniiu Rossiiskoi Konfederatsii Anarkho-Sindikalistov, *Vmesto Programmy: Rezoliutsii I i II Vserossiiskikh Konferentsii Anarkho-Sindikalistov,* Knigoizdatel'stvo Zagranichnogo Biuro Anarkho-Sindikalistov, Berlin, 1922 (henceforth referred to as *Vmesto Programmy*), p. 7.

35. For the Anarchist claim to having dispersed the Constituent Assembly, see *Goneniia Na Anarkhizm,* p. 18 and p. 53. See also Goldman, Emma, *My Disillusionment in Russia,* Doubleday, New York, 1923 (henceforth referred

to as Goldman, Emma, *My Disillusionment in Russia*), p. 46.

36. Maximov, G. P., *Sovety Rabochikh, Soldatskikh i Krestianskikh Deputatov i Nashe k Nim Otnoshenie,* Federatsiia Soiuzov Russkikh Rabochikh Soed Shtatov i Kanady, New York, 1919 (first appeared on 22 December 1917/4 January 1918 in No. 22 *Golos Truda* issued in Petrograd), (henceforth referred to as Maximov, G., *Sovety i Nashe k Nim Otnoshenie*), p. 8.

37. Iakovlev, Ia, *Russkii Anarkhizm*, p. 9.

38. *Ibid.*, p. 80.

39. *Goneniia Na Anarkhizm,* p. 16.

40. Pankratova, A., *Fabzavkomy i Profsoiuzy,* p. 64 and p. 97.

41. *Goneniia Na Anarkhizm,* p. 16.

42. Lenin, V. I., "A Letter to the Comrades," October 29-30/November 16-17, 1917, in *Selected Works, 6*, p. 305.

43. *Goneniia Na Anarkhizm*, p. 16.

44. *Ibid.*, p. 17.

45. Maximov, G., *Sovety i Nashe k Nim Otnoshenie,* p. 1.

46. *Loc. cit.*

47. *Ibid.*, pp. 1-2.

48. *Ibid.*, p. 2.

49. *Loc. cit.*

50. *Loc. cit.*

51. *Loc. cit.*

52. *Ibid.*, p. 3.

53. *Ibid.*, p. 4.

54. *Loc. cit.*

55. *Ibid.*, pp. 4-5.

56. *Ibid.*, p. 5.

57. *Ibid.*, p. 6.

58. *Ibid.*, pp. 7-8.

59. *Ibid.*, p. 8.

60. For the reaction of Russian, and of non-Russian Anarchists as well, to the Bolshevik regime, and the action they took toward it, see Goldman, Emma, *My Disillusionment in Russia, passim,* and her *My Further Disillusionment in Russia,* Doubleday Page, New York, 1924 (henceforth referred to as Goldman, Emma, *My Further Disillusionment in Russia*), *passim.* See also Berkman, Alexander, *The Bolshevik Myth* (*Diary 1920-1922*), Boni and Liveright, New York, 1925 (henceforth referred to as Berkman, A., *Bolshevik Myth*), *passim.* For a statement of the Anarchist policy on the Soviets similar to Maximov's see Voline, *The Unknown Revolution (Kronstadt 1921, Ukraine 1918-1921),* (Trans. Holley Cantine), Freedom Press, London, 1955 (henceforth referred to as Voline, *The Unknown Revolution*), fn. 1, p. 11.

61. Iakovlev, Ia, *Russkii Anarkhizm,* p. 89.

62. *Ibid.*, p. 4.

63. *Loc. cit.*

64. *Ibid.*, p. 89.

65. An example of the possible importance of the international labor movement for the Bolshevik treatment of the Russian Anarchists may be found in Maximov, G. P., *Za Chto i Kak Bol'sheviki Izgnali Anarkhistov Iz Rossii?,* Anarkho-Kommun Gruppy, 1922, pp. 10-17. Maximov claims that a

group of hunger-striking anarchist prisoners were freed by the Russians because of the presence in Russia in 1921 of European Anarchists for the International Congress of Red Trade Unions.

66. *Rezoliutsii 1 S"ezda Konfederatsii Anarkhistkikh Organizatsii Ukrainy 'Nabat'* (Elizavetgrad 2-7 Aprelia 1919), Rabochei Izdatel'skoi Gruppy v Resp. Argentine, Buenos Aires, 1923 (henceforth referred to as *Rezoliutsii 1 S"ezda Konfederatsii Anarkhistkikh Organizatsii Ukrainy 'Nabat'*), p. 14.

67. *Golos Anarkhista,* 15 March 1918.

68. For the Black Guards and their suppression, see Iakovlev, Ia, *Russkii Anarkhizm,* pp. 9-11, and Berkman, A., *Bolshevik Myth,* pp. 68-69. Iakovlev charges that the Black Guards were overrun by thieves and bandits. There may have been some truth in this accusation. Emma Goldman in her *My Further Disillusionment in Russia,* p. 86, states: "Unfortunately, as was unavoidable under the circumstances, some evil spirits had found entry into the Anarchist ranks—debris washed ashore by the Revolutionary tide. They were types to whom the Revolution meant only destruction, occasionally even for personal advantage. They engaged in shady pursuits. . . ." The association of anti-statism with banditism, interestingly enough, may also be found in Nechaev's (or Bakunin's) *Catechism of a Revolutionary.* See Steklov, Iu, *Bakunin,* p. 473, and Nomad, Max, *Apostles of Revolution,* p. 233.

69. Trotsky, L., *A Paradise in This World,* p. 22.

70. *Loc. cit.*

71. *Ibid.,* p. 23.

72. *Loc. cit.*

73. *Loc. cit.*

74. *Ibid.,* p. 24.

75. The word *ideinyi* has a fuller connotation than is conveyed simply by the word idealist. It is an adjective indicating the basic, essential principles of a world conception. See *Tolkovy Slovar'.*

76. Goldman, Emma, *My Disillusionment in Russia,* p. 108. In *My Further Disillusionment in Russia,* p. 92, Emma Goldman charges: "It had become the established policy of the Bolshevik Government to mask its barbaric procedure against Anarchists with the uniform charge of banditism." This accusation was made practically against all arrested Anarchists and frequently even against sympathizers with the movement." Voline, in his *La Révolution Inconnue,* p. 290, also asserts that criminal charges brought against Fanny Baron and Lev Chernyi (Turchaninov) by the Bolsheviks in 1921, for which they suffered the death penalty, were later proved false. Voline, however, presents no documentation for his assertion.

77. Maximov on the 3rd day, 9/22 January 1918 of the First All-Russian Congress of Trade Unions in *1 S"ezd Profsoiuzov,* p. 85.

78. *Loc. cit.*

79. Maximov on the 3rd day, 9/22 January 1918 of the First All-Russian Congress of Trade Unions in *ibid.,* p. 84.

80. *Loc. cit.*

81. Maximov on the 3rd day, 9/22 January 1918 of the First All-Russian Conference of Trade Unions, in *ibid.,* p. 85.

82. Karelin, A., *Chto Takoe Anarkhiia?* p. 1.

83. *Ibid.,* p. 4.

84. Maximov on the 7th day, 13/26 January 1918 of the First All- Russian Congress of Trade Unions in *1 S"ezd Profsoiuzov,* p. 216.

85. Resolution of the Anarcho-Syndicalists, presented by Maximov, 7th day, 13/26 January 1918 in *ibid.,* p. 216.

86. Maximov on the 7th day, 13/26 January 1918 of the First All-Russian Congress of Trade Unions, in *ibid.,* p. 214.

87. Resolution of the Anarcho-Syndicalists, 7th day, 13/26 January 1918, of the First All-Russian Congress of Trade Unions, *ibid.,* p. 217.

88. *Loc. cit.*

89. *Loc. cit.*

90. *Loc. cit.*

91. Maximov on the Regulation of Industry, 8th day, 14/27 January 1918 of the First All-Russian Congress of Trade Unions in *ibid.,* p. 239.

92. Maximov on the 7th day, 13/26 January 1918 of the First All-Russian Congress of Trade Unions in *ibid.,* p. 215.

93. For the Anarchist attitudes to law and authority, see Kropotkin, Peter, *Law and Authority, An Anarchist Essay by Pierre Kropotkine,* International Publishers, London, 1886.

94. For Anarchism in the Ukraine, see Voline, *The Unknown Revolution,* pp. 75ff.

95. Resolution on the Growth and Tasks of the Anarchist Movement in General in Rezoliutsii *1 S"ezda Konfederatsii Anarkhistskikh Organizatsii Ukrainy 'Nabat',* pp. 12-13. See also *Vmesto Programmy,* pp. 9ff.

96. Resolution on the Growth and Tasks of the Anarchist Movement in General in Rezoliutsii *1 S"ezda Konfederatsii Anarkhistskikh Organizatsii Ukrainy 'Nabat',* p. 13.

97. Resolution on the Current Moment in *ibid.,* p. 11.

98. For the work of the Anarchists where thay had the opportunity of implementing their ideas for a time—or as the Anarchists themselves would put it—of allowing the workers and peasants to create freely their own order, see Voline, *The Unknown Revolution,* pp. 105-115. The contradiction in the idea of the spontaneous creation of a movement which is being propagated is illustrated by Voline's statement: "All these communes were created freely, by a spontaneous impulse of the peasants themselves, with the help of a few good organizers. . . ." *Ibid.,* p. 106.

99. Anarchist faith in the revolutionary aptitude of the masses may be illustrated by the following statement in *Goneniia Na Anarkhizm,* p. 10. "The revolutionary masses of the people instinctively feel and defend the essence of the true revolution." The Anarchists regard themselves as having less knowledge of the revolutionary situation than the masses. Nevertheless, they regard their role as one of ideological assistance. The pamphlet continues: "Out of such a concept of social revolution there naturally arises the idea not of the power oriented leadership of the masses, but only of ideological (*ideinyi*) assistance to them in their future free and creative revolution. . . ." *Loc. cit.*

100. Resolution on the Current Moment in *Rezoliutsii 1 S"ezda Konfederatsii Anarkhistkikh Organizatsii Ukrainy 'Nabat',* p. 10.

CHAPTER VI

1. See Gorki, Maxim, "January 22, 1905 and January 18, 1918, in *Novaia Zhizn'*, No. 6, January 23, 1918, p. 3, translated in Bunyan and Fisher, *Bolshevik Revolution*, pp. 387-388; Kefali, on the 1st day, 19 January, of the First All-Russian Congress of Trade Unions, in *1 S"ezd Profsoiuzov*, and Spiridonova, on the same day, same congress, *ibid.*, p. 23.

2. Lozovsky in the *Professional'nyi Vestnik*, 2 January 1918, p. 3.

3. Kozelev, 7th day, 26 January 1918, in *1 S"ezd Profsoiuzov*, and Spiri-

4. *Loc. cit.*

5. Kozelev, 7th day, 26 January 1918 in *ibid.*, p. 222.

6. Osinskii, N. (Oblenskii), *Stroitel'stvo Sotzializma, Obshchiia Zadachi Organizatsiia Proizvodstva*, Kommunist, Moscow, 1918 (henceforth referred to as Osinskii, N., *Stroitel'stvo Sotsializm*), p. 88.

7. Lozovsky, 6th day, 25 January 1918, of the First All-Russian Congress of Trade Unions, in *1 S"ezd Profsoiuzov*, p. 192.

8. Lozovsky, 7th day, 26 January 1918, *ibid.*, p. 230.

9. Adopted Resolution on Workers' Control at the First All-Russian Congress of Trade Unions, *ibid.*, p. 369.

10. Gastev on the Demobilization of Industry, 6th day, 25 January 1918, of the First All-Russian Congress of Trade Unions, in *ibid.*, p. 165.

11. Riazanov, 8th day, 27 January 1918, of the First All-Russian Congress of Trade Unions, in *ibid.*, p. 235.

12. *Loc. cit.*

13. *Loc. cit.*

14. Lozovsky, "Rabochii Kontrol'," in *Professional'nyi Vestnik*, No. 9-10, 18 January 1918, p. 4.

15. *Loc. cit.*

16. Cherevanin, Speech on the Regulation of Industry and Workers' Control, 7th day, 26 January 1918, at the First All-Russian Congress of Trade Unions, in *1 S"ezd Profsoiuzov*, p. 204.

17. Lozovsky on the Regulation of Industry, 6th day, 25 January 1918, of the First All-Russian Congress of Trade Unions, in *ibid.*, p. 193.

18. Lozovsky, *1 S"ezd Tektil'shchikov, Protokoly*, p. 30.

19. *Ibid.*, p. 31.

20. *Loc. cit.*

21. Lozovsky on the Regulation of Industry, 6th day, 25 January 1918, of the First All-Russian Congress of Trade Unions, *1 S"ezd Profsoiuzov*, p. 195.

22. *Ibid.*, p. 196.

23. *Loc. cit.*

24. *Loc. cit.*

25. Adopted Resolution on Workers' Control, First All-Russian Congress of Trade Unions, January 1918, in *ibid.*, p. 371. See also Plan of Instructions for Workers' Control, Article 2, Paragraph 8 in *Narodnoe Khziaistvo*, No. 1, March 1918, p. 27. The preface to the Instructions states: "The first meeting of the All-Russian Council of Workers' Control decided to issue a compulsory decree on Workers' Control. A commission was elected to draw up the plan. The Commission consisted of the representatives of the Central Executive Committee of the Soviet of Workers', Soldiers' and Peasants' Deputies, of the

All-Russian Council of Trade Unions, of the All-Russian Center of Factory Committees, and of the Economic Branch of the Moscow Soviet of Workers' Deputies (Miliutin, Larin, Antipov, Smidovich, and others). This commission unanimously adopted the plan of instructions published here.

"It will be examined in the next plenary meeting of the Council [the All-Russian Council of Workers' Control]." *Loc. cit.*

27. *Okt. Rev. i Fabzavkomy, 2,* p. 193.

28. *Loc. cit.*

29. *Ibid.,* p. 105.

30. *Loc. cit.*

31. *Ibid.,* pp. 105-106.

32. *Ibid.,* p. 107. See also Arskii, R., "Professionalnye Soiuzy i Zavodskie Komitety," in *Vestnik NKT,* No. 2-3, February-March 1918, p. 128 for a similar view.

33. Riazanov, 8th day, 27 January 1918, of the First All-Russian Conference of Trade Unions, in *1 S"ezd Profsoiuzov,* p. 234.

34. Lozovsky, 2nd day, 21 January 1918, of the First All-Russian Congress of Trade Unions, *ibid.,* pp. 33-34.

35. Riazanov, 8th day, 27 January 1918, of the First All-Russian Congress of Trade Unions, *ibid.,* p. 234.

36. Riazanov, on the Relations between the Factory Committees and the Trade Unions, 8th day, 27 January 1918, of the First All-Russian Congress of Trade Unions, *ibid.,* p. 237. Weinberg, speaking on the Regulation of Industry and Workers' Control on the 8th day, 27 January 1918, at this congress, stated: "The factory committees are interested in the people's economy only insofar as it serves the interest of the given factory." *Ibid.,* p. 242.

37. Lozovsky on the Regulation of Industry, 6th day, 25 January 1918, *ibid.,* p. 196.

38. Lozovsky, "Rabochii Kontrol'," in *Professional'nyi Vestnik,* No. 9-10, 5 January 1918, p. 5.

39. *Loc. cit.*

40. *Loc. cit.*

41. Weinberg on the Regulation of Industry and Workers' Control, 8th day, 27 January 1918, of the First All-Russian Congress of Trade Unions, in *1 S"ezd Profsoiuzov,* p. 243.

42. *Loc. cit.*

43. *1 S"ezd Tekstil'shchikov, Rezoliutsii,* p. 5. Paragraph 7 of the section on Organizational Structure of the same statute states: "The factory committees serve as the bases of the union locally. They are its executive organs each subordinate to the individual organ of the union standing above it and they carry out all the decisions of the Union." *Ibid.,* p. 3.

44. Tomsky in *1 S"ezd Profsoiuzov,* p. ix.

45. *Loc. cit.*

46. *Loc. cit.*

47. Adopted Resolution on the Trade Unions and Factory Committees, in *1 S"ezd Profsoiuzov,* p. 374.

48. *Loc. cit.*

49. *Loc. cit.* See also R. Arskii who, in his "Professional'nye Soiuzy i Zavodskie Komitety," in *Vestnik NKT,* No. 2-3, February-March 1918, p.

127, wrote: "In the life of the enterprise and of the proletarian organization there cannot be a diarchy: there cannot be institutions carrying out one and the same work. One of them must yield. . . . In virtue of this, the factory committees must become organs of the unions in the localities."

50. Adopted Resolution on the Trade Unions and Factory Committees, in *1 S"ezd Profsoiuzov,* p. 374.

51. Adopted Resolution on Workers' Control, First All-Russian Congress of Trade Unions, January 1918, in *ibid.,* p. 370.

52. *Ibid.,* pp. 369-370.

53. *Loc. cit.*

54. Arskii, "Professionalnye Soiuzy i Zavodskie Komitety," in *Vestnik NKT,* No. 2-3, February-March 1918, p. 125.

55. Tomsky in *1 S"ezd Profsoiuzov,* p. vi.

56. Gastev, meeting of 26 October 1918 of the Tariff Conference of Metal Workers, in *1 Vseros. Konf. Metallistov,* p. 8.

57. Lozovsky at the First All-Russian Congress of Trade Unions and Factory Committees of Textile Workers, 1918, in *1 S"ezd Tekstil'shchikov, Protokoly,* p. 29. See also Lozovsky's speech on the Regulation of Industry, 6th day, 25 January 1918, of the First All-Russian Congress of Trade Unions, in *1 S"ezd Profsoiuzov,* p. 192.

58. Adopted Resolution on the Regulation of Industry, First All-Russian Congress of Trade Unions, January 1918, in *ibid.,* p. 368.

59. *Loc. cit.*

60. *Loc. cit.*

61. Paragraph 10, *Loc. cit.*

62. Lozovsky on Workers' Control, the First All-Russian Congress of Trade Unions and Factory Committees of Textile Workers, 1918, in *1 S"ezd Tekstil'shchikov, Protokoly,* p. 30.

63. Cherevanin, speech on the Regulation of Industry and Workers' Control, 7th day, 21 January 1918, First All-Russian Congress of Trade Unions, in *1 S"ezd Profsoiuzov,* p. 201.

64. *Loc. cit.*

65. Resolution on the Regulation of Industry proposed by the supporters of the independence of the trade unions, 7th day, 21 January 1918, First All-Russian Congress of Trade Unions, in *ibid.,* p. 206.

66. Cherevanin, speech on the Regulation of Industry and Workers' Control, 7th day, 26 January 1918, First All-Russian Congress of Trade Unions, *ibid.,* p. 203.

67. Belousov on the Regulation of Industry, 7th day, 26 January 1918, First All-Russian Congress of Trade Unions, *ibid.,* p. 221.

68. *Loc. cit.*

69. *Ibid.,* p. 222.

70. *Loc. cit.*

71. Lozovsky at the First All-Russian Congress of Trade Unions and Factory Committees of Textile Workers, 1918, in *1 S"ezd Tekstil'shikov, Protokoly,* p. 33. For this same point of view expressed elsewhere by Lozovsky, see his "Rabochii Kontrol'," in *Professional'nyi Vestnik,* No. 9-10, January 1918, p. 5.

CHAPTER VII

1. Resolution concerning the problem of the trade unions and political parties in *Professional'nyi Vestnik,* 20 December 1917/2 January 1918, No. 8.
2. *Loc. cit.*
3. *Loc. cit.*
4. *Loc. cit.*
5. *Loc. cit.*
6. When this resolution was published Lozovsky was still a member of the party.
7. A Resolution of the Bolshevik Central Committee on 11 January 1918 states in Paragraph 3 ". . . the general political behavior of Comrade Lozovsky, especially his articles in *Professional'nyi Vestnik* Nos. 7-8, testifies to his complete departure from the basic principles of socialism on the question of the role of the proletariat in the socialist revolution." Bunyan and Fisher, *Bolshevik Revolution,* p. 638.
8. *Professional'nyi Vestnik,* 20 December 1917, No. 8.
9. *Loc. cit.*
10. *Ibid.,* pp. 1-2.
11. *Ibid.,* p. 2.
12. *Loc. cit.*
13. *Loc. cit.*
14. *Loc. cit.*
15. *Loc. cit.*
16. *Loc. cit.*
17. *Loc. cit.*
18. *Loc. cit.*
19. *Ibid.,* p. 3.
20. *Loc. cit.*
21. *Loc. cit.*
22. Lozovsky, "A Letter to the Bolshevik Group in the Central Executive Committee," November 4/17 1917 published in *Novaia Zhizn',* No. 172, November 4/17 1917, pp. 1-2, translated in Bunyan and Fisher, *Bolshevik Revolution,* p. 205.
23. See Lozovsky, "A Letter to the Bolshevik Group in the Central Executive Committee," published in *Novaia Zhizn',* No. 172. November 4/17 1917, pp. 1-2, translated in *ibid.,* pp. 204-206. See also the "Statement of the Minority Group of Trade Unions Leaders," April 29, 1918 (signed by Lozovsky), in *Novaia Zhizn',* No. 80, April 30, in *ibid.,* pp. 647-648 and also Lozovsky in *Professional'nyi Vestnik,* No. 8, 20 December 1917, pp. 1-3.
24. Lozovsky at the 2nd meeting 8/21 January 1918 of the First All-Russian Congress of Trade Unions in *1 S"ezd Profsoiuzov,* p. 205.
25. *Loc. cit.*
26. *Loc. cit.*
27. Strazhevskii on the 3rd day, 9/22 January 1918 of the First All-Russian Congress of Trade Unions in *ibid.,* p. 88.
28. *Loc. cit.*
29. *Loc. cit.*
30. *Loc. cit.*

31. Grinevich on the 4th day, 10/23 January 1918 of the First All-Russian Congress of Trade Unions in *ibid.,* p. 103.

32. Maiskii speaking in the name of the Russian Social Democratic Workers Party, United, at the 1st meeting 7/20 January 1918 of the First All-Russian Congress of Trade Unions in *ibid.,* p. 10.

33. Cherevanin on the 7th day, 13/26 January of the First All-Russian Congress of Trade Unions in *1 S"ezd Profsoiuzov,* p. 205.

34. Resolution on the Regulation of Industry proposed by the supporters of the independence of the trade unions on the 7th day, 13/26 January 1918 of the First All-Russian Congress of Trade Unions in *ibid.,* p. 207.

35. Resolution of the Menshevik Fraction on the 4th day, 10/23 January 1918 of the First All-Russian Congress of Trade Unions in *ibid.,* p. 122.

36. *Loc. cit.*

37. *Loc. cit.*

38. Zinoviev on the Current Moment on the 3rd day, 9/22 January 1918 of the First All-Russian Congress of Trade Unions in *ibid.,* p. 73.

39. *Loc. cit.*

40. Zinoviev on the Current Moment on the 3rd day, 9/22 January 1918 of the First All-Russian Congress of Trade Unions in *ibid.,* p. 74.

41. Weinberg on the 4th day, 10/23 January 1918 of the First All-Russian Congress of Trade Unions in *ibid.,* p. 99.

42. Weinberg on the 4th day, 10/23 January 1918 of the First All-Russian Congress of Trade Unions in *ibid.,* p. 100.

43. *Loc. cit.*

44. *Loc. cit.*

45. *Loc. cit.*

46. See, for example, Weinberg on the 4th day, 10/23 January 1918 of the First All-Russian Congress of Trade Unions in *ibid.,* pp. 98-99.

47. See Lozovsky at the First All-Russian Congress of Textile Workers in *1 S"ezd Tekstil'shchikov Protokoly,* p. 11.

48. Adopted Resolution of the Bolshevik Fraction on the independence of the trade unions, 4th day, 10/23 January 1918 of the First All-Russian Congress of Trade Unions in *1 S"ezd Profsoiuzov,* p. 119.

49. *Loc. cit.*

50. Paragraph 3 of the Adopted Resolution of the Bolshevik Fraction on the independence of the trade unions, 4th day, 10/23 January 1918 of the First All-Russian Congress of Trade Unions in *1 S"ezd Profsoiuzov,* p. 119.

51. *Loc. cit.*

52. Resolution of the Bolshevik Fraction on the independence of the trade unions on the 4th day, 10/23 January 1918 of the First All-Russian Congress of Trade Unions in *ibid.,* pp. 119-120.

53. Paragraph 7, Adopted Resolution of the Bolshevik Fraction on the independence of the trade unions on the 4th day, 10/23 January of the First All-Russian Congress of Trade Unions in *ibid.,* p. 120.

54. Paragraph 8, *loc. cit.*

55. Paragraph 9, *loc. cit.*

56. Resolution of the Left Social Revolutionary Fraction (Internationalists) on the Current Moment, 4th day, 10/23 January 1918 in *ibid.,* p. 121.

57. Paragraph 9 of the Adopted Resolution of the Bolshevik Fraction on

the independence of the trade unions on the 4th day, 10/23 January 1918 of the First All-Russian Congress of Trade Unions in *ibid.,* p. 120. The author does not intend to relegate the communist international trade union movement to the adventitious function presented here. However, the international trade union movement, as such, does not enter into the scope of this work.

58. For the conversion of the Provisional Government's Ministry of Labor into the Commissariat of Labor in the Soviet State, see Bunyan and Fisher, *Bolshevik Revolution,* p. 228.

59. Lenin, V. I., "State and Revolution," in *Collected Works,* 21, Part 2, p. 226.

60. Paragraph 4, part 13 of the Theses on the Soviet Power, *7 S"ezd Partii,* p. 205.

61. Theses on the Soviet Power in *ibid.,* p. 208.

62. Adopted Resolution on the Regulation of Industry in *1 S"ezd Profsoiuzov,* p. 368.

63. Tomsky's Resolution on the Relationship between the Trade Unions and the Commissariat of Labor adopted by the Fourth Conference of Trade Unions 12-17 March 1918, Komissiia Po Izucheniiu Istorii Professional'nogo Dvizheniia v Rossii Pri V.Ts.S.P.S. (1st prof.) Seriia Istoricheskikh Dokumentov, *IV Vserossiisskaia Konferentsiia Professional'nykh Soiuzov 12-17 Marta 1918, V.Ts.S.P.S.* (Istprof.), Moscow, 1923 (henceforth referred to as *4 Konferentsiia Profsoiuzov*), p. 27.

64. *Loc. cit.*

65. *Loc. cit.*

66. *Loc. cit.*

67. *Loc. cit.*

68. *Loc. cit.*

69. *Loc. cit.*

70. *Loc. cit.*

71. Tomsky's Resolution on the Relationship Between the Trade Unions and the Commissariat of Labor adopted by the Fourth Conference of Trade Unions, 12-17 March 1918 in *ibid.,* p. 28.

72. *Loc. cit.*

73. According to a Statute of the Second *Oblast'* Congress of Commissars of Labor with Representatives of the Labor Exchanges, proposed at their 3rd meeting on 12 March 1918, the *collegia* were to be composed not of trade-union representatives alone but of various workers' organizations. The members of the *collegia* were to be appointed by the local Soviets of Deputies. These *collegia* were to decide all problems of principle, and all current matters submitted to the commissars of labor or to members of the *collegia* for their decision. See *Vestnik NKT,* February-March 1918, No. 2-3, p. 334.

74. Paragraph 3 of the Resolution of the Second All-Russian Congress of Commissars of Labor, Representatives of the Labor Exchange and Insurance Funds, 18-25 May 1918, Moscow, Concerning the Relationship of the Commissariat of Labor to the Council of the People's Economy, to the Executive Committee of the Soviet of Deputies and to the Trade Unions in *Vestnik NKT,* April-May 1918, No. 4-5, p. 356.

75. Resolution of the Second All-Russian Congress of Commissars of Labor, Representatives of the Labor Exchange and Insurance Funds, 18-25 May 1918,

Moscow, Concerning the Relationship of the Commissariat of Labor to the Council of the People's Economy, to the Executive Committee of the Soviet of Deputies and to the Trade Unions in *ibid.*, p. 357.

76. For the popularity of the Soviets as opposed to the party, see Chapter III.

77. Tomsky's Resolution on the Relationship between the Trade Unions and the Commissariat of Labor in *4 Konferentsiia Profsoiuzov,* p. 28.

78. *Loc. cit.*

79. Smirnov on the 1st day, 7/20 January 1918 of the First All-Russian Congress of Trade Unions in *1 S"ezd Profsoiuzov,* p. 9.

80. Kammermacher on the 2nd day, 8/21 January 1918 of the First All-Russian Congress of Trade Unions in *ibid.*, p. 38.

81. Lozovsky's Resolution on the Relationship between the Trade Unions and the Commissariat of Labor at the Fourth All-Russian Conference of Trade Unions 12-17 March 1917 in *4 Konferentsiia Profsoiuzov,* p. 38.

82. *Loc. cit.*

83. *Loc. cit.*

84. Paragraph 4, *loc. cit.*

85. Paragraph 5, *loc. cit.*

86. *Loc. cit.*

87. Paragraph 9, *loc. cit.*

88. *Loc. cit.*

89. *Loc. cit.*

90. Paragraphs 10 and 11, Lozovsky's Resolution on the Relationship between the Trade Unions and the Commissariat of Labor at the All-Russian Conference of Trade Unions 12-17 March 1918 in *4 Konferentsiia Profsoiuzov,* p. 39.

91. *Loc. cit.*

92. Paragraph 14, *loc. cit.*

CHAPTER VIII

1. For the support by the Metal Workers' Union of the Bolsheviks, see Pankratova, A., *Politicheskaia Bor'ba v Rossiiskom Profdvizhenii* 1917-1918, Leningradskii Profsovet, Leningrad, 1927 (henceforth referred to as Pankratova, A., *Polit. Bor'ba Profdvizhenii*), p. 101. See also Abolin, A., *October Revolution and Trade Unions,* p. 9. For the textile workers, see *1 S"ezd Tekstil'shchikov Protokoly, passim.*

2. For the attempt of Vikzhel to bring about a coalition, see Bunyan and Fisher, *Bolshevik Revolution,* pp. 153-160, and Schapiro, L., *Communist Autocracy,* pp. 70ff.

3. See Gorki, Maxim, "January 22, 1905 and January 18, 1918" in *Novaia Zhizn',* No. 6, January 23, 1918, p. 3, translated in Bunyan and Fisher, *Bolshevik Revolution,* pp. 387-388; Kefali on the 1st day, January 7/20 of the First All-Russian Congress of Trade Unions in *1 S"ezd Profsoiuzov,* p. 7; and Spiridonova on the same day of the same congress in *ibid.*, p. 23.

4. Lozovsky, in the *Professional'nyi Vestnik,* 20 December 1917/2 January 1918, No. 8, p. 3.

5. *Loc. cit.*

6. Riazanov at the 3rd meeting, 20 January of the Second All-Russian Congress of Trade Unions in Vserossiiskii Tsentral'nyi Sovet Professional'nyk Soiuzov, *Vtoroi Vserossiiskii S"ezd Professional'nykh Soiuzov 16-25 Ianvaria 1919 Stenograficheskii Otchet Chast' 1 Plenumy,* Gosudarstvennoe Izdatel'stvo Moscow, 1921 (henceforth referred to as *2 S"ezd Profsoiuzov Plenumy*), p. 68.

7. Declaration of the Social Democratic (Menshevik) Fraction, read at the meeting 12/25 June of the Moscow Soviet of Workers' Deputies. From *Nash Vek,* 15/28 March 1918, in the Nikolaevskii Collection, Vol. 13, at the Hoover Institution on War, Revolution, and Peace, Stanford, California.

8. From *Nash Golos,* 13/26 May 1919, in the Nikolaevskii Collection, Vol. 12, at the Hoover Institution on War, Revolution, and Peace, Stanford, California.

9. From the *Iskra* of 14/27 June 1918, No. 2, in the Nikolaevskii Collection, Vol. 5, at the Hoover Institution on War, Revolution, and Peace, Stanford, Calif.

10. From the material available to this writer, the circumstances and conditions under which the arrests were made is not clear. There is no doubt, however, that Briansk and Tula were centers of workers' resistance to Bolshevik policy. This declaration is presented as an example of Menshevik labor leadership in opposition to the Bolsheviks.

11. From the Menshevik *Iskra,* 14/27 June 1918, No. 2, in the Nikolaevskii Collection, Vol. 5, at the Hoover Institution on War, Revolution, and Peace, Stanford, Calif.

12. *Loc. cit.*

13. *Loc. cit.*

14. Resolution of the Conference of the Moscow Organization of the Russian Social Democratic Workers' Party, 26 June 1918. From *Iskra* of 15/28 June 1918, No. 3, in the Nikolaevskii Collection, Vol. 5, at the Hoover Institution on War, Revolution, and Peace, Stanford, Calif.

15. Paragraph 2, *loc. cit.*

16. *Loc. cit.*

17. Tomsky at the 3rd meeting, 20 January 1919 of the Second All-Russian Congress of Trade Unions in *2 S"ezd Profsoiuzov Plenumy,* p. 84. Tomsky is here talking about the use of violence against the bourgeoisie, but the Mensheviks would also qualify for its use.

18. From *Iskra,* 15/28 June 1918, No. 3, in the Nikolaevskii Collection, Vol. 5, at the Hoover Institution on War, Revolution, and Peace, Stanford, Calif.

19. Martov at the 20th meeting, 14 June 1918 of the All-Russian Central Executive Committee in Rossiiskaia Sotsialisticheskaia Federativnaia, Sovetskaiia Respublika, *Chetvertyi Vserossiiskii S"ezd Sovetov Rabochikh, Krestianskikh, Soldatskikh i Kazach'ikh Deputatov. Stenograficheskii Otchet,* Gosudarstvennoe, Moscow, 1919 (henceforth referred to as *4 S"ezd Sovetov*), p. 420.

20. *4 S"ezd Sovetov,* p. 420.

21. *Loc. cit.*

22. *Loc. cit.*

23. Lenin on the Tasks of the Trade Unions at the 3rd meeting, 20 June 1919 of the Second All-Russian Congress of Trade Unions in *2 S"ezd Profsoiuzov Plenumy,* p. 46.

24. Sosnovskii at the 1st meeting, 7/20 January 1918 of the First All-Russian Congress of Trade Unions in *1 S"ezd Profsoiuzov,* p. 9.

25. Statutes of the All-Russian Central Soviet of Trade Unions adopted at the First All-Russian Congress of Trade Unions, January 1918, in *ibid.,* p. 377.

26. The People's Commissar of Labor, Shliapnikov, at the First All-Russian Congress of Commissars of Labor in *Vestnik NKT,* February-March 1918, Nos. 2-3, p. 213.

27. Adopted Resolution on Workers' Control of the First All-Russian Congress of Trade Unions, January 1918 in *1 S"ezd Profsoiuzov,* p. 369.

28. Arskii, R., "Povyshenie Proizvoditel'nosti Truda i Sdel'naia Plata," p. 21 in *Narodnoe Khoziaistvo,* March 1919, No. 3, pp. 18-22.

29. *Ibid.,* p. 19.

30. Peshekonov, A. V., *Krestiane i Rabochie v Ikh Vzaimnykh Otnosheniakh,* Russkoe Bogatstvo, St. Petersburgh, 1906, first published in *Russkoe Bogatstvo,* 1898. Peshekonov's stand was an anti-Marxist one. For the validity of his investigations, observations and opinions, see his statistical tables in *ibid., passim.* For close connection of Russian labor with its rural background, see also Schwarz, Solomon, *Labor in the Soviet Union,* Praeger, New York, 1951 (henceforth referred to as Schwarz, Solomon, *Labor in the Soviet Union*), pp. 1-5.

31. *Ibid.,* p. 5.

32. Rudzutak at the 6th meeting, 24 January 1919 of the Second All-Russian Congress of Trade Unions in *2 S"ezd Profsoiuzov Plenumy,* p. 138.

33. Lenin, V. I., "A Great Beginning," *Selected Works 9,* p. 433.

34. All these figures are taken from the Report of the Mandate Commission on the 5th day, 10/23 January 1918 of The First All-Russian Congress of Trade Unions in *1 S"ezd Profsoiuzov,* p. 134.

35. Lozovsky on the Statutes of the All-Russian Soviet of Trade Unions and the Statutes of the Congress at the First All-Russian Congress of Trade Unions in *ibid.,* p. 265.

36. Arskii, R., "Povyshenie Proizvoditel'nosti Truda i Sdel'naia Plata" in *Narodnoe Khozaistvo,* March 1919, No. 3, p. 19.

37. Paragraph 1, part 2 of the Adopted Resolution on Organizational Problems at the Second All-Russian Congress of Trade Unions, January 1919, in *2 S"ezd Profsoiuzov,* p. 127.

38. *Loc. cit.*

39. *Loc. cit.*

40. Adopted Resolution of the Second All-Russian Congress of Trade Unions, January 1919 in *ibid.,* p. 128.

41. Tomsky at the morning meeting of 28 September 1918 at the First All-Russian Congress of Communist Railwaymen in Vserossiiskaia Konferentsiia Zheleznodorozhnikov Kommunistov, *I Konferentsiia, Protokoly,* Kommunist, Moscow, 1919, p. 72.

42. Tomsky's report on the All-Russian Central Soviets of Trade Unions at the second meeting, 18 January 1919 of the Second All-Russian Congress

of Trade Unions in *2 S"ezd Profsoiuzov Plenumy,* p. 20.

43. Adopted Resolution on Organizational Structure at the First All-Russian Congress of Trade Unions, January 1918 in *1 S"ezd Profsoiuzov,* p. 374.

44. *Loc. cit.*

45. Paragraph 4, *loc. cit.*

46. Paragraph 5, *loc. cit.*

47. *Loc. cit.*

48. Adopted Resolution on the Organizational Structure at the First All-Russian Congress of Trade Unions, January 1918, in *ibid.,* p. 375.

49. Tomsky's Report on the All-Russian Central Soviet of Trade Unions at the 1st meeting, 16 January 1919 of the Second All-Russian Congress of Trade Unions in *2 S"ezd Profsoiuzov Plenumy,* p. 22.

50. *Ibid.,* p. 23.

51. *Ibid.,* p. 22.

52. See the speech of Tomsky at the 2nd meeting of the Second All-Russian Congress of Trade Unions, 18 January 1919 in *ibid.,* p. 42, and the speech of Lozovsky at the same meeting, same congress in *ibid.,* p. 43. See also the speech of Zinoviev on the Current Moment on the 3rd day, 9/22 January 1918 of the First All-Russian Congress of Trade Unions in *1 S"ezd Profsoiuzov,* p. 75 for promise of financial assistance to the unions by the Soviet Government.

53. Chirkin at the 2nd meeting, 18 January 1919 of the Second All-Russian Congress of Trade Unions in *2 S"ezd Profsoiuzov Plenumy,* p. 35.

54. Kammermacher on Tomsky's speech on the All-Russian Central Soviet of Trade Unions at the 2nd day, January 18, 1919 of the Second All-Russian Congress of Trade Unions in *ibid.,* p. 30.

55. Paragraphs 21, 22 and 23 of the Adopted Resolution on Organizational Structure of the First All-Russian Congress of Trade Unions, January 1918 in *1 S"ezd Profsoiuzov,* p. 375.

56. Paragraph 24 in *ibid.,* p. 376.

57. For the Bolshevik policy of uniting lower and higher personnel, technicians, foremen and administrative personnel into the same unions, see Vserossiiskii Tsentral'nyi Sovet Professional'nykh Soiuzov *Ocherednyia Zadachi Professional'nykh Soiuzov (Organizatsionnyi Vopros, Tarif, Trudovaia Distsiplina), Pervoe Tsirkularnoe Pismo Vserossiiskogo Tsentral'nogo Soveta Professional'nykh Soiuzov,* Moscow, 1918 (henceforth referred to as *Ocherednyia Zadachi*), p. 10.

58. *1 S"ezd Tekstil'shchikov Rezoliutsii,* p. 7.

59. Paragraph 3, Section C, Part 1 of the Adopted Resolution on the Organizational Problems at the Second All-Russian Congress of Trade Unions in *2 S"ezd Profsoiuzov,* p. 124.

60. *Loc. cit.*

61. Adopted Resolution on the Organizational Problems at the Second All-Russian Congress of Trade Unions in *ibid.,* p. 125.

62. See Lozovsky's warning against workers' control in government departments in *VTSIK II Protokoly,* p. 62.

63. For the use of the terms trade union—political and public law, see Lozovsky on the Organizational Question on the 5th day, 11 January 1918

of the First All-Russian Congress of Trade Unions in *1 S"ezd Profsoiuzov,* pp. 143-144. For the use of these terms and also for *Vikzhedor,* see Paragraph 6 of the Resolution of the Social-Democratic International Fraction on the Tasks of the Trade Unions introduced by Lozovsky at the 4th meeting, 21 January 1919 of the Second All-Russian Congress of Trade Unions in *2 S"ezd Profsoiuzov Plenumy,* p. 94, and Riazanov at the third meeting, 20 January 1919 of the Second All Russian Congress of Trade Unions in *ibid.,* p. 69. For *Vikzhedor,* see also Bunyan and Fisher, Bolshevik Revolution, pp. 652-656.

64. Rossiiskaia Sotsialisticheskaia Federativnaia Sovetskaia Respublika, *Sed'moi Vserossiiskii S"ezd Sovetov Krest'ianskikh, Krasnoarmeiskikh i Kazach'ikh Deputatov Stenograficheskii Otchet* (*22-29 Dekabria 1920*) Gosudarstvennoe, Moscow, 1921 (henceforth referred to as *7 S"ezd Sovetov*), p. 205.

65. Chirkin on the 2nd day, January 18, 1919 of the Second All-Russian Congress of Trade Unions in *2 S"ezd Profsoiuzov Plenumy,* p. 34.

66. See Goldman, Emma, *My Disillusionment in Russia,* where she cites examples from the Bakers' Union and a Moscow factory, pp. 136 and 139.

67. Kossior *Nashi Raznoglasiia* (*o Roli i Zadachakh Profsoiuzov*), Gosudarstvennoe Izdatel'stvo, n.p. 1920. (henceforth referred to as *Kossior Nashi Raznoglasiia*), p. 24.

68. Perkon on the Trade Unions and the Commissariat of Labor at the 4th Meeting, 21 January 1919, of the Second All-American Congress of Trade Unions in *2 S"ezd Profsoiuzov Plenumy,* p. 103.

69. Speech of the Commissar of Labor A. G. Shliapnikov on 14/27 January 1918 at the First All-Russian Congress of the Commissars of Labor in *Vestnik NKT,* February-March 1918, Nos. 2-3, p. 214.

70. Schmidt, *Professional'nyi Vestnik,* 20 January 1919, No. 1(27), p. 3.

71. "The Independents and the Press" in British Labour Delegation to Russia 1920, *Report,* London, 1920 (henceforth referred to as *Report of the British Labour Delegation to Soviet Russia 1920*), p. 65.

72. Lenin, V. I., "The Trade Unions, the Present Situation and the Mistakes of Comrade Trotsky" December 30, 1920 in *Selected Works, 9,* p. 17.

73. "The Independents and the Press" in *Report of the British Labour Delegation to Soviet Russia 1920,* p. 65.

74. Rubtsov at the 3rd meeting, 7 April 1919, of the Third All-Russian Congress of Trade Unions in Vserossiiskii Tsentral'nyi Sovet Professional'nykh Soiuzov, *Tretii Vserossiiskii S"ezd Professional'nykh Soiuzov 6-13 Aprelia 1920, Stenograficheskii Otchet Chast' I Plenumy,* Gosudarstvennoe Izdatel'stvo, Moscow, 1921 (henceforth referred to as *3 S"ezd Profsoiuzov*), p. 43.

75. Kossior at the 3rd meeting, 7 April 1920 of the Third All-Russian Congress of Trade Unions, *loc. cit.*

76. Antsilovich at the 2nd meeting, 18 January 1919, of the Second All-Russian Congress of Trade Unions in *2 S"ezd Profsoiuzov Plenumy,* p. 31.

77. *Loc. cit.*

78. Adopted Resolution on the Regulation of Industry at the First All-Russian Congress of Trade Unions in *1 S"ezd Profsoiuzov,* p. 369.

79. Antsilovich at the 2nd meeting, 18 January 1919, of the Second All-Russian Congress of Trade Unions in *2 S"ezd Profsoiuzov Plenumy,* p. 31.

80. *Loc. cit.*

81. *Loc. cit.*
82. *Loc. cit.*
83. For this meeting see *Report of the British Labour Delegation to Russia 1920,* pp. 64-65.
84. See the documents given to C. R. Buxton, the last member of the British Labour Delegation to pass through Moscow on June 23, 1920 in *ibid.,* pp. 68-72.
85. *Ibid.,* p. 71.
86. *Ibid.,* p. 72.
87. *Loc. cit.*
88. *Loc. cit.*
89. *Loc. cit.*
90. Matrozov at the 5th day, 11/24 January 1918 of the First All-American Congress of Trade Unions in *1 S"ezd Profsoiuzov,* p. 155.
91. *Loc. cit.*
92. *Loc. cit.*
93. Matrozov on the 2nd day, 8/21 January 1918, of the First All-Russian Congress of Trade Unions in *ibid.,* p. 53.
94. See the 4th day, 10/23 January 1918 of the First All-Russian Congress of Trade Unions in *ibid.,* p. 95.
95. Grinevich on the 2nd day, 8/21 January 1918 of the First All-Russian Congress of Trade Unions in *ibid.,* p. 49.
96. Schmidt, "O Vzaimnootnosheniakh Narodnago Komissariata Truda s Vserossiiskim Tsentral'nym Sovetom Professional'nykh Soiuzov" in *Vestnik NKT,* February 1918, No. 2, pp. 26-28.
97. Welcoming speech of the Chairman of the Third International, Comrade Zinoviev, read by Comrade Antsilovich on 6 April 1918 at the Third All-Russian Congress of Trade Unions in *3 S"ezd Profsoiuzov,* p. 14.

CHAPTER IX

1. Schmidt, "Professional'nyie Soiuzy i Komissariat Truda," *Professional'nyi Vestnik,* 20 January 1919, No. 1. (27), p. 3.
2. *Loc. cit.*
3. *Loc. cit.*
4. *Loc. cit.*
5. *Ibid.,* p. 4.
6. *Ibid.,* p. 3.
7. *Loc. cit.*
8. *Ibid.,* p 4.
9. *Ibid.,* p. 3.
10. *Ibid.,* p. 4.
11. *Loc. cit.* (Italic mine.)
12. *Loc. cit.*
13. *Loc. cit.*
14. *Ibid.,* p. 5.

15. *Loc. cit.*
16. *Loc. cit.*
17. *Ibid.*, p. 6.
18. *Loc. cit.*
19. Rudzutak at the 6th meeting, 24 January 1919 of Second All-Russian Congress of Trade Unions in *2 S"ezd Profsoiuzov Plenumy,* p. 139.
20. *Loc. cit.*
21. Martov at the 3rd meeting, 20 January 1919 of the Second All-Russian Congress of Trade Unions in *ibid.*, p. 57.
22. Schmidt at the 3rd meeting, 20 January 1919 of the Second All-Russian Congress of Trade Unions in *ibid.*, p. 73.
23. Adopted Resolution on the Tasks of the Trade Unions at the Second All-Russian Congress of Trade Unions, January 1919, in *2 S"ezd Profsoiuzov,* p. 108.
24. *Loc. cit.*
25. Tomsky at the 3rd meeting, 20 January 1919 of the Second All-Russian Congress of Trade Unions in *2 S"ezd Profsoiuzov Plenumy,* p. 82.
26. Adopted Resolution on the Tasks of the Trade Unions at the Second All-Russian Congress of Trade Unions, January 1919 in *2 S"ezd Profsoiuzov,* p. 108.
27. Schmidt at the 3rd meeting, 20 January 1919 of the Second All-Russian Congress of Trade Unions in *2 S"ezd Profsoiuzov Plenumy,* p. 73.
28. *Loc. cit.*
29. Paragraph 8 of the Resolution of the Social Democratic Internationalist Fraction on the Tasks of the Trade Unions, introduced by Lozovsky at the 4th meeting, 21 January 1919 of the Second All-Russian Congress of Trade Unions in *ibid.*, p. 95.
30. Lozovsky at the 3rd meeting, 20 January 1919 of the Second All-Russian Congress of Trade Unions in *ibid.*, p. 66.
31. *Loc. cit.*
32. Resolution of the Social Democratic Internationalists on the Tasks of the Trade Unions, introduced by Lozovsky at the 4th meeting, 21 January 1919 of the Second All-Russian Congress of Trade Unions in *ibid.*, pp. 95-96.
33. Lozovsky at the 6th meeting, 24 January 1919 of the Second All-Russian Congress of Trade Unions in *ibid.*, p. 144.
34. Adopted Bolshevik Resolution on the Trade Unions and the Commissariat of Labor, introduced by Schmidt at the Second All-Russian Congress of Trade Unions in *2 S"ezd Profsoiuzov,* p. 109.
35. *Loc. cit.*
36. *Loc. cit.*
37. *Loc. cit.*
38. *Loc. cit.*
39. Resolution of the Fraction of Independents on the Commisariat of Labor and the Trade Unions proposed at the 4th meeting, 22 January 1919 of the Second All-Russian Congress of Trade Unions in *2 S"ezd Profsoiuzov Plenumy,* p. 104.
40. *Loc. cit.*
41. *Loc. cit.*
42. *Loc. cit.*

43. Resolution of the Internationalists on the Trade Unions and the People's Commissariat of Labor at the 4th meeting, 22 January 1919 of the Second All-Russian Congress of Trade Unions in *ibid.,* p. 107.

44. *Loc. cit.*

45. For the establishment of V.S.N.Kh. and of the Heads and Centers see especially Larin, Iu., "U Kolybeli" in *Narodnoe Khoziaistvo,* November 1918, No. 11, p. 18. See also Kritsman, L., *Geroicheskii Period Velikoi Russkoi Revoliutsii,* Gosudarstvennoe Izdatel'stvo, Moscow, n.d. (henceforth referred to as Kritsman, L., *Geroicheskii Period*), p. 102 and Rosenfeld, R., *Promyshlennaia Politika,* p. 94.

46. For the conflict between the Heads and Centers and the Soviet structure, see the excerpt from the speech of the chairman of the Supreme Soviet of the People's Economy Rykov, in *Narodnoe Khoziaistvo,* November 1918, No. 11, p. 34; Kaktyn, A., "Osnovnoi Nedostatok Nashei Sistemy Upravleniia," in *Narodnoe Khoziaistvo,* April 1919, No. 4, pp. 16-19; and Bazhanov's reply to Kaktyn in his "Organizatsiia Upravleniia Promyshlennost'iu," in *Narodnoe Khoziaistvo,* September-October, Nos. 9-10, pp. 11-15 and November-December, Nos. 11-12, 1919, pp. 3-7.

47. Zinoviev at the 2nd meeting, 21 March 1919 of the Eighth Congress of the Russian Communist Party (Bolshevik) in Rossiiskaia Kommunisticheskaia Partiia (Bol'shevikov), *VIII S"ezd Rossiiskoi Kommunisticheskoi Partii (Bol'shevikov) Moscow 18-23 Marta 1919 Stenograficheskii Otchet,* Kommunist, Moscow, 1919 (henceforth referred to as *8 S"ezd Partii*), p. 191.

48. Osinskii's Resolution on the Party Structure at the 2nd meeting, 21 March 1919 of the Eighth Congress of the Russian Communist Party (Bolshevik) in *ibid.,* p. 167.

49. Lunacharsky at the 7th meeting, 22 March 1919 of the Eighth Congress of the Communist Party in *ibid.,* p. 275.

50. *Loc. cit.*

51. Zinoviev on Party Organization at the 6th meeting, 22 March 1919 of the Eighth Congress of the Russian Communist Party (Bolshevik) in *ibid.,* p. 242.

52. Adopted Resolution on the Organization Program, Eighth Congress of the Russian Communist Party, March 1919 in *ibid.,* p. 369.

53. *Loc. cit.*

54. *Loc. cit.*

55. *Loc. cit.*

56. *Loc. cit.*

57. *Loc. cit.*

58. *Loc. cit.*

59. *Loc. cit.*

60. *Loc. cit.*

61. *Loc. cit.*

62. *Loc. cit.*

63. Bogolepov at the 7th meeting, 8 April 1918, of the Fourth All-Russian Congress of Soviets, 20 March-18 June 1918, in *4 S"ezd Sovetov,* p. 137. This seems to be true of the party organizations as well. Krestinskii, speaking at the 9th Party Congress of March and April 1920, stated that "If at the Eighth Congress, March 1919, our Central Committee had connection with

almost all *guberniia* organizations, it had connection with not more than half of the *uezd,* and the remaining never had any direct connection with the Ts.K., however after eight months of work . . . we could already say that out of 400 *uezd* only 20, 5% in all, did not have direct connection with the central committee. But now after a year, at this congress, only 5 of the *uezd* enumerated . . . do not have direct connection with the center . . ." Krestinskii at the 1st meeting, 29 March 1920, of the 9th Congress of the Bolshevik Party in Rossiiskaia Kommunisticheskaiia Partiia (Bol'shevikov), *Deviatyi S"ezd Rossiiskoi Kommunisticheskoi Partii 29 Marta 4 Aprelia 1920, Stenograficheskii Otchet,* Gosudarstvennoe, M. P., 1920.

64. For the lack of clarity in defining the Soviet structure by the Soviet Constitution, see the speeches of Sapronov and Vladimirskii at the 1st meeting of the Organizational Section, 8 December 1919 of the Seventh Congress of Soviets in *7 S"ezd Sovetov,* pp. 77 and 104.

65. Sapronov at the 1st meeting of the Organizational Section, 8 December 1919, at the Seventh Congress of Soviets in *ibid.,* p. 197.

66. *Loc. cit.*

67. *Loc. cit.*

68. See Larin, "U Kolybeli," in *Narodnoe Khoziaistvo,* No. 11, November 1918, p. 18. For the structure of V.S.N.Kh., see also Bronskii, "Khronika Deiatel'nosti VSNKH. i Ego Otdelov," *ibid.,* No. 1, March 1918, pp. 9-10. For the Statutes on the Supreme Council of the People's Economy see *ibid.,* No. 11, 1918, p. 64 or the *Biulleten' Narodnago Komissariata Truda,* Nos. 3-4, February 1919, pp. 9-10.

69. Sapronov at the 1st meeting of the Organizational Section, 8 December 1919, at the Seventh Congress of Soviets in *7 S"ezd Sovetov,* p. 197.

70. Bazhanov, "Organizatsiia Upravleniia Promyshlennost'iu," in *Narodnoe Khoziaistvo,* November 1919, Nos. 9-10, p. 12.

71. Arskii, "Itogi S"ezda Sovnarkhozov," in *Narodnoe Khoziaistvo,* Nos. 1-2, p. 13, January 1919.

72. Arskii in *ibid.,* p. 14.

73. Instructions defining the mutual relations between the individuals dispatched by the Supreme Council of People's Economy and the local councils of the people's economy in the Appendix to *Narodnoe Khoziaistvo,* December 1918, No. 12, p. 15.

74. *Loc. cit.*

75. *Loc. cit.*

76. *Loc. cit.*

77. For V.S.N.Kh. as an organization embracing old and new syndicates and trusts, see Kaktyn, "Osnovnoi Nedostatok Nashei Sistemy Upravleniia Promyshlennost'iu," in *Narodnoe Khoziaistvo,* No. 4, no month given, 1919, p. 16. See also Kritsman, L., "Ob Ocherednoi Zadache Proletarskoi Revoliutsii v Rossii," in *Narodnoe Khoziaistvo,* No. 5, July 1918, pp. 3-4.

78. Bronskii, "Iz Deiatel'nosti V.S.N.Kh. i Ego Otdelov," *Narodnoe Khoziaistvo,* No. 1, March 1918, p. 9.

79. Kritsman, L., *Geroicheskii Period,* p. 101.

80. For the description of the branch organization of V.S.N.Kh. used here, see Bronskii, "Khronika Deiatel'nosti V.S.N.Kh. i Ego Otdelov," in *Narodnoe Khoziaistvo,* March 1918, No. 1, p. 10.

81. For the Praesidium of V.S.N.Kh., see Kritsman L., *Geroicheskii Period,* p. 102.

82. *1 S"ezd Tekstil'shchikov Rezoliutsii,* p. 9.

83. *Ibid.,* p. 10.

84. *Ibid.,* p. 11.

85. Kaktyn, "Osnovnoi nedostatok Nashei Sistemy Upravleniia Promyshlennost'iu," in *Narodnoe Khoziastvo,* No. 4, 1919, p. 18.

86. *Loc. cit.*

87. Rudzutak at the 6th meeting, 24 January 1919 of the Second All-Russian Congress of Trade Unions in *2 S"ezd Profsoiuzov Plenumy,* p. 138.

88. *Loc. cit.*

89. *Loc. cit.*

90. Osinskii, "Iz Pervykh Dnei Vyshego Soveta Narodnago Khoziaistva," in *Narodnoe Khoziaistvo,* November 1918, No. 11, p. 12.

91. Statute of 10 April 1918 of the Praesidium of the Supreme Soviet of the Peoples Economy concerning the order of publication of all statutes of V.S.N.Kh. in *Narodnoe Khoziaistvo,* May 1918, No. 3, p. 39.

92. Adopted Resolution on the Character and Formation of the Participation of the Unions in the Administration and Organization of the People's Economy at the 6th meeting, 12 April 1920 of the Third All-Russian Congress of Trade Unions in *3 S"ezd Profsoiuzov,* p. 108.

CHAPTER X

1. Adopted Resolution on the organizational question proposed by Rykov at the 6th meeting, 28 December 1920, at the Eighth Congress of Soviets in Rossiiskaia Sotsialisticheskaia Federativnaia Respublika, *Vos'moi Vserossiiskii S"ezd Sovetov Rabochikh Krest'ianskikh Krasnoarmeiskikh i Kazach'ikh Deputatov Stenograficheskii Otchet (22-28 Dekabr')* 1920, Gosudarstvennoe, Moscow, 1921 (henceforth referred to as *8 S"ezd Sovetov*), p. 187.

2. *Loc. cit.*

3. *Loc. cit.*

4. Theses of Rykov on the Position of Industry and the Measures to Restore It, at the Eighth Congress of Soviets, December 1920 in *ibid.,* p. 117.

5. *Loc. cit.*

6. Theses of Rykov on the Position of Industry and the Measures to Restore It, at the Eighth Congress of Soviets in *ibid.,* p. 118.

7. Zinoviev at the 6th meeting, 28 December 1920 at the Eighth Congress of Soviets in *ibid.,* p. 209.

8. Zinoviev at the 6th meeting, 28 December 1920 of the Eighth Congress of Soviets in *ibid.,* p. 221.

9. Kaktyn, "Osnovnoi Nedostatok Nashei Sistemy Upravleniia Promyshlennost'iu," in *Narodnoe Khozaistvo,* 1919, No. 4, p. 18.

10. *Loc. cit.*

11. *Loc. cit.*

12. *Loc. cit.*

13. Tomsky at the 4th meeting, 8 April 1920 of the Third All-Russian Congress of Trade Unions in 3 *S"ezd Profsoiuzov*, p. 62.

14. Trotsky, Leon, *O Zadachakh Profsoiuzov Doklad Prochitannyi na Sobranii 30 Dekabria 1920*, Gosudarstvennoe Izdatel'stvo, n.p., 1921 (henceforth referred to as Trotsky, L., *O Zadachakh Profsoiuzov*), p. 15.

15. *Ibid.*, p. 14.

16. *Ibid.*, p. 17.

17. Trotsky, L., *Rol' i Zadachi Profsoiuzov*, p. 24 quoted in Zinoviev, G., *O Roli Professional'nykh Soiuzov, Doklad i Zakliuchitel'noe Slovo Na Diskussionnom Sobranii v Moskve 30go Dekabria 1920 v Sostave Fraktsii VIII S"ezda Sovetov i V.Ts.S.P.S. Sodokladchikom Vystupil T. Trotskii* (henceforth referred to as Zinoviev, G., *O Roli Professional'nykh Soiuzov*), p. 43.

18. Lenin, V. I., "O Professional'nykh Soiuzakh, O Tekushchem Momente i Ob Oshibkakh Trotskogo," 30 Dekabria 1920, in *Sochineniia, 32*, p. 10.

19. Trotsky, L., *O Zadachakh Profsoiuzov*, p. 5.

20. See this decree of the Ninth Party Congress quoted in Zinoviev, G., *O Roli Professional'nykh Soiuzov*, pp. 31-32. See also Rossiiskaia Kommunisticheskaia Partiia (Bol'shevikov), *Deviatyi S"ezd Rossiiskoi Kommunisticheskoi Partii Stenograficheskii Otchet 29 Marta—4 Aprelia 1920*, Gosudarstvennoe Izdatel'stvo, no place given, 1920 (henceforth referred to as *9 S"ezd Partii*), pp. 378-379. See also *Izvestiia Tsentral'novo Komiteta Rossiiskoi Kommunisticheskoi Partii* (Bol'shevikov), (henceforth referred to as *Izvestiia Ts.K. R.K.P.*), No. 16, 28 March 1920.

21. Schapiro, L., *Communist Autocracy*, p. 257, and Daniels, R. V., *The Conscience of the Revolution, Communist Opposition in Soviet Russia*, Harvard University Press, Cambridge, 1960 (henceforth referred to as Daniels, R. V., *Conscience of the Revolution*), pp. 129-132.

22. For the policy of *Tsektran*, see Kossior, *Nashi Raznoglasiia*, pp. 23-24.

23. For Trotsky's policy toward the abolition of *Glavpolitput'*, see his *O Zadachakh Profsoiuzov*, p. 6ff. See also Lenin, V. I., "The Party Crisis," 19 January 1921 in *Selected Works*, 9, p. 29ff, and also Lenin's "Once Again on the Trade Unions, The Present Situation and the Mistakes of Comrades Trotsky and Bukharin," 25 January 1921 in *ibid.*, p. 49. The *Malaia Sovetskaia Entsikopediia* claims that *Tsektran* was established in March of 1921. It was created, however, some time before 1920. For a contemporary defense of Trotsky, see Kossior, *Nashi Raznoglasiia*. For an account of *Tsektran* and *Glavpolitput'* as a focus of dispute within the Central Committee of the Party, see Schapiro, L., *Communist Autocracy*, pp. 273-290 and pp. 256-259.

24. For Trotsky's alleged proposal on joint representation, see Lenin, V. I., "Once Again on the Trade Unions, the Present Situation and the Mistakes of Comrades Trotsky and Bukharin," in *Selected Works, 9*, p. 15.

25. See *ibid.*, p. 60.

26. The animosity between Lenin and Trotsky in this dispute may be illustrated by the following accusation leveled at Lenin by Trotsky. ". . . Comrade Lenin wants to deprive and rob us of any kind of discussion concerning the essence of this problem, he is trying to terrorize, to frighten us a little. . . ." *O Zadachakh Profsoiuzov*, p. 19.

27. For the abolition of *Glavpolitput'* and *Glavpolitvod* and the calling

of new elections for Tsektran see *Izvestiia Ts.K. R.K.P.*, No. 26, 20 December 1920, pp. 16-17 and 3.

28. Kossior, *Nashi Raznoglasiia,* p. 22.

29. *Ibid.,* p. 25.

30. For an excellent account of the political alignment within the Party on the problem of *Tsektran,* see Daniels, R. V., *Conscience of the Revolution,* p. 131.

31. Lenin V. I., "O Professilonal'nykh Soiuzakh, O Tekushchem Momente i Ob Oshibkakh Trotskogo," *Sochineniia, 32,* p. 11.

32. *Ibid.,* p. 2.

33. *Ibid.,* p. 3.

34. Lenin, V. I., "Once Again on the Trade Unions, The Present Situation and the Mistakes of Comrades Trotsky and Bukharin," in *Selected Works, 9,* p. 70.

35. Lenin, V. I., "O Professional'nykh Soiuzakh, O Tekushchem Momente i Ob Oshibkakh Trotskogo," in *Sochineniia, 32,* p. 2.

36. Zinoviev, G., *O Roli Professional'nykh Soiuzov,* p. 8.

37. Lenin, V. I., "Ob Oshibkakh Trotskogo," in *Sochineniia, 32,* p. 3.

38. Zinoviev, G., *O Roli Professional'nykh Soiuzov,* p. 9.

39. Lenin, V. I., "O Professional'nykh Soiuzakh, O Tekushchem Momente i Ob Oshibkakh Trotskogo," in *Sochineniia, 32,* pp. 2-3.

40. Zinoviev, G., *O Roli Professional'nykh Soiuzov,* p. 44. In *The Communist Party and Industrial Unions,* The Workers' Socialist Federation, London, 1920, p. 10, Zinoviev states: "And just because the transformation of State Departments takes place gradually, and quite normally, there is no present necessity of forcing this process, there is no need to proclaim from one minute to another the transformation of Industrial into State Departments. . . ."

41. Zinoviev, G., *O Roli Professional'nykh Soiuzov,* p. 44.

42. Lenin, V. I., "O Professional'nykh Soiuzakh, O Tekushchem Momente i Ob Oshibkakh Trotskogo," 30 December 1920 in *Sochineniia, 32,* p. 2.

43. Zinoviev, G., *O Roli Professional'nykh Soiuzov,* p. 9.

44. Kossior, *Nashi Raznoglasiia,* pp. 26-27.

45. *Ibid.,* p. 28.

46. *Izvestiia Ts.K. R.K.P.,* No. 26, 20 December 1920, p. 17.

47. Zinoviev at the 6th meeting, 28 December 1920 of the Eighth Congress of Soviets in *8 S"ezd Sovetov,* p. 221.

48. Zinoviev at the 6th meeting, 28 December 1920 of the Eighth Congress of Soviets in *ibid.,* p. 213.

49. Zinoviev at the 6th meeting, 28 December 1920 of the Eighth Congress of Soviets in *ibid.,* p. 214.

50. *Loc. cit.*

51. *Loc. cit.*

52. *Loc. cit.*

53. *Loc. cit.*

54. See Chapter XII.

55. Zinoviev at the 6th meeting, 28 December 1920 of the Eighth Congress of Soviets in *8 S"ezd Sovetov,* pp. 214-215.

56. *Ibid.,* p. 222.

57. See Gerasimovich, V. E., *Gosudarstvennaia Sluzhba* Iuridicheshkaia Biblioteka (Izdanie Neofitsial'noe), Komiteta Pomoshchi Invalidam Voiny, Moscow, 1923, pp. 43-44. The punishments ranged from reprimand to two weeks' arrest. A record of the punishment was entered in the personal dossier of the offender and in a book kept for that purpose by the employing institution.

58. See Chapter IX *supra*.

59. Zinoviev at the 6th metting, 28 December 1920 of the Eighth Congress of Soviets in *8 S"ezd Sovetov,* p. 222.

60. *Ibid.*, p. 219.

61. For the Worker-Peasant Inspections, see *7 S"ezd Sovetov,* p. 212.

62. *Izvestiia Tsentral'nogo Komiteta Rossiiskoi Kommunisticheskoi Partii (Bol'shevikov)*, 30 March 1920, No. 17.

63. For this argument, see also Kalinin's welcoming speech on 6 April 1920 at the Third All-Russian Congress of Trade Unions in *3 S"ezd Profsoiuzov,* p. 3.

64. *Izvestiia Tsentral'nogo Komiteta Rossiiskoi Kommunisticheskoi Partii (Bol'shevikov)*, 30 March 1920, No. 17.

65. *Loc. cit.*

66. *Loc. cit.*

67. *Loc. cit.*

68. *Loc. cit.*

69. *Loc. cit.*

70. *Loc. cit.*

71. *Loc. cit.*

72. See, for example, Trotsky's assertion that those opposing him attacked first those who carried out his decisions, Trotsky, L., *O Zadachakh Profsoiuzov,* p. 7.

73. *Izvestiia Glavnogo Komiteta Vseobshchei Trudovoi Povinnosti,* March 1920, No. 1, p. 28.

74. For an excellent general discussion of rule by decree, see Arendt, H., *The Origins of Totalitarianism,* pp. 243-244.

75. Lenin, V. I., "Once Again the Trade Unions, The Present Situation and the Mistakes of Comrades Trotsky and Bukharin," *Selected Works, 9,* p. 54.

CHAPTER XI

1. Bukharin, N., *Programma Kommunistov,* p. 31. The English translation *The Program of the Communists,* p. 43, is not true to the Russian in its translation of this paragraph.

2. Adopted Resolution on Workers' Control at the First All-Russian Congress of Trade Unions in *1 S"ezd Profsoiuzov,* p. 370. See also Paragraph 7 of the Plan of Instructions on Workers' Control drawn up by a commission consisting of Representatives of the Central Executive Committee of the Soviet of Workers', Soldiers' and Peasants' Deputies of the All-Russian Soviet of Trade Unions, of the All-Russian Center of Factory Committees and of the

Moscow Soviet of Workers' Deputies, and published in *Narodnoe Khoziaistvo,* March 1918, No. 1, p. 27.

3. *Loc. cit.,* and Adopted Resolution on Workers' Control at the First All-Russian Congress of Trade Unions in *1 S"ezd Profsoiuzov,* p. 370.

4. Paragraph 11, *loc. cit.*

5. Paragraph 15, *ibid.,* p. 372.

6. Paragraph 16, Adopted Resolution on Workers' Control of the First All-Russian Congress of Trade Unions in *1 S"ezd Profsoiuzov,* p. 372.

7. Lenin, V. I., "Once Again the Trade Unions, the Present Situation and the Mistakes of Comrades Trotsky and Bukharin," in *Selected Works, 9,* p. 54.

8. See Paragraph 5, *loc. cit.*

9. Paragraph 5 of the Resolution on Workers' and State Control of the Second All-Russian Congress of the Soviets of the People's Economy in *Narodnoe Khoziaistvo,* March 1919, No. 3, p. 69.

10. *Loc. cit.*

11. Paragraph 10, *ibid.,* pp. 69-70.

12. Paragraph 10, *ibid.,* p. 70. See also Adopted Resolution on Workers' Control at the Second All-Russian Congress of Trade Unions, 16-25 January 1919, in *2 S"ezd Profsoiuzov,* p. 112.

13. Lenin, V. I., on the "Tasks of the Trade Unions," speech of 20 January 1919 at the Second All-Russian Congress of Trade Unions in his *Collected Works, 33,* p. 516.

14. *Ibid.,* p. 517.

15. *Ibid.,* pp. 514-515.

16. *Ibid.,* p. 517.

17. Arskii, R., "Rabochii Kontrol' Natsionalizovannykh Predpriiatiakh," in *Narodnoe Khoziaistvo,* 1919, Nos. 1-2, pp. 23-25.

18. *Loc. cit.*

19. *Loc. cit.*

20. See, for example, Glebov, "Rabochii Kontrol'," in *Professional'nyi Vestnik,* 20 January 1919, No. 1(27), p. 9. See also Gastev at the meeting of 15 October of the First All-Russian Tariff Conference of the Union of Metallists with Representatives of the Factory Committees in Vserossiiskii Soiuz Rabochikh Metallistov, *Protokoly Pervoi Vserossiiskoi Tarifnoi Konferentsii Soiuzov Metallistov Sovmestno c Predstavitelem Zavodskikh Komitetov,* Tsentral'nyi Komitet, Petrograd, 1918 (henceforth referred to as *1 Vseros. Konf. Metallistov Protokoly*), p. 5; and Glebov on Workers' Control at the 5th meeting 23 January 1919 of the Second All-Russian Congress of Trade Unions in *2 S"ezd Profsoiuzov Plenumy,* p. 109.

21. *Okt. Rev. i Fabzavkomy,* 1, p. 32.

22. See Chapters VII, IX, X *supra.*

23. For a definition of *edinovlastie,* see the speech of Comrade Rykov at the 5th meeting, 9 April 1920 of the Third All-Russian Congress of Trade Unions in *3 S"ezd Profsoiuzov,* p. 87.

24. Lenin, V. I., "State and Revolution," in *Collected Works, 21,* Part 2, p. 211.

25. Trotsky, L., *Trud, Ditsiplina, Poriadok, Spasut Sotsialisticheskuiu Sovetskuiu Respubliku. Doklad Na Moskovskoi Gorodskoi Konferentsii Rossiiskoi Kommunisticheskoi Partii, 28 Marta 1918,* Zhizn' i Znanie, Moscow, 1918

(henceforth referred to as Trotsky, L., *Trud, Ditsiplina, Poriadok*), p. 17.

26. *Loc. cit.*

27. Lenin, V. I., "Left-Wing Childishness and Petty Bourgeois Mentality," May 1918, in *Selected Works, 7,* p. 374.

28. *Loc. cit.*

29. Sapronov at the 1st meeting of the organizational section, 8 December 1919 of the Seventh Congress of Soviets in *7 S"ezd Sovetov,* p. 201.

30. *Loc. cit.*

31. *Loc. cit.*

32. *Loc. cit.*

33. Adopted Resolution on the Character and Form of Participation of the Unions in the Administration and Organization of the People's Economy, 12 April 1920, at the Third All-Russian Congress of Trade Unions in *3 S"ezd Profsoiuzov,* p. 108.

34. Paragraph 2, *loc. cit.*

35. *Loc. cit.*

36. *Loc. cit.*

37. Subparagraph b, Paragraph 7, *loc. cit.*

38. *Loc. cit.*

39. *Loc. cit.*

40. *Loc. cit.*

41. Lozovsky at the morning meeting of 13 April 1920 at the Third All-Russian Congress of Trade Unions in *3 S"ezd Profsoiuzov,* p. 131.

42. Glebov at the 6th meeting 12 April 1920 of the Third All-Russian Congress of Trade Unions in *ibid.,* p. 107.

43. Subparagraph f, Paragraph b of the Adopted Resolution on the Character and Form of Participation of the Union in the Administration and Organization of the People's Economy, 12 April 1920 at the Third All-Russian Congress of Trade Unions in *ibid.,* p. 108.

44. Paragraph 4a, *loc. cit.*

45. Paragraph b, Section 13, *loc. cit.*

46. Paragraph 6, Section B, *loc. cit.*

47. Vserossiiskii Soiuz Rabochikh Metallistov *Ustav* Ts.K.V.S.R.M., March 1919 (henceforth referred to as Vserossiiskii Soiuz Rabochikh Metallistov, *Ustav*), p. 9.

48. *Loc. cit.*

49. Rykov at the 5th meeting, 9 April 1920 of the Third All-Russian Congress of Trade Unions in *3 S"ezd Profsoiuzov,* p. 88.

50. Trotsky at the 5th meeting, 8 April 1920 of the Third All-Russian Congress of Trade Unions in *ibid.,* p. 95.

51. *Loc. cit.*

52. *Loc. cit.*

53. See Chapter X.

54. Lenin at the 1st meeting, 29 March 1920 of the Ninth Congress of the Bolshevik Party in *9 S"ezd Partii,* p. 20.

55. Lenin at the 1st meeting 29 March of the Third All-Russian Congress of Trade Unions in *3 S"ezd Profsoiuzov,* p. 20.

56. *Loc. cit.*

57. *Ibid.,* p. 19.

58. See Chapter III.

59. Adopted Resolution on the Military Problem, 8th Congress of the Russian Communist Party (Bolshevik), March 1919 in *8 S"ezd Partii*, p. 358.

60. *Loc. cit.*

61. *Loc. cit.*

62. *Loc. cit.*

63. *Loc. cit.*

64. *Loc. cit.*

CHAPTER XII

1. Rykov at the 5th meeting, 9 April 1920 of the Third All-Russian Congress of Trade Unions in *3 S"ezd Profsoiuzov*, p. 87.

2. Weinstein at the 1st meeting, 6 April 1920 of the Third All-Russian Congress of Trade Unions in *ibid.*, p. 10.

3. Vserossiiskii Tsentral'nyi Sovet Professional'nykh Soiuzov, *Konferentsiia Fabrichno-Zavodskikh i Professional'nykh Soiuzov IV, 1918 Protokoly*, Moscow 1919 (henceforth referred to as *4 Konf. Fabzav. Prof. Protokoly*), p. 114. For these Statutes, see also *Narodnoe Khoziaistvo*, November 1918, No. 11, p. 64.

4. *4 Konf. Fabzav. Prof. Protokoly*, p. 114.

5. *Ibid.*, p. 115.

6. Tomsky, 2 July 1918, at the Fourth Conference of Factory Committees and Trade Unions. *Loc. cit.*

7. For the difficulties in food supply, see, for example, the Resolution of Antsilovich on Food Supply at the 7th meeting, 25 January 1919 of the Second All-Russian Congress of Trade Unions in *2 S"ezd Profsoiuzov Plenumy*, pp. 173-174 and his speech on p. 171.

8. *4 Konf. Fabzav. Prof. Protokoly*, p. 115.

9. *Ibid.*, p. 114.

10. Vserossiiskii Soiuz Rabochikh Metallistov, *Ustav*, p. 4.

11. *Ibid.*, p. 5.

12. *Loc. cit.*

13. *Loc. cit.*

14. *Loc. cit.*

15. Tomsky at *4 Konf. Fabzav. Prof. Protokoly*, p. 117.

16. For the comradely courts and their functions see *Ocherednaia Zadachi*, p. 48.

17. *Loc. cit.*

18. Kozelev in *Izvestiia*, 13 April 1918.

19. *Loc. cit.*

20. *Loc. cit.*

21. Adopted Resolution on the Normalization of Wages and Labor at the Second All-Russian Congress of Trade Unions, 16-25 January 1919 in *2 S"ezd Profsoiuzov*, pp. 113-114.

22. Adopted Resolution on the Normalization of Wages and Labor at the

Second All-Russian Congress of Trade Unions, 16-25 January 1919 in *ibid.*, p. 114.

23. *Ibid.*, p. 115.

24. *Loc. cit.*

25. *Loc. cit.*

26. Adopted Resolution on the Normalization of Wages and Labor at the Second All-Russian Congress of Trade Unions, 16-25 January 1919 in *ibid.*, p. 113.

27. Schmidt on the Wage Problem at the 6th meeting, 24 January 1919 of the Second All-Russian Congress of Trade Unions in *2 S"ezd Profsoiuzov Plenumy*, p. 153. According to Margaret Dewar in her *Labour Policy in the U.S.S.R. 1917-28,* Royal Institute of International Affairs, London, 1956, pp. 26-27: "This principle of equalization [of wages] was first broken when the need for specialists became acute, and when, in order to promote higher productivity of labour, bonuses and collective payment in kind and piece rates were introduced in 1920." Miss Dewar's statement, however, does not agree with the facts. The situation which she describes as taking place in 1920 actually took place at least two years earlier, in 1918.

28. Lozovsky at the 6th meeting, 24 January 1919 of the Second All Russian Congress of Trade Unions in *2 S"ezd Profsoiuzov,* p. 165.

29. Seniushkin at the 6th meeting of the Second All-Russian Congress of Trade Unions in *ibid.,* p. 158.

30. *Loc. cit.*

31. Resolution on the Tasks of the Tariff Policy of the Third All-Russian Congress of Trade Unions in *3 S"ezd Profsoiuzov,* p. 114.

32. *Loc. cit.*

33. Rubtsov at the 6th meeting, 12 April 1920 of the Third All-Russian Congress of Trade Unions in *ibid.*, p. 115.

34. Lenin, V. I., *State and Revolution,* pp. 76ff.

35. *Ibid.*, p. 76.

36. *Ibid.*, p. 77.

37. Lenin, V. I., "Economics and Politics in the Era of the Dictatorship of the Proletariat," October 30, 1919, *Selected Works, 8,* p. 13.

38. Resolution on the Tasks of the Tariff Policy of the Third All-Russian Congress of Trade Unions in *3 S"ezd Profsoiuzov,* p. 113.

39. *Loc. cit.*

40. *Loc. cit.*

41. *Loc. cit.*

42. See, for example, the bonus payments for wood cutters, carters, and loaders according to the Russian Code of Labor Laws of 1919 Article 7, Ordinance No. 1708. The bonuses were as follows:

"(a) For the cutting of 1 cube:
1/2 lb. of salt
1/2 of tissue arshine
1/8 lb. tobacco
1/2 box of matches;

(b) For the carriage of 1 cube:
1/2 lb. salt
1/2 arshine of tissue

1/8 lb. of tobacco
1/2 box of matches;
(c) For the loading of one truck:
1/8 lb. salt
1/8 arshine of tissue
1/16 lb. tobacco
1/4 box of matches."

International Labour Office, *Labour Conditions in Soviet Russia, Systematic Questionnaire and Bibliography Prepared for the Mission of Enquiry in Russia,* Harrison and Sons, London, n.d., p. 51.

43. Resolution on the Tasks of the Tariff Policy of the Third All-Russian Congress of Trade Unions in *3 S"ezd Profsoiuzov,* p. 113.

44. *Loc. cit.*

45. *Loc. cit.*

46. Lenin, at the 3rd meeting, 7 April 1920 of the Third All-Russian Congress of Trade Unions in *ibid.,* p. 46.

47. Buksin at the 4th meeting, 8 April 1920 of the Third All-Russian Congress of Trade Unions in *ibid.,* p. 57.

48. *Loc. cit.*

49. *Loc. cit.*

50. *Loc. cit.*

51. *Loc. cit.*

52. *Loc. cit.*

53. *Loc. cit.*

54. For descriptions of various types of premium payment see Dobb, Maurice, *Wages,* Cambridge University Press, London, 1947, pp. 65ff.

55. Trotsky at the 5th meeting, 9 April 1920 of the Third All-Russian Congress of Trade Unions in *3 S"ezd Profsoiuzov,* p. 90.

56. *Loc. cit.*

57. *Loc. cit.*

58. Trotsky at the 5th meeting, 9 April 1920 of the Third All-Russian Congress of Trade Unions in *ibid.,* p. 88.

59. Abramovich at the 5th meeting, 9 April 1920 of the Third-All Russian Congress of Trade Unions, in *ibid.,* p. 97.

60. Theses of the Central Committee of the Russian Communist Party on the Mobilization of the Industrial Proletariat, Labor Service, the Militarization of the Economy and the Use of Military Units for Economic Needs in Glavnyi Komitet po Vseobshchei Trudovoi Povinnosti, *Izvestiia,* March 1920, No. 1, p. 6.

61. For the adaptation of the Labor Exchanges to the Soviet state, see the speech of Comrade Schmidt at the 4th meeting, 8 April 1920 of the Third All-Russian Congress of Trade Unions in *3 S"ezd Profsoiuzov,* p. 49.

62. Schmidt at the 4th meeting, 8 April 1920 of the Third All-Russian Congress of Trade Unions in *ibid.,* pp. 49-50.

63. Schmidt at the 4th meeting, 8 April 1920 of the Third All-Russian Congress of Trade Unions in *ibid.,* p. 50.

64. *Loc. cit.*

65. *Loc. cit.*

66. *Loc. cit.*

67. Schmidt at the 4th meeting, 8 April 1920 of the Third All-Russian Congress of Trade Unions in *ibid.,* p. 51.

68. *Loc. cit.*

68[a]. For the conversion of the Third Army into the First Labor Army, see Zinoviev, G., *Novye Zadachi Nashei Partii ot Voiny k Khoziaistvu, Rech' Proiznossenaia na Obshchem Sobranii Chlenov Partii, Kandidatov i Sochuvstviushihikh Petrogradskogo Raiona 28 Ianvaria 1920 Goda, Moscow* Gozizdat, 1920. Zinoviev presents the formation of the Labor army as deriving from the initiative of the soldiers of the Third Army. For Trotsky's plans for the reorganization of his army for labor service, see Trotsky telegram Tr. 408, The Trotsky Archive, Houghton Library, Harvard University.

68[b]. *Ibid.,* par. 4, p. 2.

69. Decree of the Soviet of Worker-Peasant Defense in Glavnyi Komitet po Vseobshchei Trudovoi Povinnosti, *Izvestiia,* March 1920, No. 1, p. 35.

70. Trotsky at the 5th meeting, 9 April 1920 of the Third All-Russian Congress of Trade Unions in *3 S"ezd Profsoiuzov,* p. 91.

71. Theses of the Central Committee of the Russian Communist Party on the Mobilization of the Industrial Proletariat, Labor Service, the Militarization of the Economy and the Use of Military Units for Economic Needs in Glavnyi Komitet po Vseobshchei Trudovoi Povinnosti, *Izvestiia,* March 1920, No. 1, p. 9.

72. *Loc. cit.*

73. *Loc. cit.*

74. *Vestnik NKT,* March-April 1918, Nos. 4-5.

75. Rykov at the 5th meeting, 9 April 1920 of the Third All-Russian Congress of Trade Unions in *3 S"ezd Profsoiuzov,* p. 83.

76. For the criticism of the Printers' Union representative and Schmidt's reply to it, see Buksin at the 4th meeting, 8 April 1920 of the Third All-Russian Congress of Trade Unions in *ibid.,* p. 57 and Schmidt, *loc. cit.*

77. For the labor code, see Labry, Raoul, *Une Legislation Communiste, Recueil Des Lois, Decrets, Arretes Principaux Du Gouvernemente Bolsheviste,* Payot, Paris, 1920, pp. 173-203.

78. Schmidt at the 4th meeting, 8 April 1920 of the Third All-Russian Congress of Trade Unions in *3 S"ezd Profsoiuzov,* p. 51.

79. Schmidt at the 4th meeting, 8 April 1920 of the Third All-Russian Congress of Trade Unions in *ibid.,* p. 52.

80. *Loc. cit.*

81. *Loc. cit.*

82. Seniushkin on 24 January 1919 at the Second All-Russian Congress of Trade Unions in *2 S"ezd Profsoiuzov,* p. 164.

83. Decree of the Soviet of People's Commissars of 29 January 1920 in Gerasimovich, V., *Gosudarstvennaia Sluzhba,* p. 50.

84. Molotov, V. M., "Eshche Odin Shag k Osvobozhdeniu Truda" in Molotov, V. M. (Ed.), *Pervomaiskii Sbornik Nizhegorodskoi Gubernskii Komitet Organizatsii Truda,* 1920 (henceforth referred to as *Pervomaiskii Sbornik*), p. 5.

85. Paragraph 3, Subparagraph 5 of the Regulations on *Subbotniks* in Glavnyi Komitet Po Vseobshchei Trudovoi Povinnost', *RKP i Trudovaia Povinnost' Sbornik Materialov,* Moscow, 1920 (henceforth referred to as *RKP i Trudovaia Povinnost'*), p. 10.

86. *Malaia Entsiklopediia Professional'nogo Dvizhenie i Truda,* p. 56.
87. *Pervomaiskii Sbornik,* p. 6.
88. See Paragraph 2, Subparagraph 8 on Regulations on *Subbotniks* in *RKP i Trudovaia Povinnost',* p. 11.
89. *Ibid.,* p. 9.
90. Ugleb, D., "Nabliudeniem vo Vremia Rabot (Kommunisty i Bezpartiinye)," in *Pervomaiskii Sbornik,* p. 76.
91. Molotov in *Pervomaiskii Sbornik,* p. 6.
92. Paragraph 1, Subparagraph 1 of the Regulations on *Subbotniks* in *RKP i Trudovaia Povinnost',* p. 9.
93. Paragraph 1, Subparagraph 2 of the Regulations on *Subbotniks in ibid.,* p. 8.
94. Lenin, V. I., "A Great Beginning," in *Selected Works, 9,* p. 439.
95. *Loc. cit.*
96. *Ibid.,* p. 438.
97. *Loc. cit.*
98. *Loc. cit.*
99. Lenin, V. I., "From the First Subbotnik on the Moscow Kazan Railway to the All-Russian May Day Subbotnik," in *ibid., 8,* p. 244.
100. *Ibid.,* p. 243.
101. Molotov, V. M., in *Pervomaiskii Sbornik,* p. 7.
102. *Loc. cit.*
103. Resolution of the *Guberniia* Commission for the First of May *Subbotnik* of Nizhegorodskaia Guberniia in *ibid.,* pp. 111 and 113.
104. See, for example, Lenin, quoting an article by N. R. in *Pravda,* May 20 "A Great Beginning," *Selected Works, 9,* p. 426 and Molotov, V. M., "Eshche Odin Shag k Osvobozhdeniu Truda" in *Pervomaiskii Sbornik,* p. 15.
105. *RKP i Trudovaia Povinnost',* p. 9.
106. Lenin, V. I., "A Great Beginning," *Selected Works, 9,* p. 428.
107. Molotov, V. M., "Eshche Odin Shag k Osvobozhdeniu Truda" in *Pervomaiskii Sbornik,* p. 17.
108. Spontaneous here does not refer to *soznatel'nost* but is used in the English language sense.
109. Paragraph 1, Subparagraph 2 of the Regulations on *Subbotniks* in *RKP i Trudovaia Povinnost',* p. 9.
110. Paragraph 2, Subparagraph 4 of the Regulations on *Subbotniks, loc. cit.*
111. Paragraph 2, Subparagraph 5 of the Regulations on *Subbotniks, loc. cit.*
112. Paragraph 2, Subparagraph 6 of the Regulations on *Subbotniks, ibid.,* pp. 9-10.
113. Paragraph 2, Subparagraph 7 of the Regulations on *Subbotniks, ibid.,* p. 10.
114. Paragraph 2a, Subparagraph 8 of the Regulations on *Subbotniks, loc. cit.*
115. Paragraph 3, Subparagraph 1 of the Regulations on *Subbotniks, loc. cit.*
116. Paragraph 3, Subparagraph 2 of the Regulations on *Subbotniks, loc. cit.*
117. Paragraph 3, Subparagraph 3 of the Regulations on *Subbotniks, loc. cit.*

118. Paragraph 3, Subparagraph 7 of the Regulations on *Subbotniks, ibid.*, p. 11.
119. Paragraph 3, Subparagraph 7 of the Regulations on *Subbotniks, loc. cit.*
120. Paragraph 5, Subparagraphs 1, 2 and 3 of the Regulations on *Subbotniks, ibid.*, p. 12.
121. Paragraph 5, Subparagraphs 5, 6 and 7 of the Regulations on *Subbotniks, loc. cit.*
122. Paragraph 4, Subparagraph 1 of the Regulations on *Subbotniks, loc. cit.*
123. Paragraph 4, Subparagraph 3, Note 1, of the Regulations on *Subbotniks, loc. cit.*
124. Lenin, V. I., "From the First *Subbotnik* on the Moscow Kazan Railway to the All-Russian May Day *Subbotnik*" in *Selected Works, 8,* p. 243. See also "A Great Beginning," *ibid., 9,* p. 444.
125. Paragraph 4, Subparagraph 3, Note 2 of the Regulations on *Subbotniks* in *RKP i Trudovaia Povinnost',* p. 12.
126. Molotov, V. M., in *Pervomaiskii Sbornik,* p. 13.
127. Gusman, B., "Trud Prazdnik," in *ibid.,* p. 27.
128. Zinoviev in *ibid.,* p. 23.
128[a]. *Pravda,* 15 November 1920.
129. Lenin, V. I., "How to Organize Competition," in *Selected Works, 9,* p. 414.
130. Lenin, V. I., "A Great Beginning," in *ibid.,* p. 445.
131. Lenin, V. I., "From the Destruction of the Ancient Social System to the Creation of the New," in *ibid.,* p. 447. See also Molotov, V. M., "Eshche Odin Shag k Osvobozhdeniu Truda," in *Pervomaiskii Sbornik,* p. 12.
132. Schmidt at the 4th meeting, 8 April 1920 of the Third All-Russian Congress of Trade Unions in *3 S"ezd Profsoiuzov,* p. 54.
133. *Loc. cit.*
134. *Loc. cit.*
135. Kozelev at the 5th meeting 12 April 1920 of the Third All-Russian Congress of Trade Unions in *3 S"ezd Profsoiuzov,* p. 121.

CHAPTER XIV

1. The indebtedness of the author to the Weber Thesis in Weber, Max, *The Protestant Ethic and the Spirit of Capitalism* (Trans. Talcott Parsons), Allen and Unwin, London, 1930, will be apparent in his discussion of the Ethics of Soviet Labor. It is not within the scope of this work to discuss the merits or faults of Weber's work, but some essential differences between what Weber described as the Protestant ethic and what this writer regards as the ethics of Soviet labor be mentioned. Protestantism is other-worldly oriented; Communism "this-worldly," although future-oriented. The Protestant ethic was subsumed under religion, the Communist under politics or, more accurately, the social. Weber claims that Protestantism, although its founders and bearers did not consciously associate it with capitalism, functioned to develop capitalism and its concomitant rationalization and industrialization of production. Bol-

shevism, on the other hand, consciously fostered industrialization, labor discipline and increased productivity. The Protestant ethic tended to suppress the chiliastic outburst; communism tended consciously to make use of it.

2. Lenin, V. I., "How to Organize Competition," *Selected Works, 9,* p. 414.

3. Lenin, V. I., "From the Destruction of the Ancient Social System to the Creation of the New," *ibid.,* p. 447.

4. Gladkov, F. W., *Cement* (Trans. Arthur, A. S., and Ashleigh, C.), International Publishers, New York, n.d. (henceforth referred to as Gladkov, F., *Cement*), p. 229.

5. *Ibid.,* p. 266-267.

6. Lenin, V. I., "From the Destruction of the Ancient Social System to the Creation of the New," in *Selected Works, 9,* p. 447.

7. Lenin, V. I., "A Great Beginning," *ibid.,* p. 433.

8. Lenin, V. I., "How to Organize Competition," *Selected Works, 9,* p. 421.

9. *Ibid.,* p. 418.

10. Lenin, V. I., "A Great Beginning," *ibid.,* p. 439.

11. Lenin, V. I., "The Immediate Tasks of the Soviet Government," (henceforth referred to as "Immediate Tasks"), *ibid., 7,* p. 348.

12. Interview with A. S. Batova in Kor, I. (Ed.), *Kak my Zhili Pri Tsare i Kak Zhevem Teper', Vospominaniia Starykh Kadrovykh Rabochikh Trekhgornoi Manufaktury,* Moskovskii Rabochii, Moscow, 1934 (henceforth referred to as Kor, *Kak my Zhili i Zhivem*), p. 10. Although there is no way of determining the authenticity of the reminiscences presented by Kor or the sincerity of the ideas expressed in them, it is important for this study merely that they serve as an ideal or model for behavior and attitudes approved for labor by the Soviet State and Communist Party. However, during the academic year 1960-1961 which this author spent in the Soviet Union, he heard such ideas expressed freely by Soviet workers. This identification of the worker with the state, and of his productivity with the state's productivity, may represent the communist answer to the alienated capitalist labor of which Marx spoke. For the latter, see Marx, K., *Economic and Philosophic Manuscripts of 1844,* Foreign Languages Publishing House, Moscow, 1961, pp. 64-83 and Tucker, R., *Philosophy and Myth in Karl Marx,* Cambridge University Press, Cambridge, 1961, especially pp. 123-135.

13. *Ibid.,* p. 13.

14. *Loc. cit.*

15. Lenin, V. I., "Immediate Tasks," *Selected Works, 7,* p. 318.

16. Glavnyi Komitet po Vseobshchei Trudovoi Povinnosti, *Izvestiia,* No. 1, March 1920, p. 8.

17. Lenin, V. I., "Immediate Tasks," *Selected Works, 7,* p. 340.

18. Lenin, V. I., "A Great Beginning," *ibid., 9,* p. 431.

19. Lenin, V. I., "How to Organize Competition," *ibid.,* p. 421.

20. Trotsky, L., *A Paradise in This World,* p. 15.

21. *Ibid.,* p. 21.

22. *Ibid.,* p. 20.

23. Gladkov, F., *Cement,* p. 285.

24. Kataev, Valentin P., *Vremia Vpered, Khronika,* Gosudarstvennoe Izdatel'stvo Khudozhestvennoi Literatury, Moscow, 1960.

25. Lenin, V. I., "Immediate Tasks," *Selected Works, 7,* p. 343.

26. See for example Tomsky at the Fourth Conference of Factory Committees and Trade Unions in *4 Konf. Favkom. i Profsoiuzov,* p. 112.

27. Lenin, V. I., "Immediate Tasks," *Selected Works, 7,* p. 343.

28. *Ibid.,* p. 344.

29. Bogdanov, A., *Elementy Proletarskoi Kultury v Razvitie Rabochego Klassa. Lektsii Prochitannye v Moskovskom Proletkul'te Vesnoi 1919 Goda,* Gosudarstvennoe Izdatel'stvo, Moscow, 1920 (henceforth referred to as Bogdanov, A., *Elementy Proletarskoi Kultury*), p. 75. In the early years of the Soviet state, especially in 1919 and 1920, Bogdanov played a leading role as an exponent of the new proletarian culture. See, for example, Shcheglov, A. V., *Bor'ba Lenina Protiv Bogdanovskoi Revizii Marksizma,* Gosudarstvennoe Sotsial'no Ekonomicheskoe Izdatel'stvo, Moscow, 1937 (henceforth referred to as Shcheglov, A., *Bor'ba Lenina*), p. 212, and Daniels, R. V., *Conscience of the Party,* p. 161. It was not until October 1920 that the organization he headed, Proletarian Culture, or Proletkul't, evoked the antagonism of Lenin, largely, it seems, on the question of the relationship of Proletkul't to state and party. See Lenin, V. I., "Proletarian Culture," *Selected Works, 9,* pp. 484-485. Charges were made against Bogdanov alleging he repudiated the previous bourgeois culture and, unlike Lenin, wanted to start a proletarian culture upon a new foundation. However, the weakness of this allegation is suggested by an attacker's admission that Bogdanov did not do this openly or in words. See Shcheglov, A., *Bor'ba Lenina,* p. 215. Schapiro suggests, in his *Communist Party of the Soviet Union,* Random House, New York, 1960, p. 344 that the suppression of Proletkul't may be attributed to Lenin's detestation of Bogdanov's views. Although this may be true, Lenin had clarified his theoretical differences with Bogdanov in *Materialism and Empirio-Criticism,* and if he entrusted Bogdanov with the headship of Proletkul't, he must have conceded, at least at the time, that insofar as the formulation of labor ethics were concerned the differences between him and Bogdanov were not insurmountable. Also, Bogdanov may have made some modifications in his views to bring them closer to those of Lenin. The conflict between Lenin and Bogdanov over proletarian culture, however, seems to have centered upon the function of consciousness. Bogdanov seems to have emphasized the necessity of changing the consciousness of labor rather than leading labor intransigently toward Bolshevik goals. The distinction is a subtle one but it would seem that Bogdanov emphasized teaching rather than leading, guiding rather than directing. This is associated with his former equating of social consciousness with social being. It tends to place the authority of the mediator in social being, whereas Lenin, by insisting that the proletariat acquire its consciousness through experience in the revolutionary struggle, emphasized performance rather than thought, placed the authority of the mediator beyond social being or the collective consciousness, and anchored it in the natural and historical law determining social being and consciousness themselves.

However, in spite of Bogdanov's repudiation by the Party and in spite of the fate of Proletkul't, Bogdanov's teaching must be recognized as part of the ideas presented to labor and the intelligentsia officially by the Party during the period under study.

30. Bogdanov, A., *Elementary Proletarskoi Kultury,* p. 76.

31. *Ibid.,* p. 79.

32. *Ibid.,* p. 80.
33. *Loc. cit.*
34. *Loc. cit.*
35. *Loc. cit.*
36. *Loc. cit.*
37. *Ibid.,* p. 75.
38. Unfortunately for him, Bogdanov, by rooting expediency in the collective rather than in nature or history, became liable to charges of unorthodoxy, with more serious consequences than in pre-revolutionary days.
39. Bogdanov, A., *Elementy Proletarskoi Kultury,* p. 55.
40. *Loc. cit.*
41. Efimova, P. P., in Kor, *Kak my Zhili i Zhivem,* p. 55.
42. Bogdanov, A., *Elementy Proletarskoi Kultury,* pp. 34-35.
43. Gladkov, F., *Cement,* p. 116.
44. *Ibid.,* p. 115.
45. *Ibid.,* p. 116.
46. Bogdanov, A., *Elementy Proletarskoi Kultury,* p. 35.
47. *Loc. cit.*
48. *Ibid.,* p. 38.
49. *Ibid.,* p. 34.
50. *Ibid.,* p. 35.
51. *Ibid.,* p. 39.
52. *Loc. cit.*
53. Bukharin, N. and Preobrazhensky, E., *The ABC of Communism: A Popular Exposition of the Program of the Communist Party (The Bolsheviks)* (Trans. from the German by P. Lavin), Socialist Labor Press, Glasgow, 1921, p. 94.
54. Trotsky, L., *A Paradise in This World,* p. 17.
55. *Ibid.,* pp. 17-18.
56. For the political significance of immortality in life and the world see, Arendt, Hannah, "The Concept of History" in *Between Past and Future,* pp. 63-75.
57. Aleshin, S. in "Vse Ostaetsia Liudiam," *Pesy Sovetskii Pisatel',* Moscow, 1962, p. 75.
58. For a discussion of the relationship between labor and consumption, see Arendt, Hannah, *The Human Condition, A Study of the Central Dilemmas Facing Modern Man,* Doubleday Anchor, Garden City, 1959.

APPENDIX

1. I am indebted to James Bogen, Department of Philosophy, Pitzer College, Claremont, California, for pointing out to me these arguments.

2. For Lenin on sensations, see *Materialism and Empirio-Criticism,* pp. 99 and 100.

3. See Berkeley, George, "A Treatise Concerning the Principles of Human Knowledge," in *A New Theory of Vision and Other Writings,* Everymans Library, E. P. Dutton, New York, 1945 (henceforth referred to as Berkeley, George, *Theory of Vision*), pp. 121-122.

4. Wittengenstein, Ludwig, *Philosophical Investigations,* Macmillan, New York, 1953, Sec. 265.

5. Lenin, V. I., *Materialism and Empirio-Criticism,* p. 99.

6. For this argument, cf. Berkeley, George, "The First Dialogue," in *Theory of Vision,* p. 237.

7. *Ibid.,* p. 213.

8. *Loc. cit.*

9. Berkeley, George, "Principles of Human Knowledge," in *ibid.,* p. 216.

10. It will be remembered that Lenin claims the accuracy of our perceptions can be tested by action, "that the proof of the pudding is in the eating." G. A. Paul, in his "Lenin's Theory of Perception," in *Philosophy and Analysis,* a selection of articles published in *Analysis* between 1939-40 and 1947-53, edited with a note and introduction by Margaret Macdonald, Philosophical Library, New York, 1954, says on pp. 285-286 that "Lenin's account of perception allows only of indirect comparison of reflection and the thing: there is no mention of any direct comparison of them. So what is the use of saying: 'Success in practice shows us that our perception was a reflection of the thing when there is no independent way of finding whether there is a reflection or not?' "

BIBLIOGRAPHICAL NOTE

The books included in this bibliography have been selected from collections housed in various libraries of America and Europe. In America I have consulted the collections of the University of California at Berkeley, the Hoover Institution of War, Revolution and Peace at Stanford, The Columbia University Library, the New York Public Library, the Library of Congress, the Widener and Houghton Libraries of Harvard University, and the Yale University Library. In Europe I have had access to the libraries of the University of Helsinki in Finland, the Russian Institute at the University of Stockholm, the Institute for Social History of Amsterdam, The Feltrinelli Library in Milan and the British Museum at London. The most complete collection for my purposes is that of the Hoover Institution, and it is there that I have done most of my work. Needless to say, all the libraries at which I Ihave researched have yielded something additional of value, and of the European collections I found that of the University of Helsinki the richest in holdings on Russian labor for 1917 to 1920.

The reasons for my selection of the books presented here are various. Many have been chosen for their value to the field, some for their interest, others for their rarity. The reader should bear in mind that many books which might be of interest to him, I have not chosen to include in this bibliography.

SELECTED BIBLIOGRAPHY

DOCUMENTS, OFFICIAL REPORTS, AND SPEECHES

General and Collections of Laws

Aleksandrov, N. G., *Sovetskoe Trudovoe Pravo,* Gosudarstvennoe Izdatel'stvo Iuridicheskoi Literatury, Moscow, 1954.

Arkhiv Oktiabr'skoi Revoliutsii, *Robachee Dvizhenie v 1917 Godu,* (ed. Miller, V.L.) Gosudarstvennoe Izdatel'stvo, Moscow, 1926.

British Labor Delegation to Russia 1920, *Report, London,* VTBJ.

Bunyan, James, *Intervention, Civil War and Communism in Russia, April-December, 1918, Documents and Materials,* John Hopkins Press, Baltimore, 1936.

Bunyan, and Fisher, H., *The Bolshevik Revolution 1917-1918, Documents and Materials,* Stanford University Press, Stanford, 1934.

Dogadov, V. M., *Ocherki Trudovogo Prava,* Priboi, Moscow, 1927.

Glavnyi Komitet po Vseobshchei Trudovoi Povinnosti, *Borb'a s Trudovym Dezertirstvom* (*Sbornik Ofitsial'nykh Polozhenii*), Moscow, 1920.

Glavnyi Komitet po Vseobshchei Trudovoi Povinnosti, R.K.P. *R.K.P. i Trudovaia Povinnost'* (*Sbornik Materialov*), Moscow, 1920 (?).

Golder, F.A., *Documents of Russian History 1914-1917* (*trans.* Aronsberg, E., Century, New York and London, 1927.

International Labor Office, *Labour Conditions in Soviet Russia, Systematic Questionnaire and Bibliography Prepared for the Mission of Enquiry in Russia,* Harrison and Sons, London, n.d.

International Labor Office, *L'Evolution des Conditions du Travail dans la Russie des Soviets, Geneva,* n.d.

International Labor Office, *Organization of Industry and Labour Conditions in Soviet Russia,* Geneva, 1922.

Ivnitskia, T. V. (ed.), *Dokumentry Trudogo Entuziazma,* Profizdat, n.p., 1961.

Labry, Raoul, *Une Legislation Communiste—Recueil des Lois, Decrets, Arretes Principaux du Gouvernement Bolcheviste,* Payot, Paris, 1920.

Ministerstvo Vnutrennikh Del, *Otchet Vserosiiskago Tsentral'nago Soveta Professional'nykh Soiuzov Za Iiul'—Dekabr' 1917,* Petrograd, 1918.

Orakhelashvili, M.D. and Sorin, V. G., *Dekrety Oktiabrskoi Revoliutsii* (*Pravitel'stvennye akty Podpisannye ili Utverzhdennye Leninym kak Predsedatelem Sovnarkoma*) *Oktiabr'skogo Perevorota do Rospuska Uchreditel'nogo Sobraniia,* Partinnoe Izdatel'stvo, Moscow, 1923.

Popov, A. and Rozhkov ed., *Arkhiv Revoliutsii 1917, Oktiabriskii Perevorot—Fakty i Dokumentry,* Novaia Evropa, Petrograd, 1918.

Sbornik Dekretov i Postanovlenii po Narodnomu Khoziaistvu 25/9/17-25/9/18), (Ed. Iuridicheskii Otdel), VSNKh, Moscow, 1919.

Sobranie uzakonenii i Rasporiazhenii po Narodnomu Komissariatu Sotsial'nago Obespecheniia, Ianvar'-Sentabr' 1918 g.

Sovet Narodnykh Komissarov, Narodnyi Komissariat Truda, *Sobranie Zakonov, Polozhenii, Dekretov, Vyrabotannykh Narodnym Komissariatom Truda i Utverzhdennykh Organami Pravitel'stva 26 Oktiabria-17 Dekabria 1917,* Petrograd, 1917.

Stroitel'stvo Krasnoi Armii, (Sbornik Statei k S'ezdy Sovetov pod Redaktsiei Voennogo Komissara Vseross. Glavnogo Shtaba Tov. V. G. Sharmanova i s Presdisloviem Zam. Predsedatelia Respubliki E. Shlianskogo), Gosizdtt, Petrograd, 1919.

United States Department of State, *Memorandum on Certain Aspects of the Bolshevist Movement in Russia,* Government Printing Office, Washington, 1919.

Vserossiiskii Tsentral'nii Sovet Professional'nykh Soiuzov, *Kodeks Zakonov o Trude i Declaratsiia Prav Trudiaschchegosia i Eksploatiruemovo Naroda,* Moscow, 1920.

CONGRESSES AND CONFERENCES OF THE FACTORY COMMITTEES AND TRADE UNIONS

Conferences

Komissia po Izucheniiu Istorii Professional'nogo Dvizheniia v SSSR, *Oktiabr'skaia Revoliutsiia i Fabzavkomy I, II,* VTsSPS, Moscow, 1927.

Komissiia po Izucheniiu Istorii Professional'nogo Dvizheniia v *SSSR* (Istprof VTs SPS), *Tret'ia Vserossiiskaia Konferentsiia Professional'nykh Soiuzov, 20-28 Iunia 3-11 Iulia 1917g, Stenograficheskii Otchet,* VTsSPS, Moscow, 1927.

Tretia Vserossiiskaia Konferentsiia Professional'nkh Soiuzov, *Rezoliutsii, Priniatiia na Zasedaniiakh Konferentsii 20-28 Iunia 1917 G.,* Petrograd, n.d.

Vserossiiskii Tsentral'nyi Sovet Professional'nykh Soiuzov, *Konferentsiia Fabrichno-Zavodskikh i Professional'nykh Soiuzov IV, 1918 Protokoly,* Moscow, 1919.

Komissiia po Izucheniiu Istorii Professional'nogo Dvizheniia v Rossii pri VTsSPS (istprof.) Seriia Istoricheskikh Dokumentov, *IV Vserossiiskaia Konferentsiia Professional'nykh Soiuzov 12-17 Marta 1918,* VTsSPS, Moscow, 1923.

Vsesoiuznyi Tsentral'nyi Sovet Professional'nykh Soiuzov 5go, *Piataia Vserossiiskaia Konferentsiia Professional'nykh Soiuzov 3-7 Noiabria 1920 G. Stenograficheskii Otchet,* Moscow, 1921.

Vsesoiuznyi Tsentral'nyi Sovet Professional'nykh Soiuzov 5go, *Rezoliutsii V Vserossiiskoi Konferentsii Profsoiuzov 2-6 Noiabria 1920 G.,* Moscow, 1920.

Vserossiiskogo Tsentral'nogo Ispoonitel'nogo Komiteta Sovetov R.S.K. i K. Deputatov, *Voedinennoe Zasedanie Vserossiiskogo Tsentral'nogo Komiteta, Moskovskogo Soveta Predstavitelei Fabrichnozavodskih Komitetov, Professional'nykh Soiuzov g. Moskvy i Vserossiiskogo S'ezda Predsedatelei Sovetov 28 Iulia 1918 G.,* Moscow, 1918.

Postanovleniia i Protokoly Vserossiiskoi Konferentsii Soiuza Stroitel'nykh Rabochikh, Moscow, 1918.

CONGRESSES OF THE ALL-RUSSIAN TRADE UNIONS

Vsesoiuznyi Tsentral'nyi Sovet Professional'nykh Soiuzov,, *Pervyi Vserossiiskii S"ezd Professional'nykh Soiuzov 7-14 Ianvaria 1918 Stenograficheskii Otchet s Predisloviem M. Tomskago,* Moscow, 1918.

Vsesoiuznyi Tsentral'nyi Sovet Professional'nykh Soiuzov, *Vtoroi Vserossiiskii S"ezd Professional'nykh Soiuzov 16-25 Ianvaria 1919 Stenograficheskii Otchet Chast' 1 (Plenumy),* Gosudarstvennoe Izdatel'stvo, Moscow, 1921.

Vserossiiskii Tsentral'nyi Sovet Professional'nykh Soiuzov, *Vtoroi Vserossiiskii S"ezd Professional'nykh Soiuzov,* Moscow, 1919.

Vserossiiskii Tsentral'nyi Sovet Professional'nykh Soiuzov, *Tretii Vserossiiskii S"ezd Professional'nykh Soiuzov 6-13 Aprelia 1920. Stenograficheskii Otchet Chast' 1 Plenumy,* Gosudarstvennoe Izdatel'stvo, Moscow, 1921.

Vserossiiskii S"ezd Professional'nykh Soiuzov, *Rezoliutsii i Postanovleniia III Go. Vseross. S"ezda Profess. Soiuzov s Predisloviem A. Lozovkogo,* Vserossiiskii Tsentral'nyi Sovet Professional'nykh Soiuzov, Moscow, 1920.

Rezoliutsii III Go. Vserossiiskogo S"ezda Professional'nykh Soiuzov, Izdanie Ivanovo-Voznesenskogo Gubernskogo Soveta Proizvodstvennykh Soiuzov, 1920.

Publications of Individual Unions

RSFSR, *All-Russian Builders's Union,* All Russian Central Council of Trade Unions, Moscow, 1920.

———, *All-Russian Industrial Union of Glass, China, and Porcelain Workers,* All-Russian Central Council of Trade Unions, Moscow,

———, *All-Russian Union of Workers in the Food Manufacturing Inustry,* All-Russian Central Council of Trade Unions, Moscow, 1920.

———, *All-Russian Agricultural Workers' Union,* Moscow, 1920.

———, *All-Russian Metal Workers' Union,* All-Russian Central Council of Trade Unions, Moscow, 1920.

Tsentral'nyi Komitet Vserossiiskogo S"ezda Rabotnikov Vodnago Transporta, *Trudy Chrezvychainogo Vserossiiskogo S"ezda Rabotnikov Vodnago Transporta Respubliki 14-27 Fevralia 1918,* Petrograd, 1918.

Vserossiiskaia Konferentsiia Zheleznodorozhnikov-Kommunistov, *I Konferentsiia, Protokoly,* Kommunist, Moscow, 1919.

Vserossiiskaia Konferentsiia Zheleznodorozhnikov-Kommunistov, *Proto-*

koly Pervoi Vserossiiskoi Konferentsii Zheleznodorozhnikov, Kommunsitov 24-25 Sentiabria 1918, Kommunist, Moscow, 1918.
Vserossiiskii Soiuz Bumazhnykh Proizvodstv, *Protokoly Zasedanii Konferentsii Rabochikh Bumazhnykh Proizvodstv Severnoi Oblasti ot 4go po 6go Noiabria 1918 G.*, Soiuz Bum. Prom. Sev Oblasti, Petrograd, 1918.
Vserossiiskii Soiuz Rabochikh Metallistov, Komitet Severnoi Oblasti, *Polozheniia o Normakh Zarabotnoi Platy Rabochikh i Sluzhashchikh Metallisticheskoi (Metallcobratyvaiushchei) Promyshlennosti Severnogo Petrogradskogo Raiona,* Petrograd, 1918.
Vserosiiskii Soiuz Rabochikh Metallistov, *Protokoly Vserossiiskogo Uchreditel'nogo S"ezda Soiuzov Rabochikh Metallistov 15-19 Ianvaria 1919 G.*, Tsentral'nyi Komitet Vserossiiskogo Soiuza Rabochikh Metallistov, Moscow, 1919.
———, *Protokoly Vserossiiskogo Uchreditel'nogo S"ezda Soiuzov Rabochikh Metallistov 15-19 Ianvaria 1918 G.*, Moscow, 1919.
Vserossiiskii Soiuz Rabochikh Metallistov, *Ustav,* TsKVSRM, Moscow, Mart 1919.
Vserossiiskii Soiuz Rabochikh Metallistov, *Ustav,* 1921.
Vserossiiskii Soiuz Stroitel'nykh Rabochikh Leningradskogo Gubernskogo Otdela, *Sbornik Materialov po Istorii Souiza Stroitelei 1906-1926.*
Vserossiiskii Soiuz Rabochikh Metallistov, *Protokoly Pervoi Vserossiiskoi Tarifnoi Konferentsii Soiuzov Metallistov Sovmestno c Predstavitelem Zavodskikh Komitetov,* Tsentral'nyi Komitet, Petrograd, 1918.
Shliapnikov, A. *Tarifnyi Dogovor Zakliuchennyi Mezhdu Petrogradskim Soiuzom Rabochikh Metallistov i Obshchestvom Zavodchikov i Fabrikantov s Dopolneniiami i Raz'iasneniami,* n.d.
Vserossiiskii Sovet Normirovaniia Truda v Metallisticheskoi Promyshlennosti, *Polozhenie o Normakh Zarabotnoi Platy i Sluzhahchikh Metallisticheskoi Promyshlennosti,* Moscow, 1918.
Vserossiiskii Soiuz Rabochikh Poligraficheskogo Proizvodstva, Tsentral'nyi Komitet, *Polozhenie o Fabrichno-Zavodshikh Komitetakh v Predpriatiakh Poligraficheskogo Proizvodstva, II, Instruktsiia Delegatam Predpriatiakh Poligraficheskogo Proizvodstva,* Moscow, 1921.
Vserossiiskii S"ezd Professional'nykh Soiuzov Sluzhaschikh lgo, *Resoliutsii lgo Vserossiiskogo S"ezda 22-23 Iliulia 1918,* Moscow, 1918.
Vsesoiuznyi S"ezd Professional'nykh Soiuzov Tekstil'shchikov i Fabrichnykh Komitetov, *Protokoly lgo Vserossiiskogo S"ezda Professional'nykh Soiuzov Tekstil'shchikov i Fabrichnykh Komitetov,* Vserossiiskii Sovet Professional'nykh Soiuzov Tekstil'shchikov, Moscow, 1918.
Vsesoiuznyi S"ezd Professional'nykh Soiuzov Tekstil'shchikov i Fabrich-

nykh Komitetov, *Rezoliutsii lgo Vserossiiskogo S"ezda Rabochikh i Rabotnits Tekstil'shchikov Sostoiavshegosia v Moskve, 28, Ianvaria—1 Fevralia 1918, Vserossiiskii Sovet Soiuzov Tekstil'shchikov,* Moscow, 1918.

PARTY CONGRESSES AND DECREES OF THE CENTRAL COMMITTEE

Rossiiskai Kommunisticheskaia Partiia (Bol'shevikov), *Protokoly VI S"ezda RSDRP (Bol'shevikov) 26 June—3 August 1917,* Kommunist, Moscow, 1919.

Institut Marksizma-Leninizma pri TsK KPSS, *Protokoly i Stenograficheskie Otchety S"ezdov i Konferentsii Kommunisticheskoi Partii Sovetskogo Soiuza, Shestoi S"ezd RSDRP (Bolshevikov) August 1917 G.,* Moscow, 1958.

Rossiiskaia Kommunisticheskaia Partiia (Bol'shevikov), *VIII S"ezd Rossiisskoi Kommunisticheskoi Partii (Bol'shevikov) Moscow, 18-23 Marta 1919, Stenograficheskii Otchet,* Kommunist, Moscow, 1919.

Tsentral'nyi Komitet RKP (bol'shevik), Komissiia po Istorii Oktiabr'skoi Revoliutsii i RKP (bol'shevik) (Istpart), *Sed'moi S"ezd Rossiiskoi Kommunisticheskoi Partii. Stenograficheskii Otchet 6-8 Marta 1918,* Gosudarstvennoe Izdatel'stvo, Moscow, 1923.

Institut Marksizma-Leninizma pri TsK KPSS, *Sedmaia (Aprel'skai) Vserossiiskaia Konferentsiia RSDRP (Bolshevikov) Protokoly,* Gosudarstvennoe Izdatel'stvo Politicheskoi Literatury, Moscow, 1958.

———, *Protokoly Tsentralnogo Komiteta RSDRP(B) Avgust 1917-Fevral' 1918,* Gosudarstvennoe Izdatel'stvo Politicheskoi Literatury, Moscow, 1958.

Institut Marksa-Engelsa-Lenina pri Tsk VKP(B), *Protokoly S"ezdov i Konferentsii Vsesouiznoi Kommunisticheskoi Partii (B), Vos'moi S"ezd RKP(B) 18-23 March 1919,* (Ed Iaroslavskii), Partinoe Izdatel'stvo, Moskva, 1933.

Rossiiskaia Kommunisticheskaia Partiia (Bol'shevikov), *Deviatyi S"ezd Rossiiskoi Kommunisticheskoi Partii 29 Marta—4 Aprelia 1920, Stenograficheskii Otchet,* Gosudarstvennoe, (n.p.), 1920.

Kommunisticheskaia Partiia Sovetskogo Soiuza, *Kommunisticheskaia Partiia Sovetskogo Soiuza-Rezoliutsiiakh i Resheniakh S"ezdov, Konferentsii, i Plenumov TsK, 1898-1954,* Gosudarstvennoe Izdatel'stvo Polit. Literatury, 1954.

Vsesoiuznaia Kommunisticheskaia Partiia Sovetskogo Soiuza, *Rossiiskaia Kommunisticheskaia Partiia (Bol'shevikov) v Rezoliutsiiakh ee S"ezdov i Konferentsii (1898-1922 G.),*Gosudarstvennoe, 1923.

Kommunisticheskaia Akademiia TsIK SSSR. Institut Istorii, *VKP (B) o Profsoiuzakh, Izdanie 2oe Ispravlennoe i Dopolnennoe, Sbornik Reshenii i Postanovlenii S"ezdov, Konferentsii i Plenumov TsK VKP (B)*, Profizdat, Moscow, 1934.

CONGRESSES AND MEETINGS OF THE SOVIETS

Tsentrarkhiv—1917 God v Dokumentakh i Materialakh (ed. Pokrovskii), *Vserossiiskoe Soveshchanie Sovetov Rabochikh i Soldatskikh Deputatov, Stenograficheskii Otchet,* Gosudarstvennoe Izdatel'stvo, Moscow, 1927.

Tsentrarkhiv, 1917 God v Dokumentakh i Materialakh, *Petrogradskii Sovet Rabochikh i Soldatskikh Deputatov Protokoly Zasedanii Ispolnitel'nogo Komiteta i Biuro I.K.* Gosudarstvennoe Izdatel'stvo, Moscow, 1925.

Rossiiskaia Sotsialisticheskaia Federativnaia Respublika, *Protokoly Zasedanii Vserossiiskago Tsentral'nogo Ispoln. Komiteta Soveta RSK i. Kaz. Deputatov II Sozyva,* VTsIK RSKiKD, Moscow, 1918.

Tsentrarkhiv—1917 God v Dokumentakh i Materialiakh (ed. Pokrovskii), *Vtoroi Vserossiiskii S"ezd Sovetov RiSD,* Gosudarstvennoe Izdatel'stvo, Moscow, 1928.

Rossiiskaia Sotsial-Demokraticheskaia Rabochaia Partiia, *Tretii Vserossiiskii S"ezd Sovetov Rabochikh, Soldatskikh i Krestianskikh Deputatov,* Petersburgh, 1918.

Rossiiskaia Sotsialisticheskaia Federativnaia Sovetskaia Respublika, *Chetvertyi Vserossiiskii S"ezd Sovetov Rabochikh, Krestianskikh, Soldatskihk i Kasach'ikh Deputatov, Stenograficheskii Otchet,* Gosudarstvennoe, Moscow, 1919.

Rossiiskaia Sotsialisticsheskaia Federativnaia Sovetskaia Respublika, *Piatyi Vserosssk S"ezd Sovetov Rabochikh Krestianskikh Soldatskikh i Kazach'ikh Deputatov Stenograficheskii Otchet* Moskva 4-10 Iulia 1918, VTSIK Sovetov RSKiK Deputatov, Moscow, 1918.

RSFSR, Shestoi Vserossiiski Chrezvychainyi S"ezd Sovetov, *Moscow* 6-9 *Noiabria 1918, Stenograficheskii Otchet,* VTsIK Sovetov RSKiK Deputatov, Moscow, 1919.

Rossiiskaia Sotsialisticheskaia Federativnaia Sovetskaia Respublika, *Sed'moi Vserossiiskii S"ezd Sovetov Rabochikh Krest'ianskikh, Krasnoarmeiskikh i Kazach'ikh Deputatov, Stenograficheskii Otchet,* Gosudarstvennoe, Moscow, 1921.

Rossiisskaia Sotsialistichiskaia Federativnaia Sovetskaia Respublika, *Vos'moi S"ezd Sovetov Rabochikh Krestianskikh, Krasnoarmeiskikh i Kazach'ikh Deputatov, Stenograficheskii Otchet (22-29 Dekabria 1920)*, Gosudarstvennoe, Moscow 1921.

RSFSR, *Postanovleniia i Rezoliutsii VIII Vserossiikogo S"ezda Sovetov (23-29 Dekabria 1920)*, Politotdel Kavfront, n.p., 1921.

CONGRESSES AND COMMUNICATIONS OF THE COMMISSARS OF LABOR AND THE SOVIETS OF PEOPLE'S ECONOMY

Narodnyi Komissariat Truda, *Protokoly Vsesossiiskogo S"ezda Komissarov Truda, Predstavitelei Birzh Truda i Strakhovykh Kass 18-25 Maia 1918*, Moscow 1918.

Vtoroi S"ezd Komissarov Truda i Predstavitelei Birzh Truda Moskovskoi Oblasti 10-13 Marta 1918, Moscow, 1918.

Trudy I Vserossiiskogo S"ezda Sovetov Narodnogo Khoziaistva (25 Maia-4 Iunia 1918) Stenograficheskii Otchet, VSNKH, Moscow, 1918.

Rezoliutsii Pervago Vserossiiskogo S"ezda Sovetov Narodnogo Khoziaistva s Vstupitel'noi Statei V. P. Miliutina, Itogi S"ezda Sovetov Narod-Khoziaistva, Narodnoe Khoziaistvo, Moscow, 1918.

Trudi II Vserossiiskogo S"ezda Sovetov Narodnogo Khoziaistva Stenografisheskii Otchet, VSNKh, Moscow, (n.d.).

OTHER CONGRESSES AND CONFERENCES

Moskovskii Proletkult, *Pervaia Moskovskaia Obschegorodskaia Konferentsiia Proletarskikh Kulturno-Prosvetitel'nykh Organizatsii 23-28 Fevralia 1918 G. Tezisy, Rezoliutsii, Ustav Moskovskogo Proletkul'ta*, (n.p., n.d.).

Sovet Narodnogo Khoziaistva Severnogo Raiona, *Pervyi S"ezd Sovetov Narodnogo Khoziaistva Severnoi Oblasti. Stenograficheskii Otchet*, Petrograd; Novyi Put', 1918.

Rezoliutsiia Pervogo S"ezda Konfederatsii Anarkhistskikh Organizatsii Ukrainy 'Nabat' (Sostoiavshegosia v. g. Elizavetgrade 2-7 Aprelia 1919). Rabochei Izdatel'skoi Gruppy v Resp. Argentine, 1923.

Sovet Narodnogo Khoziaistva Severnogo Raiona, *Primer Sotsialisticheskogo Stroitel'stva Khoziaistva' Zasedanie Plenuma Soveta Narodnogo Khoziaistva Severnogo Raiona*, Petrograd, 1918.

Vserossiiskii Sovet Proletkulta, *Protokoly Pervoi Vserossiiskoi Konferentsii Proletarskikh Kulturno-Prosvetitel'nykh Organizatsii 15-20 Sentiabria 1918 G.*, Prolestarskaia Kultura, Moscow, 1918.

Vsesoiuznyi Tsentral'nyi Sovet Professional'nykh Soiuzov. Petrogradskii Gubernskii Sovet, 1 Konferentsii 1919, *Pervaia Petrogradskaia Gu-*

bernskaia Konferentsiia Professional'nykh Soiuzov (11-13 Sentiabria 1919) Stenograficheskii Otchet, Leningrad, 1930.

Zagranichnoe Biuro po Sozdaniiu Rossiiskoi Konfederatsii Anarkho-Sindikalistov, *Vmesto Programmy: Rezoliutsii I i II Vserossiiskikh Konferentsii Anarkho-Sindikalistov,* Knigoizdatel'stvo Zagranichnogo Biuro Anarkho-Sindikalistov, Berlin, 1922.

OFFICIAL SPEECHES AND COMMUNICATIONS CONCERNING LABOR

Biuro Fraktsii RKP. Vserossiskogo Tsentral'nogo Soveta Professional'nykh Soiuzov, *Tol'ko dlia Chlenov RKP. O Roli Professional'nykh Soiuzov v Proizvodstve.* Doklady T.T. Zinovieva i Trotskogo, Rech' T. Lenina, so Doklady T.T. Bukharina, Nogina, Shliapnikova, i Riazanova i Zakliuchitel'nie Slova T.T. Trotskogo i Zinovieva na Soedinenom Zasedanii Delegatov 8go S"ezda Sovetov, VTs SPS i MGSRS —Chlenov RKP 30 Dekabria 1920, Moscow, 1921.

Da Zdravstvuiet loe Maia k Vsem Rabochim, Rabotnitsam, Krasnoarmeitsam, Matrosam, Zheleznodorozhnikam, ko vsem Trudiashchimsia, n.p., Petersburgh, 1920.

Glavkomtrud, *Instruktsia po Proizvodstvu Mobilizatsii i Rasperedeleniu Kvalifikatsionykh Rabochikh Soglasno Postanovleniu Soveta Truda i Oborony ot 7 Iiulia 1920 G.,* Glavkomtrud, Moscow, 1920.

Glavnyi Komitet Po Vseobshchei Trudovoi Povinnost', *RKP i Trudovaia Povinnost', Sbornik Materialov,* Moscow, 1920.
tel'stvo, Moscow, 1920.

Kamenev, L., *Rech' k Rabochim i Krestianam,* Gosudarstvennoe Izdatel'stvo, Moscow, 1920.

Kollantai, A., *The Workers Opposition in Russia, Industrial Workers of the World,* Chicago, 1921 (?).

———, *Rabochaia Oppozitsiia Tol'ko Dlia Chlenov Xgo S"ezda RKP,* Moscow, 1921.

Kossior, *Nashi Raznoglasiia (O Roli i Zadachakh Profsoiuzov),* (written by hand on the cover: "Only for Responsible Members of the Party"), Gosudarstvennoe Izdatel'stvo, 1920.

Lenin, N., *O Professional'nykh Soiuzakh, o Tekushchem Momente i ob Oshibkakh Tov. Trotskogo,* Petersburgh, 1921.

———, *Eshche Raz o Profsoiuzakh, o Tekushchem Momente i ob Oshibkakh T. Trotskogo i Bukharina,* Gosudarstvennoe Izratel'stvo, 1921.

Moskovskii Sovet Rabochikh i Soldatskikh Deputatov; Otdel Truda, *Kak*

Organizovat' Zavodskii (Fabrichnyi) Rabochii Komitet, Mamontov, Moscow, 1917.

Otchet Tsektrana k Vserossiiskomu Soveshchaniu Rabotnikov Soiuza Narodnyi Komissariat Putei Soobshchenia, Moscow, 1920.

Otchet Vserossiiskogo Tsentral'nogo Soveta Professional'nykh Soiuzov, (Mart 1920-Aprel 1921 G.) Moscow, 1921.

Proekt Postanovleniia X S"ezda RKP po Voprosu o Roli i Zadachi Professional'nykh Soiuzov. Vnesennyi na Rassmotrenie TsKRKP Gruppoi Chlenov TsK i Chlenov Professionalnoi Komissii pri TsK, Gosudarstvennoe Izdatel'stvo, Moscow, 1921.

RSFSR, *Obshchaia Instruktsiia po Raboche-Krestianskoi Inspektsii,* (*Osnovye Polozheniia*) *Utverzhdena Zamestitelem Narodnogo Komissara V. Avakesovym 20go Fevralia 1920,* Rostov no Donu, 1920.

Sovet Rabochego Kontrolia Tsentral'noi Promyshlennoi Oblasti, Rukovodstvo po Rabochemu Kontroliu Tsentral'noi Promyshlennoi Oblasti, *Rukovodstvo po Rabochemu Kontroliu. Izdanie Vtoroe, Vnov' Pererabotannoe i Dopolnennoe s Predlozheniem o Natsionalizatsii Fabrik i Postanovlenii o Likvidatsii Predpriatti,* Moscow, 1918.

Sovet Rabochego Kontrolia Tsentral'noi Promyshlennoi Oblasti, *Spravochnik dlia Fabrichnykh Komitetov, Kontrol'nykh Komisii i Mestnykh Sovetov Narodnogo Khoziaistva,* Moscow, 1918.

Sovet Naradnogo Khoziaistva Severnogo Raiona, *Opyt Proletarskoi Programmy Organizatsii Proizvodstva,* Petrograd, 1918.

———, *Skhema Organizatsii Soveta Narodnogo Khoziaistva Severnogo Raiona, i ego Mestnykh Organov* (*S Ustavom SNKhSR*), Petrograd, 1918.

Tettenborn, Z., *Sovetskoe Zakonodatel'stvo o Trude* (*Lektsii Prochitannye na Kursakh dlia Inspektorov Truda*), *Gosizdat,* Moscow, 1920.

Tomskii, *Rech' o Zadachakh Soiuzov v Teatre Zimina, Stenograficheskii Otchet,* Gosudarstvennoe Izdatel'stvo, 1921.

Trotsky, Leon, *A Paradise in This World,* (An address delivered to a working class audience on April 14, 1918.), British Socialist Party, London, 1918.

———, *Krasanaia Armiia, Rech' L. D. Trotskogo Na Zasedanii Tsentral'nogo Ispol'nitel'nogo Komiteta 22 Aprelia 1918,* VTsIK RSKiK Deputatov, Voennyi Otdel, 1918.

———, *Mezhdunarodnoe Polozhenie i Krasnaia Armiia; Lektsiia, Prochitannaia, L. Trotskim v Sergievskom Narodnom Dome 16 Iunia 1918,* VTsIK, Voennyi Otdel, Moscow, 1918.

———, *Mobilizatsiia Truda, Doklad na Obiedinennom Zasedanii III S"ezda Narod-Khoziaistva i Moskovskogo Soveta Rabochikh i Krasnoarmeiskikh Deputatov,* Moscow, 1920.

Trotsky, *Trud, Distsiplina, Poriadok, Spasut' Sotsialisticheskuiu Sovetskuiu Respubliku, Doklad na Moskovskoi Gorodskoi Konferentsii Rossiiskoi Kommunisticheskoi Partii 28 Marta 1918,* Zhizn' i Znanie, Moscow, 1918.

———, *Na Bor'bu s Golodom. Rech' Proiznesennaia 9 Iunia 1918 G. Na Naradnom Sobranii v Sokol'nikakh,* Kommunist, 1918.

———, *Na Proizvodstvennyi Put', Doklad na Partiinom Sobranii v Moskve,* Gosudarstvennoe Izdatel'stvo, 1921.

———, *O Zadachakh Profsoiuzov, Doklad Prochitannyi na Sobranii 30 Dekabria 1920,* Gosudarstvennoe Izdatel'stvo, 1921.

———, *Petrogradskie Rabochie, o Roli i Zadachakh Professional'nykh Soiuzov, 2 Pisma Petrogradskoi Organizatsii RKP i Otvet Tov. Trotskogo,* Gosudarstvennoe Izdatel'stvo, 1921.

———, *Rech' na III Vserossiiskom S''ezde Sovetov Naradnogo Khoziaistva,* VSNKh-Otdel Redaktsionno-Izdatelskii.

———, *Rol' i Zadachi Professional'nykh Soiuzov (K 10mu S''ezdu Partii),* Gosudarstvennoe Izdatel'stvo, Moscow, 1920.

———, *Slovo Russkim Rabochim i Krestianam o Nashikh Druziakh i Vragakh i o Tom, Kak Uberech' i Uprochit' Sovietskuiu Respubliku. Rech' Proiznosena na Rabochem Sobranii 14 Aprelia 1918 G.,* Vtoroe Izdanie Petrograd, Soveta Rabochikh, 1918.

Tsent, Sovet Professional'nykh Soizuv, *Tarif Rabochikh i Sluzhashcikh Derevoobratyvaiuschei i Lesnoi Promyshlennosti,* Moscow, 1919.

Vserossiiskii Tsentral'nyi Sovet Professional'nykh Soiuzov, *Deleproizvodstvo Shchetovdstvo i Otchetnost' Professional'nykh,* Moscow, 1918.

———, *Ocherednyia Zadachi Professional'nykh Soiuzov (Organizatsionnyi Vopros, Tarif, Trudovaia Distsiplina) Pervoe Tsirkularnoe Pismo Vserossiiskogo Tsentral'nogo Soveta Professional'nykh, Soiuzov,* Moscow, 1918.

———, *O Roli Professional'nykh Soiuzov v Proizvodstve 1920,* Moscow, 1921.

———, *Polozhenie o Mestnykh Komitetakh (Kollektivakh) Sluzhashchikh (Utverzhden Presidiumom TSSPS), Moscow,* 1919.

Vserossiiskii Tsentral'nyi Sovet Professional'nykh Soiuzov, *Proekt Kollektivnogo Dogovora,* Moscow, 1919.

Vyshaia Shkola Profdvizheniia VTsSPS, *Osnovy Marksistsko-Leninskogo Ucheniia o Profsoiuzakh, Vypusk II, Profizdat,* Moscow, 1934.

Zinoviev, G., *Bespartiinyi ili Kommunist,* Gosudarstvennoe Iz-vo, Moscow, 1919.

———, *Iiulskie Dni. Rech' na Mitinge v Morskom Korpuse 20 Iiulia 1919 G,* Gosudartvennoe Izdatel'stvo, Petrograd, 1919.

Zinoviev, *Novye Zadachi Nashei Partii k X S"ezdu,* Petrogradskii Soiuz i Sektsiia Poligraficheskogo Proizvodstva, 1921.

———, *Novye Zadachi Nashei Partii ot Voiny k Khoziaistvu, Rech' Proiznosennaia na Obshchem Sobranii Chlenov Partii, Kandidatov i Sochuvstvuiushchikh Petrogradskogo Raiona 28 Ianvaria 1920 G,* Gosizdat, Moscow, 1920.

———, *Partiia i Soiuzy,* Gosudarstvennoe Izdatel'stvo, Petersburgh, 1921.

———, *Rabochaia Partiia i Professional'nye Soiuzy. O Neitralizme Professional'nogo Dvizheniia,* Petrogradskii Sovet Rabochikh i Krasnoarmeishikh Deputatov, 1918.

———, *O Roli Professional'nykh Soiuzov, Doklad i Zakliuchitel'noe Slovo na Diskussionnom Sobrani v Moskve 30 Dekabria 1920 v Sostave Fraktsii VIII S"ezda Sovetov i VTsSPS Sodokladchikom Vystupil T. Trotskii,* Gosudarstvennoe Izdatel'stvo, Petersburgh, 1921.

———, *Spor o Professional'nykh Soiuzov (Doklad v Peterburge),* Gosizdat, Petersburgh, 1921.

———, *Stroitel'stvo, Zhizn' i Sovetskaia Vlast'. Rech' na Obshchergorodskom Soveshchanii Predstavitelei Fabrik i Zavodov 13 Aprelia 1921, Petrograd Sovet Profsoiuzov,* 1921.

GOVERNMENT SERIALS

Ekonomicheskaia Zhizn' Severa, Organ Ekonomicheskikh Komissariatov Narodnogo Khoziaistva Severnoi Oblasti. No. 1, Dec. 8, 1918; No. 2, Dec. 15, 1918; No. 3, Dec. 22, 1918.

Ezhenedel'nik Soveta Narodnogo Khoziaistva Severnogo Raiona i Ekonomicheskikh Uchrezhdenii Petrogradskogo Sovdepa. No. 24, July 27, 1919; No. 25, Aug. 3, 1919; No. 27, Aug. 17, 1919; No. 28, Aug. 24, 1919; No. 29, Aug. 31, 1919; No. 31, Sept. 14, 1919.

Glavnyi Komitet po Vseobshchei Trudovoi Povinnosti, *Izvestiia* No. 1-7 March-Oct., 1920 (Not to be confused with the following).

Izvestiia Glavnogo Komiteta po Vseobshchei Trudovoi Povinnosti i Narodnogo Komissariata Truda. (Only one issue, undated.) (1920?).

Narodnyi Komissariat Truda, *Biulleten' Otdela Sotsial'nogo Strakhovaniia i Okhrany Truda pri Narodnom Komissariate Truda Vykhodit pri Blizhaishem Uchastii Rabochei Gruppy, No. 1-4* August September 1918; No. 5-6 October-November 1918; No. 7 December 1918.

———, *Biulleten' Narodnogo Komissariata Truda,* No. 1-6, January-March 1919; No. 8-9, August-September 1919; No. 11-12, November-December 1919; No. 1-6, 1920.

Narodnyi Komissariat Truda, *Vestnik*, January-April-May 1918.

———, i Glavkomtruda, *Biulleten' Trudovogo Fronta,* No. 1-3, 1921; 5-9, 1921; 11-20, 1921; 23-27, 1921.

———, Otdel Strakhovaniia i Okhrany Truda, *Biulleten'* No. 1-4, 1918.

Proletarskaia Kul'tura, Ezhemesiachnyi Zhurnal, Organ Vserossiiskogo Soveta Proletarskikh Organizatsii, No. 1-10 Iiul' 1918-Iiul' 1919; No. 11-12 Dekabr' 1919; No. 13-14 Ianvar'-Mart 1920; No. 15-16 Aprel'-Iiul' 1920; No. 17-19 Avgust-Dekabr' 1920, Gosudartsvennoe Izdatel'stvo, Moscow.

Vysshii Sovet Narodnogo Khoziaistva, *Narodnoe Khoziaistvo-Organ Vysshego* Soveta Narodnogo Khoziaistva, 1918-1920. (Published through 1922.)

TRADE UNION SERIALS

Professional'nyi Vestnik, Organ Vserossuskogo Soveta Professional'nykh Souizov, 1917-1920.

Vestnik Truda, 1920.

Vestnik Professional'nykh Soiuzov, Organ Petrogradskogo Soveta Professional'nykh Soiuzov, No. 1, May 4, 1918; No. 2, July 15, 1918; No. 4, Nov. 7, 1918; No. 1 (5), Jan. 1, 1919, No. 2-4, May 1, 1919.

Vestnik Metallista. Vserossiiskii Soiuz Rabochikh Metallistov. One issue 1917- Petrograd; No. 2, Jan. 1918 (Petrograd); No. 3, May 18 (Moscow); Nos. 3, 4, 5, 6, June-August 1918 (Moscow).

COMMUNIST PARTY SERIALS

Vsesoiuznaia Kommunisticheskaia Partia (B) Tsentral'nyi Komitet, 1919-1920, *Izvestiia,* No. 17, March 30, 1920, is especially valuable.

ARCHIVES

Trotsky Archive, Houghton Library, Harvard University.

BOOKS AND PAMPHLETS

Abel', G., *Vsekh i Seichas -Zhe na Pomoshch' Rodine, Vsoebshchaia Trudovaia Povinnost',* Marii Malykh, Petrograd, 1917.

Abolin, A., *The October Revolution and the Trade Unions.* Cooperative Publishing Society of Foreign Workers in the USSR, Moscow, 1933.

Acton, H. B., *The Illusion of the Epoch Marxism-Leninism As a Philosophical Creed,* Beacon Press, Boston, 1957.

Adoratsky, V., *Dialectical Materialism, The Theoretical Foundation of Marxism-Leninism,* International Publishers, New York, 1934.

Adorno, et al., *The Authoritarian Personality,* Harper, New York, 1950.

Akademiia Obshchestvennykh Nauk pri TsK KPSS, *Voprosy Dialekticheskogo i Istoricheskogo Materializma,* Moscow, 1956.

Akademiia Nauk SSSR Institut Filosofii, *Osnovy Marksistkoi Filosofii,* Politliteratury, Moscow, 1959.

———, *O Dialekticheskom Materializme Sbornik Statei,* Gosudarstvennoe Izdatelistvo Politicheskoi Literatury, (n.p.) 1953.

———, *Voprosy Marksistko-Leninskoi Filosofii Sbornik Statei,* Akademiia Nauk, Moscow, 1950.

Aluf. A., *The Development of Socialist Methods and Forms of Labor From the First Subbotnik to the Present Vast Scope of Socialist Competition,* Cooperative Publishing Society of Foreign Workers in the USSR, Moscow, 1932.

Andreev, I. D., *Osnovnye Zakoni i Kategorii Materialisticheskoi Dialektiki,* Moskovskii Rabochii, Moscow, 1959.

Anet, Claude, *Through the Russian Revolution, Notes of an Eye-Witness, From 12 March-30 May,* Hutchinson, London, 1917.

Aniket, A., *Organizatsiya Rynka Truda za Dva Goda Sovetskoi Vlasti, Kratkii Ocherk,* Narodnyi Komissariat Truda, Moscow, 1920.

Anikst, A. (ed.), *Spravochnik po Birzham Truda,* Narodnyi Komissariat Truda Otdel Rynka Truda, Moscow, 1918.

———, *Stat'i i Doklady za 1918-1920 po Organizatsii Raspredelniia Rabochei Sily,* Narodnyi Komissariat Truda, Moscow, 1921.

Anskii, A. (ed.), *Professional'noe Dvizhenie v Petrograde v 1917g Ocherki i Materiali,* Istprof Leningradskogo Oblastnogo Soveta Prof. Soiuzov, Leningrad, 1928.

Antonov-Saratovskii, V. P. (ed.), *Sovety v Epokhu Voennogo Kommunizma, Sbornik Dokumentov, Chast' 1-2,* Kommunisticheskaia Akademiia, Moscow, 1928-1929.

Antoshkin, A., *Professional'noe Divzhenie Sluzhashchikh 1917-1924,* Ts.K. Sovtorg Sluzhashchikh, Moscow, 1927.

Arendt, Hannah, *The Origins of Totalitarianism,* Harcourt Brace, New York, 1951.

Arkelian, A. A., *Zhiznennaia Sila V. I. Lenina o Proizvoditel'nosti Truda,* Znanie, Moscow, 1955.

Arskii, R., *Le Controle Ouvrier,* B. F. Manuel sur le Controle Ouvrier, (n.p), (n.d.).

———, *Primiritel'nyia Kamery,* Sotsialist, Petersburgh, 1917.

Arskii, *Zarabotnaia Plata, Tarifnaya Politika,* Institut Ekonomicheskikh Issledovanii Pri Narodnom Komissariate Finansov, Petrograd, 1919.

Astapovich, Z. Z., *Pervyie Meropriyatiya Sovetskoi Vlasti v Oblasti Truda (1917-1918 G),* Gospolitizdat, Moscow, 1958.

Astrov, W., Slepikov, A. and Thomas, J., *An Illustrated History of the Russian Revolution,* (trans. Freda Utley), 1 and 2, International Publishers, New York, March 1928.

Austin, J. L., *Philosophical Papers,* Clarendon Press, Oxford, 1961.

Avdeev, N., *Revoliutsiia 1917 Goda (Khronika Sobytii),* 1-3 Gosudarstvennoe Izdatel'stvo, Moscow, 1923.

Bakunin, Michael, *Izbrannye Sochineniia, 1, Anarkhiia,* Golos Truda, St. Petersburgh, 1922.

———, *Marxism Freedom and the State* (trans. and ed. by K. J. Kenafic), London Press, London, 1950. Translations from Bakunin's work from 1870-1872.

———, *Parizhkaia Kommuna i Poniatie Gosudarstvennosti s Pis'mom P. A. Kropotkina, K Izdateliam Anarkhicheskoi Biblioteki,* Novaiia Russkaiia Tipografiia, Geneva, 1892.

———, *Polnoe Sobranie Sochinenii,* 1 and 2 (ed. A. I. Bakunin), Balshov, n.p., n.d.

———, *Rechi i Vozzvaniia,* Balshov, n.p., 1906.

Balabanov, M. S., *Ocherki Po Istorii Rabochego Klassa v Rossii,* Ekonomicheskaia Zhizn, Moscow, 1925-1926.

Bauer, Raymond, *The New Man in Soviet Psychology,* Harvard University Press, Cambridge, 1952.

Baykov, Alexander, *The Development of the Soviet Economic System,* Macmillan, New York, 1948.

Beliakov-Gorskov, H. H., Senatov, B. G., Thegubov, I. M., *Kommunisty i Sektanty, Bronnaia,* Moscow, 1919.

Berdayev, *The Origins of Russian Communism,* (trans. R. M. French), Goeffrey Bles, London, 1948.

———, *The Russian Idea,* Macmillan, New York, 1948.

———, *The Russian Revolution,* (trans. D. B. London), Sheed and Ward, 1935.

Bergman, Henrikh, *Rossiiskaya Sotsialisticheskaya Armiya,* Gosudarstvennoe Izdatel'stvo, 1919.

Beriushina, A., *Pochemu Ia Stala Kommunistkoi?* Gosudarstvennoe Izdatel'stvo, Moscow, 1919.

Berkeley, George, *A New Theory of Vision and Other Writings,* Dutton, New York, 1954.

Berkman, Alexander, *The Bolshevik Myth (Diary 1920-1922),* Boni and Liveright, New York, 1925.

———, *The Russian Revolution and the Communist Party,* (written in Moscow, June 1921). Published in 1922, no publisher, n.d.

Bezrabotnyi, I., *Dve Revoliutsii,* Rossisskaia Sotsial'-Demokraticheskaia Rabochaia Partia, Petrograd, 1918.

Bibikov, T. and Moskalev, S., *Profsoyuzy Leningrada v Gody Sovetskoi Vlasti 1917-1959,* Profizdat, Moscow, 1960.

Blakeley, Thomas J., *Soviet Scholasticism,* D. Reidel, Dordrecht, 1961.

Blonina, E., *Pochemu Ia Stala Zashchitnitsei Sovetskoi Vlasti.* Gosizdat, Moscow, 1919.

Blonskii, P. P., *Trudovaia Shkola,* Chast' l, Izdanie Vtoroe, Gosizdat, Moscow, 1919.

Bochenski, J. M., *Soviet Dialectical Materialism,* Reidel, Dordrecht, 1963.

Bogdanov, A. (Malinowskii), *A Short Course of Economic Science,* Revised and Supplemented by S. M. Dvolartsky in conjunction with the Author. (trans. J. Fineberg), Communist Party of Great Britain, n.p. 1927.

———, *Elementy Proletarskoi Kultury v Razvitii Rabochego Klassa Lektsii Prochitannye v Moskovskom Proletkul'te Vesnoi* 1919g, Gosudarstvennoe Izdate'stvo, Moscow, 1920.

Bogdanov, A., *Empiriomonism, Stati po Filosofii,* Voronov, Moscow, 1904.

———, *Filosofiia Zhivogo Opyta, Popularnye Ocherki,* Gosudarstvennoe Izdatel'stvo, Moscow, 1920.

———, *Iz Psikhologii Obshchestva,* Petersburgh, 1906.

———, *Novyi Mir. Izdanie Vtoroe Dopolnennoe,* Kommunist, Moscow, 1918.

———, *Uroki Pervykh Shagov Revoliutsii,* Moscow, 1917.

Bogdanov, H., (Fedosov), *Organizatsiia Stroiitel'nykh Rabochikh Rossii i Drugikh Stran,* V.Ts.I. K.S.R.S. i K. Deputatov, Moscow, 1919.

Borisov, S., *Sed'moi S"ezd RKP(b),* Gospolizdat, (n.p.), 1952.

Borchchenko, I. L., *Poiavlenie Sovremennogo Promyshlennogo Proletariata i Rabochee Dvizhenie v Rosii do Pervoi Russkoi, Revoliutsii,* VTSSPS Profizdat, 1952.

Broshyrg, L. and Yakushev I., *Bol'sheviki-Organizatory Razgroma Kornilovshchiny.* Gospolitizdat, Moscow, 1957.

Brusilov, A. A., *Moi Vospominaniia,* Moscow, 1921.

Bukharin, N., *Ekonomika Perekhodnogo Perioda,* Gosudarstvennoe Izdatel'stvo, Moscow, 1920.

Bukharin, N., *Klassovaia Bor'ba i Revoliutsiia v Rossii,* Kommunist, Petrograd, 1919.

———, Lenin as a Marxist, Communist Party of Great Britain, London, 1925.

———, *Program of the Communists (Bolshevists),* Communist Labor Party of America—imprint blocked over; stamped above is United Communist Party of America, (n.p), (n.d.). This is a translation of the following.

———, *Programma Kommunistov (Bol'shevikov)*, Petrogradskii Sovet Rabochikh i Krasnoarmeiskikh Deputatov, (n.p.), 1919 (originally published 1918).

———, *Diktatura Proletariata,* Federatsiia Russkikh Otdelov Kommunisticheskoi Rabochei Partii v Amerike, (n.p.), 1920.

———, *Historical Materialism, A System of Sociology,* International Publishers, New York, 1925.

———, *Novyi Kurs Ekonomicheskoi Politiki,* Gosudarstvennoe, Petersburgh, 1921.

———, *The Communist Program, An Analysis of the Principles of the Russian Communist Party,* Contemporary Publishing Association, New York, 1920.

———, *Trudovaia Povinnost' i Zadachi Rabotnits i Krest'ianok,* Gosudarstvennoe, Moscow, 1920.

———, *Vseobshchaia Delezha ili Kommunistcheskoe Proizvodstvo,* Vserossiiskago Tsentral'nago Ispolnitel'nago Komiteta R., S., K. and K. Deputatov, Moscow, 1918

———, and Preobrazhensky, E., *The ABC of Communism, A Popular Exposition of the Program of the Communist Party (the Bolsheviki),* (trans. from German by P. Lavin), Socialist Labor Press, Glasgow, 1921.

Burmistrova T. Yu, *Borba Bol'sheviskoi Partii za Internatsional'noe Splochenie Trudyashchikhsya Mass Rossii v 1917 Godu,* Izdatel'stvo Leningradskogo Universiteta, 1957.

Cameron, J., *Scrutiny of Marxism,* SCM Press, London, 1948.

Carr, Edward Hallett, The *Bolshevik Revolution* 1917-1923, Vol. 1, 2, 3, Macmillan, New York, 1951.

Chamberlain, William Henry, *The Russian Revolution 1917-1921.* Vol. 1 and 2, Macmillan, New York, 1935.

Chernov, Viktor M., *Filosofskie i Sotsiologicheskie Etiudy,* Russkoe Tovarishchestvo, Moscow, 1907.

———, *The Great Russian Revolution,* (trans. and abridged by Philip E. Mosely), Yale University Press, New Haven, 1936.

Chernov, *Mes tribulations en Russie Sovietique,* (traduit par V.U.), Povolozky, Paris, 1921.

———, *Rozhdenie Revoliutsionnoi Rossii (Fevral'skaia Revoliutsiia),* Iubileinyi Komitet po Izdaniu Trudov V. M. Chernova, Paris, Prague, New York, 1934.

Ciliga, Anton, *The Russian Enigma* (English version by Fernand G. Renier and Anne Cliff), Routledge, London, 1940.

Communist Party of the Soviet Union, Central Committee, *History of the Communist Party of the Soviet Union, Short Course,* Foreign Languages Publishing House, 1951.

Cornforth, Maurice C., *Dialetical Materialism, An Introductory Course,* Lawrence and Wishart, London, 1952.

———, *Dialetical Materialism and Science,* Lawrence and Wishart, London, 1949.

Dallin, D., *Posle Voin i Revoliutsii,* Grani, Berlin, 1922.

Dan, F. I., *Dva Goda Skitanii* (*1919-1921*), Berlin, 1922.

———, *Gewerkshaften und Politik in Sowjetrusland,* Dietz Nachfolger, Berlin, 1923.

———, *Politique Économique et la Situation de la Classe Ouvrière en Russie Sovietique,* (trad. de l'Allemand par Entuine), L'Eglantine, Bruxeles, 1923.

Dan, F. I., *Proiskhozhdenie Bol'shevizma; K Istorii Demokraticheskikh i Sotsialisticheskikh Idei v Rossii Posle Osvobozhdeniia Krest'ian,* Novaia Demokratiia, New York, 1946.

Daniels, R. V., *The Conscience of the Revolution, Communist Opposition in Soviet Russia,* Harvard University Press, Cambridge, 1960.

Deborin, A. M., *Filosofiia i Politika,* Akademiia Nauk, Moscow, 1961.

Deutscher, Isaac, *Stalin, A Political Biography* Oxford University Press, London, 1949.

———, *The Prophet Armed*: *Trotsky 1879-1921,* Oxford University Press, New York, 1954.

———, *Soviet Trade Unions, Their Place in Soviet Labour Policy,* Royal Institute of International Affairs, London and New York, 1950.

Dewar, Margaret, *Labour Policy in the USSR 1917-1918,* Royal Institute of International Affairs, London, 1956.

Dietzgen, J., *Filosofiia Sotsialdemokratii, Sbornik Melkikh Filosofskikh Statei,* Skirmunt, Moscow, 1907.

Dobb, Maurice, *Soviet Economic Development Since 1917,* International Publishers, New York, 1948.

Dobbs, Maurice, *Wages,* Cambridge University Press, London, 1947.

Drezena (ed.), *Bol'shevizatsiia Petrogradskogo Garnizona, Shornik Materialov i Dokumentov,* Leningradskoe Oblastnoe Izdatel'stvo, Leningrad, 1932.

Dorprofsozh Mosk-Kaz. Zh. D., *Professional'noe Dvizhenie na Moskovsko-Kazanskoi Zheleznoi Doroge 1917-1927G,* Moscow, 1928.

Dunn, Robert W., *Soviet Trade Unions,* Vanguard, New York, 1928.

Dvinov, B., *Ot Legal'nosti k Podpol'yu* (*1921-1922*), Zapiski, New York, 1955.

Egorov, K., *Moskovskie Ditsiplinarnye Sudy za 1920 Goda, (Materialy k X S"ezdu R. K. P. i IVmu S"ezdu Profsoiuzov*), c Predisloviem A. Lozovskogo, M. G. S. P. S., Moscow, 1921.

Egorova, A. G., *Profsoiuzy i Fabzavkomy v Bor'be Za Pobedu Oktiabria* (*Mart-Oktiabr' 1917 Goda*), Profizdat, (n.p.), 1960.

El'nitskii A., *Pervyie Shagi Rabochago Dvizhenia v Rossii,* Belopl'skago, Petrograd, 1917.

Engels, Friedrich, *Dialectics of Nature* (trans. Clemens Dutt), Foreign Languages Publishing House, Moscow, 1954.

———, *Herr Eugen Duhring's Revolution in Science (Anti-Duhring),* International Publishers, New York, 1939.

———, *Ludwig Feuerbach and the End of Classical German Philosophy,* Foreign Languages Publishing House, Moscow, 1949.

Erykalov, E., *Krasnaya Gvardiya v Bor'be za Vlast' Sovetov,* Gospolitizdat, Moscow, 1957.

Fainsod, Merle, *How Russia is Ruled,* Harvanrd University Press, Cambridge, 1953.

Faire S. (ed.), *Encyclopedie Anarchiste, Oeuvre Internationale des Editions Anarchistes,* A. L., Paris, 1926.

Farbman, Michael S., *Bolshevism in Retreat,* W. Collins Sons, London, 1923.

Federation of Russian Anarchist Communist Groups of U. S. and Canada, Ukrainian Anarchist Communist Groups of U. S. and Canada, *Manifesto of the Russian Revolution* Issued by the Anarchist Communist Groups of U. S. and Canada, (n.p.), 1922.

Federn, Karl, *The Materialist Conception of History, A Critical Analysis,* Macmillan, New York, 1939.

Federov, K., *V. Ts. I. K. V Pervye Gody Sovetskoi Vlasti* (*1917-1920*), Gosudarstvennoe Izdatel'stvo Yuridicheskoi Literatury, Moscow, 1957.

Fedotoff-White, D., *The Growth of the Red Army,* Princeton University Press, Princeton, 1944.

Ferdman, I. U., *Rabochii Vopros v Rossii v Proshlom i Nastoiza-shchem,* Obshchestvo Narodnago Izdatel'stva Imeni A. Hertsena, Lausanne, 1918.

Fleyer, M. G., *Rabochee Dvizhenie v Gody Voiny,* Voprosy Truda, 1925.

Garvy, N. and Chatskii I., *Professional'nye Soiuzy, ikh Organizatsiia i Deiatel'nost',* (Vtoroe Izdanie), Rabochaia Biblioteka Tsentral. Komiteta R. S. D. R. P., Petrograd, 1917.

Garvy, F. A., *Professional'nye Soiuzy v Rossii v Pervye Gody Revoliutsii (1917-1921),* (ed. Aronson, G. A.), n.p., New York, 1958.

Gel'fer, D. A., *Chto Takoe Sotsial'noe Strakhovanie Dlia Chego Ono Nuzhno i Kak Ego Provodit' v Zhizn',* Narodnyi Komissariat Truda Otdel Sotsialnogo Strakhovaniia, Moscow, 1918.

Gerasimovich, V. E., *Gosudarstvennaia Sluzhba,* Iuridicheskaia Biblioteka (Izdanie Neofitsial'noe, Komiteta Pomoshchi Invalidam Voiny), Moscow, 1923.

Girinis, S., *Chto Takoe Professional'nyi Proizvodstvennyi Soiuz,* MGSPS Trud i Kniga, Moscow, 1924.

Glebov, A., *Les Syndicats Russes et la Revolution,* Preface Boris Souvarine, Bibliotheque Communiste, Paris, 1920.

Gelbov, N., *Le Role des Syndicats Ouvriers Dans la Revolution Russe,* Edition des Jeunesses Socialistes Romandes, (n.p.), (n.d.).

Goikhbarg, A. G., *Stotsial'noe Zakonodatel'stvo Sovetskoi Respubliki,* (Vvedenie), Narodny Komissariata Yustitsii, Moscow, 1919.

Goldman, Emma, *My Disillusionment in Russia,* Doubleday, Garden City, 1923.

———, *My Further Disillusionment in Russia,* Doubleday, Garden City, 1924.

Goldschmidt, Alfons, *Die Wirtschaftsorganisation Sowjetruslands,* Rowohlt, Berlin, 1920.

Gol'tsman, A. (Ia. Boiarkov) *Reguliarovanie i Naturalizatsiia Zarabotnoi Platy,* Tsentralny Komitet Vseross, Soiuza Rabochikh Metallistov, Moscow, 1918.

Gompers, Samuel, *Out of Their Own Mouths,* E. P. Dutton, New York, 1921.

Gordon, Manya, *Workers Before and After Lenin,* E. P. Dutton, New York, 1941.

Gordon, M. I., *Ocherk Ekonomicheskoi Bor'by Rabochikh v Rossii Iz Istorii Volnenii i Zabastovok,* Petrograd. Soviet Profsoiuzov, Petrograd, 1924.

Gorer, Geoffrey, *The People of Great Russia,* Cresset, New York, 1950.

Gorev, B. I., *Kto Takie Lenintsy i Chego oni Khotiat?* 'Rabochaia Biblioteka' Organizatsionnago Komiteta R. S. D. R. P., Petrograd, 1917.

Gorin, D., *Proletariat v 1917 v Bor'be Za Vlast'*, Gos-izdat, Moscow, 1927.

Gorkii, et al. (ed.), *Istoriia Grazhdanskoi Voiny v SSSR,* 1, 2, Ogiz, Moscow, 1935.

Gosudarstvennyi Soviet Vtorogo Departmenta, *Obzor Deiatel'nosti Vtorago Departamenta Gosudarstvennago Soveta po Razsmotreniiu Del o Chastnykh Zheleznykh Dorogakh za Vremiia s 1906 do 1913 g,* Gosudarstvennaia Tipografiia, St. Petersburgh, 1914.

Greiner, J. E., (Member of the American Railway Commission to Russia) "The Russian Railway Situation and Some Personal Observations." Reprinted from the *Monthly Journal* of the Engineers Club of Baltimore, Vol. VIII, 7 (January, 1918).

Grinevetskii, V. J., *Poslevoenniya Perspektivy Russkoi Promyshlennosti,* Vserossiiskii Tsentral'nyi Soiuz Potrebitel'nykh Obshchestv, Moscow, 1919.

Grishin, P. P., *Men'sheviki i Oktiabr'skaia Revoliutsiia,* Partiinoe Izdatel'stvo, Moscow, 1932.

Gronsky, P. and Astrov, N., *The War and the Russian Government,* Yale University Press, New Haven, 1929.

Groupe d'Anarchistes Russes a l'Étranger, *Response de Quelques Anarchistes Russes la Platforme,* Librairie Internationale, Paris, 1927.

Gruppy Russkikh Anarkhistov v Germanii, *Goneniia na Anarkhizm v Sovetskoi Rossii,* Berlin, 1922.

Gudvan, A. M., *Normirovka Truda Torgovo-Promyshlennykh Sluzhashikh,* (8 mi Chasovoi Rabochii Den' Dlia Prikazchikov i 6ti Chasovoi Dlia Kontorovchikov) s prilozheniem proekta zakona, Kapbasnikov, Petrograd, 1917.

Gulevich, K. and Mikhailov, E., *Profsoiuzy SSSR v Sozdanii Krasnoi Armii 1918-1920,* Profizdat, Moscow, 1939.

Gusev, *Teoriia Proletariata,* (Nauchnyi Sotsialism) Petrogradskii Sovet Rabochikh i Krasnoarmeiskikh Deputatov, Petrograd, 1919.

Hammond, Thomas, *Lenin on Trade Unions and Revolution 1893-1917,* New York, 1957.

Harper, S. N., *The New Electoral Law for the Russian Duma,* University of Chicago Press, Chicago, 1908.

Hegel, George Wilhelm, *Hegel's Philosophy of Right Translated* with Notes by T. M. Knox, Oxford, 1945.

———, George William, *The Logic of Hegel,* Translated from the Encyclopedia of the Philosophical Sciences with Prolegomena by William Wallace, Clarendon Press, Oxford, 1914.

Hegel, George, (trans. Wallace William), *Philosophy of Mind,* Oxford Press, New York, London, 1894.

Hume, David, (ed. Yalden Tomonson, D. C.), *Theory of Knowledge Containing the Enquiry Concerning Human Understanding,* the Abstract and Selected Passages From Book 1 of *A Treatise of Human Nature,* Nelson, Edinburgh, 1951.

Iakovlev, Ia, *Les 'Anarchistes-Syndicalistes' Russes Devant le Tribunal du Proletariat Mondial,* La Presse de la Internationale Communiste, Moscow, 1921.

———, "Russkii Anarkhizm v Velikoi Russkoi Revoliutsii," Iskra, New York, 1921.

Iaroslavskii, E., (Yaroslavsky), *History of Anarchism in Russia,* International Publishers, New York, 1937.

———, (ed.), *Istoriia VKP(b),* 4, Gosudarstvennoe Izdatel'stvo, Moscow, 1930.

———, *Protiv Oppozitsii, Sbornik Statei,* Gosudarstvennoe, Moscow, 1928.

Iastrzhembskii, V. Ia. *Kak Rabochie Sozdaiut Novyi Stroi Sektsiia po Metallu Soveta Narodnogo Khoziaistva Severnogo Raiona,* Sovet Narodnogo Khoziaistva Severnogo Raiona, Petrograd, 1918.

———, *Rabochie i Sozidanie Narodnogo Khozaistva v Sektsii po Metallu Soveta Narodnogo Khozaistva Severnogo Raiona s Predisloviem Tov. Molotova,* Sovet Narodnogo Khozaistva, Petrograd, 1918.

Institut Filosofii Akademii Nauk BSSR—Belorusskii Gosudarstvennyi Universitet V. I. Lenina, *O Filosofskikh Tetradiakh V. I. Lenina,* Sotsial'no-Economicheskoi Literatury, (n.p.), 1959.

Internationale Rat Der Gewerkschaften und Industrieverbande, *Die Textilarbeiter in Sowjetrussland,* Seehof, Berlin, 1920.

Jackson, T. A., Dialectics, *The Logic of Marxism and Its Critics—An Essay in Exploration,* Lawrence and Wishart, London, 1936.

Kamenev, Lev, *The Dictatorship of the Proletariat by L. Kameneff,* Marxian Educational Society, Detroit, 1920.

———, *Stat'i i Rechi, 1905-1923,* 1, 10, 12, Gosudarstvennoe, Leningrad, 1925-1927.

———, Central and Local Authorities—*A Report on Soviet Construction* Read at the VII All-Russian Congress of Soviets, All Russian Central Council of Trade Unions, Moscow, 1920.

Kant, Immanuel, *Immanuel Kant's Critique of Pure Reason* (trans. by Norman Kemp Smith), Macmillan, London, 1929.

Kaplun, S. *The Protection of Labor in Soviet Russia,* Russian Soviet Government Bureau, New York, 1920.

Karelin, A., *Chto Takoe Anarkhiia?* Vserossiiskaia Federatsiia Anarkh.—Kommunistov, Moscow, 1923.

Kazskov, A., *Pervii S"ezd Profsoiuzov, Profizdat,* (n.p.), 1933.

Kerensky, Alexander F., *The Catastrophe, Kerensky's Own Story of the Russian Revolution,* Appleton, New York, 1927.

———, *Delo Kornilova,* Zadruga, Moscow, 1918.

———, *Izdaleka: Sbornik Statei (1920-1921), Russkoe Knigoizdatel'stvo,* Paris, 1922.

———, *The Prelude to Bolshevism,* Fisher Unwin, London, 1919.

Kerzhentsev, V., *Kak Vesti Sobraniia,* Petrogradskii Sovet Rabochikh i Krasnoarmeiskih Deputatov, Petrograd, 1919.

Khaskhachikh, *Materiia i Soznanie,* Gospolitizdat, 1951.

Kissileff, A., *Die Gewerkschaftsbewegung der Bergarbeiter in Sowjet-Russland,* Frankes Verlag G. m. b. H., Leipzig, 1920.

Kleinbort, *Professionalnye Soiuzy v Rossii, Kniga,* Petrograd, 1917.

Koch, Woldemar, *Die Bolschewistischen Gewerkschaften Eine Herrschafts-soziologische Studie,* Fischer, Jena, 1932.

Kohn, Hans (ed.), *The Mind of Modern Russia, Historical and Political Thought of Russia's Great Age,* Rutgers University Press, New Brunswick, 1955.

Kollontai, A., *Novaia Moral' i Rabochii Klass,* Vserossiiskii Tsentralnyi Ispolnitel'nyi Komitet Sovetov R. K. i Kr. Deputatov, Moscow, 1918.

———, *Rabotnitsa-mat'* V. Ts. I, K. Sovetov R. S. Kr. i Kazach, Deputatov, Moscow, 1918.

———, *Rabotnitsa Za God Revoliutsii,* Kommunist, Moscow, 1918.

Kolokol'nikov, P. (K. Dmitriev), *Professional'noe Dvizhenie v Rossii, I Organizatsiia Soiuzov,* Rabochaia Biblioteka Tsentral'nago Komi-*teta* R.S.-D.R.P. (obedin), Petrograd, 1917.

———, *Professional'nye Soiuzy v Moskve,* Novyi Mir, Petersburgh, n.d., pp. 46-48.

Kon, I. S., *Filosofskii Idealizm i Krizis Burzhuaznoi Istoricheskoi Mysli,* Sotsekgiz, 1959.

Konstantinov, F. V., *Istoricheskii Materializm,* Gosudarstvennoe Izdatel'stvo Politicheskoi Literatury, Moscow, 1954.

Kor, I. (ed.), *Kak My Zhili Pri Tsare i Kak My Zhivem Teper'* Moskovskii Rabochii, 1934.

Kornilov, A., *Modern Russia History,* 2, Knopf, New York, 1917.

Kornilov, *Partiia Narodnoi Svobody (Istoricheskii Ocherk)*, Partiia Narodnoi Svobody, Petrograd, 1917.

Korol'shuk, E., *Rabochee Dvizhenie Semidesiatykh Godov—Sbornik Arkhivnykh Dokumentov c Stateii Dopolneniiami po Literature*, Moscow, 1934.

Kostomarev, Grigori, *Kommunisticheskii Subbotnik v Moskve i Moskovskoi Gubernii v 1919-1920*, Moscovskii Rabochii, Moscow, 1950.

———, (ed.), *Oktiabr' v Moskve, Materialy i Dokumenty*, Gosudarst, Sotsial'no Ekonomicheskoe Izdat., Moscow, 1932.

Koval'chuk, A. S., *Osobennosti Perekhoda Kolichestva v Kachestvo v Obshchestvennom Razvitii*, Znanie, Moscow, 1958.

Kozlovskii, V. E., *V. I. Lenin O Dialektike Protivorechii*, Znanie, 1960.

Krasnyi Internatsional Professional'nykh Soiuzov, *Krasnyi Soiuz Rabochikh i Sluzhaschikh Pishchevoi Promishlenosti v Sovetskoi Rossii (Kratkii Istoricheskii Ocherk)*, Moscow, 1921.

Kritsman, L., *Geroicheskii Period Velikoi Russkoi Revoliutsii*, Gosudarstvennoe, Izdatel'stvo, Moscow, (n.d.).

Krivitsky, M. M. (ed.), *Voprosy Truda v Rabotakh Lenina*, Moscow, 1933.

Kropotkin, Peter, *Anarchist Communism, Its Basis and Principles*, Freedom Press, London, 1913.

———, *Anarkhiia*, Petersburgh, 1919.

———, *Ethics, Origin and Development*, (trans. S. Friedland and Joseph Piroshnikov), Dial Press, New York, 1924.

———, *K Chemu i Kak Prilagat' Trud Ruchnoi i Umstvennyi, Sokrashchennoe Izlozhenie Knigi 'Polia, Fabriki i Masterskiia*, Golos Truda, Petrograd, 1919.

———, *Kommunizm i Anarkhiia*, Petersburg, 1919.

———, *Law and Authority*, International Publishing, London, 1886.

———, *Revolutionary Government*, Freedom Press, London, 1943, (first published 1890).

———, *Velikaia Revoliutsiia*, (Perevod s Frantsuzkago), Moskovskaia Federatsiia Anarkhistskikh Grupp, Moscow, 1917.

Kukushkin, Iu, Shelestov, D., *Pervye Kommunisticheskie Subbotniki*, Moskovskii Rabochii, 1959.

Kuusinen, O. V., (Chief ed.), *Osnovy Marksizma-Leninizma Uchebnoe Posobie*, Polit. Literatury, Moscow, 1959.

Larin, Iu, *Inteligentsiia i Sovety: Khoziaistvo, Burzhuaziia, Revoliutsiia,*

Gosapparat, Gosudarstvennoe Izdatel'stvo, Moscow, (n.d.).

Larin, *Trudovaia Povinnost' i Rabochii Kontrol',* Kniga, (n.p.), 1918.

Leites, Nathan, *The Operational Code of the Politburo,* McGraw Hill, New York, 1951.

———, *A Study of Bolshevism,* Free Press, Glencoe, Illinois, 1953.

Lenin, V. I., *Materialism and Empirio-Criticism, Critical Comments on a Reactionary Philosophy,* Foreign Languages Publishing House, Moscow, 1947.

———, *The Teachings of Karl Marx,* Martin Lawrence, London, 1931.

———, *Collected Works of V. I. Lenin,* International Publishers, New York, 1932.

———, *Lenin v Pervye Mesiatsy, Sovetskoi Vlasti, Sbornik Statei i Vospominanii,* Moscow, 1933.

———, *The Paris Commune,* International Publishers, New York, 1931.

———, *Selected Works,* International Publishers, New York, (n.d.).

———, *Sochineniia* (2nd ed.), 30 vols., Gosudarstvennoe Izdatel'stvo, Moscow, 1926-1932.

———, *Sochineniia* (3rd ed.), 30 vol., Partizdat Ts. K. VKP(b), Moscow, 1928-1937.

———, Sochineniia (4th ed.), 35 vols., Gosudarstvennoe Izdatel'stvo Politicheskoi Literatury, Moscow, 1941-1952.

———, *Spravochnik k II i III Izdaniiam Sochinenii V. I. Lenina,* Partizdat Ts. K. VKP(b), Moscow, 1935.

———, *The Teachings of Karl Marx,* International Publishers, New York, 1930.

——— and Stalin, Joseph, *Lenin, Stalin, 1917,* Foreign Languages Publishing House, 1938.

Lenin, V. I. and Stalin, Joseph, *The Russian Revolution by V. I. Lenin and Joseph Stalin; Writings and Speeches from the February Revolution to the October Revolution, 1917,* International Publishers, New York, 1938.

Lenin, V. I. and Trotsky, Leon, *The Proletarian Revolution in Russia by N. Lenin and Leon Trotsky* (ed. Louis Fraina), Communist Press, New York, 1918.

Leningradskii Gubprofsovet, *Leningradskiye za Desiat' Let 1917-1927, Sbornik Vospominanii,* Leningradskii Gubprofsovet, 1927.

Leningrad Universitet, *Natsionalizatsiia Promishlennosti i Drganizatsiia Sotsialisticheskogo Proizvodstva v Petrograde 1917-1920 G; Tom I,* Leningradskii Universitet, Leningrad, 1958.

Lesevich, Vladimir Viktorovich, *Chto Takoe Nauchnaia Filosofiya?* Skorokhodov, St. Petersburgh, 1891.

———, *Opyt Kriticheskago Issledovaniia Osnovonachal Positivnoi Filosofii,* Published by the Author, St. Petersburgh, 1877.

Lewis, C. I., *Mind and the World Order, Outline of a Theory of Knowledge,* Dover, New York, 1956.

Liubomirov, P. T., *Ocherki po Istorii Russkoi Promyshlennosti XVII, XVIII i Nachala XIX Vekov,* Gosudarstvennoe, Moscow, 1947.

Lozovsky, A. (Dridzo), *Aims and Tactics of the Trade Unions (Drafted by Comrade Lozovsky),* Press Bureau of the International Congress of the Red Trade and Industrial Unions, 1921.

———, *Anarkho-Sindikalizm i Kommunizm,* Krasnaia, Moscow, November 1923.

———, *The International Council of Trade and Industrial Unions,* Union Publishing Association, New York, 1920.

———, *Lenin and the Trade Union Movement,* Trade Union Education League, Chicago, 1920.

———, *Marx and the Trade Unions,* International Publishers, New York, 1942.

———, *Professional'nye Soiuzy v Sovetskoi Rossii.* Vserossiiskogo Tsentral'nogo Soveta Professional'nykh Soiuzov, Moscow, 1920.

———, *Rabochii Kontrol',* Sotsialist, Petersburgh, 1918.

———, *The Role of the Labour Unions in the Russian Revolution,* Union Publishing Association, New York, 1921 (?).

Lozovsky, A. (Dridzo), *The Trade Unions in Soviet Russia,* All-Russian Central Council of Trade Unions, Moscow, 1920.

Lunacharsky, A. *Kulturnyia Zadachi Rabochego Klassa,* Ts. V.I.K. Sovetov R.S.Kr. i Kazach, Deputatov, Moscow, 1918.

Macdonald, Margaret (ed.), *Philosophy and Analysis,* Philosophical Library, New York, 1954.

Makhno, Nestor, *Makhnovshchina i ee Vcherashnie Soiuzniki-Bol'sheviki,* Biblioteka Makhnovtsev, Paris 1928.

———, *Pod Udarami kontr-revoliutsii,* Kniga II (Aprel'Iun') Pod Redaktsiei s Predisloviem i Primechaniyami Tov. Volina, Paris, 1936.

———, *Russkaia Revoliutsiya na Ukraine,* (*Ot Marta 1917 po Aprel' 1918 God*), Biblioteka Makhnovtsev-Federatsiya Anarkho-Kommunistichekikh Grupp Severnoi Ameriki i Kanady, Paris, 1929.

Mamai, N., *Kommunisticheskaya Partiya v Bor'be za Ideinopoliticheskoe Vospitanie Mass v Pervye Gody NEPA,* n.p., Gospolitizdat, 1954.

Mamontov, Savva Ivanovich, *O Zhelezno-Dorozhnom Khoziaistve v Rossii,* Kushnerev, Moscow, 1909.

Mannheim, Karl, *Essays on the Sociology of Knowledge* (ed. Paul Kecskemeti), Oxford University Press, New York, 1953.

———, *Essays on Sociology and Social Psychology* (ed. Paul Kecskemeti), Oxford University Press, New York, 1953.

———, *Ideology and Utopia, An Introduction to the Sociology of Knowledge,* Harcourt Brace, New York, 1949.

Marinskii Komitet Partiia Sotsialistov-Revoliutsionerov, *Chego Trebuiut Sotsialisty Revoliutsionery,* Mariinsk, 1917.

Martov, Iu (Tsederbaum, Iu), *Obshchestvennye i Umstvennye Techeniia v Rossi,* Kniga, Leningrad, 1924.

———, (L), *Proletarskaia Bor'ba v Rossii* Glagolev, St. Petersburgh, 1904.

———, *Zapiski Sotsial-Demokrata,* Book 1, Grzhebina, Berlin, 1922.

———, (J), *The State and the Socialist Revolution* (trans. by Integer), International Review, New York, 1938.

Marx, Karl, *Capital* (trans. Eden and Cedar Paul), J. M. Dent, London, 1933.

———, *Economic and Philosophic Manuscripts of 1844,* Foreign Languages Publishing House, Moscow, 1961.

———, Engels, F. Lenin, V., *On the Paris Commune,* Tovarishchestvo Inostrannykh Rabochikh v SSSR, Moscow, 1932.

Masaryk, Thomas Garrigue, *The Spirit of Russia, Studies in History, Literature and Philosophy* (trans. from German by Eden and Cedar Paul), 1, 2, Allen and Unwin, London, 1919.

Mason, E. S., *The Paris Commune,* Macmillan, New York, 1930.

Matlock, Jack F., *An Index to the Collected Works of J. V. Stalin,* External Research Staff, Office of Intelligence Research, Department of State, Washington, 1955.

Mavor, James, *An Economic History of Russia,* Vols. 1 and 2, Dutton, New York, 1935.

———, *The Russian Revolution,* Allen and Unwin, London, 1928.

Maximov, G. P., *Sovety Rabochikh, Soldatskikh i Krestianskikh Deputatov i Nashe k Nim Otnoshenie,* Federatsiia Soiuzov Russkikh Rabochikh Soed. Shtatov i Kanady, 1919, First appeared on 22 December 1917 in No. 22 *Golos Truda* issued in Petrograd, New York.

———, *Za Chto i Kak Bolsheviki Izgnali Anarkhistov iz Rossii? Anarkho-Kommun Gruppy,* (n.p.), 1922.

Mel'gunov, S. P., *Zolotoi Nemetskii Kliuch Bol'shevikov,* Dom Knigi, Paris, 1940.

Menitskii, I., *Rabochee Dvizhenie i Sotsial-Demokraticheskoe Podpol'e Moskvy v Voiennye Gody (1917-1919)*, Moskovskii Rabochii, 1923.

Meyer, Alfred G., *Marxism, The Unity of Theory and Practice,* Harvard University Press, Cambridge, 1954.

Miliutin, V. P., *Die Organisation der Volkswirtschaft in Sowjet-Russland,* Hoym Nachf. L. Cahnbley, Hamburg, 1921.

———, *The Economic Organization of Soviet Russia; A Brief Sketch of the Organization and the Present Situation of Industry in Russia,* Communist Party of Great Britain, London, 1920.

———, *Istoriia Ekonomicheskogo Razvitia SSSR 1917-1927,* Gosudarstvennoe, Moscow, 1927.

———, *Sovremennoe Ekonomicheskoe Razvitie Rossii i Diktatura Proletariata (1914-1918)*, VTs. I. Sovetov R.S.Kp.iK Deputatov, Moscow, 1918.

Milonov, Iu K. (ed.), *Istoriia i Praktika Rossiiskogo Professional'nogo Dvizhenia, Khrestomatiia Dlia Profkruzhkov i Profkursov,* MGSPS "Trud i Kniga," Moscow, 1925.

Mindlin, Z., *Putevoditel' po Rabochim Organizatsiam,* Moscow, 1919.

Mitel'man, M., *Bor'ba Partii Bol'shevikov Za Uprochnenie Sovetskoi Vlasti (1917-1918)*, Politizdat Ts.K.V.K.P.(b) 1940.

Molotov, V. M. (ed.), *Pervomaiskii Sbornik,* Nizhegorodskii Gubernskii Komitet Organizatsii Truda, 1920.

———, *Kak Rabochie Stroiat Sotsialisticheskoe Khoiziaistvo,* Sovet Narodnogo Khoziaistva Severnogo Raiona, Petrograd, 1918.

Monnerot, Jules, *Sociology and Psychology of Communism* (trans. by Jane Degras and Richard Rees), Beacon Press, Boston, 1953.

Moore, Barrington, *Soviet Politics the Dilemma of Power,* Harvard University Press, Cambridge, 1950.

Moroz, K. V., *Zakon Edinstva i Bor'by Protivopolozhnostei* Znanie, n.p., 1957.

Moskovskii Komitet RKP(b), Gubernskoe Biuro Komissii po istorii Oktiabr'skoi Revoliutsii i RKP (Isparta), *Ot Fevralia k Oktiabriu (v Moskve) Sbornik Statei, Vospominanii i Dokumentov,* Novaia Moscow, 1923.

Moskovskii Sovet R. K. i Kr. D., *Krasnaia Moskva 1917-1920,* Moscow, 1920.

Moskovskii Sovet Rabochikh, Krestianskikh i Krasnoarmeiskikh Deputatov, *Kratkii Obzor Deiatel'nosti Moskovskogo Soveta,* Gosudarstvennoe Izdatel'stvo, n.d.

Moskovskii Sovet Rabochikh Soldatskikh Deputatov Otdel Truda, *Kak*

Organizovat' Zavodskii (Fabrichnyi) Rabochii Komitet, Mamontov, Moscow, 1917.

Moskovskoe Biuro Isparta Komissiia po Istorii Oktiabr'skoi Revoliutsii i R.K.P., *Nakanune Revoliutsii, Sbornik Statei, Zametok i Vospominanii pod. red. Ovsiannikova, N.* Moskovskoe Otdelenie Gosudarstvennoe Izdatel'stvo, Moscow, 1922.

Murashov, S., *Kak Rabochie i Krest'iane Pod Rukovodstvom Bol'shevistskoi Partii Ustanovili Sovetskuiu Vlast',* Molodaia Gvardia, 1947.

Mutovkin, N., *'Soldatskaya Pravda' v Oktyabr'skoi Revoliutsii,* Gospolizdat, Moscow, 1957.

Nechkina, M. V., *Obshchestvo Soedinennykh Slavian,* Gosudarstvennoe, Moscow, 1927.

Nesteianov, A. N., *Lenin i Nauka,* Asademiia Nauk SSSR, Moscow, 1960.

Nevskii, V. I., *Prezhde i Teper' (ot Mraka k Sovetu),* Gosudarstvennoe Izdatel'stvo, Moscow, 1919.

Nikulikhin, Ia, *Novye Printsipy Professional'nogo Dvizheniia,* Petersburgh, 1918.

Nomad, Max, *Apostles of Revolution,* Little Brown, Boston, 1939.

Novomirskii, D., *Iz Programma Sindikal'nago Anarkhizma,* Golos Truda, Odessa, 1907.

———, *Manifest Anarkhistov-Kommunistov, Svobodnaya Kommuna,* (n.d.).

Oberoucheff, S. M., *Soviets vs. Democracy,* Russian Information Bureau, New York, 1919.

———, *Sovety i Sovetskaia Vlast' v Rossii,* Narodpravstvo, New York, 1919.

Ogden, C. K. and Richards, I. A.,*The Meaning of Meaning; A Study of the Influence of Language Upon Thought and of the Science of Symbolism by C. K. Ogden and I. A. Richards with Supplementary Essays by B. Malinowski and F. G. Crookshank,* Harcourt Brace, New York, 1938.

Okulov, A. F., *Bor'ba V. I. Lenina Protiv Filosofii Reformizma i Revizionizma,* Sotsial'no-Ekonomicheskoi Literatury, Moscow, 1959.

Oppenheim, K. A., *Rossiia v Dorozhnom Otnoshenii,* Vyshii Sovet Narodnago Khoziaistva, Moscow, 1920.

Ordzhonikidze, G. K., *Izbrannye Stat'i i Rechi 1911-1937,* Gosudarstvennoe Izdatel'stvo Politicheskoi Literatury, Moscow, 1939.

Osinskii, N., (Obolenskii), *Stroitel'stvo Sotsializma, Obshchiia Zadachi, Organizatsiia Proizvodstva,* Kommunist, Moscow, 1918.

Pankratova, A. M., *Fabzavkomy i Profsoiuzy v Revoliutsii 1917 Goda,* Gosudarstvennoe, Moscow, 1927.

Pankratova, *Fabzavkomy Rossii v Borbe Za Sotsialisticheskuiu Fabriku,* Krasnaya Nov', Moscow, 1923.

———, *Politicheskaia Bor'ba v Rossiiskom Profdvizhenii 1917-1918,* Leningradskii Profsovet, Leningrad, 1917.

Pares, Bernard, *The Fall of the Russian Monarchy; A Study of Evidence,* Knopf, New York, 1939.

Partiia Narodnoi Svobody, *Rezoliutsiia VIII Delegatskago S"ezda Partii Narodnoi Svobody 9-12 Maia 1917 v Petrograde,* Svoboda, 1917.

Partinnie Organizatsii Professional'nykh Souizov, *Spravochnik Tsentral'nykh i Mestnykh Uchrendenii RSFSR,* Moscow, 1920.

Pavliuchenko, *Profsoiuzy i Krasnaia Armiia,* Profizdat, Moscow, 1933.

Pervyi Tsentral'nyi Sotsiotekhnikum Vremenyii Tekhnikum Agitatsii i Propagandy, *Rechi Anarkhista,* n.p., 1919.

Peshekonov, A. V., *Krestiane i Rabochie v Ikh Vzaimnykh Otnosheniakh,* Russkoe Bogatstvo, St. Petersburgh, 1906.

Pestrzeckij, D., *Rabochii Vopros v Sovetskoi Rossii,* Berlin, 1922.

Petrovich, D., *Proletarii Vsekh Stran Soediniaites',* Soiuz Kommun. Severnoi Oblasti, Petrograd, 1919.

Petrunkevitch, A., Harper, S. N., Golder, F. A., *The Russian Revolution,* Harvard University Press, Cambridge, 1918.

Plamenatz, John, *German Marxism and Russian Communism,* Longmans Green, New York, 1954.

Plekhanov, G., *The Development of the Marxist View of History,* Foreign Languages Publishing House, Moscow, 1959.

———, *Le Materialisme Militant,* (trans. S. Engelson), Les Revues, Paris, 1930.

———, *Russkii Rabochii v Revoliutsionnom Dvizhenii (po Lichnom Vospominaniiam'),* Moskovski Sovet R.I.K.D., Moscow, 1919.

———, *Sotsializm i Proletarskaia Bor'ba Esche Raz Sotsializm i Politicheskaia Bor'ba,* Petrogradskii Sovet Rabochikh i Krasnoaremiskikh Deputatov, 1918.

Pogolyanin, *Sovremennyi Anarkhizm,* Molodaya Rossiya, Moscow, 1906.

Pokrovskii, M. N., *Oktiabr'skaia Revoliutsiia, Sbornik Statei, 1917-1927,* Kommunisticheskaia Akademiia, Moscow, 1929.

Polianskii, N. N., *Narodnicheskii Sotsializm,* Zadruga, Moscow, 1918.

Popper, Karl R., *The Open Society and Its Enemies,* Princeton University Press, Princeton, 1950.

———, *The Poverty of Historicism,* Routledge and Kegan Paul, London, 1960.

Prawdin, Michael, *The Unmentionable Nechaev,* George Allen and Unwin, London, 1961.

Pribcevic, Branko, *The Shop Stewards Movement and Workers' Control 1910-1922,* Oxford, 1959.

Price, H. H. *Perception,* Methuen, London, 1961.

Price, M. Philips, *My Reminiscences of the Russian Revolution,* George Allen and Unwin, 1921.

———, *The Origin and Growth of the Russian Soviets,* People's Information Bureau, London, 1919.

———, *The Soviet, The Terror and the Intervention,* Socialist Publication Society, Brooklyn, n.d.

Rabinovich, A. I., *Trud i Byt Rabochego,* V.S.N.Kh., Moscow, 1923.

Ransome, Arthur, *The Crisis in Russia* Huebsch, New York, 1921.

Rashin, A. G., *Formirovanie Promyshlennogo Proletariata v Rossii,* Gosudarstvennoe, Moscow, 1940.

———, *Formirovanie Rabochego Klassa Rossii, Istorikoekonomicheskie Ocherki,* Akad. Nauk SSSR, Institut Istorii, Moscow, 1958.

Razumovich, N. N., *Organizatsionno-pravovye Formy Sotsialisticheskogo Obobshchestvleniya Promishlennosti v SSSR 1917-1920 g.,* Akad. Nauk SSSR, Moscow, 1959.

Reed, John, *Ten Days That Shook the World,* Modern Library, New York, 1935.

Reswick, William, *I Dreamt Revolution,* H. Regnery, Chicago, 1952.

Riazanov, D. (Goldendach, D.), *Zadachi Profsoiuzov do i v Epochu Diktatury Proletariata,* Gosudarstvennoe, Moscow, 1921.

Rogdaev, N. (N. I. Muzul'), *Mezhdunarodnii Anarkhicheskii Kongres v Amsterdame 1907,* Pazgrad, 1909.

Romanov, F. A., *Rabochee i Professional'noe Dvizhenie v Gody Pervoi Mirovoi Voiny i Vtoroi Russkoi Revoliutsii,* V.Ts.S.P.S. Profizdat, Moscow, 1949.

Rosenfeld, R. S., *Promyshlenaia Politika SSSR,* Moscow, 1926.

Rosmer, Alfred, *Le Mouvement Ouvrier Pendant la Guerre, De L'union Sacree a Zimmerwald,* Travail, Paris, 1936.

———, *Moscou Sous Lenine: Les Origines du Communisme,* P. Horay, Paris, 1953.

Ross, Edward Alsworth, *The Russian Bolshevik Revolution,* Century, New York, 1921.

Rozenblum, D. S., *O Professional'nykh Soiuzakh,* Partiia Sotsialistov-Revoliutsionerov, Petrograd, 1917.

Rudin, I., *Primiritel'nyia Kamery i Treteiskii Sud,* Moskovskii Sovet Rabochikh Deputatov, Moscow, 1917.

Russian Information Bureau, *The Case of Russian Labor Against Bolshevism,* Facts and Documents, ew York, n.d.

Russia-Tsentrarkhiv, *Rabochee Dvizhenie v 1917 Godu,* Moscow, 1920.

Sarab'ianov, V. N., *Revoliutsiia i Professionalnye Soiuzy,* No. 9, Kooperativnyi Mir, Moscow, 1917.

Savinkov, B. V., *Bor'ba s Bol'shevikami,* Izdanie Russkago Politicheskago Komiteta, 1920.

———, *Memoirs of a Terrorist* (trans. by Joseph Shaplen), A. and C. Boni, New York, 1931.

Schapiro, Leonard, *The Communist Party of the Soviet Union,* Random House, New York, 1960.

———, *The Origin of the Communist Autocracy, Political Opposition in the Soviet State: First Phase 1917-1922,* Harvard University Press, Cambridge, 1955.

Schwarz, Solomon, *Heads of Russian Factories,* Research Project of the Graduate Faculty of Political and Social Science, New York, 1942.

———, *Lenine et le Movement Syndical,* Nouveau Promehtee, Paris, 1935.

———, *Ruckblick und Ausblick Uber Die Russische Gewerkschaftsbewegung,* Internationaler Gewerkschaftsbund, Amsterdam, 1923.

———, *Trade Unions in the USSR,* New York, 1953.

———, *Labor in the Soviet Union,* Praeger, New York, 1952.

———, Bienstock, G. and Yugow, A., *Management in Russian Industry and Agriculture* (ed. by Arthur Reiler and Jacob Marshak), Oxford, 1944.

Somonov-Bulkin, *Soiuzov Metallistov i Department Politsii,* Leningradskii Raikomitet VsRM, Leningrad, 1926.

Seton-Watson, Hugh, *The Decline of Imperial Russia 1855-1914,* Praeger, New York, 1952.

Shatilova, T., *Ocherk Istorii Leningradskogo Soiuza Khimikov* (*1905-1918g*), Leningradskii Gubotdel Soiuza Khimikov, 1927.

Shatunovskii, Ia, *Vosstanovlenie Puti Soobshcheniia i Puti Revoliutsii,* S Predisloviem L. Trotsky, N.K.P.S., Moscow, 1920.

Shchap, Z., *Moskovskie Metallisty v Professional'nom Dvizhenii, Ocherki po Istorii Moskovskogo Siouza Metallistov,* Izdanie Moskovskogo Raionnogo Komiteta Vsesoiuznogo Soiuza Rabochikh Metallistov, 1926.

Shcheglov, A. V., *Bor'ba Lenina Protiv Bogdanovskoi Revizii Marksizma,* Gosudarstvennoe Sotsial'no Ekonomicheskoe Izdatel'stvo, Moscow, 1937.

Shliapnikov, *Kanun Semnadtsatogo Goda,* Gosudarstvennoe Izdatel'stvo, Moscow, 1920.

———. *Les Syndicats Russes,* Bibliotehque du Travil, Paris, 1921.

———, *Semnadtsatyi God,* Gosudarstvennoe Izdatel'stvo, Moscow, 1923.

Shpovalon, A. I., *Po Doroge K Markhsizmu, Vospominaniia Rabochego Revoliutsionera,* Gosudarstvennoe Izdatel'stvo, 1922.

Shub, David, *Lenin, A Biography,* Doubleday New York, 1951.

Silant'yev, *Rabochii Kontrol'-Proiavlenie Tvorchestva Narodnykh Mass v Bor'be za Vlast' Sovetov (1917-1918),* Znanie, Moscow, 1954.

Smilga, N., *Na Povorote. Zametki k Xmu S"ezdy Partii, Tol'ko Dlia Chlenov Partii,* Gosudarstvenoe Izdatel'stvo, 1921.

Soiuz Sots. Rev. Maksimalistov, *Zadachi Maksimalizma (Materialy k Postroeniiu Programmy),* Vypusk II, Maksimalist, Moscow, 1918.

Sokolov, B., *Bol'sheviki o Bol'shevikakh,* Franko-Slavianskoe, Paris, 1919.

Sorokin, Pitrim, *Leaves From a Russian Diary,* Dutton, New York, 1924.

Souvarine, Boris, *Stalin, A Critical Survey of Bolshevism,* Longmans Green, New York, 1939.

Spirkin, A., *Proiskhozhdenie Soznaniia,* Akademiia Nauk SSSR Politliteratury, Moscow, 1960.

Stalin, Joseph, *Anarkhizm ili Sotsializm?* Gospolizdat, Leningrad, 1951.

———, Dialectical and Historical Materialism, International Publishers, New York, 1940.

———, *God Velikogo Pereloma: K XII Godovshchine Oktiabria,* Ogiz, Leningrad, 1947.

———, *Foundations of Leninism,* International Publishers, n.p., 1934.

———, et al, *Lenin in Action; the Early Days of the Soviet Power; Personal Reminiscences of Lenin in the Soviet Revolution of October 1917 by J. Stalin and Others,* M. Lawrence, London, 1934.

———, *Mastering Bolshevism,* Workers Library, New York, 1938.

———, *O Lenine i Leninisme,* Gosudarstvennoe Izdatel'stvo, Moscow, 1924.

———, *The October Revolution, A Collection of Articles and Speeches,* International Publishers, New York, 1934.

———, *Problems of Leninism,* Foreign Languages Publishing House, Moscow, 1940.

———, *Sochineniia,* Gosudarstvennoe Izdatel'stvo Politicheskoi Literatury, Moscow, 1946-1951.

———, *The Road to October,* International Publishers, New York, 1937.

———, *Voprosy Leninisma,* Gospolitizdat, Moscow, 1952.

Stanislav, (A. Vol'skii), *Teoriia i Praktika Anarkhizma,* Gosudarstvennoe Izdatel'stvo, 1919.

Steinberg, I. N., *In the Workshop of the Revolution, Rinehart,* New York, 1953.

Steinberg, I. Z., *Ot Fevralia po Oktiabr' 1917 G,* Skify, Berlin, 191(?).

Steklov, Iu. *Mikhail Aleksandrovich Bakunin Ego Zhizn' i Deiatel'nost',* 3 Gosudarstvennoe, Moscow, 1927.

Sternberg, Fritz, *The End of Revolution, Soviet Russia from Revolution to Reaction,* Day, New York, 1953.

Strumilin, S. G., *Problemy Ekonomiki Truda Ocherki i Etiudy,* Voprosy Truda, Moscow, 1925.

Struve (ed.), Zaitsev, Dolinsky, and Demosthenov, *Food Supply in Russia During the World War,* Yale University Press, New Haven, 1930.

Sukhanov, N., *The Russian Revolution, 1917, A Personal Record* (ed., abridged and trans. by Joel Carmichael from *Zapiski o Revoliutsii*), Oxford University Press, New York, 1955.

———, *Zapiski o Revoliutsii,* Vols. 1-7, Grzhebina, Berlin, 1922-1923.

Sverdlov, Ia M., *Izbrannye Stat'i i Rechi 1917-1919,* Gosudarstvennoe Izdatel'stvo Polit. Literatury, Moscow, 1939.

Sviatlovskii, V. V., *Istoriia Professional'nogo Dvizheniia v Rossii ot Vozniknovennia Rabochego Klassa do Kontsa 1917 Goda,* Izdanie Leningradskogo Gubernskogo Soveta Professinal'nykh Soiuzov, 1924.

Taylor, Frederick W., *The Principles of Scientific Management,* Harper and Brothers, New York, 1929.

———, *Two Papers on Scientific Management, A Piece Rate System and Notes on Belting,* Routledge & Sons, London, 1919.

Tomskii, M. P., *Izbrannye Stat'i i Rechi 1917-1927,* VTsSPS, 1928.

———, *Ocherki Professional'nogo Dvizhenia v Rossii,* VTsSPS, Moscow, 1920.

———, *Printsipy Organizatsionnogo Stroitel'stva Professional'nykh Soiuzov,* VTsSPS, Moscow, 1919.

———, *Profdvizhenie SSSR za Desiat' Let Diktatury Proletariata; Doklad na Plenume Moskovskogo Gubernskogo Soveta Professional'nykh Soiuzov Sovmestno c Predisloviem Fabzavkomov i Mestkomov 5 Noiabria 1927,* VTsSPS, Moscow, 1927.

Towster, Julian, *Political Power in the USSR, 1917-1947* Oxford, New York, 1948.

Trotsky, Leon, *Chto Zhe Dal'she? (Itogi i Perspektivy)*, Rossiskaia Sotsial'-Demokraticheskaia Rabochaia Partia, 1917.

———, *The Deciding Night of the Russian Revolution,* Socialist Labour Party of Australia, Sydney, 1937.

Trotsky, *The Defence of Terrorism* (*Terrorism and Communism*), A Reply to Karl Kautsky by L. Trotsky with a Preface by H. N. Brailsford, Labour Publishing and George Allen and Unwin, London, 1921.

———, *From October to Brest-Litovsk,* Authorized translation from the Russian, Socialist Publication Society, New York, 1919.

———, *Gody Velikago Pereloma,* Kommunist, Moscow, 1919.

———, *The History of the Russian Revolution* (trans. Max Eastman), 3 vols. in one, Simon and Schuster, New York, 1932.

———, *Itogi i Perspektivy-Dvizhushchie Sily Revoliutsii,* Sovetskii Mir, Moscow, 1919.

———, *K Istorii Oktabr'skoi Revoliutsii,* Russkaia Sotsialistcheskaia Federatsiia, New York, 192(?).

———, *The Lessons of October* 1917 (trans. Susan Lawrence and I. Olshan), Labour Publishing Co., London, 1925.

———, *My Life: An Attempt at an Autobiography,* Scribners, New York, 1930.

———, *Novyi Etap. Mirovoe Polozhenie i Nashi Zadachi,* Gosudarstvennoe Izdatel'stvo, Moscow, 1920.

———, *The Permanent Revolution,* Pioneer Publishers, New York, 1931.

———, *Problems of Life* (trans. Z. Vengorova), Methuen, London, 1924.

———, *Sochinenniia,* 2, 3, 9, 12, 15, 20 and 21, Gosudarstvennoe Izdatel'stvo, Moscow, 1925-1927.

———, *1917 Uroki Oktiabria, Kamanev i Stalin, Leninism ili Trotskizm otvet Trotskomu,* Berlinskoe Knigoizdatel'stvo, 192(4?).

———, and Zinoviev, G., *Petrograd 1917-1919,* Internationale Communiste, Petrograd, 1920.

———, *The Paris Commune,* Lanka Samasamja, Colombo, 1955.

Tsverkezov, V., *Predtechi Internationala, Doktrina Marksizma,* Golos Truda, Moscow, 1919.

Tsyperovich, G. V., *Chemu Uchit Opyt Petrogradskii Soiuz Rabochikh Shveinoi Promyshlennosti i Ego Uchastie v Proizvodstve,* Gosudarstvennoe Izdatel'stvo, Petersburgh, 1921.

———, *Zadachi Professional'nago Dvizheniia,* Petrograd,1918.

Tucker, Robert C., *Philosophy and Myth in Karl Marx,* Cambridge, 1961.

Tugan-Baranovskii, M. I., *Russkaia Fabrika v Proshlom i Nastoiaschem: Istoricheskoe Razvitie Russkoi Fabriki v XIX Veke,* Nasha Zhizn', St. Petersburgh, 1907.

Tugarinov, V. P., *Marksistkaia Dialektika Kak Teoriia Poznaniia i Logika,* Znanie, Leningrad, 1952.

Turin, Sergiei, *From Peter the Great to Lenin, a History of the Russian Labour Movement with Special Reference to Trade Unionism,* S. P. King, London, 1935.

Tyrkova-Williams, Ariadna, *From Liberty to Brest-Litovsk, The First Year of the Russian Revolution,* Macmillan, London, 1919.

Ullrich, Richard, *Die Stellung des Monarchen im Russischen Staatsrecht,* Druck von W. Drugulin, Leipzig, 1910.

Uspenskii, Iu I., *Budushchee Zheleznodorozhnogo Stroitel'stva Ego Razmery i Poriadok Osushchestvleniia, Doklad Chitannyi v Sobranii Inzhenerov Putei Sodbshcheniia 15 May 1915,* Ministerstva Putei Soobshcheniia, Petrograd, 1916.

Ustinov, G., *Intelligentsiia i Oktiabr'skii Perevorot,* V.Ts.I.K. Sovetov R.S.K. i Kazach. Deputatov, Moscow, 1918.

Vardin, Il, *Revoliutsiia i Menshevizm,* Gosudarstvennoe, Moscow, 1925.

Vartanian, G. M., *Razvitie V. I. Leninym Marksistkoi Teorii Otrazheniia,* Gosudarstvennoe Izdatel'stvo Armenii, Erevan, 1960.

Vatin, M., *Ne Politsiia a Vsenarodnaia Militsiia,* Rossiiskaia Sotsial-Demokratcheskaia Rabochiia Partiia, Petrograd, 1917.

Vinokurov, A., *Sotsial'noe Obespechenie v Sovetskoi Rossii (Sbornik Statei k S"ezdu Sovetov pod Redaktsiei i s Predisloviem Narodnogo Komissara Sotsial'nogo Obespecheniia A. Vinokurova),* Gosizdat, Moscow, 1919.

Vladimorova, Vera, *Revoliutsiia 1917 Goda (Khronika Sobytii),* 3 (June-July), 4 (August-September), Gosudarstvennoe, Moscow, 1923-1924.

Vladimirskii, M., *Organizatsiia Sovetskoi Vlasti na Mestakh,* Gosudarstvennoe Izdatel'stvo, Moscow, 1919.

Voline, (V. M. Eichenbaum), *La Revolution Inconnue (1917-1921), Documentation Inedite Sur la Revolution Russe,* Les Amis de Voline, Paris, 1947.

———, (Volin), *The Unknown Revolution (Kronstadt 1921, Ukraine 1918-1921* (trans. Holly Cantine), Freedom Press, London, 1955. A translation of the above.

Vucinich, Alexander, *Soviet Economic Institutions, The Social Structure of Production Units,* Hoover Institution Studies, Stanford, 1952.

Webb, Sidney and Beatrice, *Soviet Communism: A New Civilization?* 1 and 2, Scribners, New York, 1938.

Weber, Max, *The Protestant Ethic and the Spirit of Capitalism* (trans. Talcott Parsons), Allen and Unwin, London, 1930.

Weidle, Wladimer, *Russia: Absent and Present* (trans. by A. Gordon Smith), Hollis and Carter, London, 1952.

Weter, Gustave, *Dialectical Materialism, A Historical and Systematic Survey of Philosophy in the Soviet Union* (trans. Peter Heath), Praeger, New York, 1960.

Wild, John, *Plato's Modern Enemies and the Theory of Natural Law,* University of Chicago Press, Chicago, 1953.

Williams, Albert Rhys, *Through the Russian Revolution,* Boni and Liveright, New York, 1921.

Witt-Hansen, *Historical Materialism:The Method, The Theories, Exposition, and Critique, Book 1, The Method,* Munksgaard, Copenhagen, 1960.

Wittgenstein, Ludwig, *Philosophical Investigations,* Macmillan, New York, 1959.

Wolfe, Bertram, *Three Who Made a Revolution,* Dial Press, New York, 1948.

Yugoff, A., *Economic Trends in Soviet Russia* (trans. Eden and Cedar Paul), Richard R. Smith, New York, 1930.

Zagorsky, S., *La Republique des Soviets,* Payot, Paris, 1921.

———, *L'Evolution Actuelle du Bolchevisme Russe,* Povolozky, Paris, 1921.

Zagorsky, S., *Rabochii Vopros v Sovetskoi Rossii,* Biblioteka Izd-a Svbodnaia Rossia, n.p., 1925.

———, *State Control of Industry in Russia During the War,* Yale, University Press, New Haven, 1928.

Zenkovich, V. A., *Sotsial'noe Obespechenie i Sudokhodnye Rabochie i Sluzhashchie,* Narodnyi Komissariat Truda, Moscow, 1918.

Zenkovsky, V. V., *A History of Russian Philosophy* (trans. by George L. Kline), 1 and 2, Routledge and Kegan Paul, London, 1953.

Zinoviev, Grigorii, *God Revoliutsii, Fevral'* 1917-*Mart* 1918, Gosudarstvennoe Izdatel'stvo, Leningrad, 1925.

———, (preface), *La Commune de Paris, Actes et Documents, Episodes de la Semaine Sanglante,* Editions de l'Internationale Communiste, 44, Petrograd, 1920.

———, *The Communist Party and Industrial Unionism,* The Workers' Socialist Federation, London, (n.d.-after 1919).

———, *Kontr-Revoliutsiia i Zadachi Rabochikh, June 1918,* Moscow.

———, *O 8-mi-Chasom Rabochem Dne,* Priboi, Petrograd, 1917. (This was written before 1917 and republished in 1917.)

———, *O Roli Professional'nykh Soiuzov,* Gosudarstvennoe Izdatel'stvo, Petersburgh, 1921.

———, (ed.), *Partiia i Soiuzy, K Diskussii o Roli i Zadachakh Profsoiuzov, Sbornik Statei i Materialov,* Gosudarstvennoe, Petersburgh, 1921.

Zinoviev, *Protiv Techeniia—Sbornik Statei iz Sotsial-Demokrata,* Kommunist, Petrograd, 1918.

———, *Rabochaiia Partiia i Professional'nye Soiuzy: O Neitralisme Professional'nogo Dvizhenia,* Petrogradskogo Soveta Rabochikh i Krasnoarmeiskikh Deputatov, Petrograd, 1918.

———, *Rabochaia Partiia i Professional'nye Soiuzy* (*o "Tsentralisme" Professionalnogo Dvizheniia*), Petrogradskago Soveta Rabochikh i Krasnoarmeiskikh Deputatov, Petrograd, 1918.

——— and Lenin, N., *Sotsializm i Voina* (*Otnoshenie R.S.-D.R.P. k Voine*), Sotsialdemokrat, Geneva, 1915.

Zlodeev, N. I., *Krasnaya Gvardiya,* Voennoe Izdatel'stvo Ministerstva Oborony Soiuza SSR, Moscow, 1957.

Zmeul, A., *Ot Fevralia k Oktiabriu. Profsoiuzy i Fabzavkomy v 1917 Godu,* Profizdat, 1934.

SELECTED ARTICLES

Arskii, R., "Itogi S"ezda Sovnarkhozov," *Narodnoe Khoziaistvo,* Nos. 1-2, 1919, pp. 10-15.

———, "Povyshenie Proizvoditel'nosti Truda i Sdel'naia Plata," *Narodnoe Khoziaistvo,* No. 3, 1919, pp. 18-22.

———, "Professional'nye Soiuzy i Zavodskie Komitety," *Vestnik Narodnago Komissariata Truda,* Nos. 2-3, February-March 1918.

———, "Rabochii Kontrol' v Natsionalizovannykh Predpriatiiakh," *Narodnoe Khoziaistvo,* Nos. 1-2, January 1919, pp. 23-25.

Ascher, Abraham, "The Kornilov Affair," *Russian Review* Vol. 12, No. 4, pp. 235-252.

Avrich, P.H., "The Bolshevik Revolution and Workers Control in Russian Industry," *Slavic Review* Vol. 22, No. 1, March 1963, pp. 47-63.

———, "Russian Factory Committees in 1917," *Jahrbuecher Fuer Geschichte Osteuropas,* Vol. II, No. 2, June 1963, pp. 161-182.

Bazhanov, "Organizatsiia Upravleniia Promyshlennost'iu," *Narodnoe Khoziaistvo,* Nos. 9-10, September-October 1919, pp. 11-15 and *Narodnoe Khoziaistvo,* Nos. 11-12, November-December 1919, pp. 3-7.

Bronskii, "Iz Deiatel'nosti VSNKh i Ego Otdelov," *Narodnoe Khoziaistvo,* No. 1, March 1918, pp. 9-11.

Chubar', "Rol' Tsentral'novo Soveta Fabrichno-Zavodskikh Komitetov v Organizatsii Vyshego Soveta Narodnogo Khoziaistva," *Narodnoe Khosiaistvo,* No. 11, November 1918, pp.d 7-9.

Dicks, Henry V., "Observations on Contemporary Russian Behaviour,"

Human Relations, Studies Toward the Integration of the Social Sciences, pp. 111-176.
"Doklad i Preniia po Voprosu o Leninskikh Zamechaniiakh na Knigu Bukharina 'Ekonomika Perekhodnogo Perioda'," *Proletarskaiia Revoliutsiia,* No. 12 (95), 1929, pp. 176-187.
Glebov, "Otdel Normirovaniia Zarabotnoi Platy," *Vestnik Narodnago Komissariata Truda,* No. 2, February 1918.
———, "Rabochii Kontrol'," *Professional'nyi Vestnik,* No. 1 (27), 20 January 1919.
Gorki, Maxim, "January 22, 1905 and January 18, 1918," from *Novaia Zhizn',* No. 6 January 23, 1918, p. 3, translated by Bunyan and Fisher, *Bolshevik Revolution,* pp. 387-388.
Greiner, J.E. "The Russian Railway Situation and Some Personal Observations," reprinted from the *Monthly Journal of the Engineers Club* of Baltimore, Vol. 7, No. 7,January 1918.
Kaktyn, A., "Osnovnoi Nedostakok Nashei Sistemy Upravleniia Promyshlennost'iu," *Narodnoe Khoziaistvo,* No. 4, 1919, pp. 16-19.
Kritsman, L., "Ob Ocherednoi Zadache Proletarskoi Revoliutsii v. Rossii," *Narodnoe Khoziaistvo,* No. 5, July 1918, pp. 1-4.
Larin, Iu., "U Kolybeli," *Narodnoe Khoziaistvo,* No. 11, November 1918, pp. 16-23.
Lozovsky, *Professional'nyi Vestnik,* No. 8, 20 December 1917.
———, "Rabochii Kontrol'," *Professional'nyi Vestnik,* Nos. 9-10, 5 January 1918.
Macdonald, Margaret, "Things and Processes," *Philosophy and Analysis,* Philosophical Library, New York, 1954.
Miliutin, V., "Ekonomicheskaia Programma Kommunistov," *Narodnoe Khoziaistvo,* No. 4, 1919, pp. 1-5.
———, "K Voprosu o Natsionalizatsii Promyshlennosti," *Narodnoe Khoziaistvo,* No. 5, July 1918, pp. 5-7.
Osinski, "Iz Pervykh Dnei Vyshego Soveta Narodnago Khoziaistva," *Narodnoe Khoziaistvo,* November 1918, No. 11.
———, "Predposylki Sotsialisticheskoi Revoliutsii," *Narodnoe Khoziaistvo,* Nos. 6-7, August 1918, pp. 1-7.
Paul, G. A., "Lenin's Theory of Perception" in Margaret Mcdonald's *Philosophy and Analysis,* Philosophical Library, New York, 1954.
Schmidt, V., "Profesesional'nye Soiuzy i Komissariat Truda," *Professional'nyi Vestnik,* No. 1 (27), 20 January 1919.
———, "Professional'nye Soiuzy i Vysshii Sovet Narodnogo Khozaistva," *Narodnoe Khoziaistvo,* No. 11, November 1918, pp. 9-11.
Schmidt, V., "O Vzaimnootnosheniakh Narodnago Komissariata Truda s

Vserossiiskim Tsentral'nym Sovetom Professional'nykh Soiuzov," *Vestnik Narodnago Komissariata Truda,* No. 2, February 1918.

Serge, Victor, "The Danger Was Within. I War Communism," *Politics, March* 1945, pp. 74-78.

Strakhovsky, L.I., "Was there a Kornilov Rebellion—A Re-Appraisal of the Evidence," *The Slavonic and East European Review* Vol. 33, No. 8, pp. 372-395.

Tseretelli, Irakli, "Reminiscences of the February Revolution," Parts 1, 2, 3, and 4. *The Russian Review,* Vol. 14, No. 2, April 1955; Vol. 14, No. 3, July 1955; Vol. 14, No. 4, October 1955; Vol 15, No. 1, January 1956.

Ward, B., "Wild Socialism in Russia: The Origins," *California Slavic Studies,* Vol. III, 1964, pp. 127-148.

PERIODICALS

The American Slavic and East European Review.

Human Relations, Studies Toward the Integration of the Social Sciences.

Krasny Arkhiv.

Politics.

Proletarskaia Revoliutsiia, 1921-.

The Russian Review.

The Slavic Review.

The Slavonic and East European Review.

Voprosy Istorii.

Voprosy Filosofii.

NEWSPAPERS

(*Particularly for* 1917 *and* 1918) *at Hoover Library*

Delo Naroda (Social Revolutionary)

Edinstvo (Edinstvo group)

Novoe Vremia (Conservative)

Novyi Luch' (Menshevik)

Rabochaia Gazeta (Menshevik)

Rabochii Put' (Bolshevik)

Rech' (Cadets)

Russkaia Vedomsti (Liberal)

Russkaia Volia (Protopopov)

Russkoe Slovo (Liberal)

From the Nikolaevskii Collection of Menshevik Newspapers Deposited at the Hoover Library

Den'
Iskra
Delo Naroda

Menshevik Newspapers at the Columbia University Library

Rabochaia Gazeta—issues from year 1917.
Rabochee Delo—issues from year 1917.
Sotsial Demokrat—issues from year 1917.
Soldatskaia Pravda—issues from year 1917.
Vsegda Vpered—issues from year 1919.

Anarchist Newspapers at the New York Public Library

Biulleten' Initsiativoi Gruppy Anarkhistov Molodezhi Ukrainy Nabat, April 1919.

Biulleten' No. 3, Izdaetsia Vremennym Vsedomitel'nym Biuro Anarkhistov Rossii, 15 December 1917.

Biulletin' Kievskoi Gruppy Anarkhistov Molodiezhi, March 1920.

Burevestnik—Kollegiia Propagandy Sotsial'nago Soznaniia Pri Ob'edinenykh Anarkhicheskikh Organizatsii g. Odessa, Issues from the Month of February 1920.

Ekaterinoslavskii Nabat, Organ Ekaterinoslavskoi Federatsii Anarkhistskikh Grupp Nabat, 6 November 1919.

Ekaterinoslavskii Nabat, Organ Ekaterinoslavskoi Gruppy Anarkhistov Nabat, 7 November 1920.

Elisavetgradskii Nabat Organ Elisavetgradskoi Federatsii Anarkhistkikh Grupp Nabat, 30 March 1919.

Golos Anarkhista (Ekaterinoslav), 17 March 1918 and 18 March 1918. (Hoover Library also has issues of this.)

Guliaipol'skii Nabat Organ Guliaipol'skoi Gruppy Anarkhistov 'Nabat'. Issues from February, March and April 1919.

K Svete, Organ Assotsiatsii Anarkhistov Kharkov, 1 February 1918 and Issues from February and March 1919.

Khark*ovskii Nabat Organ Kharkovskoi Gruppy Anarkhistov Nabat,* 19 January 1919.

Kommuna, Organ Federatsii Petrogradskikh Anarkhistov Kommunistov, September 1917, (1 issue).

Nabat, Organ Federatsii Anarkhistov Sibiri, 25 April 1920.

Nabat, Organ Konfederatsii Anarkhistskikh Organizatsii Ukrainy, Issues from January, February, May, June, July, and December 1919.

Nabat, Organ Guliaipol'skoi Gruppy Anarkhistov 'Nabat', 31 January 1919. (Same as *Guliaipol'skii 'Nabat'*)

Nabat, Organ Sekretariata Konfederatsii Anarkhistikikh Organizatsii Ukrainy Nabat i Kharkovskoi Federatsii Nabat, November 1920.

Odesskii Nabat, Organ Obedinennykh Anarkhistov, 16 February 1920.

Odesskii Nabat, Organ Odesskoi Federatsii Anarkhistskikh Grupp Nabat, 26 May 1919, 16 June 1919 and February 1920.

Put' k Svobode, Organ Revoliutsionnykh Povstantsev i Guliaipol'skogo Soiuza Anarkhistov, 24 May 1919 and 4 June 1919.

Put' k Svobode, Organ Revoliutsionnnykh Povstantsev i Voisk Imeni Bat'-ko-Makhno, 17 May 1919.

Trud i Volia, Organ Soiuza Anarkho-Sindikalistov-Kommunistov G. Moskvy, 30 January 1919, 17 February 1919, 14 April 1919, 9 May 1919 and 20 May 1919.

Vol'nyi Golos Elizavetgradskoi Federatsii Anarkhistskikh Grupp Nabat, 19 February 1919.

COMMUNIST NEWSPAPERS

Izvestiia
Pravda

DICTIONARIES AND ENCYCLOPEDIAS

Aleksandrov, G., Galianov, V. and Rubinstein, N., *Politicheskii Slovar',* Gosudarstvennoe Izdatel'stvo Politicheskoi Literatury, (n.p.), 1940.

Dal' Vladimir, *Tolkovyi Slovar' Zhivogo Velikorusskago Iazyka,* 3rd edition, M. O. Wol'f, St. Petersburgh, 1903-1909.

Bol'shaia Sovetskaia Entsiklopediia, Moscow, 1926.

Gordon, M. Ia, et al, *Malaia Entsiklopediia Professionalnogo Dvizheniia i Truda,* Leningradskii Guberniskii Sovet Professional'nykh Soiuzov, 1925.

Malaiia Sovetskaiia Entsiklopediia, Moscow, 1919.

Narodnyi Politicheskii Slovar', *Posobie pri Chtenii Gazet, Zhurnal, Broshiur i Politicheskoi Literatury,* Reznikov, Petrograd, 1917.

Tolkovyi Slovar' Russkogo Iazyka (ed. Ushakov), Ogiz, Moscow, 1935.

Index